History of the Family and Kinship

History of the Family and Kinship: A Select International Bibliography

EDITED BY GERALD L. SOLIDAY

with Tamara K. Hareven, Richard T. Vann, and
Robert Wheaton, Associate Editors

A Project of the
Journal of Family History,
The National Council on Family Relations

KRAUS INTERNATIONAL PUBLICATIONS
Millwood, New York

A U.S. Division of Kraus-Thomson Organization Ltd.

First printing

Printed in the United States of America

The research for and the assembling and editing of this bibliography was supported by a grant from the Research Tools Program of the Research Grants Division, the National Endowment for the Humanities.

Library of Congress Cataloging in Publication Data

Main entry under title:

History of the family and kinship.

Includes index.
  1. Family--History--Bibliography. 2. Kinship--History--Bibliography. I. Soliday, Gerald Lyman.
II. Journal of family history.
Z7164.M2H57   [HQ503]   016.3068'09   80-11782
ISBN 0-527-84451-9

Contents

THE MIDDLE EAST AND NORTH AFRICA

AFRICA SOUTH OF THE SAHARA

SOUTH ASIA

SOUTHEAST ASIA

List of Contributors

GENERAL WORKS
Compiled by Howard Litwak
Reviewed by Glen Elder (Cornell University),
    Tamara K. Hareven (Clark University), and
    Robert Wheaton (*Journal of Family History*)

EUROPE
Compiled by Howard Litwak
Reviewed by Robert Wheaton

GREAT BRITAIN AND IRELAND
Compiled by James R. Davis
Reviewed by Richard T. Vann (Wesleyan University)

FRANCE
Compiled by Lee Shai Weissbach (University of
    Louisville)
Reviewed by Robert Wheaton

CENTRAL EUROPE
Compiled by Gerald L. Soliday (University of
    Texas at Dallas)

THE NETHERLANDS AND BELGIUM
Compiled by Jay R. Kaufman
Reviewed by Robert Wheaton

NORTHERN EUROPE
Compiled by David Gaunt (Uppsala University)

THE IBERIAN PENINSULA
Compiled by Stanley Brandes (University of
California at Berkeley)

CLASSICAL ANTIQUITY
Compiled by Sarah B. Pomeroy (Hunter College of
the City University of New York)

ITALY
Compiled by Ruth Liebowitz (Radcliffe Seminars)

GREECE
Compiled by Jill Dubisch (University of
North Carolina at Charlotte)

EASTERN EUROPE, RUSSIA, AND THE BALKANS
Compiled by Andrejs Plakans (Iowa State University)

THE MIDDLE EAST AND NORTH AFRICA
Compiled by Elizabeth Warnock Fernea (University of
Texas at Austin) with James M. Malarkey and
Sabra J. Webber

AFRICA SOUTH OF THE SAHARA
Compiled by Kennell A. Jackson, Jr. (Stanford University)
Reviewed by Ivan Karp (Indiana University)

SOUTH ASIA
Compiled by Sylvia Vatuk (University of Illinois at
Chicago Circle)

SOUTHEAST ASIA
Compiled by David K. Wyatt (Cornell University)

OCEANIA
Compiled by Mac Marshall (University of Iowa)

AUSTRALIA AND NEW ZEALAND
Compiled by Harold Scheffler (Yale University)

CHINA
Compiled by Charlotte Ikels (University of
    Massachusetts at Boston)

JAPAN
Compiled by Laurel L. Cornell (Johns Hopkins University)

KOREA
Compiled by Laurel L. Cornell

CANADA
Compiled by Chad Gaffield (McGill University)

THE UNITED STATES
Compiled by Blanche M. G. Linden
Reviewed by Linda Auwers (Temple University), Glen Elder,
    Harvey J. Graff (University of Texas at Dallas), and
    Tamara K. Hareven

LATIN AMERICA
Compiled by Donald Ramos (Cleveland State University)

Foreword

This bibliography is intended to serve a wide, interdisciplinary, and international community of scholars by making available an extensive yet selective bibliography of secondary works on family history and related areas. The need for such a bibliography has become acute because of the rapid development of research in family history over the past ten years, and because writings in the field are widely dispersed in monographs and periodicals in a variety of disciplines and languages. Our hope is that this work will provide bibliographic control over these scattered resources and will prove useful to researchers, teachers, and students in social, economic, cultural, and legal history, as well as demography, sociology of the family, anthropology, and psychology.

In 1976, we conceived the idea of producing a retrospective bibliography on family history, which was to be published in a special issue of the *Journal of Family History*. We then applied to the National Endowment for the Humanities, and Clark University was awarded a grant for the project from the NEH's Research Tools Program. We subsequently invited Professor Gerald Soliday to coordinate the project and to act as its chief editor. Professor Richard Vann, who had already been compiling a bibliography on the subject, generously contributed the titles which he had gathered as a base upon which to proceed. Professor Soliday engaged scholars to expand and to update these initial lists and to assemble others for areas not covered.

As the bibliography grew in size, we decided to publish it as a separate book rather than in an issue of the journal. The volume remains, however, a special project of the *Journal of Family History*.

We are grateful to Clark University, especially to its President, Dr. Mortimer Appley, to the National Council on Family Relations, and to its Executive Officer, Dr. Ruth Jewson, for their support of the *Journal of Family History* and its work. We are indebted to the National Endowment for the Humanities for its generosity in funding this project with the initial grant as well as with a supplemental grant which made expansion of the bibliography possible. We are especially grateful to Gail Halkias, Gerald P. Tyson, and George F. Farr of the NEH Research Tools Division for their support and encouragement.

This book would not have been possible without the initiative, encouragement, and expert advice of Mrs. Marion Sader, who graciously invited us to publish the volume with Kraus International Publications. We are grateful to Jerry Soliday for his meticulous and patient execution of this project, and for his persistence in solving a large number of problems which arose in the course of its completion; to Richard Vann for his contributions and helpful suggestions; and to the many research assistants, compilers, and consultants, whose names and contributions are listed at the front of this volume.

We are also much indebted to Joyce Ingham and James Smith Allen for their contribution to smooth office management.

Tamara K. Hareven,
Editor, *Journal of
Family History*

Robert Wheaton,
Associate Editor, *Journal of
Family History*

Preface

This work seeks to provide its users with a selection of the best and most important scholarship on the history of kinship and the family. Its coverage is worldwide and includes all time periods from prehistory to the present. Such an ambitious undertaking has been possible only as a collaborative project between the editors and various experts in regional or national research on the family and kinship. For several European areas and for the United States, the editors first hired graduate students to make initial compilations of appropriate titles; these were then reviewed by researchers active in those national fields. For other areas of the world, the editors turned directly to scholars publishing works on the history of kinship and the family and requested that they prepare selective bibliographies for their regions. The resulting volume contains approximately 6200 entries, which the editors hope will be the most authoritative guide to past scholarship as well as a useful aid to future research.

The major issue for our contributors was, of course, selection of the most important publications on the family and kinship in their respective fields. The general "Statement of Purpose" in the first issue of the *Journal of Family History* was used to define the focus of the bibliography: "the study of the internal structure and processes of family and kinship as well as their interaction with the larger society and with community, economic, legal, religious, and educational institutions."

Clearly, the best work in this rapidly expanding field is analytical in thrust and interdisciplinary in character. Yet the quantity, quality, and emphasis of research in the various regional or national areas vary considerably.

The editors and contributors have observed some basic guidelines in the compilation of this bibliography. Historical concern is the chief criterion; items from disciplines other than history are included only if they have general theoretical value or particular relevance to the history of family experience. Items of strictly local or purely genealogical interest which do not address the general issues of family history have been omitted, whereas sociological studies having historical relevance are included. Examinations of American family structure from the Second World War to the present are appropriate, for example, but current debates over childrearing practices or speculation about the future of current marital customs have no place in this bibliography. Demographic work involving family reconstitution, age at marriage, fertility, and infant mortality are included, but aggregate population studies are not relevant here. It was the editors' hope that all disciplinary or methodological perspectives would be represented in each compilation, but the diversity of research developments from region to region has meant that substantive and temporal emphases can change from list to list. Anthropological studies predominate in Oceania, while historical demography is more highly developed in France or Northern Europe than, for example, North Africa and the Middle East. Hence, the most sensible editorial strategy has been to rely on the good judgment of scholars who know the individual fields well.

Their selections reflect, therefore, the state of research in the fields in which they work. Coverage of the literature is systematic through 1976, with the addition of some studies published in 1977 and 1978 which the contributors think will shape future historical studies on the family and kinship.

One major restriction has been placed on our contributors to the sections on non-Western areas. Bibliographic items in non-Western languages are included only if they have summaries in a Western European language.

ORGANIZATION OF THE VOLUME

The organization of the entire volume and of the individual lists follows the historian's usual division of the world into regional or national units as well as his proclivity for chronological subdivisions within those areas. Of course, flexibility has been necessary. Professor Marshall prefers no temporal subdivisions for Oceania, and the lists for some complex regions like Eastern Europe or Southeast Asia have only geographical or political rather than chronological refinements. The editorial assumption has been that compilers should decide the internal organization of their lists. Most of the bibliographies do contain chronological divisions, however, and the reader should note that whenever an individual item cuts across two time periods, it has been placed in the earlier one. An entry dealing with a particular subject from the seventeenth century to the present, in a list subdivided at the year 1800 into early modern and modern periods, is placed in the early modern period. Lists usually begin with works of a more general nature (for example, surveys of an entire field or collections of essays), and most also include bibliographic entries useful for more detailed exploration of regional research on topics related to the history of kinship and the family.

The citation of individual entries has been kept, like the organization of the entire volume, as clear and simple as possible. The main goal is to provide sufficient information to facilitate the user's further location of bibliographic items. We hope this aim has been achieved in all cases. The editors have preferred the traditional style of citation to the newer format used by many social scientists, but they have not hesitated to modify the usual stylistic conventions in the interests of greater simplicity. We have paid particular attention to establishing the correct names of authors, titles, and places and dates of publication. Publishers and the series in which many (especially European) monographs appear are not identified, a decision made originally because of space limitations, but justified as well by the fact that most library cataloging or verification does not hinge on that information. Subtitles are cited only when they give essential information about the nature of the work. Because it is most accessible, citation is usually to the latest edition but the date of first publication is added for old or historic works recently reissued. Edited collections are listed by title rather than by editor, a practice which facilitates the citation of individual articles and permits consistency with the many European collections published without named editors. Should the user already know a collection by its editor, however, the citation is found easily through the name index. Within the various sections, works by the same author have been arranged alphabetically, chronologically, or in ranked order of importance, depending upon the preference of the section's compiler.

ACKNOWLEDGEMENTS

A collaborative project such as this bibliography places its general editor in the debt of many scholars, both in the United States and abroad, who have been kind enough to offer suggestions for its organization or to propose contributors for specific fields. There have been so many helpful colleagues over the past two and a half years of work on the volume that naming all of them is simply not possible here. I hope they will accept my sincerest thanks, nonetheless, and will approve the final result which they aided so generously.

Detailed work with a large number of contributors has its frustrations and its rewards, though I believe that the latter outweigh the former. I have been most impressed, on balance, by the professional spirit and personal courtesy displayed by the contributors. The associate editors and I are very grateful for their willingness to participate in this difficult but, we trust, worthwhile venture.

For their kind help with my own contribution, the bibliography on Central Europe, I wish to thank Professors Arthur Imhof (Berlin) and Michael Mitterauer (Vienna), men who combine genuine personal warmth with their high scholarly stature. Joyce Ingham's friendly and efficient management of our financial affairs at Clark University has benefitted the project in countless ways, and I am also grateful to Donna Soliday and Eileen Tollett for their cheerful acceptance of typing assignments. Two Dallas colleagues and friends, Professors Donna Maier and Harvey Graff, were especially supportive during this project, and I thank them both sincerely for their advice and encouragement.

The bibliography on the Iberian Peninsula was compiled, in part, with the use of General Research Funds from the University of California at Berkeley. Professor Brandes would like to thank David Fogerty, Richard Herr, and Temma Kaplan for providing helpful bibliographic leads.

Dr. Laurel L. Cornell extends her thanks to Professors Charles Goldberg, Cornelius J. Kiley, and Robert J. Smith for their valuable suggestions and criticisms concerning her lists on Japan and Korea.

Professor Kennnell A. Jackson, Jr., wishes to thank Ms. Jessica Glicken for her assistance with the bibliography on Africa South of the Sahara.

The editors and Dr. Donald Ramos greatly appreciate the advice and helpful suggestions of Professors Peter Smith and Esteban Egea on the Latin American list.

Gerald L. Soliday

Dallas, Texas
June, 1979

History of the Family and Kinship

General Works

BIBLIOGRAPHIES

1 Besterman, Theodore, *Family History: A Bibliography of Bibliographies.* Totowa, N.J., 1971.
2 Chasteland, Jean-Claude, *Démographie: bibliographie et analyse d'ouvrages et d'articles en français.* Paris, 1961.
3 Freedman, Ronald, "The Sociology of Human Fertility: A Trend Report and Bibliography," *Current Sociology* 10-11 (1961-62), 35-121.
4 Hill, Reuben, "Sociology of Marriage and Family Behaviour, 1945-56: A Trend Report and Bibliography," *Current Sociology* 7 (1958-59), 1-98.
5 *International Bibliography of Research in Marriage and the Family.* v. 1: *1900-1964*, ed. Joan Aldous and Reuben Hill. Minneapolis, 1967.
6 *International Bibliography of Research in Marriage and the Family.* v. 2: *1965-1972*, ed. Joan Aldous and Nancy S. Dahl. Minneapolis, 1974.
7 *Inventory of Marriage and Family Literature.* v. 3:*1973-74*, ed. David H. L. Olson and Nancy S. Dahl. St. Paul, Minn., 1975.
8 *Inventory of Marriage and Family Literature.* v. 4: *1975 and 1976*, ed. David H. Olson and Nancy S. Dahl. St. Paul, Minn., 1977.
9 Legeard, Claud, *Guide de recherches documentaires en démographie.* Paris, 1966.
10 Lopez, Manuel D., "A Guide to the Interdisciplinary Literature of the History of Childhood," *History of Childhood Quarterly* 1 (1973-74), 463-494.
11 Milden, James Wallace, *The Family in Past Time: A Guide to the Literature.* New York and London, 1977.
12 Zimmerman, Carle, *Bibliography of Studies of Family Living in Asia, Australia, New Zealand, Peru, Mexico, and the Islands of the Pacific.* Washington, D.C., 1934.

GENERAL THEORETICAL, METHODOLOGICAL, OR COMPARATIVE WORKS

13   Adams, Bert N., "Interaction Theory and the Social Network," *Sociometry* 30 (1967), 64-78.

14   Adams, Bert N., *Kinship in an Urban Setting.* Chicago, 1968.

15   Adams, Bert N., "Kinship Systems and Adaptation to Modernization," *Studies in Comparative International Development* 4 (1968-69), 47-60.

16   *Adulthood,* ed. Erik Erikson. New York, 1978.

17   Ariès, Philippe, *Western Attitudes Toward Death from the Middle Ages to the Present.* Baltimore, 1974.

18   *Aspects of the Analysis of Family Structure,* ed. Ansley J. Coale et al. Princeton, 1965.

19   Bachofen, Johann Jakob, *Das Mutterrecht.* Stuttgart, 1861. Also as *Myth, Religion, and Mother Right: Selected Writings,* tr. Ralph Manheim. Princeton, 1967.

20   Bairoch, Paul, *et al., La population active et sa structure.* Brussels, 1968.

21   Bardis, Panos D., "Family Forms and Variations Historically Considered," *Handbook of Marriage and the Family,* ed. Harold T. Christensen (Chicago, 1964), 403-461. (See #124)

22   Bardis, Panos D., *Studies in Marriage and the Family.* Lexington, Mass., 1975.

23   Barnes, John A., "Measures of Divorce Frequency in Simple Societies," *Journal of the Royal Anthropological Institute* 79 (1951), 37-62.

24   Barnes, John A., *Three Styles in the Study of Kinship.* London, 1971.

25   Becker, Gary, *The Economic Approach to Human Behavior.* Chicago, 1977.

26   Berkner, Lutz K., "The Use and Misuse of Census Data for the Historical Analysis of Family Structure," *Journal of Interdisciplinary History* 5 (1974-75), 721-738.

27   Biraben, Jean-Noël, "Evolution récente de la fécondité des mariages dans les pays occidentaux," *Population* 16 (1961), 49-70.

28   *Birth Control in Asia,* ed. Michael Fielding. London, 1935.

29   Blitsten, Dorothy R., *The World of the Family: A Comparative Study of Family Organizations in Their Social and Cultural Settings.* New York, 1963.

30   Bogue, Donald J., *Principles of Demography.* New York, 1969.

31   Bott, Elizabeth, *Family and Social Network.* 2nd ed.; New York and London, 1971.

32   Bourgeois-Pichat, Jean, *La mesure de la fécondité des populations.* Paris, 1950.

33   Bourgeois-Pichat, Jean, "La mesure de la mortalité infantile," *Population* 6 (1951), 233-248, 459-480.

34   Briffault, Robert, *The Mothers: A Study of the Origins of Sentiments and Institutions.* New York, 1927.

35 Buchler, Ira R., and Henry A. Selby, *Kinship and Social Organization: An Introduction to Theory and Method*. New York, 1968.

36 Burch, Thomas K., "The Size and Structure of Families: A Comparative Analysis of Census Data," *American Sociological Review* 32 (1967), 347-363.

37 Burgess, Ernest W., and Harvey J. Locke, *The Family from Institution to Companionship*. 3rd ed.; New York, 1960.

38 *Les Carnets de l'enfance* 10 (1969).

39 Chaianov, Aleksandr Vasil'evich, *The Theory of Peasant Economy*, ed. Daniel Thorner, Basile Kerblay, and R.E.F. Smith. Homewood, Ill., 1966. Russian original, Moscow, 1925.

40 *The Character of Kinship*, ed. Jack Goody. London, 1973.

41 Chevalier, Louis, *Démographie générale*. Paris, 1951.

42 Chevalier, Louis, "Pour une histoire de la population," *Population* 2 (1946), 245-256.

43 Chez, Gilbert, and Gary S. Becker, *The Allocation of Time and Goods Over the Life Cycle*. New York, 1975.

44 *Childhood in Contemporary Cultures*, ed. Margaret Mead and Martha Wolfenstein. Chicago, 1955.

45 Choi, Jai-seuk, "Comparative Study on the Traditional Families in Korea, Japan, and China," *Families in East and West...* , ed. Reuben Hill and René König (The Hague, 1970), 202-210. (See #76)

46 Coale, Ansley J., *The Growth and Structure of Human Populations*. Princeton, 1975.

47 Collomp, Alain, "Ménage et famille: études comparatives sur la dimension et le structure du groupe domestique (note critique)," *Annales E.S.C.* 29 (1974), 777-786.

48 Comhaire, Jean L., "Economic Change and the Extended Family," *Annals of the American Academy of Political and Social Science* 305 (1956), 45-52.

49 *Comparative Family Systems*, ed. Meyer F. Nimkoff. Boston, 1965.

50 Cooper, J. M., "The Early History of the Family," *Primitive Man* 3 (1930), 56-68.

51 Cooper, J. M., "Incest Prohibitions in Primitive Culture," *Primitive Man* 5 (1932), 1-20.

52 Cutright, Phillips, "Historical and Contemporary Trends in Illegitimacy," *Archives of Sexual Behavior* 2 (1972), 97-118.

53 Delcourt, Jacques, "Influence of Urbanization on the Diverse Phases of Development in the Family Cycle," *Current Sociology* 12 (1963), 34-45.

54 DeMause, Lloyd, "The Evolution of Childhood," *History of Childhood Quarterly* 1 (1973-74), 503-575. Also in the *History of Childhood*, ed. Lloyd DeMause (New York, 1974), 1-74. (See #154)

55 Demos, John, "Developmental Perspectives on the History of Childhood," *Journal of Interdisciplinary History* 2 (1971-72), 315-327. Now in *The*

Family in History, ed. Theodore K. Rabb and Robert I. Rotberg (New York, 1973), 127-139. (See #80)

56 *The Developmental Cycle in Domestic Groups,* ed. Jack Goody. Cambridge, England, 1971. Originally 1958.

57 Dick, Ernst S., "Bridesman in Indo-European Tradition: Ritual and Myth in Marriage Ceremonies," *Journal of American Folklore* 79 (1966), 338-347.

58 Draper, Elizabeth, *Birth Control in the Modern World.* London, 1965.

59 Dumond, Don, "The Limitation of Human Population: A Natural History," *Science* 187 (1975), 713-721.

60 Dupâquier, Jacques, "De l'animal à l'homme: le mécanisme autorégulateur des populations traditionelles," *Revue de l'Institut de sociologie* [Brussels] (1972), 177-211.

61 Durkheim, Emile, "La prohibition de l'inceste et ses origines," *Année sociologique* 1 (1898), 1-70. English translation as *Incest: The Nature and Origin of the Taboo.* New York, 1963.

62 Duvall, Evelyn M., *Marriage and Family Development.* 5th ed.; Philadelphia, 1977.

63 Easterlin, Richard A., "Implications of the Demographic History of Developed Countries for Present-Day Underdeveloped Nations," *Comparative Studies in Society and History* 2 (1959-60), 374-378.

64 *Economic Factors in Population Growth,* ed. Ansley J. Coale. New York, 1976.

65 *Economics of the Family: Marriage, Children, and Human Capital,* ed. Theodore Schultz. Chicago, 1974.

66 Elder, Glen H., "Age Differentiation and the Life Course," *Annual Review of Sociology* 1 (1975), 165-190.

67 Elder, Glen H., "Approaches to Social Change and the Family," *Turning Points,* ed. John Demos and Sarane Spence Boocock (Chicago, 1978), 1-38. (See #262)

68 Elder, Glen H., "Family History and the Life Course," *Journal of Family History* 2 (1977), 279-304.

69 Ellul, Jacques, "Position des églises protestantes à l'égard de la famille," *Renouveau des idées sur la famille,* ed. Robert Prigent (Paris, 1954), 269-274.

70 Engels, Friedrich, *Der Ursprung der Familie, des Privateigentums und des Staates.* Zurich, 1884. Reissued in Karl Marx–Friedrich Engels, *Werke,* v. 21 (Berlin, 1962), 25-173. The book appears in English as *The Origin of the Family, Private Property and the State.* New York, 1972.

71 Erikson, Erik, *Childhood and Society.* New York, 1950.

72 Erikson, Erik, *Identity and the Life Cycle.* New York, 1959.

73 Erikson, Erik, *Identity, Youth and Crisis.* New York, 1968.

74 Erikson, Erik, *Life History and the Historical Moment.* New York, 1975.

75 Evans-Pritchard, E. E., "The Study of Kinship in Primitive Societies," *Man* 29 (1969), 190-193.

76 *Families in East and West: Socialization Process and Kinship Ties*, ed. Reuben Hill and René König. The Hague, 1970.

77 *Family and Society: Selections from the Annales*, ed. Robert Forster and Orest Ranum. Baltimore, 1976.

78 *The Family and the State: Select Documents*, ed. Sophonisba Preston Breckinridge. Chicago, 1934. Reprint, New York, 1972.

79 *The Family in History*, ed. Charles E. Rosenberg. Philadelphia, 1975.

80 *The Family in History: Interdisciplinary Essays*, ed. Theodore K. Rabb and Robert I. Rotberg. New York, 1973.

81 *The Family in Various Cultures*, ed. Stuart A. Queen, Robert W. Habenstein, and John B. Adams. Chicago, 1961.

82 *The Family: Its Functions and Destiny*, ed. Ruth Nanda Anshen. rev. ed.; New York, 1959.

83 *Family Law in Asia and Africa*, ed. James N. D. Anderson. London and New York, 1968.

84 *Family, Marriage, and Parenthood*, ed. Howard Becker and Reuben Hill. Boston, 1955.

85 Farber, Bernard, *Family and Kinship in Modern Society*. Glenview, Ill., 1973.

86 Finch, Bernard, and Hugh Green, *Contraception Through the Ages*. London, 1963.

87 Fortes, Meyer, "Introduction," *The Developmental Cycle in Domestic Groups*, ed. Jack Goody (Cambridge, England, 1971), 1-14. Originally 1958. (See #56)

88 Fortes, Meyer, *Kinship and the Social Order: The Legacy of Lewis Henry Morgan*. Chicago, 1969.

89 Fortes, Meyer, "Structure of Unilineal Descent Groups," *American Anthropologist* 55 (1953), 17-41.

90 Fortes, Meyer, *Time and Social Structure and Other Essays*. London and New York, 1970.

91 Fortes, Meyer, *The Web of Kinship Among the Talensi*. London, 1969.

92 Fox, Robin, *Kinship and Marriage: An Anthropological Perspective*. Harmondsworth, 1967.

93 Freeman, J. D., "On the Concept of the Kindred," *Journal of the Royal Anthropological Institute* 91 (1961), 192-220.

94 Freud, Sigmund, *Totem and Taboo*, tr. and ed. James Strachey. London, 1953. Original German edition, Leipzig, 1913.

95 Fried, M. H., "The Classification of Corporate Unilineal Descent Groups," *Journal of the Royal Anthropological Institute* 87 (1957), 1-29.

96 Géraud, Roger, *La limitation des naissances. Histoire, biologie, psychologie, démographie, législation, doctrine*. Paris, 1968.

97 Gilbert, John B., and Eugene Hammel, "Computer Simulation and Analysis of Problems in Kinship and Social Structure," *American Anthropologist* 68 (1966), 71-93.

98   Godelier, Maurice, "Modes de production, rapports de parenté et structures démographiques," *La pensée* new series 172 (1973), 7-31.

99   Goldschmidt, Walter, and Evalyn Jacobson Kunkel, "The Structure of the Peasant Family," *American Anthropologist* 73 (1971), 1058-1076.

100 Goode, William J., *The Family*. Englewood Cliffs, N.J., 1964.

101 Goode, William J., *Family and Mobility*. New York, 1963. Reprinted in *Class, Status, and Power: Social Stratification in Comparative Perspective*, ed. Reinhard Bendix and Seymour M. Lipset. 2nd ed.; (New York, 1966), 582-601.

102 Goode, William J., "Family Cycle and Theory Construction," *The Family Life Cycle...*, ed. Jean Cuisenier and Martine Segalen (The Hague, 1977), 59-76. (See #297)

103 Goode, William J., "Family Systems and Social Mobility," *Families in East and West...*, ed. Reuben Hill and René König (The Hague, 1970), 120-131. (See #76)

104 Goode, William J., "Industrialization and Family Change," *North American Conference on the Social Implications of Industrialization and Technological Change*, ed. Bert Hoselitz and Wilbert E. Moore (Paris, 1963), 237-255.

105 Goode, William J., "The Theory and Measurement of Family Change," *Indicators of Social Change*, ed. Eleanor H. Sheldon and Wilbur E. Moore (New York, 1968), 295-348.

106 Goode, William J., *World Revolution and Family Patterns*. New York and London, 1963.

107 Goodsell, Willystine, *A History of the Family as a Social and Educational Institution*. New York, 1915.

108 Goodsell, Willystine, *A History of Marriage and the Family*. New York, 1934.

109 Goody, Jack [i.e., John Rankine], "A Comparative Approach to Incest and Adultery," *British Journal of Sociology* 7 (1956), 286-305.

110 Goody, Jack, *Death, Property, and the Ancestors*. London, 1962.

111 Goody, Jack, "The Evolution of the Family," *Household and Family...*, ed. Peter Laslett and Richard Wall (Cambridge, England, 1972), 103-124. (See #156)

112 Goody, Jack, "Inheritance, Property and Marriage in Africa and Eurasia," *Sociology* 3 (1969), 55-76.

113 Goody, Jack, "Inheritance, Property and Women: Some Comparative Considerations," *Family and Inheritance...*, ed. Jack Goody, Joan Thirsk, and E. P. Thompson (Cambridge, England, 1976), 10-36. (See #296)

114 Goody, Jack, *Production and Reproduction: A Comprative Study of the Domestic Domain*. Cambridge, England, 1976.

115 Goody, Jack, "Strategies of Heirship," *Comparative Studies in Society and History* 15 (1973), 3-20.

116 Gough, Kathleen, "The Origin of the Family," *Journal of Marriage and the Family* 33 (1971), 760-771.

117 Greenfield, S. M., "Industrialization and the Family in Sociological Theory," *American Journal of Sociology* 67 (1961), 312-322.

118 Gruenberg, Sidonie M., "Changing Conceptions of the Family," *Annals of the American Academy of Political and Social Science* 251 (1947), 128-136.

119 Guillaume, Pierre, and Jean-Pierre Poussou, *La démographie historique.* Paris, 1970.

120 Hajnal, John, "Analyses of Changes in the Marriage Pattern by Economic Groups," *American Sociological Review* 19 (1954), 295-302.

121 Hall, G. Stanley, *Adolescence.* New York, 1969. Originally, New York, 1904.

122 Hallowell, A. Irving, and Earle L. Reynolds, "Biological Factors in Family Structure," *Marriage and the Family*, ed. Howard Becker and Reuben Hill (Boston, 1942), 25-46.

123 Hammel, Eugene, and Peter Laslett "Comparing Household Structure over Time and Between Cultures," *Comparative Studies in Society and History* 16 (1974), 73-109.

124 *Handbook of Marriage and the Family*, ed. Harold T. Christensen. Chicago, 1964.

125 Hareven, Tamara K., "Cycles, Courses and Cohorts: Reflections on Theoretical and Methodological Approaches to the Historical Study of Family Development," *Journal of Social History* 12 (1978-79), 97-109.

126 Hareven, Tamara K., "The Family as Process: The Historical Study of the Family Cycle," *Journal of Social History* 7 (1973-74), 322-329.

127 Hareven, Tamara K., "The Family in Historical Perspective: The Development of a New Field, Report on Work in Progress in England and the United States," *Geschichte und Gesellschaft* 1 (1975), 370-386.

128 Hareven, Tamara K., "Family Time and Historical Time," *Daedalus* 106 (1977), 57-70.

129 Hareven, Tamara K., "Historical Changes in the Life Course and the Family: Policy Implications," *Major Social Issues: A Multidisciplinary View*, ed. Milton Yinger and Stephen Cutler (New York, 1978), 338-345.

130 Hareven, Tamara K., "The History of the Family as an Interdisciplinary Field," *Journal of Interdisciplinary History* 2 (1971-72), 399-414. Also in *The Family in History*, ed. Theodore K. Rabb and Robert I. Rotberg (New York, 1973), 211-226. (See #80)

131 Hareven, Tamara K., "Modernization and Family History: Reflections on Social Change," *Signs* 2 (1976), 190-206.

132 Harper, Fowler, *Problems of the Family.* Indianapolis, 1952.

133 Hartland, Edwin S., *The Beginnings of the Family and the Reckoning of Descent.* London, 1921.

134 Hartland, Edwin S., *Primitive Paternity: The Myth of Supernatural Birth in Relation to the History of the Family.* London, 1910.

135 Hausen, Karin, "Familie als Gegenstand historischer Sozialwissenschaft:

Bemerkungen zu einer Forschungsstrategie," *Geschichte und Gesellschaft* 1 (1975), 171-209.

136   Henry, Louis, "L'apport des témoignages et de la statistique," *La prévention des naissances...*, ed. Hélène Bergues (Paris, 1960), 361-376. (See #215)

137   Henry, Louis, "Approximations et erreurs dans les tables de nuptialité de générations," *Population* 18 (1963), 737-776.

138   Henry, Louis, *Fécondité des mariages. Nouvelle méthode de mesure.* Paris, 1953.

139   Henry, Louis, "Fécondité et famille. Modèles mathématiques," *Population* 12 (1957), 413-444.

140   Henry, Louis, "Historical Demography," *Daedalus* 97 (1968), 385-396.

141   Henry, Louis, "Intervalle entre le mariage et la première naissance," *Population* 28 (1973), 261-284.

142   Henry, Louis, *Manuel de démographie historique.* Geneva and Paris, 1970.

143   Henry, Louis, "Mesure de la fréquence des divorces," *Population* 7 (1952), 267-282.

144   Henry, Louis, *On the Measurement of Human Fertility: Selected Writings*, tr. and ed. Mindel C. Sheps and Evelyne Lapierre-Adamcyk. Amsterdam and New York, 1972.

145   Henry, Louis, "Simulation d'une reconstitution de familles par ordinateur," *Annales de démographie historique* (1972), 303-309.

146   Henry, Louis, "Vues sur la statistique des familles," *Population* 8 (1953), 473-490.

147   Hill, Reuben, *Family Development in Three Generations.* Cambridge, Mass., 1970.

148   Hill, Reuben, "Social Theory and Family Development," *The Family Life Cycle...*, ed. Jean Cuisenier and Martine Segalen (The Hague, 1977), 9-39. (See #297)

149   Hill, Reuben, "The Three Generation Research Design: Method for Studying Family and Social Change," *Families in East and West*, ed. Reuben Hill and René König (The Hague, 1970), 536-555. (See #76)

150   Himes, Norman, "Contraceptive Technique in Islam and Europe During the Middle Ages," *Marriage Hygiene* 1 (1934-35), 156-171.

151   Himes, Norman, *Medical History of Contraception.* Baltimore, 1936.

152   Himes, Norman, "Medical History of Contraception," *New England Journal of Medicine* (1934), 567-581.

153   *Historical Studies of Changing Fertility*, ed. Charles Tilly. Princeton, N.J., 1978.

154   *The History of Childhood*, ed. Lloyd DeMause. New York, 1974.

155   Hollingsworth, Thomas Henry, *Historical Demography.* Ithaca, New York, 1969.

156   *Household and Family in Past Time*, ed. Peter Laslett and Richard Wall. Cambridge, England, 1972. (See the reviews #26 and #135.)

157 Howard, George G., *A History of Matrimonial Institutions*. 3 v. New York, 1964. Originally, Chicago, 1904.

158 *Identifying People in the Past*, ed. E. Anthony Wrigley. London, 1973.

159 Inkeles, Alex, and David Smith, *Becoming Modern*. Cambridge, Mass., 1974.

160 Kenniston, Kenneth, "Psychological Development and Historical Change," Journal of Interdisciplinary History 2 (1971-72), 329-346. Reprinted in *The Family in History*, ed. Theodore K. Rabb and Robert I. Rotberg (New York, 1973), 141-158. (See #80)

161 Keyfitz, Nathan, *Applied Mathematical Demography*. New York, 1977.

162 *Kinship and Family Organization*, ed. Bernard Farber. New York, 1966.

163 *Kinship and Social Organization*, ed. Paul Bohannan and John Middleton. New York, 1968.

164 *Kinship: Selected Readings*, ed. Jack Goody. Harmondsworth, 1971.

165 Kohn, Melvin L., *Class and Conformity*. 2nd ed.; Chicago, 1977.

166 König, René, "Alte Probleme und neue Fragen in der Familiensoziologie," *Kölner Zeitschrift für Soziologie* 18 (1966), 1-20.

167 König, René, *Die Familie der Gegenwart: ein interkultureller Vergleich*. München, 1974.

168 König, René, "Soziologie der Familie," *Handbuch der empirischen Sozialforschung*, v. 7, ed. René König. 2nd ed.; (Stuttgart, 1976), 1-217.

169 Krause, John T., "Some Implications of Recent Research in Demographic History," *Comparative Studies in Society and History* 1 (1958-59), 164-188.

170 Laing, Ronald D., *The Politics of the Family and Other Essays*. London, 1971.

171 Landry, Adolphe, et al., *Traité de démographie*. 2nd ed.; Paris, 1949.

172 Langer, William L., "American Foods and Europe's Population Growth 1750-1850," *Journal of Social History* 8 (1974-75), 51-65.

173 Laslett, Peter, "Characteristics of the Western Family Considered Over Time," *Journal of Family History* 2 (1977), 89-115.

174 Laslett, Peter, "The Comparative History of Household and Family," *Journal of Social History* 4 (1970-71), 75-87. Now in *The American Family in Social-Historical Perspective*, ed. Michael Gordon (New York, 1973), 19-33.

175 Laslett, Peter, "La famille et le ménage: approches historiques," *Annales E.S.C.* 27 (1971), 847-872.

176 Laslett, Peter, "The History of Population and Social Structure," *International Social Science Journal* 17 (1965), 582-593.

177 Laslett, Peter, "Introduction: The History of the Family," *Household and Family...*, ed. Peter Laslett and Richard Wall (Cambridge, England, 1972), 1-89. (See #156)

178 Laslett, Peter, "Societal Development and Aging," *Handbook of Aging and the Social Sciences*, ed. Robert Binstock and Ethel Shanas (New York, 1976), 87-126.

179 Lautman, Françoise, "Différences ou changement dans l'organisation familiale," *Annales E.S.C.* 27 (1972), 1190-1196.

180   Layard, J., "The Family and Kinship," *The Institutions of Primitive Society*, ed. E. E. Evans-Pritchard (Oxford, 1954), 50-65.

181   Le Bras, Hervé, "Parents, grands-parents, bisaïeux," *Population* 28 (1973), 9-38.

182   Le Play, Pierre Guillaume Frédéric, *L'organisation de la famille selon le vrai modèle signalé par l'histoire de toutes les races et de tous le temps.* Paris, 1871. 3rd rev. ed.; Tours, 1884.

183   Lestapis, Stanislas de, "Evolution de la pensée exprimé de l'Eglise Catholique," *Renouveau des idées sur la famille*, ed. Robert Prigent (Paris, 1954), 254-268.

184   Lestapis, Stanislas de, *La limitation des naissances.* Paris, 1959.

185   Letourneau, Charles J. M., *The Evolution of Marriage and the Family.* London, 1911.

186   Levine, Robert, "Comparative Notes on the Life Course," *Transitions*, ed. Tamara K. Hareven (New York, 1978), 287-297. (See #261)

187   Levine, Robert, *Culture, Behavior, and Personality.* Chicago, 1973.

188   Lévi-Strauss, Claude, "The Family," *Man, Culture and Society*, ed. Harry L. Shapiro. rev. ed. (New York, 1971), 333-357.

189   Lévi-Strauss, Claude, *Les structures élémentaires de la parenté.* Paris, 1949. In English as *The Elementary Structure of Kinship.* Boston, 1969.

190   Levy, Marion J., Jr., "Aspects of the Analysis of Family Structure," *Aspects of the Analysis of Family Structure*, ed. Ansley J. Coale et al. (Princeton, 1965), 1-63. (See #18)

191   Linton, Ralph, "The Natural History of the Family," *The Family: Its Functions...*, ed. Ruth Nanda Anshen. rev. ed. (New York, 1959), 18-38. (See #82)

192   McKeel, H. Scudder, "Preliterate Family Patterns," *Marriage and the Family*, ed. Howard Becker and Reuben Hill (Boston, 1942), 47-58.

193   McLennan, John F., *Primitive Marriage: An Inquiry into the Origins of the Form of Capture in Marriage Ceremonies*, ed. Peter Riviere. Chicago, 1970. Originally, Edinburgh, 1865. Also published as *Studies in Ancient History.* London and New York, 1886.

194   Malinowski, Bronislaw, *The Family Among the Australian Aborigines: A Sociological Study.* London, 1913.

195   Manheim, Ernst, "Beiträge zu einer Geschichte der autoritären Familie," *Autorität und Familie*, ed. Erich Fromm, Max Horkheimer, et al. (Paris, 1936), 523-574.

196   Marwick, M. C., "The Modern Family in Social Anthropological Perspective," *African Studies* 17 (1958), 137-158.

197   *Matrilineal Kinship*, ed. David M. Schneider and E. Kathleen Gough. Berkeley, 1961.

198   Mead, Margaret, *Sex and Temperament in Three Primitive Societies.* New York, 1935.

199 Mitterauer, Michael, and Reinhard Sieder, *Vom Patriarchat zur Partner-schaft: Zum Strukturwandel der Familie*. München, 1977.

200 *A Modern Introduction to the Family*, ed. Norman W. Bell and Ezra F. Vogel. Glencoe, Ill., 1960.

201 Morgan, Lewis Henry, *Systems of Consanguinity and Affinity of the Human Family*. Washington, 1871. Reprint, Oosterhout, 1970.

202 Murdock, George P., "Family Stability in Non-European Cultures," *Annals of the American Academy of Political and Social Science* 272 (1950), 195-201.

203 Murdock, George P., *Social Structure*. New York, 1949.

204 Nash, Arnold S., "Ancient Past and Living Present," *Family, Marriage, and Parenthood*, ed. Howard Becker and Reuben Hill (Boston, 1955), 84-103. (See #84)

205 Nimkoff, Meyer F., "Evolution of Family Structure Within the World," *Redis-covery of the Family*, ed. International Union of Family Organizations (Paris, 1958), 7-21.

206 Nimkoff, Meyer F., and R. Middleton, "Types of Family and Types of Economy," *American Journal of Sociology* 66 (1960), 215-225.

207 Noonan, John T., *Contraception: A History of Its Treatment by the Catholic Theologians and Canonists*. Cambridge, Mass., 1966. In French as *Contra-ception et mariage, évolution ou contradiction dans la pensée chrétienne*. Paris, 1969. See review by Jean-Louis Flandrin in *Annales de démographie historique* (1969), 337-359.

208 Noonan, John T., "Intellectual and Demographic History," *Daedalus* 97 (1968), 463-485.

209 Noonan, John T., *Power to Dissolve: Lawyers and Marriages in the Courts of the Roman Curia*. Cambridge, Mass., 1972.

210 Parsons, Elsie, *The Family: An Ethnographical and Historical Outline*. New York and London, 1906.

211 Parsons, Talcott, "The Social Structure of the Family," *The Family: Its Functions...*, ed. Ruth Nanda Anshen. rev. ed. (New York, 1959), 241-274. (See #82)

212 Parsons, Talcott, and Robert Bales, *Family, Socialization and Interaction Process*. Glencoe, Ill., 1960.

213 Pomerai, Ralph de, *Marriage, Past, Present and Future: An Outline of Human Sexual Relationships*. London, 1930.

214 *Population in History: Essays in Historical Demography*, ed. David V. Glass and D.E.C. Eversley. London, 1965.

215 *La prévention des naissances dans la famille: ses origines dans les temps modernes*, ed. Hélène Bergues. Paris, 1960.

216 *Problèmes de mortalité: méthodes, sources et bibliographie en démographie historique. Actes du colloque international de démographie historique, Liège, 18-20 Avril, 1963*, ed. Paul Harsin and Etienne Hélin. Liège, 1965.

217 Radcliffe-Brown, A. R., "Introduction," *African Systems of Kinship and*

Marriage, ed. A. R. Radcliffe-Brown and Daryll Ford. London, 1950.

218 Radcliffe-Brown, A. R., *Structure and Function in Primitive Society*. New York, 1965.

219 Reinhard, Marcel R., André Armengaud, and Jacques Dupâquier, *Histoire générale de la population mondiale*. Paris, 1968.

220 Rémy, Jean, "La famille dans la dynamique culturelle contemporaine," *Recherche sociale* 26 (1969), 24-32.

221 *Research in Family Planning*, ed. Clyde V. Kiser. Princeton, 1962.

222 *Revue de droit canonique* 21:1-4 (1971): "Le lien matrimonial."

223 Riquet, Michel, "Christianisme et population," *Population* 4 (1949), 615-630. English translation in *Popular Attitudes...*, ed. Orest and Patricia Ranum (New York, 1972), 21-44. (See #316)

224 Riley, Matilda White, Anne Finer, et al., *Aging and Society*. 3 v. New York, 1968-72.

225 Rodgers, Roy H., "The Family Life Cycle Concept: Past, Present, and Future," *The Family Life Cycle...*, ed. Jean Cuisenier and Martine Segalen (The Hague, 1977), 39-59. (See #297)

226 Rosenbaum, Heidi, *Familie als Gegenstruktur zur Gesellschaft*. Stuttgart, 1973.

227 Rosenbaum, Heidi, *Familie und Gesellschaftsstruktur: Materialien zu den sozio-ökonomischen Bedingungen von Familienformen*. Frankfurt, 1974. 2nd expanded edition entitled *Seminar: Familie und Gesellschaftsstruktur*. Frankfurt, 1978.

228 Rosenbaum, Heidi, "Zur neueren Entwicklung der historischen Familien-forschung," *Geschichte und Gesellschaft* 1 (1975), 210-225.

229 Rossi, Alice S., "A Biosocial Perspective on Parenting," *Daedalus* 106 (1977), 1-31.

230 Ryder, Norman B., "The Cohort as a Concept in the Study of Social Change," *American Sociological Review* 30 (1965), 845-846.

231 Sauvy, Alfred, "Les études de population avec recherches sur le dévelopement des sociétés et leur évolution profonde," *Vie économique et sociale* 30 (1959), 1-10.

232 Schermerhorn, Richard A., "Family Carry-overs of Western Christendom," *Family, Marriage, and Parenthood*, ed. Howard Becker and Reuben Hill (Boston, 1955), 104-130. (See #84)

233 Scheffler, Harold W., and Floyd G. Lounsbury, *A Study in Structural Seman-tics. The Siriono Kinship System*. New York, 1971.

234 Schmelz, Oscar, *Infant and Early Childhood Mortality Among Jews of the Diaspora*. Jerusalem, 1971.

235 Schmidt, Wilhelm, *Gebräuche des Ehemannes bei Schwangerschaft und Geburt: Mit Richtigstellung des Begriffes der Couvade*. Wien, 1955.

236 Schofield, Roger S., "La reconstitution de la famille par ordinateur," *Annales E.S.C.* 27 (1972), 1071-1082.

237 Schwägler, Georg, *Soziologie der Familie*. Tübingen, 1970.

238 *Selected Studies in Marriage and the Family*, ed. Robert Winch. New York, 1974.

239 Shorter, Edward, *The Making of the Modern Family*. New York, 1975.

240 *Six Cultures: Studies of Child Rearing*, ed. Beatrice B. Whiting. New York and London, 1963.

241 Skolnick, Arlene, "The Family Revisited: Themes in Recent Social Science Research," *Journal of Interdisciplinary History* 5 (1974-75), 703-720.

242 Smith, Rockwell, "Hebrew, Greco-Roman, and Early Christian Family Patterns," *Marriage and the Family*, ed. Howard Becker and Reuben Hill (Boston, 1942), 59-71.

243 *Social Structure and the Family*, ed. Ethel Shanas and Gordon F. Streib. n. p., 1965.

244 Söderberg, B., "An Ethno-Historic Survey of Family Planning," *Ethnos* 36 (1971), 163-180

245 Sommerville, John C., "Towards a History of Childhood and Youth," *Journal of Interdisciplinary History* 3 (1972-73), 438-447.

246 Sonnabend, H., "Demographic Samples in the Study of Backward and Primitive Populations," *South African Journal of Economics* 2 (1934), 306-333.

247 Sorokin, Pitirim A., *Social and Cultural Dynamics*. 4 v. New York, 1937-41. One-volume edition, Boston, 1957.

248 Sorokin, Pitirim A., and Carle Zimmerman, *Principles of Rural-Urban Sociology*. New York, 1929. Reprint, New York, 1969.

249 *Soziologie der Familie*, ed. Günther Lüschen and Eugen Lupri. Opladen, 1970.

250 Spencer, Herbert, *Principles of Sociology*. London, 1876.

251 Spengler, Joseph J., "Aging Populations: Mechanics, Historical Emergence, Impact," *Law and Contemporary Problems* 27 (1962), 2-21.

252 Spitzer, Alan B., "The Historical Problem of Generations," *American Historical Review* 78 (1973), 1353-1385.

253 Starcke, Carl Nicolai, *The Primitive Family in its Origin and Development*, ed. Rodney Needham. Chicago and London, 1976. German original, Leipzig, 1888.

254 Straus, Murray A., and Bruce W. Brown, *Family Measurement Techniques: Abstracts of Published Instruments, 1935-1974*. Minneapolis, 1978.

255 Sussman, Marvin B., and Lee Burchinal, "Kin Family Network: Unheralded Structure in Current Conceptualization of Family Functioning," *Marriage and Family Living* 24 (1962), 231-240.

256 Taylor, G. Rattray, *Sex in History*. New York, 1954. Rev. ed.; London, 1959.

257 Thomlinson, Ralph, *Population Dynamics: Causes and Consequences of World Demographic Change*. New York, 1965.

258 Tietze, Christopher, "History and Statistical Evaluation of Intrauterine Contraceptive Devices," *Public Health and Population Change: Current*

Research Issues, ed. M. C. Sheps and J. C. Ridley (Pittsburgh, 1965), 432-440.

259 Tilly, Charles, "The Historical Study of Vital Processes," *Historical Studies of Changing Fertility*, ed. Charles Tilly (Princeton, N.J., 1978), 3-55. (See #153)

260 Tilly, Charles, "Questions and Conclusion," *ibid.*, 335-350.

261 *Transitions: The Family and the Life Course in Historical Perspective*, ed. Tamara K. Hareven. New York, 1978.

262 *Turning Points: Historical and Sociological Essays on the Family*, ed. John Demos and Sarane Spence Boocock. Chicago, 1978. A Supplement to the *American Journal of Sociology* 84 (1978).

263 Tylor, E. B., "On a Method of Investigation of the Development of Institutions: Applied to Laws of Marriage and Descent," *Journal of Anthropological Institute* 18 (1889), 245-269.

264 Vann, Richard T., "History and Demography," *History and Theory* 9 (1969), 64-78.

265 Vincent, Paul, "Comment déterminer la tendance de la fécondité," *Population* 2 (1947), 465-480.

266 Voeltzel, R., "Le lien matrimonial en climat protestant," *Revue de droit canonique* 21 (1971), 149-179.

267 Wake, Charles Staniland, *The Development of Marriage and Kinship*, ed. with an introduction by Rodney Needham. Chicago and London, 1967. Originally, London, 1889.

268 Westermarck, Edvard A., *The History of Human Marriage*. London and New York, 1891. 5th ed. rewritten in 3 v.; London, 1921. Latter ed. reprinted, New York, 1971.

269 Wickes, I. G., "A History of Infant Feeding," *Archives of Disease in Childhood* 28 (1953), 151-158, 232-240, 332-340, 416-422, 495-502.

270 Winch, Robert, and Margaret Gordon, *Familial Structure and Function As Influence*. Lexington, Mass., 1974.

271 Winch, Robert, et al., *Familial Organization*. New York, 1978.

272 Witkowski, Gustave Joseph, *Histoire des accouchements chez tous les peuples*. Paris, 1887.

273 Wittfogel, Karl A., "Wirtschaftsgeschichtliche Grundlagen der Familien-authorität," *Studien über Autorität und Familie*, ed. Erich Fromm, Max Horkheimer, et al. (Paris, 1936), 473-522.

274 Wrigley, E. Anthony, *Population and History*. London and New York, 1959.

275 Wrigley, E. Anthony, "Reflections on the History of the Family," *Daedalus* 106 (1977), 71-85.

276 Wrong, D. H., "Class Fertility Differentials Before 1850," *Social Research* 25 (1958), 70-86.

277 Wrong, D. H., "Trends in Class Fertility in Western Nations," *Canadian Journal of Economics and Political Science* 24 (1958), 216-229.

278 Yokor, K., "Historical Trends in Home Discipline," *Families in East and West...*, ed. Reuben Hill and René König (The Hague, 1970), 175-186. (See #76)

279 Young, Michael, and Peter Willmott, *The Symmetrical Family*. London, 1973.

280 Zimmerman, Carle, *Consumption and Standards of Living*. New York, 1936.

281 Zimmerman, Carle, *Family and Civilization*. New York, 1947.

See also   #3290, #4357, #4628, #4900, #4927, #4951, #4952, #5028, #5139, #5289, and #5299

Europe

GENERAL WORKS AND COLLECTIONS

282 Anderson, Robert T., "Changing Kinship in Europe," *Kroeber Anthropological Society Papers* 28 (1963), 1-48.

283 Anderson, Robert T., *Traditional Europe: A Study in Anthropology and History*. Belmont, Calif., 1971.

284 *Annales de démographie historique* (1973): "Enfants et Sociétés."

285 *Annales E.S.C.* 27:4-5 (1972): "Famille et Société."

286 Ariès, Philippe, "Interpretation pour une histoire des mentalités," *Prévention des naissances...*, ed. Hélène Bergues (Paris, 1960), 311-327. (See #215) English translation in *Popular Attitudes...*, ed. Orest and Patricia Ranum (New York, 1972), 100-125. (See #316)

287 Berkner, Lutz K., "Recent Research on the History of the Family in Western Europe," *Journal of Marriage and the Family* 35 (1973), 395-405.

288 Berkner, Lutz K., and Franklin Mendels, "Inheritance Systems, Family Structure and Demographic Patterns in Western Europe (1700-1900)," *Historical Studies of Changing Fertility*, ed. Charles Tilly (Princeton, N.J., 1978), 200-224. (See #153)

289 *Biology of Man in History*, ed. Robert Forster and Orest Ranum. Baltimore, 1975.

290 Cooper, J. P., "Patterns of Inheritance and Settlement by Great Landowners from the Fifteenth to the Eighteenth Centuries," *Family and Inheritance*, ed. Jack Goody, Joan Thirsk, and E. P. Thompson (Cambridge, England, 1976), 192-327. (See #296)

291 Cuisenier, Jean, M. Segalen, and M. de Virville, "Pour l'étude de la parenté dans la société européenne, le programme d'ordinateur, archives," *L'homme* 10:3 (1970), 27-74.

292 *Le droit des gens mariés (Mémoires de la Société pour l'histoire du droit et des institutions des anciens pays bourguignons, comtois, et romands)* 27 (1966).

293 Duby, Georges, *L'économie rurale et la vie des campagnes dans l'occident mediéval.* 2 v. Paris, 1962. English translation, London and Columbia, S.C., 1968.

294 Esmein, Adhémer, *Le mariage en droit canonique.* 2 v. Paris, 1891. Reprint, New York, 1968.

295 Eversley, D.E.C., "Population, Economy and Society," *Population in History*, ed. David V. Glass and D.E.C. Eversley (London, 1965), 23-69. (See #214)

296 *Family and Inheritance: Rural Society in Western Europe 1200-1800*, ed. Jack Goody, Joan Thirsk, and E. P. Thompson. Cambridge, England, 1976.

297 *The Family Life Cycle in European Societies (Le cycle de la vie familiale dans les sociétés européennes)*, ed. Jean Cuisenier and Martine Segalen. The Hague, 1977.

298 Flandrin, Jean-Louis, "L'attitude à l'égard du petit enfant et les conduites sexuelles dans la civilisation occidentale: structures anciennes et évolution," *Annales de démographie historique* (1973), 143-210.

299 Flandrin, Jean-Louis, "La cellule familiale et l'oeuvre de procréation dans l'ancienne société," *XVIIe siècle* 102-103 (1974), 3-14.

300 Flandrin, Jean-Louis, "Contraception, mariage et relations amoureuses dans l'Occident chrétien," *Annales E.S.C.* 24 (1969), 1370-1390. English translation in *Biology of Man...*, ed. Robert Forster and Orest Ranum (Baltimore, 1975), 23-47. (See #289)

301 Flandrin, Jean-Louis, *L'église et le contrôle des naissances.* Paris, 1970.

302 Flandrin, Jean-Louis, *Familles: parenté, maison, sexualité dans l'ancienne société.* Paris, 1976.

303 Foucault, Michel, *Histoire de la sexualité.* v. 1. Paris, 1976.

304 Gaudemet, Jean, "Législation canonique et attitudes séculières a l'égard du lien matrimonial au XVIIe siècle," *XVIIe siècle* 102-103 (1974), 15-30.

305 Genestal, Robert, *Histoire de la légitimation des enfants naturels en droit canonique.* Paris, 1905.

306 Gilles, Henri, "Mariages de princes et dispenses pontificales," *Mélanges Louis Falletti...* (Lyon, 1971), 295-308. (See #1231)

307 Hajnal, John, "Age at Marriage and Proportions Marrying," *Population Studies* 7 (1953-54), 111-136.

308 Hajnal, John, "European Marriage Patterns in Perspective," *Population in History*, ed. David V. Glass and D.E.C. Eversley (London, 1965), 101-143. (See #214)

309 Kühn, Joachim, *Ehen zur linken Hand in der europäischer Geschichte.* Stuttgart, 1968.

310 Lavergne, Bernard, "Le mystère des oscillations de la natalité en France et

dans les pays occidentaux," *Année politique et économique* 44 (1971), 435-443.

311 Melia, E., "Le lien matrimonial à la lumière de la théologie sacramentaire et de la théologie morale de l'Eglise orthodoxe," *Revue de droit canonique* 21 (1971), 180-197.

312 Mols, Roger, *Introduction à la démographie historique des villes d'Europe du XIVe au XVIIIe siècle.* 3 v. Gembloux, 1954-56.

313 Ortigues, Edmond, "La psychanalyse et les institutions familiales," *Annales E.S.C.* 27 (1972), 1091-1104.

314 Phillpotts, Bertha Surtees, *Kindred and Clan in the Middle Ages and After: A Study in the Sociology of the Teutonic Races.* Cambridge, 1913.

315 Piers, M. W., "Kindermord: Ein historischer Rückblick," *Psyche* 30 (1976), 418-435.

316 *Popular Attitudes toward Birth Control in Pre-Industrial France and England,* ed. Orest and Patricia Ranum. New York, 1972.

317 Riquet, Michel, "Point de vue d'historien et de théologien catholique," *Prévention des naissances...*, ed. Hélène Bergues (Paris, 1960), 329-340. (See #215)

318 Rosambert, André, *La Veuve en droit canonique.* Paris, 1923.

319 Sauvy, Alfred, "Essai d'une vue d'ensemble," *Prévention des naissances...*, ed. Hélène Bergues (Paris, 1960), 377-391. (See #215)

320 Wheaton, Robert, "Family and Kinship in Western Europe: The Problem of the Joint Family Household," *Journal of Interdisciplinary History* 5 (1974-75), 601-628.

ANCIENT AND MEDIEVAL PERIODS (TO c.1500)

321 Amundsen, Darrel W., and Carol J. Diers, "The Age of Menarche in Medieval Europe," *Human Biology* 45 (1973), 363-369.

322 Amundsen, Darrel W., and Carol J. Diers, "The Age of Menopause in Medieval Europe," *Human Biology* 45 (1973), 605-612.

323 Bardis, Panos D., "Early Christianity and the Family," *Sociological Bulletin* 13 (1964), 1-23.

324 Biraben, Jean-Noël, "La médecine et l'enfant au Moyen Age," *Annales de démographie historique* (1973), 73-75.

325 Brundage, James A., "Concubinage and Marriage in Medieval Canon Law," *Journal of Medieval History* 1 (1975), 1-17.

326 Bullough, Vern L., "Medieval Medical and Scientific Views of Women," *Viator* 4 (1973), 485-501.

327 Dauvillier, Jean, *Le mariage en droit classique de l'église, dupuis le Décret de Gratien (1140) jusqu'à la mort de Clément V (1314).* Paris, 1933.

328 Donaldson, E. Talbot, "The Myth of Courtly Love," *Ventures* 5 (1965), 16-23.

329 Duby, Georges, "The Diffusion of Cultural Patterns in Feudal Society," *Past and Present* 39 (1968), 3-10.

330 Duby, Georges, "Structures familiales dans le Moyen Age occidental," *XIIIe Congrès International des Sciences Historiques 16-23 août, 1970* 1:4 (1973), 152-161.

331 Etienne, Robert, "La conscience médicale antique et la vie des enfants," *Annales de démographie historique* (1973), 15-46.

332 Fransen, Gérard, "La formation du lien matrimonial au Moyen Age," *Revue de droit canonique* 21 (1971), 106-126.

333 Garnier, F., "L'iconographie de l'enfant au Moyen Age," *Annales de démographie historique* (1973), 135-136.

334 Gaudemet, Jean, "Le lien matrimonial: les incertitudes du haut Moyen Age," *Revue de droit canonique* 21 (1971), 81-105.

335 Gimpel, Jean, "Population and Environment in the Middle Ages," *Environment and Change* 2 (1973), 233-242.

336 Goodich, Michael, "Childhood and Adolescence Among the Thirteenth-Century Saints," *History of Childhood Quarterly* 1 (1973-74), 285-309.

337 Heaney, Seamus P., *The Development of the Sacramentality of Marriage from Anselm of Laon to Thomas Aquinas.* Washington, D.C., 1963.

338 Heers, Jacques, "Les limites des méthodes statistiques pour les recherches de démographie médiévale," *Annales de démographie historique* (1968), 43-72.

339 Heers, Jacques, *Le clan familial au Moyen Age: étude sur les structures politiques et sociales des milieux urbains.* Paris, 1974.

340 Helleiner, Karl F., "Population Movement and Agrarian Depression in the Later Middle Ages," *Canadian Journal of Economics and Political Science* 15 (1949), 368-377.

341 Herlihy, David, "Life Expectancies for Women in Medieval Society," *Role of Woman in the Middle Ages*, ed. Rosemarie Thee Morewedge (Albany, 1975), 1-22.

342 Herlihy, David, "Land, Family and Women in Continental Europe, 701-1200," *Traditio* 18 (1962), 89-120. Also in *Women in Medieval Society*, ed. Susan Mosher Stuard (Philadelphia, 1976), 13-45. (See #369)

343 Howarth, W. D., "Droit du Seigneur: Fact or Fantasy?" *Journal of European Studies* 1 (1971), 291-312.

344 Hughes, Diane Owen, "Toward Historical Ethnography: Notarial Records and Family History in the Middle Ages," *Historical Methods Newsletter* 7 (1973-74), 61-71.

345 Kaufman, Michael W., "Spare Ribs: The Conception of Women in the Middle Ages and Renaissance," *Soundings* 56 (1973), 139-163.

346 Lawy, S., "The Extent of Jewish Polygamy in Talmudic Times," *Journal of Jewish Studies* 9 (1958), 115-138.

347 LeBras, Gabriel, "Le mariage dans la théologie et le droit de l'Eglise du XIe au XIIIe siècle," *Cahiers de civilisation médiévale* 11 (1968), 191-202.

348 LeGoff, Jacques, "Petits enfants dans la littérature des XIIe-XIIIe siècles," *Annales de démographie historique* (1973), 129-132.

349 Lyman, Richard B., Jr., "Barbarism and Religion: Late Roman and Early Medieval Childhood," *The History of Childhood*, ed. Lloyd DeMause (New York, 1974), 75-100. (See #154)

350 McLaughlin, Mary Martin, "Survivors and Surrogates: Children and Parents from the Ninth to the Thirteenth Centuries," *The History of Childhood*, ed. Lloyd DeMause (New York, 1974), 101-182. (See #154)

351 McNamara, Jo Anne, and Suzanne Wemple, "The Power of Women Through the Family in Medieval Europe: 500-1100," *Clio's Consciousness Raised*, ed. Mary Hartman and Lois Banner (New York, 1974), 103-118.

352 *The Meaning of Courtly Love*, ed. F. X. Newman. Albany, 1969.

353 Moller, Herbert, "The Meaning of Courtly Love," *Journal of American Folklore* 73 (1960), 39-52.

354 Moller, Herbert, "The Social Causation of the Courtly Love Complex," *Comparative Studies in Society and History* 1 (1958-59), 137-163. Now in *Sociology and History: Theory and Research*, ed. Werner Cahnman and Alvin Boskoff (New York, 1964), 484-503.

355 Noonan, John T., "Power to Choose," *Viator* 4 (1973), 419-434.

356 Parmisano, Fabian, "Love and Marriage in the Middle Ages," *New Blackfriars* 50 (1969), 599-608, 649-660.

357 Post, J. B., "Ages at Menarche and Menopause: Some Medieval Authorities," *Population Studies* 25 (1971), 83-87.

358 Riché, Pierre, "Problèmes de démographie historique du Haut Moyen Age (Ve-VIIIe siècles)," *Annales de démographie historique* (1966), 37-55.

359 Riché, Pierre, "L'enfant dans le Haut Moyen Age," *Annales de démographie historique* (1973), 95-98.

360 Ritzer, Korbinian, *Formen, Riten und religiöses Brauchtum der Eheschliessung in den christlichen Kirchen des ersten Jahrtausends*. Münster, 1962.

361 Rosenthal, Joel T., "Marriage and the Blood Feud in 'Heroic' Europe," *British Journal of Sociology* 17 (1966), 133-144.

362 Russell, Josiah Cox, "Aspects démographiques des débuts de la féodalité," *Annales E.S.C.* 20 (1965), 1118-1127.

363 Russell, Josiah Cox, "Demographic Pattern in History," *Demographic Analysis: Selected Readings*, ed. Joseph J. Spengler and Otis Dudley Duncan (Glencoe, Ill., 1956), 52-68.

364 Russell, Josiah Cox, "The Ecclesiastical Age: A Demographic Interpretation of the Period A.D. 200-900," *Review of Religion* 5 (1941), 137-147.

365 Russell, Josiah Cox, *Late Ancient and Medieval Population*. Philadelphia, 1958.

366 Russell, Josiah Cox, "Late Medieval Population Patterns," *Speculum* 20 (1945), 157-171.

367 Smith, Charles E., *Papal Enforcement of Some Medieval Marriage Laws*.

Reprint, Port Washington, New York, 1972. Originally 1940.

368 Thurston, H., "Mediaeval Matrimony," *Dublin Review* 171 (1922), 44-57.

369 *Women in Medieval Society*, ed. Susan Mosher Stuard. Philadelphia, 1976.

EARLY MODERN PERIOD (c.1500–c.1800)

370 Bardet, Jean-Pierre, "La démographie des villes de la modernité (XVIe–XVIIIe siècles): mythes et réalités," *Annales de démographie historiques* (1974), 101-126.

371 Berkner, Lutz K., "Rural Family Organization in Europe: A Problem in Comparative History," *Peasant Studies Newsletter* 1 (1972), 145-156. (See #399)

372 Burguière, André, "De Malthus à Max Weber: le mariage tardif et l'esprit d'entreprise," *Annales E.S.C.* 27 (1972), 1128-1138. English translation in *Family and Society*, ed. Robert Forster and Orest Ranum (Baltimore, 1976), 237-250.

373 Bastelo García del Real, Francisco, "Economía y población en las sociedades preindustriales: al siglo XVIII europeo," *Estudios Geograficos* 35 (1974), 25-51.

374 Cohen, Joel, "Childhood Mortality, Family Size, and Birth Order in Pre-Industrial Europe," *Demography* 12 (1975), 35-55.

375 Depoid, Pierre, *Reproduction nette en Europe depuis l'origine des statistiques de l'état civil*. Paris, 1941.

376 Drake, Michael, "Age at Marriage in the Pre-Industrial West," *Population Growth and the Brain Drain*, ed. Frank Bechhofer (Edinburgh, 1969), 196-207.

377 Flandrin, Jean-Louis, "Mariage tardif et vie sexuelle: Discussions et hypothèses de recherche," *Annales E.S.C.* 27 (1972), 1351-1378.

378 Flinn, M. W., "The Stabilisation of Mobility in Preindustrial Western Europe," *Journal of European Economic History* 3 (1974), 285-318.

379 Friedlander, Dov, "Demographic Responses and Population Change," *Demography* 6 (1969), 359-381.

380 Gille, H., "The Demographic History of the Northern European Countries in the Eighteenth Century," *Population Studies* 3 (1949-50), 3-65.

381 Habakkuk, H. J., *Population Growth and Economic Development Since 1750*. Leicester, 1971.

382 Haffter, Carl, "The Changeling: History and Psychodynamics of Attitudes to Handicapped Children in European Folklore," *Journal of the History of the Behavioral Sciences* 4 (1968), 55-61.

383 Heer, David M., "Economic Development and the Fertility Transition," *Population and Social Change*, ed. David V. Glass and Roger Revelle (New York and London, 1972), 99-113.

384 Helleiner, Karl F., "The Vital Revolution Reconsidered," *Population in History*, ed. David V. Glass and D.E.C. Eversley (London, 1965), 79-86. (See #214)

385 Hornstein, Walter, *Jugend in ihrer Zeit: Geschichte und Lebensformen des jungen Menschen in der europäischen Welt*. Hamburg, 1966.

386 Houdaille, Jacques, "Fécondité des familles souveraines du XVIᵉ au XVIIIᵉ siècle, influence de l'âge du père sur la fécondité," *Population* 31 (1976), 961-970.

387 Katz, Jacob, "Family, Kinship and Marriage Among Ashkenazim in the Sixteenth to Eighteenth Centuries," *Jewish Journal of Sociology* 1 (1959), 3-22.

388 Krause, John T., "Some Aspects of Population Change, 1690-1790," *Land, Labour and Population in the Industrial Revolution*, ed. Eric L. Jones and G. E. Mingay (London, 1967), 187-205.

389 Langer, William L., "Checks on Population Growth: 1750-1850," *Scientific American* 226:2 (1972), 93-99.

390 Langer, William L., "Europe's Initial Population Explosion," *American Historical Review* 69 (1963-64), 1-17.

391 Langer, William L., "Further Notes on the History of Infanticide," *History of Childhood Quarterly* 2 (1974-75), 129-134.

392 Langer, William L., "Infanticide: A Historical Survey," *History of Childhood Quarterly* 1 (1973-74), 353-365.

393 Laslett, Peter, "Age at Menarche in Europe Since the Eighteenth Century," *The Family in History*, ed. Theodore K. Rabb and Robert I. Rotberg (New York, 1973), 28-47. (See #80)

394 Lorence, Bogna W., "Parents and Children in Eighteenth Century Europe," *History of Childhood Quarterly* 2 (1974-75), 1-30.

395 Malkin, H. J., "Observations on Social Conditions, Fertility and Family Survival in the Past," *Proceedings of the Royal Society of Medicine* 53 (1960), 117-132.

396 McArdle, Frank, "Another Look at 'Peasant Families East and West,'" *Peasant Studies Newsletter* 3 (1974), 11-14. (See #371)

397 Morineau, Michael, "Démographie ancienne: monotonie ou variété des comportments?" *Annales E.S.C.* 20 (1965), 1185-1197.

398 Peller, Sigismund, "Births and Deaths Among Europe's Ruling Families Since 1500," *Population in History*, ed. David V. Glass and D.E.C. Eversley (London, 1965), 87-100.

399 Plakans, Andrejs, "Peasant Families East and West: A Comment on Lutz K. Berkner's 'Rural Family Organization in Europe: A Problem in Comparative History,'" *Peasant Studies Newsletter* 2 (1973), 11-16. (See #371)

400 *Population Movements in Modern European History*, ed. Herbert Moller. London, 1964.

401 Sabean, David, "Aspects of Kinship Behaviour and Property in Rural Western Europe before 1800," *Family and Inheritance*, ed. Jack Goody, Joan

Thirsk, and E. P. Thompson (Cambridge, England, 1976), 96-111. (See #296)

402 Schofield, Roger S., "The Relationship between Demographic Structure and Environment in Pre-industrial Western Europe," *Sozialgeschichte der Famile...*, ed. Werner Conze (Stuttgart, 1976), 147-160. (See #450)

403 Solé, Jacques, *L'amour en Occident a l'époque moderne.* Paris, 1976.

404 Spengler, Joseph J., "Demographic Factors and Early Modern Economic Development," *Population and Social Change*, ed. David V. Glass and Roger Revelle (London and New York, 1972), 87-98.

405 Thirsk, Joan, "The European Debate on Customs of Inheritance, 1500-1700," *Family and Inheritance*, ed. Jack Goody, Joan Thirsk, and E. P. Thompson (Cambridge, England, 1976), 177-191. (See #296)

406 Utterström, Gustav, "Climatic Fluctuations and Population Problems in Early Modern History," *Scandinavian Economic History Review* 3 (1955), 3-47.

407 van de Walle, Etienne, and Francine van de Walle, "Allaitement, stérilité et contraception: les opinions jusqu'au XIXe siècle," *Population* 27 (1972), 685-701.

408 Wikman, Karl Robert Villehad, *Die Einleitung der Ehe: Eine vergleichend ethno-soziologische Untersuchung über die Vorstufe der Ehe in den Sitten des schwedischen Volkstums.* Åbo, 1937.

MODERN PERIOD (c.1800 TO THE PRESENT)

409 Andorka, R., "Peasant Family Structure in the Eighteenth and Nineteenth Centuries," *Ethnographica* 86 (1975), 341-365.

410 Armengaud, André, "L'attitude de la société à l'égard de l'enfant au XIXe siècle," *Annales de démographie historique* (1973), 303-312.

411 Backman, Gaston, "Die Beschleunigte Entwicklung der Jugend," *Acta Anatomica* 4 (1947-48), 421-480.

412 Battara, Pietro, "Le curve della natalità nei paesi agricoli ed industriali," *Rivista de Economia Corporativa e di Scienze Sociali* 15 (1935), 409-438.

413 Campbell, Arthur A., "Beyond the Demographic Transition," *Demography* 11 (1974), 549-561.

414 Carlsson, Gösta, "The Decline of Fertility: Innovation or Adjustment Process?" *Population Studies* 20 (1966), 149-174.

415 Carlsson, Gösta, "Nineteenth-Century Fertility Oscillations," *Population Studies* 24 (1970), 413-422.

416 Coale, Ansley J., "The Decline of Fertility in Europe from the French Revolution to World War II," *Fertility and Family Planning: A World View*, ed. Samuel J. Behrman et al. (Ann Arbor, Mich., 1969), 3-24.

417 Coale, Ansley J., "Factors Associated with the Development of Low Fertility: An Historic Summary," *Proceedings* of the [Second] World Population Conference [Belgrade, 1965] v. 2 (New York, 1966-67), 205-209.

418 Cox, P. R., "International Variations in the Relative Ages of Brides and Grooms," *Journal of Biosocial Science* 2 (1970), 111-121.

419 Daric, Jean, "Place de la famille dans les textes constitutionnels des états modernes," *Renouveau des idées sur la famille*, ed. Robert Prigent (Paris, 1954), 185-196.

420 Fischer, Wolfram, "Rural Industrialization and Population Change," *Comparative Studies in Society and History* 15 (1973), 158-170.

421 Gerhartz, J. G., "L'indissolubilité du mariage et la dissolution du mariage dans la problématique actuelle," *Revue de droit canonique* 21 (1971), 198-234.

422 Gillis, John R., *Youth and History: Tradition and Change in European Age Relations, 1770-Present.* New York, 1974.

423 Glass, David V., "Family Limitation in Europe: A Survey of Recent Studies," *Research in Family Planning*, ed. Clyde V. Kiser (Princeton, 1962), 231-262.

424 Glass, David V., "Fertility Trends in Europe Since the Second World War," *Fertility and Family Planning: A World View*, ed. Samuel Behrman et al. (Ann Arbor, Mich., 1969), 25-74.

425 Glass, David V., *Population Policies and Movements in Europe.* London, 1940. Reprint, New York, 1967.

426 Habakkuk, H. J., "Family Structure and Economic Change in Nineteenth Century Europe," *Journal of Economic History* 15 (1955), 1-12.

427 Habakkuk, H. J., "Population Problems and European Economic Development in the Late Eighteenth and Nineteenth Centuries," *American Economic Review* 53 (1963), 607-618.

428 Hausen, Karin, "Die Polarisierung der 'Geschlechtscharaktere'—Eine Spiegelung der Dissoziation von Erwerbs- und Familienleben," *Sozialgeschichte der Familie...*, ed. Werner Conze (Stuttgart, 1976), 363-393. (See #450)

429 Knodel, John, and Hallie Kinter, "The Impact of Breast Feeding Patterns on the Biometric Analysis of Infant Mortality," *Demography* 14 (1977), 391-409.

430 Kuczynski, R. R., "The International Decline of Fertility," *Political Arithmetic*, ed. Lancelot Hogben (London, 1938), 47-72.

431 Kunzel, Renate, "The Connection Between the Family Cycle and Divorce Rates: An Analysis Based on European Data," *Journal of Marriage and the Family* 36 (1974), 379-388.

432 Laslett, Peter, "Familie und Industrialisierung," *Sozialgeschichte der Familie...*, ed. Werner Conze (Stuttgart, 1976), 13-31. (See #450)

433 Le Play, Frédéric, *Les ouvriers européens: études sur les traveaux, la vie domestique et la condition morale des populations ouvrières de l'Europe, précédées d'un exposé de la méthode d'observation.* 6 v. Paris, 1855-78.

434 Lestaeghe, L., "Le dossier de la transition démographique," *European Demographic Information Bulletin* 1 (1970), 218-229.

435 Linde, Hans, "Familie und Haushalt als Gegenstand bevölkerungsgeschichtlicher Forschung," *Sozialgeschichte der Familie...*, ed. Werner Conze (Stuttgart, 1976), 32-52. (See #450)

436 Maitron, Jean, "Les thèses révolutionnaires sur l'évolution de la famille du milieu du XIXe siècle à nos jours," *Renouveau des idées sur la famille*, ed. Robert Prigent (Paris, 1954), 131-148.

437 McKeowan, Thomas, R. G. Brown, and R. G. Record, "An Interpretation of the Modern Rise of Population in Europe," *Population Studies* 27 (1972), 345-383.

438 Medick, Hans, "Bevölkerungsentwicklung, Familienstruktur und Proto-Industrialisierung," *Sozialwissenschaftliche Informationen für Unterricht und Studium* 3 (1974), 33-38.

439 Medick, Hans, "The Proto-Industrial Family Economy: The Structural Function of Household and Family during the Transition from Peasant Society to Industrial Capitalism," *Social History* 3 (1976), 291-316. Also in German in *Sozialgeschichte der Familie...*, ed. Werner Conze (Stuttgart, 1976), 254-282. (See #450)

440 Michels, Robert, *Sittlichkeit in Ziffern? Kritik der Moralstatistik*. München and Leipzig, 1928.

441 Prigent, Robert, "Notion moderne du couple humain uni par le mariage," *Renouveau des idées sur la famille*, ed. Robert Prigent (Paris, 1954), 304-318.

442 Robertson, Priscilla, "Home as a Nest: Middle Class Childhood in Nineteenth-Century Europe," *The History of Childhood*, ed. Lloyd De Mause (New York, 1974), 407-431. (See #154)

443 Schomerus, Heilwig, "Sozialer Wandel und generatives Verhalten: Diskussionsbeitrag zur brauchenspezifischen Untersuchung generativen Verhaltens," *Sozialgeschichte der Familie...*, ed. Werner Conze (Stuttgart, 1976), 173-182. (See #450)

444 Scott, Joan W., and Louise A. Tilly, "Women's Work and the Family in Nineteenth-Century Europe," *Comparative Studies in Society and History* 17 (1975), 36-64.

445 Shorter, Edward, "Capitalism, Culture, and Sexuality: Some Competing Models," *Social Science Quarterly* 53 (1972), 338-356.

446 Shorter, Edward, John Knodel, and Etienne van de Walle, "The Decline of Non-Marital Fertility in Europe, 1880-1940," *Population Studies* 25 (1971), 375-393.

447 Shorter, Edward, "Female Emancipation, Birth Control, and Fertility in European History," *American Historical Review* 78 (1973), 605-640.

448 Shorter, Edward, "Illegitimacy, Sexual Revolution, and Social Change in Modern Europe," *Journal of Interdisciplinary History* 2 (1971-72), 237-272.

Also in *The Family in History*, ed. Theodore K. Rabb and Robert I. Rotberg (New York, 1973), 48–84. (See #80)

449 Shorter, Edward, "Sexual Change and Illegitimacy: The European Experience," *Modern European Social History*, ed. Robert Bezucha (Lexington, Mass., 1972), 231–269.

450 *Sozialgeschichte der Familie in der Neuzeit Europas*, ed. Werner Conze. Stuttgart, 1976.

451 Stengers, J., "Les pratiques anticonceptionnelles dans le mariage au XIXe siècle: problèmes humains et attitudes religieuses," *Revue belge de philologie et d'histoire* 49 (1971), 403–481, 1119–1174.

452 Sutter, Jean, "Fréquence de l'endogamie et ses facteurs au XIXe siècle," *Population* 23 (1968), 305–324.

453 Tanner, J. M., "The Trends towards Earlier Physical Maturation," *Biological Aspects of Social Problems*, ed. James E. Meade and Alan S. Parkes (Edinburgh and New York, 1965), 40–65.

454 Tilly, Louise A., and Joan W. Scott, *Women, Work, and Family*. New York, 1978.

455 Tilly, Louise A., Joan W. Scott, and Miriam Cohen, "Women's Work and European Fertility Patterns," *Journal of Interdisciplinary History* 6 (1975–76), 447–476.

456 van de Walle, Etienne, "Marriage and Marital Fertility," *Daedalus* 97 (1968), 486–501.

457 van de Walle, Etienne, "Problèmes de l'étude du déclin de la fécondité européene," *Recherches économiques de Louvain* 35 (1969), 271–287.

458 van de Walle, Etienne, and John Knodel, "Demographic Transition and Fertility Decline," *Contributed Papers*, Sydney Conference of the International Union for the Scientific Study of Population, 1967 (Canberra, Australia, 1967), 47–55.

Great Britain and Ireland

GENERAL SURVEYS AND COLLECTIONS

459 Barley, M. W., *The House and Home: A Review of 900 Years of House Planning and Furnishing in Britain.* New York, 1971.

460 Braun, Hugh, *The Story of the English House.* London, 1940.

461 Cleveland, Arthur Rackman, *Woman under the English Law from the Time of the Saxons to the Present Time.* London, 1896.

462 Clifton-Taylor, Alec, *The Pattern of English Building.* new ed.; London, 1972.

463 Cook, Olive, *The English House through Seven Centuries.* London, 1968.

464 Coveney, Peter, *The Image of Childhood: The Individual and Society: A Study of the Theme in English Literature.* Baltimore, 1967.

465 Cunnington, P., and A. Buck, *Children's Clothes in England.* New York, 1965.

466 Flinn, M. W., *An Economic and Social History of Britain, 1066–1939.* London, 1962.

467 Fraser, A., *A History of Toys.* London, 1972.

468 Gloag, John, *The Englishman's Castle, a History of Houses, Large and Small, in Town and Country, from A.D. 100 to the Present Day.* London, 1945.

469 Gloag, John, and Walker Thompson, *Home Life in History: Social Life and Manners in Britain, 200 B.C.–A.D. 1926.* New York, 1928.

470 Hardwick, Elizabeth, *Seduction and Betrayal: Women in Literature.* London, 1974.

471 Harrison, Molly, *The Kitchen in History.* New York, 1973.

472 Henderson, A., *The Family House in England.* London, 1964.

473 Hill, Georgiana, *Women in English Life from Medieval to Modern Times.* 2 v. London, 1896.

474 Hoskins, William George, *Provincial England: Essays in Social and Economic History.* London, 1964.

475   *Images of Women in Fiction: Feminist Perspectives*, ed. Susan Koppelman. Bowling Green, 1972.

476   *An Introduction to English Historical Demography*, ed. Peter Laslett, D.E.C. Eversley, and W. A. Armstrong. London, 1966.

477   Kamm, Josephine, *Hope Deferred: Girls' Education in English History*. London, 1965.

478   Kenny, Courtney Stanhope, *The History of the Law of England as to the Effects of Marriage on Property and on the Wife's Legal Capacity*. London, 1879.

479   Laslett, Peter, *Family Life and Illicit Love in Earlier Generations*. Cambridge, England, 1977.

480   Lloyd, Nathaniel A., *A History of the English House from Primitive Times to the Victorian Period*. London, 1931.

481   Marshall, Dorothy, *The English Domestic Servant in History*. London, 1949.

482   Ohlin, G., "Mortality, Marriage and Growth in Pre-Industrial Populations," *Population Studies* 14 (1960), 190–197.

483   O'Mattey, I., *Women in Subjection: A Study of the Lives of English Women before 1832*. London, 1933.

484   *Perspectives in English Urban History*, ed. Alan M. Everitt. New York, 1973.

485   Phillips, M., and W. S. Tomkinson, *English Women in Life and Letters*. Oxford, 1926.

486   Stenton, Doris, *The English Woman in History*. London, 1957.

487   *Studies in Building History*, ed. E. M. Jope. London, 1961.

488   Thirsk, Joan, "The Family," *Past and Present* 23 (1964), 116–122.

489   Wrigley, E. Anthony, "Family Reconstitution," *An Introduction to English Historical Demography*, ed. Peter Laslett, D.E.C. Eversley, and W.A. Armstrong (London, 1931), 96–159. (See #476)

490   Yarwood, D., *The English Home*. London, 1956.

491   Rennie, James A., *The Scottish People. Their Clans, Families and Origins*. London, 1960.

BIBLIOGRAPHIES, REVIEW ESSAYS, AND METHODOLOGICAL ARTICLES

492   Brown, W. Newman, "Wider Reconstitution," *Local Population Studies* 7 (1971), 44–56.

493   Chaloner, W. H., and R. C. Richardson, *British Economic and Social History: A Bibliographical Guide*. Manchester, 1976.

494   Cox, J. C., *The Parish Registers of England*. London, 1910.

495   Duffy, K. S., "An Approach to Parish Register and Census Work," *Local Population Studies* 5 (1970), 44–52.

496 Johnston, J. A., "Family Reconstitution and the Local Historian," *The Local Historian* 9 (1970), 9–15.

497 Lancaster, Lorraine, "Some Conceptual Problems in the Study of the Family and Kin in the British Isles," *British Journal of Sociology* 12 (1961), 317–333.

498 Levine, David, "The Reliability of Parochial Registration and the Representativeness of Family Reconstruction," *Population Studies* 30 (1976), 107–122.

499 McGregor, O. R., "The Social Position of Women in England 1850–1914: A Bibliography," *British Journal of Sociology* 6 (1955), 48–59.

500 McGregor, O. R., "Some Research Possibilities and Historical Materials for Family and Kinship Study in Britain," *British Journal of Sociology* 12 (1961), 310–317.

501 O'Brien, Jo, "Writing Women Back into English History," *International Socialist Review* 32 (1971), 19–22.

502 Pryce, W.T.R., "Parish Registers and Visitation Returns as Primary Sources for the Population Geography of the Eighteenth Century," *Transactions of the Honourable Society of Cymmrodorion* (1971), 271–293.

503 Schofield, Roger S., "The Representativeness of Family Reconstitution," *Local Population Studies* 8 (1972), 13–17.

504 Smith, Valerie, "The Analysis of Census-Type Documents," *Local Population Studies* 2 (1969), 12–24.

505 Steel, D. J., *National Index of Parish Registers.* v. 1: *Sources of Births, Marriages and Deaths before 1837.* London, 1968.

506 Stephens, William Brewer, *Sources for the History of Population and Their Uses.* Manchester, 1973.

507 Teitelbaum, M. S., "Birth Under-Registration in the Constituent Counties of England and Wales: 1841–1910," *Population Studies* 28 (1974), 329–343.

508 Thirsk, Joan, *Sources of Information on Population 1500–1760 and Unexplored Sources in Local Records.* Canterbury, 1965.

509 Thomas, Keith, "The History of the Family," *Times Literary Supplement* 3: 943 (1977), 1226–1227.

510 Tillott, P. M., "An Approach to Census Returns," *Local Population Studies* 2 (1969), 25–28.

511 Tillott, P. M., "The Analysis of Census Returns," *The Local Historian* 8 (1968), 2–10.

512 Tillott, P. M., "Sources of Inaccuracy in the 1851 and 1861 Censuses: Appendices 1 and 2," *Nineteenth-Century Society*, ed. E. A. Wrigley (Cambridge, 1972), 82–133.

513 Turner, Derek, "The Effective Family," *Local Population Studies* 2 (1969), 47–52.

ANCIENT AND MEDIEVAL PERIODS
(TO 1500)

514 Addyman, P. V., "The Anglo-Saxon House: A New Review," *Anglo-Saxon England* 1 (1972), 273–308.

515 Alcock, N. W., "The Medieval Cottages of Bishops Clyst, Devon," *Medieval Archaeology* 9 (1965), 146–149.

516 Altschul, M., *A Baronial Family in Medieval England: The Clares, 1217–1314.* Baltimore, 1965.

517 "The Anglo-Saxon Family Law," *Essays in Anglo-Saxon Law* (Boston, 1976), 121–182.

518 Arnold, Ralph, *A Social History of England 55 B.C. to A.D. 1215.* London, 1967.

519 Baker, A.R.H., "Open Fields and Partible Inheritance on a Kent Manor," *Economic History Review* 2nd series 17 (1964–65), 1–23.

520 Bandel, Betty, "The English Chronicler's Attitude Toward Women," *Journal of the History of Ideas* 16 (1955), 113–118.

521 Bennett, M. J., "A County Community: Social Cohesion amongst the Cheshire Gentry 1400–1425," *Northern History* 8 (1973), 24–44.

522 Binchy, Daniel, "The Legal Capacity of Women in Regard to Contracts," *Essays in Early Irish Law,* ed. Nancy P. Thurneysen et al. (London, 1936), 207–234. (See #615)

523 Birley, Anthony R., *Life in Roman Britain.* New York, 1964.

524 Britton, Edward, *The Community of the Vill: A Study in the History of the Family and Village Life in Fourteenth-Century England.* Toronto, 1977.

525 Britton, Edward, "The Peasant Family in Fourteenth-Century England," *Peasant Studies* 5 (1976), 2–7.

526 Buck, J. T., "Pre-Feudal Women," *Journal of the Rutgers University Library* 34 (1971), 46–51.

527 Buckstaff, Florence, "Married Woman's Property in Anglo-Saxon and Anglo-Norman Law and Origin of the Common Law Power," *Annals of the American Academy of Political and Social Science* 4 (1894), 233–264.

528 Chadwick, N. K., "Pictish and Celtic Marriage in Early Literary Tradition," *Scottish Gaelic Studies* 8 (1958), 56–155.

529 Charles-Edwards, T. M., "Kinship, Status, and the Origins of the Hide," *Past and Present* 56 (1972), 3–33.

530 Charles-Edwards, T. M., "Some Celtic Kinship Terms," *Bulletin of the Board of Celtic Studies* 24 (1970–72), 107–111.

531 Collis, Louise, *The Memoirs of a Medieval Woman: The Life and Times of Margery Kempe.* New York, 1964.

532 Darton, F.J.H., *Children's Books in England: Five Centuries of Social Life.* Cambridge, England, 1956.

533 DeWindt, E., *Land and People in Holywell-Cum-Needingworth*. Toronto, 1975.

534 Dillon, Miles, "The Relationship of Mother and Son, of Father and Daughter, and the Law of Inheritance with Regard to Women," *Essays in Early Irish Law,* ed. Nancy P. Thurneysen et al. (London, 1936), 129–186. (See #615)

535 Dodwell, Barbara, "Holdings and Inheritance in Medieval East Anglia," *Economic History Review* 2nd series 20 (1967), 53–66.

536 Engdahl, David E., "Medieval Metaphysics and English Marriage Laws," *Journal of Family Law* 8 (1968), 381–397.

537 Faith, Rosamond, "Peasant Families and Inheritance Customs in Medieval England," *Agricultural History Review* 14 (1966), 77–95.

538 Faulkner, P. A., "Domestic Planning from the Twelfth to the Fourteenth Century," *Archaeological Journal* 115 (1958), 150–183.

539 Field, R. K., "Worcestershire Peasant Buildings, Household Goods and Farming Equipment in the Later Middle Ages," *Medieval Archaeology* 9 (1965), 105–145.

540 Fox, C. F., *Monmouthshire Houses: A Study of Building Techniques and Smaller House-Plans in the Fifteenth to Seventeenth Centuries.* Cardiff, 1954.

541 François, Martha Ellis, "Adults and Children: Against Evil or against Each Other," *History of Childhood Quarterly* 1 (1973–74), 164–177.

542 Gransden, A., "Childhood and Youth in Medieval England," *Nottingham Medieval Studies* 16 (1972), 3–19.

543 Hallam, Herbert Enoch, *Settlement and Society: A Study of the Early Agrarian History of South Lincolnshire.* London, 1965.

544 Hallam, Herbert Enoch, "Some Thirteenth-Century Censuses," *Economic History Review* 2nd series 10 (1957–58), 340–361.

545 Hanawalt, Barbara A., "Childrearing among the Lower Classes of Late Medieval England," *Journal of Interdisciplinary History* 8 (1977–78), 1–22.

546 Haskell, Anne S., "The Paston Women on Marriage in Fifteenth-Century England," *Viator* 4 (1973), 459–471.

547 Helmholz, R. H., "Infanticide in the Province of Canterbury during the Fifteenth Century," *History of Childhood Quarterly* 2 (1974–75), 379–390.

548 Helmholz, R. H., *Marriage Litigation in Medieval England.* New York, 1975.

549 Hilton, R. H., *The English Peasantry in the Later Middle Ages.* Oxford, 1975.

550 Holms, D. T., *Daily Living in the Twelfth Century.* Madison, Wis., 1962.

551 Holmes, G. A., *The Estates of the Higher Nobility in Fourteenth Century England.* Cambridge, England, 1957.

552 Homans, George C., *English Villagers of the Thirteenth Century.* 2nd ed.; London, 1970.

553 Homans, George C., "Partible Inheritance of Villagers' Holdings," *Economic History Review* 8 (1937–38), 48–56.

554 Howell, Cicely, "Stability and Change, 1300–1700: The Socio-Economic Con-

text of the Self-Perpetuating Family Farm in England," *Journal of Peasant Studies* 2 (1974-75), 468-482.

555 Howell, Cicely, "Peasant Inheritance Customs in the Midlands, 1280-1700," *Family and Inheritance*, ed. Jack Goody, Joan Thirsk, and E. P. Thompson (Cambridge, England, 1976), 112-155. (See #296)

556 Jack, R. I., "Entail and Descent: The Hastings Inheritance, 1370 to 1436," *Bulletin of the Institute of Historical Research* 38 (1965), 1-19.

557 Kellum, Barbara A., "Infanticide in England in the Later Middle Ages," *History of Childhood Quarterly* 1 (1973-74), 367-388.

558 Kelly, Henry Ansgar, "Clandestine Marriage and Chaucer's Troilus," *Viator* 4 (1973), 435-458.

559 Kendall, Paul Murray, *The Yorkist Age: Daily Life during the Wars of the Roses*. New York, 1962.

560 Krause, John T., "The Medieval Household, Large or Small?" *Economic History Review* 2nd series 9 (1956-57), 420-432.

561 Labarge, Margaret W., *A Baronial Household of the Thirteenth Century*. New York, 1965.

562 Laithwaite, Michael, "The Buildings of Burford: A Cotswold Town in the Fourteenth to Nineteenth Centuries," *Perspectives in English Urban History*, ed. Alan M. Everitt (New York, 1973), 60-90. (See #484)

563 Lancaster, Lorraine, "Kinship in Anglo-Saxon Society," *British Journal of Sociology* 9 (1958), 230-250, 359-377.

564 Lander, J. R., "Marriage and Politics in the Fifteenth Century: The Nevilles and the Wydevilles," *Bulletin of the Institute of Historical Research* 36 (1963), 119-152.

565 Loyn, H. R., "Kinship in Anglo-Saxon England," *Anglo-Saxon England* 3 (1974), 197-210.

566 McFarlane, Kenneth B., *The Nobility of Later Medieval England*. Oxford, 1973.

567 Maitland, Frederic William, "The Laws of Wales, the Kindred and the Blood Feud," *Collected Papers*. v. 1 (Cambridge, England, 1911), 202-229.

568 Mathew, Gervase, "Marriage and *Amour courtois* in Late Fourteenth-Century England," *Essays Presented to Charles Williams* (Oxford, 1947), 128-135.

569 Miles, A.E.S., "Assessment of the Ages of a Population of Anglo-Saxons from Their Dentition," *Proceedings of the Royal Society of Medicine* 55 (1962), 881-886.

570 Naughton, K. S., *The Gentry of Bedfordshire in the Thirteenth and Fourteenth Centuries*. Leicester, 1976.

571 Painter, Sidney, "The Family and the Feudal System in Twelfth-Century England," *Speculum* 25 (1960), 1-16.

572 Pantin, W. A., "Medieval English Town House Plans," *Medieval Archaeology* 6-7 (1962-63), 209-239.

573 Pantin, W. A., "The Merchants' Houses and Warehouses of King's Lynn,"

Medieval Archaeology 6-7 (1962-63), 173-181.

574 Pantin, W. A., "Some Medieval English Town Houses," *Culture and Environment,* ed. Doris Llewelyn Foster and L. Alcock (London, 1963), 445-478.

575 Pitkin, Donald S., "Partible Inheritance and the Open Fields," *Agricultural History* 35 (1961), 65-69.

576 Platt, Colin, *The English Medieval Town.* London, 1976.

577 Portman, Derek, *Exeter Houses, 1400-1700.* Exeter, 1966.

578 Post, J. B., "Another Demographic Use of Inquisitions Post Mortem," *Journal of the Society of Archivists* 5 (1974), 110-114.

579 Raftis, John A., "Changes in an English Village after the Black Death," *Medieval Studies* 29 (1967), 158-177.

580 Raftis, John A., "Geographical Mobility in Lay Subsidy Rolls," *Medieval Studies* 38 (1976), 385-403.

581 Raftis, John A., "Social Structures of Five East Midland Villages: A Study in Possibilities in the Use of Court Roll Data," *Economic History Review* 2nd series 18 (1965), 83-100.

582 Raftis, John A., *Tenure and Mobility: Studies in the Social History of the Medieval English Village.* Toronto, 1964.

583 Rivers, Theodore John, "Widows' Rights in Anglo-Saxon Law," *American Journal of Legal History* 19 (1975), 208-215.

584 Roden, D., "Inheritance Customs and Succession to Land in the Chiltern Hills in the Thirteenth and Fourteenth Centuries," *Journal of British Studies* 7 (1967), 1-11.

585 *The Roman Villa in Britain*, ed. A.L.F. Rivet. New York, 1969.

586 Rosenthal, Joel T., "Mediaeval Longevity and the Secular Peerage, 1350-1500," *Population Studies* 27 (1973), 287-293.

587 Rosenthal, Joel T., *Nobles and Noble Life, 1295-1500.* London, 1976.

588 Russell, Josiah Cox, *British Mediaeval Population.* Albuquerque, 1948.

589 Russell, Josiah Cox, "Medieval Midland and Northern Migrants to London, 1100-1365," *Speculum* 34 (1959), 341-345.

590 Russell, Josiah Cox, "The Preplague Population of England," *Journal of British Studies* 5 (1966), 1-21.

591 Scammell, Jean, "Freedom and Marriage in Medieval England," *Economic History Review* 2nd series 27 (1974), 523-537.

592 Scammell, Jean, "Wife-Rents and Merchet," *Economic History Review* 2nd series 29 (1976), 487-490.

593 Searle, Eleanor, "Freedom and Marriage in Medieval England: An Alternative Hypothesis," *Economic History Review* 2nd series 29 (1976), 482-486.

594 Sheehan, Michael M., "The Formation and Stability of Marriage in Fourteenth-Century England: Evidence of an Ely Register," *Mediaeval Studies* 33 (1971), 228-263.

595 Sheehan, Michael M., "The Influence of Canon Law on the Property Rights of Married Women in England," *Mediaeval Studies* 25 (1963), 109-124.

596 Sheehan, Michael M., "Marriage and Family in English Conciliar and Synodal Legislation," *Essays in Honor of Anton Charles Pegis,* ed. Reginald O'Donnell (Toronto, 1974), 205-214.

597 Sheehan, Michael M., *The Will in Medieval England: From the Conversion of the Anglo-Saxons to the End of the Thirteenth Century.* Toronto, 1963.

598 *A Small Household of the Fifteenth Century,* ed. K. L. Wood-Legh. Manchester, 1956.

599 Squibb, G. D., *Founder's Kin: Privilege and Pedigree.* Oxford, 1972.

600 Stenton, Frank M., "The Place of Women in Anglo-Saxon Society," *Transactions of the Royal Historical Society* 4th series 25 (1943), 1-113.

601 Stenton, Frank M., "The Place of Women in Anglo-Saxon Society," *Preparatory to Anglo-Saxon England,* ed. Frank M. Stenton (Oxford, 1970), 314-324.

602 Thompson, A. Hamilton, "The English House," *Social Life in Early England,* ed. Geoffrey Barraclough (London, 1960), 139-178.

603 Thrupp, John, *The Anglo-Saxon Home: A History of the Domestic Institutions and Customs of England from the Fifth to the Eleventh Century.* London, 1862.

604 Thrupp, Sylvia, *The Merchant Class of Medieval London 1300-1500.* 2nd ed.; Ann Arbor, 1962.

605 Thrupp, Sylvia, "The Problem of Replacement Rates in Late Medieval English Population," *Economic History Review* 2nd series 18 (1965), 101-119.

606 Titow, J. Z., *English Rural Society, 1200-1350.* London, 1969.

607 Titow, J. Z., "Some Evidence of the Thirteenth-Century Population Increase," *Economic History Review* 2nd series 14 (1961-62), 218-224.

608 Tucker, M. J., "The Child as Beginning and End: Fifteenth and Sixteenth Century English Childhood," *The History of Childhood,* ed. Lloyd De Mause (New York, 1974), 229-258. (See #154)

609 Walker, Sue Sheridan, "Widow and Ward: The Feudal Law of Child Custody in Medieval England," *Feminist Studies* 3 (1976), 104-116. Now in #369, 159-172.

610 Westman, Barbara H., "The Peasant Family and Crime in Fourteenth Century England," *Journal of British Studies* 13 (1974), 1-18.

611 Whitelock, D., *Anglo-Saxon Wills.* Cambridge, England, 1930.

612 Wood, Margaret E., *The English Mediaeval House.* London, 1965.

613 Wood, Margaret E., *Thirteenth-Century Domestic Architecture in England.* London, 1950.

614 Woods, William, *England in the Age of Chaucer.* New York, 1976.

615 Young, Ernst, "The Anglo-Saxon Family Law," *Essays in Anglo-Saxon Law,* ed. Henry Adams (Boston, 1876), 121-182.

Ireland

616 *Essays in Early Irish Law*, ed. Nancy P. Thurneysen et al. London, 1936.

617 Mulchrone, Kathleen, "The Rights and Duties of Women with Regard to the Education of Their Children," ibid., 187–206.

618 Power, Nancy, "Classes of Women Described in the *Senchas Mar*," ibid., 81–108.

EARLY MODERN PERIOD
(1500–1750)

619 *The Agrarian History of England and Wales.* v. 4: *1500–1640*, ed. Joan Thirsk. Cambridge, England, 1967.

620 Airs, Malcolm, *The Making of the English Country House, 1500–1640.* Reprint, New York, 1976.

621 Alcock, N. W., "Devon Farm Houses," *The Devonshire Association. Report and Transactions* 100 (1968), 13–28; 101 (1969), 83–106.

622 Alleman, G. E., *Matrimonial Law and the Materials of Restoration Comedy.* Wallingford, Pa., 1942.

623 Allison, K. J., "An Elizabethan Village 'Census'," *Bulletin of the Institute of Historical Research* 36 (1963), 91–103.

624 Ashley, Maurice, "Love and Marriage in Seventeenth-Century England," *History Today* 8 (1958), 667–675.

625 Ashley, Maurice, *The Stuarts in Love, with Some Reflections on Love and Marriage in the Sixteenth and Seventeenth Centuries.* New York, 1964.

626 Ashmore, Owen, "Household Inventories of the Lancashire Gentry, 1550–1700, *Transactions of the Historical Society of Lancashire and Cheshire* 110 (1958), 59–105.

627 Aveling, Hugh Dom, "The Marriages of Catholic Recusants, 1559–1642," *Journal of Ecclesiastical History* 14 (1963), 68–83.

628 Barley, M. W., *The English Farmhouse and Cottage.* London, 1961.

629 Barley, M. W., "Farmhouses and Cottages, 1550–1725," *Economic History Review* 2nd series 7 (1954–55), 291–306.

630 Barley, M. W., "Rural Housing in England," *The Agrarian History of England...*, ed. Joan Thirsk (Cambridge, England, 1967), 696–766. (See #619)

631 Bayne-Powell, Rosamond, *Eighteenth Century London Life.* London, 1937.

632 Bayne-Powell, Rosamond, *The English Child in the Eighteenth Century.* London, 1939.

633 Bayne-Powell, Rosamond, *Housekeeping in the Eighteenth Century.* London, 1956.

634 Beattie, J. M., "The Criminality of Women in Eighteenth-Century England,"

Journal of Social History 8 (1974-75), 80-116.

635   Bedford, Jessie [= Elizabeth Godfrey], *English Children in the Olden Time.* London, 1907.

636   Bedford, Jessie [= Elizabeth Godfrey], *Home Life Under the Stuarts, 1603-1699.* London, 1903.

637   Berry, Boyd M., "The First English Pediatricians and Tudor Attitudes toward Childhood," *Journal of the History of Ideas* 35 (1974), 561-577.

638   Bingham, Caroline, "Seventeenth-Century Attitudes toward Deviant Sex," *Journal of Interdisciplinary History* 1 (1970-71), 447-472.

639   Blackman, Janet M., "Seventeenth Century Midland Midwifery—A Comment," *Local Population Studies* 9 (1972), 47-48.

640   Blackwood, B. G., "The Marriages of the Lancashire Gentry on the Eve of the English Civil War," *Genealogists Magazine* 16 (1970), 321-327.

641   Bradley, Leslie, "An Inquiry into Seasonality in Baptisms, Marriages and Burials. Part 1: Introduction. Methodology and Marriages," *Local Population Studies* 4 (1970), 21-40.

642   Bradley, Leslie, "An Inquiry into Seasonality in Baptisms, Marriages and Burials. Part 2. Baptism Seasonality," *Local Population Studies* 5 (1970), 18-35.

643   Bradley, Leslie, "An Inquiry into Seasonality in Baptisms, Marriages and Burials. Part 3. Burial Seasonality," *Local Population Studies* 6 (1971), 15-31.

644   Bradley, Rose M., *The English Housewife in the 17th and 18th Centuries.* London, 1912.

645   Braun, Hugh, *Old English Houses.* London, 1962.

646   Bridenbaugh, Carl, *Vexed and Troubled Englishmen.* New York, 1968.

647   Buckatzsch, E. F., "The Constancy of Local Populations and Migration in England before 1800," *Population Studies* 5 (1951), 62-69.

648   Buckatzsch, E. F., "Places of Origin of a Group of Immigrants into Sheffield 1624-1799," *Economic History Review* 2nd series 2 (1950), 303-306.

649   Burn, W. L., *The Age of Equipoise.* London, 1964.

650   Burton, Elizabeth, *The Elizabethans at Home.* London, 1958.

651   Burton, Elizabeth, *The Georgians at Home, 1714-1830.* London, 1967.

652   Burton, Elizabeth, *The Jacobeans at Home.* London, 1962.

653   Byrne, Muriel St. Clare, *Elizabethan Life in Town and Country.* 2nd ed.; London, 1961.

654   Camden, Caroll, *The Elizabethan Woman.* London, 1952.

655   Chalklin, C. W., *Seventeenth-Century Kent: A Social and Economic History.* London, 1965.

656   Chambers, Jonathan D., *Nottinghamshire in the Eighteenth Century.* 2nd ed.; London, 1966.

657   Chambers, Jonathan D., "Population Change in a Provincial Town, Nottingham 1700-1800," *Studies in the Industrial Revolution: Essays Presented to*

T. S. Ashton, ed. L. S. Pressnell (London, 1960), 97–124.

658   Chambers, Jonathan D., *Population Economy and Society in Preindustrial England.* Oxford, 1972.

659   Chambers, Jonathan D., "The Vale of Trent, 1670–1800. A Regional Study of Economic Change," *Economic History Review* Supplement 3 (1957).

660   Chapman, Richard A., "Leviathan Writ Small: Thomas Hobbes on the Family," *American Political Science Review* 69 (1975), 76–90.

661   Charles, F.W.B., and Kevin Down, "A Sixteenth Century Drawing of a Timber-Framed Town House," *Transactions of the Worcestershire Archaeological Society* 3 (1970–72), 67–79.

662   Chesher, V. M., and F. J. Chesher, *The Cornishman's House: An Introduction to the History of Traditional Domestic Architecture in Cornwall.* Truro, 1968.

663   Cheyney, E. P., "Some English Conditions Surrounding the Settlement of Virginia," *American Historical Review* 12 (1907), 507–528.

664   *Child Marriages, Divorces, and Ratifications in the Diocese of Chester, 1561–66,* ed. Frederick J. Furnivall. Millwood, 1973. Reprint of 1897 original.

665   Clark, Alice, *The Working Life of Women in the Seventeenth Century.* 2nd ed.; London, 1968.

666   Clark, Cumberland, *Shakespeare and Home Life.* London, 1935.

667   Clark, Peter, "The Migrant in Kentish Towns, 1580–1640," *Crisis and Order in English Towns, 1500–1700,* ed. Peter Clark and Paul Slack (London, 1972), 117–163.

668   Clay, C., "Marriage, Inheritance and the Rise of Large Estates in England, 1660–1815," *Economic History Review* 2nd series 21 (1968), 503–518.

669   Cliffe, J. T., *The Yorkshire Gentry 1540–1648.* London, 1969.

670   Coate, Mary, *Social Life in Stuart England.* London, 1924.

671   Collas, V. J., "Some Vale Houses and Families," *Transactions de la Société guernesiaise* 17 (1960), 60–69.

672   Cook, Olive, *English Cottages and Farmhouses.* London, 1954.

673   Cook, Olive, *The English Country House.* New York, 1974.

674   Cornwall, Julian, "Evidence of Population Mobility in the Seventeenth Century," *Bulletin of the Institute of Historical Research* 40 (1967), 143–152.

675   Coward, B., "Disputed Inheritances: Some Difficulties of the Nobility in the Late Sixteenth and Early Seventeenth Centuries," *Bulletin of the Institute of Historical Research* 44 (1971), 194–215.

676   Cowgill, Ursula, "Life and Death in the Sixteenth Century in the City of York," *Population Studies* 21 (1967), 53–62. See also comment by Louis Henry, ibid. 22 (1968), 165–169.

677   Cowgill, Ursula, "The People of York, 1538–1812," *Scientific American* 222 (1970), 104–113.

678   Crafts, N.F.R., and N. J. Ireland, "A Simulation of the Impact of Changes in

Age at Marriage before and during the Advent of Industrialisation in England," *Population Studies* 30 (1976), 495–511.

679   Cressy, David, "Occupations, Migration and Literacy in East London 1580–1640," *Local Population Studies* 5 (1970), 53–60.

680   Cunningham, Carole, "Christ's Hospital: Infant and Child Mortality in the Sixteenth Century," *Local Population Studies* 18 (1977), 37–40.

681   DeGaris, Marie, "A Brehaut Family Some 400 Years Ago," *Transactions de la Société guernesiaise* 17 (1962), 319–330.

682   *Devon Inventories of the Sixteenth and Seventeenth Centuries*, ed. Margaret Cash. Torquay, 1966.

683   Dickens, A. G., "Estate and Household Management in Bedfordshire, c. 1540," *Bedfordshire Historical and Record Society Publications* 36 (1955), 38–45.

684   Dulley, A.J.E., "People and Homes in the Medway Towns: 1687–1785," *Essays in Kentish History*, ed. Margaret Roake and John Whyman (London, 1973), 101–117.

685   Eden, Peter, *Small Houses in England 1520–1820*. London, 1969.

686   Emmison, F. G., *Elizabethan Life: Disorder*. Chelmsford, 1970.

687   Emmison, F. G., *Elizabethan Life: Home, Work, and Land*. Chelmsford, 1976.

688   Emmison, F. G., *Elizabethan Life: Morals and the Church Courts*. Chelmsford, 1973.

689   Eshleman, Michael K., "Diet During Pregnancy in the Sixteenth and Seventeenth Centuries," *Journal of the History of Medicine and Allied Sciences* 30 (1975), 23–39.

690   Everitt, Alan, *The Community of Kent and the Great Rebellion, 1640–1660*. Leicester, 1966.

691   Everitt, Alan, "Farm Labourers," *The Agrarian History of England...*, ed. Joan Thirsk (Cambridge, England, 1967), 396–465. (See #619)

692   Everitt, Alan, "Kentish Family Portrait: An Aspect of the Rise of the Pseudo-gentry," *Rural Change and Urban Growth 1500–1800*, ed. C. W. Chalklin and M. A. Havinden (London, 1974), 167–199.

693   Eversley, D.E.C., "Population and Economic Growth in England Before the 'Take Off,' " *Communications of the First International Conference of Economic History, Stockholm* (Stockholm, 1960), 457–473.

694   Eversley, D.E.C., "A Survey of Population in an Area of Worcestershire from 1660–1850 on the Basis of Parish Records," *Population Studies* 10 (1957), 253–279.

695   *Farm and Cottage Inventories of Mid-Essex, 1635–1749*, ed. Francis W. Steer. Chelmsford, 1950.

696   Finch, M. E., *The Wealth of Five Northamptonshire Families, 1540–1640*. Oxford, 1956.

697   Finch, Pearl, "Notes on Household Management in the Eighteenth Century,"

Notes and Queries 203 (1958), 349–351; 204 (1959), 97–99, 144–147, 168–172.

698 Fleming, Sandford, *Children and Puritanism.* New Haven, Conn., 1933.

699 Fletcher, Anthony, *A County Community in Peace and War: Sussex, 1600–60.* London, 1975.

700 Flinn, M. W., *British Population Growth 1700–1850.* London, 1970.

701 Forbes, Thomas R., *Chronicle from Aldgate: Life and Death in Shakespeare's London.* New Haven, 1971.

702 Forbes, Thomas R., "The Regulation of English Midwives in the Sixteenth and Seventeenth Centuries," *Medical History* 8 (1964), 235–236.

703 Fussell, George Edwin, *Village Life in the Eighteenth Century.* Worcester, 1947.

704 Fussell, George Edwin, and K. R. Fussell, *The English Countryman: His Life and Work, 1500–1900.* London, 1955.

705 Fussell, George Edwin, and K. R. Fussell, *The English Countrywoman: A Farmhouse Social History, 1500–1900.* London, 1953.

706 Gagen, J. E., *The New Woman: Her Emergence in the English Drama, 1600–1730.* New York, 1954.

707 Gardiner, D., *English Girlhood at School.* London, 1929.

708 Garside, B., *People and Homes in Hampton-on-Thames in the Sixteenth and Seventeenth Centuries.* n. p., 1956.

709 George, M. Dorothy, *London Life in the 18th Century.* 2nd ed.; London, 1965.

710 George, Margaret, "From 'Goodwife' to 'Mistress': The Transformation of the Female in Bourgeois Culture," *Science and Society* 37 (1973), 152–177.

711 Glass, David V., "Population and Population Movements in England and Wales, 1700 to 1850," *Population in History*, ed. David V. Glass and D.E.C. Eversley (London, 1965), 221–246. (See #214)

712 Goode, William J., "Marriage among the English Nobility in the Sixteenth and Seventeenth Centuries: A Comment," *Comparative Studies in Society and History* 3 (1960–61), 207–214.

713 Habakkuk, H. J., "English Population in the Eighteenth Century," *Economic History Review* 2nd series 6 (1953–54), 117–133.

714 Habakkuk, H. J., "Marriage Settlements in the Eighteenth Century," *Transactions of the Royal Historical Society* 4th series 32 (1950), 15–30.

715 Hair, P.E.H., *At the Bawdy Court.* London, 1972.

716 Hair, P.E.H., "Bridal Pregnancy in Earlier Rural England, Further Examined," *Population Studies* 24 (1970), 59–70.

717 Hair, P.E.H., "Bridal Pregnancy in Rural England in Earlier Centuries," *Population Studies* 20 (1966), 233–244.

718 Hair, P.E.H., "Homicide, Infanticide, and Child Assault in Late Tudor Middlesex," *Local Population Studies* 9 (1972), 43–46.

719 Halkett, J., *Milton and the Idea of Matrimony.* New Haven, 1970.

720   Haller, William, " 'Hail Wedded Love,' " *ELH: A Magazine of English Literary History* 13 (1946), 79–97.

721   Hardy, E., "Life on a Suffolk Manor in the 16th and 17th Centuries," *Suffolk Review* 3 (1965–70), 225–237.

722   Harvey, Nigel, *A History of Farm Buildings in England and Wales*. Newton Abbot, 1970.

723   Haw, R., *The State of Matrimony*. London, 1952.

724   Hecht, J. Jean, *The Domestic Servant Class in Eighteenth-Century England*. London, 1956.

725   Henry, Louis, "Démographie de la noblesse britannique," *Population* 20 (1965), 692–704.

726   Herford, Charles H., *Shakespeare's Treatment of Love and Marriage*. London, 1921.

727   Hewett, C. A., "The Development of the Post Medieval House," *Post-Medieval Archaeology* 7 (1973), 60–78.

728   Hey, David G., *An English Rural Community: Myddle under the Tudors and Stuarts*. Leicester, 1974.

729   Hill, Christopher, "The Spiritualization of the Household," *Society and Puritanism in Pre-Revolutionary England* (London, 1964), 443–481.

730   Hogrefe, Pearl, "Legal Rights of Tudor Women and the Circumvention by Men and Women," *Sixteenth-Century Journal* 3 (1972), 97–105.

731   Hole, Christina, *English Home Life, 1500–1800*. New York, 1947.

732   Hole, Christina, *The English Housewife in the Seventeenth Century*. London, 1953.

733   Hollingsworth, Thomas H., "A Demographic Study of the British Ducal Families," *Population Studies* 11 (1957), 4–26.

734   Hollingsworth, Thomas H., *The Demography of the British Peerage*. Supplement to *Population Studies* 18 (1965).

735   Holman, J. R., "Orphans in Pre-Industrial Towns—the Case of Bristol in the Late Seventeenth Century," *Local Population Studies* 15 (1975), 40–44.

736   Hoskins, William George, *Devon and Its People*. Exeter, 1959.

737   Hoskins, William George, "The Farm-Labourer through Four Centuries," *Devonshire Studies* (London, 1952), 419–441. (See #741)

738   Hoskins, William George, *Industry, Trade and People in Exeter, 1688–1800*. Manchester, 1935. Reprint, Exeter, 1968.

739   Hoskins, William George, "The Rebuilding of Rural England 1570–1640," *Past and Present* 4 (1953), 44–59.

740   Hoskins, William George, "Three Studies in Family History," *Devonshire Studies* (London, 1952), 78–119. (See #741)

741   Hoskins, William George, and H.P.R. Finberg, *Devonshire Studies*. London, 1952.

742   *Household and Farm Inventories in Oxfordshire, 1550–1590*, ed. M. A. Havinden. London, 1965.

743 Hurstfield, Joel, *The Queen's Wards: Wardship and Marriage under Elizabeth I.* London, 1958.

744 Hussey, C.E.C., *English Country Houses: Early Georgian, 1715–1760.* London, 1955.

745 Inglis-Jones, E., "A Pembrokeshire County Family in the Eighteenth Century," *Journal of the National Library of Wales* 17 (1971), 136–160, 217–237, 321–342.

746 Jackson, S., and P. Laxton, "Of Such as Are of Riper Years? A Note on Age at Baptism," *Local Population Studies* 18 (1977), 30–36.

747 James, Mervyn, *Family, Lineage, and Civil Society: A Study of Society, Politics, and Mentality in the Durham Region, 1500–1640.* New York, 1974.

748 Jekyll, Gertrude, *Old English Household Life: Some Account of Cottage Objects and Country Folk.* London, 1975. Originally 1925.

749 Johnson, James Turner, "The Covenant Idea and the Puritan View of Marriage," *Journal of the History of Ideas* 32 (1971), 107–118.

750 Johnson, James Turner, "English Puritan Thought on the Ends of Marriage," *Church History* 38 (1969), 429–436.

751 Johnson, James Turner, *A Society Ordained by God: English Puritan Marriage Doctrine in the First Half of the Seventeenth Century.* Nashville, 1970.

752 Johnston, J. A., "Probate Inventories and Wills of a Worcestershire Parish 1676–1775," *Midland History* 1 (1971), 20–33.

753 Jones, G. J., "Some Population Problems Relating to Cumberland and Westmorland in the Eighteenth Century," *Transactions of the Cumberland and Westmorland Archaeological Society* 58 (1958), 123–139.

754 Jones, R. E., "Infant Mortality in Rural North Shropshire 1561–1810," *Population Studies* 30 (1976), 305–318.

755 Jones, R. E., "Population and Agrarian Change in an Eighteenth Century Shropshire Parish," *Local Population Studies* 1 (1968), 6–29.

756 Kelshall, A. F., "The London House Plan in the Later 17th Century," *Post-Medieval Archaeology* 8 (1974), 80–91.

757 Kenny, C., "Wife-Selling in England," *Law Quarterly Review* 45 (1929), 494–497.

758 Kerridge, Eric, *The Farmers of Old England.* London, 1973.

759 Krause, John T., "Some Aspects of Population Change, 1690–1790," *Land, Labour and Population...,* ed. E. L. Jones and G. E. Mingay (London, 1967), 187–205. (See #1011)

760 Laslett, Peter, "Le brassage de la population en France et en Angleterre au XVIIe et au XVIIIe siècles," *Annales de démographie historique* (1968), 99–109.

761 Laslett, Peter, "Mean Household Size in England Since the Sixteenth Century," *Household and Family...,* ed. Peter Laslett and Richard Wall (Cambridge, England, 1972), 125–158. (See #156)

762 Laslett, Peter, "Parental Deprivation in the Past: A Note on the History of

Orphans in England," *Local Population Studies* 13 (1974), 11–18. See now #479, 160–173.

763   Laslett, Peter, "Size and Structure of the Household in England over Three Centuries," *Population Studies* 23 (1969), 199–224.

764   Laslett, Peter, *The World We Have Lost*. London, 1965. 2nd ed.; London, 1971.

765   Laslett, Peter, and John Harrison, "Clayworth and Cogenhoe," *Historical Essays 1600–1750, Presented to David Ogg*, ed. H. E. Bell and R. L. Ollard (London, 1962), 157–184. Revised version now in #479, 50–101.

766   Laslett, Peter, and Karla Oosterveen, "Long-term Trends in Bastardy in England: A Study of the Illegitimacy Figures in the Parish Registers and in the Reports of the Registrar-General, 1561–1960," *Population Studies* 27 (1973), 255–286. See now #479, 102–159.

767   Latham, Jean, *Happy Families: Growing up in the Eighteenth and Nineteenth Centuries*. New York, 1974.

768   Law, C. M., "Local Censuses in the 18th Century," *Population Studies* 23 (1969), 87–100.

769   Lee, Ronald, "Estimating Series of Vital Rates and Age Structures from Baptisms and Burials: A New Technique, with Applications to Pre-Industrial England," *Population Studies* 28 (1974), 495–512.

770   Lloyd, Howell A., *The Gentry of South-West Wales 1540–1640*. Cardiff, 1968.

771   Lloyd, L. C., "Multiple Births in Shropshire, 1601-1800," *Local Population Studies* 3 (1969), 29–37.

772   Lloyd, Rachel, *Dorset Elizabethans at Home and Abroad*. London, 1967.

773   Loschky, David J., and Donald F. Krier, "Income and Family Size in Three Eighteenth-Century Lancashire Parishes: A Reconstitution Study," *Journal of Economic History* 29 (1969), 429–448.

774   Macfarlane, Alan, *The Family Life of Ralph Josselin: An Essay in Historical Anthropology*. Cambridge, England, 1970.

775   McLaren, Dorothy, "The Marriage Act of 1653: Its Influence on the Parish Registers," *Population Studies* 28 (1974), 319–328.

776   Maltby, Bessie, "Easingwold Marriage Horizons," *Local Population Studies* 2 (1969), 36–39.

777   Maltby, Bessie, "Parish Registers and the Problem of Mobility," *Local Population Studies* 6 (1971), 32–42.

778   Marshall, Dorothy, *English People in the Eighteenth Century*. London, 1956.

779   Marshall, Dorothy, *The English Poor in the Eighteenth Century*. London, 1926.

780   Marshall, T. H., "The Population Problem during the Industrial Revolution," *Population in History*, ed. David V. Glass and D.E.C. Eversley (London, 1965), 247–268. (See #214)

781   Martin, J. M., "Marriage and Economic Stress in the Felden of Warwickshire during the Eighteenth Century," *Population Studies* 31 (1977), 519–535.

782 Massey, Margaret, "Seasonality, Some Further Thoughts," *Local Population Studies* 8 (1972), 48–54.

783 Mercer, E., "The Houses of the Gentry," *Past and Present* 5 (1954), 11–32.

784 Mills, Dennis R., "The Christening Custom at Melbourn, Cambs.," *Local Population Studies* 11 (1973), 11–22.

785 Mingay, Gerald E., *English Landed Society in the 18th Century.* London, 1963.

786 Morell, C. C., "Tudor Marriages and Infantile Mortality," *Journal of State Medicine* 43 (1935), 173–181.

787 Mueller, Gerhard J. W., "Inquiry into the State of a Divorceless Society: Domestic Relations, Law and Morals in England from 1660–1857," *University of Pittsburgh Law Review* 18 (1957), 545–578.

788 Notestein, Wallace, "The English Woman, 1580 to 1650," *Studies in Social History,* ed. J. H. Plumb (London, 1955), 69–107.

789 Outhwaite, R. B., "Age at Marriage in England from the Late Seventeenth to the Nineteenth Century," *Transactions of the Royal Historical Society* 23 (1973), 55–70.

790 Owen, G. R., "Illegitimacy at Ilsington, 1558–1820," *Devon and Cornwall. Notes and Queries* 31 (1968–70), 220–221.

791 Patten, John, *Rural-Urban Migration in Pre-Industrial England.* Oxford, 1973.

792 Pearson, Lu Emily, *Elizabethans at Home.* Stanford, 1957; 2nd ed., 1967.

793 Peate, Iorwerth C., *The Welsh House.* 3rd ed.; Liverpool, 1946.

794 Peate, Iorwerth C., "The Welsh Long-House: A Brief Reappraisal," *Culture and Environment,* ed. Idris Llewelyn Foster and L. Alcock (London, 1963), 439–444.

795 Pinchbeck, Ivy, and Margaret Hewitt, *Children in English Society.* 2 v. Toronto, 1971–73.

796 Pinchbeck, Ivy, "The State and the Child in Sixteenth Century England," *British Journal of Sociology* 7 (1956), 273–285; 8 (1957), 59–74.

797 Plumb, J. H., "The New World of Children in Eighteenth-Century England," *Past and Present* 67 (1975), 64–95.

798 Portman, Derek, "Vernacular Building in the Oxford Region in the Sixteenth and Seventeenth Centuries," *Rural Change...,* ed. C. W. Chalklin and M. A. Havinden (London, 1974), 135–168. (See #805)

799 Powell, Chilton L., *English Domestic Relations, 1487–1653.* 2nd ed.; New York, 1971. Originally 1917.

800 Prest, W. R., "Stability and Change in Old and New England: Clayworth and Dedham," *Journal of Interdisciplinary History* 6 (1975–76), 359–374.

801 Quaife, G. R., "The Consenting Spinster in a Peasant Society: Aspects of Pre-marital Sex in 'Puritan' Somerset 1645–1660," *Journal of Social History* 11 (1977), 228–244.

802 Razzell, P. E., "Population Growth and Economic Change in Eighteenth- and

Early Nineteenth-Century England and Ireland," *Land, Labour and Population...*, ed. E. L. Jones and G. E. Mingay (London, 1967), 260-281. (See #1011)

803   Richards, E., "Women in the British Economy Since about 1700: An Interpretation," *History* 59 (1974), 337-357.

804   Rowse, A. L., *Simon Forman: Sex and Society in Shakespeare's Age.* London, 1974.

805   *Rural Change and Urban Growth 1500-1800,* ed. C. W. Chalklin and M. A. Havinden. London, 1974.

806   Saffady, William, "The Effects of Childhood Bereavement and Parental Remarriage in Sixteenth-Century England: The Case of Thomas More," *History of Childhood Quarterly* 1 (1973-74), 310-336.

807   Saunders, Beatrice, *The Age of Candlelight: The English Social Scene in the 17th Century.* London, 1959.

808   Sayer, M. J., "Norfolk Visitation Families: A Short Social Structure," *Norfolk Archaeology* 36 (1975), 176-182.

809   Schafer, Jurgen, "When They Marry, They Get Wenches," *Shakespeare Quarterly* 22 (1971), 203-211.

810   Schnucker, Robert V., "Elizabethan Birth Control and Puritan Attitudes," *Journal of Interdisciplinary History* 5 (1974-75), 655-667.

811   Schnucker, Robert V., "The English Puritans and Pregnancy," *History of Childhood Quarterly* 1 (1973-74), 637-658.

812   Schocket, Gordon J., "Patriarchalism, Politics, and Mass Attitudes in Stuart England," *Historical Journal* 12 (1969), 413-441.

813   Schofield, Roger S., "Perinatal Mortality in Hawkshead, Lancashire, 1581-1710," *Local Population Studies* 4 (1970), 11-16.

814   Schücking, Levin L., *The Puritan Family: A Social Study from the Literary Sources.* London, 1969. Original German, Leipzig, 1929.

815   Seth, Ronald, *Children against Witches.* London, 1969.

816   Slater, Miriam, "The Weightiest Business: Marriage in an Upper-Gentry Family in Seventeenth-Century England," *Past and Present* 72 (1976), 25-54.

817   Smith, J. T., "Timber Framed Building in England," *Archaeological Journal* 122 (1965), 133-158.

818   Smith, Peter, "Rural Housing in Wales," *The Agrarian History of England...*, ed. Joan Thirsk (Cambridge, England, 1967), 767-813. (See #619)

819   Smith, Steven R., "Growing Old in Early Stuart England," *Albion* 8 (1976), 125-141.

820   Smith, Steven R., "The London Apprentices as Seventeenth-Century Adolescents," *Past and Present* 61 (1973), 149-161.

821   Smith, Steven R., "Religion and the Conception of Youth in Seventeenth-Century England," *History of Childhood Quarterly* 2 (1974-75), 493-516.

822   Sogner, Solvi, "Aspects of the Demographic Situation in Seventeen Parishes in

Shropshire 1711–1760: An Exercise Based on Parish Registers," *Population Studies* 17 (1963), 126–146.

823 Spufford, Margaret, *Contrasting Communities: English Villagers in the Sixteenth and Seventeenth Centuries*. Cambridge, England, 1974.

824 Spufford, Margaret, "Peasant Inheritance Customs and Land Distribution in Cambridgeshire from the Sixteenth to the Eighteenth Centuries," *Family and Inheritance*, ed. Jack Goody, Joan Thirsk, and E. P. Thompson (Cambridge, England, 1976), 156–176. (See #296)

825 Spufford, Peter, "Population Mobility in Pre-Industrial England," *Genealogists Magazine* 17 (1973), 420–429, 475–481, 537–543.

826 Spufford, Peter, "Population Movement in Seventeenth Century England," *Local Population Studies* 4 (1970), 41–50.

827 Stannard, David E., "Death and the Puritan Child," *American Quarterly* 26 (1974), 456–476.

828 Stone, Lawrence, *Family and Fortune: Studies in Aristocratic Finance in the Sixteenth and Seventeenth Centuries*. New York, 1973.

829 Stone, Lawrence, *The Family, Sex and Marriage in England 1500–1800*. London, 1977.

830 Stone, Lawrence, "Marriage among the English Nobility in the Sixteenth and Seventeenth Centuries," *Comparative Studies in Society and History* 3 (1960–61), 182–206. Comment by William J. Goode, ibid., 207–215.

831 Stone, Lawrence, "Patriarchy and Paternalism in Tudor England: The Earl of Arundel and the Peasant Revolt of 1549," *Journal of British Studies* 13 (1974), 19–23.

832 Stone, Lawrence, "The Rise of the Nuclear Family in Early Modern England," *The Family in History*, ed. Charles E. Rosenberg (Philadelphia, 1975), 13–57. (See #79)

833 Styles, Philip H., "A Census of a Warwickshire Village in 1698," *University of Birmingham Historical Journal* 3 (1951–52), 33–51.

834 Summerson, John, *Georgian London: An Architectural Survey*. New York, 1970.

835 Taylor, C. C., "Population Studies in 17th Century and 18th Century Wiltshire," *Wiltshire Archaeological and Natural History Magazine* 60 (1965), 100–108.

836 Taylor, R., "Town Houses in Taunton, 1500–1700," *Post-Medieval Archaeology* 8 (1974), 63–79.

837 Thirsk, Joan, "Younger Sons in the Seventeenth Century," *History* 54 (1969), 358–377.

838 Thomas, David, "The Social Origins of Marriage Partners of the British Peerage in the 18th and 19th Centuries," *Population Studies* 26 (1972), 99–112.

839 Thomas, Keith, "The Double Standard," *Journal of the History of Ideas* 20 (1959), 195–216.

840 Thompson, Roger, "Seventeenth-Century English and Colonial Sex Ratios: A

Postscript," *Population Studies* 28 (1974), 153–165.

841   Thompson, Roger, *Women in Stuart England and America: A Comparative Study*. Boston, 1974.

842   Thomson, Gladys Scott, *Life in a Noble Household, 1641–1700*. 2nd ed.; London, 1940.

843   Trumbach, Randolph, *The Rise of the Egalitarian Family: Aristocratic Kinship and Domestic Relations in Eighteenth-Century England*. New York, 1978.

844   Tucker, G.S.L., "English Pre-Industrial Population Trends," *Economic History Review* 2nd series 16 (1963–64), 205–218.

845   Urwin, Alan Charles Bell, *Population and Housing in 1664: An Analysis of the Hearth Tax Return for Ladyday 1664 for Twickenham, Hampton, Teddington, Isleworth, Heston and Hounslow*. Twickenham, 1967.

846   Vann, Richard T., "Nurture and Conversion in the Early Quaker Family," *Journal of Marriage and the Family* 31 (1969), 639–643.

847   *The Voices of Children 1700–1914*, ed. Irina Strickland. Oxford, 1974.

848   Wall, Richard, "Mean Household Size in England from Printed Sources," *Household and Family...*, ed. Peter Laslett and Richard Wall (Cambridge, England, 1972), 159–204. (See #156)

849   West, F., "Infant Mortality in the East Fen Parishes of Leake and Wrangle," *Local Population Studies* 13 (1974), 41–44.

850   Whitbread, Nanette, *The Evolution of the Nursery-Infant School*. London, 1972.

851   Wiener, Carol Z., "Sex Roles and Crime in Late Elizabethan Hertfordshire," *Journal of Social History* 8 (1974–75), 38–60.

852   Winchester, B., *Tudor Family Portrait*. London, 1955.

853   Wood-Jones, R. B., *Traditional Domestic Architecture of the Banbury Region*. London, 1963.

854   Wrightson, Keith, "Infanticide in Earlier Seventeenth-Century England," *Local Population Studies* 15 (1975), 10–22.

855   Wrightson, Keith, "Villages, Villagers and Village Studies (16th-Century England)," *Historical Journal* 18 (1975), 632–639.

856   Wrigley, E. Anthony, "Clandestine Marriage in Tetbury in the Late 17th Century," *Local Population Studies* 10 (1973), 15–21.

857   Wrigley, E. Anthony, "Family Limitation in Pre-Industrial England," *Economic History Review* 2nd series 19 (1966), 82–109.

858   Wrigley, E. Anthony, "Mortality in Pre-Industrial England: The Example of Colyton, Devon, over Three Centuries," *Daedalus* 97 (1968), 546–580.

Scotland

859   Bingham, Madeleine, *Scotland under Mary Stuart: An Account of Everyday Life*. London, 1971.

860 Carter, Ian, "Marriage Patterns and Social Sectors in Scotland before the Eighteenth Century," *Scottish Studies* 17 (1973), 51-60.

861 Fenton, A., "Farm Servant Life in the Seventeenth to Nineteenth Centuries," *Scottish Agriculture* 44 (1965), 281-285.

862 Guthrie, Charles John, "The History of Divorce in Scotland," *Scottish Historical Review* 8 (1910), 39-52.

863 Kermack, W. R., "Did the Marriage Age of Scottish Brides Decrease in the Eighteenth Century?" *Scottish Genealogist* 18 (1971), 21-22.

864 Lochhead, M., *The Scots Household in the Eighteenth Century*. Edinburgh, 1948.

865 MacInnes, J., "Clan Unity and Individual Freedom," *Transactions of the Gaelic Society of Inverness* 47 (1971-72), 338-373.

866 O'Dell, A. C., "The Population of Scotland, 1755-1931: A General Survey," *Scottish Geographical Magazine* 48 (1932), 282-290.

867 Plant, Marjorie, *The Domestic Life of Scotland in the Eighteenth Century*. Edinburgh, 1952.

868 Warrack, J., *Domestic Life in Scotland, 1488-1688*. London, 1920.

869 Whyte, I. D., "Rural Housing in Lowland Scotland in the Seventeenth Century," *Scottish Studies* 19 (1975), 55-68.

Ireland

870 Danachair, Caoimhin O., "Traditional Forms of the Dwelling House in Ireland," *Journal of the Royal Society of Antiquaries of Ireland* 102 (1972), 77-96.

871 Jackson, Donald, *Intermarriage in Ireland, 1550-1650*. Montreal, 1970.

872 Tucker, G.S.L., "Irish Fertility Ratios before the Famine," *Economic History Review* 2nd series 23 (1970), 267-284.

MODERN PERIOD (1750 TO THE PRESENT)

873 Acworth, Evelyn, *The New Matriarchy*. London, 1965.

874 Adam, Ruth, *A Woman's Place 1910-1975*. London, 1975.

875 Ambler, R. W., "Baptism and Christening. Custom and Practice in Nineteenth Century Lincolnshire," *Local Population Studies* 12 (1974), 25-27.

876 Ambrose, Peter, *The Quiet Revolution: Social Change in a Sussex Village, 1871-1971*. London, 1974.

877 Anderson, Michael, *Family Structure in Nineteenth Century Lancashire*. Cambridge, England, 1971.

878   Anderson, Michael, "Household Structure and the Industrial Revolution: Preston in Comparative Perspective," *Household and Family...*, ed. Peter Laslett and Richard Wall (Cambridge, England, 1972), 215-235. (See #156)

879   Anderson, Michael, "A National Sample from the 1851 Census of Great Britain: A Summary of Aims and Procedure," *Historical Methods Newsletter* 6 (1973), 49-52.

880   Anderson, Michael, "Standard Tabulation Procedures for the Census Enumerators' Books 1851-1891," *Nineteenth-Century Society*, ed. E. Anthony Wrigley (Cambridge, England, 1972), 134-145. (See #1054)

881   Anderson, Michael, "The Study of Family Structure," ibid., 47-81.

882   Anderson, Olive, "The Incidence of Civil Marriage in Victorian England and Wales," *Past and Present* 69 (1975), 50-87.

883   Anderson, Stanley, *Britain in the Sixties: Housing.* London, 1962.

884   Armstrong, Alan [= W. A.], *Stability and Change in an English County Town: A Study of York 1801–51.* London, 1974.

885   Armstrong, W. A., "A Note on the Household Structure of Mid-Nineteenth-Century York in Comparative Perspective," *Household and Family...*, ed. Peter Laslett and Richard Wall (Cambridge, England, 1972), 205-214. (See #156)

886   Armstrong, W. A., "La population de L'Angleterre et du Pays de Galles (1789-1815)," *Annales de démographie historique* (1965), 135-189.

887   Askwith, Betty, *Two Victorian Families.* London, 1971.

888   Auerbach, Nina, "Alice and Wonderland: A Curious Child," *Victorian Studies* 17 (1973-74), 31-47.

889   Avery, Gillian, *Nineteenth Century Children: Heroes and Heroines in English Children's Stories, 1780–1900.* London, 1965.

890   Baack, Bennett D., and Robert Paul Thomas, "The Enclosure Movement and the Supply of Labour during the Industrial Revolution," *Journal of European Economic History* 3 (1974), 401-423.

891   Bain, George Sayer, Robert Bacon, and John Pimlott, "The Labour Force," *Trends in British Society Since 1900*, ed. A. H. Halsey (London, 1972), 97-128.

892   Baker, David, "The Inhabitants of Cardington in 1782," *Bedfordshire Historical Record Society* 52 (1973).

893   Banks, Joseph Ambrose, *Feminism and Family Planning in Victorian England.* Liverpool, 1964.

894   Banks, Joseph Ambrose, *Prosperity and Parenthood: A Study of Family Planning among the Victorian Middle Classes.* London, 1954.

895   Basch, Françoise, *Relative Creatures: Victorian Women in Society and the Novel.* New York, 1974.

896   Beales, H. L., "The Victorian Family," *Ideas and Beliefs of the Victorians,* ed. British Broadcasting Corporation (London, 1949), 343-350.

897   Beales, H. L., and Edward Glover, "Victorian Ideas of Sex, " ibid., 351-357.

898 Beaver, M. A., "Population, Infant Mortality and Milk," *Population Studies* 27 (1973), 243–254.

899 Bedarida, François, *L'Angleterre triomphante, 1832–1914*. Paris, 1974.

900 Bedarida, François, *La société anglaise, 1851–1975*. Paris, 1976.

901 Bell, Colin R., *Middle-Class Families*. London, 1968.

902 Beresford, Maurice W., "The Unprinted Census Returns of 1841, 1851, 1861 for England and Wales," *Amateur Historian* 5 (1963), 260–269.

903 Bevan-Evans, M., *Farmhouses and Cottages: An Introduction to Vernacular Architecture in Flintshire*. Hawarden, Flintshire, 1964.

904 Blackmore, J. S., and F. C. Mellonie, "Family Endowment and the Birth Rate in the Early Nineteenth Century," *Economic History* 1 (1926–29), 205–213, 412–418.

905 Blease, W. L., *The Emancipation of English Women*. London, 1913.

906 Blunden, Edmund, "Country Childhood," *Edwardian England, 1901–1914*, ed. Simon Nowell-Smith (London, 1964), 139–212.

907 Blythe, Ronald, *Akenfield: Portrait of an English Village*. London, 1969.

908 Bott, Elizabeth, *The Family and the Social Network: Roles, Norms, and External Relationships in Ordinary Urban Families*. London, 1957.

909 Bowley, Marian, "The Housing Statistics of Great Britain," *Journal of the Royal Statistical Society* Series A (General) 113 (1950), 396–411.

910 Bracey, Howard E., *English Rural Life: Village Activities, Organisations and Institutions*. London, 1959.

911 Bracey, Howard E., *Neighbors: Subdivision Life in England and the U.S.* London, 1964.

912 Branca, Patricia, *Silent Sisterhood. Middle Class Women in the Victorian Home*. Pittsburg, 1975.

913 Branson, William H., "Social Legislation and the Birth Rate in Nineteenth Century Britain," *Western Economic Journal* 6 (1968), 134–144.

914 Buer, Mabel, *Health, Wealth, and Population in the Early Days of the Industrial Revolution*. London, 1926.

915 Burnett, John, *Annals of Labour. Autobiographies of British Working-Class People 1820–1920*. Bloomington, Ind., 1974.

916 Burton, Elizabeth, *The Early Victorians at Home 1837–1861*. London, 1972.

917 Busfield, Joan, and Geoffrey Hawthorn, "Some Social Determinants of Recent Trends in British Fertility," *Journal of Biosocial Science* Supplement 3 (1971), 65–77.

918 Calder, Jenni, *Women and Marriage in Victorian Fiction*. New York, 1976.

919 Carrier, N. H., "An Examination of Generation Fertility in England and Wales," *Population Studies* 9 (1955), 3–23.

920 Chastenet, Jacques, *La vie quotidienne en Angleterre au début du règne de Victoria 1837–1851*. Paris, 1961.

921 Checkland, S. G., *The Gladstones, a Family Biography 1764–1851*. Cambridge, England, 1971.

922 Clephane, Irene, *Our Mothers...Late Victorian Women*. London, 1932.

923 Colby, Vineta, *Yesterday's Woman: Domestic Realism in the English Novel*. Princeton, 1974.

924 Collier, Francis, *The Family Economy of the Working Classes in the Cotton Industry, 1784–1833*. Manchester, 1965.

925 Cominos, Peter T., "Late-Victorian Sexual Respectability and the Social System," *International Review of Social History* 8 (1963), 18–48, 216–250.

926 Conway, Jill, "Stereotypes of Femininity in a Theory of Sexual Evolution," *Victorian Studies* 14 (1970–71), 47–62.

927 Cornforth, John, "Some Early Victorians at Home," *Country Life* 158 (1975), 1530–1535.

928 Cox, P. R., "Studies in the Recent Marriages and Fertility Data of England and Wales," *Population Studies* 5 (1951), 132–152.

929 Crafts, N.F.R., and N. J. Ireland, "Family Limitation and the English Demographic Revolution: A Simulation Approach," *Journal of Economic History* 36 (1977), 598–623.

930 Cross, George C., "Mary Cowden Clarke, 'The Girlhood of Shakespeare's Heroines,' and the Sex Education of Victorian Women," *Victorian Studies* 16 (1972–73), 37–58.

931 Crow, Duncan, *The Victorian Woman*. London, 1971.

932 Cullingworth, J. B., "Household Formation in England and Wales," *Town Planning Review* 31 (1960–61), 5–26.

933 Curle, A., "Kinship Structure in an English Village," *Man* 52 (1952), 68–69.

934 Daley, Allen, and B. Benjamin, "London as a Case Study," *Population Studies* 17 (1964), 249–262.

935 Davidoff, Lenore, *The Best Circles: Women and Society in Victorian England*. London, 1973.

936 Davidoff, Lenore, "Mastered for Life: Servant and Wife in Victorian and Edwardian England," *Journal of Social History* 7 (1973–74), 406–428.

937 Davies, Agnes M., *A Book with Seven Seals: A Victorian Childhood*. London, 1974.

938 Davies, Clarice Stella, *North Country Bred: A Working-Class Family Chronicle*. London, 1963.

939 Davies, Stella, *Living through the Industrial Revolution*. London, 1966.

940 Dawes, Francis Edward, *Not in Front of the Servants: Domestic Service in England 1850–1939*. London, 1973.

941 Dennis, N., F. Henriques, and C. N. Slaughter, *Coal is Our Life: An Analysis of a Yorkshire Mining Community*. London, 1956.

942 Desai, Rashmi, *Indian Immigrants in Britain*. London, 1963.

943 Ditchfield, Peter, *The Cottages and Village Life of Rural England*. London, 1912.

944 Donnelly, J. S., *The Land and People of Nineteenth Century Cork*. London, 1975.

945 Douglas, J.W.B., and G. Rowntree, *Maternity in Great Britain*. London, 1948.

946 Dunbar, Janet, *The Early Victorian Woman: Some Aspects of Her Life*. London, 1953.

947 Dutton, R., *The Victorian Home: Some Aspects of Nineteenth-Century Taste and Manners*. London, 1954.

948 Dyos, H. J., "The Slums of Victorian London," *Victorian Studies* 11 (1967–68), 5–40.

949 Dyos, H. J., *Victorian Suburb. A Study of the Growth of Camberwell*. Leicester, 1966.

950 Eversley, D.E.C., and V. Jackson, "Population, Employment and Housing Trends in the West Midlands," *Town and Country Planning* 29 (1961), 307–308.

951 Farid, S. M., "Cohort Nuptiality in England and Wales," *Population Studies* 30 (1976), 137–152.

952 Farid, S. M., "The Current Tempo of Fertility in England and Wales," *Population Studies* 28 (1974), 69–84.

953 Findlay, Joseph J., *Children of England: A Contribution to Social History and to Education*. London, 1973.

954 Firth, Raymond, et al., *Families and Their Relatives: Kinship in a Middle-Class Section of London*. New York, 1969.

955 Firth, Raymond, "Family and Kin Ties in Britain and Their Social Implications: Introduction," *British Journal of Sociology* 12 (1961), 305–309.

956 Fletcher, R., *The Family and Marriage in Britain*. London, 1966.

957 Floud, R. C., and R. S. Schofield, "Social Structure from the Early Census Returns," *Economic History Review* 2nd series 21 (1968), 607–609. Rejoinder by W. A. Armstrong, ibid., 609–613.

958 Frankenberg, Ronald, *Communities in Britain: Social Life in Town and Country*. London, 1965.

959 Franklin, Jill, "Troops of Servants: Labour and Planning in the Country House 1840–1914," *Victorian Studies* 19 (1975–76), 211–240.

960 Friedlander, Dov, "Demographic Patterns and Socio-Economic Characteristics of the Coal Mining Population in England and Wales in the Nineteenth Century," *Economic Development and Cultural Change* 22 (1973–74), 39–51.

961 Fussell, George Edwin, *The English Rural Labourer*. London, 1949.

962 Gathorne-Hardy, Jonathan, *The Rise and Fall of the British Nanny*. London, 1972.

963 Gauldie, Enid, *Cruel Habitations: A History of Working-Class Housing, 1780–1918*. London, 1974.

964 Gibbs, Mary Ann, *The Years of the Nannies*. London, 1960.

965 Gibson, A.V.B., "Huguenot Weavers' Houses in Spitalfields," *East London Papers* 1 (1958), 3–14.

966 Gibson, Colin, "The Association between Divorce and Social Class in England and Wales," *British Journal of Sociology* 25 (1974), 79–93.

967 Gibson, Colin, "A Note on Family Breakdown in England and Wales," *British Journal of Sociology* 22 (1971), 322–325.

968 Girouard, Mark, *The Victorian Country House.* London, 1971.

969 Girouard, Mark, "A Victorian Country Household," *Listener* 86 (1971), 397–399.

970 Gornall, J.F.G., "Marriage, Property, and Romance in Jane Austen's Novels," *Hibbert Journal* 65 (1967), 151–156; 66 (1967), 24–29.

971 Griffith, Grosvenor, *Population Problems of the Age of Malthus.* Cambridge, England, 1926.

972 Habakkuk, H. J., *Population Growth and Economic Development since 1750.* Leicester, 1971.

973 Haines, Michael R., "Fertility, Nuptiality, and Occupation: A Study of Coal Mining Populations and Regions in England and Wales in the Mid-Nineteenth Century," *Journal of Interdisciplinary History* 8 (1977–78), 245–280.

974 Hajnal, John, "Aspects of Recent Trends in Marriage in England and Wales," *Population Studies* 1 (1947), 72–98.

975 Hare, F. H., "A Note on the Distribution of Family Sizes in the Adult Population of Great Britain, 1972," *Journal of Biosocial Science* 6 (1974), 343–346.

976 Harrison, G.A., R. W. Hiorns, and C. F. Kuchemann, "Social Class Relatedness in Some Oxfordshire Parishes," *Journal of Biosocial Science* 2 (1970), 71–80.

977 Harrison, G. A., R. W. Hiorns, and C. F. Kuchemann, "Social Class and Marriage Patterns in Some Oxfordshire Populations," *Journal of Biosocial Science* 3 (1971), 1–12.

978 Harrison, Molly, *People and Furniture: A Social Background to the English Home.* Totowa, N.J., 1971.

979 Hartman, Mary S., "Child-Abuse and Self-Abuse: Two Victorian Cases," *History of Childhood Quarterly* 2 (1974–75), 221–248.

980 Hartwell, R. M., "Children as Slaves," *Industrial Revolution and Economic Growth* (London, 1971), 390–408.

981 Henstock, Adrian, "Group Projects in Local History: House Repopulation in the Mid-Nineteenth Century," *Bulletin of Local History, East Midlands Region* 6 (1971), 11–20.

982 Henstock, Adrian, "House Repopulation from the Census Returns of 1841 and 1851," *Local Population Studies* 10 (1973), 37–52.

983 Hewitt, M., *Wives and Mothers in Victorian Industry.* London, 1959.

984 *The History of Working Class Housing: A Symposium*, ed. Stanley Chapman. Newton Abbot, 1971.

985 Holcombe, Lee, *Victorian Ladies at Work: Middle-Class Working Women in England and Wales, 1850–1914.* Hamden, Conn., 1973.

986   Hole, W. Vere, and W. V. Poutrey, *Trends in Population, Housing and Occupancy Rates 1861–1961.* London, 1971.

987   Hopkin, W.A.B., and J. Hajnal, "Analysis of the Births in England and Wales, 1939, by Father's Occupation," *Population Studies* 1 (1947), 187–201, 275–300.

988   Hopkins, Eric, "The Decline of the Family Work Unit in Black Country Nailing," *International Review of Social History* 22 (1977), 184–197.

989   Horn, Pamela, "Child Workers in the Pillow Lace and Straw Plait Trades of Victorian Buckinghamshire and Bedfordshire," *Historical Journal* 17 (1974), 776–796.

990   Horn, Pamela, "The Country Child, 1850–1870," *Cake and Cockhorse* 4 (1970), 163–171.

991   Horn, Pamela, "Domestic Service in Northhamptonshire, 1830–1914," *Northhamptonshire Past and Present* 5 (1975), 267–275.

992   Horn, Pamela, *The Rise and Fall of the Victorian Servant.* New York, 1975.

993   Horn, Pamela, *The Victorian Country Child.* London, 1974.

994   Hubert, J., "Kinship and Geographical Mobility in a Sample from a London Middle-Class Area," *International Journal of Comparative Sociology* 6 (1965), 61–80.

995   Higgett, F. E., *A Day in the Life of A Victorian Farm Worker.* London, 1972.

996   Hughes, Molly V., *A London Family.* London, 1973.

997   Hussey, C.E.C., *English Country Houses: Late Georgian, 1800–1840.* London, 1958.

998   Hussey, C.E.C., *English Country Houses: Mid-Georgian, 1760–1800.* London, 1956.

999   Innes, J. W., *Class Fertility Trends in England and Wales.* Princeton, 1938.

1000   Innes, Kennet, "The Ruined Maid and Her Prospect: Some Victorian Attitudes in Life and Art," *Albion* 4 (1974), 115–124.

1001   James, Alan G., *Sikh Children in Britain.* London, 1974.

1002   Jasper, Albert Stanley, *A Hoxton Childhood–Life in an East End London Borough.* London, 1969.

1003   Jenkins, David, *The Agricultural Community in South-West Wales at the Turn of the Twentieth Century.* Cardiff, 1971.

1004   Johnson, Wendell Stacy, *Sex and Marriage in Victorian Poetry.* Ithaca, New York, 1975.

1005   Kern, Stephen, "Explosive Intimacy: Psychodynamics of the Victorian Family," *History of Childhood Quarterly* 1 (1973–74), 437–461.

1006   Kerr, B., *Bound to the Soil: A Social History of Dorset, 1750–1918.* London, 1968.

1007   Klein, Viola, *Britain's Married Women Workers.* London, 1965.

1008   Krause, John T., "Changes in English Fertility and Mortality, 1781–1850," *Economic History Review* 2nd series 11 (1958–59), 52–70.

1009   Krause, John T., "Some Neglected Factors in the English Industrial Revolution," *Journal of Economic History* 19 (1959), 528–540.

1010   Kuchemann, C., "A Demographic and Genetic Study of a Group of Oxford-shire Villages," *Human Biology* 39 (1967), 251–276.

1011   *Land, Labour and Population in the Industrial Revolution*, ed. E. L. Jones and G. E. Mingay. London, 1967.

1012   Langer, William L., "The Origins of the Birth Control Movement in England in the Early Nineteenth Century," *Journal of Interdisciplinary History* 5 (1974–75), 669–686.

1013   Laqueur, T., *Religion and Respectability: Sunday Schools and Working Class Culture, 1780–1850*. London, 1976.

1014   Laski, Marghanita, "Domestic Life," *Edwardian England, 1901–1914*, ed. Simon Nowell-Smith (London, 1964), 139–212.

1015   Leach, Edmund, "Complementary Filiation and Bilateral Kinship," *The Character of Kinship*, ed. Jack Goody (Cambridge, England, 1973), 53–58.

1016   Lee, Robert, "Probleme der Bevölkerungsgeschichte in England, 1750–1850: Fragestellungen und vorläufige Ergebnisse," *Vierteljahrschrift für Sozial-und Wirtschaftsgeschichte* 60 (1973), 289–310.

1017   Lerner, Jeffrey C., "Attitudes toward Death: The Widow in Great Britain in the Early Twentieth Century," *Bereavement: Its Psychosocial Aspects*, ed. Bernard Schoenberg (New York, 1975), 91–118.

1018   Leser, C.E.V., "The Supply of Women for Gainful Work in Britain," *Population Studies* 9 (1955), 142–147.

1019   Leslie, Anita, *Edwardians in Love*. London, 1972.

1020   Lewis, G. J., "The Demographic Structure of a Welsh Rural Village during the Mid-Nineteenth Century," *Ceredigion* 5 (1966), 290–304.

1021   Lochhead, Marion, *The First Ten Years: Victorian Childhood*. London, 1956.

1022   Lochhead, Marion, *The Victorian Household*. London, 1964.

1023   Lochhead, Marion, *Young Victorians*. London, 1959.

1024   Loudon, J. B., "Kinship and Crisis in South Wales," *British Journal of Sociology* 12 (1961), 333–350.

1025   McBride, Theresa, *The Domestic Revolution. The Modernisation of House-hold Service in England and France, 1820–1920*. London, 1976.

1026   McEwan, J. A., Carol Owens, and J. R. Newton, "Pregnancy in Girls under Seventeen: A Preliminary Study in a Hospital District in South London," *Journal of Biosocial Science* 6 (1974), 357–382.

1027   McGregor, O. R., *Divorce in England*. London, 1957.

1028   McGregor, O. R., "Family Breakdown and Social Policy," *Proceedings of the British Academy* 59 (1973), 65–81.

1029   McKendrick, Neil, "Home Demand and Economic Growth: A New View of the Role of Women and Children in the Industrial Revolution," *Historical Perspectives: Studies in English Thought and Society, in Honour of J. H. Plumb*, ed. Neil McKendrick (London, 1974), 152–210.

1030   McKeown, Thomas, and R. G. Record, "Reasons for the Decline of Mortality in England and Wales during the Nineteenth Century," *Population Studies* 16 (1962), 94-122.

1031 McLaren, Angus, "Contraception and the Working Classes: The Social Ideology of the English Birth Control Movement in Its Early Years," *Comparative Studies in Society and History* 18 (1976), 236-251.

1032 Marris, Peter, *Widows and Their Families*. London, 1958.

1033 Marsh, David C., *The Changing Social Structure of England and Wales, 1871-1951*. 2nd rev. ed.; London, 1958.

1034 Marshall, T. H., "The Population of England and Wales from the Industrial Revolution to the First World War," *Economic History Review* 5 (1934-35), 65-78.

1035 Martin, Ernest Walter, *The Secret People: English Village Life after 1750*. London, 1954.

1036 Martin, Ernest Walter, *The Shearers and the Shorn: A Study of Life in a Devon Community*. London, 1965.

1037 Matras, J., "Social Strategies of Family Formation: Data for British Female Cohorts Born 1831-1906," *Population Studies* 19 (1965), 167-182.

1038 May, Margaret, "Innocence and Experience: The Evolution of the Concept of Juvenile Delinquency in the Mid-Nineteenth Century," *Victorian Studies* 17 (1973-74), 7-29.

1039 Middleton, Nigel, *When Family Failed. The Treatment of Children in the Care of the Community during the First Half of the Twentieth Century*. London, 1971.

1040 Miller, F.J.W., S.D.M. Court, W. S. Walton, and E. G. Knox, *Growing Up in Newcastle on Tyne*. London, 1960.

1041 Millett, Kate, "The Debate over Women: Ruskin versus Mill," *Victorian Studies* 14 (1970-71), 63-82.

1042 *A Minority in Britain. Social Studies of the Anglo-Jewish Community*, ed. M. Freedman. London, 1955.

1043 Mogey, John M., "Changes in Family Life Experienced by English Workers Moving from Slums to Housing Estates," *Marriage and Family Living* 17 (1955), 123-128.

1044 Mogey, John M., *Family and Neighborhood: Two Studies in Oxford*. London, 1956.

1045 Moindrot, Claude, "Les vagues d'immigration en Grande-Bretagne," *Population* 20 (1965), 633-650.

1046 Moore, Katherine, *Victorian Wives*. London, 1974.

1047 *Multi-Storey Living: The British Working-Class Experience*, ed. Anthony Sutcliffe. London, 1974.

1048 Musgrove, F., "Middle Class Families and Schools, 1780-1880," *Sociological Review* 7 (1959), 169-178.

1049 Musgrove, F., "Population Changes and the Status of the Young in England since the Eighteenth Century," *Sociological Review* 11 (1963), 69-83.

1050 Nalson, John S., *Mobility of Farm Families*. Manchester, 1968.

1051 Newson, John, and Elizabeth Newson, *Four Years Old in an Urban Community*. London, 1968.

1052 Newson, John, and Elizabeth Newson, *Infant Care in an Urban Community*. London, 1963.

1053 Nicholson, J. L., "Variations in Working Class Family Expenditure," *Journal of the Royal Statistical Society* Series A (General) 112 (1949), 359-418.

1054 *Nineteenth-Century Society*, ed. E. Anthony Wrigley. Cambridge, England, 1972.

1055 Ohren, Laura, "The Welfare of Women In Laboring Families: England, 1860-1950," *Feminist Studies* 1 (1973), 107-125.

1056 O'Keefe, Dennis J., "Some Economic Aspects of Raising the School Leaving Age in England and Wales in 1947," *Economic History Review* 2nd series 28 (1975), 500-516.

1057 Olsen, Donald J., "Victorian London: Specialization, Segregation, and Privacy," *Victorian Studies* 17 (1974), 265-278.

1058 O'Neill, William L., *The Woman Movement: Feminism in the United States and England*. New York, 1969.

1059 Ovenden, Graham, and Robert Melville, *Victorian Children*. New York, 1973.

1060 Page, Robin, *The Decline of an English Village*. London, 1974.

1061 Parker, Vanessa, *The English House in the Nineteenth Century*. London, 1970.

1062 Parreaux, Andre, *Daily Life in England in the Reign of George III*. London, 1969.

1063 Pearce, Carol G., "Expanding Families. Some Aspects of Fertility in a Mid-Victorian Community," *Local Population Studies* 10 (1973), 22-35.

1064 Pearsall, Ronald, *The Worm in the Bud: The World of Victorian Sexuality*. New York, 1969.

1065 Peel, C. S., *The Stream of Time: Social and Domestic Life in England 1805-1861*. London, 1931.

1066 Peel, Dorothy C., *How We Lived Then, 1914-1918: A Sketch of Social and Domestic Life in England during the War*. London, 1929.

1067 Peel, Dorothy C., *A Hundred Wonderful Years: Social and Domestic Life of a Century, 1820-1920*. London, 1926.

1068 Penny, N. B., "England Church Monuments to Women Who Died in Childbed between 1780 and 1835," *Journal of the Warburg and Courtauld Institutes* 38 (1975), 314-332.

1069 Penrose, David, and Peter Hill, "Suffolk Timber Houses," *Suffolk Review* 3 (1965-70), 3-7.

1070 Perry, P. J., "Working Class Isolation and Mobility in Rural Dorset 1837-1936. A Study in Marriage Distances," *Transactions of the Institute of British Geographers* 46 (1969), 121-142.

1071 Peterson, M. J., "The Victorian Governess: Status Incongruence in Family and Society," *Victorian Studies* 14 (1970-71), 7-26.

1072 Pinchbeck, Ivy, *Women Workers and the Industrial Revolution*. London, 1930.

1073 Rattray Taylor, Gordon, *The Angel Makers*. London, 1958.

1074 Rice, M. Spring, *Working-Class Wives*. London, 1939.

1075 Rimmer, W. G., "Working Men's Cottages in Leeds, 1770-1840," *Thoresby Society* 46 (1961), 165-199.

1076 Roberts, Robert, *The Classic Slum: Salford Life in the First Quarter of the Century*. Manchester, 1971.

1077 Roe, Frederick Gordon, *The Georgian Child*. London, 1961.

1078 Roe, Frederick Gordon, *The Victorian Child*. London, 1959.

1079 Rollett, Constance, "Housing," *Trends in British Society Since 1900*, ed. A. H. Halsey (London, 1974), 284-320.

1080 Rollett, Constance, and Julia Parker, "Population and Family," ibid., 20-63.

1081 Rosenberg, Rosalind, "In Search of Woman's Nature, 1850-1920," *Feminist Studies* 3 (1975), 1-11, 141-154.

1082 Rosser, Colin, and Christopher Harris, *The Family and Social Change: A Study of Family and Kinship in a South Wales Town*. London, 1965.

1083 Rover, Constance, *Love, Morals and the Feminists*. London, 1972.

1084 Rowntree, Griselda, "Some Aspects of Marriage Breakdown in Britain during the Last Thirty Years," *Population Studies* 18 (1964), 147-164.

1085 Rowntree, Griselda, and Norman H. Carrier, "The Resort to Divorce in England and Wales 1858-1957," *Population Studies* 11 (1958),188-233.

1086 Rowntree, Griselda, and Rachel M. Pierce, "Birth Control in Britain," *Population Studies* 15 (1961), 3-31, 121-160.

1087 Rubinstein, David, *Victorian Homes*. Newton Abbot, 1975.

1088 Ryder, Judith, and Harold Silver, *Modern English Society: History and Structure, 1850-1970*. London, 1970.

1089 Salway, Lance, *A Peculiar Gift: Nineteenth Century Writings on Books for Children*. London, 1976.

1090 Saville, J., *Rural Depopulation in England and Wales 1851-1951*. London, 1957.

1091 Scannell, Dorothy, *Mother Knew Best—An East End Childhood in London*. London, 1974.

1092 Schofield, Roger S., "Age Specific Mobility in an Eighteenth Century Rural English Parish," *Annales de démographic historique* 6 (1970), 261-274.

1093 Schupp, Harriet Warm, "Single Women and Social Reform in Mid-Nineteenth Century England: The Case of Mary Carpenter," *Victorian Studies* 17 (1973-74), 301-317.

1094 Seear, Nancy, "The Economic Position of Women in the United Kingdom," *American Economic Review* 66 (1976), 213-221.

1095   Shaw, L. A., "Impressions of Family Life in a London Suburb," *Sociological Review* 2 (1954), 179-194.

1096   Sheppard, J. A., "Rural Population Changes Since 1851: Three Sample Studies," *Sociological Review* 10 (1962), 81-95.

1097   Shiman, Lilian Lewis, "The Band of Hope Movement: Respectable Recreation for Working-Class Children," *Victorian Studies* 17 (1973-74), 49-74.

1098   Showalter, Elaine, and English Showalter, "Victorian Women and Menstruation," *Victorian Studies* 14 (1970-71), 83-92.

1099   Silver, Morris, "Births, Marriages, and Income Fluctuations in the United Kingdom and Japan," *Economic Development and Cultural Change* 14 (1965-66), 302-315.

1100   Smelser, Neil J., *Social Change in the Industrial Revolution.* London, 1959.

1101   Smelser, Neil J., "Sociological History: The Industrial Revoution and the British Working-Class Family," *Journal of Social History* 1 (1967-68), 17-35. Also in *Essays in Social History*, ed. M. W. Flinn and T. C. Smout (London, 1974), 23-38.

1102   Smith, F. B., "Sexuality in Britain, 1800-1900," *University of Newcastle Historical Journal* 2 (1974), 19-32.

1103   Smith, J. T., "The Long-House in Monmouthshire: A Re-Appraisal," *Culture and Environment*, ed. Idris Llewelyn Foster and L. Alcock (London, 1963), 389-414.

1104   Smith, Peter, "The Long-House and the Laithe House: A Study of the House-and-Byre Homestead in Wales and the West-Riding," ibid., 415-437.

1105   Smith, Roger, "Early Victorian Household Structure: A Case Study of Nottinghamshire," *International Review of Social History* 15 (1970), 69-84.

1106   Spengler, Joseph John, *Population Problems in the Victorian Age.* 2 v. Farnborough, Hants., 1973.

1107   Stacey, Margaret, et al., *Power, Persistence and Change: A Second Study of Banbury.* London, 1975.

1108   Stacey, Margaret, *Tradition and Change: A Study of Banbury.* Oxford, 1960.

1109   Stanford, Jean, and A. T. Patterson, *The Condition of the Children of the Poor in Mid-Victorian Portsmouth.* Portsmouth, 1974.

1110   Stevenson, T.H.C., "The Fertility of Various Social Classes in England and Wales from the Middle of the Nineteenth Century to 1911," *Journal of the Royal Statistical Society* 83 (1920), 401-444.

1111   Sutcliffe, Anthony, "Working-Class Housing in Nineteenth-Century Britain: A Review of Recent Research," *Bulletin of the Society for the Study of Labour History* 24 (1972), 40-51.

1112   Tarn, John, *Five Per Cent Philanthropy—An Account of Housing in Urban Areas between 1840 and 1914.* New York, 1974.

1113   Tarn, John, *Working Class Housing in 19th-Century Britain.* London, 1971.

1114   Thomis, Malcolm I., *The Town Laborer and the Industrial Revolution.* London, 1974.

1115 Thompson, F.M.L., *English Landed Society in the 19th Century*. Toronto, 1963.

1116 Titmuss, Richard, "The Position of Women: Some Vital Statistics," *Essays on the Welfare State* (London, 1963), 88-103. Now in *Essays in Social History*, ed. M. W. Flinn and T. C. Smout (Oxford, 1974), 277-289.

1117 Townsend, Peter, and Brian Rees, *The Personal, Family, and Social Circumstances of Old People*. London, 1960.

1118 Tranter, N. L., "Population and Social Structure in a Bedfordshire Parish: The Cardington Listing of Inhabitants, 1782," *Population Studies* 21 (1967), 261-282.

1119 Tranter, N. L., *Population Since the Industrial Revolution: The Case of England and Wales*. New York, 1973.

1120 Tranter, N. L., "The Social Structure of a Bedfordshire Parish in the Mid-Nineteenth Century," *International Review of Social History* 18 (1973), 90-106.

1121 Trudgill, Eric, *Madonnas and Magdalens: The Origins and Development of Victorian Sexual Attitudes*. New York, 1976.

1122 Trudgill, Eric, "Prostitution and Paterfamilias," *The Victorian City*, ed. H. J. Dyos and Michael Wolff (London, 1973), 693-705.

1123 Turner, Christopher, *Family and Kinship in Modern Britain*. London, 1969.

1124 Turner, Michael, "Parliamentary Enclosure and Population Change in England, 1750-1830," *Explorations in Economic History* 13 (1976), 463-468.

1125 *Two Studies of Kinship in London*, ed. Raymond Firth. London, 1956.

1126 Tyack, Geoffrey, "The Victorian Country Houses of Warwickshire," *Warwickshire History* 2 (1972), 3-19.

1127 Verrière, Jacques, "L'Evolution récente de l'émigration irlandaise," *Population* 20 (1965), 233-252.

1128 Vicinus, Martha, *Suffer and Be Still: Women in the Victorian Age*. Bloomington, Ind., 1972.

1129 Wadsworth, A. P., "The First Manchester Sunday Schools," *Essays in Social History*, ed. M. N. Flinn and T. C. Smout (London, 1974), 100-122.

1130 Ward, D., "Living in Victorian Towns," *Geographical Magazine* 43 (1971), 574-581.

1131 Weaver, M. E., "Industrial Housing in West Cornwall," *Industrial Archaeology* 3 (1966), 23-45.

1132 Wertheim, Albert, "Childhood in John Leech's 'Pictures of Life and Character,' " *Victorian Studies* 17 (1973-74), 75-87.

1133 West, Trudy, *The Timber-Frame House in England*. London, 1971.

1134 Williams, M. W., "The Social Study of Family Farming," *Geographical Journal* 129 (1963), 63-75.

1135 Williams, William Morgan, *Gosforth: The Sociology of an English Village*. Glencoe, Ill., 1956.

1136 Williams, William Morgan, "Kinship in an English Village," *Man* 52 (1952), 143–144.

1137 Williams, William Morgan, *A West Country Village: Ashworthy: Family, Kinship and Land.* London, 1963.

1138 Willmott, Peter, *The Evolution of a Community. A Study of Dagenham after Forty Years.* London, 1963.

1139 Willmott, Peter, and Michael Young, *Family and Class in a London Suburb.* London, 1960.

1140 Willmott, Peter, and Michael Young, *Family and Kinship in East London.* London, 1957.

1141 Winter, J. M., "Some Aspects of the Demographic Consequences of the First World War in Britain," *Population Studies* 30 (1976), 539–552.

1142 Wise, M. J., "Some Notes on the Growth of Population in the Cannock Chase Coalfield," *Geography* 36 (1951), 235–248.

1143 Wohl, A. S., et al., *The History of Working-Class Housing: A Symposium.* Totowa, N.J., 1971.

1144 Wolf, Howard R., "British Fathers and Sons, 1773–1913," *Psychoanalytic Review* 52 (1965–66), 53–70.

1145 Wrigley, E. Anthony, "Baptism Coverage in Early 19th Century England: The Colyton Area," *Population Studies* 29 (1975), 299–315.

1146 Wrigley, E. Anthony, "A Note on the Life-Time Mobility of Married Women in a Parish Population in the Later Eighteenth Century," *Local Population Studies* 18 (1977), 22–29.

1147 Young, Michael, "Kinship and Family in East London," *Man* 54 (1954), 137–139.

Scotland

1148 Dunlop, James C., "The Fertility of Marriage in Scotland: A Census Study," *Journal of the Royal Statistical Society* 77 (1914), 259–288.

1149 Gaily, R. A., "Peasant Houses of the South-West Highlands of Scotland," *Gwerin* 3 (1960–62), 227–242.

1150 Littlejohn, James, *Westrigg: The Sociology of a Cheviot Parish.* London, 1963.

1151 Macpherson, A. G., "An Old Highland Parish Register: Survival of Clanship and Social Change in Laggan, Inverness-shire, 1775–1854," *Scottish Studies* 11 (1967), 149–192.

1152 Rehfisch, F., "Marriage and the Elementary Family among the Scottish Tinkers," *Scottish Studies* 5 (1961), 121–148.

1153 Soulsby, E. M., "Changing Sex Ratios in the Scottish Border Counties," *Scottish Geographical Magazine* 88 (1972), 5–18.

Ireland

1154 Aalen, F.H.A., "A Review of Recent Irish Population Trends," *Population Studies* 17 (1963), 73–78.

1155 Arensberg, Conrad M., *The Irish Countryman: An Anthropological Study.* London, 1937.

1156 Arensberg, Conrad M., and Solon T. Kimball, *Family and Community in Ireland.* 2nd ed.; Cambridge, Mass., 1968.

1157 Butler, Hubert, "The Country House — The Life of the Gentry," *Social Life in Ireland, 1800–1845,* ed. R. B. McDowell (Dublin, 1957), 28–42.

1158 Compton, Paul A., Lorna Goldstrom, and J. M. Goldstrom, "Religion and Legal Abortion in Northern Ireland," *Journal of Biosocial Science* 6 (1974), 493–500.

1159 Connell, Kenneth Hugh, "Catholicism and Marriage in the Century after the Famine," *Irish Peasant Society...* (Oxford, 1968), 113–161. (See #1161)

1160 Connell, Kenneth Hugh, "Illegitimacy before the Famine," ibid., 51–86.

1161 Connell, Kenneth Hugh, *Irish Peasant Society: Four Historical Essays.* Oxford, 1968.

1162 Connell, Kenneth Hugh, "Land and Population in Ireland, 1750–1845," *Economic History Review* 2nd series 2 (1949–50), 278–289.

1163 Connell, Kenneth Hugh, "Marriage in Ireland after the Famine: The Diffusion of the Match," *Journal of the Statistical and Social Inquiry Society of Ireland* 19 (1955–56), 82–103.

1164 Connell, Kenneth Hugh, "Peasant Marriage in Ireland after the Great Famine," *Past and Present* 12 (1957), 76–91.

1165 Connell, Kenneth Hugh, "Peasant Marriage in Ireland, Its Structures and Development since the Famine," *Economic History Review* 2nd series 14 (1961–62), 502–523.

1166 Connell, Kenneth Hugh, "Population," *Social Life in Ireland, 1800–1845,* ed. R. B. McDowell (Dublin, 1957), 85–97.

1167 Connell, Kenneth Hugh, "The Population of Ireland in the Eighteenth Century," *Economic History Review* 16 (1946), 111–124.

1168 Connell, Kenneth Hugh, *The Population of Ireland, 1750–1845.* London, 1950.

1169 Connell, Kenneth Hugh, "Some Unsettled Problems in English and Irish Population History, 1750–1845," *Irish Historical Studies* 7 (1951), 225–234.

1170 Cowens, S. H., "Population Trends in Ireland at the Beginning of the Twentieth Century," *Irish Geography* 5 (1964–68), 387–401.

1171 Cullen, L. M., "Irish History without the Potato," *Past and Present* 40 (1968), 72–83.

1172 Drake, Michael, "Marriage and Population Growth in Ireland, 1750–1845," *Economic History Review* 2nd series 16 (1963–64), 301–313.

1173 Fraser, Morris, *Children in Conflict. Growing Up in Northern Ireland.* New York, 1977.

1174 Freeman, Thomas Walter, *Pre-Famine Ireland.* Manchester, 1957.

1175 Froggatt, P., "The Census in Ireland of 1813-15," *Irish Historical Studies* 14 (1964-65), 227-235.

1176 Hannan, D., "Kinship, Neighbourhood and Social Change in Irish Rural Communities," *Economic and Social Review* 3 (1971-72), 163-188.

1177 Humphreys, Alexander J., *New Dubliners: Urbanization and the Irish Family.* London, 1966.

1178 Hutchinson, Bertram, "Observations on Age at Marriage in Dublin, Related to Social Status and Social Mobility," *Economic and Social Review* 2 (1970-71), 209-222.

1179 Johnson, James, "Marriage and Fertility in Nineteenth Century Londonderry," *Journal of the Statistical and Social Inquiry Society of Ireland* 20 (1958), 99-117.

1180 Johnson, James, "Population Changes in Ireland, 1951-1961," *Geographical Journal* 129 (1963), 167-174.

1181 Johnson, James, "Population Change in Ireland, 1961-1966," *Irish Geography* 5 (1964-68), 470-477.

1182 Kane, Eileen, "Man and Kin in Donegal: A Study of Kinship Functions in a Rural Irish and an Irish-American Community," *Ethnology* 7 (1968), 245-257.

1183 Kennedy, Hugh L., "Love and Famine, Family and Country in Trollope's *Castle Richmond,*" *Eire-Ireland* 7 (1972), 48-66.

1184 Kennedy, Robert E., Jr., *The Irish: Emigration, Marriage, and Fertility.* Berkeley, 1973.

1185 Lee, J., "Marriage and Population in Pre-Famine Ireland," *Economic History Review* 2nd series 21 (1968), 283-295.

1186 Lees, Lynn, "Mid-Victorian Migration and the Irish Family Economy," *Victorian Studies* 20 (1976), 25-43.

1187 Messenger, John C., "Types and Causes of Disputes in an Irish Community," *Eire-Ireland* 3 (1968), 27-37.

1188 Park, A. T., "An Analysis of Human Fertility in Northern Ireland," *Journal of the Statistical and Social Inquiry Society of Ireland* 21 (1962-63), 1-13.

1189 Quinn, Gerard, "The Changing Pattern of Irish Society, 1938-51," *Ireland in the War Years and After,* ed. Kevin B. Nowlan and T. Desmond Williams (Notre Dame, Ind., 1970), 120-133.

1190 Robinson, Alan, "The Geography of Human Fertility in Northern Ireland," *Irish Geography* 5 (1964-68), 302-310.

1191 *Social Life in Ireland, 1800-45,* ed. R. B. McDowell. Dublin, 1957.

1192 Streib, Gordon F., "Old Age in Ireland: Demographic and Sociological Aspects," *Gerontologist* 8 (1968), 227-235.

1193 Symes, D. G., "Farm Household and Farm Performance: A Study of Twentieth

Century Changes in Ballyferriter, Southern Ireland," *Ethnology* 11 (1972), 25-38.

1194 Wallace, Martin, *The Irish: How They Live and Work*. London, 1972.

1195 Walsh, Brendan M., "An Empirical Study of the Age Structure of Irish Population," *Economic and Social Review* 1 (1969-70), 259-279.

1196 Walsh, Brendan M., "Ireland's Demographic Transformation 1958-1970," *Economic and Social Review* 3 (1971-72), 251-275.

1197 Walsh, Brendan M., "Marriage Rates and Population Pressure: Ireland, 1871 and 1911," *Economic History Review* 2nd series 23 (1970), 148-162.

1198 Walsh, Brendan M., "A Perspective on Irish Population Patterns," *Eire-Ireland* 4 (1969), 3-21.

1199 Walsh, Brendan M., "Some Irish Population Problems Reconsidered," ed. The Economic and Social Research Institute Dublin. Paper 42 (1968).

1200 Walsh, Brendan M., "A Study of Irish County Marriage Rates, 1961-66," *Population Studies* 24 (1970), 205-216.

1201 Wilson-Davis, Keith, "The Contraceptive Situation in the Irish Republic," *Journal of Biosocial Science* 6 (1974), 483-492.

France

GENERAL SURVEYS AND COLLECTIONS

1202 *Annales de démographie historique* (1969): "Villes et villages de l'ancienne France."

1203 Aubenas, Roger, *Cours d'histoire du droit privé.* 3 v. Aix-en-Provence, 1954.

1204 Audiat, Pierre, *Vingt-cinq siècles de mariage.* Paris, 1961.

1205 Baehrel, René, "Sur des communes-échantillons," *Annales E.S.C.* 15 (1960), 702–741.

1206 Benjamin, Roger, "De la famille traditionnelle à la famille moderne," *Recherche sociale* 26 (1969), 20–23.

1207 Biraben, Jean-Noël, Michel Fleury, and Louis Henry, "Inventaire pour sondage des registres paroissiaux de France," *Population* 15 (1960), 25–59.

1208 Bourgeois-Pichat, Jean, "De la mesure de la mortalité infantile," *Population* 1 (1946), 53–68.

1209 Calvet, Jean, *L'enfant dans la littérature française.* 2 v. Paris, 1931.

1210 Chamoux, Antoinette, "La reconstitution des familles: espoirs et réalités," *Annales E.S.C.* 27 (1972), 1083–1090.

1211 Chaunu, Pierre, "Histoire et prospective: l'exemple démographique," *Revue historique* 507 (1973), 131–148.

1212 Cherel, Albert, *La famille française. Pages choisies de nos bons écrivains de 825 à 1924: le moyen âge et le XVIe siècle.* Paris, 1924.

1213 Daubeze, Yvette, and Jean-Claude Perrot, "Un programme d'étude démographique sur ordinateur," *Annales E.S.C.* 27 (1972), 1047–1070.

1214 Delzons, Louis, *La famille française et son évolution.* Paris, 1913.

1215 Dion, Roger, *Essai sur la formation du paysage rural français.* Tours, 1934.

1216 *XVIIe siècle* 102–103 (1974): "Le XVIIe siècle et la famille."

1217 *Le droit des gens mariés...* (1966). (See #292)

1218   *Droit privé et institutions régionales: études historiques offertes à Jean Yver.*
       Paris, 1976.

1219   Dupâquier, Jacques, *Introduction à la démographie historique.* Paris, 1974.

1220   Dupâquier, Jacques, "Problèmes de représentativité dans les études fondées sur
       la reconstitution des familles," *Annales de démographie historique* (1972),
       83-91.

1221   Dupâquier, Jacques, and M. Demonet, "Ce qui fait les familles nombreuses,"
       Annales E.S.C. 27 (1972), 1025-1045.

1222   Fleury, Michel, and Louis Henry, *Nouveau manuel de dépouillement et de
       l'exploitation de l'état civil ancien.* Paris, 1965.

1223   Guerdan, René, *La femme et l'amour en France à travers les âges.* Paris, 1965.

1224   Guillaume, Pierre, "La comportement au mariage de différents groups sociaux
       bordelais," *Sur la population française...* (Paris, 1973), 325-340. (See
       #1239)

1225   Guillaume, Pierre, and Jean-Pierre Poussou, *La démographie historique.*
       Paris, 1970.

1226   Henry, Louis, "Une richesse démographique en friche: les registres parois-
       siaux," *Population* 8 (1953), 281-290.

1227   *Histoire des paysans français du XVIIIe siècle à nos jours,* ed. J.-P. Houssel et
       al. Roanne, 1976.

1228   Jeanniere, Able, *Anthropologie sexuelle.* Paris, 1969.

1229   Lepointe, Gabriel, *Droit romain et ancien droit français, régimes matrimo-
       niaux, libéralités, successions.* Paris, 1958.

1230   Maranda, Pierre, *French Kinship: Structure and History.* The Hague, 1974.

1231   *Mélanges offerts au Professeur Louis Falletti: annales de la faculté de droit et
       des sciences économiques de Lyon.* Lyon, 1971.

1232   *Mélanges Roger Aubenas (Recueil de mémoires et travaux publié par la société
       d'histoire du droit et des institutions des anciens pays de droit écrit)* 9 (1974).

1233   Ourliac, Paul, and J. de Malafosse, *Histoire du droit privé.* v. 3: Le droit
       familial. Paris, 1968.

1234   Pernoud, Régine, "La famille bourgeoise et son évolution," *Recherche sociale*
       26 (1969), 5-12.

1235   Peronnet, Michel, "Généalogie et histoire: approches méthodiques," *Revue
       historique* 239 (1968), 111-122.

1236   Perrot, Michelle, "Travaux universitaires [diplômes d'études supérieures d'his-
       toire concernant les problèmes démographiques et les mouvements ouvriers
       dans la seconde moitié du XIXe siècle]," *Mouvement social* 43 (1963),
       139-146.

1237   *Renouveau des idées sur la famille,* ed. Robert Prigent. Paris, 1954.

1238   Spengler, Joseph John, *France Faces Depopulation.* Durham, N.C., 1938.

1239   *Sur la population française au XVIIIe et au XIXe siècles: hommage à Marcel
       Reinhard.* Paris, 1973.

1240   Valmary, Pierre, "L'état civil ancien et les généalogies au service du la démographie historique," *Concours médical* 79 (1957), 3293-3298.

1241 van de Walle, Etienne, and Francine van de Walle, "Allaitement, stérilité et contraception: les opinions jusqu'au XIXe siècle," *Population* 27 (1972), 685-701.

1242 Vialleton, Henri, *Les successions.* Paris, 1963.

1243 Villers, Robert, "Note sur l'immutabilité des conventions matrimoniales dans l'ancien droit français (origines de l'article 1895 du ancien code civil)," *Droit privé et institutions regionales...* (Paris, 1976), 679-689. (See #1218)

1244 Vincent, Paul, "L'utilisation des statistiques des familles," *Population* 1 (1946), 143-148.

1245 Wismes, Armel de, *Ainsi vivaient les Français, des croisades à la troisième Republique, d'après les archives d'une très ancienne famille.* Paris, 1962.

BIBLIOGRAPHIES AND
REVIEW ESSAYS

1246 *Bibliographie annuelle de l'histoire de France du cinquième siècle à 1939.* Paris, 1955 ff.

1247 *Les femmes: guide bibliographique*, ed. Direction de la documentation. Paris, 1974.

1248 Vallin, Pierre, "La famille en France, esquisse d'histoire religieuse," *Etudes* 339 (1973), 283-301.

ANCIENT AND MEDIEVAL PERIODS
(TO c.1450)

1249 Armstrong, C.A.J., "La politique matrimoniale des ducs de Bourgogne de la maison de Valois," *Annales de Bourgogne* 40:1 (1968), 5-58; 40: 2 (1968), 1-139.

1250 Aubenas, Roger, "L'adoption en Provence au moyen âge," *Revue historique de droit français et étranger* 4th series 13 (1934), 700-726.

1251 Aubenas, Roger, "La famille dans l'ancienne Provence," *Annales d'histoire économique et sociale* 8 (1936), 523-540.

1252 Aubenas, Roger, "Note sur quelques aspects de la recherche de la paternité naturelle en pays de droit écrit à la fin du Moyen Age," *Recueil de mémoires et travaux publiés par la Société d'histoire du droit et des institutions des anciens pays du droit écrit* 3 (1955), 1-3.

1253 Aubenas, Roger, "Reflexions sur les 'fraternités artificielles' au Moyen Age," *Etudes historiques à la mémoire de Noël Didier* (Paris, 1960), 1-10.

1254 Baratier, Edouard, *La démographie provençale du XIIIe au XVIe siècle.* Paris, 1961.

1255 Baudoux, L. A., "A propos de l'évolution démographique des communes de la région du centre," *Annales [du] Cercle archéologique et folklorique de la Louvière et du Centre* 4 (1966), 105-129.

1256 Bart, Jean, *Recherche sur l'histoire des successions "ab intestat" dans le droit du duché de Bourgogne du XIIIe siècle à la fin du XVIe siècle (coutume et pratique).* Dijon, 1966.

1257 Batany, Jean, "Regards sur l'enfance dans la littérature moralisante," *Annales de démographie historique* (1973), 123-127.

1258 Bautier, Robert-Henri, "Feux, population et structure sociale au milieu du XVe siècle: l'exemple de Carpentras," *Annales E.S.C.* 14 (1959), 255-268.

1259 Beech, George T., *Rural Society in Medieval France: The Gâtine of Poitou in the Eleventh and Twelfth Centuries.* Baltimore, 1964.

1260 Bernard, Jacques, *Navires et gens de mer à Bordeaux.* Paris, 1968.

1261 Berthe, Maurice, *Le Comté de Bigorre: un milieu rural au bas Moyen Age.* Paris, 1976.

1262 Billot, Claudine, "Les enfants abandonnés à Chartres à la fin du Moyen Age," *Annales de démoraphie historique* (1975), 167-186.

1263 Biraben, Jean-Noël, "La population de Toulouse au XIVe et au XVe siècles," *Journal des Savants* (1964), 284-300.

1264 Bizet, J.-A., *Suso et le minnesang: ou, la morale de l'amour courtois.* Paris, 1948.

1265 Bloch, Marc, *La société féodale.* Paris, several editions between 1939 and 1968. English translation by L. A. Manyon, *Feudal Society.* Chicago, 1961.

1266 Bloch, Marc, *Les caractères originaux de l'histoire rurale française.* 2 v. 2nd ed.; Paris, 1964. English translation by Janet Sondheimer, *French Rural History.* Berkeley, 1966.

1267 Bocquet, André, *Recherches sur la population rurale de l'Artois et du Boulonnais pendant la période bourguignonne (1384–1477).* Arras, 1969.

1268 Bonnecorse de Lubières, Gabriel de, *La condition des gens mariés en Provence aux XIVe, XVe et XVIe siècles.* Paris, 1929.

1269 Bonney, Françoise, "Jean Gerson: un nouveau regard sur l'enfance," *Annales de démographie historique* (1973), 137-142.

1270 Boutruche, Robert, *La crise d'une société: seigneurs et paysans du Bordelais pendant la guerre de cent ans.* Paris, 1963.

1271 Brissaud, Y.-B., "L'Infanticide à la fin du Moyen Age: ses motivations psychologiques et sa répression," *Revue historique de droit français et étranger* 4th series 50 (1972), 229-256.

1272 Burgues, Jean, *Les garanties de restitution de la dot en Languedoc, des invasion barbares à la fin de l'Ancien Régime.* Paris, 1937.

1273 Carpentier, Elisabeth, and Jean Glénisson, "Bilans et méthodes: la démographie française au XIVe siècle," *Annales E.S.C.* 17 (1962), 109-129.

1274 Charbonnier, Pierre, *Guillaume de Murol, un petit seigneur auvergnat au début du XVe siècle*. Clermont-Ferrand, 1973.

1275 Chedéville, André, *Chartres et ses campagnes (XIe–XIIIe siècles)*. Paris, 1973.

1276 Chevailler, Laurent, "Note sur le testament du bâtard dans les coutumes du Nord," *Revue du Nord* 40 (1958), 207–211.

1277 Chevailler, Laurent, "Observations sur le droit de bâtardise dans la France coutumière du XIIe au XVe siècle," *Revue historique de droit français et étranger* 4th series 35 (1957), 376–411.

1278 Chevailler, Laurent, "Remarques sur la condition juridique du bâtard en droit valdôtain et en droit coutumier français," *31° Congresso storico subalpino, Aosta, 1956* (Torino, 1959), I,187–197.

1279 Chevrier, Georges, "Les aspects familiaux du parage comtois," *Etudes d'histoires du droit privé, offertes à Pierre Petot* (Paris, 1959), 79–95.

1280 Chevrier, Georges, "Autorité communale et vie familiale à Dijon aux XIVe et XVe siècles," *Annales de Bourgogne* 16 (1944), 7–14; 17 (1945), 131–138; 18 (1946), 251–257.

1281 Chevrier, Georges, "Sur quelques caractères de l'histoire du régime matrimonial dans la Bourgogne ducal aux diverses phases de son développement," *Le droit des gens mariés...* (1966), 257–284. (See #292)

1282 Coleman, Emily R., "L'infanticide dans le haut Moyen Age," *Annales E.S.C.* 29 (1974), 315–335.

1283 Coleman, Emily R., "Medieval Marriage Characteristics: A Neglected Factor in the History of Medieval Serfdom," *Journal of Interdisciplinary History* 2 (1971–72), 205–219. Also: *The Family in History*, ed. Theodore K. Rabb and Robert I. Rotberg (New York, 1973), 1–15. (See #80)

1284 Comet, Georges, "Quelques remarques sur la dot et les droits de l'épouse dans la région d'Arles au XIIe et XIIIe siècles," *Mélanges offerts à René Crozet...*, ed. Pierre Gallais and Yves-Jean Riou (Poitiers, 1966), II, 1031–1034.

1285 Conon, Marguerite, *La vie familiale en Forez au XIVe siècle et son vocabulaire d'après les testaments*. Paris, 1961.

1286 Coudert, Jean, "L'aînesse roturière en Lorraine: les vicissitudes de la coutume de Void," *Droit privé et institutions régionales...* (Paris, 1976), 157–167. (See #1218)

1287 Daudet, Pierre, *Etudes sur l'histoire de la jurisdiction matrimoniale*. Paris, 1933.

1288 Demolon, Pierre, *Le village mérovingien de Brebières (VIe–VIIe siècles)*. Arras, 1972.

1289 Devailly, Guy, *Le Berry du Xe siècle au milieu du XIIIe*. Paris, 1973.

1290 Du Plessis de Grenadan, Joachim, *Histoire de l'autorité paternelle et de la société familiale en France avant 1789*. Paris, 1900.

1291 Dubled, Henri, "Conséquences économiques et sociales des mortalités du XIVe siècle, essentiellement en Alsace," *Revue d'histoire économique et sociale* 37 (1959), 273–294.

1292 Duby, Georges, *Hommes et structures au Moyen Age.* Paris, 1973.

1293 Duby, Georges, "Dans la France du Nord-Ouest au XIIe siècle: les 'Jeunes' dans la société aristocratique," *Annales E.S.C.* 19 (1964), 835–846. Also in #1292, 213–225; English translations as "Northwest France: The 'Young' in Twelfth-Century Aristocratic Society," *Social Historians in Contemporary France,* ed. Marc Ferro (New York, 1972), 87–99; "In Northwestern France: The 'Youth' in Twelfth Century Aristocratic Society," *Lordship and Community in Medieval Europe,* ed. F. L. Cheyette (New York, 1968), 198–209.

1294 Duby, Georges, "Lignage, noblesse et chevalerie au XIIe siècle dans la région mâconnaise: une révision," *Annales E.S.C.* 27 (1972), 803–823. Also in #1292, 395–422. English translation as "Lineage, Nobility, and Chivalry in the Region of Mâcon during the Twelfth Century," *Family and Society,* ed. Robert Forster and Orest Ranum (Baltimore, 1976), 16–40. (See #77)

1295 Duby, Georges, "La noblesse dans la France médiévale: une enquête à poursuivre," *Revue historique de droit français et étranger* 226 (1961), 1–22. Also in #1292, 145–166.

1296 Duby, Georges, "Remarques sur la littérature généalogique en France aux XIe et XIIe siècles," *Comptes rendus des séances de l'année 1967* of the Académie des inscriptions et belles-lettres (Paris, 1967), 335–345. Also in #1292, 287–298.

1297 Duby, Georges, "Structures de parenté et noblesse dans la France du Nord aux XIe et XIIe siècles," *Miscellanea Mediaevalia in Memoriam Jan Frederik Niermeyer* (Groningen, 1967), 149–165. Also in #1292, 267–285.

1298 Duby, Georges, "Structures familiales aristocratiques en France du XIe siècle en rapport avec les structures de l'état," *L'Europe aux IXe–XIe siècles: aux origines des états nationaux,* ed. T. Manteuffel and A. Gieysztor (Warsaw, 1968), 57–62.

1299 Duby, Georges, *La société aux XIe et XIIe siècles dans la région mâconnaise.* Paris, 1953.

1300 Dufresne, Jean-Luc, "Les comportements amoureux d'après les registres de l'officialité de Cerisy (XIVe–XVe siècle)," *Bulletin philologique et historique du comité des travaux historiques et scientifiques 1973* (1976), 131–156.

1301 Du Moriez, S., *L'avortement. Etude historique, philosophique, sociale, médicale, légale et de droit comparé. Ses conséquences du point de vue de la dépopulation de la France.* Paris, 1912.

1302 Dumas, Auguste, *La condition des gens mariés dans la famille périgourdine.* Paris, 1908.

1303 Etienne, Robert, "La démographie de la famille l'Ausone," *Etudes et chronique de démographie historique* (1964), 15–25, and *Actes du 87e Congrès de la Société des savantes, Poitiers, 1962* (1965), 531–538.

1304 Falletti, Louis, *Le retrait liquager en droit coutumier français.* Paris, 1923.

1305 Farnsworth, William Oliver, *Uncle and Nephew in the Old French Chansons de Gest: A Study in the Survival of Matriarchy*. New York, 1913. Reprint, New York, 1966.

1306   Favarger, Dominique, *Le régime matrimonial dans le comté de Neuchâtel du XVe au XIXe siècle*. Neuchâtel, 1970.

1307   Fédou, René, "Une famille aux XIVe et XVe siècles: les Jossard de Lyon," *Annales E.S.C.* 9 (1954), 461–480.

1308   Feuchère, Pierre, "La bourgeoisie lilloise au moyen âge," *Annales E.S.C.* 4 (1949), 421–430.

1309   Feuchère, Pierre, "La noblesse du Nord de la France," *Annales E.S.C.* 6 (1951), 306–318.

1310   Fiétier, Roland, "Le droit des gens mariés à Besançon au Moyen Age (XIIIe–XVe siècle)," *Le droit des gens mariés...* (1966), 221–253. (See #292)

1311   Flandrin, Jean-Louis, "Repression and Change in the Sexual Life of Young People in Medieval and Early Modern Times," *Journal of Family History* 2 (1977), 196–210.

1312   Fossier, Robert, *La terre et les hommes en Picardie*. Louvain, 1968.

1313   Fourquin, Guy, *Les campagnes de la région parisienne à la fin du Moyen Age*. Paris, 1964.

1314   Galy, Charles, *La famille à l'époque mérovingienne*. Paris, 1901.

1315   Gaudemet, Jean, *Les communautés familiales*. Paris, 1963.

1316   Gauvard, Claude, and Gokalp, Altan, "Les conduites de bruit et leur signification à la fin du Moyen Âge: le Charivari," *Annales E.S.C.* 29 (1974), 693–704.

1317   Gay, Jean-L., "Contribution aux origines du droit des gens mariés dans le Comté de Bourgogne," *Le droit des gens mariés...* (1966), 197–220. (See #292)

1318   Gay, Jean-L., *Les effets pécuniaires au mariage en Nivernais du XIVe au XVIIIe siècle*. Paris, 1953.

1319   Genestal, R., "La femme mariée dans l'ancien droit normand," *Revue historique de droit français et étranger* 4th series 9 (1930), 472–505.

1320   Genestal, R., "La formation du droit d'aînesse," *Normannia* 1 (1928), 157–179.

1321   Genicot, Léopold, *L'économie rurale namuroise au bas Moyen Age (1199–1429). II: Les hommes. La noblesse*. Louvain, 1960.

1322   Gilissen, John, "Le privilège de masculinité dans le droit coutumier de la Belgique et du Nord de la France," *Revue du Nord* 43 (1961), 201–216.

1323   Gilissen, John, "Puissance paternelle et majorité émancipatrice dans l'ancien droit de la Belgique et du nord de la France," *Revue historique de droit français et étranger* 4th series 38 (1960), 5–57.

1324   Girard, René, "Marriage in Avignon in the Second Half of the Fifteenth Century," *Speculum* 28 (1953), 485–498.

1325   Gonon, Marguerite, "Les dots en Forez au XVe siècle, d'après les testaments enregistrés en la chancellerie de Forez," *Mélanges Pierre Tisset: Recueil de mémoires et travaux publiés par la Société d'histoire du droit et des institutions des anciens pays de droit écrit* 7 (1970), 247-265.

1326 Gonon, Marguerite, *Testaments foréziens, 1305-1316.* n. p., 1951.

1327 Gonon, Marguerite, *La vie familiale en Forez au XIVe siècle et son vocabulaire d'après les testaments.* Paris, 1961.

1328 Gouron, André, "Pour une géographie de l'augment de dot," *Le droit de gens mariés...* (1966), 113-131. (See #292)

1329 Guérin, Isabelle, *La vie rurale en Soloque aux XIVe et XVe siècles.* Paris, 1960.

1330 Harsgor, Mikhaël, "L'essor des bâtards nobles au XVe siècle," *Revue historique* 253 (1975), 319-354.

1331 Hilaire, Jean, *Le régime des biens entre époux dans la région de Montpellier du début du XIIIe siecle à la fin du XVIe siècle.* Montpellier, 1957.

1332 Hilaire, Jean, "Les aspects communautaires du droit matrimonial des régions situées autour du Massif Central à la fin du XVe siècle et au debut du XVIe," *Recueil des mémoires et travaux publiés par la Société d'histoire du droit et des institutions des anciens pays du droit écrit* 4 (1958-60), 99-109.

1333 Hilaire, Jean, "Les régimes matrimoniaux aux XIe et XIIe siècles dans la région de Montpellier," ibid. 3 (1955), 15-37.

1334 Hilaire, Jean, "Vie en commun, famille et esprit communautaire [dans le Midi de la France]," *Revue historique de droit français et étranger* 4th series 51 (1973), 8-53.

1335 Imbert, Jean, "Le régime matrimonial de la coutume de la cité de Metz," *Revue historique de droit francais et étranger* 4th series 36 (1958), 304-305.

1336 Imbert, Jean, "Une coutume de lisière: la famille à Aire-sur-la-Lys," *Droit privé et institutions régionales...* (Paris, 1976), 389-399. (See #1218)

1337 Jarriand, E., "La succession coutumière dans les pays de droit écrit," *Revue historique de droit français et étranger* 3rd series 14 (1890), 30-69.

1338 Joris, A., *La ville de Huy au Moyen Age.* Paris, 1959.

1339 Kaiser-Guyot, Marie-Thérèse, *Le berger en France aux XIVe et XVe siècles.* Paris, 1974.

1340 Lafon, Jacques, *Régimes matrimoniaux et mutations sociales. Les époux bordelais (1450-1550).* Paris, 1972.

1341 Laribière, Genevieve, "Le mariage à Toulouse aux XIVe et XVe siècles," *Annales du Midi* 79 (1967), 335-361.

1342 Legohérel, H., "Le parage en Touraine-Anjou au Moyen Age," *Revue historique de droit français et étranger* 4th series 43 (1965), 222-246.

1343 Lehmann, Andrée, *Le rôle de la femme dans l'histoire de France au moyen âge.* Paris, 1952.

1344 Lemaire, André, "Les origines de la communauté de biens entre époux dans le droit coutumier français," *Revue historique de droit français et étranger* 4th series 7 (1928), 584-643.

1345 Le Mené, Michel, "La population nantaise à la fin du XVe siècle," *Annales de Bretagne* 71 (1964), 189-220.

1346 Lévy, Jean-Philippe, "L'officialité de Paris et les questions familiales à la fin du XIVe siècle," *Etudes d'histoire de droit canonique dédiées à Gabriel Le Bras* (Paris, 1965), II, 1265-1294.

1347 Lorcin, Marie-Thérèse, "Pratique successorale et conjoncture démographique," *Bulletin du Centre d'histoire économique et sociale de la région lyonnaise* 3 (1975), 39-61.

1348 Lorcin, Marie-Thérèse, "Retraite des veuves et filles au couvent: quelques aspects de la condition féminine à la fin du Moyen Age," *Annales de démographie historique* (1975), 187-204.

1349 McLaughlin, T. P., "The Formation of the Marriage Bond according to the *Summa parisiensis*," *Mediaeval Studies* 15 (1953), 208-212.

1350 Maillet, Jean, "De l'exclusion coutumière des filles dotées à la renonciation à succession future dans les coutumes de Toulouse et Bordeaux," *Revue historique de droit français et étranger* 4th series 30 (1952), 514-544.

1351 Maillet, Jean, "Les anciens coutumiers bourguignons et la dévolution successorale ab intestat," ibid. 4th series 40 (1962), 153-179.

1352 Malaussena, Paul-Louis, *La vie en Provence orientale aux XIVe et XVe siècles.* Paris, 1969.

1353 Marin-Muracciole, Madeleine-Rose, *L'honneur des femmes en Corse, du XIIIe siècle à nos jours.* Paris, 1964.

1354 Molin, Jean-Baptiste, and Protais Mutembe, *Le rituel du mariage en France du XIIe au XVIe siècle.* Paris, 1974.

1355 Moore, John C., "Love in Twelfth-Century France: A Failure in Synthesis," *Traditio* 24 (1968), 429-443.

1356 Mutel, André, "Recherches sur les coutumes d'aînesse absolue: Ponthieu et Boulonnais," *Revue historique de droit français et étranger* 4th series 54 (1976), 321-347.

1357 Neveux, Hugues, "Démographie et habitat en Cambrésis (XVe-XVIe siècles)," *Annales de démographie historique* (1975), 25-28.

1358 Ourliac, Paul, "La famille pyrénéenne au Moyen Age," *Recueil d'études publiées à la mémoire de Frédéric Le Play* (Paris, 1956), 50-58.

1359 Ourliac, Paul, "Le mariage à Avignon au XVe siècle," *Recueil de mémoires et travaux publiés par la Société d'histoire du droit et des institutions des anciens pays de droit écrit* 1 (1948), 55-61.

1360 Ourliac, Paul, "Le retrait lignagier dans le sud-ouest de la France," *Revue historique de droit français et étranger* 4th series 30 (1952), 328-355.

1361 Paillot, Pierre, *Etude sur la représentation successorale et sa place dans le droit familial du Nord de la France.* Paris, 1935.

1362 Pernoud, Régine, "La vie de famille du moyen âge à l'ancien régime," *Renouveau des idées sur la famille*, ed. Robert Prigent (Paris, 1954), 27-32.

1363 Perrin, Charles-Edmund, "Note sur la population de Villeneuve-Saint-Georges au IXe siècle," *Le Moyen Age* 69 (1963), 75–86.

1364 Petitjean, Michel, *Essai sur l'histoire des substitutions du IXe au XVe siècle dans la pratique et la doctrine, spécialement en France méridionale.* Dijon, 1975.

1365 Petot, P., and A. Vandenbossche, "Le statut de la femme dans les pays coutumiers français du XIIIe au XVIIe siècle," *La Femme. Recueils de la société Jean Bodin* 12 (1962), 243–254.

1366 Poumarède, Jacques, "Puissance paternelle et esprit communautaire dans les coutumes du Sud-Ouest de la France au Moyen Age," *Mélanges Roger Aubenas* (1974), 651–663. (See #1232)

1367 Poumarède, Jacques, *Les successions dans le Sud-Ouest de la France au Moyen Age.* Paris, 1972.

1368 Renardet, Etienne, *Vie et croyances des gaulois avant la conquête romaine.* Paris, 1975.

1369 Renouard, Yves, *Bordeaux sous les rois d'Angleterre.* Bordeaux, 1965.

1370 Richardot, H., "Tutelle, curatelle et émancipation des enfants légitimes en Forez au XIIIe siècle," *Revue historique de droit français et étranger* 4th series 24 (1945), 29–79.

1371 Riché, Pierre, "L'enfant dans la société monastique aux XIe et XIIe siècles," *Actes du Colloque Pierre Abelard-Pierre le Vénérable, Cluny, 1972* (1975), 689–701.

1372 Rossiaud, Jacques, "Fraternités de jeunesse et niveaux de culture dans les villes du Sud-Est à la fin du moyen-âge," *Cahiers d'histoire* 21 (1976), 67–102.

1373 Rossiaud, Jacques, "Prostitution, jeunesse et société dans les villes du sud-est au XVe siècle," *Annales E.S.C.* 31 (1976), 289–325. English translation in *Deviants and the Abandoned in French Society*, ed. Robert Forster and Orest Ranum (Baltimore, 1978), 1–31.

1374 Rousiers, Paul de, *Une famille de hobereaux pendant six siècles.* Paris, 1934.

1375 Shatzmiller, Joseph, *Recherches sur la communauté de manosque au moyen âge, 1241–1329.* Paris, 1973.

1376 Timbal, René-Clément, "La belle-mère, le gendre et le facteur: un mariage parisien au XIVe siècle," *Etudes d'histoire du droit privé, offertes à Pierre Petot* (Paris, 1959), 543–552.

1377 Timbal, Pierre-Clément, "La dévolution successorale 'ab intestat' dans la coutume de Toulouse," *Revue historique de droit français et étranger* 4th series 33 (1955), 51–82.

1378 Timbal, Pierre-Clément, "La tutelle dans la famille des Comtes de Foix au XIVe siècle," *Recueil de mémoires et travaux publiés par la Société du droit et des institutions des anciens pays de droit écrit* 1 (1948), 69–76.

1379 Turlan, Juliette-M., "Une licence du mariage au XIVe siècle. Survivance ou exaction?" *Etudes d'histoire du droit canonique, dediées à Gabriel Le Bras* v. 2 (Paris, 1965), 1447–1457.

1380 Turlan, Juliette-M., "Recherches sur le mariage dans la pratique coutoumière (XIIe–XVIe siècle)," *Revue historique de droit français et étranger* 4th series 35 (1957), 477–528.

1381 Valous, Guy de, *Le patriciat lyonnais aux XIIIe et XIVe siècles.* Paris, 1973.

1382 Weinberger, Stephen, "Peasant Households in Provence: ca. 800–1100," *Speculum* 47 (1973), 247–257.

1383 Wolff, Philippe, "Une famille, du XIIIe au XVIe siècle: les Ysalquier de Toulouse," *Mélanges d'histoire sociale* 1 (1942), 35–58.

1384 Wolff, Philippe, "Quelques actes notariés concernant famille et mariage (XIVe–XVe siècles)," *Annales du Midi* 78 (1966), 115–123.

1385 Wolff, Philippe, "Quelques données sur la société de Rodez autour de 1420," *Rouergue et confins* (1958), 121–133.

1386 Yver, Jean, "Les caractères originaux de la coutume de Normandie," *Mémoires de l'Académie nationale des Sciences, Arts et Belles-Lettres de Caen* 12 (1952), 307–356.

1387 Yver, Jean, "Les caractères originaux du groupe de coutumes de l'ouest de la France," *Revue historique de droit français et étranger* 4th series 30 (1952), 18–79.

1388 Yver, Jean, "Coutume et droit écrit: la puissance paternelle en Poitou," *Mélanges Pierre Tisset (Recueil de mémoires et travaux publiés par la société d'histoire du droit et des institutions des anciens pays de droit écrit)* 7 (1970), 473–486.

1389 Yver, Jean, "Les deux groupes de coutumes du Nord," *Revue du Nord* 35 (1953), 197–220; 36 (1954), 5–36.

1390 Yver, Jean, "Le droit de jouissance du survivant des parents sur les biens de ses enfants dans les trois coutumes de Bourbonnais, Nivernais, Berry," *Mélanges Roger Aubenas...* (1974), 799–814. (See #1232)

1391 Yver, Jean, *Égalité entre héritiers et exclusion des enfants dotés: essai de géographie coutumière.* Paris, 1966.

1392 Yver, Jean, "Note sur quelques textes coutumiers relatifs à l'exclusion successorale des filles dotées," *Etudes historiques à la mémoire de Noël Didier* (Paris, 1960), 351–361.

1393 Yver, Jean, "Sur deux jugements du Maître-Echevin de Metz (1361 et 1376) concernant le partage successoral entre enfants de plusieurs lits," *Mélanges... Falletti* (Lyon, 1971), 591–600. (See #1231)

EARLY MODERN PERIOD
(1450–1789)

1394 Adam, Paul, "Une famille bourgeoise à Sélestat aux XVe et XVIe siècles: les Ergersheims," *La Bourgeoisie alsacienne* (Strasbourg, 1954), 197–202.

1395 Ainson, Vera, "Enquête sur la société et la famille vers 1640 d'après les testaments," *Recherches régionales*, Centre de documentation des Alpes-Maritimes 3:4 (1963), 1-9.

1396 Aleil, Pierre-François, "Enfants illégitimes et enfants abandonnés à Clermont dans la seconde moitié du XVIIIᵉ siècle," *Cahiers d'histoire* 21 (1976), 307-333.

1397 Allieu, Nicole, and Jacqueline Pendino, *Suresnes, 1735-1850. Aspects démographiques et sociaux*. Paris, 1972.

1398 Ariès, Philippe, "Attitudes devant la vie et devant la mort du 17ᵉ au 19ᵉ siècle," *Population* 4 (1949), 463-470.

1399 Ariès, Philippe, "La famille hier et aujourd'hui," *Counterpoint* 11 (1973), 89-97.

1400 Ariès, Philippe, *L'enfant et la vie familiale sous l'ancien régime*. Paris, 1960. 2nd ed.; Paris, 1973. Translated by Robert Baldick as *Centuries of Childhood*. London, 1962.

1401 Ariès, Philippe, "Les familles d'Ancien Régime," *Revue des travaux de l'Académie des sciences morales et politiques* 4th series 109 (1956), 46-55.

1402 Ariès, Philippe, *Histoire des populations françaises et de leurs attitudes devant la vie depuis le XVIIIᵉ siècle*. Paris, 1976. Originally 1948.

1403 Ariès, Philippe, "Le rôle nouveau de la mère et de l'enfant dans la famille moderne," *Les Carnets de l'enfance* 10 (1969), 35-46.

1404 Ariès, Philippe, "Sur les origines de la contraception en France," *Population* 8 (1953), 465-472. Translated as "On the Origins of Contraception in France," *Popular Attitudes toward Birth Control...*, ed. Orest and Patricia Ranum (New York, 1972), 10-20. (See #316)

1405 Armengaud, André, *La famille et l'enfant en France et en Angleterre du XVIᵉ au XVIIIᵉ siècle: aspects démographiques*. Paris, 1975.

1406 Arrighi, Paul, *La vie quotidienne en Corse au XVIIIᵉ siècle*. Paris, 1970.

1407 Aubry, Marie-Elisabeth, "La congrégation de Notre Dame à Nancy et l'éducation des filles aux XVIIᵉ et XVIIIᵉ siècles," *Annales E.S.C.* 26 (1974), 75-96.

1408 Baehrel, René, *Une croissance: la basse Provence rurale*. Paris, 1961.

1409 Bardet, Jean-Pierre, "Enfants abandonnés et enfants assistés à Rouen dans la second moitié du XVIIIᵉ siècle," *Sur la population française...* (Paris, 1973), 19-48. (See #1239)

1410 Basdevant, Jules, *Des rapports de l'Eglise et de l'Etat dans la législation du mariage du concile de Trente au Code civil*. Paris, 1900.

1411 Baulant, Micheline, "La famille en miettes: sur un aspect de la démographie du XVIIIᵉ siècle," *Annales E.S.C.* 27 (1972), 959-968. Translated as "The Scattered Family: Another Aspect of Seventeenth-Century Demography," *Family and Society*, ed. Robert Forster and Orest Ranum (Baltimore, 1976), 104-116. (See #77)

1412 Baulant, Micheline, "Niveaux de vie paysans autour de Meaux en 1700 et 1750," *Annales E.S.C.* 30 (1975), 505-518.

1413 Beaud, Jacques, and Georges Bouchart, *La population de Saint-Denis-en-France (1670-1792).* Paris, 1971.

1414 Becker, Georges, "La bienséance au Grand Siècle: naissance, éducation, amours, mariage," *Aesculape* 54:2 (1971), 2-62; 54:3 (1971), 1-62; 54:4 (1971), 41-59; 54:5 (1971), 2-57.

1415 Bels, Pierre, "La formation du lien de mariage dans l'église protestante française (XVIe et XVIIe siècle)," *Le droit des gens mariés...* (1966), 331-344. (See #292)

1416 Bels, Pierre, *Le mariage des protestants français jusqu'en 1685.* Paris, 1968.

1417 Berthet, M., "Un réactif social: le parrainage du XVIe siècle à la révolution," *Annales E.S.C.* 1 (1946), 43-50.

1418 Berthieu, René, "Les nourrissons à Cormeilles-en-Parisis (1640-1789)," *Annales de démographie historique* (1975), 259-289.

1419 Bideau, Alain, "La population de Thoissey aux XVIIIe et XIXe siècles," *Bulletin du Centre d'histoire économique et sociale de la région lyonnaise* 2 (1972), 23-42.

1420 Bideau, Alain, "L'envoi des jeunes enfants en nourrice. L'exemple d'une petite ville: Thoissey-en-Dombes (1740-1840)," *Sur la population française...* (Paris, 1973), 49-58. (See #1239)

1421 Biraben, Jean-Noël, "A Southern French Village: The Inhabitants of Montplaisant in 1644," *Household and Family...*, ed. Peter Laslett and Richard Wall (Cambridge, England, 1972), 237-254. (See #156)

1422 Biraben, Jean-Noël, "Travaux et recherches sur la démographie de la France au XVIIIe siècle," *Union internationale pour l'étude de la population: conférence internationale de New York en 1961*, v. 1 (1963), 556-564.

1423 Bitton, Davis, *The French Nobility in Crisis, 1560-1640.* Stanford, 1969.

1424 Blacker, C. P., "Social Ambitions of the Bourgeoisie in 18th Century France, and Their Relation to Family Limitation," *Population Studies* 11 (1957), 46-63.

1425 Blanc, Marcel, *Les communautés familiales dans l'ancien droit et leur survivance en Limousin.* Paris, 1905.

1426 Blayo, Yves, and Louis Henry, "Données démographiques sur la Bretagne et l'Anjou de 1740 à 1829," *Annales de démographie historique* (1967), 91-171.

1427 Bluche, François, *La vie quotidienne de la noblesse française au XVIIIe siècle.* Paris, 1973.

1428 Bongert, Yvonne, "Délinquance juvénile et responsabilité penale du mineur au XVIIIe siècle," *Crime et criminalité en France, 17e–18e siècles*, ed. A. Abbiateci et al. (Paris, 1971), 49-90.

1429 Borne, Louis, "Natalité à Boussières (Doubs) de 1673 à 1935," *Procès-verbaux et mémoires de l'Académie des sciences, belles-lettres et arts de Besançon* 172 (1958), 146-157.

1430 Bouchard, Gérard, *Le village immobile: Sennely-en-Sologne au XVIIIe siècle.* Paris, 1972.

1431 Bourdin, Jacques and Anne-Marie, "Brenat au XVIIIe siècle: étude démographique," [*Actes du*] *88e Congrès national des sociétés savants, Clermont-Ferrand, 1963* (Paris, 1964), 763-782.

1432 Bourdin, Pierre-Marie, "La plaine d'Alençon et ses bordures forestières: essai d'histoire démographique et médicale (XVIIe-XVIIIe siècles)," *Cahier des Annales de Normandie* 6 (Caen, 1968), 205-520.

1433 Bourgeois-Pichat, Jean, "Evolution générale de la population française depuis le XVIIIe siècle," *Population* 6 (1951), 635-662. Also as "The General Development of the Population of France since the Eighteenth Century," *Population in History*, ed. David V. Glass and D.E.C. Eversley (London, 1965), 474-506. (See #214)

1434 Bourrachot, Lucile, "Une famille protestante de l'Agenais et ses cousins allemands: les Digeon de Monteton," *Annales du Midi* 81 (1969), 55-71. (See #214)

1435 Bousquet, Jacques, "Un père abusif (Rodez, 1788)," *Revue du Rouerque* 8 (1954), 25-43.

1436 Bouvet, Michel, "Thoarn: étude de démographie historique (XVIIe-XVIIIe siècle)," *Cahier des Annales de Normandie* 6 (Caen, 1968), 17-202.

1437 Boyer, Laurent, "Les assemblées de parents de mineurs en Forez à la fin de l'ancien régime," *Mélanges...Falletti* (Lyon, 1971), 37-57. (See #1231)

1438 Brejon de Lavergnée, Jacques, "Un curieux acte de mariage des registres paroissiaux de Pleuruit en Bretagne (1675)," *Mélanges Pierre Petot* (1959), 49-59.

1439 Brémond, Henri, *Histoire littéraire du sentiment religieux en France depuis la fin des guerres de religion jusqu'à nos jours.* 11 v. Paris, 1916-1959.

1440 Brown, Irene Q., "Philippe Ariès on Education and Society in Seventeenth- and Eighteenth-Century France," *History of Education Quarterly* 7 (1967), 357-368.

1441 Bugler, Georges, "Enquête historique sur la clandestinité matrimoniale et les mariages mixtes dans le pays de Montbéliard," *Société d'émulation de Montbéliard. Bulletin et mémoires* 65 (1966), 35-46.

1442 Burgière, André, "De Malthus à Max Weber: le mariage tardif et l'esprit d'enterprise," *Annales E.S.C.* 27 (1972), 1128-1138. English translation in *Family and Society,* ed. Robert Forster and Orest Ranum (Baltimore, 1976), 237-250. (See #77)

1443 Burgière, André, "Endogamia e comunità contadine: sulla practica matrimoniala a Romainville nel XVIII secolo," *Quaderni storici* 11 (1976), 1073-1094.

1444   Butel, Paul, "Comportements familiaux dans le négoce bordelais au XVIIIe siècle," *Annales du Midi* 88 (1976), 139-157.

1445   Canestrier, Paul, "La dot en Provence au XVIe siècle d'après des documents dialectaux," *Bulletin philologique et historique du Comité des travaux historiques et scientifiques 1955* (1953-54), 279-292.

1446   Carabie, Robert, "La nature du droit de la femme mariéee aux conquêts faits dans les bourgages normands," *Droit privé...* (Paris, 1976), 125-136. (See #1218)

1447   Caspard, Pierre, "Conceptions prénuptiales et développement du capitalisme dans la Principauté de Neuchâtel (1678-1820)," *Annales E.S.C.* 29 (1974), 989-1008.

1448   Castan, Nicole, "La criminalité familiale dans le ressort du Parlement de Toulouse, 1690-1730," *Crimes et criminalité en France sous l'ancien régime, XVIIe-XVIIIe siècles,* ed. A. Abbiateci et al. (Paris, 1971), 91-107.

1449   Castan, Yves, *Honnêteté et relations sociales en Languedoc, 1715-1780.* Paris, 1974.

1450   Castan, Yves, "Pères et fils en Languedoc à l'époque classique," *XVIIe siècle* 102-103 (1974), 31-43.

1451   Chamoux, Antoinette, "L'enfance abandonnée à Reims à la fin du XVIIIe siècle," *Annales de démographie historique* (1973), 263-285.

1452   Chamoux, Antoinette, "Town and Child in Eighteenth-Century Rheims," *Local Population Studies* 13 (1974), 45-46.

1453   Chamoux, Antoinette, and Cécile Dauphin, "La contraception avant la Révolution française: l'exemple Chârillon-sur-Seine," *Annales E.S.C.* 24 (1969), 662-684.

1454   Charbonneau, Hubert, *Tourouve-au-Perche aux XVIIe et XVIIIe siècles: étude de démographie historique.* Paris, 1969.

1455   Charpentier, Jehanne, *Le droit de l'enfance abandonnée; son évolution sous l'influence de la psychologie (1552-1791).* Paris, 1967.

1456   Charpy, André, "Registres paroissiaux et démographie en Bugey et Valromey (1660-1860)," *Visages de l'Ain* 28 (1975), 32-36.

1457   Charrin, Louis de, *Les testaments dans la région de Montpellier.* Montpellier, 1961.

1458   Chatelain, Abel, "Migrations et domesticité féminine urbaine en France, XVIIIe siècle-XXe siècle," *Revue d'histoire économique et sociale* 47 (1969), 506-528.

1459   Chaunu, Pierre, "Les éléments de longue durée dans la société et la civilisation du XVIIe siècle: la démographie," *XVIIe siècle* 106-107 (1975), 3-22.

1460   Chaunu, Pierre, "Reflexions sur la démographie normande," *Sur la population française...* (Paris, 1973), 97-117. (See #1239)

1461   Chaussinand-Nogaret, Guy, *La noblesse au XVIIIe siècle.* Paris, 1976.

1462   Chevrier, Georges, "Caractères méconnus de la tutelle des mineurs dans le droit coutumier récent," *Revue historique de droit français et étranger* 4th series 22 (1943), 217-235.

1463 Chevrier, Georges, "Le régime matrimonial en Mâconnais aux XVIIe et XVIIIe siècles," *Mémoires de la Société pour l'histoire du droit et des institutions des anciens pays bourguignons, comtois et romands* 25 (1964), 77-95.

1464 Chevrier, Georges, "La vieille famille comtoise," *Nouvelle revue francomtoise* 1 (1954), 73-78.

1465 Chrisman, Miriam O., "Women and the Reformation in Strasbourg 1490-1530," *Archiv für Reformationsgeschichte* 63 (1972), 143-167.

1466 Collier, Raymond, *La vie en Haute-Provence de 1600 à 1850.* Gap, 1973.

1467 Collomp, Alain, "Famille nucléaire et famille élargie en Haute Provence au XVIIIe siècle (1703-1734)," *Annales E.S.C.* 27 (1972), 969-975.

1468 Colombet, A., "Types de maisons rurales du Châtillonnais: vieilles maisons de Beaunotte," *Travaux de linguistique et de folklore de Bourgogne* 5 (1958), 34-38.

1469 Coudert, J., "Le mariage dans le diocèse de Toul au XVIe siècle," *Annales de l'Est* 5th series 3 (1952), 61-92.

1470 Courtès, Georges, "Un village du Condomois aux XVIIe et XVIIIe siècles: Gazaupouy. Etude démographique et sociale," *Bulletin de la Société archéologique, historique, littéraire et scientifique du Gers* 67 (1966), 7-55.

1471 Couturier, Marcel, *Recherches sur les structures sociales de Châteaudun 1525-1789.* Paris, 1969.

1472 Croix, Alain, and C. Dauphin, "La contraception avant la révolution," *Annales E.S.C.* 24 (1969), 662-684.

1473 Croix, Alain, "La démographie du pays nantais au XVIe siècle," *Annales de démographie historique* (1967), 63-90.

1474 Croix, Alain, *Nantes et le Pays Nantais au XVIe siècle: étude demographique.* Paris, 1974.

1475 Cros, Claude, "Les mouvements saisonniers des conceptions et des mariages, paroisse de Saint-Priest-le-Betoux (1700-1820) en Lemosin (Haute-Vienne)," *Etudes limousines* 60-61 (1976), 37-42.

1476 Crump, Lucy, *Nursery Life Three Hundred Years Ago: The Story of a Dauphin of France, 1601-1610, Taken from the Journal of Dr. Jean Herourd, Physician-in-Charge, and from Other Sources.* London, 1929.

1477 Davis, Natalie Zemon, "Ghosts, Kin, and Progeny: Some Features of Family Life in Early Modern France," *Daedalus* 106 (1977), 87-114.

1478 Davis, Natalie Zemon, "The Reasons of Misrule: Youth Groups and Charivaris in Sixteenth-Century France," *Past and Present* 50 (1971), 41-75. Now in next entry, 97-123.

1479 Davis, Natalie Zemon, *Society and Culture in Early Modern France.* Stanford, 1975.

1480 Daumard, Adeline, and François Furet, *Structures et relations sociales à Paris au milieu du XVIIIe siècle.* Paris, 1961.

1481   DeHaussy, Jacques, *L'assistance publique à l'enfance; les enfants abandonnés.* Paris, 1951.

1482   Delasselle, Claude, "Les enfants abandonnés à Paris au XVIIIe siècle," *Annales E.S.C.* 30 (1975), 187–218.

1483   Delumeau, Jean, "Démographie d'un port français sous l'ancien régime: Saint-Malo, 1651–1750," *XVIIe siècle* 86–87 (1970), 3–19.

1484   Deniel, Raymond, and Louis Henry, "La population d'un village du Nord de la France: Sainghin-en-Melantois, de 1665 à 1851," *Population* 20 (1965), 563–602.

1485   Depauw, Jacques, "Amour illégitime et société à Nantes au XVIIIe siècle," *Annales E.S.C.* 27 (1972), 1155–1182. English translation in *Family and Society,* ed. Robert Forster and Orest Ranum (Baltimore, 1976), 145–191. (See #77)

1486   Depauw, Jacques, "Immigration féminine, professions féminines et structures urbaines à Nantes au XVIIIe siècle," *Université de Nantes Centre de recherches sur l'histoire de la France Atlantique. Enquêtes et documents* (Nantes, 1972), 37–60.

1487   Depauw, Jacques, "Pauvres, pauvres mendiants, mendiants valides ou vagabonds? Les hésistations de la législation royal," *Revue d'histoire moderne et contemporaine* 21 (1974), 401–418.

1488   Desportes, Pierre, "La population de Reims au XVe siècle," *Le Moyen Age* 72 (1966), 463–509.

1489   Devyver, André, *La sang épuré. Les préjugés de race chez les gentilshommes français de l'ancien régime (1560–1720).* Brussels, 1973.

1490   Deyon, Pierre, *Amiens, capitale provinciale: étude sur la société urbaine au 17e siècle.* Paris, 1967.

1491   Dinet, D., "Quatre paroisses du Tonnerrois," *Annales de démographie historique* (1969), 62–84.

1492   Doyle, William, *The Parlement of Bordeaux and the End of the Old Regime 1771–1790.* New York, 1974.

1493   Drake, T.G.H., "Infant Welfare Laws in France in the Eighteenth Century," *Annals of Medical History* 7 (1935), 49–61.

1494   Drake, T.G.H., "The Wet Nurse in France in the Eighteenth Century," *Bulletin of the History of Medicine* 8 (1940), 934–948.

1495   Dravasa, Etienne, "Les classes sociales au XVIIIe siècle à Bordeaux, d'après les contrats de mariage," *Revue juridique et économique du Sud-Ouest* série économique 12 (1963), 961–1012. (See critique #1719)

1496   Dreyer-Roos, Suzanne, *La population strasbourgeoise sous l'ancien régime.* Strasbourg, 1969.

1497   Drouot, Henri, "Un père de famille sous Henri IV: lettres domestiques d'Etienne Bernard (1598–1609)," *Annales de Bourgogne* 24 (1952), 160–175.

1498 Duchêne, Roger, "La famille au XVIIe siècle: à propos de quelques mots d'enfants," *Information historique* 37 (1975), 211-216.

1499 Dupâquier, Jacques, "Croissance démographique régionale dans le Bassin parisien au XVIIIe siècle," *Sur la population française...* (Paris, 1793), 231-250. (See #1239)

1500 Dupâquier, Jacques, "Des roles de tailles à la démographie historique: l'exemple du Vexin français," *Annales de démographie historique* (1965), 31-42.

1501 Dupâquier, Jacques, "Habitat rural et démographie: l'exemple de l'Ile-de-France," *Annales de démographie historique* (1975), 65-68.

1502 Dupâquier, Jacques, "Les caractères originaux de l'histoire démographique française au XVIIIe siècle," *Revue d'histoire moderne et contemporaine* 23 (1976), 182-202.

1503 Dupâquier, Jacques, "Sur la population française au XVIIe et au XVIIIe siècle," *Revue historique* 239 (1968), 43-79.

1504 Dupâquier, Jacques, and Louis Jadin, "Structure of Household and Family in Corsica 1769-1771," *Household and Family...*, ed. Peter Laslett and Richard Wall (Cambridge, England, 1972), 283-298. (See #156)

1505 Dupâquier, Jacques, and M. Lachiver, "Sur les débuts de la contraception en France, ou les deux malthusianismes," *Annales E.S.C.* 24 (1969), 1391-1406.

1506 Durand, Bernard, "Aut nubere, aut dotare," *Mélanges...Aubenas* (1974), 281-293. (See #1232)

1507 Dussourd, Henriette, *Au même pot et au même feu: étude sur les communautés familiales agricoles du centre de la France.* Moulins, 1962.

1508 Dussourd, Henriette, "Les dissolutions des communautés familiales agricoles dans le centre de la France depuis le XVIIIe siècle iusqu'au Code civil," [*Actes du*] *89e Congrès national des sociétés savantes, Lyon, 1964* (Paris, 1964), 309-319.

1509 El Kordi, Mohamed, *Bayeux aux XVIIe et XVIIIe siècles.* Paris, 1970.

1510 Emmanuelli, François-Xavier, " 'Ordres du Roi' et lettres de cachet en Provence à la fin de l'ancien régime. Contribution a l'histoire du climat social et politique," *Revue historique* 252 (1974), 357-392.

1511 Estienne, Pierre, "Démographie ancienne d'une paroisse haute-alpine (1629-1822)," *Cahiers d'histoire* 15 (1970), 215-222.

1512 Faigniez, Georges, *La femme et la société française dans la première moitié du XVIIe siècle.* Paris, 1929.

1513 Fauchon, Max, "A propos des actes de baptême des enfants naturels dans l'ancien régime," *Revue de l'Avranchin et du pays de Granville* 43 (1966), 88-97.

1514 Faure-Soulet, Jean-François, *La vie quotidienne dans les Pyrénées sous l'ancien régime, du XVIe au XVIIIe siècle.* Paris, 1974.

1515 Ficatier, G., "Quels étaient les usages et les coutumes concernant la famille et le mariage dans l'Auxerrois au XVIe siècle?" *L'echo d'Auxerre* 62 (1966), 7–11.

1516 Filhol, René, "Protestantisme et droit d'aînesse au XVIe siècle (resumé)," *Revue historique de droit français et étranger* 4th series 5 (1960), 618–622.

1517 Filhol, René, "L'application de l'édit des secondes noces en pays coutumier," *Mélanges...Aubenas* (1974), 295–299. (See #1232)

1518 Filhol, René, and Michel Brunet, "Autour de l'arrêt du 'sang damné': l'abrogation de la coutume normande d'exclusion successorale des enfants de condamnés," *Droit privé...* (Paris, 1976), 209–241. (See #1218)

1519 Flandrin, Jean-Louis, *Les amours paysannes: amour et sexualité dans les campagnes de l'ancienne France, XVIe–XIXe siècle.* Paris, 1975.

1520 Flandrin, Jean-Louis, "Enfance et société," *Annales E.S.C.* 19 (1964), 322–329.

1521 Flandrin, Jean-Louis, *Familles: parenté, maison, sexualité dans l'ancienne société.* Paris, 1976.

1522 Flandrin, Jean-Louis, "Sentiments et civilisation: sondage au niveau des titres d'ouvrages," *Annales E.S.C.* 20 (1965), 939–966.

1523 Fleury, Michel, and Louis Henry, "Pour connaître la population de la France depuis Louis XIV," *Population* 13 (1958), 663–686.

1524 Fontez, Petro, *Les diverses étapes de la laïcisation du mariage en France.* Perpignan, 1972.

1525 Forestier, H., "Le 'droit de garçons' dans la communauté villageoise aux XVIIe et XVIIIe siècles," *Annales de Bourgogne* 13 (1941), 109–114.

1526 Forster, Robert, *The House of Saulx-Tavanes: Versailles and Burgundy, 1700–1830.* Baltimore, 1971.

1527 Fourastié, Jean, "De la vie traditionnelle à la vie tertiaire," *Population* 14 (1959), 417–432.

1528 Fresel-Lozey, Michel, *Histoire démographique d'un village en Béarn: Bilhères d'Ossau.* Bordeaux, 1969.

1529 Funck-Brentano, Frantz, *L'ancien régime.* Paris, 1926. Translated as *The Old Regime in France.* New York, 1929.

1530 Gabet, Camille, "Etude démographique dans une paroisse rurale au XVIIIe siècle: les mariages à Thaire d'Aunis," *Actes du 90e Congrès de la Société des savantes, Nice, 1965,* v. 1 (1966), 151–157.

1531 Galliano, Paul, "La mortalité infantile (indigènes et nourrissons) dans la banlieue Sud de Paris à la fin du XVIIIe siècle (1774–1794)," *Annales de démographie historique* (1966), 139–177.

1532 Galliot, Simone, *Le régime matrimonial franc-comtois de 1459 à la Révolution.* Besançon, 1953.

1533 Galliot, Simone, "Le trousseau de la mariée en France-Comte aux XVIe, XVIIe et XVIIIe siècles," *Nouvelle revue franc-comtoise* 1 (1954), 102–107.

1534 Ganghoffer, Roland, "Les régimes matrimoniaux du centre de l'Alsace aux XVIe et XVIIe siècles," *Droit privé...* (Paris, 1976), 267–283. (See #1218)

1535   Ganiage, Jean G., "Aux confins de la Normandie: structures de la natalité dans cinq villages du Beauvaisis," *Annales de Normandie* 23 (1973), 57-90.

1536   Ganiage, Jean G., "Nourrissons parisiens en Beauvais," *Sur la population française...* (Paris, 1973), 271-287. (See #1239)

1537   Ganiage, Jean G., *Trois villages d'Ile-de-France au XVIIIe siècle: étude démographique.* Paris, 1963.

1538   Garden, Maurice, "Les verriers de Givors au XVIIIe siècle," *Sur la population française...* (Paris, 1973), 291-304. (See #1239)

1539   Garden, Maurice, *Lyon et les lyonnais au XVIIIe siècle.* Paris, 1970. Abridged edition, Paris, 1975.

1540   Garden, Maurice, "Quelques remarques sur l'habitat urbain: l'example de Lyon au XVIIIe siècle," *Annales de démographie historique* (1975), 29-35.

1541   Gaudemet, J., "Législation canonique et attitudes séculières a l'égard du lien matrimonial au XVIIe siècle," *XVIIe siècle* 102-103 (1974), 15-30.

1542   Gautier, Etienne, and Louis Henry, *La population de Crulai, paroisse normande.* Paris, 1958.

1543   Gayot, Gérard, "A propos des structures sociales ardennaises aux XVIIIe et XIXe siècles, fiscalité et relations familiales," *Etudes ardennaises* 53-54 (1968), 7-28.

1544   Geisendorf, P., *Histoire d'une famille du refuge français: les Des Gouttes.* Geneva, 1941.

1545   Ghestin, Jacques, "L'action des parlements contre les 'mésalliances' aux XVIIe et XVIIIe siècles," *Revue historique de droit français et étranger* 4th series 34 (1956) 74-110, 196-224.

1546   Giacchetti, Jean-Claude, and Michel Tyvaert, "Argenteuil (1740-1790)," *Annales de démographie historique* (1969), 40-61.

1547   Gigot, Jean-Gabriel, "Enfants abandonnés à Perpignan au XVIIe siècle," *Centre d'études et de recherches catalanes des archives* 17 (1962), 263-276.

1548   Gille, Bertrand, *Les sources statistiques de l'histoire de France, des enquêtes du XVIIe siècle à 1870.* Geneva, 1964.

1549   Gilles, H., "Mariages de princes et dispenses pontificales," *Mélanges...Falletti* (Lyon, 1971), 295-308. (See #1231)

1550   Gintrac, Alain, *Histoire démographique d'un village corrézien: Soudeilles, 1610-1859.* 2 v. n. p., 1970.

1551   Girard, Pierre, "Aperçus de la démographie de Sotteville-les-Rouen vers la fin du XVIIIe siècle," *Population* 14 (1959), 485-508.

1552   Gonnet, Paul, *L'adoption lyonnaise des orphelins légitimes (1531-1793).* 2 v. Paris, 1935.

1553   Goubert, Pierre, *L'ancien régime,* v. 1. Paris, 1969. English translation as *The Ancien Régime: French Society, 1600-1750.* London, 1973. New York, 1974.

1554   Goubert, Pierre, *Beauvais et le Beauvaisis de 1600 à 1730.* Paris, 1960.

1555 Goubert, Pierre, *Cent mille provinciaux au XVIIe siècle: Beauvais et le Beauvaisis de 1600 à 1730.* Paris, 1968.

1556 Goubert, Pierre, "En Beauvaisis: problèmes démographiques du XVIIe siècle," *Annales E.S.C.* 7 (1952), 453-468.

1557 Goubert, Pierre, *Familles marchandes sous l'ancien régime: les Danse et les Motte, de Beauvais.* Paris, 1959.

1558 Goubert, Pierre, "Family and Province: A Contribution to the Knowledge of Family Structure in Early Modern France," *Journal of Family History* 2 (1977), 179-197.

1559 Goubert, Pierre, "Historical Demography and the Reinterpretation of Early Modern French History: A Research Review," *Journal of Interdisciplinary History* 1 (1970-1971), 37-48. Also in *The Family in History,* ed. Theodore K. Rabb and Robert I. Rotberg (New York, 1973), 16-28. (See #80)

1560 Goubert, Pierre, "La famille française au XVIIIe siècle," *Saggi di demografia storica, serie Ricerche empiriche* 2 (1969), 35-50.

1561 Goubert, Pierre, "Legitimate Fecundity and Infant Mortality in France during the Eighteenth Century: A Comparison," *Daedalus* 97 (1968), 593-603.

1562 Goubert, Pierre, "Recent Theories and Research in French Population between 1500 and 1700," *Population in History,* ed. David V. Glass and D.E.C. Eversley (London, 1965), 457-473. (See #214)

1563 Goubert, Pierre, "Registres paroissiaux et démographie dans la France du XVIe siècle," *Annales de démographie historique* (1965) 43-48.

1564 Gouesse, Jean-Marie, "En Basse-Normandie aux XVIIe et XVIIIe siècles: le refus de l'enfant au tribunal de la pénitence," *Annales de démographie historique* (1973), 231-261.

1565 Gouesse, Jean-Marie, "La formation du couple en Basse-Normandie," *XVIIe siècle* 102-103 (1974), 45-58.

1566 Gouesse, Jean-Marie, "Parenté, famille et mariage en Normandie aux XVIIe et XVIIIe siècles: Presentation d'une source et d'une enquête," *Annales E.S.C.* 27 (1972), 1139-1154.

1567 Gouhier, Pierre, *Port-en-Bessin, 1597-1792. Etude d'histoire démographique.* Caen, 1962.

1568 Goy, Gérard, "Esquisse de l'évolution démographique de la Brede et des ses environs dans la deuxième moitié du XVIIIe siècle," *Revue historique de Bordeaux et du département de la Gironde* 21 (1972), 71-77.

1569 Grenouiller, J.-F., "Communautés et familles en Bas-Dauphiné: les côtes d'Arey et sa région (XVIIe siècle-1815)," *Bulletin du centre d'histoire économique et sociale de la région lyonnaise* 2 (1972), 62-68.

1570 Gresset, Maurice, *Le monde judiciaire à Besançon de la conquête par Louis XIV à la Révolution (1674-1789).* Lille, 1975.

1571 Guery, Alain, "La population du Rouergue, de la fin du Moyen Age au XVIIIe siècle," *Annales E.S.C.* 28 (1973), 1555-1576.

1572 Guilleux, Joseph, "Etude démographique mancelle, les mariages célébrés à l'intérieur de la ville du Mans durant les années 1775-1804: les influences économiques, politiques et religieuses," *Bulletin de la Société d'agriculture, science et arts de la Sarthe* 4th series 8 (1971-72), 125-158.

1573   Gutton, Jean-Pierre, *La société et les pauvres: l'exemple de la généralité de Lyon, 1534-1789.* Paris, 1971.

1574   Gutton, Jean-Pierre, *L'état et la mendicité dans la première moitié du XVIIIe siècle: Auvergne, Beaujolais, Forez, Lyonnais.* Lyon, 1973.

1575   Henry, Louis, "Ducs et pairs sous l'Ancien Régime: charactéristiques démographiques d'une caste," *Population* 15 (1960), 807-830.

1576   Henry, Louis, "Evolution de la fécondité légitime à Meulan de 1660 à 1860," *Population* 25 (1970), 875-885.

1577   Henry, Louis, and J. Houdaille, "Fécondité des mariages dans le quart nord-ouest de la France de 1670 à 1829," *Population* 28 (1973), 873-924.

1578   Henry, Louis, "Fécondité des mariages dans le quart sud-ouest de la France de 1720 à 1829," *Annales E.S.C.* 27 (1972), 612-640, 977-1023.

1579   Henry, Louis, "La nuptialité à la fin de l'Ancien Régime," *Population* 9 (1954), 542-546.

1580   Henry, Louis, "Monographie paroissiale sur la population française au XVIIIe siècle. Un faubourg du Havre: Ingouville," *Population* 16 (1961), 285-300.

1581   Henry, Louis, "The Population of France in the Eighteenth Century," *Population in History,* ed. David V. Glass and D.E.C. Eversley (London, 1965), 434-456. (See #214)

1582   Henry, Louis, and Claude Lévy, "Quelques données sur la région autour de Paris au XVIIIe siècle," *Population* 17 (1962), 297-326.

1583   Higonnet, Patrice L.-R., *Pont-de-Montvert: Social Structure and Politics in a French Village, 1700-1914.* Cambridge, Mass., 1972.

1584   Hilaire, Jean, "L'évolution des régimes matrimoniaux dans la région de Montpellier aux XVIIe et XVIIIe siècles," *Le droit des gens mariés...* (1966), 133-194. (See #292)

1585   Hildesheimer, Françoise, "L'organisation familiale à Nice au XVIIe siècle," *Revue historique de droit français et étranger* 4th series 54 (1976), 177-202.

1586   Hildesheimer, Françoise, "Nice au XVIIe siècle (économie, famille, société)," *Recherches régionales* 14 (1974), 23-30.

1587   Houdaille, Jacques, "Analyse démographique de deux ouvrages de généalogie sur les descendants de Mme. de Sévigné, Bussy-Rabutin et Jean Racine," Population 26 (1971), 953-955.

1588   Houdaille, Jacques, "La population de Boulay (Moselle) avant 1850," *Population* 22 (1967), 1055-1084.

1589   Houdaille, Jacques, "La population de sept villages des environs de Boulay (Moselle) aux XVIIIe et XIXe siècles," *Population* 26 (1971), 1061-1072.

1590   Houdaille, Jacques, "Un village du Morvan: Saint-Agnan," *Population* 16 (1961), 301-312.

1591　Houdaille, Jacques, "Trois paroisses de Saint Domingue au XVIIIe siècle: étude démographique," *Population* 18 (1963), 93–110.

1592　Huet, Alain, "Annebault et Bourgeauville aux XVIIe et XVIIIe siècles: contribution a l'étude démographique du pays d'Auge," *Annales de Normandie* 22 (1972), 277–300.

1593　Hufton, Olwen, "Women and the Family Economy in Eighteenth-Century France," *French Historical Studies* 9 (1975), 1–23.

1594　Hufton, Olwen, *The Poor of Eighteenth-Century France 1750–1789.* New York, 1974.

1595　Hunt, David, *Parents and Children in History: The Psychology of Family Life in Early Modern France.* New York, 1970.

1596　Jacquart, Jean, *La crise rurale en Ile-de-France 1550–1670.* Paris, 1974.

1597　Jarriot, Jacques, "Une famille de 'bons ménagers': la branche nivernaise des Menou de Charnizay aux XVIIe et XVIIIe siècles," *Revue d'histoire moderne et contemporaine* 23 (1976), 80–101.

1598　Joly, Danielle, *Démographie d'Anet au XVIIIe siècle.* Paris, 1970.

1599　Jouan, Marie-Hélène, "Les originalités démographiques d'un bourg artisanal normand au XVIIIe siècle: Villedieu-les-Poëles (1711–1790)," *Annales de démographie historique* (1969), 87–124.

1600　Jurgens, Madeleine, and Pierre Couperie, "Le logement à Paris aux XVIe et XVIIe siècles: une source, les inventaires après décès," *Annales E.S.C.* 17 (1962), 488–500.

1601　Kintz, Jean-Pierre, "Démographie en pays lorrains au XVIe siècle: présentation partielle d'une thèse de doctorat d'Etat," *Annales de démographie historique* (1975), 409–415.

1602　Kintz, Jean-Pierre, "Deux études alsaciennes," *Annales de démographie historique* (1969), 261–292.

1603　Kunstler, Charles, *La vie quotidienne sous la Régence.* Paris, 1960.

1604　Kunstler, Charles, *La vie quotidienne sous Louis XV.* Paris, 1953.

1605　Kunstler, Charles, *La vie quotidienne sous Louis XVI.* Paris, 1950.

1606　Labatut, Jean-Pierre, *Les ducs et pairs de France au XVIIe siècle.* Paris, 1972.

1607　Lachiver, Marcel, "En Touraine et en Berry: une étude et quelques esquisses," *Annales de démographie historique* (1969), 215–240.

1608　Lachiver, Marcel, "Fecondité légitime et contraception dans la région parisienne," *Sur la population française...* (Paris, 1973), 383–402. (See #1239)

1609　Lachiver, Marcel, *La population de Meulan du XVIIe au XIXe siècle (vers 1600–1870).* Paris, 1969.

1610　Laget, Mireille, "Province et insalubrité: morts d'enfants dans le Languedoc Côtier sous Louis XIV," *les provinciaux sous Louis XIV, colloque, Marseille, 1975* (Marseille, 1975), 78–86.

1611　Lajonchère, Lucien, and Jean-Pierre Poussou, "Les actes de mariage des villes corréziennes à la veille de la Révolution et leurs apports: Essai méthodologique," *Annales du Midi* 85 (1973), 403–422.

1612   Landraud, Micheline, "Observations sur un contrat de mariage passé en Dauphiné au XVIIIe siècle," *Mélanges...Falletti* (Lyon, 1971), 355-370. (See #1231)

1613   Lannes, Xavier, "Le XVIIIe siècle: l'évolution des idées," *Renouveau des idées sur la famille,* ed. Robert Prigent (Paris, 1954), 34-49.

1614   Le Roy Ladurie, Emmanuel, *Les paysannes de Languedoc.* 2 v. Paris, 1966. 2nd ed.; Paris, 1974. Abridged English translation: *The Peasants of Languedoc.* Urbana, Ill., 1974.

1615   Le Roy Ladurie, Emmanuel, "Système de la coutume: structures familiales et coutume d'héritage en France au XVIe siècle," *Annales E.S.C.* 27 (1972), 825-846. Also in his *Territoire de l'historien* (Paris, 1973), 222-251. English translations in *Family and Inheritance...,* ed. Jack Goody, Joan Thirsk, and E. P. Thompson (Cambridge, England, 1976), 37-70, and *Family and Society,* ed. Robert Forster and Orest Ranum (Baltimore, 1976), 75-103. (See #296)

1616   Lebrun, François, "Angers sous l'ancien régime: introduction à l'étude démographique de la population," *Annales de Bretagne* 81 (1974), 151-166.

1617   Lebrun, François, "Démographie et mentalités: le mouvement des conceptions sous l'ancien régime," *Annales de démographie historique* (1974), 45-50.

1618   Lebrun, François, "Une famille Angevine sous l'ancien régime d'après son 'papier mémorial,' " *Annales de Bretagne et des pays de l'ouest* 82 (1975), 48-67.

1619   Lebrun, François, *Les hommes et la mort en Anjou aux XVIIe et XVIIIe siècles: essai de démographie et psychologie historiques.* Paris, 1971.

1620   Lebrun, François, "Naissances illégitimes et abandons d'enfants en Anjou au XVIIIe siècle," *Annales E.S.C.* 27 (1972), 1183-1189.

1621   Lebrun, François, *La vie conjugale sous l'ancien régime.* Paris, 1975.

1622   Lefebvre-Teillard, Anne, *La population de Dôle au XVIIIe siècle.* Paris, 1969.

1623   ˙Le Goff, Armelle, "Bilan d'une étude de démographie historique: Auray au XVIIIe siècle (vers 1740-1789)," *Annales de démographie historique* (1974), 197-229.

1624   Lelièvre, Jacques, *La pratique des contrats de mariage chez les notaires du Châtelet de Paris de 1769 à 1804.* Paris, 1959.

1625   Lelong, Jacques, "Saint-Pierre-Eglise, 1657-1790," *Annales de démographie historique* (1969), 125-135.

1626   Lenglet, P., *La population de Verneuil-Vernouillet de 1740 à 1820.* Paris, 1971.

1627   Le Pesant, Michel, "Les nourrissons parisiens dans les campagnes de l'Eure sous l'ancien régime," *Cahiers Léopold Delisle* 6 (1957), 137-145.

1628   Le Pesant, Michel, "Origines sociales des familles bourgeoises à Coutances sous l'ancien régime," *Revue historique de droit français et étranger* 4th series 37 (1959), 270-272.

1629 Lestocquoy, Jean, and A. de Selliers de Moranville, *Les patriciens d'Arras sous la Renaissance.* Arras, 1950.

1630 *Lettres et mémoires adressés au Chancelier Séguier (1633–1649),* ed. Roland Mousnier. 2 v. Paris, 1964.

1631 Lévy, Claude, "Nuptialité, natalité, limitation des naissances à la cour de Versailles (1650–1800)," *Concours médical* 83 (1961), 5755–5763.

1632 Lévy, Claude, and Louis Henry. "Ducs et pairs sous l'ancien régime," *Population* 15 (1960), 807–830.

1633 Lick, Richard, "Les inférieurs domestiques dans la seconde moité du XVIIIe siècle d'après les inventaires après décès de Coutances," *Annales de Normandie* 20 (1970), 293–316.

1634 Lottin, Alain, *La désunion du couple sous l'ancien régime: l'exemple du Nord, Lille.* Paris, 1975.

1635 Lottin, Alain, "Naissances illégitimes et filles-mères à Lille au XVIIIe siècle," *Revue d'histoire moderne et contemporaine* 17 (1970), 278–322.

1636 Lottin, Alain, "Vie et mort du couple: difficultés conjugales et divorces dans le nord de la France aux XVIIe et XVIIIe siècles," *XVIIe siècle* 102–103 (1974), 59–78.

1637 Lougee, Carolyn C., "Domesticity and Social Reform: The Education of Girls by Fenelon and Saint-Cyr," *History of Education Quarterly* 14 (1974), 87–113.

1638 Luppé, Albert Marie Pierre, *Les jeunes filles [de l'aristocratie et de la bourgeoisie] à la fin du XVIIIe siècle.* Paris, 1924.

1639 McLaren, Angus, "Some secular attitudes towards sexual behavior in France, 1760–1860," *French Historical Studies* 8 (1973–74), 604–625.

1640 Malgorn, Bernadette, "La population d'Ouessant au XVIIIe siècle: étude démographique," *Annales de Bretagne* 80 (1973), 289–315.

1641 Mandrou, Robert, *Introduction à la France moderne 1500–1640.* Paris, 1961. English ed.; London, 1975.

1642 Marin-Muracciole, Madeleine-Rose, "Le mariage par procuration dans ancien régime droit corse," *Revue d'études corses* 1:3 (1961), 15–18.

1643 Marin-Muracciole, Madeleine-Rose, "Les mariages coutumiers dans la Corse ancienne," *Corse historique* 3 (1963), 35–63.

1644 Marvick, Elizabeth Wirth, "Childhood History and Decisions of State: The Case of Louis XIII," *History of Childhood Quarterly* 2 (1974–75), 135–180. Comment and Reply: Orest Ranum, Edward D. Joseph, and A. Lloyd Moote, ibid., 181–199.

1645 Marvick, Elizabeth Wirth, "Nature versus Nurture: Patterns and Trends in Seventeenth-Century French Child-Rearing," *The History of Childhood,* ed. Lloyd De Mause (New York, 1974), 259–302. (See #154)

1646 Maudvech, Gérard, "Conceptions prénuptiales et naissances illégitimes dans la région de Carentan (1670–1970)," *Revue du département de la Manche* 13 (1971), 43–60.

1647 Mémin, Marcel, "Conventions de mariage dans la région mancelle en 1780," *Revue historique de droit français et étranger* 4th series 43 (1965), 247-271.

1648 Mercier, Roger, *L'enfant dans la société du XVIIIe siècle (avant "l'Emile").* Paris, 1961.

1649 Meuvret, Jean, "Les crises de subsistances et la démographie de la France d'Ancien Régime," *Population* 1 (1946), 643-650. Now in his *Etudes d'histoire économique: recueil d'articles* (Paris, 1971), 271-278. English translation as "Demographic Crisis in France from the Sixteenth to the Eighteenth Century," *Population in History*, ed. David V. Glass and D.E.C. Eversley (London, 1965), 507-522. (See #214)

1650 Meyer, Jean, "Le XVIIe siècle et sa place dans l'évolution à long terme," *XVIIe siècle* 106-107 (1975), 23-57.

1651 Meyer, Jean, *La noblesse bretonne au XVIIIe siècle.* 2 v. Paris, 1966.

1652 Millon, Patricia, "L'individu et la famille dans la région de Grasse, d'après les procedures criminelles de la Sénéchaussée (1748-1763)," *Bulletin d'histoire économique et sociale de la Révolution française* (1974), 43-62.

1653 Mogensen, N. W., "Structures et changements démographiques dans vingt paroisses normandes sous l'Ancien Régime: une analyse sociale," *Annales de démographie historique* (1975), 343-367.

1654 Molinier, Alain, "Enfants trouvés, enfants abandonnés et enfants illégitimes en Languedoc aux XVIIe et XVIIIe siècles," *Sur la population francaise...* (Paris, 1973), 445-473. (See #1239)

1655 Molinier, Alain, *Une paroisse du bas Languedoc: Sérignan, 1650-1792.* Montpellier, 1968.

1656 Moreel, Léon, "La notion de famille dans le droit de l'ancien régime," *Renouveau des idées sur la famille*, ed. Robert Prigent (Paris, 1954), 20-26.

1657 Moulin, Raymond, "Petite étude démographique: les mariages à Saint-Jeannet de 1667 à 1900," *Annales de Haute-Provence* 41 (1971), 263-270.

1658 Mousnier, Roland, *La famille, l'enfant, et l'éducation en France et en Grande-Bretagne du XVIe au XVIIIe siècle.* 3 v. Paris, 1974.

1659 Mousnier, Roland, *Les institutions de la France sous la monarchie absolue, 1598-1789.* v. 1: *Société et Etat.* Paris, 1974.

1660 Mousnier, Roland, "Les survivances médiévales dans la France du XVIIe siècle," *XVIIe siècle* 106-107 (1975), 59-79.

1661 Mousnier, Roland, *Paris au XVIIe siècle.* Paris, 1962.

1662 Muchembled, Robert, "Famille, amour et marige: mentalités et comportements des nobles artésiens a l'époque de Philippe II," *Revue d'histoire moderne et contemporaine* 22 (1975), 233-261.

1663 Muchembled, Robert, "Famille et histoire des mentalités (XVIe-XVIIIe siècles). Etat présent des recherches," *Revue des études sud-est européennes* 12 (1974), 349-369.

1664 Noël, Raymond, "L'état de la population de Mostuejouls (Aveyron) en 1690," *Sur la population française...* (Paris, 1973), 505-522. (See #1239)

1665 Noël, Raymond, "La population de la paroisse d'Inières, d'après un recensement nominatif du diocèse du Rodez en 1690," *Annales du Midi* 80 (1968), 139-156.

1666 Noël, Raymond, "La population de la paroisse de Laquiole d'après un recensement de 1691," *Annales de démographie historique* (1967), 197-223.

1667 Perrot, Jean-Claude, *Genèse d'une ville moderne: Caen au XVIIIe siecle.* 2 v. Paris, 1975.

1668 Petit, A. M., "Mariages et contrats de mariage à Agen en 1785 et 1786," *Annales du Midi* 72 (1960), 215-229.

1669 Petot, Pierre, "La famille en France sous l'ancien régime," *Sociologie comparée de la famille contemporaine* (Paris, 1955), 9-18.

1670 Peyronnet, Jean-Claude, "Les enfants abandonnés et leurs nourrices à Limoges au XVIIIe siècle," *Revue d'histoire moderne et contemporaine* 23 (1976), 418-441.

1671 Phan, Marie-Claude, "Les déclarations de grossesse en France (XVIe-XVIIIe siècles): essai institutionnel," *Revue d'histoire moderne et contemporaine* 22 (1975), 61-88.

1672 Pieri, Georges, "Les particularités de la puissance paternelle dans le duché de Bourgogne de la rédaction officielle de la coutume à la fin de l'ancien régime," *Mémoires de la Société pour l'histoire du droit et des institutions des anciens pays bourguignons, comtois, et romands* 26 (1968), 51-90.

1673 Pilon, Edmond, *La vie de famille au dix-huitième siècle.* Paris, 1923.

1674 Poitrineau, Abel, *La vie rurale en Basse-Auvergne au XVIIIe siècle, 1726-1789.* Paris, 1965.

1675 Polge, H., "Cycles saisonniers et hebdomadaires de la nuptialité rurale gersoise sous l'ancien régime," *Bulletin de la Société archéologique, historique, littéraire et scientifique du Gers* 59 (1958), 438-445.

1676 Polton, J.-C., "Coulommiers et Chailly-en-Brie," *Annales de démographie historique* (1969), 14-32.

1677 Ponsot, Philippe, "Douveres-la-Délivrande (1650-1792): une inversion démographique?" *Annales de Normandie* 14 (1964), 455-477.

1678 Poussou, Jean-Pierre, "Les actes de mariage de Langon, Bazas et La Réole à la veille de la Révolution (1777-1786) et leurs apports," *Cahiers du Bazadais* 11 (1971), 91-106.

1679 Poussou, Jean-Pierre, "Experience aquitaine et méthodologie des contrats de mariage au XVIIIe siècle," *Annales du Midi* 76 (1964), 61-76.

1680 Proust, Raymond, "Contribution à l'histoire de la population de Chef-Boutonne," *Bulletin de la Société des antiquaries de l'Ouest* 4th series 7 (1964), 569-635.

1681 Ribbe, Charles de, *Les familles et la société en France avant la Révolution, la vie domestique, ses modèles et ses règles.* 2 v. Tours, 1879. Originally 1877.

1682 Richard, Jules Marie, *La vie privée dans une province de l'Ouest: Laval aux XVIIe et XVIIIe siècles.* Paris, 1922.

1683 Richard, Paul, "Les avantages réservés aux familles nombreuses de 1667 à 1720," *Echo de Saint-Pierre d'Auxerre* 25 (1960), 14-18.

1684 Rives, Jean, "L'évolution démographique de Toulouse: 1750-1792," *Bulletin d'histoire économique et social de la Révolution francaise* (1968), 85-146.

1685 Robert, Patrice, "Rumont, 1720-1790," *Annales de démographie historique* (1969), 32-40.

1686 Robida, Michel, *Ces bourgeois de Paris: trois siècles de chronique familiale de 1675 à nos jours.* Paris, 1955.

1687 Robine, M., "Les archives notariales, complément des registres paroissiaux: étude de la distribution statistique de délai entre contrat de mariage et mariage aux XVIIᵉ, XVIIIᵉ et XIX siècles, dans un village du Bazadais," *Annales de démographie historique* (1974), 59-97.

1688 Roelker, Nancy L., "The Appeal of Calvinism to French Noblewomen in the Sixteenth Century," *Journal of Interdisciplinary History* 2 (1971-1972), 391-418.

1689 Roelker, Nancy L., "The Role of Noblewomen in the French Reformation," *Archiv für Reformationsgeschichte* 63 (1972), 168-195.

1690 Rollet, Catherine, "Généalogies et démographie: quelques exemples récents," *Sur la population française...* (Paris, 1973), 547-557. (See #1239)

1691 Rousseau, R., "Les registres paroissiaux et l'état civil de Digny en Vauche (Haute-Savoie) au XVIIIᵉ siècle," *[Actes du] 85ᵉ Congrès national des sociétés savantes, Chambery-Annecy, 1960* (Paris, 1961), 439-468.

1692 Roussier, Jules, "Le problème des longues grossesses dans notre ancien droit. Doctrine et jurisprudence des trois derniers siècles de l'ancien régime," *Etudes historiques à la mémoire de Noël Didier* (Paris, 1960), 275-282.

1693 Saint-Jacob, Pierre de, *Les paysans de la Bourgogne du nord au dernier siècle de l'ancien régime.* Paris, 1960.

1694 Scherer, Jacques, "Pour une sociologie des obstacles au mariage dans le theâtre français du XVIIᵉ siècle," *Dramaturgie et Société*, ed. Jean Jacquot et al. (Paris, 1968), I, 297-305.

1695 Sheppard, Thomas F., *Loumarin in the Eighteenth Century: A Study of a French Village.* Baltimore, 1971.

1696 Shorter, Edward, "Différences de classe et sentiment depuis 1750: l'example de la France (sentiment et vie conjugale)," *Annales E.S.C.* 29 (1974), 1034-1057.

1697 Sicard, Germain, "Notes sur la famille en Gascogne toulousaine à la fin du XVIIIᵉ siècle," *Mélanges...Aubenas* (1974), 683-696. (See #1232)

1698 Sicard, Germain, and Mireille Sicard, "Les contrats de mariage de la noblesse toulousaine en 1786," *Droit privé...* (Paris, 1976), 623-653. (See #1218)

1699 Sicard, Mireille, "Mariage et famille dans la vallee de Luchon à la vielle de la Révolution," *Mélanges...Aubenas* (1974), 697-710. (See #1232)

1700 Snyders, Georges, *La pédagogie en France au XVIIᵉ et XVIIIᵉ siècles.* Paris, 1965.

1701 Solé, Jacques, "Passion charnelle et société urbaine d'ancien régime: amour venal, amour libre et amour fou à Grenoble au milieu du règne de Louis XIV," *Annales de la faculté des lettres et sciences humaines de Nice* 9-10 (1969), 211-232.

1702 Soulet, Jean François, *La vie quotidienne dans les Pyrénées sous l'ancien régime du XVIe au XVIIIe siècle.* Paris, 1974.

1703 Sudré, M., "Aspects démographiques de la paroisse Saint-Miches de Bordeaux (1660-1680)," *Annales de démographie historique* (1974), 231-248.

1704 Sussman, George D., "The Wet-Nursing Business in Paris, 1769-1876," *Proceedings of the First Annual Meeting of the Western Society for French History,* ed. Edgar Leon Newman (Las Cruces, N.M., 1974), 179-194.

1705 Tardy, P., "Mariages et moeurs dans l'Iie de Ré du XVIIe au XIXe siècle," *Bulletin de l'association des amis de l'Ile de Ré* 41 (1971), 30-60; 42 (1971), 31-65; 43 (1971), 24-61.

1706 Terrisse, Michel, "Méthode de recherches démographiques en milieu urbain ancien (XVIIe-XVIIIe)," *Annales de démographie historique* (1974), 249-262.

1707 Terrisse, Michel, "Le rattrapage de nuptialité d'après peste à Marseille (1720-1721)," *Sur la population francaise...* (Paris, 1973), 565-580. (See #1239)

1708 Terrisse, Michel, "Un faubourg du Havre: Ingouville," *Population* 16 (1961), 285-296.

1709 Tilly, Charles, "Population and Pedagogy in France," *History of Education Quarterly* 13 (1973), 113-128.

1710 Timbal, P. C., "L'esprit du droit privé au XVIIe siècle," *XVIIe siècle* 58-59 (1963), 30-39.

1711 Todd, Emmanuel, "Mobilité géographique et cycle de vie en Artois et Toscane au XVIIIe siècle," *Annales E.S.C.* 30 (1975), 726-744.

1712 Valmary, Pierre, *Familles paysannes au XVIIIe siècle en Bas-Quercy.* Paris, 1965.

1713 Van Hille, W., "Contrats de mariage à Dunkerque [1706-1790]," *Vlaamse Stam* 2 (1966), 229-238.

1714 Vincent, Paul E., "French Demography in the Eighteenth Century," *Population Studies* 1 (1947-48), 44-71.

1715 Vivier, Em., "Les pactions de mariage des paysannes de l'Avranchin aux XVIIe et XVIIIe siècles," *Annales de Normandie* 3 (1953), 149-161.

1716 Vovelle, Michel, "Chartres et le pays chartrain: quelques aspects démographiques," *Contributions à l'histoire démographique de la Révolution française,* ed. M. Bouloiseau (Paris, 1962), 129-159.

1717 Vovelle, Michel, "Y a-t-il un modèle de la famille méridionale?" *Provence historique* 25 (1975), 487-507.

1718 Wallon, Simone, "Une famille paysanne en Poitou aux XVIIIe et XIXe siècles: les Coirault," *Revue de Bas-Poitou* 76 (1966), 5-18.

1719 Wheaton, Robert, "Notes critiques sur les classes sociale au XVIIIe siècle à

Bordeaux d'après les contrats de mariage," *Revue historique* 241 (1969), 99-114. (A critique of #1495)

1720   Wiel, Philippe, "Une grosse paroisse du Cotentin aux XVIIe et XVIIIe siècles: Tamerville. Démographie, société, mentalité," *Annales de démographie historique* (1969), 136-189.

1721   Zink, Anne, *Azereix: la vie d'une communauté rurale à la fin du XVIIIe siècle.* Paris, 1969.

See also   #290 and #370.

MODERN PERIOD
(1789 TO THE PRESENT)

1722   Abensour, Léon, *La féminisme sous le règne de Louis-Philippe et en 1848.* Paris, 1913.

1723   Adler, Alfred, "Children in the *Juste Milieu*," *Romanische Forschungen* 79 (1967), 345-377.

1724   Armengaud, André, *La population française au XIXe siècle.* Paris, 1971.

1725   Armengaud, André, "L'attitude de la société à l'égard de l'enfant au XIXe siècle," *Annales de démographie historique* (1973), 303-312.

1726   Armengaud, André, "L'attitude de la société a l'égard de l'enfant au XIXe siècle: elements de bibliographie," *Annales de démographie historique* (1973), 345-352.

1727   Armengaud, André, "Les mariages de 1813 à Toulouse," *Sur la population française...* (Paris, 1973), 11-18. (See #1239)

1728   Armengaud, André, "Les nourrices du Morvan au XIXe siècle," *Etudes et chronique de démographie historique* (1964), 131-139.

1729   Armengaud, André, "Mariages et naissances sous le Consultat et l'Empire," *Revue d'histoire moderne et contemporaine* 17 (1970), 373-389.

1730   Arsac, Pierre, "Le comportement juridique des individus d'après les contrats de mariage au XIXe siècle (Grenoble, 1813-1860)," *Revue d'histoire économique et sociale* 49 (1971), 550-591.

1731   Arsac, Pierre, "Le comportement juridique des individus d'après les contrats de mariage (Grenoble, 1886-1939)," *Revue d'histoire économique et sociale* 51 (1973), 380-422.

1732   Banwens, P., and M. Debanqué, "La démographie de la hestre au XIXe siècle (1798-1900)," *Annales [du] cercle archéologique et folklorique de la Louvière et du Centre* 5 (1967), 269-347.

1733   Bart, Jean, "La pratique des contrats de mariage dans la région dijonnaise à la fin du XVIIIe et au début du XIXe siècle," *Le droit des gen mariés...* (1966), 285-313. (See #292)

1734   Beauvoir, Simone de, *La vieillesse.* Paris, 1970. Appeared also as *The Coming of Age.* New York, 1972, and as *Old Age.* London, 1972.

1735 Bernot, Lucien, and René Blancard, *Nouville, un village français.* Paris, 1953.

1736 Bertaux, Jean-Jacques, "Familles de bateliers à Tribehou (Manche), 1838-1931," *Annales de Normandie* 19 (1969), 329-359.

1737 Blayo, Chantal, "Natalité, fecondité," *Population* 29 (1974), 51-80.

1738 Blayo, Yves, "Size and Structure of Households in a Northern French Village between 1836 and 1861," *Household and Family...,* ed. Peter Laslett and Richard Wall (Cambridge, England, 1972), 255-266. (See #156)

1739 Bongaarts, J., "Intermediate Fertility Variables and Marital Fertility Rates," *Population Studies* 30 (1976), 227-242.

1740 Boudet, Robert, "La famille bourgeoise," *Sociologie comparée de la famille contemporaine* (Paris, 1955), 141-155.

1741 Bourdieu, Pierre, "Célibat et condition paysanne," *Etudes rurales* 5-6 (1962), 32-135.

1742 Bourdieu, Pierre, "Les stratégies matrimoniales dans le système de reproduction," *Annales E.S.C.* 27 (1972), 1105-1125. English translation as "Marriage Strategies as Strategies of Social Reproduction," *Family and Society,* ed. Robert Forster and Orest Ranum (Baltimore, 1976), 117-144. (See #77)

1743 Bourgeois-Pichat, Jean, "Le mariage, coutume saisonnière," *Population* 1 (1946), 623-642.

1744 Bouteiller, Marcelle, "Les types sociaux décrits à propos de l'orphelin dans la littérature 'enfantine' de 1800 à 1890," *Ethnographie* 60-61 (1966-67), 16-25.

1745 Brassard, Jean-Pierre, "Le conseil familial. Etude comparée des premières realisations françaises et de l'expérience britannique," *Pour la vie* 113 (1969), 133-177.

1746 Brasseur, A., "La mortalité infantile dans la région du Nord," *Hommes et terres du Nord* (1965), 7-36.

1747 Brant, André, "Une famille de fabricants mulhousiens au début du XIXe siècle: Jean Koechlin et ses fils," *Annales E.S.C.* 6 (1951), 314-330.

1748 Breil, Jacques, and Vincent Fonsagrive, *Tables nouvelles relatives à la population française vers 1936 (mortalité, nuptialité, fécondité).* Paris, 1945.

1749 Brekilien, Yann, *La vie quotidienne des paysans en Bretagne au XIXe siècle.* Paris, 1966.

1750 Brinton, C. Crane, *French Revolutionary Legislation on Illegitimacy, 1789-1804.* Cambridge, Mass., 1936.

1751 Brooke, Michael Z., *Le Play: Engineer and Social Scientist: The Life and Work of Frédéric Le Play.* London, 1970.

1752 Brun, Jean-Pierre, "La population de Montjoy, esquisse démographique 1813-1912." *Bulletin de la Société d'études des Haute-Alpes* (1969), 49-58.

1753 Buriez-Duez, Marie-Pascale, "Le mouvement de la population dans le département du Nord au XIXe siècle," *L'homme, la vie et la mort dans le Nord au XIXe siècle, études presentées par Marcel Gillet* (Lille, 1972), 15-39.

1754 Cabaj, Stanislas, "La mortalité infantile dans le Pas-de-Calais de 1919 à 1970," *Revue du Nord* 56 (1974), 411–420.

1755 Calot, G., and J.-C. Deville, "Nuptialité et fécondité selon le milieu socio-culturel," *Economie et Statistique* 27 (1971), 3–42.

1756 Camp, Wesley D., *Marriage and the Family in France since the Revolution.* New York, 1961.

1757 Cazaurang, Jean-Jacques, "La naissance et le premier âge en Béarn," *Revue régionaliste des Pyrénées* 49 (1965), 72–96.

1758 Ceccaldi, Dominique, *Histoire des prestations familiales en France.* Paris, 1957.

1759 Chaline, Jean-Pierre, "Les contrats de mariage à Rouen au XIXe siècle: étude d'après l'enregistrement des actes civils publics," *Revue d'histoire économique et sociale* 48 (1970), 238–275.

1760 Chasteland, Jean-Claude, and Louis Henry, "Disparités régionales de la fécondité des mariages," *Population* 11 (1956), 653–672.

1761 Chasteland, Jean-Claude, and Roland Pressat, "La nuptialité des générations françaises depuis un siècle," *Population* 17 (1972), 215–240.

1762 Chevalier, Louis, *Classes laborieuses et classes dangereuses à Paris dans la première moitié du XIXe siècle.* Paris, 1958.

1763 Chevalier, Louis, *La formation de la population parisienne au XIXe siècle.* Paris, 1950.

1764 Chevalier, Louis, *Les parisiens.* Paris, 1967.

1765 Clancier, Georges-Emmanuel, *La vie quotidienne en Limousin au XIXe siècle.* Paris, 1976.

1766 Clark, Francis, *The Position of Women in Contemporary France.* London, 1937.

1767 Clémendot, Pierre, "Evolution de la population de Nancy, de 1788 à 1815," *Contributions à l'histoire démographique de la Révolution française: 2e série,* ed. P. Clemendot et al. (Paris, 1965), 181–220.

1768 Clémendot, Pierre, "Population de Nancy (1815–1938)," *Sur la population...* (Paris, 1973), 119–134. (See #1239)

1769 Colin, Robert, "Prémices et développement de la législation familiale française," *Renouveau des idées sur la famille,* ed. Robert Prigent (Paris, 1954), 171–176.

1770 Commaille, Jacques, and Yves Dezalay, "Les caractéristiques judiciaires du divorce en France," *Population* 26 (1971), 173–196.

1771 Cornaton, Michel, "Famille et monde modern," *Les Changements de la société française,* ed. E.-H. Lacombe (Paris, 1971), 109–128.

1772 Courgeau, Daniel, "Mobilité géographique, nuptialité et fécondité," *Population* 31 (1976), 901–914.

1773 Cox, Peter, R., "International Variations in the Relative Ages of Brides and Grooms," *Journal of Biosocial Science* 2 (1970), 111–121.

1774 Crépillon, P., "Frontières et mariages. Première approche de deux exemples manchois (1804-1962)," *Revue de l'Avranchin et du pays de Granville* 44 (1967), 145-158.

1775 Cruppi, Marcel, *Le divorce pendant la Revolution, 1792-1804.* Paris, 1909.

1776 Daumard, Adeline, *La bourgeoisie parisienne de 1815 à 1848.* Paris, 1963. Abridged as *Les bourgeois de Paris au XIXe siècle.* Paris, 1970.

1777 Daumard, Adeline, "Quelques remarques sur le logement des parisiens au XIXe siècle," *Annales de démographie historique* (1975), 49-64.

1778 Defarges, Dom Bénigne, "L'industrie des nourrices morvandelles au XIXe siècle, quelques sujets marquants," *Pays de Bourgogne* 20 (1974), 979-983; 21 (1974), 18-22; 22 (1975), 301-303, 354-357.

1779 Degraeve-Noël, Françoise, "Evolution de la femme dans la famille rurale française," *Recherche sociale* 26 (1969), 55-61.

1780 Dejace, André, *Les règles de la dévolution sucessorale sous la Révolution (1789-1794).* Brussels, 1957.

1781 Deniel, Raymond, "La famille dans sa relation à l'état et à la religion, chez les penseurs traditionnalistes de la Restauration," *Recherche sociale* 26 (1969), 13-16.

1782 Deniel, Raymond, *Une image de la famille et de la société sous la Restauration (1815-1830).* Paris, 1965.

1783 Depoid, Pierre, "Essai de détermination de la productivité des mariages suivant l'âge de l'épouse," *Bulletin de la Statistique générale de la France* 24 (1935), 457-486.

1784 Derruppé, Jean, "L'évolution du droit français de la famille du début du siècle à la guerre de 1939," *Renouveau des idées sur la famille,* ed. Robert Prigent (Paris, 1954), 149-160.

1785 Desert, Gabriel, "Aperçus sur la démographie bas-normande (XIXe-XXe siècles)," *Annales de Normandie* 23 (1973), 151-168.

1786 Desforges, Jacques, *Le divorce en France.* Paris, 1947.

1787 Desforges, Jacques, "La loi Naquet," *Renouveau des idées sur la famille,* ed. Robert Prigent (Paris, 1954), 103-110.

1788 Desmottes, Georges, "De la législation Révolutionnaire au Code Civil," ibid., 50-58.

1789 Desmottes, Georges, "Le renouveau familial dans les institutions," ibid., 177-184.

1790 Deville, Jean-Claude, "Analyse harmonique du calendrier de constitution des familles en France: disparités et évolution de 1920 à 1960," *Population* 32 (1977), 17-62.

1791 Dewaepenaere, Claude-Hélène, "L'enfance illégitime dans le département du Nord au XIXe siècle," *L'homme, la vie et la mort dans le Nord...* (Lille, 1972), 139-176. (See #1821)

1792 Dewaepenaere, Claude-Hélène, and Esther Pasqualini, "La femme et l'enfant dans le Nord (1919-1939)," *La qualité de la vie dans le région Nord-Pas-de-Calais au XXe siècle,* ed. Marcel Gillet (Lille, 1975), 135-169.

1793 Dinet, Dominique, "Statistiques de martalité infantile sous le Consulat et l'Empire," *Sur la population...* (Paris, 1973), 215-230. (See #1239)

1794 Dion-Salitot, Michele, "Endogamie et système économique dans un village français," *Sociologia Ruralis* 11 (1971), 1-18.

1795 Dombrowski-Keerle, Noëlle, "Le divorce dans le départment du Nord de 1884 à 1914: aspects démographiques et sociaux. Etude statistique," *L'homme, la vie et la mort dans le Nord...* (Lille, 1972), 177-213. (See #1821)

1796 Doublet, Jacques, "Parents et enfants dans la famille ouvrière," *Sociologie comparée de la famille contemporaine* (Paris, 1955), 157-173.

1797 Ducrocq-Mathieu, Geneviève, "Le divorce dans le district de Nancy de 1792 à l'an III," *Annales de l'Est* 5th series 6 (1955), 213-227.

1798 Dupâquier, Jacques, "Problèmes démographiques de la France Napoléonienne," *Population* 17 (1970), 339-358.

1799 Duplessis-Le Guélinel, Gérard, *Les mariages en France.* Paris, 1954.

1800 Dupy, Aimé, "Oncles et neveux dans l'histoire de France," *Information historique* 5 (1964), 210-213.

1801 Espanan, Jean-Marie, *La population de Monléon-Magnoac au XIXe siècle (1792–1870).* Paris, 1971.

1802 Fabre, Daniel, and Jacques Lacroix, *La vie quotidienne des paysans du Languedoc au XIXe siècle.* Paris, 1973.

1803 Favier, Hubert, "Variation dans le temps de la natalité et de la mortalité [dans l'Aube]," *Vie en Champagne* 6 (1958), 12-13.

1804 Febvay, Maurice, "Niveau et évolution de la fécondité par catégorie socioprofessionnelle en France," *Population* 14 (1959), 729-739.

1805 Finon, Elisabeth, *Un bourg de la Brie au XIXe siècle: Donnemarie-en-Montois.* Paris, 1972.

1806 Gaillard-Bans, Patricia, "Maison longue et famille étendue en Bretagne," *Etudes rurales* 62 (1976), 73-87.

1807 Garrier, Gilbert, *Paysans du Beaujolais et du Lyonnais 1800–1970.* Grenoble, 1973.

1808 Gautier, Etienne, "Aspects démographiques de l'évolution d'une localité du pays d'Ouche: Crulai dans la première moitié du XIXe siècle," *Annales de Normandie* 18 (1968), 61-87.

1809 Gemaehling, P., "Démographie et structures familiales en France," *Sociologie comparée de la famille contemporaine* (Paris, 1955), 31-54.

1810 Girard, Alain, "Aspects statistiques du problème familial," *Sociologie comparée de la famille contemporaine* (Paris, 1955), 55-72.

1811 Guerrand, Roger-H., *La libre maternité, 1896–1969.* Paris, 1971.

1812 Guigou, J., "Sociologie du mariage dans les villages du Languedoc méditerranéen," *L'économie meridionale* 48 (1964), 1-15.

1813 Guillaume, Pierre, *La population de Bordeaux au XIXe siècle.* Paris, 1972.

1814 Halbwachs, Maurice, "Taux de natalité, esquisse de statistique comparée," *Annales d'histoire sociale* 3 (1941), 136-142.

1815 Hardach, Gerd H., *Der soziale Status des Arbeiters in der Frühindustrial-isierung. Eine Untersuchung über die Arbeitnehmer in der französischen eisenchaffender Industrie zwischen 1800 und 1870.* Berlin, 1969.

1816 Hellerstein, Erna Olafson, "French Women and the Orderly Household, 1830-1870," *[Proceedings of the] Third Meeting of the Western Society for French History, Denver 1975,* ed. Brison D. Gooch (1976), 378-389.

1817 Henry, Louis, "Evolution de la fécondité en France au XIXe siècle," *Population* 30 (1975), 905-914.

1818 Henry, Louis, "Pertubation de la nuptialité resultant de la guerre 1914-1918," *Population* 21 (1966), 273-332.

1819 Henry, Louis, "Schéma d'évolution des mariages après de grandes variations des naissances," *Population* 30 (1975), 759-780.

1820 Hilaire, Marie-Magdeleine, "Démographie et qualité de la vie dans la région du Nord au XXe siècle," *Revue du Nord* 56 (1974), 285-295.

1821 *L'homme, la vie et la mort dans le Nord au 19e siècle: études presentées par Marcel Gillet.* Lille, 1972.

1822 Houdaille, Jacques, "Les descendants des grands dignitaires du Ier Empire au XIXe siècle," *Population* 29 (1974), 263-274.

1823 Hubscher, R. H., "Une contribution à la connaissance des milieux populaires ruraux au XIXe siècle: le livre de compte de la famille Flahaut, 1811-1877," *Revue d'histoire économique et sociale* 47 (1969), 361-403.

1824 Hudry, Marius, "Relations sexuelles prénuptiales en Tarentaise et dans le Beaufortin d'après les documents ecclésiastiques," *Le monde alpin et rhoda-nien, revue régionale d'ethnologie* 2 (1974), 95-100.

1825 Ibarrola, Jésus, *Les incidences des deux conflits mondiaux sur l'évolution démographique française.* Paris, 1964.

1826 Ibarrola, Jésus, *Recherches sur la société grenobloise vers le milieu du 19e siècle à partir des tables des successions et des absences.* Paris, 1971.

1827 Ibarrola, Jésus, *Structures d'une population active de type traditionnel, Grenoble 1848.* The Hague, 1968.

1828 Ibarrola, Jésus, *Structure sociale et fortune dans la campagne proche de Grenoble en 1847.* Paris, 1966.

1829 Ibarrola, Jésus, *Structure sociale et fortune mobilière et immobilière à Grenoble en 1847.* Paris, 1965.

1830 Jan, Isabelle, "Children's Literature and Bourgeois Society in France since 1860," *Yale French Studies* 41 (1968), 57-72.

1831 Jaulerry, Elaine, "Les dissoultions d'union en France, étudiées à partir des minutes de jugement," *Population* 26 (1971), 143-172.

1832 Johnston, R. J., and P. J. Ferry, "Déviation directionnelle dans les aires de con-tact: deux exemples de relations matrimoniales dans la France rurale du XIXe siècle," *Etudes rurales* 46 (1972), 23-33.

1833 Kahane, Eric, *Un mariage parisien sous le Directoire.* Paris, 1961.

1834 Karnoouh, Claude, "L'oncle et le cousin," *Etudes rurales* 42 (1971), 7-51.

1835 Lagroua Weill-Hallé, M.-A., "Le contrôle des naissances à l'étranger et la loi française de 1920," *Semaine Hôpitaux (Semaine médicale)* 29 (1953), 145-152.

1836 Lambert-Dansette, Jean, *Quelques familles du patronat textile de Lille-Armentières [1789-1914]*. Lille, 1954.

1837 Le Roy Ladurie, Emmanuel, "Démographie et funestes secrèts: le Languedoc (fin XVIIIe-début XIXe siècles)," *Annales historique de la Révolution française* 37 (1965), 385-399.

1838 Le Bras, Hervé, "Géographie de la fécondité française depuis 1921," *Population* 26 (1971), 1093-1124.

1839 *Ledermann, Sully, "Les divorces et les séparations de corps en France,"* *Population* 3 (1948), 313-344.

1840 Lemaitre, Nicole, "Familles complexes en Bas-Limousin: Ussel au début de XIXe siècle," *Annales du Midi* 88 (1976), 219-224.

1841 Le Moigne, Y., "Evolution de la population de Strasbourg, de 1789 à 1815," *Contributions à l'histoire démographique de la Révolution française: 2e série*, ed. P. Clemendot et al. (Paris, 1965), 235-255.

1842 Léon, Pierre, *Géographie de la fortune et structures sociales à Lyon au XIXe siècle*. Lyon, 1974.

1843 Léridon, Henri, *Natalité, saisons et conjoncture économique*. Paris, 1973.

1844 Lesaege, Aline, "La mortalité infantile dans le département du Nord de 1815 à 1914," *Revue du Nord* 52 (1970), 238-244.

1845 Lesaege-Dugied, Aline, "La mortalité infantile dans le département du Nord de 1815 à 1914," *L'homme, la vie et la mort dans le Nord...* (Lille, 1972), 79-137. (See #1821)

1846 Lévi-Strauss, Laurent, "Pouvoir municipal et parenté dans un village bourguignon," *Annales E.S.C.* 30 (1975), 149-159.

1847 Lévy, Cl., "Les empêchements au mariage et leurs dispenses civiles en France depuis 1800," *Concours médical* 82 (1960), 1433-1439.

1848 Lévy, Jean-Philippe, "L'évolution du droit familial depuis 1789," *Mélanges... Aubenas* (1974), 485-504. (See #1232)

1849 Lévy-Leboyer, Maurice, "Le patronat français, a-t-il été malthusien?" *Mouvement social* 88 (1974), 3-50.

1850 Lhôte, Jean, "Le divorce à Metz sous la Révolution et l'Empire," *Annales de l'Est* 3 (1952), 175-183.

1851 McBride, Theresa, "Social Mobility for the Lower Class: Domestic Servants in France," *Journal of Social History* 8 (1974-75), 63-78.

1852 Madaule, Jacques, "La famille dans la littérature française (1900-1925)" *Renouveau des idées sur la famille*, ed. Robert Prigent (Paris, 1954), 120-129.

1853 Maison, Dominique, and Elisabeth Millet, "La nuptialité," *Population* 29 (1974), 31-50.

1854 Maitron, Jean, "Les penseurs sociaux et la famille dans la première moitié du

XIXe siècle," *Renouveau des idées sur la famille,* ed. Robert Prigent (Paris, 1954), 81-102.

1855   Maitron, Jean, "Les thèses révolutionnaires sur l'évolution de la famille du milieu du XIXe siècle à nos jours," ibid., 131-148.

1856   Magaud, Jacques, and Louis Henry, "Le rang de naissance dans les phéno-mènes démographiques," *Population* 23 (1968), 879-920.

1857   *Mari et femme dans la France rurale traditionnelle* [catalogue of exposition at the Musée national des arts et traditions populaires, 22 September-19 November 1973], ed. Martine Segalen. Paris, 1973.

1858   Martin, Olivier, *La crise du mariage dans la législation intermediarie, 1789-1804.* Paris, 1901.

1859   Maspétiol, Roland, "Sociologie de la famille rurale de type traditionnel en France," *Sociologie comparée de la famille contemporaine* (Paris, 1955), 129-140.

1860   Michel, A., "Les aspects sociologiques de la notion de famille dans la législa-tion française," *Année sociologique* (1960), 79-107.

1861   *Moi, Pierre Rivière, ayant égorgé ma mère, ma soeur et mon frère...un cas de parricide au XIXe siècle,* ed. Michel Foucault. Paris, 1973. English ed.; New York, 1975.

1862   Murtin, M.-Cl., "Les abandons d'enfants à Bourg et dans le département de l'Ain à la fin du XVIIIe siècle et dans la première moitié du XIXe siècle," *Cahiers d'histoire* 10 (1965), 135-166, 233-248.

1863   Nadot, Robert, "Evolution de la mortalité infantile endogène en France dans la deuxième moitié du XIXe siècle," *Population* 25 (1970), 49-58.

1864   Naurois, L. de, "Le problème du divorce en France," *Revue de droit canon-ique* 15 (1965), 139-163.

1865   Nizard, Alfred, "Droit et statistique de filiation en France: le droit de la filia-tion depuis 1804," *Population* 32 (1977), 91-122.

1866   O'Brien, Justin, *The Novel of Adolescence in France.* New York, 1937.

1867   Ogden, Philip, "Patterns of Marriage Seasonality in Rural France," *Local Population Studies* 10 (1973), 53-69.

1868   Paillat, Paul, "Influence du nombre d'enfants sur le niveau de vie de la famille: évolution en France de 1950 à 1970. Comparison avec quelque pays européens en 1969," *Population* 26 (1971), 13-36.

1869   Parish, William J., and Moshe Schwartz, "Household Complexity in Nine-teenth-Century France," *American Sociological Review* 37 (1972), 154-173.

1870   Parker, Clifford, *The Defense of the Child by French Novelists.* Menasha, Wisc., 1925.

1871   Perrot, Jean-Claude, "La population du département du Calvados sous la Révolution et l'Empire," *Contributions à l'histoire démographique de la Révolution française: 2e série,* ed. P. Clemendot et al. (Paris, 1965), 115-178.

1872 Perrot, Marguerite, "La famille bourgeoise à la fin du XIXe siècle," *Recherche sociale* 26 (1969), 17-19.

1873 Perrot, Marguerite, *La mode de vie des familles bourgeoises 1873-1954.* Paris, 1961.

1874 Peyronnet, Jean-Claude, "Famille élargie ou famille nucléaire? L'exemple du Limousin au début de XIXe siècle," *Revue d'histoire moderne et contemporaine* 22 (1975), 568-582.

1875 Pierrard, Pierre, "Habitat ouvrier et démographie à Lille au XIXe siècle et particulièrement sous le second Empire," *Annales de démographie historique* (1975), 37-48.

1876 Pierrard, Pierre, *La vie ouvrière à Lille sous le Second Empire.* Paris, 1965.

1877 Pingaud, Marie-Claude, "Terres et familles dans un village du Châtillonnais," *Etudes rurales* 42 (1971), 52-104.

1878 Reddy, William M., "Family and Factory: French Linen Weavers in the Belle Epoque," *Journal of Social History* 8 (1974-75), 102-112.

1879 Robiquet, Jean, *La vie quotidienne au temps de la Révolution.* Paris, 1938.

1880 Rouast, André, "La transformation de la famille en France dupuis la Révolution," *Sociologie comparée de la famille contemporaine* (Paris, 1955), 19-29.

1881 Roubin, Lucienne A., "Espace masculin, espace féminin en communauté provençale," *Annales E.S.C.* 25 (1970), 537-560.

1882 Roussel, Louis, "L'attitude des diverses générations à l'égard du mariage, de la famille et du divorce en France," *Population* 26 (1971), 101-142.

1883 Roussel, Louis, "Les divorces et les séparations de corps en France (1936-1967)," *Population* 25 (1970), 275-302.

1884 Roussel, Louis, *Le mariage dans la société française: faits de population.* Paris, 1975.

1885 Salleron, Claude, "La littérature au XIXe siècle et la famille," *Renouveau des idées sur la famille,* ed. Robert Prigent (Paris, 1954), 60-80.

1886 Salleron, Claude, "L'expression littéraire de 1925 à 1952," ibid., 197-204.

1887 Sangoi, Jean-Claude, "La population de Labarthe au XIXe siècle (1808-1913)," *Annales de démographie historique* (1974), 479-497.

1888 Sarg, Freddy, *Le mariage en Alsace: études de quelques coutumes passées et présents.* Strasbourg, 1975.

1889 Segalen, Martine, "Evoluzione dei nuclei familiari di Saint-Jean-Trolimon, Sud-Finistère a partire dal 1836," *Quaderni Storici* 33 (1976), 1122-1182.

1890 Segalen, Martine, "Le mariage et la femme dans les proverbes du Sud de la France," *Annales du Midi* 87 (1975), 265-288.

1891 Segalen, Martine, *Nuptialité et alliance: le choix du conjoint dans une commune de l'Eure.* Paris, 1972.

1892 Segalen, Martine, and Albert Jacquard, "Choix du conjoint et homogamie," *Population* 26 (1970), 487-498.

1893 Segalen, Martine, and Albert Jacquard, "Isolement sociologique et isolement génétique [mariages protestants dans le Bocage normand]," *Population* 28 (1973), 551-570.

1894 Sévegrand, Martine, "La section de Popincourt pendant la Révolution française," *Contribution à l'histoire démographique de la Revolution française:* 3ᵉ série, ed. Marcel Reinhard (Paris, 1970), 9-91.

1895 Sicard, Germain, "Les contrats de mariage à Toulouse et dans la campagne toulousaine en 1812 et 1853," [Actes du] *96ᵉ Congrès national des sociétés savantes, Toulouse 1971, Section Histoire moderne* 2 (1976), 311-320.

1896 Simon, Pierre, *Rapport sur le comportement sexuel des français.* Paris, 1972.

1897 Solignac, Michel, "Monographie d'une famille paysanne et de sa ferme," *Revue du Rouergue* 19 (1965), 489-500.

1898 Sussman, George D., "The Wet-Nursing Business in Nineteenth-Century France," *French Historical Studies* 9 (1975), 304-328.

1899 Sutter, Jean, "Fréquence de l'endogamie et ses facteurs au XIXᵉ siècle," *Population* 23 (1968), 303-324.

1900 Sutter, Jean, and Jean-Michel Goux, "Evolution de la consanguinité en France de 1926 à 1958 avec des données récentes détaillées," *Population* 17 (1962), 683-702.

1901 Sutter, Jean, and Claude Lévy, "Les dispenses civiles au mariage en France depuis 1900," *Population* 14 (1959), 285-304.

1902 Sutter, Jean, and L. Tabah, "Les dispenses d'âge au mariage depuis 1889," *Population* 3 (1948), 735-736.

1903 Sutter, Jean, and L. Tabah, "Evolution des isolats de deux départements français: Loir-et-Cher et Finistère," *Population* 10 (1955), 645-673.

1904 Sutter, Jean, and L. Tabah, "Evolution de la distance séparant le domicile des futurs époux: Loir-et-Cher 1870-1954, Finistere 1911-1953," *Population* 13 (1958), 227-258.

1905 Sutter, Jean, and L. Tabah, "Fréquence et répartition des mariages consanguins en France," *Population* 3 (1948), 607-630.

1906 Talmy, Robert, *Histoire du mouvement familial en France (1896-1939).* 2 v. Paris, 1962.

1907 Tardieu, Suzanne, "Equipement domestique et contrats de mariage en Mâconnais," *Arts et Traditions populaires* 2 (1954), 35-60.

1908 Tardieu, Suzanne, *La vie domestique dans le Mâconnais rural préindustriel.* Paris, 1965.

1909 Thabaut, Jules, *L'évolution de la législation sur la famille (1804-1913).* Paris, 1913.

1910 Thuillier, Guy, "Pour une histoire des travaux ménagers en Nivernais au XIXᵉ siècle," *Revue d'histoire économique et sociale* 50 (1972), 238-264.

1911 Toledano, André Daniel, *La vie de famille sous la Restauration et la Monarchie de Juillet.* Paris, 1943.

1912 Tollu, François, *Tableau d'une famille parisienne [bourgeoise entre 1900 et 1950].* Paris, 1972.

1913 Toursch, Victor, *L'enfant français à la fin du XIXe siècle d'après ses princi-paux romanciers.* Paris, 1939.

1914 Tugault, Yves, *Fecondité et urbanisation.* Paris, 1975.

1915 Turin, Y., "Enfants trouvés, colonisation et utopie: étude d'un comportement social au XIXe siècle," *Revue historique 244* (1970), 329-356.

1916 Turlan, Juliette-M., "L'imagination et l'honneur de la famille: deux conven-tions de mariage en Rouerque aux XVIIe et XVIIIe siècles," *Etudes en souvenir de Georges Chevrier: Mémoires de la Société pour l'histoire du droit...des anciens pays bourguignons...* 30 (1970-71), 347-363.

1917 Vallot, Françoise, "Mariages et divorces à Paris: analyse des actes de mariage de quatre cohortes [mariages contractés en 1936, 1956, 1960 et 1964]," *Population 26* (1971), 67-100.

1918 van de Walle, Etienne, *The Female Population of France in the Nineteenth Century: A Reconstruction of 82 Departments.* Princeton, 1974.

1919 van de Walle, Etienne, and R. Lesthaeghe, "Facteurs économiques et déclin de la fécondité en France et en Belgique," *Les aspects économiques de la croissance démographique,* ed. H. Guitton and A. J. Coale (Paris, 1976), 345-373.

1920 van de Walle, Etienne, and Samuel H. Preston, "Mortalité de l'enfance au XIXe siècle à Paris et dans le departement de la Seine," *Population 29* (1974), 89-107.

1921 Varagnac, André, *Civilisation traditionnelle et genres de vie.* Paris, 1948.

1922 Vialleton, Henri, *L'autorité maritale sur la personne de la femme.* Mont-pellier, 1919.

1923 Vialleton, Henri, "Famille, patrimoine et vocation héréditaire en France depuis le code civil," *Mélanges offerts à Jacques Maury* v. 2 (1960), 577-594.

1924 Vidalenc, Jean, *La société française de 1815 à 1841.* Paris, 1973.

1925 Viennot, Jean-Pierre, "La population de Dijon d'après le recensement de 1851," *Annales de démographie historique* (1969), 241-260.

1926 Villermé, Louis, *Tableau de l'état phisique et moral des ouvriers employés dans les manufactures de coton, de laine, et de soie.* 2 v. Paris, 1840. New ed.; Paris, 1971.

1927 Vincent, Jacqueline, "Richesses et lacunes des actes notaires pour les connais-sances des anciennes structures sociales: les contrats de mariage à Cannes de 1785 à 1815," *Revue historique 250* (1973), 363-402.

1928 Vincent, Paul, "La famille normale," *Population 5* (1950), 251-269.

1929 Vizioz, Marguerite, "Enfants de jadis et de naguère [le costume]," *Revue de Savoie 8* (1954), 43-48.

1930 Voranger, Jacques, "Influence de la météorologie et de la mortalité sur les nais-sances," *Population 8* (1953), 93-102.

1931 Watson, C., "Birth Control and Abortion in France since 1939," *Population Studies 5* (1952), 261-286.

1932 Wylie, Laurence, *Chanzeaux: A Village in Anjou.* Cambridge, Mass., 1966.

1933 Wylie, Laurence, *Village in the Vaucluse: An Account of Life in a French Village*. Cambridge, Mass., 1964.

1934 Zehraqui, Arsène, *Les travailleurs algériens en France. Etude sociologique de quelques aspects de la vie familiale*. Paris, 1976.

1935 Zeldin, Theodore, *France: 1848–1945*. v. 1: *Ambition, Love and Politics*. Oxford, 1973.

Central Europe

GENERAL SURVEYS AND COLLECTIONS

1936 Arnold, Jürg, *Das Erbrecht der Reichsstadt Esslingen.* Stuttgart, 1965.

1937 Bächtold, Hanns, *Die Gebräuche bei Verlobung und Hochzeit mit besonderer Berücksichtigung der Schweiz.* Basel, 1914.

1938 Bayer, Dorothea, *Der triviale Familien- und Liebesroman.* 2nd ed.; Tübingen, 1971.

1939 Bennecke, Hans, *Die strafrechtliche Lehre vom Ehebruch in ihrer historisch-dogmatischen Entwicklung.* Marburg, 1884. Reprint, Aalen, 1971.

1940 Boesch, Hans, *Kinderleben in der deutschen Vergangenheit.* Leipzig, 1900. 2nd ed.; Jena, 1924.

1941 Brunner, Otto, "Das 'Ganze Haus' und die alteuropäische 'Ökonomik'," *Neue Wege der Verfassungs- und Sozialgeschichte.* 2nd ed.; (Gottingen, 1968), 103-127.

1942 Bürgin-Kreis, Hildegard, "Der Wandel der Familie in Sitte und Recht in den letzten 150 Jahren," *Schweizerisches Archiv für Volkskunde* 49 (1953), 101-131.

1943 Debus, Friedhelm, "Die deutschen Bezeichnungen für die Heiratsverwandtschaft," *Deutsche Wortforschung in europäischen Bezügen*, v. 1, ed. Ludwig Erich Schmitt (Giessen, 1958), 1-116.

1944 Demleitner, Josef, "Hofübergabe und Heirat im bayerischen Alpenvorland," *Volk und Volkstum* 3 (1938), 54-66.

1945 Deneke, Bernward, *Hochzeit.* München, 1971.

1946 Dürig, Walter, *Geburtstag und Namenstag.* München, 1954.

1947 Dunker, Hans, *Werbungs-, Verlobungs- und Hochzeitsgebräuche in Schleswig-Holstein.* Hamburg, 1930.

1948 Egner, Erich, *Entwicklungsphasen der Hauswirtschaft.* Göttingen, 1964.

1949   *Familie und Gesellschaft*, ed. Ferdinand Oeter. Tübingen, 1966.

1950   *Familiensoziologie: Ein Reader als Einführung*, ed. Dieter Claessens and Petra Milhoffer. Frankfurt, 1973.

1951   Fehrle, Eugen, *Deutsche Hochzeitsbräuche*. Jena, 1937.

1952   Feigl, Helmuth, "Bäuerliches Erbrecht und Erbgewohnheiten in Niederösterreich," *Jahrbuch für Landeskunde von Niederösterreich*. n.f. 37 (1967), 161-183.

1953   Franz, Heinrich, "Der Tod im hessischen Volksglauben," *Hessische Blätter für Volkskunde* 24 (1925), 44-63.

1954   Friedberg, Emil, *Das Recht der Eheschliessung in seiner geschichtlichen Entwicklung*. Leipzig, 1865. Reprint, Aalen, 1965.

1955   Frölich, Karl, "Rechtsgeschichte und Volkskunde im niederdeutschen Eheschliessungsbrauchtum," *Nachrichten der Giessener Hochschulgesellschaft* 20 (1951), 102-138.

1956   Knodel, John, "Ortssippenbücher als Quelle für die historische Demographie," *Geschichte und Gesellschaft* 1 (1975), 370-386.

1957   Kretschmer, Ingrid, and Josef Piegler, "Bäuerliches Erbrecht," *Österreichischer Volkskundeatlas*, ed Richard Wolfram. 2. Lieferung (1965), Blatt 17.

1958   Langner, Ingeborg, "Fragen des sozialen Connubiums," *Familie und Volk* 4 (1955), 165-168.

1959   Lüthi, Max, "Der Familiarismus der Volksballade," *Volksliteratur und Hochliteratur* (Bern, 1970), 79-89.

1960   Lüthi, Max, "Familie und Natur im Märchen," ibid., 63-78.

1961   Mitterauer, Michael, "Familiengrosse — Familientypen — Familienzyklus: Probleme quantitativer Auswertung von österreichischem Quellenmaterial," *Geschichte und Gesellschaft* 1 (1975), 226-255.

1962   Neidhart, Freidhelm, *Die Familie in Deutschland: Gesellschaftliche Stellung, Struktur und Funktion*. 4th ed.; Opladen, 1975.

1963   Peuckert, Will-Erich, *Ehe*. Hamburg, 1955.

1964   Pfeiffer, Gerhard, "Familiengeschichte und Soziologie," *Blätter für fränkische Familienkunde* 10 (1972-73), 270-285.

1965   Reichhardt, Rudolf, *Geburt, Hochzeit und Tod im deutschen Volksbrauch und Volksglauben*. Jena, 1913.

1966   Riehl, Wilhelm Heinrich, *Die Familie*. Stuttgart, 1855.

1967   Rüdin-Bader, Sylvia, *Die erbrechtliche Stellung der Stiefkinder und Halbgeschwister nach den zürcherischen Rechtsquellen*. Aarau, 1959.

1968   Sauermann, Dietmar, "Hofidee und bäuerliche Familienverträge in Westfalen," *Rheinland-westfälische Zeitschrift für Volkskunde* 17 (1970), 58-78.

1969   Schaub, Walter, "Sozialgenealogie — Probleme und Methoden," *Blätter für deutsche Landesgeschichte* 110 (1974), 1-28.

1970   Schmidt, Karl, *Gutsübergabe und Ausgedinge: Eine agrarpolitische Untersuchung mit besonderer Berücksichtigung der Alpen- und Sudetenländer*. Wien, 1920.

1971 Schmitz, Carl August, *Grundformen der Verwandschaft.* Basel, 1964.

1972 Sohm, Rudolf, *Das Recht der Eheschliessung aus dem deutschen und canon-ischen Recht geschichtlich entwickelt.* Weimar, 1875. Reprint, Aalen, 1966.

1973 *Die Vererbung des ländlichen Grundbesitzes im Königreich Preussen,* ed. Max Sering. 4 v. Berlin, 1899-1910.

1974 Vischer, Eberhard, *Jugend und Alter in der Geschichte.* Basel, 1938.

1975 Weber-Kellermann, Ingeborg, *Die deutsche Familie: Versuch einer Sozial-geschichte.* Frankfurt, 1974.

1976 Welti, Erika, *Taufbräuche im Kanton Zürich.* Zürich, 1967.

1977 Wiegelmann, Günter, *Alltags- und Festspeisen.* Marburg, 1967.

1978 Wittich, Werner, *Die Grundherrschaft in Nordwestdeutschland.* Leipzig, 1896.

1979 Wolf, Eric, "Inheritance of Land among Bavarian and Tyrolese Peasants," *Anthropologica* new series 12 (1970), 99-114.

BIBLIOGRAPHIES AND REVIEW ESSAYS

1980 Dahlmann, Friedrich C., and George Waitz, *Quellenkunde der deutschen Geschichte.* 10th ed. prepared by Hermann Heimpel and Herbert Geuss; Stuttgart, 1969 ff.

1981 Friederichs, Heinz F., *Familienarchive in öffentlichem und privatem Besitz.* Neustadt (Aisch), 1972.

1982 Imhof, Arthur E., "Généalogie et démographie historique en Allemagne," *Annales de démographie historique* (1976), 77-107.

1983 *Jahresberichte für deutsche Geschichte.* 1927-40. 1949 ff.

ANCIENT AND MEDIEVAL PERIODS (TO c.1500)

1984 Arnold, Carl, *Das Kind in der deutschen Literatur des XI.–XV. Jahrhunderts.* Griefswald, 1905.

1985 Bell, Clair Hayden, "The Sister's Son in the Medieval German Epic: A Study in the Survival of Matriliny," *University of California Publications in Modern Philology* 10 (1920-25), 67-182. Issued 1922.

1986 Bosl, Karl, "Die 'familia' als Grundstruktur der mittelalterlichen Gesellschaft," *Zeitschrift für bayerische Landesgeschichte* 38 (1975), 403-424.

1987 Brauneder, Wilhelm, *Die Entwicklung des Ehegüterrechts in Österreich.* Salz-burg, 1973.

1988 Brunner, Heinrich, "Die fränkisch-romanische dos," *Abhandlungen zur Rechtsgeschichte*, v. 2, ed. Karl Rauch (Weimar, 1931), 78-116.

1989 Brunner, Heinrich, "Die Geburt eines lebenden Kindes und das eheliche Vermögensrecht," ibid., 117-164.

1990 Brunner, Heinrich, "Kritische Bemerkungen zur Geschichte des germanischen Weibererbrechts," ibid., 198-217.

1991 Brunner, Heinrich, "Die uneheliche Vaterschaft in den älteren germanischen Rechten," ibid., 165-197.

1992 Bücher, Carl, *Die Bevölkerung von Frankfurt am Main im 14. und 15. Jahrhundert.* Tübingen, 1886.

1993 Bücher, Carl, *Die Frauenfrage im Mittelalter.* 2nd ed.; Tübingen, 1910.

1994 Bullough, D. A., "Early Medieval Social Groupings: The Terminology of Kinship," *Past and Present* 45 (1969), 3-18. (See #2010)

1995 Daudet, Pierre, *Etudes sur l'histoire de la jurisdiction matrimoniale.* Paris, 1933.

1996 Demelius, Heinrich, *Eheliches Gütterecht im spätmittelalterlichen Wien.* Wien, 1970.

1997 Eisenmann, Hartmut, *Konstanzer Institutionen des Familien- und Erbrechts von 1370–1521.* Konstanz,1964.

1998 Escher, Katherine, "The Germanic Family of the *Leges Burgundionum*," *Medievalia et Humanistica* 15 (1963), 5-14.

1999 Fehr, Hans, *Die Rechtsstellung der Frau und der Kinder in den Weistümern.* Jena, 1912. Reprint, Niederwalluf bei Wiesbaden, 1971.

2000 Feilzer, Heinrich, *Jugend in der mittelalterlichen Ständegesellschaft.* Wein, 1971.

2001 Frölich, Karl, "Die Eheschliessung des deutschen Frühmittelalters im Lichte der neueren rechtsgeschichtlichen Forschung," *Hessische Blätter für Volkskunde* 27 (1928), 144-194.

2002 Gellinek, Christian, "Marriage by Consent in Literary Sources of Medieval Germany," *Studia Gratiana* 12 [*Collectanea Stephan Kuttner* 2] (1967), 555-579.

2003 Hazeltine, Harold Dexter, *Zur Geschichte der Eheschliessung nach angelsächsischen Recht.* Berlin, 1905.

2004 Jegel, August, "Altnürnberger Hochzeitsbrauch und Eherecht, besonders bis zum Ausgang des 16. Jahrhunderts," *Mitteilungen des Vereins für die Geschichte der Stadt Nürnberg* 44 (1953), 238-274.

2005 Koebner, Richard, "Die Eheaffassung des ausgehenden deutschen Mittelalters," *Archiv für Kulturgeschichte* 9 (1911), 136-198, 279-318.

2006 Köstler, Rudolf, "Raub-, Kauf- und Friedelehe bei den Germanen," *Zeitschrift der Savigny-Stiftung für Rechtsgeschichte   Germanistische Abteilung* 63 (1943), 92-136.

2007 Krauz, Eberhard, *Die Vormundschaft im mittelalterlichen Lübeck.* Kiel, 1967.

2008 Kroeschell, Karl, "Die Sippe im germanischen Recht," *Zeitschrift der Savigny-Stiftung für Rechtsgeschichte   Germanistische Abteilung* 77 (1960), 1-25.

2009 Kroeschell, Karl, *Haus und Herrschaft im frühen deutschen Recht.* Göttingen, 1968.

2010 Leyser, K., "The German Aristocracy from the Ninth to the Early Twelfth Century: A Historical and Cultural Sketch," *Past and Present* 41 (1968), 25-53. (See #1194)

2011 Leyser, K., "Maternal Kin in Early Medieval Germany: A Reply," *Past and Present* 49 (1970), 126-134. (A reply to #1194)

2012 Mahrenholtz, Hans, "Die Vererbung von Vornamen (Taufnamen) in der Zeit von 1150 bis 1650," *Familie und Volk* 3 (1954), 2-7.

2013 Mayer-Maly, Theo, "Die Morgengabe im Wiener Privatrecht des Spätmittelalters," *Festschrift Hans Lentze,* ed. Nikolaus Grass and Werner Ogris (Innsbruck, 1969), 381-395.

2014 Merschberger, Gerda, *Die Rechtstellung der germanischen Frau.* Leipzig, 1937.

2015 Meyer, Herbert, "Friedelehe und Mutterrecht," *Zeitschrift der Savigny-Stiftung für Rechtsgeschichte   Germanistische Abteilung* 47 (1927), 198-286.

2016 Mikat, Paul, "Die Inzestverbote des Konzils von Epaon: Ein Beitrag zur Geschichte des fränkischen Eherechts," *Rechtsbewahrung und Rechtsentwicklung: Festschrift für Heinrich Lange...,* ed. Kurt Kuchinke (München, 1970), 63-84.

2017 Mitterauer, Michael, "Produktionsweise, Siedlungsstruktur und Sozialformen im österreichischen Montanwesen des Mittelalters und der frühen Neuzeit," *Österreichisches Montanwesen,* ed. M. Mitterauer (München, 1974), 234-315.

2018 Mitterauer, Michael, "Zur Frage des Heiratsverhaltens im österreichischen Adel," *Beiträge zur neueren Geschichte Österreichs: Festschrift für Adam Wandruszka,* ed. Heinrich Fichtenau and Erich Zollner (Wien, 1974), 176-194.

2019 Neubecker, Friedrich Karl, *Die Mitgrft in rechtsvergleichender Darstellung.* Leipzig, 1909.

2020 Portmann, Marie-Louise, *Die Darstellung der Frau in der Geschichtsschreibung des früheren Mittelalters.* Basel, 1958.

2021 Rivers, Theodore J., "The Legal Status of Freewomen in the Lex Alamannorum," *Zeitschrift der Savigny-Stiftung für Rechtsgeschichte Germanistische Abteilung* 91 (1974), 175-179.

2022 Roller, Otto Konrad, "Die Kinderehen im ausgehenden deutschen Mittelalter," *Sozialhygienische Mitteilungen* 9 (1925), 3-29.

2023 Schadelbauer, Karl, *Die Kopfzahl der bäuerlichen Familien in Tirol im 15. Jahrhundert.* Innsbruck, 1939.

2024 Schmid, Karl, "Zur Problematik von Familie, Sippe und Geschlecht, Haus und

Dynastie beim mittelalterlichen Adel," *Zeitschrift für die Geschichte des Oberrheins* n.f. 66 (1957), 1-62.

2025   Störmer, Wilhelm, *Früher Adel: Studien zur politischen Führungsschicht im fränkisch-deutschen Reich vom 8. bis 11. Jahrhundert.* 2 v. Stuttgart, 1973.

2026   Weigand, Rudolf, "Die Rechtsprechung des Regensburger Gerichts in Ehesachen unter besonderer Berücksichtigung der bedingten Eheschliessung nach Gerichtsbüchern aus dem Ende des 15. Jahrhunderts," *Archiv für katholisches Kirchenrecht* 137 (1968), 403-463.

2027   Winterer, Hermann, "Die Stellung des unehelichen Kindes in der langobardischen Gesetzgebung," *Zeitschrift der Savigny-Stiftung für Rechtsgeschichte Germanistische Abteilung* 87 (1970), 32-56.

2028   Weinhold, Karl, *Die deutschen Frauen in dem Mittelalter.* 2 v. 3rd ed.; Wien, 1897.

EARLY MODERN PERIOD
(c. 1500–c. 1800)

2029   Berkner, Lutz K., "Inheritance, Land Tenure, and Peasant Family Structure: A German Regional Comparison," *Family and Inheritance*, ed. Jack Goody, Joan Thirsk, and E. P. Thompson (Cambridge, England, 1976), 71-95. (See #296)

2030   Berkner, Lutz K., "The Stem Family and the Developmental Cycle of a Peasant Household: An Eighteenth-Century Austrian Example," *American Historical Review* 77 (1972), 398-418.

2031   Bielmann, Jürg, *Die Lebensverhältnisse im Urnerland während des 18. und zu Beginn des 19. Jahrhunderts.* Basel, 1972.

2032   Blaschke, Karlheinz, *Bevölkerungsgeschichte von Sachsen bis zur Industriellen Revolution.* Weimar, 1967.

2033   Bogatzky, Carl Heinrich v., *Der christliche Haus- und Ehestand.* Halle, 1756.

2034   Braun, Rudolf, "The Impact of Cottage Industry on an Agricultural Population," *The Rise of Capitalism*, ed. David Landes (New York, 1966), 53-64.

2035   Braun, Rudolf, *Industrialisierung und Volksleben: Die Veränderungen der Lebensformen in einem ländlichen Industriegebiet vor 1800 (Züricher Oberland).* Erlenbach–Zürich, 1960.

2036   Brenne, Dieter, *Erbanfall- und Erbantrittsprinzip in der neueren deutschen Privatrechtsgeschichte.* Münster, 1959.

2037   Bucher, Silvio, *Bevölkerung und Wirtschaft des Amtes Entlebuch im 18. Jahrhundert.* Luzern, 1974.

2038   Burri, Hans-Rudolf, *Die Bevölkerung Luzerns im 18. und Frühen 19. Jahrhundert: Demographie und Schichtung einer Schweizer Stadt im Ancien Régime.* Luzern, 1975.

2039 Conrad, Hermann, "Die Rechtsstellung der Ehefrau in der Privatrechtsgesetz-gebung der Aufklärungszeit," *Aus Mittelalter und Neuzeit: Gerhard Kallen zum 70. Geburtstag...*, ed. Josef Engel and Hans Martin Klinkenberg (Bonn, 1957), 253–270.

2040 Conrad, Hermann, "Staatliche Theorie und kirchliche Dogmatik im Ringen um die Ehegesetzgebung Josephs II.," *Wahrheit und Verkündigung: Michael Schmaus zum 70. Geburtstag*, ed. Leo Scheffczyk, Werner Dettloff, and Richard Heinzmann (München, 1967), 1171–1190.

2041 Conrad, Hermann, "Das tridentinische Konzil und die Entwicklung des kirch-lichen und weltlichen Eherechts," *Das Weltkonzil von Trient*, ed. G. Schreiber (Freiburg, 1951), I, 297–324.

2042 Daw, S. F., "Age of Boys' Puberty in Leipzig, 1727–49, as Indicated by Voice Breaking in J. S. Bach's Choir Members," *Human Biology* 42 (1970), 87–89.

2043 Deiterich, Hartwig, *Das protestantische Eherecht in Deutschland bis zur Mitte des 17. Jahrhunderts.* München, 1970.

2044 Drägert, Erich, "Recht und Brauch in Ehe und Hochzeit im hamburgischen Amt Ritzebüttel nach der Reformation," *Jahrbuch der Männer vom Morgenstein* 43 (1962), 20–65.

2045 Dufour, Alfred, *Le mariage dans l'école allemande du droit naturel moderne au XVIIIe siècle.* Paris, 1972.

2046 Erbe, Günther, "Das Ehescheidungsrecht im Herzogtum Württemberg seit der Reformation," *Zeitschrift für württembergische Landesgeschichte* 14 (1955), 95–144.

2047 Fichtner, Paula Sutter, "Dynastic Marriage in Sixteenth-Century Habsburg Diplomacy and Statecraft," *American Historical Review* 81 (1976), 243–265.

2048 Fick, Ludwig, *Die bäuerliche Erbfolge im Gebiet des bayerischen Landrechtes.* München, 1895.

2049 Freudenthal, Margarete, *Gestaltwandel der städtischen bürgerlichen und pro-letarischen Hauswirtschaft unter besonderer Berücksichtigung des Typen-wandels von Frau und Familie, vornehmlich in Südwest-Deutschland zwischen 1760 und 1933.* Würzburg, 1934.

2050 Friedrichs, Christopher R., "Marriage, Family and Social Structure in an Early Modern German Town," *Historical Papers,* ed. Canadian Historical Associ-ation (1975), 17–40.

2051 Gaerte, Wilhelm, *Volksglaube und Brauchtum Ostpreussens.* Würzburg, 1956.

2052 Hartinger, Walter, "Bayerisches Dienstbotenleben auf dem Lande vom 16. bis ins 18. Jahrhundert," *Zeitschrift für bayerische Landesgeschichte* 38 (1975), 598–638.

2053 Hartinger, Walter, "Zur Bevölkerungs- und Sozialstruktur von Oberpfalz und Niederbayern in vorindustrieller Zeit," *Zeitschrift für bayerische Landesge-schichte* 39 (1976), 785–822.

2054   Henning, Freiderich-Wilhelm, *Dienste und Abgaben der Bauern im 18. Jahrhundert*. Stuttgart, 1969.

2055   Hess, Rolf-Dieter, *Familien- und Erbrecht im württembergischen Landrecht von 1555 unter besonderer Berücksichtigung des älteren württembergischen Rechts*. Stuttgart, 1968.

2056   Hesse, Hans Gert, *Evangelisches Ehescheidungsrecht in Deutschland*. Bonn, 1960.

2057   *Historische Demographie als Sozialgeschichte: Giessen und Umgebung vom 17. zum 19. Jahrhundert*, ed. Arthur E. Imhof. Darmstadt and Marburg, 1975.

2058   Hoffmann, Julius, *Die "Hausväterliteratur" und die "Predigten über den christlichen Hausstand."* Weinheim-Berlin, 1959.

2059   Hofmann, Johann Andreas, *Handbuch des deutschen Eherechts....* Jena, 1788.

2060   Hornstein, Walter, *Vom "jungen Herrn" zum "hoffnungsvollen Jüngling": Wandlungen des Jugendlebens im 18. Jahrhundert*. Heidelberg, 1965.

2061   Imhof, Arthur E., "Landliche Familienstrukturen an einem hessischen Beispiel: Heuchelheim 1690-1900," *Sozialgeschichte der Familie...*, ed. Werner Conze (Stuttgart, 1976), 197-230. (See #450)

2062   Kirstein, Roland, *Die Entwicklung der Sponsalienlehre und der Lehre vom Eheschluss in der deutschen protestantischen Eherechtslehre bis zu J. H. Böhmer*. Bonn, 1966.

2063   *Kleinkinderpädagogik in Deutschland im Zeitalter der Aufklarung*, ed. Günter Ulbricht. Berlin, 1955.

2064   Kluckhohn, Paul, *Die Auffassung der Liebe in der Literatur des 18. Jahrhunderts und in der deutschen Romantik*. 3rd ed.; Tübingen, 1966.

2065   Knodel, John, and Etienne van de Walle, "Breast Feeding, Fertility, and Infant Mortality: An Analysis of Some Early German Data," *Population Studies* 21 (1967), 109-131.

2066   Knodel, John, "Two and a Half Centuries of Demographic History in a Bavarian Village," *Population Studies* 24 (1970), 353-376.

2067   Kramer, Karl-Sigismund, "Das Haus als geistiges Kraftfeld im Gefüge der alten Volkskultur," *Rheinland-westfälische Zeitschrift für Volkskunde* 11 (1964), 30-43.

2068   Kramer, Karl-Sigismund, *Bauern und Bürger im nachmittelalterlichen Unterfranken*. Würzburg, 1957.

2069   Kramer, Karl-Sigismund, *Volksleben in Fürstentum Ansbach und seinen Nachbargebieten (1500–1800)*. Würzburg, 1961.

2070   Kramer, Karl-Sigismund, *Volksleben im Hochstift Bamberg und im Fürstentum Coburg (1500–1800)*. Würzburg, 1967.

2071   Lehners, Jean-Paul, "Haus und Familie im Markt Stockerau am Ende des 17. Jahrhunderts," *Unsere Heimat: Zeitschrift des Vereins für Landeskunde von Niederösterreich und Wien* 45 (1974), 222-235.

2072   *Leichenpredigten als Quelle historischer Wissenschaften*, ed. Rudolf Lenz. Köln-Wien, 1975.

2073 Lenz, Rudolf, and Gundolf Keil, "Johann Christoph Donauer (1669-1718): Untersuchungen zur Soziographie und Pathographie eines Nördlinger Rats-konsulenten aufgrund der Leichenpredigt," *Zeitschrift für bayerische Landesgeschichte* 38 (1975), 317-355.

2074 Mitterauer, Michael, "Vorindustrielle Familienformen: Zur Funktionsentlast-ung des 'ganzen Hauses' im 17. und 18. Jahrhundert," *Fürst, Bürger, Mensch*, ed. Friedrich Engel-Janosi, Grete Klingenstein, and Heinrich Lutz (München, 1975), 123-185.

2075 Mitterauer, Michael, "Zur Familienstruktur in ländlichen Gebieten Österreichs im 17. Jahrhundert," *Beiträge zur Bevölkerungs- und Sozialgeschichte Österreichs*, ed. Heimold Helczmanovski (Wien, 1973), 167-221.

2076 Möller, Helmut, *Die kleinbürgerliche Familie im 18. Jahrhundert*. Berlin, 1969.

2077 Muchow, Hans Heinrich, *Jugendund Zeitgeist: Morphologie der Kultur-pubertät*. Reinbek bie Hamburg, 1962.

2078 Mühlsteiger, Johannes, *Der Geist des josephinischen Eherechtes*. Wien-München, 1967.

2079 Müller, Ilse, "Bevölkerungsgeschichtliche Untersuchungen in drei Gemeinden des württembergischen Schwarzwaldes," *Archiv für Bevölkerungswissen-schaft* 9 (1939), 185-206, 247-264.

2080 Richarz, Irmintraut, *Herrschaftliche Haushalte in vorindustrieller Zeit im Weserraum*. Berlin, 1971.

2081 Roller, Otto Konrad, *Die Einwohnerschaft der Stadt Durlach im 18. Jahr-hundert in ihren wirtschaftlichen und kulturgeschichtlichen Verhältnissen dargestellt aus ihren Stammtafeln*. Karlsruhe, 1907.

2082 Sabean, David, "Family and Land Tenure: A Case Study of Conflict in the German Peasants' War (1525)," *Peasant Studies Newsletter* 3 (1974), 1-15. Also in French in *Annales E.S.C.* 27 (1972), 903-922.

2083 Sabean, David, *Landbesitz und Gesellschaft am Vorabend des Bauernkrieges*. Stuttgart, 1972.

2084 Sabean, David, "Verwandschaft und Familie in einem württembergischen Dorf 1500 bis 1870: Einige methodische Überlegungen," *Sozialgeschichte der Familie...*, ed. Werner Conze (Stuggart, 1976), 231-246. (See #450)

2085 Saller, Karl, "Sexualität und Sitte in der vorindustriellen Zeit," *Familie und Gesellschaft*, ed. Ferdinand Oeter (Tübingen, 1966), 113-140.

2086 Schaub, Walter, "Städtische Familienformen in sozialgenealogischer Sicht (Oldenburg 1743/1870)," *Sozialgeschichte der Familie...*, ed. Werner Conze (Stuggart, 1976), 292-345. (See #450)

2087 Scheidt, Walter, *Niedersächsische Bauern II: Bevölkerungsbiologie der Elbinsel Finkenwarder vom dreissigjährigen Kriege bis zur Gegenwart*. Jena, 1932.

2088 Schmelzeisen, Gustaf Klemens, *Polizeiordnungen und Privatrecht*. Münster-Köln, 1955.

2089   Schneider, Lothar, *Der Arbeiterhaushalt im 18. und 19. Jahrhundert*. Berlin, 1967.

2090   Schubart-Fikentscher, Gertrud, *Die Unehelischen-Frage in der Frühzeit der Aufklärung*. Berlin, 1967.

2091   Schubnell, Hermann, *Der Kinderreichtum bei Bauern und Arbeitern: Untersuchungen aus Schwarzwald und Rheinebene*. Freiburg im Breisgau, 1941.

2092   Schurmann, M., *Bevölkerung, Wirtschaft und Gesellschaft in Appenzell Innerrhoden im 18. und frühen 19. Jahrhundert*. Appenzell, 1974.

2093   Schwab, Dieter, *Grundlagen und Gestalt der staatlichen Ehegesetzgebung in der Neuzeit bis zum Beginn des 19. Jahrhunderts*. Bielefeld, 1967.

2094   Schwarz, Ingeborg, *Die Bedeutung der Sippe für die Öffentlichkeit der Eheschliessung im 15. und 16. Jahrhundert*. Neustadt/Aisch, 1959.

2095   Sperling, Hans, "400 Jahre sozio-demographische Entwicklung einer Familie," *Jahrbuch der Sozialwissenschaft* 24 (1973), 218–236.

2096   Stephan, G., *Die häusliche Erziehung in Deutschland während des achtzehnten Jahrhunderts*. Wiesbaden, 1891.

2097   Strieder, Jakob, "Die Geschäfts- und Familienpolitik Jakob Fugger des Reichen," *Zeitschrift für die gesamte Staatswissenschaft* 82 (1927), 337–348.

2098   Suppan, Klaus, *Die Ehelehre Martin Luthers*. Salzburg-München, 1971.

2099   Walter, Emil J., "Kritik einiger familien-soziologischer Begriffe im Lichte der politischen Arithmetik des 18. Jahrhunderts," *Schweizerische Zeitschrift für Volkswirtschaft und Statistik* 97 (1961), 64–75.

2100   Walter, Emil J., *Zur Soziologie der Alten Eidgenossenschaft: Eine Analyse der Sozial- und Berufsstruktur von der Reformation bis zur französischen Revolution*. Bern, 1966.

2101   Wesener, Gunter, *Geschichte des Erbrechtes in Österreich seit der Rezeption*. Graz-Köln, 1957.

2102   Wopfner, Hermann, *Bergbauernbuch: Von Arbeit und Leben des Tiroler Bergbauern in Vergangenheit und Gegenwart*. 3 v. Innsbruck, 1951-60.

MODERN PERIOD (c.1800 TO THE PRESENT)

2103   Adolphs, Lotte, *Industrielle Kinderarbeit im 19. Jahrhundert unter Berücksichtigung des Duisburger Raumes*. Duisburg, 1972.

2104   Arnold, Klaus, "Der Umbruch des generativen Verhaltens in einem Bergbauerngebiet," *Beiträge zur Bevölkerungs- und Sozialgeschichte Österreichs*, ed. Heimold Helczmanovski (Wien, 1973), 404-448.

2105   Bäumer, Gertrud, *Die Frau in Gesellschaft und Staatsleben in der Gegenwart*. Stuttgart, 1914.

2106   Baumert, Gerhard, "Changes in the Family and the Position of Older Persons in Germany," *International Journal of Comparative Sociology* 1 (1960), 202–210.

2107 Baumert, Gerhard, "Einige Beobachtungen zur Wandlung der familialen Stellung des Kindes in Deutschland," *Jugend in der modernen Gesellschaft,* ed. Ludwig von Friedeburg (Köln-Berlin, 1965), 309–320.

2108 Baumert, Gerhard, and Edith Hünninger, *Deutsche Familien nach dem Kriege.* Darmstadt, 1954.

2109 Bergmann, Helmut, *Strukturwandel der Familie.* Hamburg, 1960. 2nd ed.; Witten, 1966.

2110 Bergmann, Theodor, "Der bäuerliche Familienbetrieb—Problematik und Entwicklungstendenzen," *Zeitschrift für Agrargeschichte und Agrarsoziologie* 17 (1969), 215–230.

2111 Bertlein, Hermann, *Jugendleben und soziales Bildungsschicksal: Reifungsstil und Bildungserfahrung werktätiger Jugendlicher 1860–1910.* Hannover, 1966.

2112 Blochmann, Elisabeth, *Das "Frauenzimmer" und die "Gelehrsamkeit."* Heidelberg, 1966.

2113 Bosse, R., *Das Familienwesen oder Forschungen über seine Natur, Geschichte und Rechtsverhältnisse.* Stuttgart, 1835.

2114 Braun, Rudolf, *Sozialer und kultureller Wandel in einem ländlichen Industriegebiet im 19. und 20. Jahrhundert.* Zürich, 1965.

2115 Braun, Rudolf, "Probleme des sozio-kulturellen Wandels im 19. Jahrhundert," *Kulturelle Wandel im 19. Jahrhundert,* ed. Rolf W. Brednich (Göttingen, 1973), 11–23.

2116 Brepohl, Wilhelm, *Der Aufbau des Ruhrvolkes im Zuge der Ost-West-Wanderung.* Recklinghausen, 1948.

2117 Brepohl, Wilhelm, *Industrievolk im Wandel der agraren zur industriellen Daseinsform, dargestellt am Ruhrgebiet.* Tübingen, 1957.

2118 Bridenthal, Renate, "Beyond *Kinder, Küche, Kirche:* Weimar Women at Work," *Central European History* 6 (1973), 148–166.

2119 Conrad, Hermann, "Die Grundlegung der modernen Zivilehe durch die französische Revolution," *Zeitschrift der Savigny-Stiftung für Rechtsgeschichte Germanistische Abteilung* 67 (1950), 336–372.

2120 Crew, David, "Definitions of Modernity: Social Mobility in a German Town 1880–1901," *Journal of Social History* 7 (1973–74), 51–74.

2121 Deenen, Bernd van, *Bäuerliche Familien im sozialen Wandel.* Bonn, 1970.

2122 Deenen, Bernd van, and Albert Valtmann, *Die ländliche Familie unter dem Einfluss von Industrienähe und Industrieferne.* Berlin, 1961.

2123 Demeny, Paul, "Early Fertility Decline in Austria-Hungary: A Lesson in Demographic Transition," *Daedalus* 97 (1968), 502–522.

2124 Dörner, Heinrich, *Industrialisierung und Familienrecht.* Berlin, 1974.

2125 Ebel, Heinrich, "Arbeitszeit und Familienstruktur," *Arbeitswissenschaft* 3 (1964), 137–141.

2126   Engelsing, Rolf, "Das häusliche Personal in der Epoche der Industrialisierung," *Jahrbuch für Sozialwissenschaft* 20 (1969), 84–121. (Now in #2127, 225–261)

2127   Engelsing, Rolf, *Zur Sozialgeschichte deutscher Mittel- und Unterschichten.* Göttingen, 1973.

2128   *Das Familienleben der Gegenwart: 192 Familienmonographien,* ed. Alice Salmon and Marie Baum. Berlin, 1930.

2129   Fischer, Wolfram, "Rural Industrialization and Population Change," *Comparative Studies in Society and History* 15 (1973), 158–170.

2130   Fischer, Wolfram, *Wirtschaft und Gesellschaft im Zeitalter der Industrialisierung.* Göttingen, 1972.

2131   Fishman, Sterling, "Suicide, Sex, and the Discovery of the German Adolescent," *History of Education Quarterly* 10 (1970), 170–188.

2132   Fliri, Franz, *Bevölkerungsgeographische Untersuchungen im Unterinntal.* Innsbruck, 1948.

2133   Fonk, Friedrich Hermann, *Das staatliche Mischehenrecht in Preussen vom allgemeinen Landrecht an.* Bielefeld, 1961.

2134   Friedl, John, and Walter S. Ellis, "Celibacy, Late Marriage and Potential Mates in a Swiss Isolate," *Human Biology* 48 (1976), 23–35.

2135   Friedl, John, and Walter S. Ellis, "Inbreeding, Isonymy, and Isolation in a Swiss Community," *Human Biology* 46 (1974), 699–712.

2136   Friedl, John, *Kippel: A Changing Village in the Alps.* New York, 1974.

2137   Gillis, John R., "Conformity and Rebellion: Contrary Styles of English and German Youth 1900 to 1937," *History of Education Quarterly* 13 (1973), 249–260.

2138   Griessmair, Johannes, *Knecht und Magd in Südtirol: Dargestellt am Beispiel der bäuerlichen Dienstboten im Pustertal.* Innsbruck, 1976.

2139   Hävernick, Walter, *Schläge als Strafe: Ein Bestandteil der heutigen Familiensitte in volkskundlicher Sicht.* 2nd ed.; Hamburg, 1966.

2140   Höhn, H., "Sitte und Brauch bei Geburt, Taufe und in der Kindheit," *Württembergische Jahrbücher für Statistik und Landeskunde* (1909), 256–279.

2141   Hofman, Ernst, "Volkskundliche Betrachtungen zur proletarischen Familie in Chemnitz um 1900," *Wissenschaftliche Zeitschrift der Humboldt-Universität zu Berlin: Gesellschafts- und sprachwissenschaftliche Reihe* 20 (1971), 65–81.

2142   Hubbard, William H., "Forschungen zur städtischen Haushaltsstruktur am Ende des 19. Jahrhunderts: Das GRAZHAUS-Projekt," *Sozialgeschichte der Familie...,* ed. Werner Conze (Stuttgart, 1976), 283–291. (See #450)

2143   Karr, Chadwick, and Frank Wesley, "Comparison of German and U.S. Child-Rearing Practices," *Child Development* 37 (1966), 715–723.

2144   Khera, Sigrid, "An Austrian Peasant Village under Rural Industrialization," *Behavior Science Notes* 7 (1972), 29–36.

2145   *Kinderschaukel: Ein Lesebuch zur Geschichte der Kindheit in Deutschland*

1860-1930, ed. Marie-Luise Könneker. 2 v. Darmstadt, 1976.

2146   Kirkpatrick, Clifford, *Nazi Germany: Its Women and Family Life.* New York, 1938.

2147   Kirkpatrick, Clifford, "Recent Changes in the Status of Women and the Family in Germany," *American Sociological Review* 2 (1937), 650-658.

2148   Knodel, John, *The Decline of Fertility in Germany, 1871-1939.* Princeton, 1974.

2149   Knodel, John, "Infant Mortality and Fertility in Three Bavarian Villages: An Analysis of Family Histories from the 19th Century," *Population Studies* 22 (1968), 297-318.

2150   Knodel, John, "Law, Marriage and Illegitimacy in Nineteenth-Century Germany," *Population Studies* 20 (1966-67), 279-294.

2151   Knodel, John, "Malthus Amiss: Marriage Restrictions in 19th-Century Germany," *Social Science* 27 (1972), 40-45.

2152   Knodel, John, and Mary Jo Maynes, "Urban and Rural Marriage Patterns in Imperial Germany," *Journal of Family History* 1 (1976), 129-168.

2153   Kocka, Jürgen, "Family and Bureaucracy in German Industrial Management, 1850-1914: Siemens in Comparative Perspective," *Business History Review* 45 (1971), 133-156.

2154   Köllmann, Wolfgang, *Bevölkerung in der Industriellen Revolution: Studien zur Bevölkerungsgeschichte Deutschlands.* Göttingen, 1974.

2155   Köllmann, Wolfgang, *Sozialgeschichte der Stadt Barmen in 19. Jahrhundert.* Tübingen, 1960.

2156   Köllmann, Wolfgang, "The Population of Barmen before and during the Period of Industrialization," *Population in History,* ed. David V. Glass and D.E.C. Eversley (London, 1965), 588-607. (See #214)

2157   König, René, "Family and Authority: The German Father in 1955," *Sociological Review* 5 (1957), 107-125.

2158   König, René, *Materialien zur Soziologie der Familie.* 2nd ed.; Köln, 1974.

2159   Koomen, Willem, "A Note on the Authoritarian German Family," *Journal of Marriage and the Family* 36 (1974), 634-636.

2160   Kopp, Hannes, *Erziehung im Wandel: Kindererziehung in den Jahren um 1890 und 1970 im Spiegel einer deutschschweizerischen Familienzeitschrift.* Basel, 1974.

2161   Kreuzinger, Dieter, *Rechts- und sozialgeschichtliche Entwicklungen des ländlichen Dienstboten- und Gesellenwesens in der Steiermark.* Graz, 1969.

2162   Kuczynski, Jürgen, and Ruth Hoppe, *Geschichte der Kinderarbeit in Deutschland 1750-1939.* 2 v. Berlin, 1958.

2163   Kuhnen, Frithjof, *Lebensverhältnisse ländlicher Familien: Sozialökonomische Untersuchungen an 3000 Familien in Landkreis Horb/Neckar.* Bonn, 1961.

2164   Kyll, Nikolaus, *Das Kind in Glaube und Brauch des Trierer Landes.* Trier, 1957.

2165   Lamousse, Annette, "Family Roles of Women: A German Example," *Journal of Marriage and the Family* 31 (1969), 145-152.

2166   Landes, David, "Bleichröders and Rothschilds: The Problem of Continuity in the Family Firm," *The Family in History,* ed. Charles E. Rosenberg (Philadelphia, 1975), 95-114. (See #79)

2167   Langenmayr, Arnold, "Berufstätigkeit der Mutter und spätere Partnerwahl der Kinder," *Kölner Zeitschrift für Soziologie* 28 (1976), 728-737.

2168   Linde, Hans, "Persönlichkeitsbildung in der Landfamilie," *Familie und Gesellschaftsstruktur,* ed. H. Rosenbaum (Frankfurt, 1974), 194-206.

2169   Linse, Ulrich, "Arbeiterschaft und Geburtenentwicklung im Deutschen Kaiserreich von 1971," *Archiv für Sozialgeschichte* 12 (1972), 205-271.

2170   Ludwig, Karl-Heinz, "Die Fabrikarbeit von Kindern im 19. Jahrhundert," *Vierteljahrschrift für Sozial- und Wirtschaftsgeschichte* 52 (1965), 63-85.

2171   Lupri, Eugen, "Industrialisierung und Strukturwandlungen in der Familie," *Sociologia Ruralis* 5 (1955), 57-76.

2172   Mason, Timothy W., "Women in Germany, 1925-1940: Family, Welfare and Work," *History Workshop* 1 (1976), 74-113; 2 (1976), 5-32.

2173   McIntyre, Jill, "Women and the Professions in Germany, 1930-1940," *German Democracy and the Triumph of Hitler,* ed. Anthony Nicholls and Erich Matthias (London, 1971), 175-213.

2174   Melchers, Wilhelm, *Die bürgerliche Familie des 19. Jahrhunderts als Erziehungs-und Bildungsfaktor: Auf Grund autobiographischer Literatur.* Düren, 1929.

2175   Metraux, Rhoda, "Parents and Children: An Analysis of Contemporary German Child-Care and Youth-Guidance Literature," *Childhood in Contemporary Cultures,* ed. Margaret Mead and Martha Wolfenstein (Chicago, 1955), 204-228. (See #44)

2176   Mitterauer, Michael, "Auswirkung von Urbanisierung und Frühindustrialisierung auf die Familienverfassung an Beispielen des österreichischen Raums," *Sozialgeschichte der Familie...,* ed. Werner Conze (Stuttgart, 1976), 53-146. (See #450)

2177   Muchow, Hans Heinrich, *Jugendgenerationen im Wandel der Zeit.* Wien, 1964.

2178   Muchow, Hans Heinrich, *Sexualreife und Sozialstruktur der Jugend.* Reinbek bei Hamburg, 1959.

2179   Muth, Heinrich, "Jugendpflege und Politik: Zur Jugend- und Innenpolitik des Kaiserreiches," *Geschichte in Wissenschaft und Unterricht* 12 (1961), 597-619.

2180   Nave-Herz, Rosemarie, "Soziologische Aspekte der Frühehe," *Kölner Zeitschrift für Soziologie* 19 (1967), 484-510.

2181   Neidhardt, Friedhelm, *Schichtbedingte Elterneinflüsse in Erziehungs- und Bildungsprozess der heranwachsenden Generation: Ein Beitrag zum ersten Familienbericht der Bundesregierung.* Bonn, 1968.

2182 Nell, A. V., *Die Entwicklung der generativen Strukturen bürgerlicher und bäuerlicher Familien von 1750 bis zur Gegenwart.* Bochum, 1973.

2183 Neumann, Robert P., "Industrialization and Sexual Behavior: Some Aspects of Working Class Life in Imperial Germany," *Modern European Social History,* ed. Robert Bezucha (Lexington, 1972), 270-300.

2184 Neumann, Robert P., "The Sexual Question and Social Democracy in Germany," *Journal of Social History* 7 (1973-74), 271-286.

2185 Niemeyer, Annemarie, *Zur Struktur der Familie: Statistische Materialien.* Berlin, 1931.

2186 Niethammer, Lutz, and Franz Brüggemeier, "Wie wohnten Arbeiter im Kaiserreich?" *Archiv für Sozialgeschichte* 16 (1976), 61-134.

2187 Phayer, J. Michael, "Lower Class Morality: The Case of Bavaria," *Journal of Social History* 8 (1974-75), 79-95.

2188 Plätzer, Hans, *Geschichte der ländlichen Arbeitsverhältnisse in Bayern.* München, 1904.

2189 Planck, Ulrich, *Der bäuerliche Familienbetrieb zwischen Patriarchat und Partnerschaft.* Stuttgart, 1964.

2190 Planck, Ulrich, "Die Landfamilie in der Bundesrepublik Deutschland," *Soziologie der Familie,* ed. Günther Lüschen and Eugen Lupri (Opladen, 1970), 380-410.

2191 Rabbie, Jacob M., "A Cross-Cultural Comparison of Parent-Child Relationships in the United States and West Germany," *British Journal of Social and Clinical Psychology* 4 (1965), 298-310.

2192 Ramm, Thilo, "Eherecht und Nationalsozialismus," *Klassenjustiz und Pluralismus,* ed. Günter Doeker and Winifried Steffani (Hamburg, 1973), 151-166.

2193 Rodgers, R. R., "Changes in Parental Behavior Reported by Children in West Germany and the United States," *Human Development* 14 (1971), 208-224.

2194 Roessler, Wilhelm, *Jugend im Erziehungsfeld: Haltung und Verhalten der deutschen Jugend in der ersten Hälfte des 20. Jahrhunderts unter besonderer Berücksichtigung der westdeutschen Jugend der Gegenwart.* 2nd ed.; Dusseldorf, 1962.

2195 Rosenmayr, Leopold, *Arbeit und Familie in der ländlichen Region.* Wien, 1964.

2196 Rempf, Johann Daniel Franz, *Der Haus-, Brot- und Lehrherr in seinen ehelichen väterlichen und übrigen hausherrlichen Verhältnissen gegen Gesinde, Gesellen und Lehrlinge.* Berlin, 1823.

2197 Sabean, David, "Household Formation and Geographical Mobility: A Family Register Study for a Württemberg Village 1760-1900," *Annales de démographie historique* (1970), 275-294.

2198 Salvioni, G. B., "Zur Statistik der Haushaltungen," *Allgemeines Statistisches Archiv* 5 (1899), 191-236.

2199   Schaffner, Bertram H., *Father Land: A Study of Authoritarianism in the German Family.* New York, 1948.

2200   Schaffner, Martin, *Die Basler Arbeiterbevölkerung im 19. Jahrhundert.* Basel, 1972.

2201   Schelsky, Helmut, *Wandlungen der deutschen Familie in der Gegenwart.* 5th ed.; Stuttgart, 1967.

2202   Shmücker, Helga, *Die ökonomische Lage der Familie in der BRD.* Stuttgart, 1961.

2203   Schulze, Wally, *Kinderarbeit und Erziehungsfragen in Preussen zu Beginn des 19. Jahrhunderts.* Leipzig, 1890.

2204   Schwarz, Gerard, *"Nahrungsstand" und "erzwungener Gesellenstand." Mentalité und Strukturwandel des bayerischen Handwerks im Industrialisierungsprozess um 1800.* Berlin, 1974.

2205   *Seminar: Familie und Familienrecht,* ed. Spiros Simitis and Gisela Zenz. 2 v. Frankfurt, 1975.

2206   Shorter, Edward, " 'La vie intime': Beiträge zu seiner Geschichte am Beispiel des kulturellen Wandels in den bayerischen Unterschichten im 19. Jahrhundert," *Soziologie und Sozialgeschichte,* ed. Peter C. Ludz (Opladen, 1972), 530–549.

2207   Shorter, Edward, "Towards a History of *La Vie Intime:* The Evidence of Cultural Criticism in Nineteenth-Century Bavaria," *The Emergence of Leisure,* ed. Michael R. Marrus (New York, 1974), 38–68.

2208   Shorter, Edward, "Der Wandel der Mutter-Kind-Beziehungen zu Beginn der Moderne," *Geschichte und Gesellschaft* 1 (1975), 256–282.

2209   Spindler, George D., *Burgbach: Urbanization and Identity in a German Village.* New York, 1973.

2210   Staudt, Reinhold, *Studien zum Patenbrauch in Hessen.* Darmstadt, 1958.

2211   Stephenson, Jill, *Women in Nazi Society.* London, 1975.

2212   Storbeck, Dietrich, "Die Familienpolitik der SED und die Familienwirklichkeit in der DDR," *Kölner Zeitschrift für Soziologie* Sonderheft 8 (1964), 86–113.

2213   Toman, Walter, and Siegfried Preiser, *Familienkonstellationen und ihre Störungen.* Stuttgart, 1973.

2214   Wais, Kurt K. T., *Das Vater-Sohn Motiv in der Dichtung bis 1880.* Berlin and Leipzig, 1931.

2215   Wais, Kurt K. T., *Das Vater-Sohn Motiv in der Dichtung 1880–1930.* Berlin and Leipzig, 1931.

2216   Weber, Marianne, *Ehefrau und Mutter in der Rechtsentwicklung.* Tübingen, 1907. Reprint, Aalen, 1971.

2217   Wurzbacher, Gerhard, "Die Familie als sozialer Eingliederungsfaktor," *Das Dorf im Spannungsfeld industrieller Entwicklung,* ed. G. Wurzbacher and R. Pflaum (Stuttgart, 1961), 74–111.

2218   Wurzbacher, Gerhard, *Leitbilder gegenwärtigen deutschen Familienlebens: Methoden, Ergebnisse und sozialpädagogische Folgerungen einer soziologischen Analyse von 164 Familienmonographien.* 4th ed.; Stuttgart, 1969.

The Netherlands and Belgium

BIBLIOGRAPHIES AND PERIODICALS

2219   *A.A.G. Bijdragen* [Afdeling Agrarische Geschiedenis of the Landbouwhoge-school, Wageningen] 1958 ff.

2220   *Bevolking en gezin: Population et famille* 1-25 (1963-71). From 1972 this jour-nal was continued in two separate periodicals *Population et famille* 26 (1972) ff. and *Bevolking en gezin* 1 (1972) ff.

2221   De Buck, H., *Bibliografie der Geschiedenis van Nederland*. Leiden, 1968.

2222   Roessingh, H. K., *Historisch-Demografisch Onderzoek*. The Hague, 1959.

2223   Slicher van Bath, Bernard H., *Voorlopige systematische bibliografie van de Nederlandse demografische geschiedenis*. Wageningen, 1962.

TO THE NINETEENTH CENTURY

2224   Art, J., "Nataliteit en onwettige geboorten: Een onontgonnen onderzoekster-rein," *Bijdragen tot de Geschiedenis van Brabant* 55 (1972), 3-30.

2225   Brugmans, Hajo, *Het huiselijk en maatschappelijk leven onzer voorouders*. Amsterdam, 1931.

2226   Brugmans, Hajo, "Binnenshuis en buitenshuis in de zeventiende eeuw," *Ge-schiedenis van Amsterdam*, v. 3 (Utrecht, 1973), 305-330. Originally 1930-1933.

2227   Brugmans, Hajo, "Maatschappelijk en huiselijk leven in de achttiende eeuw," *Geschiedenis van Amsterdam*, v. 4 (Utrecht, 1973), 111-131.

2228   Cosemans, A., *Die Bevolking van Brabant in de XVIIe en XVIIIe eeuw*. Brussels, 1939.

2229   Daelemans, F., "Leiden 1581: Een socio-demografische onderzoek," *A.A.G. Bijdragen* 19 (1975), 137-218.

2230   Dalle, D., "De Volkstellingen te Veurne en in Veurne-Ambacht op het einde van de zeventiende eeuw," *Bulletin de la Commission Royale d'Histoire* 20 (1955), 1-34.

2231   Dalle, D., "Volstelling van 1697 in Veurne-Ambacht en de evolutie van het veurnse bevolkingscijfer in de XVIIe eeuw," *Handelingen van het Genootschap voor Geschiedenis 'Société d'Emulation' te Brugge* 90 (1953), 97-130.

2232   De Brouwer, J., "De demografische evolutie in enkele dorpen in de omgeving van Aalst gedurende de 17e en 18e eeuw," *Land van Aalst* 13 (1961), 14-53.

2233   De Brouwer, J., *Demografische evolutie van het land van Aalst, 1570-1800*. Brussels, 1968.

2234   Demyttenaere, B., "Vrouw en sexualiteit: een aantal kerkideologische standpunten in de vroege middeleeuwen," *Tijdschrift voor Geschiedenis* 86 (1973), 236-261.

2235   Deprez, P., "Het bevolkingscijfer in de Heerlijkheid Nevele in de 16^e, 17^e en 18^e eeuwen," *Handelingen der Maatschappij voor Geschiedenis en Oudheidkunde te Gent* new series 13 (1959), 53-98.

2236   Deprez, P., "Het gentse bevolkingscijfer in de 2^e helft van de achttiende eeuw," *Handelingen der Maatschappij voor Geschiedenis en Oudeidkunde te Gent* new series 11 (1957), 177-195.

2237   Deprez, P., "The Demographic Development of Flanders in the Eighteenth Century," *Population in History*, ed. David V. Glass and D.E.C. Eversley (London, 1965), 608-630. (See #214)

2238   De Rammelaere, C., "De bevolking van de Onze-lieve-vrouwparochie te Pamele (Oudenaarde) gedurende de XVIIIe eeuw," *Cultureel Jaarboek voor de Provincie Oostvlaanderen 1954* (Gand, 1960), 273-288.

2239   De Rammelaere, C., "De bevolkingsevolutie in het land van Schorisse (1569-1 1796)," *Handelingen der Maatschappij voor Geschiedenis en Oudheidkunde te Gent* new series 9 (1955), 50-119.

2240   De Roever, N., *Van vrijen en trouwen*. Haarlem, 1891.

2241   Desmedt, H., "Ruim een kwart eeuw historische navorsing op het vlak van de demografie van het Hertogdom Brabant: Een bibliografisch overzicht (1945-1972)," *Bijdragen tot de Geschiedenis van Brabant* 55 (1972), 264-278.

2242   De Vos van Steewijk, A. N., *Het geslacht de Vos van Steenwijk in het licht van de geschiedenis van de Drentse Adel*. Assen/Amsterdam, 1976.

2243   De Vos, A., "De Bevolkingsevolutie van Evergem, Lovendegem, Sleidinge, Waarschoot en Zomergem gedurende XVIIe en XVIIIe eeuwen," *Appeltjes van het Meetjesland* 8 (1957), 1-72.

2244   De Vries, Jan, *The Dutch Rural Economy in the Golden Age, 1500-1700*. New Haven, 1974.

2245 Den Boer, P., "Naar een geschiedenis van de dood," *Tijdschrift voor Geschiedenis* 89 (1972), 161-201.

2246 Dyck, J., *Evolutie van de bevolking, de bewoning en de landontginning in het landelijk district ten zuid-oosten van Antwerpen.* Ghent, 1943.

2247 Elias, J. E., *De Vroedschap van Amsterdam, 1578-1795.* 2 v. Haarlem, 1903.

2248 Evenhuis, R. B., *Ook dat was Amsterdam. De kerk der hervorming in de gouden eeuw.* 2 v. Amsterdam, 1967.

2249 Faber, J. A., "Drie eeuwen Friesland economische en sociale ontwikkeling van 1500 tot 1800," *A.A.G. Bijdragen* 17 (1972), 20-92.

2250 Faber, J. A., H. K. Roessingh, B. H. Slicher van Bath, A. M. van der Woude, and H. J. van Xanten, "Population Changes and Economic Developments in the Netherlands: A Historical Survey," *A.A.G. Bijdragen* 12 (1965), 47-113.

2251 Fischer, Herman F.W.D., "Het Nederlandse huwelijksrecht van de Reformatie tot de codificatie," *Gemeenebest* 16 (1955-56), 485-496.

2252 Hart, Simon, "Historisch-demografische notities betreffende huwelijken en migratie te Amsterdam in de 17e en 18e eeuw," *Maandblad Amstelodamum* 55 (1968), 63-69.

2253 Hélin, Etienne, *La démographie de Liège aux XVIIe et XVIIIe siècles.* Brussels, 1963.

2254 Kalff, G., *Amsterdam in de zeventiende eeuw. Huiselijk en maatschappelijk leven.* Amsterdam, n.d.

2255 Klep, P.M.M., *Groeidynamiek en stagnatie in een agrarisch grensgebied. De economische ontwikkeling in de Noordantwerpse Kempen en de Baronie von Breda, 1750-1850.* Tilburg, 1973.

2256 Klep, P.M.M., "Het huishouden in westelijk Noord-Brabant: Structuur en ontwikkeling, 1750-1789," *A.A.G. Bijdragen* 18 (1973), 23-94.

2257 Knappert, Laurentius, *Verloving en huwelijk in vroeger dagen.* Amsterdam, 1914.

2258 Koyen, M. H., *Gezinsverpleging van geesteszieken te Geel tot einde 18e eeuw.* Westerlo, 1973.

2259 Lottin, A., "Naissance illégitimes et filles-mères à Lille au XVIIIe siècle," *Revue d'histoire moderne et contemporaine* 17 (1970), 278-322.

2260 Meischke, R., *Het Nederlandse woonhuis van 1300-1800.* Haarlem, 1969.

2261 Mendels, Franklin F., "Industry and Marriages in Flanders before the Industrial Revolution," *Population and Economics: Proceedings of Section V of the Fourth Congress of the International Economic History Association, 1968,* ed. Paul Deprez (Winnepeg, 1970), 81-93.

2262 Mentink, G. J., and A. N. van der Woude, *De demografische ontwikkeling te Rotterdam en Cool in de XVIIe en XVIIIe eeuw.* Rotterdam, 1965.

2263 Mols, Roger, "Die Bevölkerungsgeschichte Belgiens im Licht der heutigen Forschung," *Vierteljahrschrift für Sozial- und Wirtschaftsgeschichte* 46 (1959), 491-511.

2264 Mols, Roger, "Beschouwingen over de bevolkingsgeschiedenis in de Nederlanden (15e en 16e eeuw)," *Tijdschrift voor Geschiedenis* 66 (1953), 201-219.

2265   Pecters, Henricus, *Kind en juegdige in het begin van de moderne tijd.* Antwerp, 1966.

2266   Peremans, N., "Une enquête sociale à Liège en 1776," *Leodium* (1972), 5-16.

2267   Philips, J.F.R., J.C.G.M. Jansen, and Th. J.A.H. Claessens, *Geschiedenis van de landbouw in Limburg, 1750–1914.* Assen,1965.

2268   Posthumus, N. W., "Kinderarbeid in de 17e eeuw in Delft," *Economisch-Historisch Jaarboek* 22 (1943), 48-67.

2269   Pounds, M.J.G., "Population and Settlement in the Low Countries and Northern France in the Middle Ages," *Revue belge de philologie et d'histoire* 49 (1971), 369-402.

2270   Roorda, D. J., and H. van Dyck, "Sociale mobiliteit onder regenten van de Republiek," *Tijdschrift voor Geschiedenis* 84 (1971), 306-328.

2271   Schotel, G.D.J., *Het Oud-Hollandsch huisgezin der zeventiende eeuw.* Arnhem, 1963.

2272   Slicher van Bath, Bernard H., *Een samenleving onder spanning. Geschiedenis van het platteland van Overijssel.* Assen, 1957.

2273   Slicher van Bath, Bernard H., "Historical Demography and the Social and Economic Development of the Netherlands," *Daedalus* 97 (1968), 604-621.

2274   van Apeldoorn, L. J., *Geschiedenis van het Nederlandsche huwelijksrecht voor de invoering van de Fransche wetgeving.* Amsterdam, 1925.

2275   van Braam, Aris, *Bloei en verval van het economisch-sociale leven aan de Zaan in de 17^e en 18^e eeuw.* Wormerveer, 1944.

2276   van der Woude, A. M., "De omvang en samenstelling van de huishouding in Nederland in het verleden," *A.A.G. Bijdragen* 15 (1970), 202-241.

2277   van der Woude, A. M., "Het gebruik van de familienamen in Holland in de zeventiende eeuw," *Holland* 5 (1973), 109-131.

2278   van der Woude, A. M., *Het Noorderkwartier. Een regionaal historisch onderzoek in de demografische en economische geschiedenis van Westelijk Nederland van de late middeleeuwen tot het begin van de negentiende eeuw.* Wageningen, 1972.

2279   van der Woude, A. M., "Variations in the Size and Structure of the Household in the United Provinces of the Netherlands in the Seventeenth and Eighteenth Centuries," *Household and Family...*, Peter Laslett and Richard Wall (Cambridge, England, 1972), 299-318. (See #156)

2280   van Leeuwen, Simon, *Het Roomsch Hollandsch recht, waarin de Roomse wetten met het huydend. Nederlandsrecht overeengebracht werden.* Leiden, 1664. In English as *Commentaries on Roman and Dutch Law,* ed. C. W. Decker. 2 v. London, 1881.

2281   van Nierop, L., "De bruidgoms van Amsterdam van 1578 tot 1601," *Tijdschrift voor Geschiedenis* 48 (1933), 337-359; 49 (1934), 136-160, 329-344; 52 (1937), 251-264.

2282 van Speybroeck L., "De Wijziging van het landschapsbeeld en van het leven van den mensch in het Land van Waas in de 18^e eeuw," *Annalen van den Oudheidkundigen Kring van het Land van Waas* 55 (1947-48), 5-56, 93-129.

2283 Vandenbroeke, C., "Karakteristieken van het huwelijksen voort-plantings-patroon in Vlaanderen en Brabant (17^e-18^e eeuw)," *Tijdschrift voor Sociale Geschiedenis* 5 (1976), 107-145.

2284 Vanlaere, G., "De demografische evolutie in Assende, Bassevelde, Boekhoute, Ertvelde, Oosteeklo en Watervliet gedurende de 17^e en 18^e eeuwen," *Handelingen der Maatschappij voor Geschiedenis en Oudheidkunde te Gent* new series 15 (1961), 49-105.

2285 Veraghtert, K., "De krankzinnigenverpleging te Geel, 1795-1860," *Jaarboek 11 van de Vrijheid en het Land van Geel* (1972), 5-148.

2286 Verbeemen, J., "De werking van economische factoren op de stedelijke demografie der XVIIe en der XVIIIe eeuw in de Zuidelijke Nederlanden," *Revue belge de philologie et d'histoire* 34 (1956), 680-700, 1021-1055.

2287 Verbeemen, J., "De demografische evolutie van Mechelen (1370-1800)," *Handelingen van de Koninklijke Kring voor Oudheidkunde en Kunst van Mechelen* 57 (1953), 63-97.

2288 Vermaseren, B. A., "De antwerpse koopman Martin Lopez en zijn familie in de zestiende en het begin van de zeventiende eeuw," *Bijdragen tot de Geschiedenis* 56 (1973), 3-79.

2289 Vleggeert, J. C., *Kinderarbeid in Nederland 1500-1874. Van Berusting tot Beperking.* Assen, 1964.

2290 Wyffels, A., "De omvang en de evolutie van het brugse bevolkingscijfer in de 17e en de 18e eeuw," *Revue belge de philologie et d'histoire* 36 (1958), 1243-1274.

NINETEENTH AND TWENTIETH CENTURIES

2291 André, Robert, and R. Gijselings, *La Mortalité infantile en Belgique.* Brussels, 1971.

2292 *Bedrijf en samenleving. Economisch-historisch studies over Nederland in de negentiende en twintigste eeuw,* ed. I. J. Brugmans. Brussels, 1967.

2293 *Bronnen voor de sociale geschiedenis van de XIXe eeuw (1794-1914),* ed. H. Balthazar. Paris, 1965.

2294 Brugmans, I. J., *Paardenkracht en mensenmacht: Sociaal-economische geschiedenis van Nederland, 1795-1940.* The Hague, 1961.

2295 Buissink, J. D., "Regional Differences in Marital Fertility in the Netherlands in the Second Half of the Nineteenth Century," *Population Studies* 25 (1971), 333-374.

2296   Cliquet, R. L., M. Thiery, R. Lesthaeghe, G. van Keymeulen-vanden Bogaert, H. van Kets, B. Becue, and L. Roelens, "Een interdisciplinair onderzoeks-project over vruchtbaarheid, vruchtbaarheidsregeling en partnerrelaties," *Bevolking en gezin* 21 (1970), 53-72.

2297   Cliquet, R. L., "Kennis, gebruik en effectiviteit van anticonceptie in Belgie," *Bevolking en gezin* 19 (1969), 1-62.

2298   Cliquet, R. L., "Nationale enquête over de vruchtbaarheid van de gehuwde vrow in Belgie. Anthropologische oogmerken van het onderzoek," *Bevolking en gezin* 13 (1967), 15-36.

2299   Cliquet, R. L., "De studie van de biologische fertiliteit en de anticonceptie in het raam van de nationale enquête over de huwelijksvruchtbaarheid: materiaal en methoden," *Bevolking en gezin* 14 (1968), 43-94.

2300   Cliquet, R. L., "De studie van de biologische fertiliteit en de anticonceptie in het raam van de nationale enquête over de huwelijksvruchtbaarheid: Enkele voorlopige resultaten," *Bevolking en gezin* 15 (1968), 1-38.

2301   Cosemans, A., *Bijdrage tot de demografische en sociale geschiedenis van de stad Brussel, 1796-1846.* Brussels, 1966.

2302   Damas, H., "Les Régions démographiques de la Belgique," *Population et famille* 11 (1967), 51-89.

2303   De Bie, P., "Le niveau de vie des ménages belges en 1961 en fonction du nombre d'enfants à charge," *Bevolking en gezin* 6-7 (1965), 57-100.

2304   De Bie, P., "Politique familiale et politique démographique," *Bevolking en gezin* 1 (1963), 6-17.

2305   De Saint-Moulin, Léon, *La construction et la propriété des maisons expressions des structures sociales. Seraing depuis le debut du XIXe siècle.* Brussels, 1969.

2306   Duchene, J., and R. Lesthaeghe, "Essai de reconstitution de la population belge sous la régime française: quelques caractéristiques démographiques de la population féminine," *Population et famille* 36 (1975), 1-48.

2307   Gadeyne, G., "De omvang en de demografische structur van de bevolking van Izegem tijdens de Franse overheersing, 1794-1815," *De Leiegouw* 9 (1967), 85-113.

2308   Glasbergen, P., and R. Zandanel, "Vrouwenemancipatie en fertiliteits-gedrag," *Bevolking en gezin* 3 (1974), 381-402.

2309   Hees, M., "Les processus d'évolution de la population active féminine en Bel-gique de 1947 à 1961," *Annales des sciences économiques appliquées de Louvain* 28 (1970), 132-152.

2310   Hélin, Etienne, "Size of Households before the Industrial Revolution: The Case of Liège in 1801," *Household and Family...,* ed. Peter Laslett and Richard Wall (Cambridge, England, 1972), 319-334. (See #156)

2311   Hofstee, E. W., and G. Kooy, "Traditional Household and Neighbourhood

Group: Survivals of the Genealogical-Territorial Societal Pattern in Eastern Parts of the Netherlands," *Transactions of the Third World Congress of Sociology* 4 (1956), 75-79.

2312 Ishwaran, Karigoudar, *Family Life in the Netherlands.* Den Haag, 1959.

2313 Jacquart, C., *La mortalité infantile dans les Flandres. Etudes de démographie belge.* Brussels, 1907.

2314 Kastelein, T. J., "Social Structure and Economic Growth in the Netherlands," *First International Conference of Economic History* (Stockholm, 1960), 489-493.

2315 Kerckhaert, F.A.M., and F.W.A. van Poppel, "Het verloop van de sterfte naar leeftijd, geslacht en burgerlijke staat in Nederland: periode 1850-1970," *Bevolking en gezin* 4 (1975), 75-110.

2316 Keymolen, D., "Feminisme in Belgie. De eerste vrouwelijke artsen (1873-1914)," *Bijdragen en Mededelingen betreffende de Geschiedenis der Nederlanden* 90 (1975), 38-58.

2317 Lesthaeghe, R., "Vruchtbaarheidscontrole, nuptialiteit en sociaal-economische veranderingen in Belgie, 1846-1910," *Bevolking en gezin* 2 (1972), 251-306.

2318 Lesthaeghe, R., and P. Chi, "Stabilisatie der leeftijdsstructuur in Belgie en Europa," *Bevolking en gezin* 15 (1968), 87-96.

2319 Lesthaeghe, R., and H. Damas, "Les composantes du viellissement ou du rejeunissement des populations européenes," *Bevolking en gezin* 23-24 (1971), 3-84.

2320 Magits, M., *Demografische en social structuren te Leuven (1946–1860). Bijdrage tot de stadsgeschiedenis in de 19ᵉ eeuw.* Brussels, 1974.

2321 Morsa, J., "Fecondité, nuptialité et composition par âge," *Bevolking en gezin* 5 (1965), 83-112.

2322 Morsa, J., "Tendances récentes de la fécondité belge," *Bevolking en gezin* 1 (1963), 18-50.

2323 Ockers, J., "De gezinnen in Belgie volgens de volkstelling op 31 december 1961," *Bevolking en gezin* 12 (1967), 79-144.

2324 Ockers, J., "De juridische aard van de kinderbijslag. Van liberaliteit naar sociaal recht," *Bevolking en gezin* 2 (1964), 121-140.

2325 Ockers, J., "Onderhoudsplicht en huwelijk," *Bevolking en gezin* 9-10 (1966), 103-140.

2326 Oleffe-van Dierdonck, L., "Note sur la mortalité infantile en Belgique," *Bevolking en gezin* 3 (1964), 60-82.

2327 Pichault, G., "Femmes chef de ménage de la ville de Liège," *Population et famille* 28 (1973), 1-103.

2328 Pichault, G., "Les répercussions famiales du travail professionel de la femme mariée et mère de famille," *Bevolking en gezin* 21 (1970), 17-52; 22 (1970), 1-22.

2329　*Population and Family in the Low Countries*, ed. H. G. Moors, R. L. Cliquet, G. Dooghe, and D. J. van de Kaa. Leiden, 1976.

2330　Renard, R., "Niveau de vie des familles ouvrières selon le nombre d'enfants," *Bevolking en gezin* 19 (1969), 63-112.

2331　Stassart, J., "Structure par age et croissance économique," *Bevolking en gezin* 6-7 (1965), 1-16.

2332　Stengers, J., "Les pratiques anticonceptionnelles dans le mariage au XIXe et XXe siècle," *Revue belge de philologie et d'histoire* 49 (1971), 403-481, 1119-1174.

2333　van de Put, C., *Volksleven in Tilburg rond 1900. Sociaal-historische hoofd-stukken.* Assen, 1971.

2334　van de Walle, Etienne, and Olivier Blanc, "Registres de population et démographie: La Hulpe, 1846-1880," *Population et famille* 36 (1975), 113-128.

2335　van de Walle, Etienne, "Household Dynamics in a Belgian Village, 1847-1866," *Journal of Family History* 1 (1976), 80-94.

2336　van de Walle, Etienne, "Marriage and Marital Fertility," *Daedalus* 97 (1968), 486-501.

2337　van de Walle, Etienne, "La nuptialité en Belgique de 1846 à 1930 et sa relation avec le déclin de la fécondité," *Bevolking en gezin* 6-7 (1965), 36-56.

2338　van den Brink, T., "Birth Rate Trends and Changes in Marital Fertility in the Netherlands after 1937," *Population Studies* 4 (1950), 314-332.

2339　van Nimwegen, N., and H. de Vries, "De beroepactiviteit van de gehuwde vrouw en haar vruchtbaarheid," *Bevolking en gezin* 2 (1974), 277-294.

2340　van Poppel, F.W.A., "De differentiele vruchtbaarheid in Nederland in historisch perspectief: de invloed van de sociale status," *Bevolking en gezin* 2 (1974), 223-248.

2341　van Poppel, F.W.A., "De differentiele vruchtbaarheid in Nederland in historisch perspectief: de invloed van de religie," *Bevolking en gezin* 3 (1974), 329-348.

2342　Verduin, J. A., *Bevolking en Bestaan in het oude Drenthe. Een sociaal-geografisch onderzoek naar het huwelijksen voortplantingspatroon in het 19e eeuwse Drentse zandgebeid.* Assen, 1972.

2343　Wattelar, C., and Wunsch, G., *Etude démographique de la nuptialité en Belgique.* Leuven, 1967.

2344　Wunsch, G., "Le delai entre le déclin de la mortalité et celui de la fécondité," *Population et famille* 29 (1973), 51-62.

2345　You, T. H., "L'Effet de la conjoncture économique sur la nuptialité en Belgique," *Recherches économiques Louvain* 32 (1966), 469-486.

Northern Europe

E, F, or G at the end of a citation indicates an English, French, or German summary for the entry.

GENERAL SURVEYS AND COLLECTIONS

2346 Appel, Elin, "Kvindens historiske Udvikling," *Kvinden i Danmark,* ed. L. Hindsgaul and K. Fleron (Odense, 1942), 9-44. [The Historical Development of Women in Denmark]

2347 *Aristocrats, Farmers, Proletarians: Essays in Swedish Demographic History,* ed. Kurt Ågren et al. Uppsala, 1973.

2348 Boëthius, Bertil, *Gruvornas, hyttornas och hamrarnas folk.* Stockholm, 1951. [History of Miners and Iron Workers]

2349 Braconier, Jean, "Svensk tjänstehjonspolitik fram till 1800-talet," *Statsvetenskapliga tidskrift* 48 (1945), 361-382. [Swedish Servant Legislation up to 1800]

2350 Campbell, Åke, *Ket svenska brödet.* Stockholm, 1950. [Swedish Bread]

2351 Carlsson, Sten, *Ståndssamhälle och ståndspersoner 1700-1865.* 2nd ed.; Lund, 1973. [The Society of Estates and Persons of Estate] E

2352 Charpentier, Axel, *Om sytning.* Helsingfors/Helsinki, 1896. [On Peasant Retirement Contracts]

2353 Drake, Michael, *Population and Society in Norway 1735-1865.* Cambridge, England, 1969.

2354 Ekenvall, Asta, *Manligt och kvinnligt. Idéhistoriska studier.* Gothenburg, 1966. [Manly and Womanly: Studies in the History of Ideas] E

2355 Elgeskog, Valter, *Svensk torpbebyggelse från 1500-talet till laga skiftet.* Stockholm, 1945. [The Cottars in Sweden 1500-1850]

2356 Erixon, Sigurd, *Svenskt folkliv*. Stockholm, 1938. [Swedish Folk Life]

2357 Fabritius, Albert, *Danmarks Riges Adel, dens Tilgang og Afgang 1536–1935. En studie i dansk Adelshistoria*. Lund, 1946. [The Danish Nobility: Its Rise and Fall 1536–1935] F

2358 *Familie, hushold og produktion*, ed. Orvar Löfgren. Copenhagen, 1974. [Family, Household, and Production]

2359 Fett, Harry, *Gamle norske hjem. Hus og bohave*. Christiania/Oslo, 1906. [Old Norwegian Homes: Dwellings and Furnishings]

2360 Fries, Ellen, *Teckningar ur svenska adelns familjelif i gamla tider*. Stockholm, 1901. [Family Life of the Swedish Nobility in Olden Times]

2361 Frimannslund, Rigmor, "Skikk og tro ved friing og bryllup," *Nordisk kultur*, ed. Karl Robert Villehad Wikman, v. 20 (Copenhagen, 1949), 41–87. [Practice and Belief in Courting and Marriage]

2362 Frimannslund, Rigmor, "Farm Community and Neighbourhood Community," *Scandinavian Economic History Review* 4 (1956), 62–81.

2363 Grøn, Frederik, *Om kostholdet i Norge fra omkring 1500–tallet op til vår tid*. Oslo, 1942. [Diet in Norway from 1500 to the Present]

2364 Hafström, Gerhard, *Den svenska familjerättens historia*. 6th ed.; Lund, 1969. [The History of Swedish Family Law]

2365 Heikinmäki, Maija-Liisa, *Die Gabe der Braut bei den Finnen und Esten*. Helsinki, 1970.

2366 Hellspong, Mats, and Orvar Löfgren, *Land och stad. Svenska samhällstyper och livsformer från medeltid till nutid*. Lund, 1972. [Country and City: Swedish Communities and Life Styles since the Middle Ages]

2367 Holter, Harriet, et al., *Familien i klassesamfunnet*. Oslo, 1975. [The Family in Class Society]

2368 Jutikkala, Eino, *Bonden i Finland genom tiderna*. Helsingfors/Helsinki, 1963. [History of the Peasant in Finland]

2369 Keyland, Nils, *Svensk allmogekost. Bidrag till den svenska folkhushållningens historia*. 2 v. Stockholm, 1919. [The Diet of the Swedish People]

2370 Klingberg, Göte, *Så levde barnen förr. Dokument om allvar och lek*. Stockholm, 1971. [Children's Life in the Past in Documents]

2371 Lundberg, Erik, *Herremannens bostad. Studier över nordisk och allmänt västerländsk bostadsanläggning*. Stockholm, 1935. [The Noble's Dwelling in Scandinavia] F

2372 Lundberg, Erik, *Svensk bostad. Dess utveckling och traditionsbildning*. Stockholm, 1942. [The Development of the Swedish House]

2373 Møller, J. S., *Moder og Barn i dansk Folkeoverleveringer. Fra Svangerskab til Daab og Kirkegang*. Copenhagen, 1940. [Mother and Child in Danish Folk Tradition: From Pregnancy to Baptism and Churching]

2374 Montgomery, Arthur, "Tjänstehjonsstadgan och äldre svensk arbetarpolitik," *Historisk tidskrift* (1933), 245–276. [Legislation on Servants in Swedish History]

2375 Mortensson, Ivar, *Bondeskipnad i Norig i Eldre Tid.* Christiania/Oslo, 1904. [Peasant Life in Norway]

2376 Nilen, Holger, *Familjen—förr och nu. En belysning av familjebegreppet genom tiderna.* Lund, 1973. [The concept of the Family Past and Present]

2377 Norlind, Tobias, *Gamla bröllopsseder hos svenska allmogen.* Stockholm, 1919. [Old Wedding Customs among Swedish Peasants]

2378 Nyberg, Bertel, *Kind und Erde. Ethnologische Studien zur Urgeschichte der Elternschaft und des Kinderschutzes.* Helsinki, 1931.

2379 Nylander, Ivar, *Studier rörande den svenska äktenskapsrättens historia.* Stockholm, 1961. [History of Swedish Marriage Law]   G

2380 Nylen, Anna-Maja, *Helmslöjd: den svenska hemslöjden fram till 1800–talets slut.* Lund, 1975. [Swedish Domestic Crafts and Industry to the 20th Century]

2381 Olgeirsson, Einar, *Från ättegemenskap till klasstat.* Stockholm, 1971. Translated from Icelandic original. [Clan Society to Class State in Iceland]

2382 Olsson, Alfa Sofia, *Om allmogens kosthåll. Studier med utgångspunkt från västsvenska matvanor.* Lund, 1958. [Peasant Diet in Western Sweden]

2383 Paulsson, Gregor, *Svensk stad. Liv och stil i svenska städer under 1800–talet.* 2 v. new ed.; Lund, 1973. [Life and Style in Swedish 19th-Century Towns]

2384 Pekkarinen, Maija, *Tutkimuksia maalaisväeston ravinnosta eräissä Itä- ja Länsi-Suomen pitäjissä.* Helsinki, 1962. [Rural Diet in Parts of East and West Finland]   E

2385 Pelkonen, Erkko, *Beiträge zur volkstümlichen Geburtshilfe in Finnland.* Helsinki, 1933.

2386 Pentikäinen, Juha, *The Nordic Dead-Child Tradition. Nordic Dead-Child Beings. A Study in Comparative Religion.* Helsinki, 1968.

2387 Ränk, Gustav, "Mannen, kvinnan och släkten hos nordeurasiska jägare och nomader," *Kulturspeglingar. Studier tillägnade S. O. Jansson* (Stockholm, 1966), 242-252. [Man, Woman, and Kin among North Eurasian Hunters and Nomads]

2388 Reichborn-Kjenneurd, Ingjald, *Vår gamle trolldomsmedisin.* 5 v. Kristiania/Oslo, 1927-47. [Norwegian Popular Magic Medicine]

2389 Robberstad, Knut, "Trulovingsborns rett i Noreg fyre 1854," *Tidsskrift for rettsvitenskap* 87 (1974), 3-33. [The Legal Rights before 1854 of Norwegian Children Born During Engagement]

2390 Rom, N. C., *Den danske Husflid, dens Betydning og dens Tilstand i Fortid og Nutid.* 2nd ed.; Copenhagen, 1898. [Danish Domestic Industry, Its Importance and Condition in the Past and Present]

2391 Shanas, Ethel, et al., *Old People in Three Industrial Societies.* London,1968.

2392 Siggaard, Niels, *Om den danske Befolknings Fφdemidler gennem Tiderne. Et landbrugshistorisk Studie.* Copenhagen, 1930. [History of Danish Diet]

2393 Sindballe, Kristian, *Af Testamentarvens Historie i dansk Ret.* Copenhagen, 1915. [History of Testamentary Inheritance in Danish Law]

2394 Skappel, Simen, *Om Husmandvaesenet i Norge, dets oprindelse og utvikling.* Kristiania/Oslo, 1922. [Norwegian Cottars and Their Development]

2395 Skrubbeltrang, Fridlev, *Husmand og Inderste. Studier over sjaellandske Landboforhold i perioden 1660–1800.* Copenhagen, 1944. [Cottars and Inmates on Zealand 1660–1800]

2396 Steen, Sverre, *Bisysler for bøndene—arbeid og markedsferder.* Oslo, 1933. [Peasant By-Employments: Work and Marketing]

2397 Steensberg, Axel, *Den danske Bondegaard. Fra Jordhuset til den moderne Bondebolig.* Copenhagen, 1942. [History of Danish Farm Dwellings]

2398 Steenstrup, Johannes, *Den danske Kvindes Historia fra Holbergs Tid til vor.* 2 v. Copenhagen, 1917. [History of the Danish Woman Since the Beginning of the 18th Century]

2399 *Studier i Dansk Befolkningshistorie 1750–1890,* ed. Hans Christian Johansen. Odense, 1976. [Studies in Danish Population History 1750–1890]

2400 Taranger, Absalon, *Aegteskabsstiftelsens historie i Norge.* Ringeren, 1898. [History of Marriage in Norway]

2401 Valonen, Niilo, *Zur Geschichte der finnischen Wohnstuben.* Helsinki, 1963.

2402 Visted, Kristofer, and Hilmar Stigum, *Vår gamle bondekultur.* 2 v. 3rd ed.; Oslo, 1971. [Old Norwegian Peasant Culture]

2403 Voionmaa, Väinö, *Suomen karjalaisen heimon historia.* Helsinki, 1915. [History of the Finnish Folk in Carelia]

2404 Wallin, Sigurd, *Bohag, heminredning och dräkt.* Stockholm, 1946. [Furniture, Home Decorations, and Clothes]

2405 Welander, Edvard, *Om de veneriska sjukdomarnes historia i Sverige.* Stockholm, 1898. [History of Venereal Disease in Sweden]

2406 Welander, Edvard, *Blad ur prostitutionsfrågans historia i Sverige.* Stockholm, 1904. [Contributions to the History of Prostitution in Sweden]

2407 Wikman, Karl Robert Villehad, "Tabu- och orenhetsbegrepp i nordgermansk folktro om könen," *Skrifter utgivna av Svenska litteratursällskapet i Finland* 135 (Helsingfors, 1917), 1–62. [The Concepts of Taboo and Uncleanliness in North Germanïc Popular Beliefs about the Sexes]

2408 Wikman, Karl Robert Villehad, *Die Einleitung der Ehe. Eine verglichend ethno-soziologische Untersuchung über die Vorstufe der Ehe in den Sitten des schwedischen Volkstums.* Åbo/Turku, 1937.

2409 Willebrand, Bengt Magnus von, *Den svenska adeln. En demografisk kultur-historisk undersökning av Sveriges och Finlands adel.* Stockholm, 1932. [Demographic and Cultural-Historical Investigation of the Swedish-Finnish Nobility]

2410 Winroth, Alfred Ossian, *Om tjenstehjonsförhållande enligt svensk rätt.* Uppsala, 1978. [Servents in Swedish Law]

2411 Wirilander, Kaarlo, *Herrasväkeä. Suomen säätyläistö 1721–1870.* Helsinki, 1974. [Gentlefolks: Finland's Persons of Estate 1721–1870]

2412 Wohlin, Nils Richard, *Den svenska jordstyckningspolitiken i de 18: de och*

19:de arhundradena. Stockholm, 1912. [Division of Landed Property in Sweden in the 18th and 19th Centuries]

BIBLIOGRAPHIES AND REVIEW ESSAYS

2413 Dyrvik, Ståle, "Historical Demography in Norway 1660–1801: A Short Survey," *Scandinavian Economic History Review* 20 (1972), 26–44.

2414 Prange, Knud, "Slaegt-Miljø-Samfund," *Personalhistorisk Tidsskrift* 15 (1971), 121–134. [Ancestry-Environment-Society]

2415 Szabó, Mátyás, "Barnarvete i agrarsamhället," *Fataburen* (1971), 19–38. [Child Labor in Agrarian Society]

2416 Weibust, Knut, "Ritual Coparenthood in Peasant Societies," *Ethnologia Scandinavica* (1972), 45–65.

MIDDLE AGES TO THE REFORMATION

2417 Almquist, Jan Erik, *Om ärftligt besittningsrätt till jord före det sjuttonde seklets slut.* Uppsala, 1929. [On the Inheritance of Landed Property before 1700]

2418 Almquist, Jan Erik, *Strödda bidrag till familjerättens historia.* 2nd ed.; Stockholm, 1945. [Contributions to the History of Family Law]

2419 Carlsson, Lizzie, "Sängledningen. Hednisk-borgerlig rättsakt och kristen ceremoni," *Skrifter utgivna av Kungliga vetenskapssocieteten i Lund* (1951), 57–107. [Leading to the Bed: A Heathen Practice and Christian Ceremony]

2420 Carlsson, Lizzie, *"Jag giver dig min dotter." Trolovning och äktenskap i den svenska kvinnans äldre historia.* 2 v. Stockholm, 1965 and 1972. ["I give you my daughter." Betrothal and Marriage in the Medieval History of the Swedish Woman]

2421 Hafström, Gerhard, "Ättens frändehjälp," *Nordisk tidskrift* 36 (1960), 247–255. [The Clan's Aid to Kin]

2422 Hemmer, Ragnar, "Vad förstår Östgötalagen med en gävträl?" *Tidskrift utgiven av Juridiska föreningen i Finland* 68 (1932), 229–237. [The Medieval Thralldom as a Form of Old-Age Care]

2423 Holmback, Åke, *Ätten och arvet enligt Sveriges medeltidslagar.* Uppsala, 1919. [Clan and Inheritance in Sweden's Medieval Laws]

2424 Iuul, Stig, *Faellig og Hovedlod. Studier over Formueforholdet mellem Aegtefaeller i Tiden før Christian V's Danske Lov.* Copenhagen, 1940. [Division of Wealth between Marriage Partners up to the 18th Century]

2425 Kålund, Kristian, "Familielivet på Island i den første Sagaperiode (indtil 1030)," *Aarbøger for nordisk Oldkyndighed og Historie* (1870), 269-290. [Family Life in Iceland up to 1030]

2426 Kock, Ebbe, *Om hemföljd (förtida arv) i svensk rätt t.o.m. 1734 års lag.* Lund, 1926. [The Dowry in Swedish Law up to 1734]

2427 Lehmann, Karl, *Verlobung und Hochzeit nach den nordgermanischen Rechten des früheren Mittelalters.* Munich, 1882.

2428 Litzen, Veikko, "Käsitys naisen asemasta myöhäiskeskiajalla," *Historiallinen Arkisto* (1972), 18-22. [Conception of Woman's Place in the Late Middle Ages]

2429 Nevéus, Clara, *Trälarna i landskapslagarnas samhälle. Danmark och Sverige.* Uppsala, 1974. [Thralldom in Medieval Denmark and Sweden]   G

2430 Petersson, Hans, *Morgongåvainstitutet i Sverige under tiden fram till 1734 års lag.* Lund, 1973. [Bride Gift in Sweden up to 1734]

2431 Schultze, Alfred, *Zum altnordischen Eherecht.* Leipzig, 1939.

2432 Schultze, Alfred, "Die Rechtslage des alternden Bauers nach den altnordischen Rechten," *Zeitschrift der Savigny-Stiftung für Rechtsgeschichte   Germanistische Abteilung* 51 (1931), 258-317.

2433 Stein-Wilkeshuis, Martina Wilhelmina, *Het kind in de Oudijslandse samenleving.* Groningen, 1970. [The Child in Old Icelandic Society]   E

2434 Wikman, Karl Robert Villehad, *Om de fornnordiska formerna for äktenskapets ingående. Med särskilt hänsyn till Eddadikterna Rigspúla och prymskvída.* Helsingfors/Helsinki, 1959. [On Early Nordic Forms for Initiating Marriage]

2435 Ylikangas, Heikki, "Huomenlahja Ruotsin keskiaikaisten lakien valossa," *Historiallinen Aikakauskirja* (1967), 14-25. [Bride Gift in Medieval Swedish Law]   G

EARLY MODERN PERIOD
(1560-1809)

2436 Ågren, Kurt, "Breadwinners and Dependents: An Economic Crisis in the Swedish Aristocracy during the 1600s?" *Aristocrats, Farmers, Proletarians,* ed. Kurt Ågren et al. (Uppsala, 1973), 9-27. (See #2347)

2437 Ågren, Kurt, "Rise and Decline of an Aristocracy: The Swedish Social and Political Elite in the Seventeenth Century," *Scandinavian Journal of History* 1 (1976), 55-80.

2438 Åkerman, Birger, *Bouppteckningar i Borgå stad 1740-1800.* Helsingfors/Helsinki, 1934. [Probate Records in Borgå Town]

2439 Albertsen, Kai, "Befolkningsgenealogi," *Personalhistorisk Tidsskrift* (1969), 81–98. [Genealogy of a Total Population]

2440 Bang, Gustav, *Den gamle adels forfald. Studier over de danske adelsslaegters uddøen i det 16. og 17. århundrede.* Copenhagen, 1897. [The Decline of Danish Noble Families in the 16th and 17th Centuries]

2441 Bang, Gustav, *Kirkebogsstudier. Bidrag til dansk Befolkningsstatistik og Kulturhistorie i det 17. Aarhundrede.* Copenhagen, 1906. [Contributions to Danish Population Statistics and Cultural History in the 17th Century]

2442 Bäärhielm, Gösta, "Utomäktenskapliga barns ställning," *Minneskrift ägnad 1734års lag,* v. 2 (Stockholm, 1934), 7–34. [The Legal Position of Illegitimate Children] F

2443 Bergman, Carl Gunnar, *Testamentet i 1600-talets rättsbildning.* Lund, 1918. [The Will in 17th-Century Jurisprudence]

2444 Bylund, Erik, *Koloniseringen av Pite Lappmark t.o.m. 1867.* Uppsala, 1956. [Colonisation of Lappland up to 1867]

2445 Drake, Michael, "Fertility Controls in Pre-Industrial Norway," *Population and Social Change,* ed. David Glass and Roger Revelle (London, 1972), 185–198.

2446 Dyrvik, Ståle, "Om giftarmål og sociale normer. Ein studie av Etne 1715–1801," *Tidsskrift for samfunnsforskning* 11 (1970), 285–300. [Marriage and Social Norms in Western Norway in the 18th Century]

2447 Edin, Karl Arvid, "Studier i svensk fruktsamhetsstatistik," *Ekonomisk tidskrift* 17 (1915), 251–304. [Studies in Swedish Fertility Statistics]

2448 Ekeberg, Birger, "Giftermålsbalken," *Minneskrift ägnad 1734års lag,* v. 1 (Stockholm, 1934), 203–216. [Marriage Law in the 18th Century]

2449 Ekeberg, Birger, "Ärvdabalken," ibid., 217–238. [Inheritance Law in the 18th Century]

2450 Finnsson, Hannes, "Um Barnadauda á Islandi," *Rit pess íslenzka Laerdoms-listafélags* (Copenhagen, 1785), 115–142. [Infant Mortality in Iceland]

2451 Fjellbu, Arne, *Waisenhuset. Norges eldste institusjon for barn.* Trondheim, 1971. [Norway's First Orphanage]

2452 Frederiksen, Anders V. Kaare, *Familierekonstitution. En modelstudie over befolkningsforholdene i Sejerø sogn 1663–1813.* Copenhagen, 1976. [Family Reconstitution of Sejero Parish 1663–1813]

2453 Friberg, Nils, and Inge Friberg, *Sveriges äldsta fullständiga husförhörslängd.* Stockholm, 1971. [Sweden's First *Liber Status Animarum*]

2454 Gahn, Hans, *Moralstatistiska uppgifter i frihetstidens tabellverk. En demografisk studie.* Uppsala, 1915. [Information on Morals in the 18th-Century Board-of-Census Material]

2455 Gaunt, David, "Family Planning and the Preindustrial Society: Some Swedish Evidence," *Aristocrats, Farmers, Proletarians,* ed. Kurt Ågren et al. (Uppsala, 1973), 28–59. (See #2347)

2456 Gaunt, David, "Familj, hushåll och arbetsintensitet. En tolkning av demografiska variationer i 1600- och 1700-talens Sverige," *Scandia* 42 (1976),

32-59. [Family, Household, and Intensity of Work: An Interpretation of Demographic Variations in Early Modern Sweden]   E

2457   Hansen, Georg, *Saedlighedsforhold blandt landsbefolkningen i Danmark i det 18. århundrerde.* Copenhagen, 1957. [Moral Conditions among the Rural Population of 18th-Century Denmark]

2458   Hanssen, Borje, *Österlen. En studie över social-antropologiska sammanhang under 1600- och 1700-talen i sydöstra Skåne.* Ystad, 1952. [A Social-Anthropological Study of 17th- and 18th-Century Scania]

2459   Hanssen, Börje, "Dimensions of Primary Group Structure in Sweden," *Recherches sur la famille* 1 (1957), 115-156.

2460   Hanssen, Börje, "Hushållens sammansättning i österlenska byar under 300 år. En studie i historisk strukturalism," *Rig* 59 (1976), 33-61. [Composition of Households in Scania over 300 Years]   E

2461   Høyberg, H. M., "Børnetallet i ca. 5000 Aegteskaber i det 17. og. 18. Aarhundrede," *Ugeskrift for Laeger* 100 (1938), 1353-1355. [Number of Children in 5000 Marriages in the 17th and 18th Centuries]

2462   Imhof, Arthur E., "Der Arbeitszwang für das landwirtschaftliche Dienstvolk in den nordischen Ländern im 18. Jahrhundert;" *Zeitschrift für Agrargeschichte und Agrarsoziologie* 22 (1974), 59-74.

2463   Imhof, Arthur E., *Aspekte der Bevölkerungsentwicklung in den nordischen Ländern 1720-1750.* 2 v. Bern, 1976.

2464   Jansson, Assar, "Giftermål med syskonbyte under 1700-talet," *Rig* 38 (1955), 83-88. [Marriages Involving Exchanges of Siblings in the 18th Century]

2465   Johansen, Hans Christian, "Some Aspects of Danish Rural Population Structure in 1787," *Scandinavian Economic History Review* 20 (1972), 61-70.

2466   Johansen, Hans Christian, *Befolkningsudvikling og familiestruktur i det 18. århundrede.* Odense, 1975. [Population Movement and Family Structure in 18th-Century Denmark]

2467   Johansen, Hans Christian, "The Position of the Old in the Rural Household in Traditional Society," *Scandinavian Economic History Review* 24 (1976), 129-142.

2468   Juhasz, Lajos, "Demografiske kriser," *Heimen* 15 (1971), 397-417. [Population Movements in Preindustrial Norway]

2469   Jutikkala, Eino, "Finnish Agricultural Labour in the Eighteenth and Early Nineteenth Centuries," *Scandinavian Economic History Review* 10 (1962), 203-219.

2470   Laurikkala, Saini, *Varsinais-Soumen talonpoikain asumukset ja kotitalousualineet 1700-luvulla.* Turku, 1947. [The Dwellings and Furnishings of Peasant Households in Southwestern Finland During the 18th Century]

2471   Lemche, Johan, "Kan Aftaegtskontrakter tjene til Belysning af Ernaeringsproblemer?" *Ugeskrift for Laeger* 102 (1940), 790-792. [Nutritional Problems Illustrated through Retirement Contracts from the 18th and Early 19th Centuries]

2472 Lundkvist, Sven, "Rölighet och socialstruktur i 1610-talets Sverige," *Historisk tidskrift* (1974), 192–258. [Social Structure and Mobility in Sweden in the Early 17th Century] E

2473 Mäkeläinen, Eva-Christina, *Säätyläisten seuraelämä ja tapakulttuuri 1700–luvun jälkipuoliskolla Turussa, Viaporissa ja Savon kartanoalueella.* Forssa, 1972. [Social Life and Traditional Culture among the 18th-Century Gentry in Several Places] E

2474 Nellemann, J., "Retshistoriske Bemaerkninger om kirkelig Vielse som Betingelse for lovligt Aegteskab i Danmark," *Historisk Tidsskrift* 5th series 1 (1879), 363–432. [Legal-historical Observations on the Church Wedding as the Condition of Legitimate Marriage in Denmark]

2475 Nordén, Arthur, " 'Fingren ringad, pigan tingad': Ett bidrag till den släta vigselringens historia," *Fataburen* (1931), 117–128. [History of the Engagement and Wedding Ring]

2476 Nygård Larsen, Henning, "Familie- og hustandsstrukturen på landet i det 18. århundrede," *Studier i Dansk Befolkningshistorie,* ed. Hans Christian Johansen (Odense, 1976), 121–188. [Family and Household Structure in 18th-Century Rural Denmark]

2477 Olrik, Jørgen, *Borgerlige Hjem i Helsingør for 300 Aar siden.* Copenhagen, 1903–04. [Bourgeois Homes in a Provincial Danish Town in the 17th Century]

2478 Olsen, Gunnar, "Stavnsbåndet og tjenestekarlene," *Jyske samlinger* new series 1 (1950–52), 197–218. [Servants and Serfdom in Denmark]

2479 *Oulun kaupungin perunkirjoituksia 1653–1800,* ed. Alf Brenner. 3 v. Helsinki, 1963–66. [Probate Records from a Town in Northern Finland 1653–1800]

2480 Selling, Gösta, *Svenska herrgårdshem under 1700–talet. Arkitektur och inredning 1700–1780.* Stockholm, 1937. [Swedish Manor Houses in the 18th Century: Architecture and Furnishings]

2481 Skrubbeltrang, Fridlev, "Faestegården som forsørger. Aftaeget og anden forsorg i det 18. århundrede," *Jyske samlinger* 5 (1959–61), 237–274. [Peasant Farms and Their Maintenance Duties: Retirement and Other Support in the 18th Century]

2482 Söderhjelm, Lars, "Spädbarnsuppfödning på 1750-talet," *Läkartidningen* (1967), 5100–5101. [Food for Infants in the 1750s]

2483 Söderlind, Nils, "Lysnings praxis under 1600–talet," *Kyrkohistorisk årsbok* (1967), 57–82. [Engagement Practices in the 17th Century] G

2484 Söderlind, Nils, "Sorgetiden som äktenskapshinder i kyrklig praxis fore 1686," *Forum theologicum* (1957), 52–60. [The Period of Grieving as a Hindrance to Marriage before the 18th Century]

2485 Söderlind, Nils, "Svenska prästerskapet och folkliga bröllopsseder under 1600–talet," *Kyrkohistorisk årsbok* (1951), 1–52. [The Swedish Priesthood and Popular Wedding Customs in the 17th Century]

2486   Sogner, Sølvi, "Freehold and Cottar," *Scandinavian Journal of History* 1 (1976), 181-199.

2487   Sogner, Solvi, "A Demographic Crisis Averted?" *Scandinavian Economic History Review* 24 (1976), 114-128.

2488   Suolahti, Gunnar, *Finlands prästerskap under 1600- och 1700-talen.* Helsingfors/Helsinki, 1927. [Finland's Priesthood 1600-1800]

2489   Thestrup, Poul, "Methodological Problems of a Family Reconstitution Study," *Scandinavian Economic History Review* 20 (1972), 1-26.

2490   Thomson, Arthur, *Barnkvävning. En rättshistorisk studie.* Lund, 1960. [Child Smothering: A Study in Legal History]

2491   Thomson, Arthur, *Otidigt sängelag. En rättshistorisk studie.* Stockholm, 1966. [Intercourse of Betrothed Couples: A Study in Legal History]

2492   Troels-Lund, Fredrick, *Dageligt liv i Norden i det sekstende Aarhundrede.* 14 v. 4th ed.; Copenhagen, 1914. [Daily Life in Scandinavia in the 16th Century]

2493   Turpeinen, Oiva, "Fertilitetens årliga fluktuationer och familjeplanering i Finland under den förindustriella tiden," *Historisk tidskrift för Finland* (1976), 209-218. [The Yearly Fluctuations of Fertility and Family Planning in Preindustrial Finland]

2494   Utterström, Gustav, "Labour Policy and Population Thought in Eighteenth-Century Sweden," *Scandinavian Economic History Review* 10 (1962), 262-279.

2495   Verkko, Veli, "Barnamorden och sexualmoralen i Sverige-Finland pa 1700-talet," *Nordisk tidsskrift for strafferet* (1946), 35-45. [Infanticide and Sexual Morality in 18th-Century Sweden-Finland]

2496   Villadsen, Kjeld, *Pest, skatter og priser. Befolkningsudviklingen i Køge 1629-72.* Copenhagen, 1976. [Plague, Prices and Taxes: Population in a Danish Town 1629-1672]

2497   Wennberg, Axel, "Familjeplanering på 1600-talet," *Geografiska notiser* (1967), 180-182. [Family Planning in the 17th Century]

2498   Wirilander, Kaarlo, "Itä-Suomen avioalueet 1700-luvulla," *Genealogiska samfundets i Finland årsskrift* (1946), 32-44. [Marriage Fields in Eastern Finland in the 18th Century]

2499   Ylikangas, Heikki, "Puolisonvalintaan vaikuttaneista tekijöista sääty-yhteiskunnan aikana," *Historiallinen aikakauskirja* (1968), 20-30. [On Factors Influencing Choice of Marriage Partners during the Age of Estates]

MODERN PERIOD (1809 TO THE PRESENT)

2500   Abukhanfusa, Kerstin, *Beredskapsfamiljernas försörjning. Krigsfamiljebi-*

dragen i teori och praktik. Stockholm, 1975. [Maintenance of Soldiers' Families during World War II]   E

2501 Agerholt, Anna Caspari, *Den norske kvinnevevegelses historie.* Oslo, 1973. [The History of the Norwegian Women's Movement]

2502 Allardt, Erik, *Miljöbetingade differenser i skilsmässofrekvensen. Olika norm-systems och andra sociala faktorers inverkan på skilsmässofrekvensen i Finland 1891-1950.* Helsingfors/Helsinki, 1952. [The Effect of Differing Norm Systems and Other Social Factors on the Frequency of Divorce in Finland]

2503 *Allmoge- och hemslöjd. Bidrag till en uppländsk kulturhistoria,* ed. A. Julius. Uppsala, 1915. [Domestic Crafts and Industry in Central Sweden]

2504 Allwood, Martin S., *Eilert Sundt: A Pioneer in Sociology and Social Anthropology.* Oslo, 1957.

2505 Alström, Carl Henry, "First Cousin Marriages in Sweden 1750-1844 and a Study of the Population Movement in Some Swedish Sub-Populations from the Genetic-Statistical Viewpoint," *Acta genetica et statistica medica* (1958), 295-369.

2506 Andersson, Marianne, "Böndernas bönemän," *Fataburen* (1969), 53-60. [The Peasant Wooer's Proxy]

2507 Ankarloo, Bengt, "Hemmabarn och tjänstefolk," *Historia och Samhälle Studier tillägnade Jerker Rosén* (Malmö, 1975), 117-125. [Children and Servants]

2508 Aukrust, Tor, "Seksualrevolusjonen og den kristne seksualmoral," *Tidsskrift for teologi og kirke* (1969), 272-289. [The Sexual Revolution and Christian Morals]

2509 Bentzel, Ragnar, *Den privata konsumtionen i Sverige 1931-65.* Stockholm, 1957. [Private Consumption in Sweden]

2510 Bernhardt, Eva, *Trends and Variations in Swedish Fertility. A Cohort Study.* Stockholm, 1971.

2511 Björkman, Jan Olof, *Bonde och tjänstehjon. Om social stratifiering i äldre mellansvensk agrarbygd.* Uppsala, 1974. [Peasant and Servant in 18th- and 19th-Century Central Sweden]   E

2512 Björnsson, Björn, *The Lutheran Doctrine of Marriage in Modern Icelandic Society.* Reykjavik, 1971.

2513 Bøgh, Charlotte, and Inger Tolstrup, "Københavnsbønder — to landsbyer på Amager," *Familie, hushold og produktion,* ed. Orvar Löfgren (Copenhagen, 1974), 33-40. [Two Rural Villages on Copenhagen's Outskirts]

2514 Bolstad Skjelbred, Ann Helene, *Uren og hedning. Barselkvinnen i norsk folke-tradisjon.* Oslo, 1972. [Unclean and Heathen: The New Mother in Norwegian Folk Tradition]

2515 Bringéus, Nils-Arvid, "Svenska dopseder," *Fataburen* (1971), 21-40. [Swedish Baptismal Customs]

2516 Brox, Ottar, "Natural Conditions, Inheritance and Marriage in a North Norwegian Fjord," *Folk* 6 (1964), 35-46.

2517   Buch, Carl Egil, "Ein Miethausmilieu der Jahrhundertwende," *Ethnologia Scandinavica* (1976), 42-82.

2518   Bull, Edvard, *Arbeidemiljø under det industrielle gjennombrudd*. Oslo, 1958. [Worker's Environment in the Industrial Breakthrough]

2519   Burjam, Fritz, *Den skandinaviska folktron om barnet under dess ömtålighetstillstånd i synnerhet före dopet*. Helsingfors/Helsinki, 1917. [Scandinavian Beliefs about Care for Delicate Infants Especially before Baptism]

2520   Carlsson, Gösta, "The Decline of Fertility: Innovation or Adjustment Process?" *Population Studies* 20 (1966), 149-174.

2521   Cederlund, Carl-Olof, "Undantagsinstitutionen i Mönsterås socken 1860-1960," *Stranda hembygdsförenings årsbok* (1964), 19-48. [Peasant Retirement Customs in Southern Sweden]

2522   Christensen, Johs. T., "De gamles Forsørgelse i forrige Aarhundrede. Aftaegtsforholdets Ordning i Landbohjemmene," *Aarbok for Historisk Samfund for Soro Amt* 16 (1928), 69-95. [Maintenance of Old People through Retirement Contracts in Farm Households in the 19th Century]

2523   Christiansen, Palle Ove, and Hanne Mathiesen, "Fiskere og bønder på Harboør," *Familie, hushold og produktion*, ed. Orvar Löfgren (Copenhagen, 1974), 47-58. [Fishermen and Farmers on Western Jutland]

2524   Christoffersen, Erik, and Klavs Gruno, "Lodbønder på Nyord," *Familie, hushold og produktion*, ed. Orvar Löfgren (Copenhagen, 1974), 13-24. [Peasant Pilots in South Denmark]

2525   Curman, Jöran, *Industriens arbetarbostäder*. Stockholm, 1944. [Workers' Housing Built by Industry]

2526   Dahlerup, Drude, *Socialisme og kvindefrigørelse i det 19. århundrede*. Aarhus, 1973. [Socialism and Women's Emancipation in 19th-Century Denmark]

2527   Dahlström, Edmund, and Rita Liljeström, *Kvinnors liv och arbete*. Oscarshamn, 1969. [Women's Life and Work]

2528   Damgaard, Ellen, and Poul Moustgaard, *Et hjem—en familie. En etnologisk punktundersøgelse af et bor erligt københavnsk miljø omkring 1890*. Copenhagen, 1970. [A Home—A Family: An Ethnological Case Study of a Bourgeois Copenhagen Milieu]

2529   Daun, Åke, *Förortsliv. En etnologisk studie av kulturell förändring*. Stockholm, 1974. [Surburban Life: An Ethnological Study of Cultural Change]

2530   Drake, Michael, "Malthus on Norway," *Population Studies* 20 (1966), 175-196.

2531   Edin, Karl Arvid, *Arbetarbefolkningens bostadsförhållanden i Uppsala*. Uppsala, 1908. [Housing Conditions of the Working Population in Uppsala]

2532   Edin, Karl Arvid, "Födelsekontrollens inträngande hos de breda lagren och den ekonomisk innebörden därav," *Nationalekonomiska föreningens förhandlingar* (1929), 123-152. [The Penetration of Birth Control Down to the Bottom of Society and Its Economic Consequences]

2533 Edin, Karl Arvid, and Edward Hutchinson, *Studies of Differential Fertility in Sweden.* London, 1935.

2534 Egardt, Brita, *Äkta makars fördel av askiftat bo. En studie på temat lag-sedvana.* Lund, 1970. [The Advantage of the Married Partner in an Intact Estate]

2535 Ejlersen, T., "Kronprisessegade. Et københavnsk gadeanlaeg og dets beboere," *Historiske Meddelelser om København* (1976), 48-98. [An 18th-Century Copenhagen Street and Its Inhabitants]

2536 Ek, Sven B., *Noden i Lund.* Lund, 1971. [The Noden District in Lund]   E

2537 Elklit, Jørgen, *Folketaellingen 1845.* Århus, 1969. [The Danish Census of 1845]

2538 Elmér, Åke, *Folkpensioneringen i Sverige med särskild hänsyn till ålders-pensioneringen.* Lund, 1960. [Popular Pensions Especially Old Age Pensions in Sweden]   E

2539 Erixon, Sigurd, "Gården och familjen. Bidrag till belysningen av storfamiljs-systemets föredomst i Sverige," *Etnologiska studier tillägnade N. E. Ham-marstedt* (Stockholm, 1921), 195-212. [Farm and Family: On the Existence of Extended Families in Sweden]

2540 Erixon, Sigurd, "Bonden i högsäte," *Svenska kulturbilder* 6-7 (Stockholm, 1935), 179-202. [The Place of Honor in Farm Dwellings]

2541 Eskildsen, Claus, *Den sønderjydske Befolkningens Slaegtsforbindelser.* Copen-hagen, 1942. [Kinship Relations in the South Jutland Population]

2542 Essen-Möller, Erik, "Familial Interrelatedness in a Swedish Rural Population," *Supplementum ad Acta genetica et statistica medica* (1967).

2543 Fischer, Ernst, "Linvävarefamiljen Nyman. Ett bidrag till det skånska linne-väveriets historia," *Svenska kulturbilder* new series 3 (1935), 285-108. [A Linen-Weaving Family]

2544 Flood, Johannes, "På lørdagsfriing og natteløpning," *By og Bygd* (1944), 37-54. [Bundling and Other Courtship Practices in Norway]

2545 Forsberg, Karl-Erik, "Fruktsamheten i äktenskap, ingångna i Helsingfors åren 1926, 1929 och 1932," *Ekonomiska samfundets tidskrift* 2nd series (1947), 64-88. [Fertility of Helsinki Marriages Established in 1926, 1929 and 1932]

2546 Fridlizius, Gunnar, "Some New Aspects on Swedish Population Growth," *Economy and History* 18 (1975), 3-33, 126-154.

2547 Frykman, Jonas, "Sexual Intercourse and Social Norms. A Study of Illegitimate Births in Sweden 1831-1933," *Ethnologia Scandinavica* (1975), 110-150.

2548 Furuland, Lars, *Statarna i litteraturen. En studie i svensk dikt och samhälls-debatt.* Stockholm, 1962. [Married Farm Servants in Literature and Social Debate]

2549 Gebhard, Hannes, *Bostadsförhallåndena.* Helsingfors/Helsinki, 1910. [Hous-ing Conditions in Finland]

2550 Gejvall, Birgit, *1800-talets Stockholmsbostad. En studie över den borgerliga bostadens planlösning.* Stockholm, 1954. [A Study of Bourgeois Housing in 19th-Century Stockholm]

2551   Granlund, John, "Familjoch gard," *Gruddbo på Sollerön* (Stockholm, 1938), 77–107. [A Village in Dalecarlia: Family and Farm]

2552   Granlund, John, "Dihornshållare," *Västerbotten* (1967), 232–254. [The Nursing Bottle for Infants in Farm Families]

2553   Granlund, John, "Bröllopsfunktionärer," *Fataburen* (1969), 133–148. [Wedding Officials]

2554   Grønseth, Erik, and Per Olav Tiller, "Father Absence in Sailor Families and Its Impact on the Personality and Later Social Adjustment of the Children," *Recherches sur la famillie* 2 (1957), 95–138.

2555   Grønseth, Erik, "Notes on the Historical Development of the Relation between Nuclear Family, Kinship System and the Wider Social Structure in Norway," *Families in East and West*, ed. Reuben Hill and René König (The Hague, 1970), 225–247.

2556   Grue-Sørensen, Bodil, "Hasselø—et øsamfund i Guldborgsund," *Familie, hushold og produktion*, ed. Orvar Löfgren (Copenhagen, 1974), 41–46. [A Danish Island's Family Structure]

2557   Gustavsson, Anders, *Kyrktagningsseden i Sverige*. Lund, 1972. [The Custom of Ceremonial Churching]   G

2558   Gustavsson, Anders, "Den nyblivna modern. En etnologisk beteende-studie," *Vetenskapssocieteten i Lund årsbok* (1972), 125–220. [The New Mother: An Ethnological Study of Behavior]

2559   Gustafsson, Berndt, "Det svenska prästerskapets börd och äktenskapsförbindelser vid tiden för folkrörelsernas genombrott," *Kyrkohistorisk årsskrift* 51 (1951), 156–180. [Marriage Relations of the Swedish Priesthood in the Mid-19th Century]

2560   Gustafsson, Berndt, *Manligt—kvinnligt—kyrkligt i 1800-talets svenska folkliv*. Stockholm, 1956. [Manly—Womanly—Churchly in 19th-Century Swedish Popular Life]

2561   Gustafsson, Bo, *Den norrländska sågverksindustrins arbetare 1890–1913*. Stockholm, 1965. [The Northern Swedish Sawmill Workers]   E

2562   Habekost, Kai, "Social mobilitet i Langelands søndre herred omkring midten af det 19. århundrede," *Studier i Dansk Befolkningshistorie 1750–1850*, ed. Hans Christian Johansen (Odense, 1976), 9–75. [Generational Social Mobility in Rural 19th-Century Denmark]

2563   Hagberg, Louise, "Den nyfödde världsmedborgaren," *Svenska kulturbilder* 11–12 (1935), 77–102. [Treatment of the Newborn]

2564   Hallerdt, Björn, *Leva i brukssamhälle. En studie över sociala relationer vid Surahammars bruk 1848–1920*. Stockholm, 1957. [Social Relations in a Swedish Company Town 1848–1920]

2565   Hamrin, John, *Redogörelse för vissa jorddelningsförhållanden inom Kopparbergs, Gotlands och Gävleborgs län*. Falun, 1920. [Conditions of Transfer and Division of Land in Parts of Central Sweden]

2566 Hansen, Hans Peter, *Hedebønder i tre slaegtled.* 2nd ed.; Copenhagen, 1959. [Three Generations of Heath Peasants] E

2567 Harva, Uno, "De gifta kvinnornas samfund med hithörande upptagningsriter," *Folk-liv* (1943–44), 277–285. [The Society of Married Women in Initiation Rites]

2568 Hatje, Ann-Katrin, *Befolkningsfrågan och välfärden. Debatten om familjepolitik och nativitetsökning under 1930– och 1940–talen.* Stockholm, 1974. [The Population Question and Welfare: The Debate over Family Policy and Fertility Increase during the 1930s and 40s] E

2569 Hedlund, Märta, "Barnets uppfostran och utbildning i en storfamilj," *Folk-liv* (1943–44), 72–90. [The Rearing and Education of a Child in an Extended Family] E

2570 Hellstenius, Johan, "Barnadödligheten i Västernorrlands och Jemtlands län," *Statistisk tidskrift* (1884), 153–168. [Infant Mortality in Northern Sweden]

2571 Heymowski, Adam, *Swedish "Travellers" and Their Ancestry. A Social Isolate or an Ethnic Minority?* Uppsala, 1969.

2572 Hirth, Eirik, "Giftarmal og brudlaup i gamal tid," *Land og hav* (1955–56), 116–142. [Marriage and Weddings in the Past]

2573 Högnäs, Hugo, *Sytning och arvslösen i den folkliga sedvänjan uti Pedersöre- och Nykarlebybygden 1810–1914.* Åbo/Turku, 1938. [Retirement Contracts and Inheritance in Northern Finland]

2574 Hojrup, Ole, *Landbokvinden. Rok og kaerne. Grovbrød og vadmel.* 3rd ed.; Copenhagen, 1967. [The Rural Woman and Her Tasks]

2575 Højrup, Ole, "Die Arbeitsteilung zwischen Männern und Frauen in der bäuerlichen Kultur Dänemarks," *Ethnologia Scandinavica* (1975), 23–36.

2576 Hyrenius, Hannes, *Studier rörande den utomäktenskapliga fruktsamhetens regionala variationer.* Lund, 1941 [Regional Variations in Illegitimacy]

2577 Hyrenius, Hannes, *Estlandssvenskarna.* Lund, 1942. [Family Reconstitution of Swedish-Speaking Estonians]

2578 Hyrenius, Hannes, "Fertility and Reproduction in a Swedish Population Group without Family Limitation," *Population Studies* 12 (1958), 121–130.

2579 Järnek, Martin, *Studier i hushållens inkomstförhållanden 1925–64. En undersökning av Malmö mot bakgrund av den svenska inkomstdebatten.* Lund, 1971. [Household Income in Malmö 1925–1964]

2580 Jensen, Adolf, *Befolkningsspørgsmålet i Danmark.* Copenhagen, 1937. [The Population Question in Denmark]

2581 Jirlow, Ragnar, "Nattfrierier i Skellefteådalen," *Etnologiska studier tillägnade N. E. Hammarstedt* (Stockholm, 1921), 232–236. [Courtship in Northern Sweden]

2582 Johannessen, Axel Theodor, *Dødeligheten i Norge af Børn under 1 Aar.* Christiania/Oslo, 1902. [Infant Mortality in Norway]

2583 Johansson, Levi, "Barnauppfostran i det gamala Frostviken," *Jämten* (1934), 209–219. [Childrearing in the Northern Swedish Mountains]

2584   Jonell-Ericsson, Britta, *Skinnare i Malung. Från hemarbete till fabriksindustri.* Uppsala, 1975. [Skinners: From Domestic Industry to the Factory]

2585   Källberg, Sture, *Off the Middle Way. Report from a Swedish Village.* New York, 1972.

2586   Kaukiainen, Yrjö, "Miksi kausa lisääntyi. Ajatuksia syntyvyyden ja kuolevuuden vaikutuksesta ja vuorovaikutuksesta," *Historiallinen Aikakauskirja* (1973), 103-121. [Effects and Interaction of Fertility and Mortality on Population Growth in Preindustrial Finland]   E

2587   Kiaer, Anders Nicolai, "Nogle oplysningar om forholdet mellem aegteskaber og fødsler med saerlig hensyn til aegteskabernes stiftelse tid," *Forhandlinger i videnskabsselskabet i Christiania* (1873), 180-184. [Observations on the Correspondence between Time of Marriage and the Number of Births]

2588   Kiaer, Anders Nicolai, *Nye bidrag til belysning af frugtbarhedsforholdene inden aegteskabet i Norge.* Christiania/Oslo, 1902. [Conditions of Marital Fertility in Norway]

2589   Kivialho, Kaaperi, *Maatalouskiinteistöjen omistajanvaihdokset ja hinnanmuodostus Halikon tuomiokunnassa 1851-1910.* Helsinki, 1927. [Transfers of Landed Property and Prices of Land in Southern Finland in the Late 19th Century]   G

2590   Kjellström, Rolf, *Eskimo Marriage. An Account of Traditional Eskimo Courtship and Marriage.* Lund, 1973.

2591   Kjellström, Rolf, "Eskimaiska barnamord," *Sista lasset in. Studier tillagnade Albert Eskerod* (Stockholm, 1975), 299-320. [Eskimo Infanticide]   E

2592   Kolderup-Rosenvinge, L. "Ere Børnebørn pligtige til at indføre i Bedsteforaelrenes Bo, hvad disse have givet deres Børn?" *Nyt juridisk Arkiv* 17 (1816), 140-165. [Must Grandchildren Give Back to Grandparents What They Have Given Their Children?]

2593   Koskikallio, Onni, *Maatalouskiinteistöjen eläkerasituksesta Pirkkalan ja Ruoveden tuomiokunnissa vuosina 1800-1913.* Helsinki, 1927. [Cost of Maintaining the Elderly in Central Rural Finland]   G

2594   Lahikainen, Anja-Riitta, *Perheen kehitys teollistumisen aikana.* Helsinki, 1976. [Development of the Family during Industrialization]

2595   Levander, Lars, *Barnavård i Ovre Dalarne vid 1800-talets mitt.* Stockholm, 1946. [Care of Children in 19th-Century Upper Dalecarlia]

2596   Levander, Lars, *Barnuppfostran på svenska landsbygden i äldre tid.* Stockholm, 1946. [Rearing Children in the Older Swedish Countryside]

2597   Liljeström, Rita, *A Study of Abortion in Sweden.* Stockholm, 1974.

2598   Lind, Grøttland, Kristine, *Daglig brød ob daglig dont. Fra nord-norsk husstell og hjemmeliv.* Oslo, 1962. [Daily Bread and Daily Toil in Northern Norwegian Homes]

2599   Lindgren, Jarl, *Intergeneration Farm Tranfers. A Study of Intergeneration Farm Transfers within Families in Finland.* Hämmenlinna, 1968.

2600   Lindström, Ulla, "Kvinnlig barnplanering in Sverige," *Forskare om befolk-*

ningsfrågor (Stockholm, 1975), 213-255. [Female Family Planning in Sweden]

2601 Linnarsson, Linnar, "Arbetsfordelning och livsforing i 1800-talets bondehushåll," *Västergötlands fornminnesförenings årskrift* 6 (1963), 177-200. [Division of Labor between the Sexes in 19th-Century West Sweden]

2602 Lithberg, Nils, "Bröllopsseder på Gottland," *Fataburen* (1906), 65-92; (1907), 144-178; (1908), 129-148; (1911), 145-168. [Wedding Customs in Gotland]

2603 Löfgren, Orvar, "Från nattfrieri till tonårskultur," *Fataburen* (1969), 25-52. [From Bundling to Teenage Culture]

2604 Löfgren, Orvar, "Family and Household among Scandinavian Peasants. An Exploratory Essay," *Ethnologia Scandinavica* (1974), 19-52.

2605 Löfgren, Orvar, "Arbeitsteilung und Geschlechterrollen in Schweden," *Ethnologia Scandinavica* (1975), 49-72.

2606 Lundequist, Karsten, *Socialhjälpstagande—utveckling och orsaker 1945-1965. Med en intensivundersökning av hjälptagandet i Uppsala.* Uppsala, 1976. [Taking Social Aid Especially in Uppsala after World War II]

2607 Mahkonen, Sami, *Köyhä lapsi. Selvitys lastensuojelulainsäädännön historiasta 1849-1936.* Helsinki, 1974. [The Poor Child: Investigation of Legislation to Protect Children 1849-1936]

2608 Måwe, Karl-Erik, *Studier i den sociala kontrollen i Östmark.* Uppsala, 1958. [Social Control in Western Sweden]

2609 Martinsen, Karl Anton, "Et sjømannshjem i Drøbak i 1890 årene," *By og Bygd* (1962), 75-90. [A Norwegian Sailor's Home at the Turn of the Century]

2610 Martinussen, Willy, "Prostitusjon i Norge. Levevei eller levevis?" *Tidsskrift for samfunnsforskning* (1969), 134-160. [Prostitution in Norway]

2611 Matinolli, Eero, "Kirkonkirjoista suku- ja henkilöhistoriallisen tutkimuksen lähdeaineistona ja suunnitelma niiden käytön helpottamiseksi," *Finska kyrkohistoriska samfundets handlingar* 93 (1975), 521-531. [Church Records as Sources for Family and Biographical Research] G

2612 Meijer-Granqvist, Paul, *Stockholmskt borgarfolk. Ett och annat om hufvudstadens gamla borgarfamiljer.* Stockholm, 1902. [The Family Life of Old Stockholm Patrician Families]

2613 Meurling, Anna Christina, "Studier i en skånsk husförhörslängd," *Historia och samhälle. Studier tillägnade Jerker Rosén* (Malmö, 1975), 126-140. [A Scanian *Liber Status Animarum* from the 19th Century]

2614 Minnhagen, Monika, *Bondens bostad. En studie rörande boningslängans form, funktion och förändring i sydöstra Skåne.* Lund, 1973. [The Changes in the Form and Function of Farm Dwellings in Southeastern Scania] E

2615 Moe, Ketil, and Tore Wiik, *Arbeiderboliger i Oslo 1850-1972.* Oslo, 1972. [Worker's Housing in Oslo 1850-1972]

2616 Nieminen, Armas, *Taistelu sukupuolimorallista Avioliitto- ja seksuaalikysymyksiä Suomalaisen hengenelämän ja yhteiskunnan murroksessa sääty-*

yhteiskunnan ajoilta 1910–luvulle. Helsinki, 1951. [The Battle Over Sexual Morality in Finland at the End of the 19th and Beginning of the 20th Centuries]

2617 Nikander, Gabriel, "Bebyggelsetyper och storfamiljsgårdar i Savolax," *Finskt museum* (1953), 41–72. [Settlement Patterns and Extended Family Farms in Eastern Finland]

2618 Nissen, Nis, *Den kroniske bolignød og fremtidens boligpolitik. Om boligproblemer 1848–1984.* Copenhagen, 1971. [Housing Problems in Denmark during the Mid-19th Century]

2619 Norberg, Anders, and Sune Åkerman, "Migration and the Building of Families: Studies on the Rise of the Lumber Industry in Sweden," *Aristocrats, Farmers, Proletarians,* ed. Kurt Ågren et al. (Uppsala, 1973), 88–119. (See #2347)

2620 Norsander, Göran, *Salt sill: en studie av kostvanor på sydsvensk landsbygd 1850–1940.* Lund, 1976. [Salt Herring: A Study of Diet in South Rural Sweden] E

2621 Ohlsson, Lars, "Barn och ungdomsarbete i svensk industri 1860–1970," *Scandia* 40 (1974), 228–244. [Child Labor in Swedish Industry]

2622 Olsson, Kent, *Husållsinkomst, inkomstfördelning och försörjningsbörda. En undersökning av vissa yrkesgrupper i Göteborg 1919–1960.* Gothenburg, 1972. [Household Income, Division of Income, and Maintenance Costs of Some Economic Groups in Gothenburg]

2623 Palme, Sven Ulric, "Samhället och barnen på änglamakerskornas tid," *Fataburen* (1971), 47–61. [Society and Children in the Time of the Angel-Makers]

2624 Pedersen, Jørgen, *De økonomiske Perioders Indflydelse paa Vielser, Fødsler og Børnedødsfald i Danmark i Aarene 1871–1900.* Copenhagen, 1912. [The Effect of Business Cycles on Marriages, Births, and Infant Mortality in Denmark 1871–1900]

2625 Pedersen, Ragnar, "Die Arbeitsteilung zwischen Frauen und Männern in einem marginalen Ackerbaugebiet—Das Beispiel Norwegen," *Ethnologia Scandinavica* (1975), 37–48.

2626 Persson, Birgit, "Att vara ogift mor på 1700- och 1800-talet," *Könsdiskriminering förr och nu,* ed. Karin Westmen Berg (Stockholm, 1972), 125–134. [Unwed Mothers in 18th and 19th Century]

2627 Persson, Lennart, *Samvetsäketenskap eller civiläktenskap. Samvetsäktenskapet vid Göteborgs högskola år 1904 och dess betydelse för civiläktenskapets införande i Sverige.* Gothenburg, 1971. [Marriage of Conscience in Gothenburg University 1904 and Its Importance for the Introduction of Civil Marriage]

2628 Petersen, Axel, *Samfundet og Børnene. Om Statens og Samfundets Stilling til den forsømte og forvildede Ungdom.* Copenhagen, 1904. [The Position of State and Society on Neglected and Wild Youth]

2629 Piha, Kalevi, *Suurperhe Karjalaisessa työyhteisössä. Karjalainen suurperhe sosialliantropologian ja sosiaalipsykologian valossa.* Turku, 1964. [The Extended Family in Carelia: Its Social Anthropology and Psychology] G

2630 Piirainen, Veikko, *Kylänkierrolta kunnalliskotiin Savon ja Pohjois-Karjalan maaseudun vaivaishoitotoiminta vaivaishoidon murroskautena 1800–luvun jälkipuoliskolla.* Forssa, 1958. [Care of Paupers in Rural Communities in Eastern Finland in the 19th Century] G

2631 Pleijel, Hilding, *Husandakt, husaga, husförhör och andra folklivsstudier.* Stockholm, 1965. [Domestic Prayers, Domestic Punishment, and Catechistic Examinations in Folklore]

2632 Quist, Gunnar, *Kvinnofrågan i Sverige 1809–1846. Studier rörande kvinnans näringsfrihet inom de borgerliga yrkena.* Gothenburg, 1960. [The Women's Question in Early 19th-Century Sweden: A Study of Women's Right to Pursue Bourgeois Trades] E

2633 Rajainen, Maija, *Naisliike ja sukupuolimoraali. Keskustelua ja toimintaa 1800–luvulla ja nykyisen vuosisadan alkupuolella noin vuoteen 1918 saakka.* Helsinki, 1973. [Women's Movement and Sexual Morals: Debate and Activity during the 19th Century to 1918]

2634 Rajainen, Maija, "Tidskrift för hemmet, vanhin pohjoismainen naisasialehti," *Turun Historiallinen Arkisto* 31 (1976), 120–141. [The First Journal for the Women's Movement in Scandinavia]

2635 Rasmussen, Agnete, *Dansk kvindesamfund og saedlighedsfejden 1887.* Grenå, 1972. [The Danish Women's Movement and the Battle over Morality in 1887]

2636 Refsum, Helge, " 'Lørdagsfriing og Natteløpning,' Et manuskript av Johannes Flood i Eilert Sundts samling," *By og Bygd* 2 (1944), 33–37. [Introduction to J. Flood's Manuscript on Bundling and Nightly Courtship]

2637 Refsum, Helge, "Utpågang og nattefriing i Trøndelag. En anonym rapport i Eilert Sundts samling," *By og Bygd* 6 (1948–49), 41–68. [Bundling and Nightly Courtship in Northern Norway]

2638 Reimer, Christine, *Nordfynsk bondeliv i mands minde.* 5 v. Odense, 1910–19. [Peasant Life in 19th-Century Denmark]

2639 Rössel, James, *Kvinnorna och kvinnorörelsen i Sverige 1850–1950.* Stockholm, 1950. [Women and the Women's Movement in Sweden 1850–1950]

2640 Rubin, Marcus, and Harald Westergaard, *Aegteskabsstatistik på Grundlag af den sociale Lagdelning. Efter Folketaellinger og Kirkebøger i Danmark.* Copenhagen, 1890. [Marriage Statistics by Social Class]

2641 Rung, Grete, "Gårdmaend og husmaend i Lystrup—en sjaellandsk landsby," *Familie, hushold og produktion,* ed. Orvar Löfgren (Copenhagen, 1974), 25–32. [Farmers' and Cottars' Families in a Zealand Village]

2642 Sarmela, Matti, *Reciprocity Systems of the Rural Society in the Finnish-Karelian Culture Area with Special Reference to Social Intercourse of the Youth.* Helsinki, 1969.

2643   Saugstad, Letten Fegersten, and Ørnulv Ødegård, "Naboskap og ekteskap. Giftermålsmønstret i en norsk fjellbygd 1600-1850," *Norveg* (1976), 99-115. [Neighborhood and Marriage: The Pattern of Marriage in a Norwegian Mountain Area 1600-1850]

2644   Schiøtz, Aina, "Prostitusjon og samfunn i 1870- og 1880-årenes Christiania," *St. Hallvard* (1976), 13-27. [Prostitution and Society in Oslo during the 1870s and 1880s]

2645   Schybergson, Per, "Barn- och kvinnoarbete i Finlands fabriksindustri vid mitten av 1800-talet," *Historisk tidskrift för Finland* (1974), 1-17. [Factory Work of Children and Women in Mid-19th-Century Finland]

2646   Sellerberg, Ann-Mari, *Kvinnorna på den svenska arbetsmarknaden under 1900-talet. En sociologisk analys av kvinnornas underordnade position i arbetslivet.* Lund, 1973. [Women on the Swedish Labor Market during the 20th Century]   E

2647   Sirelius, U. T., "Om gästabud i Finland för släktens samtliga avlidna," *Etnologiska studier tillägnade N. E. Hammarstedt* (Stockholm, 1921), 69-74. [On Meals for All the Defunct Kin in Finland]

2648   Smeds, Helmer, *Malaxbygden. Bebyggelse och hushållning i södra delen av Österbottens svenskbygd. En studie i människans och näringslivets geografi.* Helsingfors/Helsinki, 1935. [A Geographic and Anthropological Study of a Tract in Nothern Coastal Finland]   F

2649   Stehouwer, Jan, "Relations between Generations and the Three-Generation Household in Denmark," *Social Structure and the Family: Generational Relations,* ed. Ethel Shanas and Gordon Streib (Englewood Cliffs, N.J., 1965), 142-162.

2650   Stocklund, Bjarne, "Økologisk tilpasning i et dansk øsamfund," *Nord-Nytt* (1971), 35-42. [Ecological Adaptations on a Danish Island]

2651   Strange, Helene, *I mødrenes spor. Nordfalsterske kvinders arbejde gennem halvandet hundrede aar.* Copenhagen, 1945. [Women's Work Since 1800 in a Danish Province]

2652   Sucksdorff, Wilhelm, *Arbetarbefolkningens i Helsingfors Bostadsförhållanden.* Helsingsfors/Helsinki, 1904. [Dwelling Conditions of the Working Class in Helsinki]

2653   Sundt, Eilert, *Om saedlighedstilstanden i Norge.* 2 v. New ed.; Oslo-Gjovik, 1976. [On Morality in 19th-Century Norway]

2654   Sundt, Eilert, *Om Giftarmal i Norge.* New ed.; Oslo, 1975. [On Marriage in 19th-Century Norway]

2655   Suominen, Leena, *Perhepolitiikan perustelut Suomessa. Sisällön erittelylle rakentuva tutkimus maamme kansanedustajien vuosina 1934-1973 tekemien perhepoliittisten aloitteiden perusteluista.* Helsinki, 1975. [Motivations for Family Policy Motions of Finnish Politicians 1934-1973]

2656   Sverri, Knut, "De oäkta barnen," *Fataburen* (1971), 39-46. [Illegitimate Children]

2657 Tornberg, Matleena, "Kuusamolainen suurperhe työ- ja elinyhteisönä," *Sananjalka* 13 (1971), 104-131. [An Extended Family in Kuusamo as a Social and Work Collective before 1939] G

2658 Tornberg, Matleena, "Storfamiljeinstitutionen i Finland," *Nord-Nytt* (1972), 4-17. [Extended Families in Finland]

2659 Visuri, Elina, *Poverty and Children. A Study of Family Planning.* Helsinki, 1969.

2660 Wallin, Sigurd, "Herrgårdens vardag, såsom den skymtar i memoarerna," *Svenska kulturbilder* 3 (1935), 9-28. [Manor Life As It Appears in Memoires]

2661 Weiser-Aall, Lily, "Arbeitsteilung zwischen Männern und Frauen," *Volkskunde und Volkskultur: Festschrift für R. Wolfram*, v. 2 (Vienna, 1968), II, 428-431.

2662 Weiser-Aall, Lily, *Svangerskap og fødsel i nyere norsk tradisjon.* Oslo, 1968. [Pregnancy and Birth in Recent Norwegian Tradition]

2663 Weiser-Aall, Lily, *Omkring de nyfødtes stell i nyere norsk overlevering.* Oslo, 1973. [The Position of the Newborn in Recent Norwegian Tradition]

2664 Weiser-Aall, Lily, "Omkring lengden på die perioden ifølge nyere norske opptegnelser," *Fataburen* (1976), 221-232. [On the Length of Breast-Feeding in Norway]

2665 Westergaard, Harald, "Separationer og Skilsmisser i Danmark 1875-84," *Nationaløknomisk Tidsskrift* (1887), 1-31, 113-142. [Separations and Divorces in Denmark 1875-84]

2666 Whitaker, Ian, "First Cousinhood among the Northern Lapps," *Saga och sed* (1959), 142-146.

2667 Wicksell, Sven David, "Till frågan om den äktenskapliga fruktsamhetens regionala fördelning i Sverige," *Ekonomisk tidskrift* 20 (1918), 227-262; 21 (1919), 164-189. [Regional Distribution of Marital Fertility in Sweden]

2668 Wiegelmann, Gunter, "Bäuerliche Arbeitsteilung in Mittel- und Nordeuropa—Konstanz oder Wandel?" *Ethnologia Scandinavica* (1975), 5-22.

2669 Wikman, Karl Robert Villehad, "Människolivets högtider i svenska Österbotten," *Det svenska Finland*, v. 2, ed. Gabriel Nikander (Helsingfors/ Helsinki, 1922), 198-218. [The High Points of Human Life in Northern Finland]

2670 Willerslev, Richard, "Arbejdernes boligforhold på det københavnske Vesterbro omkring år 1900," *Erhvervshistorisk årbog* (1975), 7-30. [Housing Conditions in a Working-Class District of Copenhagen 1900]

2671 Winberg, Christer, *Folkökning och proletarisering. Kring den sociala strukturomvandlingen på Sveriges landsbygd under den agrara revolutionen.* Partille, 1975. [Population Increase and Proletarization: On the Social Structural Changes in the Swedish Countryside during the Agrarian Revolution] E

2672 Wohlin, Nils Richard, *Faran af Bondeklassens undergrävande i sammanhang med de gamla arfvejordsåskådnin arnas upplösningar, emigrationen och bondejordens mobilisering.* Stockholm, 1910. [The Decline of the Farming Class in Connection with the Dissolution of Inheritance of Farms, Emigration, and Capitalist Agriculture]

2673   Wohlin, Nils Richard, *Den äktenskapliga fruktsamhetens tillbakagång på Gottland.* Stockholm, 1915. [The Decline of Marital Fertility on Gotland]

The Iberian Peninsula

GENERAL SURVEYS AND COLLECTIONS

2674 Bergström, Magnus, *O Amor e a Saudade em Portugal*. Lisboa, 1930.

2675 Bosch Marín, J., and M. Blanco Otero, *Derecho Infantil y Familiar Español*. Madrid, 1945.

2676 Campo Urbano, Salustiano del, *La Familia Española en Transición*. Madrid, 1960.

2677 Chaves, Luis, *O Amor Português*. Lisboa, 1922.

2678 Clavero, Bartolomé, *Mayorazgo: Propiedad Feudal en Castilla, 1369–1836*. Madrid, 1974.

2679 Descamps, Paul, *Histoire sociale du Portugal*. Paris, 1959.

2680 Elorriaga, G., *La Familia en España*. Madrid, 1965.

2681 Foster, George M., "Cofradía and compadrazgo in Spain and Spanish America," *Southwestern Journal of Anthropology* 9 (1953), 1–28.

2682 Fraga Iribarne, Manuel, *La Familia Española Ante la Segunda Mitad del Siglo XX*. Madrid, 1959.

2683 Gacto Fernández, E., *La Filiación no Legítima en el Derecho Histórico Español*. Sevilla, 1969.

2684 Gacto Fernández, E., "La filiación ilegítima en la historia del derecho español," *Anuario de Historia del Derecho Español* 41 (1971), 899–944.

2685 Garcia Gallo, A., "L'évolution de la condition de la femme en droit espagnol," *Annales de la Faculté de Droit de Toulouse* 14 (1966), 73–96.

2686 Garrido, M. J., *La Mujer Rural*. Madrid, 1962.

2687 Gómez Arboleya, E., and S. del Campo Urbano, *Para una Sociología de la Familia Española*. Madrid, 1959.

2688 Hernández Márquez, M., "Antecedentes históricos y legales del servicio doméstico," *Cuadernos de Política Social* 41 (1959), 7–38.

2689 Luque Baena, Enrique, "Familia, parentesco y estratificación social," *Ethnica* 2 (1971), 99-118.

2690 Meléndez, L., *El Servicio Doméstico en España*. Madrid, 1961.

2691 Merêa, Manuel Paulo, *Evolução dos Regimes Matrimoniais*. Coimbra, 1913.

2692 Merêa, Manuel Paulo, "Notas sobre o poder paternal no direito hispânico ocidental," *Estudos de Direito Hispânico Medieval*, v. 2 (Coimbra, 1953), 83-112.

2693 Merêa, Manuel Paulo, "Sobre o casamento de juras," *Boletim da Faculdade de Direito* [Coimbra] 14 (1937-1938), 12-20.

2694 Miguel, Amando de, "La familia como unidad de análisis sociológico," *Revista de Estudios Políticos* 145 (1966), 29-44.

2695 Mintz, Sidney, and Eric R. Wolf, "An Analysis of Ritual Co-Parenthood (compadrazgo)," *Southwestern Journal of Anthropology* 6 (1950), 341-368.

2696 Moigenie, Victor de, *A Mulher em Portugal*. Porto, 1924.

2697 Morales, J. L., *El Niño en la Cultura Española*. Alcalá, 1960.

2698 Nadal, Jorge, *La Población Española (Siglos XVI a XX)*. Barcelona, 1966.

2699 Osorio, Ana de Castro, *As Mulheres Portugesas*. Lisboa, 1905.

2700 Pescatello, Ann M., *Power and Pawn: The Female in Iberian Families, Societies, and Cultures*. Westport, Conn., and London, 1976.

2701 Pizarro Rodríguez, A., "Evolución de la adopción en el derecho patrio," *Anales de la Universidad Hispalense* 25 (1964), 99-129.

2702 Revilla, Federico, *El Sexo en la Historia de España*. Barcelona, 1975.

2703 Ros Gimeno, J., *La Familia en el Panorama Demográfico Español*. Madrid, 1959.

2704 Terrades Saborit, Ignacio, "Organización ecónomica y protección de la virginidad," *Ethnica* 3 (1972), 181-197.

MIDDLE AGES AND ISLAMIC PERIOD

2705 Belmartino, S. M., "Estructura de la familia y 'edades sociales' en la aristocracia de León y Castilla...Siglos X-XIII," *Cuadernos de Historia de España* 48 (1968), 256-328.

2706 Bonnassie, Pierre, "Une famille de la campagne barcelonaise aux alentours de l'an mil," *Annales du Midi* 76 (1964), 261-304.

2707 Cabral de Moncada, Luís, "O casamento em Portugal na Idade Media," *Estudos de História do Direito*, I (Coimbra, 1948), 37-82.

2708 Caro Baroja, Julio, *Los Moriscos del Reino de Granada*, Madrid, 1957.

2709 Delacour, F., "El niño y la sociedad española de los siglos XIII a XVI," *Anales Toledanos* 7 (1973), 173-232.

2710 Figaniere, Federico Francisco de la, "Introdução," *Memorias das Rainhas de Portugal: D. Theresa-Santa Isabel* (Lisboa, 1859), xiii–xxxi.

2711 Fuertes, J., *La Familia Visigoda*. Madrid, 1951.

2712 Gibert Sánchez, R., "El consentimiento familiar en el matrimonio en el derecho medieval español," *Anuario de Historia del Derecho Español* 18 (1947), 706–761.

2713 Guichard, Pierre, *Al-Andalus: Estructura Antropológica de una Sociedad Islámica en Occidente,* tr. Nico Ancochea. Barcelona, 1976.

2714 Iglésies, Josep, "El poblament de Catalunya durant els segles XIV i XV," *Congreso de Historia de la Corona de Aragón* (Madrid, 1959), 247–270.

2715 López de Coca Castañar, José Enrique, "Aspectos demográficos de Vélez-Málaga: la nómina de huérfanos de 1496," *Cuadernos de Estudios Medievales* 1 (1973), 93–104.

2716 Martín Gijón, J., "La comunidad hereditaria y la partición de la herencia en el derecho medieval español," *Anuario de Historia del Derecho Español* 28 (1958), 221–303.

2717 Oliveira Marques, A. H., *Daily Life in Portugal in the Late Middle Ages*. Madison, Wis., and London, 1971.

2718 Sánchez Albornoz, Claudio, *La Mujer en España Hace Mil Años*. Buenos Aires, 1935.

2719 Sousa e Silva Costa Lobo, A., *Historia da Sociedade em Portugal no século XV*. Lisboa, 1903.

2720 Teres Sabada, Elías, "Linajes árabes en Al-Andalus," *Al-Andalus* 22 (1957), 55–112, 337–376.

EARLY MODERN ERA
(1500–1800)

2721 Arco, Ricardo del, "Una notable institución social: el Padre de Huérfanos," *Estudios de Historia Social* 3 (1955), 187–222.

2722 Bennassar, Bartolomé, *Valladolid au Siècle d'Or: une ville de Castille et sa campagne au XVIe siècle*. Paris, 1967.

2723 Bourland, Caroline B., "Aspectos de la vida del hogar en el siglo XVII según las novelas de Dª Mariana de Carabajal y Saavedra," *Homenaje Ofrecido a Menéndez Pidal*, v. 2 (Madrid, 1925), 331–368.

2724 Bravo, J., "Notas sobre el colegio de San Ildefonso y la sociedad del siglo XVII," *Hispania* 34 (1974), 425–434.

2725 Carril, Bonifacio del, *Los Mendoza*. Buenos Aires, 1954.

2726 Defourneaux, M., *La vie quotidienne en Espagne au Siècle d'Or*. Paris, 1964.

2727 Deleito y Pinuela, J., *La Mala Vida en la Epoca de Felipe IV*. Madrid, 1948.

2728   Domínguez Ortíz, Antonio, *La Sociedad Española en el Siglo XVIII.* Madrid, 1955.

2729   Domínguez Ortíz, Antonio, *La Sociedad Española en el Siglo XVII.* v. 1. Madrid, 1963.

2730   Fitzmaurice-Kelly, Julia, "Women in Sixteenth-Century Spain," *Revue Hispanique* 70 (1927), 557–632.

2731   González Amezúa, A., *La Vida Privada Española en el Protocolo Notorial... Siglos XVI, XVII, y XVIII.* Madrid, 1950.

2732   Iglésies, Josep, *La Població Catalana al Primer Quart del Segle XVIII.* Barcelona, 1959.

2733   Lapeyre, Henri, *Une famille de marchands, les Ruiz.* Paris, 1955.

2734   Martín Gaite, Carmen, *Usos Amorosos del Dieciocho en España.* Madrid, 1972.

2735   Nadal, Jorge, and E. Giralt, *La population catalane de 1553 à 1717.* Paris, 1960.

2736   Ruiz Almansa, J., *La Población de Galicia, 1500–1945.* v. 1. Madrid, 1948.

2737   Torras i Ribé, Josep Mª., *Evolució Social i Econòmica d'una Família Catalana de l'Antic Règim. Els Padró d'Igualada (1645–1862).* Barcelona, 1976.

MODERN ERA (1800–1939)

2738   Azcarate, Pablo de, "Tres 'Rincones' del siglo XIX leonés," *Boletín de la Real Academia de la Historia* 168 (1971), 575–614.

2739   Arbelo Curbelo, A., *La Mortalidad de la Infancia en España, 1901–1950.* Madrid, 1962.

2740   Bosch Marín, J., *El Niño Español en el Siglo XX.* Madrid, 1947.

2741   Bosch Marín, J., and A. Arbelo Curbelo, "La mortalidad de la edad preescolar en España (1900–1950)," *Revista Internacional de Sociología* 16 (1958), 73–107, 237–249.

2742   Deleito y Pinuela, J., *La Mujer, la Casa y la Moda.* Madrid, 1946.

2743   García Ramos, Alfredo, *Estilos Consuetudinarios y Prácticas Económico-familiares y Marítimas de Galicia.* Madrid, 1909.

2744   González Rothvoss, M., "Familia y emigración," *Revista Internacional de Sociología* 17 (1959), 225–258.

2745   Herculano, Alexandre, *Estudos Sobre o Casamento Civil.* Lisboa, 1866.

2746   Kaplan, Temma E., "Spanish Anarchism and Women's Liberation," *Journal of Contemporary History* 6 (1971), 101–110.

2747   Lafitte, M., *La Mujer en España, Cien Años de su Historia, 1860–1960.* Madrid, 1964.

2748   Leasure, William J., "Factors Involved in the Decline of Fertility in Spain, 1900–1950," *Population Studies* 16 (1963), 271–285.

2749 Livi Bacci, Massimo, *A Century of Portugese Fertility*. Princeton, 1971.

2750 Livi Bacci, Massimo, "Fertility and Nuptiality Changes in Spain from the Late 18th to the Early 20th Century," *Population Studies* 22 (1968), 83–102, 211–234.

2751 López Aranguren, J. L., "La mujer, de 1923 a 1963," *Revista de Occidente* 1 (1963), 231–243.

2752 Maspons i Anglasells, F., *La Llei de la Familia*. Barcelona, 1935.

2753 Nelkin, Margarita, *La Condición Social de la Mujer en España*. Barcelona, 1922.

2754 Ruiz Martín, Felipe, "La población española en los tiempos modernos," *Cuadernos de Historia* 1 (1967), 190–203.

2755 Terán Alvarez, M., "El presupuesto familiar de ingresos y gastos en España," *Estudios Geográficos* 21 (1960), 408–413.

CONTEMPORARY IBERIAN WORLD (1939 TO THE PRESENT)

2756 Andrea da Cunha e Freitas, Eugénio, "Costumes tradicionais da Maia—dotes, doações e sucessões," *Estudos e Ensaios Folclórios em Homenagem a Renato Almeida* (Lisboa, 1960), 367–392.

2757 Brandes, Stanley H., *Migration, Kinship, and Community: Tradition and Transition in a Spanish Village*. New York, 1975.

2758 Brandes, Stanley H., "La Soltería, Or Why People Remain Single in Rural Spain," *Journal of Anthropological Research* 32 (1976), 205–233.

2759 Caro Baroja, Julio, *Razas, Pueblos, y Linajes*. Madrid, 1957.

2760 Caro Baroja, Julio, *Estudios Sobre la Vida Tradicional Española*. Barcelona, 1968.

2761 Dias, A. Jorge, *Vilarinho da Furna: uma Aldeia Comunitária*. Porto, 1948.

2762 Dias, A. Jorge, *Rio de Onor, Comunitarismo Agro-Pastoril*. Porto, 1953.

2763 Douglass, William A., *Death in Murelaga: Funerary Ritual in a Spanish Basque Village*. Seattle, 1969.

2764 Douglass, William A., "Rural Exodus in Two Spanish Basque Villages: A Cultural Explanation," *American Anthropologist* 73 (1971), 1100–1114.

2765 Douglass, William A., "Serving Girls and Shepherders: Emigration and Continuity in a Spanish Basque Village," *The Changing Faces of Rural Spain*, ed. Joseph Aceves and William Douglass (Cambridge, Mass., 1976), 45–62.

2766 Ferrándiz, Alejandra, and Vicente Verdú, *Noviazgo y Matrimonio en la Burguesía Española*. Madrid, 1975.

2767 Freeman, Susan T., *Neighbors: The Social Contract in a Castilian Hamlet*. Chicago, 1970.

2768 Fuenmayor Champín, A., "El sistema matrimonial español," *Revista General de Legislación y Jurisprudencia* 37 (1958), 781-835; 38 (1959), 7-98.

2769   García de Haro, R., "La situación jurídica de la mujer en la derecho privado español," *Recueils de la Société Jean Bodin* 12 (1962), 605-688.

2770   Hansen, Edward C., "The Transformation of Family Structure in Rural Catalonia: An Essay on the Demise of a Regional Tradition," *Nord-Nytt* 2 (1972), 130-142.

2771   Iszaevich, Abraham, "Emigrants, Spinsters and Priests: The Dynamics of Demography in Spanish Peasant Societies," *The Journal of Peasant Studies* 2 (1975), 292-312.

2772   Kenny, Michael, *A Spanish Tapestry: Town and Country in Castile.* New York, 1961.

2773   *La Familia Española,* ed. M. Beltrán Villalva et al. Madrid, 1967. (Volume 14 of *Anales de Moral Social y Económica.*)

2774   Lisón Tolosana, Carmelo, *Antropología Cultural de Galicia.* Madrid, 1971.

2775   Lisón Tolosana, Carmelo, *Belmonte de los Caballeros: A Sociological Study of a Spanish Town.* Oxford, 1966.

2776   López Medel, Jesús, *La Familia Rural, la Urbana y la Industrial en España.* Madrid, 1961.

2777   Mira Casterà, Joan F., "Cambio social y organización familiar: un caso valenciano," *Ethnica* 3 (1972), 99-120.

2778   Muñoz Anatol, Jaime, *La Familia Española Migrante en Francia.* Madrid, 1972.

2779   Pérez Díaz, Víctor, *Estructura Social del Campo y Exodo Rural.* Madrid, 1966.

2780   Pitt-Rivers, Julian A., *People of the Sierra.* 2nd ed.; Chicago, 1971.

2781   Pitt-Rivers, Julian A., "Ritual Kinship in Spain," *Transactions of the New York Academy of Sciences* 2nd series 20 (1958), 424-431.

2782   Price, Richard, and Sally Price, "Noviazgo in an Andalusian Pueblo," *Southwestern Journal of Anthropology* 22 (1966), 302-322.

2783   Price, Richard, and Sally Price, "Stratification and Courtship in an Andalusian Village," *Man* new series 1 (1966), 526-533.

2784   Riegelhaupt, Joyce, "Saloio Women: An Analysis of Informal and Formal Political and Economic Roles of Portugese Peasant Women," *Anthropological Quarterly* 40 (1967), 109-126.

2785   Sancho Hazak, Roberto, "La sociedad rural hoy," *La España de los Años 70,* I. *La Sociedad,* ed. Manuel Fraga Iribarne, Juan Velarde Fuertes, Salustiano del Campo Urbano (Madrid, 1972), 219-317.

2786   Veiga de Oliveira, Ernesto, "Aspectos do compadrio em Portugal," *Actas do III Congresso Internacional de Estudos Luso-Brasileiros* 1 (1959), 154-169.

2787   Willems, Emilio, "On Portugese Family Structure," *International Journal of Comparative Sociology* 3 (1962), 65-79.

2788   Willems, Emilio, "A familia portugêsa contemporànea," *Sociologia* 17 (1955), 3-55.

2789   Willems, Emilio, "Die Familie in Portugal und Brasilien: ein strukturvergleichender Versuch," *Kölner Zeitschrift für Soziologie* 7 (1955), 24-42.

Classical Antiquity

GENERAL SURVEYS AND COLLECTIONS

2790 Fustel de Coulanges, Numa Denis, *La Cité Antique: étude sur le culte, le droit, les institutions de la Grèce et de Rome.* Paris, 1864. English translation as *The Ancient City.* Paperback reprint, New York, 1956.

2791 Maine, Henry J. S., *Ancient Law.* London, 1861.

2792 Momigliano, Arnaldo, "La Città antica de Fustel de Coulanges," *Revista storica italiana* 82 (1970), 81–98. Now in his *Quinto contributo alla storia degli studi classici e del mondo antico* (Rome, 1975), 159–178.

2793 Morgan, Lewis Henry, *Ancient Society.* Cleveland and New York, 1877. Reprint, New York, 1976.

2794 Samter, Ernst, *Familienfeste der Griechen und Römer.* Berlin, 1901. See also #70.

BIBLIOGRAPHIES

2795 Lambrino, Scarlat, *Bibliographie de l'antiquité classique.* Paris, 1896–1914.

2796 Marouzeau, Jules, *Dix années de bibliographie classique.* 2 v. Paris, 1914–24.

2797 *L'Année philologique,* ed. Jules Marouzeau et al. Paris, 1924 ff.

GREECE

Historical Background

2798   Andrewes, Antony, *The Greeks*. London, 1967. Paperback reprint as *Greek Society*. Harmondsworth, 1971.

2799   Flacelière, Robert, *La vie quotidienne en Grèce au siècle de Péricles*. Paris, 1959. Also as *Daily Life in Greece at the Time of Pericles*. New York, 1964.

Kinship, the Family and Law

2800   Alexiou, Margaret, *The Ritual Lament in Greek Tradition*. London, 1974.

2801   Asheri, D., "Tyrannie et mariage forcé," *Annales E.S.C.* 32 (1977), 21–48.

2802   Cooper, Alison Burford, "The Family Farm in Greece," *Classical Journal* 73 (1977–78), 162–175.

2803   Davies, John K., *Athenian Propertied Families 600–300 B.C.* London, 1971.

2804   Davies, John K., "Athenian Citizenship: The Descent Group and the Alternatives," *Classical Journal* 73 (1977–78), 105–121.

2805   Dover, Kenneth J., *Greek Popular Morality in the Time of Plato and Aristotle*. London, 1974.

2806   Ehrenberg, Victor, *The People of Aristophanes*. Oxford, 1943. Paperback revision, New York, 1962.

2807   Gernet, Louis, *Droit et société dans la Grèce ancienne*. Paris, 1955.

2808   Gernet, Louis, *Anthropologie de la Grèce antique*. Paris, 1968.

2809   Glotz, Gustave, *La solidarité de la famille dans le droit criminel en Grèce*. Paris, 1904. Reprint, New York, 1973. See the review by Emile Durkheim in *L'Année sociologique* 8 (1903–04), 465–472; now in his *Journal sociologique* (Paris, 1969), 519–525.

2810   Harrison, Alick R. W., *The Law of Athens: The Family and Property*. Oxford, 1968.

2811   Humphreys, Sarah C., *Anthropology and the Greeks*. London, 1978.

2812   Lacey, Walter K., *The Family in Classical Greece*. London and Ithaca, 1968.

2813   Michell, Humfrey, *Sparta*. Cambridge, England, 1964.

2814   Mulder, J.J.B., *Quaestiones Nonnullae ad Atheniensium Matrimonium Vitamque Coniugalem Pertinentes*. Utrecht, 1920.

2815   Savage, Charles Albert, *The Athenian Family: A Sociological and Legal Study Based Chiefly on the Works of the Attic Orators*. Baltimore, 1907.

2816   Thompson, Wesley E., "The Marriage of First Cousins in Athenian Society," *Phoenix* 21 (1967), 273–282.

2817   Thompson, Wesley E., "Athenian Marriage Patterns: Remarriage," *California Studies in Classical Antiquity* 5 (1972), 211–225.

2818 Wolff, H. J., "Marriage Law and Family Organization in Ancient Athens," *Traditio* 2 (1944), 43-95.

Selected Primary Sources

2819 Antiphon, "Prosecution of the Stepmother for Poisoning," *Minor Attic Orators*, v. 1 (Cambridge, Mass., 1941), 14-31.
2820 Aristophanes, *Comedies.*
2821 Aristotle, *Politics* 1; [Pseudo-Aristotle] *Oeconomicus.*
2822 Demosthenes, *Private Orations.* v. 4-6. Cambridge, Mass., 1936-39.
2823 Isaeus. Cambridge, Mass., 1927.
2824 Plato, *Laws, Republic.*
2825 Xenophon, *Constitution of Sparta, Oeconomicus.*

THE HELLENISTIC WORLD

The Family, Law

2826 Calderini, Aristide, *La composizione della famiglia secondo le schede di censimento dell'Egitto Romano.* Milan, 1923.
2827 Hombert, M., and C. Préaux, "Note sur la durée de la vie dans l'Egypte gréco-romaine," *Chronique d'Egypte* 20 (1945), 139-146.
2828 Hombert, M., and C. Préaux, "Recherches sur le recensement dans l'Egypte romaine," *Papyrologica Lugduno-Batava* 5 (1952), 156-160.
2829 Lewis, Naphtali, "On Paternal Authority in Roman Egypt," *Revue internationale des droits de l'antiquité* 17 (1970), 251-258.
2830 Montevecchi, Orsolina, "Contributi per una storia sociale ed economica della famiglia nell'Egitto greco-romano," *Actes du ve Congrès internationale de papyrologie (Oxford, 1937)* (Brussels, 1938), 300-313. Also in *Aegyptus* 17 (1937), 338-348.
2831 Samuel, Alan E., W. K. Hastings, A. K. Bowman, and R. S. Bagnall, *Death and Taxes: Ostraka in the Royal Ontario Museum*, v. 1. Toronto, 1971.
2832 Vatin, Claude, *Recherches sur le mariage et la condition de la femme mariée à l'époque hellénistique.* Paris, 1970.
2833 Winter, John Garrett, *Life and Letters in the Papyri.* Ann Arbor, 1933.
2834 Wolff, Hans Julius, *Written and Unwritten Marriages in Hellenistic and Post-classical Roman Law.* Haverford, 1939.

Selected Primary Sources

2835   Plutarch, "Advice to the Bride and Groom," *Moralia,* 138-146.
2836   Menander, *Comedies.*
2837   *Select Papyri 1: Non-Literary Papyri, Private Affairs.* Cambridge, Mass., 1932.

ROME

Historical Background

2838   Balsdon, John P.V.D., *Life and Leisure in Ancient Rome.* London, 1969.
2839   Carcopino, Jerome, *La vie quotidienne à Rome à l'apogée de l'empire.* Paris, 1939. Also as *Daily Life in Ancient Rome: The People and the City at the Height of the Empire.* Paperback reprint, New Haven, 1940.
2840   Friedländer, Ludwig, *Darstellungen aus der Sittengeschichte Roms.* 10th ed. by Georg Wissowa; Leipzig, 1922. The 7th ed. appeared in English as *Roman Life and Manners under the Early Empire.* London, 1908-13; Reprint, 1965.

Kinship, the Family, Law, and Politics

2841   Corbett, Percy Ellwood, *The Roman Law of Marriage.* Oxford, 1930.
2842   Crook, John A., *Law and Life of Rome: Aspects of Greek and Roman Life.* London, 1967.
2843   Humbert, Michel, *Le remariage à Rome.* Milan, 1972.
2844   Kaser, Max, *Das römische Privatrecht.* 6th ed.; Munich, 1968. In English as *Roman Private Law.* 2nd ed.; London, 1968.
2845   Pomeroy, Sarah B., "The Relationship of the Married Woman to Her Blood Relatives in Rome," *Ancient Society* 7 (1976), 67-79.
2846   Syme, Ronald, *The Roman Revolution.* Oxford, 1939. Paperback reprint, 1960.
2847   Veyne, P., "La famille et l'amour à Rome," *Annales E.S.C.* 33 (1978), 35-63.

Slaves and the Lower Classes

2848   Kajanto, Iiro, "On Divorce among the Common People of Rome," *Revue des études latines* 47 *bis* (1970), 99-113.
2849   Rawson, Beryl, "Family Life among the Lower Classes at Rome in the First

Two Centuries of the Empire," *Classical Philology* 61 (1966), 71–83.

2850 Rawson, Beryl, "Roman Concubinage and Other *de facto* Marriages," *Transactions of the American Philological Association* 104 (1974), 279–305.

2851 Tanzer, Helen H., *The Common People of Pompeii*. Baltimore, 1939.

2852 Treggiari, Susan, *Roman Freedmen during the Late Republic*. Oxford, 1969.

2853 Treggiari, Susan, "Family Life among the Staff of the Volussii," *Transactions of the American Philological Association* 105 (1975), 393–401.

2854 Weaver, Paul R. C., *Familia Caesaris: A Social Study of the Emperor's Freedmen and Slaves*. London, 1972.

A Selection of Primary Sources

2855 Lewis, Naphtali, and M. Reinhold, *Roman Civilization*. New York, 1951.

WOMEN

Bibliographic Surveys

2856 Arthur, Marylin B., "Classics," *Signs* 2 (1976), 382–403.

2857 Pomeroy, Sarah B., "Selected Bibliography on Women in Antiquity," *Arethusa* 6 (1973), 125–157.

2858 Pomeroy, Sarah B., "Women in Classical Antiquity," *Study-Guide of the American Philological Association* (1977).

Special Studies

2859 Balsdon, John P.V.D., *Roman Woman*. London, 1962.

2860 Pomeroy, Sarah B., *Goddesses, Whores, Wives, and Slaves: Women in Classical Antiquity*. New York, 1975.

2861 Redfield, James, "The Women of Sparta," *Classical Journal* 73 (1977–78), 146–161.

A Selection of Primary Sources

2862 Lefkowitz, Mary R., and Maureen Fant, *Women in Greece and Rome*. Toronto, 1977.

DEMOGRAPHY

Reproduction

2863 Amundsen, D. W., and C. J. Diers, "The Age of Menarche in Classical Greece and Rome," *Human Biology* 41 (1969), 125–132.

2864 Amundsen, D. W., and C. J. Diers, "The Age of Menopause in Classical Greece and Rome," *Human Biology* 42 (1970), 79–86.

2865 Cameron, A., "The Exposure of Children and Greek Ethics," *Classical Review* 46 (1932), 105–114.

2866 Etienne, R., "La conscience médicale antique et la vie des enfants," *Annales de démographie historique* (1973), 15–46.

2867 Fontanille, Marie-Thérèse, *Avortement et contraception dans la médicine gréco-romaine.* Paris, 1977.

2868 Hopkins, Keith, "Contraception in the Roman Empire," *Comparative Studies in Society and History* 8 (1965–66), 124–151.

2869 Preuss, Anthony, "Biomedical Techniques for Influencing Human Reproduction in the Fourth Century B.C.," *Arethusa* 8 (1975), 237–263.

Population Studies

2870 Beloch, Julius, *Die Bevölkerung der griechisch-römischen Welt.* Berlin, 1886.

2871 Biezunska-Malowist, I., and M. Malowist, "La procréation des esclaves comme source de l'esclavage," *Mélanges offerts à Kazimierz Michalowski,* ed. Marie-Louise Bernhard (Warsaw, 1966), 275–280.

2872 Broadbent, Molly, *Studies in Greek Genealogy.* Leyden, 1968.

2873 Gomme, Arnold W., *The Population of Athens in the Fifth and Fourth Centuries B.C.* Oxford, 1933.

2874 Hopkins, K., "On the Probable Age Structure of the Roman Population," *Population Studies* 20 (1966), 245–264.

2875 Hume, David, *Of the Populousness of Ancient Nations.* London, 1872.

2876 Raepsaet, G., "A propos de l'utilisation de statistiques en démographie grecque. Le nombre d'enfants par famille," *L'Antiquité Classique* 42 (1973), 536–543.

2877 Salmon, Pierre, *Population et dépopulation dans l'Empire romain.* Bruxelles, 1974.

See also #365.

PSYCHOANALYSIS AND PSYCHOHISTORY

Bibliographic Surveys

2878 Arthur, Marylin B., "Classics and Psychoanalysis," *Study-Guide of the American Philological Association* (1977).

2879 Caldwell, Richard D., "Selected Bibliography on Psychoanalysis and Classical Studies," *Arethusa* 7 (1974), 115-134.

2880 Glenn, Justin, "Psychoanalytic Writings on Greek and Latin Authors, 1911-1960," *Classical World* 66 (1972), 129-145.

2881 Glenn, Justin, "Psychoanalytic Writings on Classical Mythology and Religion: 1909-1960," *Classical World* 70 (1976-77), 225-247.

Special Studies

2882 Africa, Thomas W., "The Mask of an Assassin: A Psychohistorical Study of M. Junius Brutus," *Journal of Interdisciplinary History* 8 (1977-78), 599-626.

2883 Slater, Philip E., *The Glory of Hera: Greek Mythology and the Greek Family.* Boston, 1958. Paperback reprint, Boston, 1971.

Selected Primary Sources

2884 Aristides, Aelius, *Sacred Teachings.*

2885 Aurelius, Marcus, *Meditations.*

2886 Cicero, *Letters.*

2887 Fronto, *Letters.*

2888 Nepos, *Lives.*

2889 Pliny the Younger, *Letters.*

2890 Plutarch, *Lives.*

2891 *Scriptores Historiae Augustae.* [*See* Arnaldo Momigliano, "Historia Augusta," *The Oxford Classical Dictionary* (2nd ed.; Oxford, 1970), 520-521.]

2892 Suetonius, *Lives of the Caesars.*

2893 Theophrastus, *Characters.*

2894 Lattimore, Richmond, *Themes in Greek and Latin Epitaphs.* Urbana, Ill., 1943. Paperback reprint, Urbana, 1962.

HISTORY OF CHILDHOOD

The Life Cycle

2895   Belmont, Nicole, "Levana, ou comment 'élever' les enfants," *Annales E.S.C.* 28 (1973), 77-89. Now in *Family and Society,* ed. Robert Forster and Orest Ranum (Baltimore, 1976), 1-15. (See #77)

2896   Brelich, Angelo, *Paides e Parthenoi.* Rome, 1969.

2897   Charlier, Marie-Thérèse, and Georges Raepset, "Etude d'un comportement social: les relations entre parents et enfants dans la société athénienne à l'époque classique," *L'Antiquité Classique* 40 (1970), 589-606.

2898   *The Conflict of Generations in Ancient Greece and Rome,* ed. Stephan Bertman. Atlantic Highlands, N.J., 1976.

2899   Eyben, E., "Das Denken des jungen Römers and sein Suchen nach Identität," *Ancient Society* 2 (1971), 77-104.

2900   Eyben, E., "Antiquity's View of Puberty," *Latomus* 31 (1972), 678-682.

2901   Eyben, E., "The Concrete Ideal in the Life of the Young Roman," *L'Antiquité Classique* 41 (1972), 200-217.

2902   Eyben, E., "Die Einteilung des menschlichen Lebens im römischen Altertum," *Rheinisches Museum für Philologie* 116 (1973), 150-190.

2903   Eyben, E., "Roman Notes on the Course of Life," *Ancient Society* 4 (1972), 213-238.

2904   French, Valerie, "History of the Child's Influence: Ancient Mediterranean Civilizations," *Child Effects on Adults,* ed. Richard Q. Bell and Lawrence V. Harper (Hillsdale, N.J., 1977), 3-29.

2905   Gernet, Louis, "Structures sociales, et rites d'adolescence dans la Grèce antique," *Revue des études grecques* 57 (1944), 242-248.

2906   Jeanmarie, Henri, *Couroi et Courètes: essai sur l'éducation spartiate et sur les rites d'adolescence dans l'antiquité hellénique.* Lille, 1939.

2907   Kassel, R., *Quomodo Quibus Locis apud Veteres Scriptores Graecos Infantes atque Parvuli pueri Inducantur Describantur Commemorentur.* Würzburg, 1954.

2908   Klein, Anita E., *Child Life in Greek Art.* New York, 1932.

2909   Morford, M.P.O., "The Training of Three Roman Emperors," *Phoenix* 22 (1968), 57-72.

2910   Raepsaet, G., "Les motivations de la natalité à Athènes aux Ve et IVe siècles," *L'Antiquité Classique* 40 (1971), 80-110.

2911   Reinhold, M., "The Generation Gap in Antiquity," *Proceedings of the American Philosophical Society* 104 (1970), 347-365.

Education

2912 Marrou, Henri Irénée, *Histoire de l'éducation dans l'antiquité.* 7th ed.; Paris, 1965. The 3rd ed. was translated by George Lamb as *A History of Education in Antiquity.* New York, 1956.

2913 Pomeroy, Sarah B., "Technikai kai Mousikai: The Education of Women in the Fourth Century and in the Hellenistic Period," *American Journal of Ancient History* 2 (1977), 51-68.

Selected Primary Sources

2914 Aristotle, *Politics,* 1136-1338.

2915 Augustinus [St. Augustine], *Confessions,* 1.

2916 Cicero, *On Old Age.*

2917 Macrobius, *Commentaries on "The Dream of Scipio,"* 67-71.

2918 Plato, *Laws,* 694, 789-795; *Republic,* 376-412.

2919 Plutarch, *Lives;* "Letter of Consolation to His Wife on the Death of Their Baby Daughter," *Moralia,* 608-612; "The Education of Children," *Moralia,* 1-14.

2920 Quintilian, *Institutio Oratoria,* 1.

2921 Seneca, *Epistle 12* "On Old Age."

2922 Solon, Lyric poem "The Ten Ages of Man." [Diehl 19; tr. R. Lattimore in *Greek Lyrics* (2nd ed.; Chicago, 1960), 23.]

2923 Xenophon, *The Boyhood of Cyrus.*

Italy

GENERAL SURVEYS AND COLLECTIONS

2924 Bellomo, Manlio, *La condizione giuridica della donna in Italia. Vicende antiche e moderna.* Turin, 1970.

2925 Besta, Enrico, *La famiglia nella storia del diritto italiano.* Milan, 1962.

2926 *Quaderni storici* 17 (1971): "Popolazione, società, economia."

2927 *Quaderni storici* 33 (1976): "Famiglia e communità."

2928 *Saggi di demografia storica,* ed. Carlo Corsini et al. Florence, 1969.

BIBLIOGRAPHY

2929 Golini, Antonio, *Bibliografia della opere demografiche in lingua italiana (1930–1965).* Rome, 1966.

MEDIEVAL AND EARLY RENAISSANCE ITALY (TO 1500)

2930 Bellomo, Manlio, *Problemi di diritto familiare nell'età dei comuni: Beni paterni e pars filii.* Milan, 1968.

2931 Bellomo, Manlio, *Profili della famiglia italiana nell'età dei comuni,* v. 1. Catania, 1966.

2932 Bellomo, Manlio, *Ricerche sui rapporti patrmoniali tra coniugi. Contributo alla storia della famiglia medievale (12°–13°).* Milan, 1961.

2933 Cherubini, Giovanni, *Signori, contadini, borghesi: Ricerche sulla società italiana del basso medioevo*. Florence, 1974.

2934 Chojnacki, Stanley, "Dowries and Kinsmen in Early Renaissance Venice," *Journal of Interdisciplinary History* 5 (1974-75), 571-600. Also in *Women in Medieval Society*, ed. Susan Mosher Stuard (Philadelphia, 1976), 173-198. (See #369)

2935 Chojnacki, Stanley, "In Search of the Venetian Patriciate: Families and Factions in the Fourteenth Century," *Renaissance Venice*, ed. J. R. Hale (London, 1973), 47-90. (#2961)

2936 Chojnacki, Stanley, "Patrician Women in Early Renaissannce Venice," *Studies in the Renaissance* 21 (1974), 173-203.

2937 Goldthwaite, Richard A., "The Florentine Palace as Domestic Architecture," *American Historical Review* 77 (1972), 977-1012.

2938 Goldthwaite, Richard A., *Private Wealth in Renaissance Florence*. Princeton, 1968.

2939 Herlihy, David, *The Family in Renaissance Italy*. St. Charles, Mo., 1974.

2940 Herlihy, David, "Family Solidarity in Medieval Italian History," *Explorations in Economic History* 7 (1969-70), 173-184.

2941 Herlihy, David, "Mapping Households in Medieval Italy," *Catholic Historical Review* 58 (1972), 1-24.

2942 Herlihy, David, "Marriage at Pistoia in the Fifteenth Century," *Bullettino storico pistoiese* 74 (1972), 3-21.

2943 Herlihy, David, "The Population of Verona in the First Century of Venetian Rule," *Renaissance Venice*, ed. J. R. Hale (London, 1973), 91-120. (See #2961)

2944 Herlihy, David, "Population, Plague and Social Change in Rural Pistoia, 1201-1430," *Economic History Review* 2nd series 18 (1965), 225-244.

2945 Herlihy, David, "Problems of Record Linkages in Tuscan Fiscal Documents of the Fifteenth Century," *Identifying People in the Past*, ed. E. Anthony Wrigley (London, 1973), 41-56. (See #158)

2946 Herlihy, David, "Some Social and Psychological Roots of Violence in the Tuscan Cities," *Violence and Civil Disorder in Italian Cities, 1200–1500*, ed. Lauro Martines (Berkeley, 1973), 129-154.

2947 Herlihy, David, "Vieillir au Quattrocento," *Annales E.S.C.* 24 (1969), 1338-1352.

2948 Herlihy, David, and Christiane Klapisch-Zuber, *Les toscans et leurs familles: une étude du catasto florentin de 1427*. Paris, 1978.

2949 Hughes, Diane Owen, "Domestic Ideals and Social Behavior: Evidence from Medieval Genoa," *The Family in History*, ed. Charles E. Rosenberg (Philadelphia, 1975), 115-143. (See #79)

2950 Hughes, Diane Owen, "Struttura familiare e sistemi di successione ereditaria nei testamenti dell'Europa medievale," *Quaderni storici* 33 (1976), 929-952.

2951 Hughes, Diane Owen, "Urban Growth and Family Structure in Medieval Genoa," *Past and Present* 66 (1975), 3-28.

2952 Kent, Francis William, "The Rucellai Family and Its Loggia," *Journal of the Warburg and Courtauld Institutes* 35 (1972), 397-401.

2953 Kent, Francis William, *Household and Lineage in Renaissance Florence: The Family Life of the Capponi, Ginori and Rucellai.* Princeton, 1977.

2954 Klapisch, Christiane, "L'enfance en Toscane au début du 15ᵉ siècle," *Annales de démographie historique* (1973), 99-122.

2955 Klapisch, Christiane, "Fiscalité et démographie en Toscane (1427-1430)," *Annales E.S.C.* 24 (1969), 1313-1337.

2956 Klapisch, Christiane, "Household and Family in Tuscany in 1427," *Household and Family...,* ed. Peter Laslett and Richard Wall (Cambridge, England, 1972), 267-281. (See #156)

2957 Klapisch, Christiane, "Parenti, amici, vicini. Il territorio urbano d'una famiglia mercantile nel XV secolo," *Quaderni storici* 33 (1976), 953-982.

2958 Klapisch, Christiane, and Michel Demonet, " 'A uno pane e uno vino': Structure et développement de la famille rurale toscane (début du 15ᵉ siècle)," *Annales E.S.C.* 27 (1972), 873-901.

2959 Lane, Frederick C., "Family Partnerships and Joint Ventures in the Venetian Republic," *Journal of Economic History* 4 (1944), 178-196.

2960 Martines, Lauro, "A Way of Looking at Women in Renaissance Florence," *Journal of Medieval and Renaissance Studies* 4 (1974), 15-28.

2961 *Renaissance Venice,* ed. J. R. Hale. London, 1973.

2962 Ross, James Bruce, "The Middle-Class Child in Urban Italy, Fourteenth to Early Sixteenth Century," *The History of Childhood,* ed. Lloyd De Mause (New York, 1974), 183-228. (See #154)

2963 Tamassia, Nino, *La famiglia italiana nei secoli decimoquinto e decimosesto.* Milan, 1911.

2964 Trexler, Richard C., "Le célibat à la fin du Moyen Age: les religieuses de Florence," *Annales E.S.C.* 27 (1972), 1329-1350.

2965 Trexler, Richard C., "The Foundlings of Florence, 1395-1455," *History of Childhood Quarterly* 1 (1973-74), 259-284.

2966 Trexler, Richard C., "Infanticide in Florence: New Sources and First Results," *History of Childhood Quarterly* 1 (1973-74), 98-116.

2967 Watkins, Renée Neu, *The Family in Renaissance Florence.* Columbia, S.C., 1969.

See also #290 and #339.

EARLY MODERN ITALY
(1500-1800)

2968 Borelli, Giorgio, *Un patriziato della terraferma veneta tra XVII e XVIII secolo: Ricerche sulla nobiltà veronese.* Milan, 1974.

2969 Borelli, Giorgio, "Nozze e doti i una famiglia nobiliare durante la prima metà del XVIII secolo," *Economia e Storia* 18 (1971), 321–342.

2970 Cipolla, Carlo M., "Four Centuries of Italian Demographic Development," *Population in History,* ed. David V. Glass and D.E.C. Eversley (London, 1965), 570–607. (See #214)

2971 Corsini, Carlo A., "Ricerche di demografia storica nel territorio di Firenze," *Quaderni storici* 17 (1971), 371–399.

2972 Corsini, Carlo A., "Lignes d'un programme pour l'étude de la population de la Toscane aux XVIIe, XVIIIe et XIXe siècles," *Pour connaître la population...,* ed. Carlo A. Corsini (Florence, 1974), 7–71. (See #2985)

2973 Corsini, Carlo A., "Materiali per lo studio della famiglia in Toscana nei secoli XVII-XIX: gli esposti," *Quaderni storici* 33 (1976), 998–1052.

2974 Corsini, Carlo A., "Recherches de démographie historique menées au département de mathématiques et de statistiques de l'Université de Florence," *Annales de démographie historique* (1972), 59–69.

2975 Corsini, Carlo A., M. Livi Bacci, and A. Santini, "Spoglio dei registri parrocchiali e ricostruzione delle famiglie in Italia. Problemi delle ricerche di demografia storica," *Saggi di demografia storica* (Florence, 1969), 7–17. (See #2928)

2976 Davis, James C., *A Venetian Family and Its Fortune, 1500–1900: The Donà and the Conservation of Their Wealth.* Philadelphia, 1975.

2977 Delille, Gérard, "Classi sociali e scambi matrimoniali nel Salernitano: 1500–1650 circa," *Quaderni storici* 33 (1976), 983–997.

2978 Del Panta, Lorenzo, "Quelques problèmes relatifs à l'utilisation de listes fiscales nominatives en démographie historique," *Pour connaître la population...,* ed. Carlo A. Corsini (Florence, 1974), 125–136. (See #2985)

2979 Duglio, Maria Ricciarda, "Alfabetismo e società a Torino nel secolo XVIII," *Quaderni storici* 17 (1971), 485–510.

2980 Fedele, Salvatore, "Struttura e movimento della popolazione in una parrocchia della Capitanata, 1711-1750," *Quaderni storici* 17 (1971), 447–485.

2981 Levi, Giovanni, "Mobiltà della popolazione e immigrazione a Torino nella prima metà del Settecento," *Quaderni storici* 17 (1971), 510–554.

2982 Levi, Giovanni, "Terra e strutture familiari in una comunità piedmontese del '700," *Quaderni storici* 33 (1976), 1095–1117.

2983 Litchfield, R. Burr, "Demographic Characteristics of Florentine Patrician Families, Sixteenth to Nineteenth Centuries," *Journal of Economic History* 29 (1969), 191–205. Italian translation in *Saggi di demografia storica* (Florence, 1969), 19–34. (See #2928)

2984 Livi Bacci, Massimo, "Quelques problèmes dans le couplage des données nominatives en Toscane, 17e-18e siècles," *Annales de démographie historiques* (1972), 323–333.

2985   *Pour connaître la population de la Toscane aux XVIIe, XVIIIe et XIXe siècles,* ed. Carlo A. Corsini. Florence, 1974.

NINETEENTH AND TWENTIETH CENTURIES

2986   Anselmi, Sergio, *Dimensione delle famiglie e ambiente economico in un centro marchigiano. Dal "Registro del Sale" al censimento del 1853.* Bologna, 1977.

2987   Banfield, Edward C., *The Moral Basis of a Backward Society.* New York, 1958.

2988   Davis, John H. R., *Land and Family in Pisticci.* London, 1973.

2989   Livi Bacci, Massimo, "The Fertility of Marriages in Tuscany during the XIXth Century: Results and Methodology," *Saggi di demografia storica* (Florence, 1969), 51–64. (See #2928)

2990   Maraspini, A. L., *The Study of an Italian Village.* Paris, 1968.

2991   Marongiu, Antonio, *La famiglia nell'Italia meridionale.* Milan, 1944.

2992   Pitkin, Donald S., "Marital Property Considerations among Peasants: An Italian Example," *Anthropological Quarterly* 33 (1960), 33–39.

2993   Pizzorno, Alessandro, "Amoral Familism and Historical Marginality," *International Review of Community Development* 15–16 (1966), 55–66.

2994   Santini, Antonio, "Cicli economici e fluttuazioni demografiche: nuzialità e natalità in Italia, 1893–94," *Quaderni storici* 17 (1971), 555–586.

2995   Ungari, Paolo, *Il diritto di famiglia in Italia dalle costituzioni "giacobine" al Codice civile del 1942.* Bologna, 1970.

Greece

BYZANTINE EMPIRE

2996 Antoniadis-Bibicu, Hélène, "Quelques notes sur l'enfant de la moyenne époque byzantine (de VIe au XIIe siècle)," *Annales de démographie historique* (1973), 77-84.

2997 Laiou, Angeliki E., "Peasant Names in Fourteenth Century Macedonia," *Byzantine and Modern Greek Studies* 1 (1975), 71-95.

2998 Laiou, Angeliki E., *Peasant Society in the Late Byzantine Empire.* Princeton, 1977.

2999 Patlagean, Evelyne, "L'enfant et son avenir dans la famille byzantine (IVe-XIIe siècles)," *Annales de démographie historique* (1973), 85-93.

3000 Patlagean, Evelyne, "Sur la limitation de la fécondité dans la haute époque byzantine," *Annales E.S.C.* 24 (1969), 1353-1369.

MODERN GREECE

3001 Allen, Peter S., "Aspida: A Depopulated Maniat Community," *Regional Variation in Modern Greece and Cyprus: Toward a Perspective on the Ethnography of Greece*, ed. Muriel Dimen and Ernestine Friedl (New York, 1976), 168-198.

3002 Andromedas, John N., "Greek Kinship Terms in Everyday Use," *American Anthropologist* 59 (1957), 1086-1088.

3003 Andromedas, John N., "The Enduring Urban Ties of a Modern Greek Folk Sub-Culture," *Contributions to Mediterranean Sociology*, ed. J. G. Peristiany (The Hague, 1968), 269-278.

3004 Andromedas, John N., "Maniat Folk Culture and the Ethnic Mosaic in the Southeast Peloponnese," *Regional Variation in Modern Greece and Cyprus,* ed. Muriel Dimen and Ernestine Friedl (New York, 1976), 199–206.

3005 Aschenbrenner, Stanley, "Folk Model vs. Actual Practice: The Distribution of Spiritual Kin in a Greek Village," *Anthropological Quarterly* 48 (1975), 65–68.

3006 Bardis, Panos D., "Main Features of the Greek Family during the Early Twentieth Century," *Alpha Kappa Deltan* 26 (1956), 17–21.

3007 Bardis, Panos D., "The Changing Family in Modern Greece," *Sociology and Social Research* 40 (1955), 19–23.

3008 Bardis, Panos D., "Influences on the Modern Greek Family," *Social Science* 32 (1957), 155–158.

3009 Bardis, Panos D., "A Comparative Study of Familism," *Rural Sociology* 24 (1959), 362–371.

3010 Blum, Richard, and Eva Blum, *The Dangerous Hour.* New York, 1970.

3011 Bialor, Perry, "Tensions Leading to Conflict and the Resolution and Avoidance of Conflict in a Greek Farming Community," *Contributions to Mediterranean Sociology,* ed. J. G. Peristiany (The Hague, 1968), 107–126.

3012 Burgel, Guy, *Pobia: etude géograhique d'un village crétois.* Athens, 1965.

3013 Campbell, John K., "The Kindred in a Greek Mountain Community," *Mediterranean Countrymen,* ed. Julian Pitt-Rivers (The Hague, 1963), 73–96.

3014 Campbell, John K., *Honour, Family, and Patronage.* Oxford, 1964.

3015 Campbell, John K., "Honour and the Devil," *Honour and Shame: The Values of Mediterranean Society,* ed. J. G. Peristiany (Chicago, 1966), 141–170.

3016 Campbell, John K., and Philip Sherrard, *Modern Greece.* London, 1968.

3017 Casselberry, Samuel E., and Nancy Valvanes, " 'Matrilocal' Greek Peasants and a Reconsideration of Residence Terminology," *American Ethnologist* 3 (1976), 215–226.

3018 Dubisch, Jill, "The Ethnography of the Islands: Tinos," *Regional Variation in Modern Greece and Cyprus,* ed. Muriel Dimen and Ernestine Friedl (New York, 1976), 314–327.

3019 du Boulay, Juliet, *Portrait of a Greek Mountain Village.* Oxford, 1974.

3020 du Boulay, Juliet, "Lies, Mockery and Family Integrity," *Mediterranean Family Structures,* ed. J. G. Peristiany (Cambridge, England, 1976), 389–406.

3021 Friedl, Ernestine, "The Role of Kinship in the Transmission of National Culture to Rural Villages in Mainland Greece," *American Anthropologist* 61 (1959), 30–38.

3022 Friedl, Ernestine, *Vasilika: A Village in Modern Greece.* New York, 1962.

3023 Friedl, Ernestine, "Some Aspects of Dowry and Inheritance in Boeotia," *Mediterranean Countrymen,* ed. Julian Pitt-Rivers (The Hague, 1963), 113–136.

3024 Friedl, Ernestine, "The Position of Women: Appearance and Reality," *Anthropological Quarterly* 40 (1967), 97–108.

3025 Friedl, Ernestine, "Kinship, Class and Selective Migration," *Mediterranean Family Structures,* ed. J. G. Peristiany (Cambridge, England, 1976), 363–387.

3026 Hirshon, Renée and Thakurdessai, "Society, Culture and Spatial Organization: An Athens Community," *Ekistics* 30 (1970), 187–196.

3027 Gavrielides, Nicolas, "Name Days and Feasting: Social and Ecological Implications of Visiting Patterns in a Greek Village of the Argolid," *Anthropological Quarterly* 47 (1974), 48–70.

3028 Hoffman, Susan M., "The Ethnography of the Islands: Thera," *Regional Variation in Modern Greece and Cyprus,* ed. Muriel Dimen and Ernestine Friedl (New York, 1976), 328–340.

3029 Kayser, Bernard, *Margariti: Village d'Epire.* Athens, 1964.

3030 Kenna, Margaret E., "Houses, Fields and Graves: Property and Ritual Obligation on a Greek Island," *Ethnology* 15 (1976), 21–34.

3031 Kenna, Margaret E., "The Idiom of Family," *Mediterranean Family Structure,* ed. J. G. Peristiany (Cambridge, England, 1976), 347–362.

3032 Lambiri [-Dimaki], Ioanna, *Social Change in a Greek Country Town: The Impact of Factory Work on the Position of Women.* Athens, 1965.

3033 Lambiri [-Dimaki], Ioanna, "I Prika sti Sihroni Elliniki Kinonia [Dowry in Contemporary Greek Society]," *Nea Oikonomia* 11–12 (1966), 883–888.

3034 Lambiri [-Dimaki], Ioanna, "The Impact of Industrial Employment on the Position of Women in a Greek Country Town," *Contributions to Mediterranean Sociology,* ed. J. G. Peristiany (The Hague, 1968), 261–268.

3035 Lambiri [-Dimaki], Ioanna, "Dowry in Modern Greece: An Institution at the Crossroads between Persistence and Decline," *Toward a Sociology of Women,* ed. Constantina Safilios-Rothschild (Lexington, Mass., 1972), 73–83.

3036 Lee, Dorothy, "Greece," *Cultural Patterns and Technical Change,* ed. Margaret Mead (New York, 1953), 77–114.

3037 Moustaka, Calliope, *The Internal Migrant.* Athens, 1964.

3038 Pechoux, Pierre-Yves, *Les paysans de la Rive Orientale du Bas Nestos (Thrace Grecque).* Athens, 1969.

3039 Photiadis, John, "Stavropolis Revisited: The Restudy of a Mountainous Greek Village," *The Greek Review of Social Research* 14 (1975), 136–162.

3040 Photiadis, John, "Changes in the Social Organization of a Greek Village," *Sociologia Ruralis* 16 (1976), 25–40.

3041 Potamianou, A., and C. Safilios-Rothschild, "Trends of Discipline in the Greek Family," *Human Relations* 24 (1971), 387–395.

3042 Psaltis, Egly, "Greece," *Women in the Modern World,* ed. Raphael Patai (New York, 1967), 131–152.

3043 Safilios-Rothschild, Constantina, "Morality, Courtship and Love in Greek Folklore," *Southern Folklore Quarterly* 29 (1965), 297-308.

3044 Safilios-Rothschild, Constantina, "Comparison of Power Structure and Marital Satisfaction in Urban Greek and French Families," *Journal of Marriage and the Family* 29 (1967), 345-352.

3045 Safilios-Rothschild, Constantina, "Deviance and Mental Illness in the Greek Family," *Family Process* 7 (1968), 100-117.

3046 Safilios-Rothschild, Constantina, "Attitudes of Greek Spouses toward Marital Infidelity," *Extramarital Relations*, ed. Gerhard Neubeck (Englewood Cliffs, N.J., 1969), 77-93.

3047 Safilios-Rothschild, Constantina, "Fertility and Family Dynamics," *International Population Conference, London*, v. 3 (Liege, 1969), 1852-1860.

3048 Safilios-Rothschild, Constantina, and John Georgiopoulos, "A Comparative Study of Parental and Filial Roles," *Journal of Marriage and the Family* 32 (1970), 381-389.

3049 Safilios-Rothschild, Constantina, " 'Honor' Crimes in Contemporary Greece," *Toward A Sociology of Women*, ed. Constantina Safilios-Rothschild (Lexington, Mass., 1972), 84-95. Originally in *British Journal of Sociology* 20 (1969), 205-218.

3050 Safilios-Rothschild, Constantina, "The Options of Greek Men and Women," *Sociological Focus* 5:2 (1972), 71-83.

3051 Safilios-Rothschild, Constantina, "The Relationship between Work Commitment and Fertility," *International Journal of Sociology of the Family* 2 (1972), 1-8.

3052 Safilios-Rothschild, Constantina, "Family Sociology in Greece," *Sociology and Eastern European Newsletter* 6:4 (1974), 5-6.

3053 Safilios-Rothschild, Constantina, "La mobilité sociale des femmes en Grèce," *Sociologie et Sociétés* 6:1 (1974), 105-126.

3054 Safilios-Rothschild, Constantina, *The Modern Greek Family: The Dynamics of the Husband-Wife Relationship and Parent-Child Relations and Family Modernity*. 3 v. Athens, 1974-75.

3055 Safilios-Rothschild, Constantina, "The Family in Athens: Regional Variations," *Regional Variation in Modern Greece and Cyprus*, ed. Muriel Dimen and Ernestine Friedl (New York, 1976), 410-418.

3056 Safilios-Rothschild, Constantina, "A Macro- and Micro-Examination of Family Power and Love: An Exchange Model," *Journal of Marriage and the Family* 38 (1976), 355-362.

3057 Sanders, Irwin T., "Village Social Organization in Greece," *Rural Sociology* 18 (1953), 366-375.

3058 Sanders, Irwin T., *Rainbow in the Rock: The People of Rural Greece*. Cambridge, Mass., 1962.

3059 Sanders, Irwin T., "Greek Society in Transition," *Balkan Studies* 8 (1967), 317-332.

3060   Schein, Muriel Dimen, "Only on Sundays," *Natural History* 80 (1971), 52-61. Also in *Man's Many Ways,* ed. Richard A. Gould (New York, 1973), 287-298.

3061   Spinellis, C. C., Vasso Vassiliou, and George Vassiliou, "Milieu Development and Male-Female Roles in Contemporary Greece," *Sex Roles in a Changing World,* ed. G. H. Seward and R. C. Williamson (New York, 1970), 308-317.

3062   Stott, Margaret A., "Economic Transition and the Family in Mykonos," *The Greek Review of Social Research* 17 (1972), 122-133.

3063   Tavuchis, Nicholas, "Naming Patterns and Kinship among Greeks," *Ethnos* 30 (1971), 152-162.

3064   Triandis, Harry C., and Vasso Vassiliou, "A Comparative Analysis of Subjective Culture," *The Analysis of Subjective Culture,* ed. Harry Triandis et al. (New York, 1972), 299-355.

3065   Vassiliou, George, *A Preliminary Exploration of Variables Related to Family Transaction in Greece.* Athens, 1966.

3066   Vassiliou, George, "Aspects of Parent-Adolescent Transaction in the Greek Family," *Adolescent in a Changing World,* ed. G. Kaplan and S. Lebovici (New York, 1969), 122-132.

3067   Vassiliou, George, and Vasso Vassiliou, "On Aspects of Child-Rearing in Greece," *The Child in His Family,* ed. E. J. Anthony and C. Koupernik (New York, 1970), 429-444.

3068   Wace, Alan J. B., and M. S. Thompson, *The Nomads of the Balkans: An Account of Life and Customs among the Vlachs of Northern Pindus.* London, 1914. Reprint, London and New York, 1972.

CYPRUS

3069   Attalides, Michael, "Changing Configurations of Greek Cypriot Kinship," *Kinship and Modernization in Mediterranean Society,* ed. J. G. Peristiany (Rome, 1976), 73-90.

3070   Loizos, Peter, "Changes in Property Transfer among Greek Cypriot Villages," *Man* 10 (1975), 503-524.

3071   Loizos, Peter, *The Greek Gift: Politics in a Cypriot Village.* New York, 1975.

3072   Markides, K., E. Nikita, and E. Rangou, *Social Change in a Cypriot Village.* Nicosia, 1976.

3073   Peristiany, J. G., "Honour and Shame in a Cypriot Highland Village," *Honour and Shame: The Values of Mediterranean Society,* ed. J. G. Peristiany (Chicago, 1966), 171-190.

3074   Peristiany, J. G., "Introduction to a Cyprus Highland Village," *Contributions to Mediterranean Sociology,* ed. J. G. Peristiany (The Hague, 1968), 75-92.

Eastern Europe, Russia, and the Balkans

GENERAL SURVEYS AND COLLECTIONS

3075 *Communal Families in the Balkans: The Zadruga: Essays by Philip E. Mosely and Essays in His Honor,* ed. Robert F. Byrnes. Notre Dame, Ind., 1976.

3076 Czap, Peter, Jr., "Russian History from a Demographic Perspective," *Demographic Developments in Eastern Europe,* ed. Leszek A. Kosinski (New York, 1977), 120–137. (See #3078)

3077 Danyi, D., "La démographie historique hongroise après la seconde guerre mondiale," *Annales de démographie historique* (1968), 206–235.

3078 *Demographic Developments in Eastern Europe,* ed. Leszek A. Kosinski. New York, 1977.

3079 *Introduction to Soviet Ethnography,* ed. Stephen P. Dunn and Ethel Dunn. 2 v. Berkeley, 1974.

3080 *Population and Migration Trends in Eastern Europe,* ed. Huey L. Kostanick. Boulder, Colo., 1977.

3081 Seraphim, P. H., "Von Wesen und Wert der Statistik in Osteuropa," *Archiv für Landes- und Volksforschung* 3 (1939), 194–207.

3082 *Sociology in the USSR,* ed. Stephen P. Dunn. White Plains, New York, 1969.

3083 *Soviet Ethnology and Anthropology Today,* ed. Yulian Bromley. The Hague, 1974.

3084 Szulc, Stefan, "The Polish Institute for the Scientific Investigation of Population Problems," *Population* 1 (1934), 14–35.

3085 Yatsounski, V. K., "Démographie historique en URSS," *Actes du colloque internationale de démographie historique Liège 18–20 avril, 1963* (Paris, n.d.), 237–247.

BIBLIOGRAPHIES AND REVIEW ESSAYS

3086 Anderson, Barbara A., "Data Sources in Russian and Soviet Demography," *Demographic Developments in Eastern Europe,* ed. Leszek A. Kosinski (New York, 1977), 23-63. (See #3078)

3087 Demeny, Paul, "Demography," *Language and Area Studies: East Central and Southeastern Europe,* ed. Charles Jelavich (Chicago, 1969), 183-199.

3088 Demko, George, "Demographic Research on Russia and the Soviet Union: A Bibliographic Review and Evaluation," *Demographic Developments in Eastern Europe,* ed. Leszek A. Kosinski (New York, 1977), 94-119. (See #3078)

3089 Dordevic, V., and D. Popovic, *Demografska bibliografia 1945-1961.* Belgrade, 1963.

3090 Dubester, Henry J., *National Censuses and Vital Statistics in Europe 1918-1939.* Washington, D.C., 1948.

3091 Dzherova, L., and N. Toteva, *Bibliografia na bulgarskata statisticheska literatura 1878-1960.* Sofia, 1961.

3092 *Eesti ajaloolise demograafia bibliograafia,* ed. H. Palli and R. Pullat. Tallinn, 1969.

3093 Freedman, Ronald, *The Sociology of Human Fertility: An Annotated Bibliography.* New York, 1975.

3094 International Population Census Bibliography: Europe: Census Bibliography No. 6. Austin, Tex., 1967.

3095 Kosinski, Leszek A., "Sources of Demographic Statistics in East Central Europe," *Demographic Developments in Eastern Europe,* ed. Leszek A. Kosinski (New York, 1977) 64-75. (See #3078)

3096 Kosinski, Leszek A., "Population Censuses in East Central Europe in the Twentieth Century," *East European Quarterly* 5 (1971), 279-301.

3097 Kosinski, Leszek A., "Statistical Yearbooks in East Central Europe," *Zeitschrift für Ostforschung* 23 (1974), 137-147.

3098 Kovacsics, Joseph, "Information über die Quellen- und Methodenfragen der ungarischen ortsgeschichtlichen Forschungen," *Actes du colloque internationale de démographie historique Liège 18-20 avril, 1963* (Paris, n.d.), 273-282.

3099 Krallert, W., "Geschichte und Methoden der Bevölkerungszählungen im Südosten. I. Rumänien," *Deutsches Archiv für Landes- und Volksforschung* 3 (1939), 489-508.

3100 Krotki, K. J., "Fertility and KAP Surveys in Eastern Europe and the Soviet Union," *Demographic Developments in Eastern Europe,* ed. Leszek A. Kosinski (New York, 1977), 76-93. (See #3078)

3101 Pascu, Stefan, "Les sources et les recherches démographiques en Roumanie (période préstatistique)," *Actes du colloque internationale de démographie historique Liège 18–20 avril, 1963* (Paris, n.d.), 283–303.

3102   *The Study of the Soviet Family in the USSR and in the West,* ed. Stephen P. Dunn and Ethel Dunn. Columbus, Ohio, 1977.

3103   Todorov, N., "Les documents osmano-turcs de la Bibliothèque nationale de Sofia en tant que source démographique," *Annales de démographie historique* (1970), 123–132.

3104   Todorov, N., "Démographie historique et onomastique. Etudes d'auteurs bulgares 1945–1967," *Annales de démographie historique* (1969), 485–503.

GENERAL EASTERN EUROPE, RUSSIA, AND THE SOVIET UNION

3105   Ain, Abraham, "Swislocz: Portrait of a Jewish Community in Eastern Europe," *Yivo Annual of Jewish Social Science* 4 (1949), 86–114.

3106   Anderson, Robert T., "Changing Kinship in Europe," *Kroeber Anthropological Society Papers* 28 (1963), 1–48.

3107   Barlau, Stephen B., "An Outline of Germanic Kinship," *Journal of Indo-European Studies* 4 (1976), 97–130.

3108   Berent, Jerzy, "Causes of Fertility Decline in Eastern Europe and the Soviet Union," *Population Studies* 24 (1970), 35–58.

3109   Brackett, J. W., and Earl Huyck, "The Objectives of Government Policies on Fertility Control in Eastern Europe," *Population Studies* 16 (1963), 134–146.

3110   Chojnacka, Helen, "Nuptiality Patterns in an Agrarian Society," *Population Studies* 30 (1976), 203–227.

3111   David, Henry P., *Family Planning and Abortion in the Socialist Countries of Central and Eastern Europe.* New York, 1970.

3112   Friedrich, Paul, "Proto-Indo-European Kinship," *Ethnology* 5 (1966), 1–36.

3113   Gwiazdomorski, Jan, "Le statut de la femme en Europe orientale à l'époque contemporaine," *Recueils de la Société Jean Bodin* 12 (1962), 689–734.

3114   Hearn, William E., *The Aryan Household: Its Nature and Development.* London, 1897.

3115   Hurvitz, Nathan, "Courtship and Arranged Marriages among Eastern European Jews Prior to World War I," *Journal of Marriage and the Family* 37 (1975), 422–430.

3116   Katz, Jacob, "Family, Kinship, and Marriage among Ashkenazim in the Sixteenth to Eighteenth Centuries," *Jewish Journal of Sociology* 1 (1959), 4–22.

3117   Kosven, M., *Matriarkhat. Istoriia problemy.* Moscow, 1948.

3118   Kovalevski, Maxime, "Marriage among Early Slavs," *Folklore* 1 (1890), 463–480.

3119   Landes, Ruth, and Mark Zborowski, "The Context of Marriage: Family Life as a Field of Emotions," *Comparative Perspectives on Marriage and the Family,* ed. H. Kent Geiger (Boston, 1968), 77–102.

3120 LePlay, Frédéric, *Les ouvriers européens.* v. 2: *Les ouvriers de l'orient.* Paris, 1877. (See #433)

3121 Lodge, Olive, "Socio-Biological Studies in the Balkans," *Population* 1 (1934), 55–82; 2 (1935), 111–148; 2 (1937), 60–80.

3122 McIntyre, Robert, "The Fertility Response to Abortion Reform in Eastern Europe: Demographic and Economic Implications," *American Economist* 16 (1972), 45–63.

3123 Matejko, Aleksander, *Social Change and Stratification in Eastern Europe.* New York, 1974.

3124 Moore, Wilbert, *Economic Demography of Eastern and Southern Europe.* New York, 1945.

3125 Peševa, Raina, "Late Patrimonial Traditions in the Social Organization of the Slavs," *Ethnologia Slavica* 3 (1972), 159–163.

3126 Revesz, Laszlo, *Der osteuropäische Bauer: Seine Rechtslage im 17. und 18. Jahrhundert unter besonderer Berücksichtigung Ungarns.* Bern, 1964.

3127 Roman, Stanislas, "Le statut de la femme dans l'Europe oriental (Pologne et Russie) au moyen âge et aux temps modernes," *Recueils de la Société Jean Bodin* 12 (1962), 389–404.

3128 Skar, June L., "The Role of Marriage Behavior in the Demographic Transition: The Case of Eastern Europe around 1900," *Population Studies* 28 (1974), 231–247.

3129 Tekse, K., "Some Characteristics of Fertility in Central and Southern Europe before World War I," *Demografia* 1 (1969), 23–48.

3130 Tomasic, Dinko A., *Personality and Culture in Eastern European Politics.* New York, 1948.

3131 Turner, Paul, *Slavisches Familienrecht.* Strassburg, 1874.

3132 Vinogradoff, Paul, "The Joint Family," *Anthropology and Early Law,* ed. Lawrence Krader (New York, 1966), 117–128.

3133 Zborowski, Mark, and Elizabeth Herzog, *Life Is with People.* New York, 1955. *See also* #308 and #416.

RUSSIAN EMPIRE AND THE SOVIET UNION

3134 Abdushelishchvili, M. G., *The Anthropology of Georgia's Ancient and Modern Populations.* Tbilisi, 1964.

3135 Banchikov, G. G., *Brak i sem'ia v mongolov.* Ulan-Ude, 1964.

3136 Baster, Nancy, "Some Early Family Budget Studies of Russian Workers," *Slavic Review* 17 (1958), 468–480.

3137   Benet, Sula, "Some Changes in Family Structure and Personality among Peasants of Great Russia," *Transactions of the New York Academy of Sciences* 32 (1970), 51–65.

3138   Bennigsen, A., "La famille musulmane en Union soviétique," *Cahiers du monde russe et soviétique* 1 (1960), 83–108.

3139   Beskrovnyi, L. G., V. N. Kabouzan, and V. K. Iatsounski, "Bilan démographique de la Russie en 1780–1815," *Annales de démographie historique* (1965), 127–134.

3140   Beskrovnyi, L. G., *Perepisi naseleniia Rossii. Itogovyie materialy podvornykh perepisei i revizii naseleniia Rossii (1646–1858).* Moscow, 1972.

3141   Bromley, Yulian V., *The Archaic Forms of the Communal Family.* Moscow, 1968.

3142   Brower, Daniel R., "Fathers, Sons, and Grandfathers: Social Origins of Radical Intellectuals in Nineteenth-Century Russia," *Journal of Social History* 2 (1968–69), 333–356.

3143   Chaplet, Pierre, *La famille et le droit des personnes dans la législation soviétique.* Rennes, 1929.

3144   Chinn, Jeff, *Manipulating Soviet Population Resources.* London, 1977.

3145   Coquin, François Xavier, *La Sibérie: Peuplement et immigration paysanne au 19e siècle.* Paris, 1969.

3146   Darskii, L. E., *Formirovanie sem'i: demografo-statisticheskoe issledovanie.* Moscow, 1972.

3147   Demko, George, "Divorce in the USSR: Spatial and Legal Changes 1940–1960," *Soviet Union* 1 (1974), 141–146.

3148   Destefanis, Michel, "La population active soviétique: structure et évolution," *Population* 26 (1971), 241–276.

3149   Dunn, Patrick P., " 'That Enemy Is the Baby': Childhood in Imperial Russia," *The History of Childhood,* ed. Lloyd DeMause (New York, 1974), 383–405. (See #154)

3150   Dunn, Stephen P., "Structure and Functions of the Soviet Rural Family," *The Soviet Rural Community,* ed. James R. Millar (Urbana, Ill., 1971), 325–345.

3151   Dunn, Stephen P., and Ethel Dunn, *The Peasants of Central Russia.* New York, 1967.

3152   Eason, Warren W., "The Population of the Soviet Union," *Population: The Vital Revolution,* ed. Ronald Freedman (Garden City, New York, 1964), 240–255.

3153   Eaton, Henry L., "Cadasters and Censuses of Muscowy," *Slavic Review* 26 (1967), 54–69.

3154   Eck, Alexandre, "La situation juridique de la femme russe au moyen âge," *Recueils de la Société Jean Bodin* 12 (1962), 405–420.

3155   Elnett, Elaine P., *Historic Origins and Social Development of Family Life in Russia.* New York, 1927.

3156   *The Family in Imperial Russia,* ed. David L. Ransel. Urbana, Ill., 1978.

3157 Friedrich, Paul, "The Linguistic Reflex of Social Change from Tsarist to Soviet Russian Kinship," *Sociological Inquiry* 36 (1966), 159-185.

3158 Friedrich, Paul, "Semantic Structure and Social Structure: An Instance from Russian," *Explorations in Cultural Anthropology: Essays in Honor of George Peter Murdock*, ed. Ward H. Goodenough (New York, 1964), 131-166.

3159 Geiger, H. Kent, "Deprivation and Solidarity in the Soviet Urban Family," *American Sociological Review* 20 (1955), 57-68.

3160 Geiger, H. Kent, "The Family and Social Change," *The Transformation of Russian Society*, ed. Cyril Black (Cambridge, Mass., 1960), 447-459.

3161 Geiger, H. Kent, *The Family in Soviet Russia*. Cambridge, Mass., 1968.

3162 Geiger, H. Kent, "The Soviet Family," *Comparative Family Systems*, ed. Meyer F. Nimkoff (Boston, 1965), 301-328. (See #49)

3163 Goerkhe, Carsten, "Einwohnerzahl und Bevölkerungsdichte altrussischer Städte. Methodische Möglichkeiten und vorläufige Ergebnisse," *Forschungen zur osteuropäischen Geschichte* 18 (1973), 25-53.

3164 Goerkhe, Carsten, "Die Sozialstruktur des mittelalterlichen Novgorod," *Untersuchungen zur gesellschaftlichen Struktur der mittelalterlichen Städte in Europa* (Stuttgart, 1966), 357-378.

3165 Gorodetsky, Perel, *La protection maternelle et infantile en Russie soviétique*. Paris, 1928.

3166 Gsovski, Vladimir, "Family and Inheritance in Soviet Law," *Soviet Society: A Book of Readings*, ed. Alex Inkeles and H. Kent Geiger (Boston, 1961), 530-540.

3167 Heer, David M., "The Demographic Transition in the Russian Empire and the Soviet Union," *Journal of Social History* 1 (1968-69), 193-240.

3168 Kabuzan, V. M., "La colonisation paysanne de la Novorussie de 1719 à 1857," *Annales de démographie historique* (1970), 297-301.

3169 Kabuzan, V. M., *Izmemeniia v razmeshchenii naseleniia Rossii v XVIII- pervoi polovine XIX v., po materialam revizii*. Moscow, 1971.

3170 Karapetian, E. T., *Armianskaia sem'einaia obshchina*. Yerevan, 1958.

3171 Kerblay, Basile, "L'évolution de l'isba aux XIXe et XXe siècles. Etat des travaux sur l'habitation paysanne en bois," *Cahiers du monde russe et soviétique* 12 (1972), 114-136.

3172 Kerblay, Basile, *L'Isba d'hier et d'aujourdhui: l'évolution de l'habitation rurale en URSS*. Lausanne, 1973.

3173 Keussler, Johannes von, *Zur Geschichte und Kritik des bäuerlichen Gemeindebesitzes in Russland*. 3 v. Aalen, 1970. Originally, Riga, 1876; St. Petersburg, 1882-87.

3174 Kharadze, R. L., *Gruzinskaia sem'einaia obshchina*. 2 v. Tbilisi, 1960-62.

3175 Kharchev, A. G., *Brak i sem'ia v SSSR*. Moscow, 1964.

3176 Kharchev, A. G., *Sem'ia v sovetskoi obshchestve*. n. p., 1960.

3177 Kharchev, A. G., "Marriage in the USSR, *Soviet Sociology* 5 (1967), 3-25.

3178 Kharchev, A. G., "On Some Results of a Study of the Motives for Marriage," *Soviet Sociology* 2 (1964), 41-51.

3179 Knabe, Bernd, "Die Struktur der russischen Posadgemeinden und der Katalog der Beschwerden und Forderungen der Kaufmannschaft (1762-1767)," *Forschungen zur osteuropäischen Geschichte* 22 (1975), 5-396.

3180 Koenig, Samuel, "Marriage and the Family among Galician Ukrainians," *Studies in the Science of Society*, ed. George Peter Murdock (New Haven, 1937), 299-318.

3181 Koval'chenko, Ivan Dmitrievich, *Russkoe krepostnoe krest'ianstvo v pervoi polovine XIX veka*. Moscow, 1967.

3182 Kovalevsky, Maksim M., *Modern Customs and Ancient Laws of Russia*. London, 1891. Reprint, New York, 1970.

3183 Kovalevsky, Maxime, "The Modern Russian Family," *Anthropology and Early Law*, ed. Lawrence Krader (New York, 1966), 148-170.

3184 Kozyrev, Julian, "The Family and Family Relations," *Town, Country, and People*, ed. Gennadii V. Osipov (London, 1969), 65-72.

3185 Kriukov, M. V., "Types of Kinship Systems and Their Historical Interpretation," *Soviet Anthropology and Archeology* 11 (1972), 107-150.

3186 Krupianskaia, V. Iu., and N. S. Polishchuk, *Kultura i byt rabochikh gornozavodskogo Urala, konets XIX–nachalo XX veka*. Moscow, 1971.

3187 Kurganov, Ivan A., *Sem'ia v SSSR 1917–1967*. New York, 1967.

3188 Leasure, J. W., and Robert A. Lewis, "Internal Migration in Russia in the Late Nineteenth Century," *Slavic Review* 27 (1968), 375-394.

3189 Leitsch, Walter, "Die Stadtbevölkerung im Moskauer Staat in der zweiten Hälfte des 17. Jahrhunderts," *Forschungen zur osteuropäischen Geschichte* 6 (1958), 170-207.

3190 Leontovich, F. I., *Istoriia russkago prava*. Moscow, 1902.

3191 Levin, Yu., "A Description of Systems of Kinship Terminology," *Soviet Ethnology and Anthropology Today*, ed. Yulian Bromley (The Hague, 1974), 123-132. (See #3083)

3192 Levshin, A., *Family and School in the USSR*. Moscow, 1958.

3193 Lewis, Robert A., Richard H. Rowland, and Ralph S. Clem, *Nationality and Population Change in Russia and the USSR: An Evaluation of Census Data 1897–1970*. New York, 1976.

3194 Lewis, Robert A., and J. W. Leasure, "Regional Population Changes in Russia and the USSR Since 1851," *Slavic Review* 25 (1966), 663-668.

3195 Lewis, Robert A., and R. H. Rowland, "Urbanization in Russia and the USSR: 1897-1966," *Annals of the Association of American Geographers* 59 (1969), 776-796.

3196 Lorimer, Frank, *The Population of the Soviet Union*. Geneva, 1946.

3197 Lynd, Robert S., "Ideology and the Soviet Family," *American Slavic and East European Review* 9 (1950), 268-278.

3198 Mace, David R., and Vera Mace, *The Soviet Family*. Garden City, New York, 1963.

3199 Madison, Berenice, "Russia's Illegitimate Children before and after the Revolution," *Slavic Review* 22 (1963), 82–95.

3200 Matossian, Mary, "The Peasant Way of Life," *The Peasant in Nineteenth-Century Russia*, ed. Wayne S. Vucinich (Stanford, 1968), 1–40.

3201 Maurer, Rose, "Recent Trends in the Soviet Family," *American Sociological Review* 9 (1944), 242–249.

3202 Mead Margaret, and Elena Calas, "Child Training Ideals in a Postrevolutionary Context: Soviet Russia," *Childhood in Contemporary Cultures*, ed. Margaret Mead and Martha Wolfenstein (Chicago, 1955), 179–203. (See #44)

3203 Megavorian, A. *Etude ethnographique et juridique sur la famille et le mariage Arméniens*. Lausanne, 1894.

3204 Merkov, A. M., *Dvizhenie naseleniia v Evropeiskoi Rossii za 1910*. Petrograd, 1916.

3205 Morlevat, Alban, *Le Mariage et le divorce en Russie soviétique depuis 1945*. Alger, 1951.

3206 Mosely, Philip E., "The Russian Family: Old Style and New," *Communal Families in the Balkans*, ed. Robert F. Byrnes (Notre Dame, Ind., 1976), 70–84. (See #3075)

3207 Noirault, Pierre, *La famille russe sous le régime communiste*. Poitiers, 1930.

3208 Pechoux, P., "La commune rurale dans *L'Empire des Tsars* de J. H. Schnitzler," *Cahiers du monde russe et soviétique* 6 (1965), 367–399.

3209 *The Peoples of Siberia*, ed. Maksim G. Levin and L. P. Potapov. Chicago, 1964. Russian original, Moscow, 1956.

3210 Pershits, A., "Early Forms of Family and Marriage in the Light of Soviet Ethnography," *Soviet Ethnology and Anthropology Today*, ed. Yulian Bromley (The Hague, 1974), 123–132. (See #3083)

3211 *Problemy byta, braka, i sem'i*, ed. N. Solov'ev. Vilnius, 1970.

3212 *Problemy demografii: voprosy teorii i praktiki*, ed. D. L. Broner and I. G. Venetskii. Moscow, 1971.

3213 Rappaport, Angelo Solomon, *Home Life in Russia*. New York, 1913.

3214 Rashin, Adolf G., *Naselenie Rossii za 100 let, 1811–1913, gg.: statisticheskie ocherki*. Moscow, 1956.

3215 Rekunov, F. N. *Ryazanskoe selo Korablinovo*. Riazan, 1957.

3216 *The Role and Status of Women in the Soviet Union*, ed. Donald R. Brown. New York, 1968.

3217 Schlesinger, Rudolf, *The Family in the USSR: Documents and Readings*. London, 1949.

3218 Schlesinger, Rudolf, *Changing Attitudes in Soviet Russia: The Family in the USSR*. London, 1949.

3219 Semenov, Ju. I., "The Problem of the Transition from the Matrilineal to the

Patrilineal Clan," *Soviet Anthropology and Archeology* 15 (1976–77), 3–28.

3220 Shanin, Teodor, *The Awkward Class: Political Sociology of Peasantry in a Developing Society: Russia 1910–1925.* Oxford, 1972.

3221 Shinn, W. T., "The Law of the Russian Peasant Household," *Slavic Review* 20 (1961), 601–621.

3222 Smith, Robert E. F., *Peasant Farming in Muscowy.* Cambridge, England, 1977.

3223 Stscherbakiwskyj, W., "The Early Ukrainian Social Order as Reflected in Ukrainian Wedding Customs," *Slavonic and East European Review* 31 (1953), 325–352.

3224 Szeftel, Marc, "Le statut juridique de l'enfant en Russie avant Pierre Le Grand," *Recueils de la Société Jean Bodin* 36 (1976), 635–656.

3225 Teitelbaum, Salomon M., "Parental Authority in the Soviet Union," *American Slavic and East European Review* 4 (1945), 54–69.

3226 Todoroff, Radoslav, *La recherche de la paternité naturelle en droit soviétique.* Toulouse, 1928.

3227 *Town, Country, and People,* ed. Gennadii V. Osipov. London, 1969.

3228 Vakar, Nicholas P., "Society and Family in Medieval Russia." Unpublished Harvard Thesis; Cambridge, Mass., 1946.

3229 Vardumjan, D. S., and E. T. Karapetjan, *Sem'ia i semeinyi byt kolkhoznikov Armenii.* Yerevan, 1963.

3230 Vasil'eva, E. K., *Sem'ia i ee funktsiia; demografo-statisticheskii analiz.* Moscow, 1975.

3231 *The Village of Viriatino,* ed. and tr. Sula Benet. Garden City, New York, 1970. Russian original, Moscow, 1958.

3232 Vladimirskii-Budanov, M. F., *Obzor istorii russkago prava.* 6th ed.; St. Petersburg, 1909.

3233 Volin, Lazar, "The Peasant Household under the Mir and the Kolkhoz in Modern Russian History," *Cultural Approaches to History,* ed. Caroline Ware (New York, 1940), 125–139.

3234 Volkov, Theodore, "Rites et usages nuptiaux en Ukraine," *L'Anthropologie* 2 (1891), 160–184, 407–437, 537–587; 3 (1892), 541–563.

3235 Vodarsky, Y. E., "Le movement migratoire de la population russe XVIIe–XVIIIe siècles," *Annales de démographie historique* (1970), 295–301.

3236 Zhirnova, G. V., "The Russian Urban Wedding Ritual in the Late 19th and Early 20th Centuries," *Soviet Anthropology and Archeology* 14 (1975–76), 18–38.

See also #39.

THE BALTIC STATES

3237 Deichman, I., *Sem'ia i semeinyi byt kolkhoznikov Pribaltiki.* Moscow, 1962.

3238　Danilauskas, A., "A Contribution to the Study of the Culture and Mode of Life of Lithuanian Workers," *Sociology in the USSR*, ed. Stephen P. Dunn (White Plains, New York, 1969), 230-235.

3239　Dunn, Stephen P., *Cultural Processes in the Baltic Area under Soviet Rule.* Berkeley, 1966.

3240　*Ergebnisse der baltischen Volkszählung von 29. December 1881.* 3 v. Mitau, Riga, Reval, 1883-1885.

3241　Grosset, O., *Biostatik der Stadt Dorpat und ihrer Landgemeinde in den Jahren 1860 bis 1881.* Dorpat, 1883.

3242　Haller, P., *Biostatik der Stadt Narva nebst Vorstädten und Fabriken in den Jahren 1860–1885.* Dorpat, 1866.

3243　Huebner, F., *Biostatik der Stadt Dorpat und ihrer Landgemeinde in den Jahren 1834–1859.* Dorpat,1861.

3244　*Istochnikovedcheskie problemy istorii narodov Pribaltiki.* Riga,1970.

3245　Jefremova, L. S. "Krest'ianskaia sem'ia v Latgalii po dannym inventarei 1847-1849 gg.," *Izvestiia Akademii Nauk Latviiskoi SSR* 10 (1971), 66-80.

3246　Jordan, P., *Die Resultate der estländischen Volkszählung vom 29. Dez. 1881.* Reval, 1886.

3247　Jordan, P., *Die Resultate der Volkszählung der Stadt Reval am 16. Nov. 1861.* Reval, 1874.

3248　Kahk, Ju., H. Ligi, H. Palli, S. Vahtre, R. Pullat, "L'histoire démographique de l'Estonie," *Annales de démographie historique* (1972), 425-446.

3249　Kieseritzky, W., v., *Biostatik der in fellinischer Kreise gelegenen Kirchspiele Oberpahlen, Pillistfer und Klein St. Johannis in den Jahren 1834–1880.* Dorpat, 1882.

3250　Körber, B., *Die Stadt Dorpat (Jurjew) in statistischer und hygenischer Beziehung.* Jurjew (Dorpat), 1902.

3251　Körber, B., *Biostatik der im dorptschen Kreise gelegenen Kirschspiele Ringen, Randen, Nüggen und Kawelwecht in den Jahren 1834–1859.* Dorpat, 1864.

3252　Palli, Heldur, "Historical Demography of Estonia in the 17th and 18th Centuries and Computers," *Studia Historica in Honorem Hans Kruus*, ed. Ju. Kahk and A. Vasar (Tallinn, 1971), 205-222.

3253　Palli, Heldur, "Parish Registers, Revisions of Land and Souls, Family Reconstitution and Household in Seventeenth and Eighteenth Century Estonia," *Chance and Change: Social and Economic Studies in Historical Demography in the Baltic Area*, ed. Sune Åkerman, Hans Christian Johansen, and David Gaunt (Odense, 1978), 143-146.

3254　Parming, Tönu, "Population Change in Estonia 1935-1970," *Population Studies* 26 (1972), 53-78.

3255　Plakans, Andrejs, "Familial Structure in the Russian Baltic Provinces: The Nineteenth Century," *Sozialgeschichte der Familie in der Neuzeit Europas*, ed. Werner Conze (Stuttgart, 1976), 346-362. (See #450)

3256 Plakans, Andrejs, "Identifying Kinfolk beyond the Household," *Journal of Family History* 2 (1977), 3-27.

3257 Plakans, Andrejs, "Peasant Families East and West," *Peasant Studies Newsletter* 2 (1973), 11-16.

3258 Plakans, Andrejs, "Peasant Farmsteads and Households in the Baltic Littoral, 1797," *Comparative Studies in Society and History* 17 (1975), 2-35.

3259 Plakans, Andrejs, "Seigneurial Authority and Peasant Family Life: The Baltic Area in the Eighteenth Century," *Journal of Interdisciplinary History* 5 (1974-75), 629-654.

3260 Sarmela, Matti, *Reciprocity Systems of the Rural Society in the Finnish-Karelian Culture Area.* Helsinki, 1969.

3261 Schroeder, Leopold von, *Die Hochzeitsgebräuche der Esten.* Berlin, 1888. Reprint, Hannover, 1975.

3262 *Sel'skie poseleniia Pribaltiki (XIII–XX vv.),* ed. Vadim A. Aleksandrov and H. V. Shligina. Moscow, 1971.

3263 Törne, Chr., *Biostatik der im dorptschen Kreise gelegenen Kirchspiele Ringen, Randen, Nüggen, and Kawelecht in den Jahren 1860–1881.* Dorpat, 1886.

3264 Vahtre, Sulev, *Estimaa talurahvas hingeloenduste andmeil 1782–1858.* Tallinn, 1973. [German summary 269-275]

3265 Vishnjauskaite, A., "Litovskaia krest'ianskaia sem'ia v proshlom i nastoiashchem," *Trudii Instituta etnografii* 23 (1954), 66-77.

POLAND AND CZECHOSLOVAKIA

3266 Bardach, Juliusz, "L'enfant dans l'ancien droît polonais et lituanien jusqu'à la fin du XVIIIᵉ siècle," *Recueils de la Société Jean Bodin* 36 (1976), 601-643.

3267 Baš, Angelos, "The Families of Foresters and Sawyers in the Southern Pohorje during the Period of the Capitalist Exploitation of Forests," *Ethnologia Slavica* 8 (1977), 217-224.

3268 Borowski, S., "Demographic Developments and the Malthusian Problem in the Polish Territories under German Rule," *Studia Historiae Oeconomicae* 3 (1969), 159-179.

3269 Eisenbach, A., and B. Grochulska, "La population de la Pologne aux confins du XVIIIᵉ et du XIXᵉ siècle," *Annales de démographie historique* (1965), 105-126.

3270 Frolec, Vaclav, "Formen des Hofes in Mähren und Schlesien," *Ethnologia Slavica* 5 (1973), 97-116.

3271 Frumkin, Grzegorz, "Pologne: dix années d'histoire démographique," *Population* 4 (1949), 695-712.

3272 Fügedi, E. "Zur demographischen Entwicklung vier slovakischer Dörfer im

Pilis-Gebirge in 18. und 19. Jh.," *Studia Slavica Academiae Scientiarum Hungaricae* 12 (1960), 139-145.

3273 Ganckaja, O., and N. Gracianskaja, "Zur Typologie des volkstümlichen Wohnhauses bei den Westslaven," *Ethnologia Slavica* 2 (1970), 61-79.

3274 Gieysztor, I., "La démographie de la Pologne à travers les âges," *Perspectives polonaises* (1966), 35-47.

3275 Golinska, S. D., "La population des villes en Pologne avant et après la guerre mondiale," *Proceedings of the International Congress for Studies on Population...*, ed. Corrado Gini (Rome, 1933-34), 6: 357-370.

3276 Havranek, J., "Social Classes, Nationality Relations and Demographic Trends in Prague 1880-1900," *Historica* 13 (1966), 171-208.

3277 Horska, Pavla, "Au sujet des différences interrégionales dans le développement démographique en Bohème," *Annales de démographie historique* (1971), 353-361.

3278 Horska, Pavla, "L'état actuel des recherches sur l'évolution de la population dans les pays tchèques aux 18e et 19e siècles," *Annales de démographie historique* (1967), 173-196.

3279 Husa, Vaclav, "Notes d'information sur les sources et les recherches de démographie historique en Tchècoslovaquie," *Actes du colloque internationale de démographie historique Liège 18-20 avril 1963* (Paris, n.d.), 237-247.

3280 Kacprzak, M., "Family Limitation in Poland," *Population* 2 (1935), 24-60.

3281 Kos-Rabcewicz-Zubkowski, Ludwik, "Régime matrimonial en Pologne," *Etude slaves et est-européennes* 2 (1957), 94-100, 180-183.

3282 Kula, Witold, "The Seigneury and the Peasant Family in Eighteenth Century Poland," *Family and Society*, ed. Robert Forster and Orest Ranum (Baltimore, 1976), 192-203. (See #77)

3283 Kula, Witold, *Théorie économique du système féodal.* Paris, 1970.

3284 Mauldin, Wayman Parker, and Donald S. Askens, *The Population of Poland.* Washington, D.C., 1954.

3285 Pavlik, Zdenek, "Nombre désire et nombre idéal d'enfants chez les femmes rurales en Bohème," *Population* 26 (1971), 915-932.

3286 Radvanova, Senta, *Manželstvi a rodina v ČSSR.* Prague, 1964.

3287 Rubner, H., "En forêt de Bohème: immigration et émigration 1500-1960," *Annales de démographie historique* (1970), 135-142.

3288 Srb, Vladimir, "Research Regarding Marriage and Parenthood in Czechoslovakia," *International Population Conference New York, 1961,* v. 1 (London, 1963), 138-148.

3289 Srb, Vladimir, "Population Development and Population Policy in Czechoslovakia," *Population Studies* 16 (1963), 147-159.

3290 Thomas, William I., and Florian Znaniecki, *The Polish Peasant in Europe and America.* 2 v. Chicago, 1918.

3291 Wojtun, Bronislaw, "Trends in Fertility in West Poland in the Nineteenth Century," *Susquehanna University Studies* 8 (1967), 69-78.

3292   Wynne, Waller, *The Population of Czechoslovakia.* Washington, D.C., 1953.
3293   Zubrzycki, J., "Emigration from Poland in the 19th and 20th Centuries," *Population Studies* 6 (1953), 248–272.

HUNGARY AND ROMANIA

3294   Andorka, Rudolf, "La prévention des naissances en Hongrie dans la région 'Ormansag' depuis la fin du XVIIIe siècle," *Population* 26 (1971), 63–78.
3295   Andorka, Rudolf, "Une exemple de faible fécondité légitime dans une région de la Hongrie," *Annales de démographie historique* (1972), 25–54.
3296   Chirot, Daniel, "The Romanian Communal Village: An Alternative to the Zadruga," *Communal Families...,* ed. Robert F. Byrnes (Notre Dame, Ind., 1976), 139–159. (See #3075)
3297   Csizmadia, Andor, "L'enfant dans le droit hongrois depuis le moyen âge jusqu'au milieu de 19e siècle," *Recueils de la Société Jean Bodin* 36 (1976), 517–542.
3298   Demeny, Paul, "Early Fertility Decline in Austria-Hungary: A Lesson in Demographic Transition," *Daedalus* 97 (1968), 502–522.
3299   D'Eszlari, Charles, "Le statut de la femme dans le droit hongrois," *Recueils de la Société Jean Bodin* 12 (1962), 421–446.
3300   Fel, Edit, and Tamas Hofer, *Proper Peasants: Traditional Life in a Hungarian Village.* Budapest, 1969.
3301   Herlea, Alexandru, "Aspects de l'histoire du statut juridique de l'enfant en Roumanie," *Recueils de la Société Jean Bodin* 36 (1976), 543–600.
3302   Herlea, Alexandru, "Etapes de l'histoire de la délinquance juvenile en Roumanie," *Recueils de la Société Jean Bodin* 38 (1977), 325–347.
3303   Herlea, Alexandru, "Sur l'histoire du droit à l'éducation de l'enfant en Roumanie," *Recueils de la Société Jean Bodin* 35 (1975), 323–344.
3304   Horvath, R. A., "The Scientific Study of Mortality in Hungary before the Modern Statistical Era," *Population Studies* 17 (1964), 187–212.
3305   Hunyadi, I., "La population d'un comitat hongrois (Gyor) en 1550," *Annales de démographie historique* (1974), 391–402.
3306   Kovacs, Aloys, "La statistique hongroise de la fécondité des mariages," *Proceedings of the International Congress for Studies on Population...,* ed. Corrado Gini (Rome, 1933–34), 6: 371–386.
3307   Kovacsics, J., "An Account of Research Work in Historical Demography in Hungary," *Actes de colloque internationale de démographie historique Liège 18–20 avril 1963* (Paris, n.d.), 249–272.
3308   Kovacsics, J., "Quelques problèmes dans les recherches de démographie historique en Hongrie," *Annales de démographie historique* (1972), 319–322.
3309   Kovacsics, J., "Situation démographique de la Hongrie à la fin du XVIIIe

siècle," *Annales de démographie historique* (1965), 83-104.

3310 Krohn, Else, *Die Eheschliessung bei den Rumänen*. Hamburg, 1926.

3311 Manuila, Sabin, *Structure et évolution de la population rurale*. Bucharest, 1940. [Romania]

3312 Pallos, E., *Life Tables of Hungary from 1900–01 to 1967–68*. Budapest, 1971.

3313 Ramnaeatzu, Peter, "The Growth of the Population of Rumania," *Population* 2 (1935), 108-110.

3314 Siegel, Jacob S., *The Population of Hungary*. Washington, D.C., 1958.

3315 Stahl, Henri H., *Les anciennes communautés villageoises Roumaines*. Bucharest and Paris, 1969.

3316 Stefanescu, St., "Géographie historique de la Roumanie: les concentrations démographiques et leur signification historique," *Annales de démographie historique* (1971), 341-350.

3317 Stukovsky, R., "Family Size and Menarcheal Age in Constanza, Romania," *Human Biology* 39 (1967), 277-283.

3318 Szabaady, Egon, "The Social and Demographic Changes of Hungarian Society during the Last 25 Years," *Social Change in Europe*, ed. B. W. Frijling (Leiden, 1973), 13-37.

3319 Thege, Jules de Konkoly, "Population Movement in Hungary," *Population* 2 (1937), 40-46.

3320 Wellmann, Imre, "Esquisse d'une histoire rurale de la Hongrie depuis la première moitié du XVIIIe siècle jusqu'au milieu du XIXe siècle," *Annales E.S.C.* 23 (1968), 1181-1210.

YUGOSLAVIA, BULGARIA, ALBANIA

3321 Avčin, Marin, "Gypsy Isolates in Slovenia," *Journal of Biosocial Science* 1 (1969), 221-234.

3322 Balen, M., "Family Relations and Their Changes in the Village of Jalzabet," *Sociologija* 4 (1962), 254-283.

3323 Baric, Lorraine, "Traditional Groups and New Economic Opportunities in Rural Yugoslavia," *Themes in Economic Anthropology*, ed. Raymond Firth (London, 1967), 253-281.

3324 Barjaktarovic, Mirko, "Forms of Ownership as Types of Traditional Institutions in Yugoslavia," *Ethnologia Slavica* 6 (1974), 109-114.

3325 Bennett, Brian C., *Sutivan: A Dalmatian Village in Social and Economic Transformation*. New York, 1974.

3326 Bogošic, V., "D'une forme particulière de la famille rurale chez les serbes et les croates," *Revue du droit international et de la législation comparée* 16 (1884), 374-409.

3327   Davis, James C., "A Slovene Laborer and His Experience of Industrialization 1888-1976," *East European Quarterly* 10 (1976), 3-20.

3328   Dibra, Jaho, and Pasko Vako, "La population de l'Albanie d'après les recensements de 1955 à 1960," *Population* 20 (1965), 253-264.

3329   Durham, Mary E., *High Albania*. London, 1909.

3330   Durham, Mary E., *Some Tribal Origins, Laws, and Customs of the Balkans*. London, 1928.

3331   Erlich, Vera, *The Family in Transition: A Study of 300 Yugoslav Villages*. Princeton, 1966.

3332   Erlich, Vera, "Phases in the Evolution of Family Life in Jugoslavia," *Sociological Review* 37 (1945), 50-64.

3333   Erlich, Vera, "The Southern Slav Patriarchal Family," *Sociological Review* 32 (1940), 224-241.

3334   First-Dilic, Ruza, "The Life Cycle of the Yugoslav Peasant Farm Family," *The Family Life Cycle in Euopean Societies*, ed. Jean Cuisenier and Martine Segalen (The Hague, 1977), 77-92. (See #297)

3335   Georgieva, I., "The Bulgarian Kinship System," *Ethnologia Slavica* 3 (1971), 151-156.

3336   Grossmith, C. J., "The Cultural Ecology of Albanian Extended Family Households in Yugoslav Macedonia," *Communal Families...*, ed. Robert F. Byrnes (Notre Dame, Ind., 1976), 232-243. (See #3075)

3337   Halpern, Joel M., and Barbara K. Halpern, *A Serbian Village in Historical Perspective*. New York, 1972.

3338   Halpern, Joel M., "Town and Countryside in Serbia in the Nineteenth Century: Social and Household Structure as Reflected in the Census of 1863," *Household and Family...*, ed. Peter Laslett and Richard Wall (Cambridge, England, 1972), 401-427. (See #156)

3339   Halpern, Joel M., and David Anderson, "The Zadruga: A Century of Change," *Anthropologica* 12 (1970), 83-97.

3340   Hammel, Eugene A., *Alternative Social Structure and Ritual Relations in the Balkans*. Englewood Cliffs, N.J., 1968.

3341   Hammel, Eugene A., "Reflections on the Zadruga," *Ethnologia Slavica* 7 (1977), 141-149.

3342   Hammel, Eugene A., "Serbo-Croatian Kinship Terminology," *Papers of the Kroeber Anthropological Society* 16 (1957), 45-75.

3343   Hammel, Eugene A., "Social Mobility, Economic Change, and Kinship in Serbia," *Southwestern Journal of Anthropology* 25 (1969), 188-197.

3344   Hammel, Eugene A., "Some Medieval Evidence on the Serbian Zadruga: A Preliminary Analysis of the Chrysobulls of Dečani," *Communal Families...*, ed. Robert F. Byrnes (Notre Dame, Ind., 1976), 100-116. (See #3075)

3345   Hammel, Eugene A., "The Zadruga as Process," *Household and Family...*, ed. Peter Laslett and Richard Wall (Cambridge, England, 1972), 335-373. (See #156)

3346 Ilieva, N., and Vera Oshavkova, "Changes in the Bulgarian Family Cycle from the End of the 19th Century to the Present Day," *The Family Life Cycle in European Societies*, ed. Jean Cuisenier and Martine Segalen (The Hague, 1977), 381–392. (See #297)

3347 Kapor-Stamilovic, Nila, and Berislav Beric, "Family Planning in Yugoslavia, with Special Reference to the Province of the Vojvodina," *Journal of Biosocial Science* 5 (1973), 179–186.

3348 Kondov, N., "Demografische Notizen über die Landbevölkerung aus dem Gebiet des unteren Strymon im XIV. Jahrhundert," *Etudes balkaniques* (1965), 261–272.

3349 Konsulowa, N. D., *Die Grossfamilie in Bulgarien*. Erlangen, 1915.

3350 Laslett, Peter, and Marilyn Clarke, "Houseful and Household in an 18th Century Balkan City," *Household and Family...*, ed. Peter Laslett and Richard Wall (Cambridge, England, 1972), 375–400. (See #156)

3351 Lodge, Olive, *Peasant Life in Jugoslavia*. London, 1941.

3352 Moritsch, Andrea, *Das nahe Triester Hinterland: Zur wirtschaftlichen und sozialen Entwicklung vom Beginn des 19. Jahrhunderts bis zur Gegenwart*. Vienna, 1969.

3353 Mosely, Philip E., "Adaptation for Survival: The Varzic Zadruga," *Communal Families...*, ed. Robert F. Byrnes (Notre Dame, Ind., 1976), 31–57. (See #3075)

3354 Mosely, Philip E., "The Distribution of the Zadruga within Southeastern Europe," ibid., 58–69.

3355 Mosely, Philip E., "The Peasant Family: The Zadruga or Communal Joint Family in the Balkans and Its Recent Evolution," *The Cultural Approach to History*, ed. Caroline F. Ware (New York, 1940), 95–108.

3356 Myers, Paul F., and Arthur A. Campbell, *The Population of Yugoslavia*. Washington, D.C., 1954.

3357 Novakovitch, D., *La zadrouga*. Paris, 1905.

3358 Pantelic, Nikola, "Snahacestvo in Serbia and Its Origin," *Ethnologia Slavica* 3 (1972), 171–179.

3359 Radossavlievitch, M., *L'évolution de la zadruga serbe*. Belgrade, 1886.

3360 St. Kassabov, Vladimir, "La Natalité en Bulgarie: Résultats, Perspectives, Politique," *Population* 29 (1974), 275–281.

3361 Sanders, Irwin T., *Balkan Village*. Lexington, Ky., 1949.

3362 Sanders, Irwin T., "Dragalevtsy Household Members Then (1935) and Now," *Population and Migration Trends...*, ed. Huey L. Kostanick (Boulder, Colo., 1977), 125–133. (See #3080)

3363 *Selected Papers on a Serbian Village: Social Structure as Reflected by History, Demography, and Oral Tradition*, ed. B. K. Halpern and J. M. Halpern. Amherst, Mass., 1977.

3364 Sicard, Emile, "The Zadruga Community: A Phase in the Evolution of Property and Family in an Agrarian Milieu," *Communal Families...*, ed. Robert F. Byrnes (Notre Dame, Ind., 1976), 252–265. (See #3075)

3365   Sicard, Emile, *La Zadruga dans la littérature serbe 1850–1912.* Paris, 1943.

3366   Sicard, Emile, *La Zadruga sud-slave dans l'évolution du groupe domestique.* Paris, 1943.

3367   Stefanov, Ivan, "Socio-Economic Changes and Internal Migration in Bulgaria," *Social Change in Europe,* ed. B. W. Frijling (Leiden, 1973), 38–53.

3368   Vinski, Zdenko, *Die südslavische Grossfamilie in ihrer Beziehung zum asiatischen Grossraum.* Zagreb, 1938.

3369   Whitaker, Ian, "Familial Roles in the Extended Patrilineal Kin Group in Northern Albania," *Mediterranean Family Structures,* ed. J. G. Peristiany (Cambridge, England, 1976), 195–203.

3370   Whitaker, Ian, "Tribal Structure and National Politics in Albania 1910–1950," *History and Social Anthropology,* ed. I. M. Lewis (London, 1968), 253–293.

3371   Winner, Irene, *A Slovene Village: Zerovnica.* Providence, R.I., 1971.

3372   Yovanovitch, A., *L'évolution historique de la zadrouga serbe.* Belgrade, 1896.

3373   Zoricic, M., *Die bäuerlichen Hauscommunion in den Königreichen Kroatien und Slavonien.* Budapest, 1897.

The Middle East and North Africa

GENERAL WORKS

3374 'Abdal-'Ati, Hammudah, "Modern Problems, Classical Solutions: An Islamic Perspective on the Family," *Journal of Comparative Family Studies* 2 (1974), 37–54.

3375 Anderson, J.N.D., "The Islamic Law of Marriage and Divorce," *Readings in Arab Middle Eastern Societies and Cultures,* ed. Abdulla M. Lutfiyya and Charles W. Churchill (The Hague, 1970), 492–504.

3376 Beck, D. F., "The Changing Moslem Family of the Middle East," ibid., 567–577.

3377 Berger, Morroe, "Men, Women and Families," *The Arab World Today* (New York, 1964), 117–153.

3378 Daumas, Melchior Joseph Eugène, *La vie arabe et la société musulmane.* Paris, 1869.

3379 Dirks, S., *La famille musulmane: son évolution au XXe siècle.* Paris, 1969.

3380 Dodd, Peter, "Family Honor and the Forces of Change in Arab Society," *International Journal of Middle East Studies* 4 (1973), 40–54.

3381 Dudley, Kirk, "Factors Affecting Moslem Natality," *Family Planning and Population Programs,* ed. Bernard Berelson (Chicago, 1966), 561–580.

3382 El-Daghestani, K., "The Evolution of the Moslem Family in the Middle Eastern Countries," *Readings in Arab Middle Eastern Societies and Cultures,* ed. Abdulla M. Lutfiyya and Charles W. Churchill (The Hague, 1970), 554–566.

3383 El-Haddad, Tahar, "Notre femme dans la loi et dans la société," *Revue des études islamiques* 3 (1935), 202–230.

3384 Gautier, Emile F., *Moeurs et coutumes des Musulmans.* Paris, 1931.

3385 Goode, William J., "Changing Family Patterns in Arabic Islam," *World Revolution and Family Patterns* (New York, 1963), 87–163.

3386 Jeffery, Arthur, "The Family in Islam," *The Family: Its Function and Destiny,* ed. Ruth Nanda Anshen. rev. ed.; (New York, 1959), 201-238. (See #82)

3387 Levy, Reuben, *Social Structure of Islam.* New York, 1965.

3388 Lutfiyya, Abdulla M., "The Family," *Readings in Arab Middle Eastern Societies and Cultures,* ed. A. M. Lutfiyya and Charles W. Churchill (The Hague, 1970), 505-525.

3389 Mernissi, Fatima, *Beyond the Veil: Male-Female Dynamics in a Modern Muslim Society.* New York, 1975.

3390 Morand, M., *La famille musulmane.* Alger, 1903.

3391 *Muslim Attitudes toward Family Planning,* ed. Olivia Schieffelin. New York, 1967.

3392 Naqvi, Sayed Ali Raza, "Modern Reforms in Muslim Family Laws—A General Study," *Islamic Studies* 13 (1974), 235-252.

3393 Nieuwenhuijze, C.A.D., *Sociology of the Middle East.* Leiden, 1971.

3394 Patai, Raphael, *Sex and Family in the Bible and the Middle East.* New York, 1959.

3395 Patai, Raphael, *Golden River to Golden Road.* Philadelphia, 1967.

3396 Seklani, Mahmoud, "La fecondité dans les pays arabes: données numériques, attitudes et comportements," *Population* 5 (1960), 831-856.

3397 Seibert, Ilse, *Women in the Ancient Near East.* New York, 1974.

3398 Shukri, Ahmed, *Muhammedan Law of Marriage and Divorce.* New York, 1966.

3399 Siddiqi, Mohammad Mazharuddin, *Women in Islam.* Lahore, 1959.

3400 Smith, Robertson W., *Kinship and Marriage in Early Arabia.* Boston, 1903.

3401 Sweet, Louise E., "In Reality: Some Middle Eastern Women," *Many Sisters,* ed. Carolyn J. Matthiasson (London, 1974), 379-397.

BIBLIOGRAPHIES

3402 Allman, James, Ben Achour Cherifa, and Toby Stone, *A Bibliography of Recent Social Sciences Research on the Family in the Arab States.* Beirut, 1974.

3403 *Arab Culture and Society in Change: A Partially Annotated Bibliography of Books and Articles in English, French, German and Italian,* ed. Centre d'études pour le monde arabe moderne. Beirut, 1973.

3404 Atiyeh, George N., *The Contemporary Middle East 1948–1973: A Selective Annotated Bibliography.* Boston, 1975.

3405 Gray, Audrey, *Childhood, Children and Child-Rearing in the Arab Middle East: A Selected and Annotated Bibliography.* Beirut, 1973.

3406 Hopwood, Derek, and Diana Grimwood-Jones, *Middle East and Islam: A Bibliographic Introduction.* Zug, 1972.

3407 Littlefield, David N., *The Islamic Near East and North Africa: An Annotated Guide to Books in English for Non-Specialists.* Littleton, Colo., 1977.

3408 Al-Qazzazz, Ayad, *Women in the Middle East and North Africa: An Annotated Bibliography.* Austin, 1977.

3409 Selim, George D., *American Doctoral Dissertations on the Arab World, 1883–1974.* Washington, D.C., 1976.

3410 Sweet, Louise, *The Central Middle East: A Handbook of Anthropology and Published Records on the Nile Valley, the Arab Levant, Southern Mesopotamia, the Arabian Peninsula, and Israel.* New Haven, 1971.

3411 Zuwiyya, Jalal, *The Near East (Southwest Asia and North Africa): A Bibliographic Study.* Metuchen, N.J., 1973.

THEORETICAL DISCUSSIONS: ETHNOLOGICAL AND JURISPRUDENTIAL

3412 Anderson, J.N.D., "Reforms in Family Law in Morocco," *Journal of African Law* 2 (1958), 146–159.

3413 Attiyah, P. S., "Some Problems of Family Law in the Sudan Republc," *Sudan Notes and Record* 39 (1958), 88–100.

3414 Ayoub, M. R., "Parallel Cousin Marriage and Endogamy, a Study in Sociometry," *Southeastern Journal of Anthropology* 15 (1959), 266–274.

3415 Barth, F., "Father's Brother's Daughter's Marriage in Kurdistan," *Southwestern Journal of Anthropology* 2 (1954), 164–171.

3416 Barth, F., "Descent and Marriage Reconsidered," *The Character of Kinship*, ed. Jack Goody (London, 1973), 3–19. (See #40)

3417 Belghiti, Malika, "Les relations féminines et le statut de la femme dans la famille rurale—dans trois villages de la Tessaout," *Etudes sociologiques sur le Maroc*, ed. A. Khatibi (Rabat, 1971), 289–361.

3418 Berque, Jacques, *Le systeme de parenté dans les sociétés musulmanes.* Paris, 1959.

3419 Berque, Jacques, "Qu'est-ce qu'une tribu nord-africaine?" *Le Maghreb, histoire et sociétés* (Algiers, 1974), 22–34.

3420 Black-Michaud, Jacob, *Cohesive Force: Feud in the Mediterranean and the Middle East.* Oxford, 1975.

3421 Bouhdiba, Abdelwahab, *La sexualité en Islam.* Paris, 1975.

3422 Bourdieu, P., "The Sentiment of Honour in Kabyle Society," *Honour and Shame: The Values of Mediterranean Society*, ed. J. G. Peristiany (London, 1965), 191–242.

3423 Bousquet, Georges Henri, *L'éthique sexuelle de l'Islam.* Paris, 1966.

3424 Bousquet, Georges Henri, *Justice française et coutumes kabyles.* Alger, 1950.

3425   Bousser, Khelladi, "Enquête sur le trousseau *(choura)* et la dot *(sadaq)* au Maroc," *Revue africaine* (1er & 2e trim 1942), 104-155.

3426   Brown, Cecil H., and Saad Sowayan, "Descent and Alliance in an Endogamous Society: A Structural Analysis of Arab Kinship," *Social Science Information* 16 (1977), 581-599.

3427   Brown, Cecil H., and Banu Ozertug, "Semantic Structure and Social Structure in a Central Anatolian Village," *Anthropological Quarterly* 47 (1974), 345-373.

3428   Chelhod, J., "Le mariage avec la cousine parallèle dans le système arabe," *L'Homme* 4 (1964), 113-173.

3429   Coulson, Noel James, *Succession in the Muslim Family.* Cambridge, England, 1971.

3430   Cuisenier, Jean, *Economie et parenté: leurs affinités de structure dans le domaine turc et dans le domaine arabe.* Paris, 1975.

3431   Djait, Hichem, *La personnalité et le devenir arabo-islamiques.* Paris, 1974.

3432   Fanon, Frantz, *A Dying Colonialism.* New York, 1965.

3433   Favret, J., "Relations de dépendance et manipulation de la violence en Kabylie," *L'Homme* 8 (1968), 18-44.

3434   Fernea, Robert A., and James Malarkey, "Anthropology of the Middle East and North Africa: A Critical Assessment," *Annual Review of Anthropology* 4 (1975), 183-206.

3435   Feroze, M. R., "The Reform of Family Laws in the Muslim World," *Islamic Studies* 1 (1962), 107-130.

3436   Gellner, Ernest, *Saints of the Atlas.* Chicago, 1969.

3437   Guichard, Pierre, *Structures sociales 'orientales' et 'occidentales' dans l'Espagne musulmane.* Paris, 1977.

3438   Hannah, Papeneck, "Purdah: Separate Worlds and Symbolic Shelter," *Comparative Studies in Society and History* 15 (1973), 289-325.

3439   Hanoteau, Adolphe A., and A. Letourneux, *La Kabylie et les coutumes kabyles.* 3 v. Paris, 1872-73.

3440   Hilal, J., "Father's Brother's Daughter's Marriage in Arab Communities: A Problem for Sociological Explanation," *Middle East Forum* 46 (1972), 73-84.

3441   Ibn Abī Zayd al-Qayrawānī, *La risâla; ou, Epître sur les éléments du dogme et de la loi de l'Islâm selon le rite mâlikite.* 5th ed.; Alger, 1968.

3442   Idris, Hady Roger, "Le mariage en occident musulman: analyse de fawvas médiévales extraits du 'Mi'yar' al-Wancharichi'," *Revue de l'Occident musulman et de la Méditerannée* (2e sem 1972), 45-62.

3443   Keyser, J.M.B., "The Middle Eastern Case: Is There a Marriage Rule?" *Ethnology* 12 (1974), 293-309.

3444   Khuri, Fuad, "Parallel Cousin Marriage Reconsidered: A Middle Eastern Practice That Nullified the Effects of Marriage on the Intensity of Family Relationships," *Man* 5 (1970), 597-618.

3445 Lecerf, J., "Note sur la famille dans le monde arabe et islamique," *Arabica* 3 (1956), 31–60.

3446 Mamood, Syed Tahir, *Family Law Reform in the Muslim World*. Bombay, 1972.

3447 Marcais, Philippe, "Réflexions sur la structure de la vie familiale chez les indigènes de l'Afrique du Nord," *Mémorial André Basset* (Paris, 1957), 69–82.

3448 Marcy, G., "Le mariage en droit coutumier zemmour," *Revue algérienne, tunisienne et marocaine de législation et de jurisprudence* (1930), 77–92; 141–158; 208–220; 221–241.

3449 Marcy, G., "Les vestiges de la parenté maternelle en droit coutumier berbère et le régme des successions touraegues," *Revue africaine* 85 (1941), 187–211.

3450 Markarius, Raoul, "Le mariage des cousins paralleles chez les Arabes," *Des Actes du VIe Congres international des sciences anthropologiques et ethnologiques, Paris, 30 juillet–6 août 1960*, v. 2a, ed. Pierre Champion et al. (Paris, 1963), 185–190.

3451 Maunier, René, "Famille kabyle et famille romaine," *Etudes de sociologie ethnologique et juridique* 3 (1930), 7–28.

3452 Meylan, Philippe, *Les mariages mixtes en Afrique du nord*. Paris, 1934.

3453 Mohsen, Safia K., "Aspects of the Legal Status of Women among the Awlad Ali," *Peoples and Cultures of the Middle East*, ed. Louise Sweet (Garden City, 1970), 200–233.

3454 Murphy, Robert F., "Tuareg Kinship," *American Anthropologist* 69 (1967), 163–170.

3455 Murphy, Robert F., and L. Kasdan, "The Structure of Parallel Cousin Marriage," *American Anthropologist* 61 (1959), 17–29.

3456 Murphy, Robert F., and L. Kasdan, "Agnation and Endogamy: Some Further Considerations," *Southwestern Journal of Anthropology* 23 (1967), 1–14.

3457 Nelson, Cynthia, "Public and Private Politics: Woman in the Middle Eastern World," *American Ethnologist* 1 (1974), 551–563.

3458 Nicolaisen, Johannes, "The Structural Study of Kinship Behaviour with Particular Reference to Tuarag Concept," *Folk* 13 (1971), 166–194.

3459 Patai, Raphael, "Cousin-Right in Middle Eastern Marriage," *Readings in Arab Middle Eastern Societies and Cultures*, ed. Abdulla M. Lutfiyya and Charles W. Churchill (The Hague, 1970), 535–553.

3460 Patai, Raphael, "The Structure of Endogamous Unilineal Descent Groups," *Southwestern Journal of Anthropology* 21 (1965), 235–250.

3461 Pesle, Octave, *Le mariage chez les malékites de l'Afrique du Nord*. Rabat, 1936.

3462 Peters, Emrys L., "Some Structural Aspects of the Feud among the Camel-herding Bedouin of Cyrenaica," *Africa* 37 (1967), 261–282.

3463 *Psychological Dimensions of Near Eastern Studies*, ed. L. Carl Brown and Norman Itzowitz. Princeton, 1977.

3464 Ripinsky, M. M., "Middle Eastern Kinship as an Expression of a Culture-Environment System," *Muslim World* 58 (1968), 225–241.

3465 Rosenfeld, Henry, "Social and Economic Factors in Explanation of the Increased Rate of Patrilineal Endogamy in the Arab Village in Israel," *Mediterranean Family Structures*, ed. J. G. Peristiany (Cambridge, England, 1976), 115–136.

3466 Schneider, J., "Of Viligance and Virgins: Honor, Shame and Access to Resources in Mediterranean Societies," *Ethnology* 10 (1971), 1–24.

3467 Stirling, A. Paul, "Land, Marriage and the Law in Turkish Villages," *International Social Science Bulletin* 9 (1957), 21–33.

3468 Tillion, Germaine, *Le harem et les cousins*. Paris, 1966.

3469 Villot, Etienne Cecile Edouard, *Moeurs, coutumes et institutions des indigènes de l'Algérie*. Alger, 1888.

3470 Williams, Judith R., "Extended Family as a Vehicle of Culture Change," *Human Organization* 24 (1965), 59–64.

3471 Ziadeh, Farhat J., "Equality *(Kafa'ah)* in the Muslim Law of Marriage," *The American Journal of Comparative Law* 6 (1957), 503–517.

SOCIAL HISTORY

3472 Baer, Gabriel, "Women and the Family," *Population and Society in the Arab East* (New York, 1964), 34–57.

3473 Berque, Augustin, "La Bourgeoisie algérienne," *Hesperis*, 35 (1948), 1–29.

3474 Berque, Augustin, "Equisse d'une histoire de la seigneurie algérienne," *Revue de la Méditerranée* 7 (1949), 18–34, 168–180.

3475 Berque, Jacques, *Histoire sociale d'un village égyptien au XX siècle*. Paris, 1957.

3476 Boudjedra, Rachid, *La vie quotidienne en Algérie*. Paris, 1971.

3477 Bourdieu, Pierre, and Abdelmalek Sayad, *Le déracinement; la crise de l'agriculture traditionnelle en Algérie*. Paris, 1964.

3478 Boyer, Pierre, *La vie quotidienne à Alger à la veille de l'intervention française*. Paris, 1964.

3479 Brown, Kenneth L., *People of Salé: Tradition and Change in a Moroccan City, 1830–1930*. Manchester, 1976.

3480 Brown, Leon Carl, *The Tunisia of Ahmed Bey, 1837–1855*. Princeton, 1974.

3481 Charnay, Jean-Paul, *La vie musulmane en Algérie: d'après la jurisprudence de la première moitié du XXe siècle*. Paris, 1965.

3482 Cohen, Abner, *Arab Border-Village in Israel: A Study of Continuity and Change in Social Organization*. Manchester, 1965.

3483 Dirks, Sabine, *La famille musulmane turque, son évolution au 20e siècle*. Paris, 1969.

3484 Eickelman, Dale, *Moroccan Islam: Tradition and Society in a Pilgrimage Center*. Austin, 1976.

3485 Evans-Pritchard, Edward Evan, *The Sanusi of Cyrenaica*. Oxford, 1949.

3486 Fauque, L. P., *Stades d'évolution de la cellule familiale musulmane d'Algérie*. Alger, 1959.

3487 Gordon, David C., *Women in Algeria: An Essay on Change*. Cambridge, Mass., 1968.

3488 Gouvion, Marthe and Edmond, *Kitab aâyane el-Marhariba*. Algiers, 1920. [text in French]

3489 Gouvion, Marthe and Edmond, *Kitab aâyane el-Marharib 'l-akfa esquisse générale des Moghrebs de la genèse à nos jours et livre des grands du Maroc*. Paris, 1939.

3490 Keller, James F., and Lloyd A. Mendelson, "Changing Family Patterns in Iran: A Comparative Study," *International Journal of Sociology of the Family* 1 (1971), 10-20.

3491 Kongar, Emre, "A Survey of Familial Change in Two Turkish *Gecekondu* Areas," *Mediterranean Family Structures*, ed. J. G. Peristiany (Cambridge, England, 1976), 205-218.

3492 Lesne, Marcel, *Evolution d'un groupement berbère: les Zemmour*. Rabat, 1959.

3493 Le Tourneau, Roger, "L'évolution de la famille musulmane en Afrique du Nord," *La France Méditerranéenne et Africaine* 3 (1938), 5-21.

3494 Le Tourneau, Roger, *Fes avant le Protectorat: étude économique et sociale d'une ville de l'occident musulman*. Casablanca, 1949.

3495 Maher, Vanessa, *Women and Property in Morocco: Their Changing Relation to the Process of Social Stratification in the Middle Atlas*. New York, 1975.

3496 Mantran, Robert, *La vie quotidienne à Constantinople au temps de Soliman le Magnifique et de ses successeurs (XVI et XVIIe siècles)*. Paris, 1965.

3497 Mazaheri, Aly Akbar, *La vie quotidienne des Musulmans au Moyen Age, X^e au XIIIe siècle*. Paris, 1951.

3498 Morgenstern, Julian, *Rites of Birth, Marriage, Death and Kindred Occasions among the Semites*. Cincinnati, 1966. Reprint, 1973.

3499 Pastner, Carroll M., "A Social Structural and Historical Analysis of Honor, Shame and Purdah," *Anthropological Quarterly* 45 (1972), 248-260.

3500 Penzer, N. M., *The Harem. An Account of the Institution as it Existed in the Palace of the Turkish Sultans with a History of the Grand Seraglio from its Foundation to the Present Time*. London, 1936.

3501 Saadia et La Khdar, *L'aliénation colonialiste et la résistance de la famille algérienne*. Lausanne, 1961.

3502 Vinogradov, Amal Rassam, *The Ait Ndhir of Morocco: A Study of the Social Transformation of a Berber Tribe*. Ann Arbor, 1974.

3503 Zeghari, M'hammed, "Evolution des structures familiales dans les pays en voie de transformation sociale, économique, politique et institutionelle," *Familles dans le monde* (1962), 132-149. [Morocco]

ETHNOGRAPHY AND SOCIOLOGY

3504 Abdal, Kafi, *Les mariages en Tripolitaine.* Tripoli, 1964.

3505 Abu Lughod, Janet, "Egyptian Marriage Adjustment: Microcosm of a Changing Society," *Marriage and Family Living* 23 (1961), 127-138.

3506 Abu-Zahra, N., "Family and Kinship in a Tunisian Peasant Community," *Mediterranean Family Structures*, ed. J. G. Peristiany (Cambridge, England, 1976), 157-172.

3507 Adam, André, *Une enquête auprès de la jeunesse musulmane du Maroc.* Aix-en-Provence, 1962.

3508 Adam, André, *Casablanca: essai sur la transformation de la société marocaine au contact de l'occident.* 2 v. Paris, 1972.

3509 Ajami, Ismail, "Social Classes, Family Demographic Characteristics and Mobility in Three Iranian Villages," *Sociologia Ruralis* 9 (1969), 62-72.

3510 Ammar, Hammed, *Growing Up in an Egyptian Village, Silwa, Province of Aswan.* London, 1954.

3511 Antoun, Richard T., *Arab Village: A Social Structural Study of a Trans-Jordanian Peasant Community.* Bloomington, 1972.

3512 Asad, Talal, *The Kababish Arabs: Power, Authority and Consent in a Nomadic Tribe.* London, 1970.

3513 Aswad, Barbara, *Property, Control and Social Strategies: Settlers on a Middle Eastern Plain.* Ann Arbor, 1971.

3514 Aswad, Barbara, "Visiting Patterns among Women of the Elite in a Small Turkish City," *Anthropological Quarterly* 47 (1974), 9-27.

3515 Ayrout, Henry Habib, *The Egyptian Peasant.* Boston, 1963.

3516 Barclay, Harold B., *Burri al Lamaab, a Surburban Village in the Sudan.* Ithaca, 1964.

3517 Baron, Anne-Marie, "Mariages et divorces à Casablanca," *Hesperis* 15 (1953), 419-440.

3518 Baron, Anne-Marie, and H. Pirot, "La famille prolétarienne," *Faits et idées* 91 (1955), 26-54.

3519 Barth, Fredrik, *Nomads of South Persia: The Basseri Tribe of the Khamesh Confederacy.* Boston, 1961.

3520 Basagana, Ramon, and Ali Sayad, *Habitat traditionnel et structures familiales en Kabylie.* Alger, 1974.

3521 Bates, Daniel G., "Normative and Alternative Systems of Marriage among the Yoruk of Southeastern Turkey," *Anthropological Quarterly* 47 (1974), 270-287.

3522 Benedict, Peter, "Aspects of the Domestic Cycle in a Turkish Provincial Town," *Mediterranean Family Structures,* ed. J. G. Peristiany (Cambridge, England, 1976), 219-242.

3523 Behnam, D., "Nuclear Families and Kinship Groups in Iran," *Diogenes* 76 (1971), 115-131.

3524 Ben Salem, L., "Le phénomène de mobilité sociale et ses incidences sur le milieu familial," *Revue tunisienne des sciences sociales* 4 (1967), 37-52.

3525 Berque, Jacques, *Structures sociales du Haut-Atlas.* Paris, 1955. [Morocco]

3526 Bertholon, Lucien Joseph, and E. Chantre, *Recherches anthropologiques dans la Berbèrie orientale, Tripolitaine, Tunisie, Algérie.* Lyon, 1913.

3527 Bettelheim, Bruno, *The Children of the Dream.* New York, 1969.

3528 Blackman, Winifred, *The Fellahin of Upper Egypt.* London, 1927.

3529 Bouhdiba, Abdelwahab, *A la recherche des normes perdues.* Tunis, 1965. [Tunisia]

3530 Bourdieu, Pierre, *The Algerians.* Boston, 1962.

3531 Bourrilly, J., *Eléments d'ethnographie marocaine.* Paris, 1932.

3532 Briggs, Lloyd Cabot, *Tribes of the Sahara.* Cambridge, Mass., 1960.

3533 Brown, Judith L. Evans, "Household Size and Childrearing Practices: An Observational Study in Tunisia." Ph.D. Dissertation, Harvard, 1972.

3534 Busch, R. C., "In-Laws and Out-Laws: A Discussion of Affinal Components of Kinship (Turkey)," *Ethnology* 11 (1972), 127-131.

3535 Camilleri, Carmel, "Modernity and the Family in Tunisia," *Journal of Marriage and the Family* 29 (1967), 590-595.

3536 Camilleri, Carmel, *Les relations parent-enfants en Tunisie.* Paris, 1966.

3537 Camilleri, Carmel, *Jeunesse, famille et développement: essai sur le changement socio-culturel dans un pays du Tiers Monde (Tunisie).* Paris, 1973.

3538 Chatila, Khaled, *Le mariage chez les musulmans en Syrie: étude de sociologie.* Paris, 1934.

3539 Chelhod, J., "Kinship and Marriage in the Yemen," *Ethnographie* 67 (1973), 47-90.

3540 Cole, Donald Powell, *Nomads of the Nomads: The Al Murrah Bedouin of the Empty Quarter.* Chicago, 1975.

3541 *Contemporary Egyptian Nubia,* ed. Robert A. Fernea. 2 v. New Haven, 1966.

3542 Cornaton, Michel, *Les regroupements de la décolonisation en Algérie.* Paris, 1967.

3543 Crapanzano, Vincent, *The Hamadsha: A Study in Moroccan Ethnopsychiatry.* Berkeley, 1973.

3544 Cresswell, Robert, "Lineage Endogamy among Maronite Mountaineers," *Mediterranean Family Structures,* ed. J. G. Peristiany (New York, 1976), 101-114.

3545 Cuisenier, Jean, "The Domestic Cycle in the Traditional Family Organization in Tunisia," ibid., 137-156.

3546 Cunningham, D., "Dimensions of Family Loyalty in the Arab Middle East:

The Case of Jordan," *Journal of Developing Areas* 8 (1973), 55–64.

3547 Cunnison, Ian George, *Baggara Arabs: Power and the Lineage in a Sudanese Nomad Tribe.* Oxford, 1966.

3548 Daghestani, Kazem, *Etude sociologique sur la famille musulmane contemporaine en Syrie.* Paris, 1932.

3549 Demeerseman, André, *La famille tunisienne et les temps nouveaux.* 2nd ed.; Tunis, 1972.

3550 Descloitres, Robert, et al., "Organisation urbaine et structures sociales en Algérie," *Civilisations* 12 (1962), 211–230; 13 (1963), 30–81.

3551 Descloitres, Robert, and Laid Debzi, "Système de parenté et structures familiales en Algérie," *Annuaire de l'Afrique du Nord* 2 (1963), 23–59.

3552 Desparmet, Joseph, *Coutumes, institutions, croyances des Musulmans de l'Algérie.* v. 1: *L'enfance, le mariage et la famille.* Alger, 1948.

3553 Dickson, Harold R. P., *The Arab of the Desert: A Glimpse into Badawin Life in Kuwait and Saudi Arabia.* London, 1949.

3554 Duprée, Louis and Nancy, "Women and Men: Afghanistan," *Common Ground* 2 (1976), 29–36.

3555 Duvignaud, Jean, *Change at Shebika: Report from a North African Village.* Austin, 1976. Originally, 1970.

3556 Eickelmen, Dale F., "Is There an Islamic City? The Making of a Quarter in a Moroccan Town," *International Journal of Middle Eastern Studies* 5 (1974), 274–294.

3557 Elwell-Sutton, L. P., "Family Relationships in Persian Folk-Literature," *Folklore* 87 (1976), 160–166.

3558 Evans-Pritchard, Edward Evan, *The Nuer.* Oxford, 1940.

3559 Fallers, Lloyd A. and Margaret C., "Sex Roles in Edremit," *Mediterranean Family Structures,* ed. J. G. Peristiany (New York, 1976), 243–260.

3560 *Family Formation Patterns and Health: An International Collaborative Study in India, Iran, Lebanon, Philippines, and Turkey,* ed. Abdel-Rahim Omran and C. C. Standley. Geneva, 1976.

3561 Farsoun, Karen, and Samih K. Farsoun, "Class and Patterns of Association among Kinsmen in Contemporary Lebanon," *Anthropological Quarterly* 47 (1974), 93–111.

3562 Farsoun, Samih K., "Family Structure and Society in Modern Lebanon," *Peoples and Cultures of the Middle East,* ed. Louise Sweet (Garden City, 1970), 257–307.

3563 Fernea, Elizabeth Warnock, *Guests of the Sheik: An Ethnography of an Iraqi Village.* New York, 1965.

3564 Fernea, Robert A., *Nubians in Egypt: Peaceful People.* Austin, 1970.

3565 Fernea, Robert A., *Shaykh and Effendi: Changing Patterns of Authority Among the El Shabana of Southern Iraq.* Cambridge, Mass., 1970.

3566 Fiedler, M., et al., "Contribution to the Research on Egyptian Nubian Descent Groups," *Archiv Orientální* 39 (1971), 434–472.

3567 Fuller, Ann, *Buarij: Portrait of a Lebanese Muslim Village*. Cambridge, Mass., 1961.

3568 Gaudefroy-Demombynes, Maurice, *Les cérémonies du mariage chez les indigènes de l'Algérie*. Paris, 1901.

3569 Gaudry, Mathéa, *La femme chaouia de l'Aurès: étude de sociologie Berbère*. Paris, 1929.

3570 Goichon, Amelie-Marie, *La vie féminine au Mzab: étude de sociologie musulmane*. 2 v. Paris, 1927-31.

3571 Goldberg, Harvey, "FBD Marriage and Demography among Tripolitanian Jews in Israel," *Southwestern Journal of Anthropology* 23 (1967), 177-191.

3572 Goshen-Gottstein, Esther R., *Marriage and First Pregnancy: Cultural Influences on Attitudes of Israeli Women*. London, 1966.

3573 Granquist, Hilma Natalia, *Birth and Childhood among the Arabs: Studies in a Muhammedan Village in Palestine*. Helsingfors, 1947.

3574 Granquist, Hilma Natalia, *Child Problems among the Arabs: Studies in a Muhammadan Village in Palestine*. Helsinki, 1950.

3575 Gulick, John, *Social Structure and Cultural Change in a Lebanese Village*. New York, 1955.

3576 Gulick, John, and Margaret Gulick, "Kinship, Contraception and Family Planning in the Iranian City of Isfahan," *Population and Social Organization*, ed. Moni Nag (The Hague, 1975), 241-293.

3577 Haddad, Anees Adib, "The Effects of Generation, Religion and Sex on the Relationship of Family Vertical Solidarity and Mental Health in Lebanon." Ph.D. Dissertation, University of Southern California, 1971.

3578 Hansen, Henny H., *Daughters of Allah: Among the Muslim Women in Kurdistan*. London, 1960.

3579 Hansen, Henny H., *The Kurdish Woman's Life: Field Research in a Muslim Society, Iraq*. Copenhagen, 1961.

3580 Hardy, Georges, and Louis Brunot, *"L'enfant marocain, essai d'ethnographie scolaire*. Paris, 1925.

3581 Harfouche, Jamal K., *Social Structure of Low-income Families in Lebanon*. Beirut, 1965.

3582 Hart, David, *The Aith Waryaghar of the Moroccan Rif: An Ethnography and History*. Tucson, 1976.

3583 Hazelton, Elaine, "Jawazi al-Malakim, Settled Bedouin Women," *Middle Eastern Muslim Women Speak*, ed. Elizabeth W. Fernea and B. Bezirgan (Austin, 1977), 263-270.

3584 Irons, William, *The Yomut Turkmen of Iran: A Study of Social Organization among a Central Asian Turkish-Speaking Population*. Ann Arbor, 1975.

3585 Jacob, J. A., "Maximes et proverbes populaires arabes: la famille," *Mélanges de l'Institut dominicain d'études orientales du Caire* 7 (1962), 35-80.

3586 Joseph, Suad, "Zainab: An Urban Working-Class Lebanese Woman," *Middle*

Eastern Muslim Women Speak, ed. Elizabeth W. Fernea and B. Bezirgan (Austin, 1977), 359-371.

3587 Khalaf, Samir, "Primordial Ties and Politics in Lebanon," *Middle Eastern Studies* 4 (1967-68), 243-269.

3588 Khalaf, Samir, "Family Associations in Lebanon," *Journal of Comparative Family Studies* 2 (1971), 235-250.

3589 Khayat, Marie Karam, and Margaret Clark Keatinge, "Homemaking," *Man, State and Society in the Contemporary Middle East,* ed. Jacob M. Landau (New York, 1972), 432-443.

3590 Khuri, Fuad I., "Sectarian Loyalty among Rural Migrants in Two Lebanese Suburbs: A Stage between Family and National Allegiance," *Rural Politics and Social Change in the Middle East,* ed. Richard T. Antoun and Illiya Harik (Bloomington, 1972), 198-209.

3591 Khuri, Fuad I., "A Profile of Family Associations in Two Suburbs of Beirut," *Mediterranean Family Structures,* ed. J. G. Peristiany (New York, 1976), 81-100.

3592 Kiray, Mubeccel, "The New Role of Mothers: Changing Intra-Familial Relationships in a Small Town in Turkey," ibid., 261-272.

3593 Lacoste-Dujardin, Camille, *Le conte kabyle: étude ethnologique.* Paris, 1970.

3594 Lahlou, A., "Etude sur la famille traditionnelle de Fes," *Revue de l'Institut de sociologie* 3 (1968), 407-441.

3595 Lahlou, A., "Etude sur la famille traditionnelle au Maroc: le mariage à Fes," *Institut des belles lettres arabes* [Tunis] 33 (1970), 323-346.

3596 Lane, Edward William, *Manners and Customs of the Modern Egyptians.* London, 1954. First published 1860.

3597 Lapham, R., "Modernisation et contraception au Maroc central: illustration de l'analyse des données d'une enquête, C.A.P.," *Population* 26 (1971), 79-104.

3598 Layish, Aharon, "Women and Succession in the Muslim Family in Israel," *Asian and African Studies* 9 (1973), 23-62.

3599 Legrain, Georges A., *Une famille copte de Haute-Egypte.* Brussels, 1945.

3600 Lichtenstadter, I., "An Arab-Egyptian Family," *The Middle East Journal* 6 (1952), 379-399.

3601 Lizot, Jacques, *Mitidja: un village algérien de l'ouarsenis.* Algiers, 1973.

3602 Louis, André, *Tunisie du Sud: Ksars et villages de crêtes.* Paris, 1975.

3603 Lutfiyya, Abdulla B., *Baytin: A Jordanian Village.* The Hague, 1966.

3604 Magnerella, Paul J., *Tradition and Change in a Turkish Town.* Cambridge, Mass., 1974.

3605 Mansur, Fatma, *Bodrum, a Town in the Aegean.* Leiden, 1972.

3606 Marx, Emanuel, *Bedouin of the Negev.* Manchester, 1967.

3607 Mas, Marie, "La petite enfance à Fes et à Rabat. Etude de sociologie citadine," *Annales de l'Institut d'études orientales* 17 (1959), 1-44; 18-19 (1960-61), 167-275; 20 (1962), 277-400.

3608 Masqueray, Emile, *La Formation des cités chez les populations sédentaires de l'Algérie (Kabyles du Djurdjura, Chaouias d l'Aures, Beni Mzab)*. Paris, 1886.

3609 *Mediterranean Countrymen,* ed. Julian Pitt-Rivers. The Hague, 1967.

3610 Michel, Andrée, *The Modernization of North African Families in the Paris Area.* The Hague, 1974.

3611 Miner, Horace, *The Primitive City of Timbuctoo.* Garden City, 1965.

3612 Miner, Horace, and George De Vos, *Oasis and Casbah: Algerian Culture and Personality in Change.* Ann Arbor, 1960.

3613 Mohsen, Safia K., "The Egyptian Woman: Between Modernity and Tradition," *Many Sisters,* ed. Carolyn J. Matthiason (London, 1974), 37-58.

3614 Mohsen, Safia K., "La consommation des familles musulmanes d'Algérie," *Population* 16 (1961), 117-122.

3615 Montety, H. de, *Le mariage musulman en Tunisie.* Paris, 1941.

3616 M'rabet, Fadéla, *La femme algérienne. Suivi de: les Algériennes.* Paris, 1969.

3617 Musil, Alois, *The Manners and Customs of the Rwala Bedouins.* New York, 1928.

3618 Najaf, Najmeh, and Helen Hinckley, *Reveille for a Persian Village.* New York, 1958.

3619 Najaf, Najmeh, and Helen Hinckley, *A Wall and Three Willows.* New York, 1967. [Iran]

3620 Olson-Prather, Emelie, "Family Planning and Husband-Wife Relationships in Turkey," *Journal of Marriage and the Family* 38 (1976), 379-385.

3621 Omran, Abdel R., "Islam and Fertility Control," *Egypt: Population Problems and Prospects,* ed. Abdel R. Omran (Chapel Hill, N.C., 1973), 165-180.

3622 Oubouzar, Sharon O., "Dzair: Kabyle Mothers, Daughters and Granddaughters in the Urban Environment of Algiers." Ph.D. Dissertation, University of Kansas, 1974.

3623 Ougouag-Kezzal, C. "Le sadaq et le mariage suivant le 'Urf' (rite) de Sidi Ma'ammar," *Libyca* 19 (1971), 235-241.

3624 Pacques, Viviana, *L'arbre cosmique dans la pensée populaire et dans la vie quotidienne du Nord-Ouest africain.* Paris, 1964.

3625 Pascon, Paul, and Mekki Bentahar, "Ce que disent 296 jeunes ruraux," *Etudes sociologiques sur le Maroc,* ed. Abdelkebir Khatibi (Rabat, 1971), 145-287.

3626 Patai, Raphael, "The Family," *The Republic of Lebanon,* ed. Raphael Patai (New Haven, 1956), 254-296.

3627 Pehrson, Robert N., *The Social Organization of the Marri Baluch.* New York, 1966.

3628 Peters, Emrys Lloyd, "Aspects of Affinity in a Lebanese Maronite Village," *Mediterranean Family Structures,* ed. J. G. Peristiany (New York, 1976), 27-80.

3629 Peters, Emrys Lloyd, "The Proliferation of Segments in the Lineage of the

Bedouin in Cyrenaica," *Journal of the Royal Anthropological Institute of Great Britian and Ireland* 90 (1960), 29-53. Reprinted in *Peoples and Cultures of the Middle East,* ed. Louise Sweet (Garden City, 1970), 363-398.

3630   Petersen, Karen Kay, "Family and Kin in Contemporary Egypt." Ph.D. Dissertation, Columbia University, 1967.

3631   Petran, Tabitha, "South Yemen Ahead on Women's Rights," *Middle East International* 48 (1975), 24-26.

3632   Prothro, Edwin T., *Child Rearing in the Lebanon.* Cambridge, Mass., 1961.

3633   Prothro, Edwin T., and Lutfy Najib Diab, *Changing Family Patterns in the Arab East.* Beirut, 1974.

3634   Rabin, Albert I., *Growing Up in a Kibbutz: Comparison of Children Brought Up in the Kibbutz and of Family-Reared Children.* New York, 1965.

3635   Reynaud, Commandant, "Une famille, un village, un marché dans le Rif," *Le Musée Social, Mémoires et Documents, Supplement aux Annales* (Paris, 1910), 317-348.

3636   Rice, Clare Colliver Hammond, *Persian Women and Their Ways.* London, 1923. Reprint, Tehran, 1976.

3637   Rizk, Hanna, "Social and Psychological Factors Affecting Fertility in the United Arab Republic," *Marriage and Family Living* 25 (1963), 69-73.

3638   Rizk, Hanna, "Fertility Pattern in Egypt," *Actes du XIIe Congrès international de sociologie* 1 (1958), 651-666.

3639   Rosenfeld, H., "An Analysis of Marriage Statistics for a Moslem and Christian Arab Village," *International Archives of Ethnography* 48 (1957), 32-62.

3640   Rosenfeld, H., "Change, Barriers to Change, and Contradictions in the Arab Village Family," *American Anthropologist* 70 (1968), 732-752.

3641   Rosenfeld, H., "The Contradictions between Property, Kinship and Power as Reflected in the Marrige System of an Arab Village," *Contributions to Mediterranean Sociology,* ed. J. G. Peristiany (Paris, 1968), 247-260.

3642   Salim, Shakir M., *Marsh Dwellers of the Euphrates Delta.* London, 1962.

3643   Sanjana, Darab Dastur Peshotan, *Next of Kin Marriage in Old Iran.* London, 1888.

3644   Saunders, Lucy Wood, "Umm Ahmad: A Village Mother of Egypt," *Middle Eastern Muslim Women Speak,* ed. Elizabeth W. Fernea and B. Bezirgan (Austin, 1977), 219-230.

3645   Seddon, David, "Aspects of Kinship and Family Structure among the Ulad Stut of Zaio Rural Commune, Nador Province, Morocco," *Mediterranean Family Structures,* ed. J. G. Peristiany (New York, 1976), 173-194.

3646   Sertel, Ayse Kudat, "Ritual Kinship in Eastern Turkey," *Anthropological Quarterly* 44 (1971), 37-50.

3647   Servier, Jean, "Un exemple d'organisation politique traditionnelle: une tribu kabyle, les Iflissen-Lebhar," *Revue de l'occident musulman et de la Méditerranée* 2 (1966), 169-188.

3648 Spiro, Melford, *Children of the Kibbutz: A Study in Child Training and Personality*. rev. ed.; Cambridge, Mass., 1975. 1st ed.; 1958.

3649 Stirling, Paul, *Turkish Village*. London, 1965.

3650 Strouhal, E., "Marriage Pattern in Egyptian Nubia," *Annals of the Naprstek Museum* 5 (1966), 81-109.

3651 Sweet, Louise, *Tell Togaan: A Syrian Village*. Ann Arbor, 1960.

3652 Sweet, Louise, "Visiting Patterns and Social Dynamics in a Lebanese Druze Village," *Anthropological Quarterly* 47 (1974), 112-119.

3653 Sweet, Louise, "The Women of 'Ain ad Dayr,' " *Anthropological Quarterly* 40 (1967), 167-183.

3654 Sweetser, Anne T., *Family Formation Attitudes among High School Girls in Kabul, Afghanistan: A Study in Population and Social Change*. New York, 1976.

3655 Talmon-Gerber, Yonina, *Family and Community in the Kibbutz*. Cambridge, Mass., 1972.

3656 Thorne, Melvyn, and Joel Montague, "Family Planning and the Problems of Development," *Change in Tunisia*, ed. Russell A. Stone and John Simmons (New York, 1976), 201-216.

3657 al-Tikriti, Yunis Hummadi, "Industrialization, Urbanization, and Family Organization in the Middle East." Ph.D. Dissertation, University of Missouri, 1968.

3658 Touba, Jacquiline Rudolph, "Sex Role Differentiation in Iranian Families Living in Urban and Rural Areas of a Region Undergoing Planned Industrialization in Iran (Arak Shahrestan)," *Journal of Marriage and the Family* 37 (1975), 437-445.

3659 Van Dusen, Roxann A., "Changing Women's Roles and Family Planning in Lebanon," *Culture, Natality and Family Planning*, ed. John F. Marshall and Steven Polgar (Chapel Hill, 1974), 79-96.

3660 _ieille, P., and M. Kotobi, "Familles et unions de familles en Iran," *Cahiers internationaux de sociologie* (1966), 93-104.

3661 Wassink, M. W. Graeff, "Opinion Survey on Mixed Marriages in Morocco," *Journal of Marriage and the Family* 29 (1967), 578-589.

3662 Westermarck, Edward Alexander, *Marriage Ceremonies in Morocco*. London, 1914.

3663 Williams, Judith R., *The Youth of Haouch el-Harimi, a Lebanese Village*. Cambridge, Mass., 1968.

3664 Williams, Neil Vincent, "Factory Employment and Family Relationships in an Egyptian Village." Ph.D. Dissertation, University of Michigan, 1964.

3665 Yankey, D., "Some Immediate Determinants of Fertility Differences in Lebanon," *Marriage and Family Living* 25 (1963), 27-34.

3666 Youssef, Nadia H., "Differential Labor Force Participation of Women in Latin American and Middle Eastern Countries: The Influence of Family Characteristics," *Social Forces* 51 (1972), 135-153.

3667 Zghal, A., "Système de parenté et système coopératif dans les campagnes tunisiennes," *Civilisations* 19 (1969), 483–496.

AUTOBIOGRAPHY, BIOGRAPHY, AND FICTION

3668 Adivar, Halide Edib, *Memoirs of Halide Edib.* New York, 1926.

3669 Amrouche, Fadhma aith Mansour, *Histoire de ma vie.* Paris, 1968. [Algeria]

3670 Ben Cheikh, A., "Tableau de notre vie familiale," *Institut des belles lettres arabes* [Tunis] 22 (1959), 179–191.

3671 Bonjean, François J., *Confidences d'une fille de la nuit.* Tangiers, 1969. Originally, Paris, 1939.

3672 Chraibi, Driss, *Heirs to the Past.* London, 1972. [Morocco]

3673 Corrèze, Françoise, *Femmes des mechtas: témoignage sur l'Est algérien.* Paris, 1976.

3674 Dib, Mohammed, *La grande maison.* Paris, 1952. [Algeria]

3675 Diqs, Isaak, *A Bedouin Boyhood.* London, 1967.

3676 Djavidan Hanum, Princess, *Harem Life.* New York, 1801. [Egypt]

3677 Etienne, J. d', "Une famille marocaine," *Cahiers de l'Afrique et l'Asie* (Paris, 1950), 6–51.

3678 Feraoun, Mouloud, *Le fils du pauvre.* Paris, 1954. [Algeria]

3679 Fernea, Elizabeth Warnock, *A Street in Marrakech: A Personal Encounter with the Lives of Moroccan Women.* New York, 1975.

3680 Fernea, Elizabeth Warnock, "Begum Agha Kahan's Wedding Present," *A View of the Nile* (New York, 1970), 203–226.

3681 Kemal, Yashar, *The Wind from the Plain.* London, 1963. [Turkey]

3682 Kulthum, Umm, "Excerpts from the Umm Kulthum Nobody Knows as Told by Umm Kulthum, Famed Egyptian Singer, to Mahumd 'Awad," *Middle Eastern Muslim Women Speak,* ed. Elizabeth W. Fernea and B. Bezirgan (Austin, 1976), 135–166.

3683 Mahfouz, Naguib, *Midaq Alley.* London, 1975. [Egypt]

3684 Makal, Mahmut, *A Village in Anatolia.* London, 1954. 2nd ed.; London, 1972.

3685 Mehdevi, Anne Sinclair, *Persia Revisited.* New York, 1964.

3686 Mehdevi, Anne Sinclair, *Persian Adventure.* New York, 1953.

3687 Montety, Hide, *Femmes de Tunisie.* Paris, 1958.

3688 Nesin, Aziz, *Istanbul Boy.* Austin, 1976.

3689 Orga, Irfan, *Portrait of a Turkish Family.* New York, 1950.

3690 Riley, Isaac, *Syrian Home Life.* New York, 1874.

3691 Sefrioui, Ahmed, *La boîte à merveilles.* Paris, 1954. [Morocco]

3692 Zenati, R. and A., *Bou-el-nouar, le jeune algérien.* Algiers, 1945.

3693   Zerdouni, Nefissa, *Enfants d'hier: l'éducation de l'enfant en milieu tradition-nel algérien.* Paris, 1970.

Africa South of
the Sahara

GENERAL SURVEYS AND COLLECTIONS

3694 *African Systems of Kinship and Marriage,* ed. A. R. Radcliffe-Brown and
      D. Forde. London, 1950.

3695 Anderson, James, *Family Law in Asia and Africa.* London, 1968.

3696 Ardener, E., *Divorce and Fertility: An African Study.* London, 1967.

3697 Arinoala, Olagohe, *The African Wife.* London, 1965.

3698 Balandier, George, *The Sociology of Black Africa.* New York, 1970.

3699 Berhard, G., *The African Life, The Urban Family.* Paris, 1968.

3700 Boserup, Esther, *Women's Role in Economic Development.* New York, 1970.

3701 Clignet, Remi, *Many Wives, Many Powers.* Evanston, 1970.

3702 Colson, Elizabeth, and Max Gluckman, *Seven Tribes of British Central Africa.*
      Manchester, 1961.

3703 Costa, J., "The New African Family within the Rights of Independence (An
      Essay of Normative Sociology)," *L'année sociologique* 22 (1971), 153–180.

3704 *Development of the Urban Family in Africa South of the Sahara.* New York,
      1958.

3705 *Domestic Rights and Duties in Southern Ghana,* ed. Christine Oppong. Legon,
      Ghana, 1974.

3706 "Evolution and Problems of the Urban Family in Africa South of the Sahara,"
      U.S. Joint Publications Research Service 14348 (1962), 1–43.

3707 *The Family Estate in Africa,* ed. Robert F. Gray and P. H. Gulliver. London,
      1964.

3708 *French Perspectives in African Studies,* ed. Pierre Alexandre. London, 1973.

3709 Goody, Jack, *Comparative Studies in Kinship.* Stanford, 1969.

3710 Goody, Jack, "The Mother's Brother and the Sister's Son in West Africa," *Jour-
      nal of the Royal Anthropological Institute* 89 (1959), 61–88.

3711 Goody, Jack, and S. J. Tambiah, *Bridewealth and Dowry*. Cambridge, England, 1973.

3712 Kuper, Leo, *An African Bourgeoisie*. New Haven, 1965.

3713 Little, Kenneth, and Anne Price, "Some Trends in Modern Marriage among West Africans," *Africa* 37 (1967), 407–424.

3714 Mair, Lucy, *African Marriage and Social Change*. London, 1969.

3715 *Marriage in Tribal Societies*, ed. Meyer Fortes. London, 1962.

3716 Meillassoux, Claude, *Femmes, greniers et capitaux*. Paris, 1975.

3717 Murdock, George P., *Africa: Its Peoples and Their Culture History*. New York, 1959.

3718 *Slavery in Africa*, ed. Igor Kopytoff and Suzanne Miers. Madison, 1977.

3719 *Survey of African Marriage and Family Life*, ed. Arthur Phillips. London, 1953.

3720 Tuden, Arthur, and L. Plotnicov, *Social Stratification in Africa*. New York, 1970.

3721 Vincent, J. F., *African Women in Urban Environments*. Paris, 1966.

3722 Wipper, Audrey, "The Roles of African Women: Past, Present and Future," *Canadian Journal of African Studies* 6 (1972), 143–147.

3723 *Women, Culture and Society: A Theoretical Overview*, ed. Michelle Z. Rosaldo and Louise Lamphere. Stanford, 1974.

3724 *Women in Africa*, ed. Nancy Hafkin and Edna Bay. Stanford, 1976.

BIBLIOGRAPHIES

3725 Asamani, J. O., *Index Africanus*. Stanford, 1975.

3726 *Cumulative Bibliography of African Studies*, ed. International African Institute. 5 v. Boston, 1973. Cumulated from the bibliographic entries in *Africa* 1–40 (1929–70) and *International African Bibliography*.

3727 Delacourt, A., *Bibliography of Ethnographic Research in East Africa*. Leeds, 1967.

3728 Dinstel, Marion, *List of French Doctoral Dissertations on Africa, 1884–1961*. Boston, 1966.

3729 Duignan, Peter, *United States and Canadian Doctoral Dissertations on Africa*. Ann Arbor, 1973.

3730 *International African Bibliography*, ed. International African Institute. London, 1971 ff.

3731 Ita, Nduntuoni, *Bibliography of Nigeria: A Survey of Anthropological and Linguistic Writings from the Earliest Times to 1966*. London, 1971.

3732 Kratochvil, Laura, *African Women: A Select Bibliography*. Cambridge, England, 1975.

PRE-COLONIAL AND
TRADITIONAL AFRICA

3733   Aryee, A. F., "Christianity and Polygamy in Ghana: The Role of the Church as an Instrument of Social Change," *Ghana Journal of Sociology* 3 (1967), 98–105.

3734   Beattie, J.H.M., "Nyoro Kinship, Marriage, and Affinity," *Africa* 27 (1957), 317–340; 28 (1958), 1–23.

3735   Bohannan, Laura, "Dahomean Marriage: A Revaluation," *Africa* 19 (1949), 273–287.

3736   Caplan, Ann Patricia, *Choice and Constraint in a Swahili Community.* London, 1975.

3737   Chaplin, J. H., "Wiving and Thriving in Northern Rhodesia," *Africa* 32 (1962), 111–122.

3738   Childs, Stanley H., "Christian Marriage in Nigeria," *Africa* 16 (1946), 238–246.

3739   Cohen, David W., *Womunafu's Bunafu: A Study of Authority in a Nineteenth-Century African Community.* Princeton, 1977.

3740   Cunnison, Ian, "Perpetual Kinship: A Political Institution of the Luapula Peoples," *Rhodes-Livingston Journal* 20 (1956), 28–48.

3741   Davidson, J., "Protestant Missions and Marriage in the Belgian Congo," *Africa* 18 (1948), 120–128.

3742   Douglas, Mary, "Matriliny and Pawnship in Central Africa," *Africa* 34 (1964), 301–313.

3743   Driberg, J. H., "The Status of Women among the Nilotes and Nilo-Hamites," *Africa* 5 (1932), 404–421.

3744   Elam, Yitzchak, *The Social and Sexual Roles of Hima Women.* Manchester, 1973.

3745   Evans-Pritchard, Edward Evan, *Kinship and Marriage among the Nuer.* Oxford, 1951.

3746   Evans-Pritchard, Edward Evan, *The Position of Women in Primitive Societies and Other Essays in Social Anthropology.* London, 1965.

3747   Fallers, L. A., "Some Determinants of Marriage Stability in Bugosa: A Reformulation of Gluckman's Hypothesis," *Africa* 27 (1957), 106–124.

3748   Forde, Daryll, *Yako Studies.* Oxford, 1964.

3749   Fortes, Meyer, "The First Born," *Journal of Child Psychology and Psychiatry* 15 (1974), 81–104.

3750   Gluckman, Max, "Marriage Payments and Social Structure among the Lozi and Zulu," *Kinship,* ed. Jack Goody (London, 1971), 227–247.

3751   Goody, Jack, and Esther Goody, "The Circulation of Women and Children in Northern Ghana," *Man* 2 (1967), 226–249.

3752   Gough, Kathleen, "Nuer Kinship: A Re-examination," *The Translation of Culture,* ed. T. O. Beidelman (London, 1971), 79–121.

3753 Gulliver, P. H., *The Family Herds*. London, 1955.

3754 Gulliver, P. H., *Social Control in an African Society*. London, 1963.

3755 Jackson, Michael, *The Kuranko*. London, 1977.

3756 Jackson, Michael, "The Structure and Significance of Kuranko Clanship," *Africa* 44 (1974), 397-416.

3757 Kaberry, Phyllis, *Women of the Grassfields*. London, 1952.

3758 Kopytoff, Igor, "Matrilineality, Residence, and Residential Zones," *American Ethnologist* 4 (1977), 539-559.

3759 Krige, Eileen Jensen, "Woman-Marriage, With Special Reference to the Lovedu—Its Significance for the Definition of Marriage, " *Africa* 44 (1974), 11-38.

3760 Kuper, Adam, "The Kgalagari and the Jural Consequences of Marriage," *Man* 5 (1970), 466-483.

3761 Kuper, Adam, "The Social Structure of Sotho-Speaking Peoples of Southern Africa," *Africa* 45 (1975), 67-82.

3762 Lancaster, C. S., "Brideservice, Residence and Authority among the Goba (N. Shona) of the Zambezi Valley," *Africa* 44 (1974), 46-65.

3763 Laurentin, Anne, "Nzakara Women," *Women of Tropical Africa,* ed. Denise Paulme (Berkeley, 1963), 121-178.

3764 Leith-Ross, Sylvia, *African Women: A Study of the Ibo of Nigeria*. London, 1939.

3765 Lewis, I. M., *Marriage and the Family in Northern Somaliland*. Kampala, 1962.

3766 *Man and Woman among the Azande,* ed. Edward Evan Evans-Pritchard. London, 1974.

3767 Meek, C. K., "Marriage by Exchange in Nigeria—A Disappearing Institution," *Africa* 9 (1936), 64-74.

3768 Meillassoux, Claude, *Anthropologie économique des Gouro de Côte d'Ivoire*. Paris, 1964.

3769 Meillassoux, Claude, "L'économie des échanges precoloniaux en pays Gouro," *Cahier d'études africaine* 3 (1963), 551-576.

3770 Middleton, John, *Lugbara Religion*. London, 1960.

3771 Muller, Jean-Claude, "Ritual Marriage, Symbolic Fatherhood and Invitation among the Rukuba, Plateau Benue State, Nigeria," *Man* 7 (1972), 283-296.

3772 Ndeti, Kivuto, *Elements of Akamba Life*. Nairobi, 1972.

3773 Netting, Robert McC., "Household Organisation and Intensive Agriculture: The Kofyar Case," *Africa* 35 (1965), 422-428.

3774 Paulme, Denise, "The Social Condition of Women in Two West African Societies," *Man* 48 (1948), 44.

3775 Porter, R., "The Crispe Family and the African Trade in the Seventeenth Century," *Journal of African History* 9 (1968), 57-77.

3776 Priestley, Margaret, *West African Trade and Coast Society: A Family Study*. London, 1969.

3777   Reyburn, William D., "Polygamy, Economy and Christianity in the Eastern Cameroon," *Practical Anthropology* 6 (1959), 1-19.

3778   Richards Audrey I., "African Kings and Their Royal Relatives," *Journal of the Royal Anthropological Institute* 91 (1961), 135-150.

3779   Rigby, Peter, *Cattle and Kinship among the Gogo*. Ithaca, New York, 1969.

3780   Rigby, Peter, "Joking Relationships, Kin Categories, and Clanship among the Gogo," *Africa* 38 (1968), 133-156.

3781   Robin, J., "Evolution of Traditional Marriages among the Moslems of Senegal," *Africa* 17 (1947), 192-201.

3782   Shapera, I., *Married Life in an African Tribe*. London, 1940.

3783   Shorter, Aylward, "Animal Marauders and Family Morality in Africa," *Africa* 42 (1972), 1-9.

3784   Siquet, M., "Legal and Customary Status of Women," *La Promotion de la femme au Congo et en Ruanda-Urundi* (Brussels, 1956), 197-251.

3785   Skinner, E. P., "Intergenerational Conflict among the Mossi: Father and Son," *Journal of Conflict Resolution* 5 (1961), 55-60.

3786   Southall, Aidan W., *Alur Society*. Cambridge, England, 1953.

3787   Stauder, Jack, *The Majangir*. Cambridge, England, 1971.

3788   Swanzy, Henry, "A Trading Family in the Nineteenth-Century Gold Coast," *Transactions of the Gold Coast and Togoland Historical Society* 2 (1956), 87-120.

3789   Turner, Victor W., *Schism and Continuity in an African Society*. Manchester, 1957. Reprint, 1972.

3790   Uchendu, Victor C., "Concubinage among Ngwa Igbo of Southern Nigeria," *Africa* 35 (1965), 187-197.

3791   Ukaegbu, Alfred O., "The Role of Traditional Marriage Habits in Population Growth," *Africa* 46 (1976), 390-398.

3792   Wagner, G., *The Changing Family among the Bantu Kavirondo*. London, 1939.

3793   Wilks, Ivor, "Akwamu and Otublohum: An Eighteenth-Century Akan Marriage Arrangement," *Africa* 29 (1959), 391-404.

3794   Wilks, Ivor, *Asante in the Nineteenth Century*. New York, 1975.

3795   Wilson, Gordon, *Luo Customary Law and Marriage Laws Customs*. n. p., 1968.

3796   Wright, Marcia, "Family, Continuity, and Women as Reflected in 'Die Safwa' by Elise Kootz-Kretschmer," *Vision and Service: Papers in Honor of Barbro Johansson*, ed. B. Sundkler and P. A. Wahlström (Uppsala, 1977), 108-116.

COLONIAL AND POST-COLONIAL AFRICA

3797   Aldous, Joan, "Urbanization, the Extended Family, and Kinship Ties in West

Africa," *Africa: Social Problems of Change and Conflict,* ed. Pierre L. van den Berghe (San Francisco, 1960), 107–116.

3798 Arens, W., and Diana Antos Arens, "Kinship and Marriage in a Polyethnic Community," *Africa* 48 (1978), 149–161.

3799 Amoo, J. W., "The Effect of Western Influence on Akan Marriage," *Africa* 16 (1946), 228–237.

3800 Baech, L., "Social Change in Central Africa," *Bulletin de l'Institute de recherches économiques et sociales* 25 (1959), 729–768.

3801 Balandier, George, "The Urban Family in Central Africa," *Renouveau des idées sur la Famille,* ed. Robert Prigent (Paris, 1954), 295–302.

3802 Banton, Michael, *West African City.* London, 1957.

3803 Barnes, J. A., *Marriage in a Changing Society.* London, 1951.

3804 Barrett, Stanley R., *Two Villages on Stilts: Economic and Family Changes in Nigeria.* New York, 1974.

3805 Beattie, John H., "Matiyo and His Two Wives," *Africa* 35 (1965), 252–262.

3806 Bernard, Guy, "Conjugalité et rôle de la femme à Kinshasa," *Canadian Journal of African Studies* 6 (1972), 261–274.

3807 Bird, Mary, "Urbanization, Family and Marriage in Western Nigeria," *Urbanization in African Social Change,* ed. Centre of African Studies (Edinburgh, 1963), 63–79.

3808 Brain, Robert, *Bangwa Kinship and Marriage.* London, 1972.

3809 Brandel, M., "Urban Lobolo Attitudes: A Preliminary Report," *African Studies* 17 (1958), 34–50.

3810 Burness, H., "Women in Katsina Province, Northern Nigeria," *Overseas Education* 29 (1957), 116–122.

3811 Caldwell, John C., "The Erosion of the Family: A Study of the Fate of the Family in Ghana," *Population Studies* 20 (1966), 5–26.

3812 Charles, J., "Families of Working Women and Social Evolution in Thysville," *Zaire* 9 (1955), 731–739.

3813 Child, H. F., "Family and Tribal Structure: Status of Women," *Nada* 35 (1938), 65–70.

3814 Clignet, Remi, "Urbanization and Family Structure in the Ivory Coast," *Comparative Studies in Society and History* 8 (1965–66), 385–410.

3815 Clignet, Remi, and J. Sween, "Traditional and Modern Life Styles in Africa," *Journal of Comparative Family Studies* 2 (1971), 188–214.

3816 Cole, Patrick D., *Modern and Traditional Elites in the Politics of Lagos, 1884–1938.* Cambridge, England, 1975.

3817 Colson, Elizabeth, "Family Change in Contemporary Africa," *Annals of the New York Academy of Sciences* 96 (1962), 641–647.

3818 Colson, Elizabeth, *Marriage and the Family among the Plateau Tonga of Northern Rhodesia.* Manchester, 1958.

3819 Dartevelle, A., "La Femme: Etude de sa condition et de sa situation sociale chez les Ba-Vili (Congo Français)," *Bulletin de la Société royale belge d'anthropologie et de pré-histoire* 54 (1939), 99-100.

3820 Dethler, R., *An Urban Family in Katanga.* Liege, 1961.

3821 Douglas, Mary, "Is Matriliny Doomed in Africa?" *Man in Africa,* ed. Mary Douglas and Phyllis Kaberry (London, 1969), 121-135.

3822 Edgerton, Robert B., "Pokot Intersexuality: An East African Example of the Resolution of Sexual Incongruity," *American Anthropologist* 66 (1964), 1288-1299.

3823 Faladé, Solange, "Women of Dakar and the Surrounding Urban Area," *Women of Tropical Africa,* ed. Denise Paulme (Berkeley, 1963), 217-230.

3824 Forthomme, Georges, *Mariage et industrialisation: évolution de la mentalité indigène dans une cité de travasilleurs d'Elisabethville.* Liège, 1957.

3825 Gamble, David, "The Temne Family in a Modern Town (Lunsar) in Sierra Leone," *Africa* 33 (1963), 209-225.

3826 Goddard, A. D., "Changing Family Structures among the Rural Hausa," *Africa* 43 (1973), 207-218.

3827 Gomm, Roger, "Harlots and Bachelors: Marital Instability among the Coastal Digo of Kenya," *Man* new series 7 (1972), 95-113.

3828 Goody, Jack, "Class and Marriage in Africa and Eurasia," *American Journal of Sociology* 76 (1971), 585-603.

3829 Goody, Jack, " 'Normative,' 'Recollected' and 'Actual' Marriage Payments among the Lowiili of Northern Ghana," *Africa* 39 (1969), 54-61.

3830 Greenstreet, Miranda, "Social Change and Ghanian Women," *Canadian Journal of African Studies* 6 (1972), 351-356.

3831 Gugler, Josef, "The Second Sex in Town," *Canadian Journal of African Studies* 6 (1972), 289-302.

3832 Gulliver, P. H., *Neighbours and Networks: The Idiom of Kinship in Social Action among the Ndendeuli of Tanzania.* Berkeley, 1971.

3833 Gutkind, P.C.W., "The African Family and Its Adaption to Urban Life," *Diogenes* 37 (1960), 93-112.

3834 Gutkind, P.C.W., "African Urban Family Life: Comment on and Analyses of Some Rural-Urban Differences," *Cahiers d'études africaines* 3 (1962-63), 149-217.

3835 Gutkind, P.C.W., "African Urban Family Life and the Urban System," *Asian and African Studies* 1 (1966), 35-42.

3836 Gutkind, P.C.W., "Some Problems of African Urban Family Life: An Example from Kampala, Uganda, British E. Africa," *Zaire* 15 (1961), 59-74.

3837 Harrell-Bond, Barbara E., *Modern Marriage in Sierra Leone.* The Hague, 1975.

3838 Harries, Lyndon, "Christian Marriage in African Society," *Survey of African Marriage...,* ed. Arthur Phillips (London, 1953), 329-462. (See #3719)

3839 Hennin, R., "Les structures familiales en milieu urbain," *Problèmes sociaux congolais* 68 (1968), 3-90.

3840 Hoffer, Carol P., "Mende and Sherbo Women in High Office," *Canadian Journal of African Studies* 6 (1972), 151–164.

3841 Holleman, J. F., "Bantu Marriage at the Crossroads," *Race Relations Journal* 28:1 (1961),32–44; 28:2 (1961), 12–23.

3842 Hunter, M. M., "Effects of Contact with Europeans on the Status of Pondo Women," *Africa* 6 (1933), 259–276.

3843 Jackson, Kennell A., Jr., "The Family Entity and Famine among the Nineteenth-Century Akamba of Kenya," *Journal of Family History* 1 (1977), 193–216.

3844 Kabwegyere, T. B., "Family Life and Economic Change in Uganda," *International Studies in Sociology and Social Anthropology* 12 (1972), 147–159.

3845 Karp, Ivan, "New Guinea Models in the African Savannah," *Africa* 48 (1978), 1–16.

3846 Kilson, Marion, *African Urban Kinsmen*. New York, 1974.

3847 Knak, D. S., "The Influence of European Civilization on Bantu Family Life," *Africa* 4 (1931), 178–200.

3848 Knowles, O. S., "Some Modern Adaptations of Customary Law in the Settlement of Matrimonial Disputes in the Luo, Kisii and Kuria Tribes of Southern Nyanza," *Journal of African Administration* 8 (1956), 11–15.

3849 Kopytoff, Jean H., *A Preface to Modern Nigeria: The "Sierra Leonians" in Yoruba, 1830–1890*. Madison, 1965.

3850 Krige, E. S., "Changing Conditions in African Marital Relations and Parental Duties among Urbanized Natives," *Africa* 9 (1936), 1–23.

3851 Lancaster, C. S., "Women, Horticulture and Society in Sub-Saharan Africa," *American Anthropologist* new series 78 (1976), 539–564.

3852 Letney, A., "Problems in the Development of Family Relations in West Africa," *International Social Science Journal* 16 (1964), 400–410.

3853 Levine, Robert A., "Sex Roles and Economic Change in Africa," *Ethnology* 5 (1966), 186–201.

3854 Levine, Robert A., and Barbara B. Levine, "Nyansongo: A Gusii Community in Kenya," *Six Cultures*, ed. Beatrice Whiting (New York, 1963), 15–202.

3855 Little, Kenneth, *African Women in Towns*. London, 1973.

3856 Little, Kenneth, "The Changing Position of Women in the Sierra Leone Protectorate," *Africa* 18 (1948), 1–17.

3857 Little, Kenneth, "Some Traditionally Based Forms of Mutual Aid in W. African Urbanization (Voluntary Associations)," *Ethnology* 1 (1962), 197–211.

3858 Little, Kenneth, "Some Trends in Modern Marriage among West Africans," *Africa* 37 (1967), 407–424.

3859 Little, Kenneth, "Some Urban Patterns of Marriage—Domesticity in West Africa," *Sociological Review* 7 (1959), 65–82.

3860 Little, Kenneth, "Voluntary Associations and Social Mobility among West African Women," *Canadian Journal of African Studies* 6 (1972), 275–288.

3861   Lombard, J., "Cotonou, ville africaine. Tendances évolutives et réaction des coutumes traditionelles," *Bulletin de L'IFAN* 16 (1954), 341-377.

3862   Long, Norman, *Social Change and the Individual.* Manchester, 1968.

3863   Lux, Andre, "Gift Exchange and Income Redistribution between Yombe Rural Wage Earners and Their Kinsfolk in Western Zaire," *Africa* 42 (1972), 173-192.

3864   Lystad, Robert A., "Marriage and Kinship among the Ashanti and the Agni: A Study of Differential Acculturation," *Continuity and Change in African Cultures*, ed. W.Bascom and M. Herskovits (Chicago, 1959), 187-205.

3865   MacGaffey, Wyett, *Custom and Government in the Lower Congo.* Berkeley, 1970.

3866   Makonga, B., "La position sociale de la mère," *Problèmes sociaux congolais* 17 (1951), 243-259.

3867   Mann, Kristin, "Social History of the New African Elite in Lagos Colony, 1880-1913." Ph.D. Dissertation, Stanford University, 1977.

3868   Marris, Peter, "African Families and the Process of Change," *Families in East and West,* ed. Reuben Hill and René König (The Hague, 1970), 397-409. 1961. (See #76)

3869   Marris, Peter, *Family and Social Change in an African City.* London, 1961.

3870   Mayer, Philip, *Townsmen or Tribesmen.* London, 1961.

3871   Mbilinyi, Marjorie J., "The State of Women in Tanzania," *Canadian Journal of African Studies* 6 (1972), 371-377.

3872   McCall, D. F., "Trade and the Role of Wife in a Modern West African Town," *Social Change in Modern Africa,* ed. Aidan Southall (London, 1965), 286-299.

3873   Meillassoux, Claude, *Urbanization of an African Community.* Seattle, 1968.

3874   Mitchell, J. C., "Aspects of African Marriage on the Copperbelt of Northern Rhodesia," *Rhodes-Livingstone Journal* 22 (1957), 1-30.

3875   Mitchell, J. C., "Social Change and the Stability of African Marriage in Northern Rhodesia," *Social Change in Modern Africa,* ed. Aidan Southall (London, 1965), 316-329.

3876   Mookodi, R., "Women's Life in Botswana," *Canadian Journal of African Studies* 6 (1972), 357-358.

3877   Mafziger, A., "The Effect of the Nigerian Extended Family on Entrepreneurial Activity," *Economic Development and Cultural Change* 18 (1969), 25-33.

3878   Ohadike, P. O., "A Demographic Note on Marriage, Family, and Family Growth in Lagos, Nigeria," *The Population of Tropical Africa,* ed. J. C. Caldwell and C. Okonjo (London, 1968), 379-392.

3879   Okonjo, Unokanma, *The Impact of Urbanization on the Ibo Family Structure.* Göttingen, 1970.

3880   Ominde, Simeon H., *The Luo Girl from Infancy to Marriage.* New York, 1952.

3881 Osei-Kofi, E., "The Family and Social Change in Ghana," *Goteborg* 3 (1967), 3-62.

3882 Ottenberg, P. V., "The Changing Economic Position of Women among the Afikpo Ibo," *Continuity and Change in African Cultures,* ed. W. Bascom and M. Herskovits (Chicago, 1959), 205-223.

3883 Parkin, David J., "Types of Urban African Marriage in Kampala," *Africa and Change,* ed. Colin P. Turnbull (New York, 1973), 208-226.

3884 Pauw, Berthold A., *The Second Generation: A Study of the Family among Urbanized Bantu in East London.* London, 1963.

3885 Phillips, A., and H. Morns, *Marriage Laws in Africa.* London, 1971.

3886 Poewe, Karla O., "Matriliny in the Throes of Change: Kinship, Descent, and Marriage in Luapula, Zambia," *Africa* 48 (1978), 205-219.

3887 Pool, D. I., "Conjugal Patterns in Ghana," *The Canadian Review of Sociology and Anthropology* 5 (1968), 241-253.

3888 Pool, Janet E., "A Cross-Comparative Study of Aspects of Conjugal Behavior among Women of 3 West African Countries," *Canadian Journal of African Studies* 6 (1972), 233-260.

3889 Powdermaker, Hortense, *Copper Town: Changing Africa.* New York, 1963.

3890 Read, Margaret, *Migrant Labor in Africa and Its Effects on Tribal Life.* Montreal, 1943.

3891 Richards, Audrey I., *Bemba Marriage and Present Economic Conditions.* Lusaka, 1940.

3892 Shropshire, Dennis W. T., *Primitive Marriage and European Law: A South African Investigation.* London, 1970.

3893 Southall, A. W., "The Position of Women and the Stability of Marriage," *Social Change in Modern Africa,* ed. Aidan Southall (London, 1963), 46-66.

3894 Stenning, Derrick, *Savannah Nomads.* London, 1959.

3895 Sudarkasa, Niara, *Where Women Work: A Study of Yoruba Women in the Marketplace and the Home.* Ann Arbor, 1973.

3896 Symons, H. J., "The Status of African Women," *Modern Africa,* ed. Peter McEwan and R. Sutchcliffe (New York, 1965), 326-331.

3897 Tardits, Claude, *Porto-Novo: les nouvelles generations africaines entre leur traditions et l'Occident.* Paris, 1958.

3898 Van Allen, Judith, " 'Sitting on a Man': Colonialism and the Lost Political Institutions of Igbo Women," *Canadian Journal of African Studies* 6 (1972), 165-182.

3899 Van Velsen, J., *The Politics of Kinship.* Manchester, 1964.

3900 Vincent, Joan, *African Elite: The Big Men of a Small Town.* New York, 1971.

3901 Vine, V. T., "Generational Conflicts and Politics in Africa: A Paradigm," *Civilizations* 18 (1968), 399-420.

3902 Watson, William, *Tribal Cohesion in a Money Economy.* Manchester, 1958.

3903   Williamson, Kay, "Changes in the Marriage System of the Okrika Ijo," *Africa* 32 (1962), 53-60.

3904   Wilson, Monica, *For Men and Elders.* New York, 1977.

3905   Winter, Edward H., *Beyond the Mountains of the Moon.* London, 1959. See also #48 and #112.

South Asia

GENERAL SURVEYS AND COLLECTIONS

3906 *The Family in India: A Regional View,* ed. George Kurian. The Hague, 1974.

3907 *Family, Kinship and Marriage among Muslims in India,* ed. Imtiaz Ahmad. New Delhi, 1976.

3908 *Family and Social Change in Modern India,* ed. Giri Raj Gupta. New Delhi, 1976.

3909 Karve, Irawati, *Kinship Organization in India.* 2nd rev. ed.; Bombay, 1965.

3910 *Kinship and History in South Asia,* ed. Thomas R. Trautmann. Ann Arbor, 1974.

BIBLIOGRAPHIES AND REVIEW ESSAYS

3911 Abbi, Behari L., "Urban Family in India," *Contributions to Indian Sociology* new series 3 (1969), 116–127.

3912 Carroll, James J., "Field Research on Urbanization and Family Change in India," *Man in India* 55 (1975), 339–354.

3913 Dube, Leela, *Sociology of Kinship: An Analytical Survey of Literature.* Bombay, 1974.

CLASSICAL, MEDIEVAL, AND MUSLIM PERIODS (TO 1740 A.D.)

3914 Altekar, A. S., *The Position of Women in Hindu Civilization.* 3rd ed.; Delhi, 1962.

3915   Chaudhary, Roop L., *Hindu Woman's Right to Property: Past and Present.* Calcutta, 1961.

3916   Ghurye, Govind S., *Family and Kin in Indo-European Culture.* Bombay, 1963.

3917   Ghurye, Govind S., "Some Kinship Usages in Indo-Aryan Literature," *Journal of the Anthropological Society of Bombay* 1 (1946), 1-19.

3918   Hocart, A. M., "The Indo-European Kinship System," *Ceylon Journal of Science* 1 (1928), 179-204.

3919   Inden, Ronald B., *Marriage and Rank in Bengali Culture: A History of Caste and Clan in Middle Period Bengal.* Berkeley, 1976.

3920   Kapadia, K. M., *Marriage and Family in India.* 3rd ed.; Bombay, 1966.

3921   Prabhu, Pandharinath H., *Hindu Social Organization.* 4th ed.; Bombay, 1963.

3922   Raychaudhuri, Tapan, "Norms of Family Life and Personal Morality among the Bengali Hindu Elite, 1600-1850," *Aspects of Bengali History and Society,* ed. Rachel Van M. Baumer (Honolulu, 1975), 13-25.

3923   Sengupta, Nilakshi, *Evolution of Hindu Marriage: With Special Reference to Rituals.* Bombay, 1965.

3924   Tambiah, S. J., "Dowry and Bridewealth, and the Property Rights of Women in South Asia," *Bridewealth and Dowry,* ed. Jack Goody and S. J. Tambiah (Cambridge, England, 1973), 59-169.

3925   Wagle, Narendra K., "Kinship Groups in the Jātakas," *Kinship and History in South Asia,* ed. Thomas R. Trautmann (Ann Arbor, 1974), 105-143. (See #3910)

BRITISH PERIOD (1740-1947)

3926   Avalaskar, S. V., "Some Notes on the Social Life in Nagaon in the Early 19th Century," *Indian Economic and Social History Review* 3 (1966), 169-173.

3927   Chambard, Jean-Luc, "Le pothī du Jagā ou le registre secret d'un généalogiste de village en Inde centrale," *L'Homme* 3 (1963), 5-85.

3928   Desai, N. C., *Report on the Hindu Joint Family: Its Economic and Social Aspects.* Baroda, 1936.

3929   Dumont, L., "Les mariages nayar comme fait Indiens," *L'Homme* 1 (1961), 11-36.

3930   Fuller, C. J., *The Nayars Today.* Cambridge, England, 1976.

3931   Ghosh, B. R., "Changes in the Size and Composition of the Household Brought About by Urbanization in Delhi Area," *Family in India,* ed. George Kurian (The Hague, 1974), 249-261. (See #3906)

3932   Ghurye, G. S., *After a Century and a Quarter: Lonikand Then and Now.* Bombay, 1960.

3933   Goswamy, B. N., "History at Pilgrim Centers: On Pattas Held by Families of

Priests at Centers of Hindu Pilgrimage," *Sources on Punjab History,* ed. W. Eric Gustafson and Kenneth W. Jones (New Delhi, 1975), 339–373.

3934 Goswamy, B. N., "The Records Kept by Priests at Centres of Pilgrimage as a Source of Social and Economic History," *Indian Economic and Social History Review* 3 (1966), 174–184.

3935 Gough, E. Kathleen, "Changing Kinship Usages in the Setting of Political and Economic Change among the Nayars of Malabar," *Journal of the Royal Anthropological Institute* 82 (1952), 71–88.

3936 Karve, D. D., and Ellen E. McDonald, *The New Brahmans: Five Maharashtrian Families.* Berkeley, 1963.

3937 Kessinger, Tom G., "Anthropology and History: The Study of Social and Economic Change in Rural India," *Journal of Interdisciplinary History* 3 (1972–73), 313–322.

3938 Kessinger, Tom G., "Historical Materials on Rural India," *Indian Economic and Social History Review* 7 (1970), 491–492.

3939 Kessinger, Tom G., *Vilyatpur 1848–1968: Social and Economic Change in a North Indian Village.* Berkeley, 1974.

3940 Khare, R. S., "One Hundred Years of Occupational Modernization among Kanya-Kubja Brahmans: A Genealogical Reconstruction of Social Dynamics," *Entrepreneurship and Modernization of Occupational Cultures in South Asia,* ed. Milton Singer (Durham, 1973), 243–274.

3941 Kolenda, Pauline M., "Family Structure in Village Lonikand, India: 1819, 1958 & 1967," *Contributions to Indian Sociology* new series 4 (1970), 50–72.

3942 Lakshminarayana, H. D., *Analysis of Family Patterns through a Century.* Poona, 1968.

3943 Mencher, Joan P., "Changing Familial Roles among South Malabar Nayars," *Southwestern Journal of Anthropology* 18 (1962), 230–245.

3944 Mencher, Joan P., "The Nayars of South Malabar," *Comparative Family Systems,* ed. Meyer F. Nimkoff (Boston, 1965), 163–191. (See #49)

3945 Mencher, Joan P., and Helen Goldberg, "Kinship and Marriage Regulations among the Namboodiri Brahmans of Kerala," *Man* new series 2 (1967), 87–106.

3946 Nakane, Chie, "The Nayar Family in a Disintegrating Matrilineal System," *Family and Marriage,* ed. J. Mogey (Leiden, 1963), 17–28.

3947 Nath, Viswa, "Female Infanticide and the Lewa Kanbis of Gujarat in the Nineteenth Century," *Indian Economic and Social History Review* 10 (1973), 386–404.

3948 Orenstein, Henry, "The Recent History of the Extended Family in India," *Social Problems* 8 (1961), 341–350.

3949 Orenstein, Henry, and Michael Micklin, "The Hindu Joint Family: The Norms and the Numbers," *Pacific Affairs* 39 (1966), 314–325.

3950 Pakrasi, Kanti, "A Study of Some Aspects of Household Types and Family

Organization in Rural Bengal, 1946-1947," *Eastern Anthropologist* 15 (1962), 55-63.

3951 Patterson, Maureen L. P., "Chitpavan Brahman Family Histories: Sources for a Study of Social Structure and Social Change in Maharashtra," *Structure and Change in Indian Society,* ed. Milton Singer and Bernard S. Cohn (Chicago, 1968), 397-411.

3952 Pocock, David F., *Kanbi and Patidar: A Study of the Patidar Community of Gujarat.* Oxford, 1972.

3953 Rudolph, Susanne Hoeber, and Lloyd I. Rudolph, "Rajput Adulthood: Reflections on the Amar Singh Diary," *Daedalus* 105 (1976), 145-167.

3954 Srinivas, Mysore N., *Marriage and Family in Mysore.* Bombay, 1942.

3955 Srivastava, Harish C., "Marriage among the Christians of Goa: A Study Based on Parish Registers," *Indian Economic and Social History Review* 14 (1977), 247-254.

3956 Ziegler, Norman P., "Marvari Historical Chronicles: Sources for the Social and Cultural History of Rajasthan," *Indian Economic and Social History Review* 13 (1976), 217-250.

POST-INDEPENDENCE PERIOD
(1947 TO THE PRESENT)

3957 Acharya, H., "Caste and Joint Family in an Immigrant Community," *Sociological Bulletin* 4 (1955), 129-138.

3958 Agarwala, S. N., *Age at Marriage in India.* Bombay, 1962.

3959 Agarwala, S. N., *A Demographic Study of Six Urbanising Villages.* Bombay, 1970.

3960 Agarwala, S. N., "Widow Remarriages in Some Rural Areas of Northern India," *Demography* 4 (1967), 126-134.

3961 Alavi, Hamza A., "Kinship in West Punjab Villages," *Contributions to Indian Sociology* new series 6 (1972), 1-27.

3962 Ames, Michael M., "Modernisation and Social Structure: Family, Caste and Class in Jamshedpur," *Economic and Political Weekly* 4 (1969), 1217-1224.

3963 Ames, Michael M., "Structural Dimensions of Family Life in the Steel City of Jamshedpur," *Entrepreneurship and Modernization of Occupational Cultures in South Asia,* ed. Milton Singer (Durham, 1973), 107-131.

3964 Bailey, F. G., "The Joint Family in India: A Framework for Discussion," *Economic Weekly* 12 (1960), 345-353.

3965 Banerjee, Bhavani, *Marriage and Kinship of the Gangadikara Vokkaligas of Mysore.* Poona, 1966.

3966 Banerjee, Shailendra Nath, "Effect of Changes in Age Patterns of Marriage on Fertility Rates in Bihar 1961-1968," *Man in India* 53 (1973), 262-278.

3967 Conklin, George H., "Social Change and the Joint Family: The Causes of Research Biases," *Economic and Political Weekly* 4 (1969), 1445–1449.

3968 Dasgupta, Manisha, "Changes in the Joint Family in India," *Man in India* 45 (1965), 283–289.

3969 Davis, Marvin, "The Politics of Famiy Life in Rural West Bengal," *Ethnology* 15 (1976), 189–200.

3970 Derrett, John D. M., *Hindu Law Past and Present: Being an Account of the Hindu Code, the Text of the Code as Enacted and Some Comments Thereon.* Calcutta, 1957.

3971 Derrett, John D. M., "The History of the Juridical Framework of the Joint Hindu Family," *Contributions to Indian Sociology* 6 (1962), 17–47.

3972 Derrett, John D. M., "Law and the Predicament of the Hindu Family," *Economic Weekly* 12 (1960), 305–311.

3973 Desai, I. P., "Joint Family in India: An Analysis," *Sociological Bulletin* 5 (1956), 144–156.

3974 Desai, I. P., *Some Aspects of Family in Mahuva: A Sociological Study of Jointness in a Small Town.* New York, 1964.

3975 Driver, Edwin D., *Differential Fertility in Central India.* Princeton, 1963.

3976 Dumont, Louis, "Marriage in India, the Present State of the Question: I. Marriage and Alliance in South East India and Ceylon," *Contributions to Indian Sociology* 5 (1961), 75–95.

3977 Chatterjee, Mary, "Kinship in an Urban Low Caste Locality" *Eastern Anthropologist* 27 (1974), 337–350.

3978 Chekki, D. A., "Mate Selection, Age at Marriage, and Propinquity among the Lingāyats of India," *Journal of Marriage and the Family* 30 (1968), 707–711.

3979 Chekki, D. A., "Modernization and Kin Network in a Developing Society: India," *Sociologus* new series 23 (1973), 22–40.

3980 Claus, Peter J., "Determinants of Household Organization among Tenants and Landowners in the Bant Caste," *Contributions to Indian Sociology* new series 9 (1975), 89–110.

3981 Cohn, Bernard S., "Chamar Family in a North Indian Village: A Structural Contingent," *Economic Weekly* 13 (1961), 1051–1055.

3982 Collver, A., "The Family Cycle in India and the United States," *American Sociological Review* 28 (1963), 89–96.

3983 Conklin, George H., "The Extended Family as an Independent Factor in Social Change: A Case from India," *Journal of Marriage and the Family* 36 (1974), 798–804.

3984 Conklin, George H., "The Family Formation Process in India: An Overview," *Journal of Family Welfare* 14 (1968), 28–37.

3985 Conklin, George H., "Family Structure, Caste and Economic Development: An Urban-Rural Comparison from Dharwar, Karnataka," *Family and Social Change in Modern India,* ed. Giri Raj Gupta (New Delhi, 1976), 19–35.

3986 Conklin, George H., "The Household in Urban India," *Journal of Marriage and the Family* 38 (1976), 771–780.

3987 Basu, Salil Kumar, and Shibani Roy, "Change in the Frequency of Consanguineous Marriages among Delhi Muslims after Partition," *Eastern Anthropologist* 25 (1972), 21–28.

3988 Berreman, Gerald D., "Demography, Domestic Economy and Change in the Western Himalayas," *Eastern Anthropologist* 30 (1977), 157–192.

3989 Berreman, Gerald D., "Himalayan Polyandry and the Domestic Cycle," *American Ethnologist* 2 (1975), 127–138.

3990 Berrreman, Gerald D., "Pahari Polyandry: A Comparison," *American Anthropologist* 64 (1962), 60–75.

3991 Berreman, Gerald D., "Village Exogamy in Northernmost India," *Southwestern Journal of Anthropology* 18 (1962), 55–58.

3992 Bétéille, André, "Family and Social Change in India and Other South Asian Countries," *Economic Weekly* 16 (1964), 237–244.

3993 Bose, A. B., and P. C. Saxena, "Composition of Rural Household in Rajasthan," *Indian Journal of Social Research* 5 (1964), 299–308.

3994 Bose, A. B., and P. C. Saxena, "Some Characteristics of Nuclear Households," *Man in India* 45 (1965), 195–200.

3995 Burkhart, Geoffrey, "On the Absence of Descent Groups among Some Udayars of South India," *Contributions to Indian Sociology* new series 10 (1976), 31–61.

3996 Burling, Robbins, "Linguistics and Ethnographic Description [Garo Family]," *American Anthropologist* 71 (1969), 817–827.

3997 Burling, Robbins, *Rengsanggri: Family and Kinship in a Garo Village*. Philadelphia, 1963.

3998 Chambard, Jean-Luc, "Mariages secondaires et foires aux femmes en Inde centrale," *L'Homme* 1 (1961), 51–88.

3999 Dumont, Louis, "Marriage in India, the Present State of the Question: II. Marriage and Status, Nayar and Newar," *Contributions to Indian Sociology* 7 (1964), 77–98.

4000 Dumont, Louis, "Marriage in India, the Present State of the Question: III. North India in Relation to South India," *Contributions to Indian Sociology* 9 (1966), 90–114.

4001 Eglar, Zekiye, *A Punjabi Village in Pakistan*. New York, 1960.

4002 von Ehrenfels, V. R., "Matrilineal Joint Family Patterns in India," *Journal of Comparative Family Studies* 2 (1971), 54–66.

4003 Fox, Richard G., "Family, Caste and Commerce in a North Indian Market Town," *Economic Development and Cultural Change* 15 (1967), 297–314.

4004 Gallagher, Orwell R., "Endogamous Marriage in Central India," *Ethnology* 4 (1965), 72–77.

4005 Gore, M. S., "The Traditional Indian Family," *Comparative Family Systems,* ed. Meyer F. Nimkoff (Boston, 1965), 209–231. (See #49)

4006   Gore, M. S., *Urbanization and Family Change*. Bombay, 1968.

4007   Gough, E. Kathleen, "Brahman Kinship in a Tamil Village," *American Anthropologist* 58 (1956), 826–853.

4008   Gould, Harold A., "A Further Note on Village Exogamy in North India," Southwestern Journal of Anthropology 17 (1961), 297–300.

4009   Gould, Harold A., "The Micro-Demography of Marriages in a North Indian Area," *Southwestern Journal of Anthropology* 16 (1960), 476–491.

4010   Gould, Harold A., "Some Aspects of Kinship among Business and Professional Elite in Lucknow, India," *Contributions to Indian Sociology* new series 5 (1971), 116–130.

4011   Gould, Harold A., "Time Dimension and Structural Change in an Indian Kinship System: A Problem of Conceptual Refinement," *Structure and Change in Indian Society,* ed. Milton Singer and Bernard Cohn (Chicago, 1968), 413–421.

4012   Gulati, Iqbal S., and Kuldip S. Gulati, *The Undivided Hindu Family: Its Tax Privileges*. Bombay, 1962.

4013   Inden, Ronald B., and Ralph W. Nicholas, *Kinship in Bengali Culture*. Chicago, 1977.

4014   Ishwaran, K., "Kinship and Distance in Rural India," *International Journal of Comparative Sociology* 6 (1965), 81–94.

4015   Jain, S. C., "Some Features of Fraternal Polyandry in Jaunsar Bawar," *Eastern Anthropologist* 1 (1947), 27–33.

4016   Jha, J. C., and B. B. Chatterjee, "Changing Family in a Polyandrous Community," *Eastern Anthropologist* 18 (1965), 64–72.

4017   Kaldate, Sudha, "Urbanization and Disintegration of Rural Joint Family," *Sociological Bulletin* 11 (1961), 103–112.

4018   Kapadia, K. M., "Changing Patterns of Hindu Marriage and Family I," *Sociological Bulletin* 3 (1954), 131–158.

4019   Kapadia, K. M., "Changing Patterns of Hindu Marriage and Family II," *Sociological Bulletin* 4 (1955), 161–192.

4020   Kapadia, K. M., "The Family in India: The Family in Transition," *Sociological Bulletin* 8 (1959), 68–100.

4021   Kapadia, K. M., "Rural Family Patterns: A Study in Urban-Rural Relations," *Sociological Bulletin* 5 (1956), 111–126.

4022   Kapoor, Saroj, "Family and Kinship Groups among the Khatris in Delhi," *Sociological Bulletin* 14 (1965), 54–63.

4023   Khare, R. S., "Hierarchy and Hypergamy: Some Interrelated Aspects among the Kanya-Kubja Brahmans," *American Anthropologist* 74 (1972), 611–628.

4024   Khatri, A. A., "The Adaptive Extended Family in India Today," *Journal of Marriage and the Family* 37 (1975), 633–642.

4025   Khatri, A. A., "The Indian Family: An Empirically Derived Analysis of Shifts in Size and Types," *Journal of Marriage and the Family* 34 (1972), 725–732.

4026   Kolenda, Pauline M., "Region, Caste and Family Structure: A Comparative

Study of the Indian 'Joint' Family," *Structure and Change in Indian Society,* ed. Milton Singer and Bernard S. Cohn (Chicago, 1968), 339-396.

4027   Kolenda, Pauline M., "Regional Differences in Indian Family Structure," *Regions and Regionalism in South Asian Studies: An Exploratory Study,* ed. Robert I. Crane (Durham, 1967), 147-226.

4028   Korson, J. Henry, "Dower and Social Class in an Urban Muslim Community," *Journal of Marriage and the Family* 29 (1967), 527-533.

4029   Kulkarni, M. G., "Family Patterns in Gokak Taluka," *Sociological Bulletin* 9 (1960), 60-81.

4030   Kurian, George, *The Indian Family in Transition: A Case Study of Kerala Syrian Christians.* 's Gravenhage, 1961.

4031   Kutty, Abdul R., *Marriage and Kinship in an Island Society.* Delhi, 1972.

4032   Lambert, Richard D., *Workers, Factories and Social Change in India.* Princeton, 1963.

4033   Madan, T. N., *Family and Kinship: A Study of the Pandits of Rural Kashmir.* Bombay, 1965.

4034   Madan, T. N., "The Joint Family: A Terminological Clarification," *International Journal of Comparative Sociology* 3 (1962), 7-16.

4035   Mandelbaum, David G., "The Hindu Family," *The Family...,* ed. Ruth Nanda Anshen. rev. ed. (New York, 1959), 167-187. (See #82)

4036   Mandelbaum, David G., *Society in India.* v. 1: *Continuity and Change.* Berkeley, 1970.

4037   Mayer, Adrian C., *Caste and Kinship in Central India.* Berkeley, 1960.

4038   Morrison, William A., "Family Patterns in Badlapur: An Analysis of a Changing Institution in a Maharashtrian Village," *Sociological Bulletin* 8 (1959), 45-67.

4039   Mukherjee, Ramkrishna, "On the Classification of Family Structure," *Indian Anthropology,* ed. T. N. Madan and Gopala Sharana (Bombay, 1962), 352-398.

4040   Mukherjee, Ramkrishna, *The Sociologist and Social Change in India Today.* New Delhi, 1965.

4041   Nakane, Chie, *Garo and Khasi: A Comparative Study in Matriarchal Systems.* Paris, 1967.

4042   Nicholas, Ralph W., "Economics of Family Types in Two West Bengal Villages," *Economic Weekly* 13 (1961), 1057-1060.

4043   Nimkoff, M. F., and M. S. Gore, "Social Bases of the Hindu Joint Family," *Sociology and Social Research* 44 (1959), 27-36.

4044   Owens, Raymond, "Industrialization and the Indian Joint Family," *Ethnology* 10 (1971), 223-250.

4045   Ramu, G. N., *Family and Caste in Urban India.* Delhi, 1977.

4046   Ramu, G. N., "Family Structure and Entrepreneurship: An Indian Case," *Journal of Comparative Family Studies* 4 (1973), 239-256.

4047 Ramu, G. N., "Geographic Mobility, Kinship and the Family in South India," *Journal of Marriage and the Family* 34 (1972), 147–155.

4048 Ramu, G. N., "Urban Kinship Ties in South India: A Case Study," *Journal of Marriage and the Family* 36 (1974), 619–627.

4049 Rao, M.S.A., "Occupational Diversification and Joint Household Organization," *Contributions to Indian Sociology* new series 2 (1968), 98–111.

4050 Robinson, Marguerite S., "Some Observations on the Kandyan Sinhalese Kinship System," *Man* new series 3 (1968), 402–423.

4051 Ross, Aileen D., *The Hindu Family in Its Urban Setting*. Toronto, 1961.

4052 Rowe, William L., "The Marriage Network and Structural Change in a North Indian Community," *Southwestern Journal of Anthropology* 16 (1960), 299–311.

4053 Sahai, Indu, *Family Structure and Partition*. Lucknow, 1973.

4054 Sarma, Jyotirmoyee, "The Nuclearization of Joint Family Households in West Bengal," *Man in India* 44 (1964), 193–206.

4055 Shah, A. M., "Basic Terms and Concepts in the Study of the Family in India," *Indian Economic and Social History Review* 1 (1964), 1–36.

4056 Shah, A. M., "Changes in the Indian Family: An Examination of Some Assumptions," *Economic and Political Weekly* 3 (1968), 127–134.

4057 Shah, A. M., *The Household Dimension of the Family in India*. Berkeley, 1974.

4058 Shah, A. M., and R. G. Shroff, "The Vahivancha Barots of Gujarat: A Caste of Genealogists and Mythographers," *Journal of American Folklore* 71 (1958), 246–278.

4059 Shahani, Savitri, "The Joint Family: A Case Study," *Economic Weekly* 13 (1961), 1823–1828.

4060 Singer, Milton, "The Indian Joint Family in Modern Industry," *Structure and Change in Indian Society*, ed. Milton Singer and Bernard S. Cohn (Chicago, 1968), 423–452.

4061 Tambiah, S. J., "Kinship Fact and Fiction in Relation to the Kandyan Sinhalese," *Journal of the Royal Anthropological Institute* 95 (1965), 131–173.

4062 Tambiah, S. J., "Polyandry in Ceylon," *Caste and Kin in Nepal, India and Ceylon*, ed. Christoph von Fürer-Haimendorf (Bombay, 1966), 264–359.

4063 Unni, K. Raman, "Polyandry in Malabar," *Sociological Bulletin* 7 (1958), 62–79, 123–133.

4064 van der Veen, Klaas W., *I Give Thee My Daughter*. Assen, 1972.

4065 Vatuk, Sylvia, *Kinship and Urbanization: White-Collar Migrants in North India*. Berkeley, 1972.

4066 Yalman, Nur, "On the Purity of Women in the Castes of Ceylon and Malabar," *Journal of the Royal Anthropological Institute* 93 (1963), 25–58.

4067 Yalman, Nur, "The Structure of the Sinhalese Kindred: A Re-Examination of the Dravidian Terminology," *American Anthropologist* 64 (1962), 548–575.

4068 Yalman, Nur, *Under the Bo Tree*. Berkeley, 1967.

Southeast Asia

GENERAL SURVEYS AND COLLECTIONS

4069 Fisher, Charles A., "Some Comments on Population Growth in South-East Asia, With Special Reference to the Period Since 1830," *The Economic Development of Southeast Asia,* ed. Charles D. Cowan (New York, 1964), 48-71.

4070 LeBar, Frank M., *Ethnic Groups of Insular Southeast Asia.* 2 v. New Haven, 1972-75.

4071 LeBar, Frank M., Gerald C. Hickey, and John K. Musgrave, *Ethnic Groups of Mainland Southeast Asia.* New Haven, 1964.

4072 Lingat, Robert, *Les régimes matrimoniaux du Sud-est de l'Asie.* 2 v. Paris, 1952-55.

4073 Petros, Prince of Greece, *A Study of Polyandry.* The Hauge, 1963.

4074 Rajhadhon, P. Anuman, *Southeast Asian Birth Customs.* New Haven, 1965.

4075 *Social Structure in Southeast Asia,* ed. George Peter Murdock. Chicago, 1960.

4076 *Southeast Asian Tribes, Minorities, and Nations,* ed. Peter Kunstadter. 2 v. Princeton, 1966.

GENERAL BIBLIOGRAPHIES

4077 *Cumulative Bibliography of Asian Studies, 1941-1965,* ed. Association for Asian Studies. 8 v. Boston, 1969. Continued as the annual *Bibliography of Asian Studies.* Ann Arbor, 1969 ff.

4078 Embree, John F., and Lillian Ota Dotson, *Bibliography of the Peoples and Cultures of Mainland Southeast Asia.* New Haven, 1950.

4079 Kennedy, Raymond, *Bibliography of Indonesian Peoples and Cultures.* 2nd rev. ed.; New Haven, 1962.

4080 LeBar, Frank M., "The Ethnography of Mainland Southeast Asia: A Bibliographic Survey," *Behavior Science Notes* 1 (1966), 14-40.

4081 United States, Dept. of the Army, *Insular Southeast Asia: A Bibliographic Survey.* Washington, 1971.

BURMA

4082 Ba Han, "Piquant Splendours of the Burmese Family Life of Old," *Journal of the Burma Research Society* 50:1 (1967), 21-32.

4083 Brant, Charles S., and Mi Mi Khaing, "Burmese Kinship and the Life Cycle: An Outline," *Southwestern Journal of Anthropology* 7 (1951), 437-454.

4084 Gledhill, Alan, "Burmese Law in the Nineteenth Century, with Special Reference to the Position of Women," *Cahiers d'histoire mondiale* 7 (1962), 172-194.

4085 Gledhill, Alan, "The Status of Woman in Burmese Law," *Receuils de la Société Jean Bodin* 11 (1959), 269-273.

4086 Hla Aung, U, "The Effect of Anglo-Indian Legislation on Burmese Customary Law," *Family Law and Customary Law in Asia,* ed. David C. Buxbaum (The Hague, 1968), 67-88.

4087 Maung Maung, U, *Law and Custom in Burma and the Burmese Family.* The Hague, 1963.

4088 Mi Mi Khaing, *Burmese Family.* Bloomington, Ind., 1962. Originally, Bombay, 1946.

4089 Mya Sein, Daw, "Towards Independence in Burma: The Role of Women," *Asian Affairs* 59 (1972), 288-299.

4090 Nash, June, and Manning Nash, "Marriage, Family, and Population Growth in Upper Burma," *Southwestern Journal of Anthropology* 19 (1963), 251-266.

4091 Nash, Manning, *The Golden Road to Modernity: Village Life in Contemporary Burma.* New York, 1965.

4092 Ni Ni Gyi, "Patterns of Social Change in a Burmese Family," *Women in the New Asia,* ed. Barbara E. Ward (Paris, 1963), 138-148.

4093 Than Tun, "Social Life in Burma, A.D. 1044-1287," *Journal of the Burma Research Society* 41 (1958), 37-47.

CAMBODIA

4094 Chakravarti, Adhir K., "The Caste System in Ancient Cambodia," *Journal of Indian History* 4 (1970-71), 14-59.

4095   Delvert, Jean, *Le paysan cambodgien*. The Hague, 1961.

4096   Jenner, Philip N., and Saveros Pou, "Les Cpāp ou 'Codes de conduite' khmers, II: cpāp prus," *Bulletin de l'Ecole française d'Extrême-Orient* 63 (1976), 313-350.

4097   Kirsch, A. Thomas, "Kinship, Genealogical Claims, and Societal Integration in Ancient Khmer Society: An Interpretation," *Southeast Asian History and Historiography: Essays Presented to D.G.E. Hall,* ed. Charles D. Cowan and O. W. Wolters (Ithaca, 1976), 190-202.

4098   Kishore, Kaushal, "Varnas in Early Kambuja Inscriptions," *Journal of the American Oriental Society* 85 (1965), 566-569.

4099   Lewitz, Saveros, "Kpuon ābāh-bibāh,ou le livre de mariage des Khmers par Ker Nou et Nhieuk Nou," *Bulletin de l'Ecole française d'Extrême-Orient* 60 (1973), 245-328.

4100   Mestier du Bourg, Hubert de, "Remarques sur la transmission des biens à cause de mort au Cambodge ancien," *Journal Asiatique* 258:3-4 (1970), 143-147.

4101   Migozzi, Jacques, "Contribution à l'étude de la population du Cambodge: les facteurs de l'accroissement démographique au Cambodge." Thèse (Doctorat de spécialité), Université de Paris, 1969.

4102   Migozzi, Jacques, "La population du Cambodge," *Asie du Sud-est et Monde Insulinden* 3:2 (1972), 57-107.

4103   Osborne, Milton E., "History and Kingship in Contemporary Cambodia," *Journal of Southeast Asian History* 7 (1966), 1-14.

4104   O'Sullivan, Kevin, "Concentric Conformity in Ancient Khmer Kinship Organization," Academia Sinica, Institute of Ethnology, *Bulletin* 13 (1962), 87-96.

4105   Pich-Sal, *Le mariage cambodgien*. Phnom Penh, 1962.

4106   Thierry, Solange, "Contribution à une étude de la société cambodgienne," *L'ethnographie* new series 58-59 (1964-65), 50-71.

INDONESIA

4107   Alisjahbana, S. Takdir, "Customary Law and Modernization in Indonesia," *Family Law and Customary Law in Asia,* ed. David C. Buxbaum (The Hague, 1968), 3-16.

4108   Belo, Jane, "A Study of a Balinese Family," *American Anthropologist* 38 (1936), 12-32.

4109   Berg, L.W.C. van den, "De Afwijkingen van het Mohammedaansche Familie en Erfrecht op Java en Madoera," *Bijdragen tot de Taal-, Land- en Volkenkunde* 41 (1892), 454-512.

4110   Burger, Dionijs Huibert, *Structural Change in Javanese Society: The Village Sphere*. Ithaca, 1957.

4111 Geertz, Clifford, *Peddlers and Princes: Social Development and Economic Change in Two Indonesian Towns.* Chicago, 1963.

4112 Geertz, Hildred, *The Javanese Family: A Study of Kinship and Socialization.* New York, 1961.

4113 Gille, Halvor, and R. N. Pardoko, "A Family Life Study in East Java: Preliminary Findings," *Family Planning and Population Programs,* ed. International Conference on Family Planning Programs, Geneva, 1965 (Chicago, 1966), 503-521.

4114 Haar, Barend ter, *Adat Law in Indonesia.* New York, 1948.

4115 Koentjaraningrat, "Family and Religion in Indonesia," *East Asian Cultural Studies* 13 (1974), 59-68.

4116 McNicoll, Geoffrey, *Research in Indonesian Demography: A Bibliographic Essay.* Honolulu, 1970.

4117 Maretin, J. V., "Disappearance of Matriclan Survivals in Minangkabau Family Marriage Relations," *Bijdragen tot de Taal-, Land- en Volkenkunde* 117 (1961), 168-195.

4118 Palmier, Leslie H., "The Javanese Nobility under the Dutch," *Comparative Studies in Society and History* 2 (1959-60), 197-227.

4119 Pandam Guritno Siswoharsojo, "A Cross-Cultural Study of Divorce, with Special Reference to a Javanese Village in Jogjakarta, Indonesia." M.A. thesis, Cornell University, 1964.

4120 Peper, B., "Population Growth in Java in the Nineteenth Century," *Population Studies* 24 (1970), 71-84.

4121 Prins, J., "Le statut de la femme indonésienne," *Receuils de la Société Jean Bodin* 11 (1959), 329-343.

4122 Selosumardjan, *Social Changes in Jogjakarta.* Ithaca, 1962.

4123 Subandrio, Hurustiati, "The Respective Roles of Men and Women in Indonesia," *Women in the New Asia,* ed. Barbara E. Ward (Paris, 1963), 230-242.

4124 Sutherland, Heather, " 'Tempo doeloe' and 'Pudjangga Baru': Aspects of Social and Intellectual Life in Twentieth-Century Batavia, Focussing on the Indonesian Community 1933 to 1942." M.A. thesis, Australian National University, 1967.

4125 Swellengrebel, J. L., et al., *Bali: Studies in Life, Thought and Ritual.* The Hague, 1960.

4126 Van der Veur, Paul W., *The Eurasians of Indonesia: A Political-Historical Bibliography.* Ithaca, 1971.

4127 *Villages in Indonesia,* ed. Koentjaraningrat. Ithaca, 1967,

4128 Vreede-de Stuers, Cora, *The Indonesian Woman: Struggles and Achievements.* 's Gravenhage, 1960. French original, Paris, 1959.

4129 Wertheim, Willem F., *Indonesian Society in Transition: A Study of Social Change.* The Hague, 1959.

4130 Widjojo Nitisastro, *Population Trends in Indonesia.* Ithaca, 1970.

LAOS

4131 Condominas, Georges, *Essai sur la société rurale lao de la région de Vientiane*. Vientiane, 1962.

4132 Halpern, Joel M., "Observations on the Social Structure of the Lao Elite," *Asian Survey* 1:5 (1961), 25-32.

MALAYSIA, SINGAPORE, AND BRUNEI

4133 Ahmad bin Mohamed Ibrahim, "The Administration of Muslim Family Law in Malaysia," *World Muslim League Monthly Magazine* 2 (Feb. 1965), 24-44; (Mar. 1965), 22-35; (Apr. 1965), 30-46; (May 1965), 20-28; (June 1965), 45-57; (July 1965), 26-42; (Aug. 1965), 18-34; (Sept./Oct. 1965), 16-40; 3 (Nov./Dec. 1965), 35-48; (Jan. 1966), 44-60; (Feb./Mar. 1966), 26-34; (Apr. 1966), 46-57; (May 1966), 45-55; (June 1966), 39-53; (July/Aug. 1966), 32-47; (Sept. 1966), 35-49; (Oct./Nov. 1966), 27-36; (Dec. 1966), 32-46.

4134 Ahmad [bin Mohamed] Ibrahim, "Developments in the Marriage Laws in Malaysia and Singapore," *Malaya Law Review* 12 (1970), 257-276.

4135 Ahmad bin Mohamed Ibrahim, "Islam and Customary Law in the Malaysian Legal Context," *Family Law and Customary Law in Asia*, ed. David C. Buxbaum (The Hague, 1968), 107-145.

4136 Ahmad bin Mohamed Ibrahim, "The Status of Muslim Women in Family Law in Malaysia and Brunei," *Malaya Law Review* 5 (1963), 313-337; 6 (1964), 40-82, 327-352.

4137 Ahmad bin Mohamed Ibrahim, "The Status of Women in Family Law in Malaysia, Singapore, and Brunei," *Malaya Law Review* 7 (1965), 54-94, 299-313; 8 (1966), 46-85, 233-269.

4138 Beavitt, Paul, "Ngayap (Changes in the Pattern of Premarital Relations of the Iban)," *Sarawak Museum Journal* new series 15:30-31 (1967), 406-413.

4139 Caldwell, J. C., "Fertility Decline and Female Chances of Marriage in Malaya," *Population Studies* 17 (1963), 20-32.

4140 Chan, Kok Eng, "Population Growth and Migration of the Eurasians in Malacca since 1871," *Journal of Tropical Geography* 35 (1972), 17-25.

4141 Cho, Lee-Jay, James A. Palmore, and Lyle Saunders, "Recent Fertility Trends in West Malaysia," *Demography* 5 (1968), 732-744.

4142 Djamour, Judith, *Malay Kinship and Marriage in Singapore*. New York, 1965.

4143 Djamour, Judith, *The Muslim Matrimonial Court in Singapore*. London, 1966.

4144 Firth, Raymond, *Malay Fishermen: Their Peasant Economy.* 2nd rev. ed.; London, 1966.

4145 Firth, Raymond, "Relations between Personal Kin (Waris) among Kelantan Malays," *Social Organizations and the Applications of Anthropology: Essays in Honor of Lauriston Sharp,* ed. Robert J. Smith (Ithaca, 1974), 23-61.

4146 Firth, Rosemary, *Housekeeping among Malay Peasants.* 2nd rev. ed.; London, 1966.

4147 Freedman, Maurice, *Chinese Family and Marriage in Singapore.* New York, 1970.

4148 Galvin, A. D., "Leppo Tau Genealogies," *Sarawak Museum Journal* new series 12 (1965), 173-175.

4149 Minattur, Joseph, "The Nature of Malay Customary Law," *Family Law and Customary Law in Asia,* ed. David C. Buxbaum (The Hague, 1968), 17-39.

4150 Mohamed Din bin Ali, Haji, "Malay Customary Law and the Family," ibid., 181-201.

4151 Palmore, James A., and Ariffin bin Marzuki, "Marriage Patterns and Cumulative Fertility in West Malaysia, 1966-1967," *Demography* 6 (1969), 383-401.

4152 Palmore, James A., Robert E. Klein, and Ariffin bin Marzuki, "Class and Family in a Modernizing Society," *American Journal of Sociology* 76 (1970), 375-398.

4153 Roose, Hashimah, "Changes in the Position of Malay Women," *Women in the New Asia,* ed. Barbara E. Ward (Paris, 1963), 287-294.

4154 Sandin, Benedict, "Some Iban (Sea-Dayak) Customary Law in Sarawak," *Family Law and Customary Law in Asia,* ed. David C. Buxbaum (The Hague, 1968), 40-44.

4155 Saw Swee-hock, "The Changing Population Structure in Singapore during 1824-1962," *Malayan Economic Review* 9 (1964), 90-101.

4156 Saw Swee-hock, "Fertility Differentials in Early Postwar Malaya," *Demography* 4 (1967), 641-656.

4157 Saw Swee-hock, "A Note on the Fertility Levels in Malaya during 1947-1957," *Malayan Economic Review* 12 (1967), 117-124.

4158 Saw Swee-hock, *Singapore Population in Transition.* Philadelphia, 1970.

4159 Siraj, M., "The Shariah Court of Singapore and Its Control of the Divorce Rate," *Malaya Law Review* 5 (1963), 148-159.

4160 Smith, T. E., "Marriage, Widowhood and Divorce in the Federation of Malaya," *International Population Conference,* v. 2 (New York, 1961), (London, 1963), 302-310.

4161 Swift, Michael G., *Malay Peasant Society in Jelebu.* London, 1965.

4162 Swift, Michael G., "Men and Women in Malay Society," *Women in the New Asia,* ed. Barbara E. Ward (Paris, 1963), 268-286.

4163 Taylor, E. N., "Malay Family Law," *Journal of the Malayan Branch Royal Asiatic Society* 15 (1937), 1-78.

THE PHILIPPINES

4164 Angeles, Noli de los, "Marriage and Fertility Patterns in the Philippines," *Philippine Sociological Review* 13 (1965), 232-248.

4165 Arcilla, Ricardo A., "The Philippine Dowry System: A Lego-Historical Approach," *Historical Bulletin* [Manila] 11 (1967), 144-152.

4166 Atienza, Maria Fe G., "The Filipino Family—Impact of New Social and Cultural Forces on It," *Philippine Educational Forum* 13 (1964), 10-14.

4167 Carroll, John J., *Provisional Paper on Changing Patterns of Social Structure in the Philippines, 1896-1963*. Delhi, 1963.

4168 Castillo, C. T., and J. F. Pua, "Research Notes on the Contemporary Filipino Family," *Philippine Journal of Home Economics* 14 (1963), 4-35.

4169 Concepción, Mercedes B., "Fertility Differences among Married Women in the Philippines." Ph.D. Dissertation, University of Chicago, 1963.

4170 Concepción, Mercedes B., "Some Socio-Economic Correlates of Completed Family Size, 1960," *Philippine Sociological Review* 12 (1964), 16-26.

4171 Flores, Bienvenido V., "An Analysis of Philippine Family Studies, 1952-1971: A Preliminary Report of an Effort at Inventorization and Evaluation of Family Theory and Research in the Philippines," *Research Journal of St. Louis University* 5 (1974), 45-97, 199-240, 345-391.

4172 Garcia, Excelso, "Particular Discipline on Marriage in the Philippines during the Spanish Regime," *Philippiniana Sacra* 7:22 (1973), 7-85.

4173 Guthrie, George M., *The Filipino Child and Philippine Society*. Manila, 1961.

4174 Guthrie, George M., and Pepita Jimenez Jacobs, *Child Rearing and Personality Development in the Philippines*. University Park, Pa., 1966.

4175 Harman, Alvin J., *Fertility and Economic Behavior of Families in the Philippines*. Santa Monica, Calif., 1970.

4176 Infante, Teresita R., "The Woman in Early Philippines and among the Cultural Minorities," *Unitas* [Manila] 42 (1969), 1-196.

4177 Liu, William T., Arthur J. Rubel, and Elena Yu, "The Urban Family of Cebu: A Profile Analysis," *Journal of Marriage and the Family* 31 (1969), 393-402.

4178 Liu, William T., and Siok-Hue Yu, "The Lower Class Cebuano Family: A Preliminary Profile Analysis," *Philippine Sociological Review* 16 (1968), 114-123.

4179 Mendez, Paz A., "The Progress of the Filipino Woman during the Last Sixty Years," Centro Escolar University [Manila], *Graduate and Faculty Studies* 16 (1965), 1-29.

4180 Mercado, Nestor J., "The Population of the Philippines: Its Aspects and Problems," *Economic Research Journal* 11 (1964), 76-82.

4181 Palma, Rafael, "The Filipino Family," *Historical Bulletin* [Manila] 11 (1967), 132-143.

4182 Quisumbing, Lourdes R., "Characteristic Features of Cebuano Family Life

Amidst a Changing Society," *Philippine Sociological Review* 11 (1963), 135–141.

4183 Ramos, Norberto de, "The Preservation of the Filipino Family," *Unitas* [Manila] 32 (1959), 218–222.

4184 Rita, Emilio Sta., *Church and Civil Law on Marriage Separation in the Philippines*. Manila, 1963.

4185 Saito, Shiro, *Philippine Ethnography: A Critically Annotated and Selected Bibliography*. Honolulu, 1972.

4186 *Selected Bibliography of the Philippines, Topically Arranged and Annotated*, ed. Philippine Studies Program, University of Chicago. Westport, Conn., 1973. Originally 1956.

4187 Smith, Peter C., "Age at Marriage: Recent Trends and Prospects," *Philippine Sociological Review* 16 (1968), 1–16.

THAILAND

4188 Akin Rabibhadana, *The Organization of Thai Society in the Early Bangkok Period, 1782–1873*. Ithaca, 1969.

4189 Anuman Rajadhon, Phya, "The Story of Thai Marriage Custom," *Asian Culture Quarterly* 1 (1973–74), 55–62.

4190 Cruagao, Paitoon, "Changing Thai Society: A Study of the Impact of Urban Cultural Traits and Behavior upon Rural Thailand." Ph.D. Dissertation, Cornell University, 1962.

4191 deYoung, John E., *Village Life in Modern Thailand*. Berkeley, 1955.

4192 Dickinson, Pramuan, "My Life History in Thailand," *Women in the New Asia*, ed. Barbara E. Ward (Paris, 1963), 452–459.

4193 Fraser, Thomas M., *Rusembilan: A Malay Fishing Village in Southern Thailand*. Ithaca, 1960.

4194 Graham, Henry M., *Some Changes in Thai Family Life*. Bangkok, 1959.

4195 Haas, Mary R., "The Declining Descent Rule for Rank in Thailand," *American Anthropologist* 53 (1951), 585–587.

4196 Hamburger, Ludwig, "Fragmentierte Gesellschaft: die Struktur der Thai-Familie," *Kölner Zeitschrift für Soziologie* 17 (1965), 49–72.

4197 Hanks, Jane R., "Recitation of Patrilineages among the Akha," *Social Organization and the Applications of Anthropology: Essays in Honor of Lauriston Sharp*, ed. Robert J. Smith (Ithaca, 1974), 114–127.

4198 Hanks, Lucien M., Jr., and Jane Richardson Hanks, "Thailand: Equality between the Sexes," *Women in the New Asia*, ed. Barbara E. Ward (Paris, 1963), 424–451.

4199 Hawley, Amos H., and Visid Prachuabmoh, "Family Growth and Family Planning: Responses to a Family Planning Program in a Rural District of Thailand," *Demography* 3 (1966), 319–331.

4200   Kambhu, Leigh R., *Thailand Is Our Home: A Study of Some American Wives of Thais.* Cambridge, Mass., 1963.

4201   Keyes, Charles F., "Kin Groups in a Thai-Lao Community," *Change and Persistence in Thai Society: Essays in Honor of Lauriston Sharp,* ed. G. William Skinner and A. Thomas Kirsch (Ithaca, 1975), 278–297.

4202   Lingat, Robert, *L'esclavage privé dans le vieux droit siamois.* Paris, 1931.

4203   Lingat, Robert, "Le statut de la femme au Siam," *Receuils de la Société Jean Bodin* 11 (1959), 275–292.

4204   Phillips, Herbert P., *Thai Peasant Personality.* Berkeley, 1965.

4205   Piker, Steven Isaac, "An Examination of Character and Socialization in a Thai Peasant Community." Ph.D. Dissertation, University of Washington, 1964.

4206   Piker, Steven Isaac, "The Post-Peasant Village in Central Plain Thai Society," *Change and Persistence in Thai Society: Essays in Honor of Lauriston Sharp,* ed. G. William Skinner and A. Thomas Kirsch (Ithaca, 1975), 298–323.

4207   Prasert Yamklinfung, "Family, Religion and Socio-Economic Change in Thailand," *East Asian Cultural Studies* 13 (1974), 20–31.

4208   Satit Niyomyaht, "Differential Fertility in Thailand: An Analysis of Social and Economic Factors Affecting Fertility." Ph.D. Dissertation, Washington University, 1974.

4209   Skinner, G. William, *Chinese Society in Thailand: An Analytical History.* Ithaca, 1957.

4210   Skinner, G. William, *Leadership and Power in the Chinese Community of Thailand.* Ithaca, 1958.

4211   Ukrit Mongkolnavin, "La situation juridique de la femme mariée en droit thaïlandais." Thèse (Doctorat de l'Université), Université de Paris, 1966.

4212   Wyatt, David K., "Family Politics in Nineteenth Century Thailand," *Journal of Southeast Asian History* 9 (1968), 208–228.

VIETNAM

4213   Bergman, Arlene Eisen, *Women of Viet Nam.* San Francisco, 1974.

4214   Cadière, L., "La famille et la religion au Viet-Nam," *France-Asie* 13 (1958), 260–271.

4215   Dang Thi Tam, "Le divorce en droit vietnamien." Thèse (Doctorat d'Etat), Université de Paris, 1967.

4216   d'Enjoy, Paul, "La famille annamite," *Revue scientifique* [Paris] 4th series 5 (1896), 243–244.

4217   Gourou, Pierre, *The Peasants of the Tonkin Delta.* 2 v. New Haven, 1955. French original, Paris, 1936.

4218   Hoang Van Co, *La femme vietnamienne et son évolution*. Saigon, 1960.

4219   Le Kwang Kim, "A Woman of Viet-Nam in a Changing World," *Women in the New Asia,* ed. Barbara E. Ward (Paris, 1963), 462–470.

4220   Le-Phong-Thuan, Emmanuel, "La polygamie en droit vietnamien." Thèse, Pontificia Universitas Urbaniana, Roma, 1966–67.

4221   Nguyen-huy-Lai, *Les régimes matrimoniaux en droit annamite.* Paris, 1934.

4222   Nguyen-van-Phong, *La société vietnamienne de 1882 à 1902, d'après les écrits des auteurs français.* Paris, 1971.

4223   Nguyen Xuan Chanh, "The Widow's Statute in Vietnamese Customary Law," *Family Law and Customary Law in Asia,* ed. David C. Buxbaum (The Hague, 1968), 252–261.

4224   Nguyen-xuan-Linh, "Habitation et famille au Vietnam: étude socioethnologique." Thèse (Doctorat de specialité), Université de Paris, 1969.

4225   Rambo, Arthur Terry, "A Comparison of Peasant Social Systems of Northern and Southern Viet-nam: A Study of Ecological Adaptation, Social Succession and Cultural Evolution." Ph.D. Dissertation, University of Hawaii, 1972.

4226   Thanh Hoang Ngoc, "The Social and Political Development of Vietnam as Seen through the Modern Novel." Ph.D. Dissertation, University of Hawaii, 1968.

4227   Tran-van-Trai, *La famille patriarcale annamite.* Paris, 1942.

4228   Trinh Van Tao, "Portrait psycho-social du repatrié: étude d'un processus d'adaptation sociale." Thèse, Université de Paris, 1967.

4229   *Vietnamese Women in Society and Revolution,* tr. Ngo Vinh Long, ed. Paul Grace et al. Cambridge, Mass., 1974.

4230   Vu Duy Tu, "Die vietnamesische Familie im Spiegel des Ca-dao," *Oriens Extremus* 13 (1966), 85–97.

4231   *Women in Vietnam: Selected Articles from Vietnamese Periodicals,* tr. Chiem T. Keim. Honolulu, 1967.

Oceania

4232 Aginsky, Bernard William, and Peter H. Buck, "Interacting Forces in the Maori Family," *American Anthropologist* 42 (1940), 195-210.

4233 Allen, Michael, "Kinship Terminology and Marriage in Vanua Lava and East Aoba," *Journal of the Polynesian Society* 73 (1964), 315-323.

4234 Aoyagi, Machiko, "Kinship Organisation and Behaviour in a Contemporary Tongan Village," *Journal of the Polynesian Society* 75 (1966), 141-176.

4235 Barnes, J. A., "African Models in the New Guinea Highlands," *Man* 62 (1962), 5-9.

4236 Barnes, J. A., "Agnatic Taxonomies and Stochastic Variation," *Anthropological Forum* 3 (1971), 3-12.

4237 Bateson, Gregory, *Naven*. 2nd ed.; Stanford, 1958. Originally 1936.

4238 Berndt, R. M., "Kamano, Jate, Usurufa, and Fore Kinship of the Eastern Highlands of New Guinea: A Preliminary Account," *Oceania* 25 (1955), 25-53, 156-187.

4239 Biggs, Bruce G., *Maori Marriage: An Essay in Reconstruction*. Wellington, 1960.

4240 Brady, Ivan, "Kinship Reciprocity in the Ellice Islands," *Journal of the Polynesian Society* 81 (1972), 290-316.

4241 Brady, Ivan, "Problems of Description and Explanation in the Study of Adoption," *Transactions in Kinship: Adoption and Fosterage in Oceania*, ed. Ivan Brady (Honolulu, 1976), 3-27.

4242 Brady, Ivan, "Socioeconomic Mobility: Adoption and Land Tenure in the Ellice Islands," ibid., 120-163.

4243 Brady, Ivan, "Adaptive Engineering: An Overview of Adoption in Oceania," ibid., 271-295.

4244 Brooks, Candace Carleton, "Adoption on Manihi Atoll, Tuamotu Archipelago," ibid., 51-63.

4245 Brown, Paula, "Non-Agnates among the Patrilineal Chimbu," *Journal of the Polynesian Society* 71 (1962), 57-69.

4246 Brown, Paula, "Enemies and Affines," *Ethnology* 3 (1964), 335-356.

4247 Brown, Paula, "Marriage in Chimbu," *Pigs, Pearlshells, and Women: Marriage in the New Guinea Highlands,* ed. R. M. Glasse and M. J. Meggitt (Englewood Cliffs, 1969), 77-95.

4248 Burridge, K.O.L., "Descent in Tangu," *Oceania* 28 (1957), 85-99.

4249 Burridge, K.O.L., "Friendship in Tangu," *Oceania* 27 (1957), 177-189.

4250 Burridge, K.O.L., "Marriage in Tangu," *Oceania* 29 (1958), 44-61.

4251 Burridge, K.O.L., "Adoption in Tangu, New Guinea," *Oceania* 29 (1959), 185-199.

4252 Burridge, K.O.L., "Siblings in Tangu, New Guinea," *Oceania* 30 (1959), 128-154.

4253 Capell, A., and R. H. Lester, "Kinship in Fiji," *Oceania* 15 (1945), 171-200; 16 (1945-46), 109-143, 234-253, 297-318.

4254 Carroll, Vern, "Nukuoro Kinship." Ph.D. Dissertation, University of Chicago, 1966.

4255 Carroll, Vern, "Introduction: What Does 'Adoption' Mean?" *Adoption in Eastern Oceania,* ed. Vern Carroll (Honolulu, 1970), 3-17.

4256 Carroll, Vern, "Adoption on Nukuoro," ibid., 121-157.

4257 Chowning, Ann, "Cognatic Kin Groups among the Molima of Fergusson Island," *Ethnology* 1 (1962), 92-101.

4258 Chowning, Ann, "Lakalai Kinship," *Anthropological Forum* 1 (1965-66), 476-501.

4259 Cook, Edwin A., "Marriage among the Manga," *Pigs, Pearlshells, and Women: Marriage in the New Guinea Highlands,* ed. R. M. Glasse and M. J. Meggitt (Englewood Cliffs, 1969), 96-116.

4260 Cook, Edwin A., "On the Conversion of Non-Agnates into Agnates among the Manga, Jimi River, Western Highlands District, New Guinea," *Southwestern Journal of Anthropology* 26 (1970), 190-196.

4261 Craig, Ruth, "Marriage among the Telefolmin," *Pigs, Pearlshells, and Women: Marriage in the New Guinea Highlands,* ed. R. M. Glasse and M. J. Meggitt (Englewood Cliffs, 1969), 176-197.

4262 Davenport, William, "Nonunilinear Descent and Descent Groups," *American Anthropologist* 61 (1959), 557-572.

4263 Ember, Melvin, "The Non-Unilinear Descent Groups of Samoa," *American Anthropologist* 61 (1959), 573-577.

4264 Ember, Melvin, "Political Authority and the Structure of Kinship in Aboriginal Samoa," *American Anthropologist* 64 (1962), 964-971.

4265 Epling, P. J., Jerome Kirk, and John Paul Boyd, "Genetic Relations of Polynesian Sibling Terminologies," *American Anthropologist* 75 (1973), 1596-1625.

4266   Finney, Ben R., "Notes on Bond-Friendship in Tahiti," *Journal of the Polynesian Society* 73 (1964), 431–435.

4267   Firth, Raymond, *We, the Tikopia: A Sociological Study of Kinship in Primitive Polynesia.* London, 1936.

4268   Firth, Raymond, "A Note on Descent Groups in Polynesia," *Man* 57 (1957), 4–8.

4269   Firth, Raymond, "Bilateral Descent Groups: An Operational Viewpoint," *Studies in Kinship and Marriage,* ed. Isaac Schapera (London, 1963), 22–37.

4270   Firth, Raymond, "Bond Friendship," *Tikopia Ritual and Belief* (Boston, 1967), 108–115. Originally, London, 1936.

4271   Firth, Raymond, "Sibling Terms in Polynesia," *Journal of the Polynesian Society* 79 (1970), 272–287.

4272   Fischer, John L., "Avunculocal Residence on Losap," *American Anthropologist* 57 (1955), 1025–1032.

4273   Fischer, John L., "The Classification of Residence in Censuses," *American Anthropologist* 60 (1958), 508–517.

4274   Fischer, John L. "Adoption on Ponape," *Adoption in Eastern Oceania,* ed. Vern Carroll (Honolulu, 1970), 292–313.

4275   Fischer, John L., Roger Ward, and Martha Ward, "Ponapean Conceptions of Incest," *Journal of the Polynesian Society* 85 (1976), 199–207.

4276   Force, Roland W., and Maryanne Force, *Just One House: A Description and Analysis of Kinship in the Palau Islands.* Honolulu, 1972.

4277   Forster, John, "The Hawaiian Family System of Hana, Maui," *Journal of the Polynesian Society* 69 (1960), 92–103.

4278   Fortes, Meyer, "Malinowski and the Study of Kinship," *Man and Culture: An Evaluation of the Work of Bronislaw Malinowski,* ed. Raymond Firth (London, 1957), 157–188.

4279   Freeman, Derek, "Some Observations on Kinship and Political Authority in Samoa," *American Anthropologist* 66 (1964), 553–568.

4280   Gilson, Richard P., "Samoan Descent Groups: A Structural Outline," *Journal of the Polynesian Society* 72 (1963), 372–377.

4281   Glasse, Robert M., *Huli of Papua: A Cognatic Descent System.* Paris, 1968.

4282   Glasse, Robert M., "Marriage in South Fore," *Pigs, Pearlshells, and Women: Marriage in the New Guinea Highlands,* ed. R. M. Glasse and M. J. Meggitt (Englewood Cliffs, 1969), 16–37.

4283   Glick, Leonard B., "The Role of Choice in Gimi Kinship," *Southwestern Journal of Anthropology* 23 (1967), 371–382.

4284   Goldman, Irving, *Ancient Polynesian Society.* Chicago, 1970.

4285   Goodenough, Ruth G., "Adoption on Romónum, Truk," *Adoption in Eastern Oceania,* ed. Vern Carroll (Honolulu, 1970), 314–340.

4286   Goodenough, Ward H., *Property, Kin, and Community on Truk.* New Haven, 1951.

4287 Goodenough, Ward H., "A Problem in Malayo-Polynesian Social Organization," *American Anthropologist* 57 (1955), 71-83.

4288 Goodenough, Ward H., "Componential Analysis and the Study of Meaning," *Language* 32 (1956), 195-216.

4289 Goodenough, Ward H., "Residence Rules," *Southwestern Journal of Anthropology* 12 (1956), 22-37.

4290 Goodenough, Ward H., "Kindred and Hamlet in Lakalai, New Britain," *Ethnology* 1 (1962), 5-12.

4291 Goodenough, Ward H., "Rethinking 'Status' and 'Role': Toward a General Model of the Cultural Organization of Social Relationships," *The Relevance of Models for Social Anthropology,* ed. Michael Banton (London, 1965), 1-24.

4292 Goodenough, Ward H., "Epilogue: Transactions in Parenthood," *Adoption in Eastern Oceania,* ed. Vern Carroll (Honolulu, 1970), 391-410.

4293 Goodenough, Ward H., "Changing Social Organization on Romónum, Truk, 1947-1965," *Social Organization and the Applications of Anthropology,* ed. Robert J. Smith (Ithaca, 1974), 62-93.

4294 Groves, Murray, "Western Motu Descent Groups," *Ethnology* 2 (1963), 15-30.

4295 Guiart, Jean, "Marriage Regulations and Kinship in the South Central New Hebrides," *Ethnology* 3 (1964), 96-106.

4296 Hagaman, Roberta M., "Divorce, Remarriage, and Fertility in a Micronesian Population," *Micronesica* 10 (1974), 237-242.

4297 Hage, Per, "A Graph Theoretic Approach to the Analysis of Alliance Structure and Local Grouping in Highland New Guinea," *Anthropological Forum* 3 (1973-74), 280-294.

4298 Hage, Per, "The Atom of Kinship as a Directed Graph," *Man* 11 (1976), 558-568.

4299 Handy, E.S.C., and M. Pukui, *The Polynesian Family System in Ka-'U Hawaii.* Wellington, 1958.

4300 Hanson, F. Allan, "Nonexclusive Cognatic Descent Systems: A Polynesian Example," *Polynesia: Readings on a Culture Area,* ed. Alan Howard (Scranton, 1971), 109-132.

4301 Heuer, Berys, "Maori Women in Traditional Family and Tribal Life," *Journal of the Polynesian Society* 78 (1969), 448-494.

4302 Hogbin, H. Ian, "Adoption in Wogeo, New Guinea," *Journal of the Polynesian Society* 44 (1935), 208-215; 45 (1936) 17-38.

4303 Hogbin, H. Ian, "Marriage in Wogeo, New Guinea," *Oceania* 15 (1945), 324-352.

4304 Hooper, Antony, "Adoption in the Society Islands," *Adoption in Eastern Oceania,* ed. Vern Carroll (Honolulu, 1970), 52-70.

4305 Hooper, Antony, " 'Eating Blood': Tahitian Concepts of Incest," *Journal of the Polynesian Society* 85 (1976), 227-241.

4306   Howard, Alan, "Land, Activity Systems, and Decision-Making Models in Rotuma," *Ethnology* 2 (1963), 407–440.

4307   Howard, Alan, "Adoption on Rotuma," *Adoption in Eastern Oceania,* ed. Vern Carroll (Honolulu, 1970), 343–368.

4308   Howard, Alan, Robert H. Heighton, Jr., Cathie E. Jordan, and Ronald G. Gallimore, "Traditional and Modern Adoption Patterns in Hawaii," *Adoption in Eastern Oceania,* ed. Vern Carroll (Honolulu, 1970), 21–51.

4309   Huntsman, Judith W., "Concepts of Kinship and Categories of Kinsmen in the Tokelau Islands," *Journal of the Polynesian Society* 80 (1971), 317–354.

4310   Huntsman, Judith W., and Antony Hooper, "The 'Desecration' of Tokelau Kinship," *Journal of the Polynesian Society* 85 (1976), 257–273.

4311   Kaberry, Phyllis, "The Plasticity of New Guinea Kinship," *Social Organization: Essays Presented to Raymond Firth,* ed. Maurice Freedman (London, 1967), 105–124.

4312   Kay, Paul, "Tahitian Fosterage and the Form of Ethnographic Models," *American Anthropologist* 65 (1963), 1027–1044.

4313   Kay, Paul, "Aspects of Social Structure in a Tahitian Urban Neighbourhood," *Journal of the Polynesian Society* 72 (1963), 325–371.

4314   Keesing, Roger M., "Mota Kinship Terminology and Marriage: A Reexamination," *Journal of the Polynesian Society* 73 (1964), 294–301.

4315   Keesing, Roger M., "Kwaio Kindreds," *Southwestern Journal of Anthropology* 22 (1966), 346–353.

4316   Keesing, Roger M., "Statistical Models and Decision Models of Social Structure: A Kwaio Case," *Ethnology* 6 (1967), 1–16.

4317   Keesing, Roger M., "Step Kin, In-Laws, and Ethnoscience," *Ethnology* 7 (1968), 59–70.

4318   Keesing, Roger M., "Shrines, Ancestors, and Cognatic Descent: The Kwaio and Tallensi," *American Anthropologist* 72 (1970), 755–775.

4319   Keesing, Roger M., "Kwaio Fosterage," *American Anthropologist* 72 (1970), 991–1019.

4320   Keesing, Roger M., "Descent, Residence and Cultural Codes," *Anthropology in Oceania: Essays Presented to Ian Hogbin,* ed. Lester R. Hiatt and C. Jayawardena (Sydney, 1971), 121–138.

4321   Kelly, Raymond C., "Demographic Pressure and Descent Group Structure in the New Guinea Highlands," *Oceania* 39 (1968), 36–63.

4322   Kirkpatrick, John T., and Charles R. Broder, "Adoption and Parenthood on Yap," *Transactions in Kinship: Adoption and Fosterage in Oceania,* ed. Ivan Brady (Honolulu, 1976), 200–227.

4323   Kiste, Robert C., and Michael A. Rynkiewich, "Incest and Exogamy: A Comparative Study of Two Marshall Island Populations," *Journal of the Polynesian Society* 85 (1976), 209–226.

4324   Koch, Klaus-Friedrich, "Structure and Variability in the Jale Kinship Terminology: A Formal Analysis," *Ethnology* 9 (1970), 263–301.

4325 Koentjaraningrat, "Bride-Price and Adoption in the Kinship Relations of the Bgu of West Irian," *Ethnology* 5 (1966), 233-244.

4326 Korn, Shulamit R. Decktor, "Tongan Kin Groups: The Noble and the Common View," *Journal of the Polynesian Society* 83 (1974), 5-13.

4327 Korn, Shulamit R. Decktor, "Household Composition in the Tonga Islands: A Question of Options and Alternatives," *Journal of Anthropological Research* 31 (1975), 235-259.

4328 Labby, David, *The Demystification of Yap.* Chicago, 1976.

4329 Labby, David, "Incest as Cannibalism: the Yapese Analysis," *Journal of the Polynesian Society* 85 (1976), 171-179.

4330 Lambert, Bernd, "Fosterage in the Northern Gilbert Islands," *Ethnology* 3 (1964), 232-258.

4331 Lambert, Bernd, "Ambilineal Descent Groups in the Northern Gilbert Islands," *American Anthropologist* 68 (1966), 641-664.

4332 Lambert, Bernd, "Adoption, Guardianship, and Social Stratification in the Northern Gilbert Islands," *Adoption in Eastern Oceania,* ed. Vern Carroll (Honolulu, 1970), 261-291.

4333 *Land Tenure in Oceania,* ed. Henry P. Lundsgaarde. Honolulu, 1974.

4334 Lane, Barbara S., and Robert B. Lane, "Implicit Double Descent in South Australia and the Northeastern New Hebrides," *Ethnology* 1 (1962), 46-52.

4335 Lane, Robert B., "A Reconsideration of Malayo-Polynesian Social Organization," *American Anthropologist* 63 (1961), 711-720.

4336 Lane, Robert B., and Barbara Lane, "A Reinterpretation of the Anomalous Six-Section Marriage System of Ambrym, New Hebrides," *Southwestern Journal of Anthropology* 12 (1956), 406-414.

4337 Lane, Robert B., and Barbara Lane, "The Evolution of Ambrym Kinship," *Southwestern Journal of Anthropology* 14 (1958), 107-135.

4338 Langness, Lewis L, "Some Problems in the Conceptualization of Highlands Social Structures," *American Anthroplogist* 66 (1964), 162-182.

4339 Langness, Lewis L., "Marriage in Bena Bena," *Pigs, Pearlshells, and Women: Marriage in the New Guinea Highlands,* ed. R. M. Glasse and M. J. Meggitt (Englewood Cliffs, 1969), 38-55.

4340 Leach, Edmund R., "Concerning Trobriand Clans and the Kinship Category Tabu," *The Developmental Cycle in Domestic Groups,* ed. Jack Goody (Cambridge, England, 1971), 120-145. (See #56)

4341 Leach, Edmund R., "A Note on the Mangaian *Kopu* with Special Reference to the Concept of 'Nonunilineal Descent,' " *American Anthropologist* 64 (1962), 601-604.

4342 Levy, Robert I., "Child Management Structure in Tahitian Families," *Journal of the Polynesian Society* 78 (1969), 35-43.

4343 Levy, Robert I., "Tahitian Adoption as a Psychological Message," *Adoption in Eastern Oceania,* ed. Vern Carroll (Honolulu, 1970), 71-87.

4344 Lieber, Michael D., "The Nature of the Relationship between Kinship and

Land Tenure on Kapingamarangi." Ph.D. Dissertation, University of Pittsburgh, 1968.

4345   Lieber, Michael D., "Adoption on Kapingamarangi," *Adoption in Eastern Oceania,* ed. Vern Carroll (Honolulu, 1970), 158-205.

4346   Lounsbury, Floyd G., "Another View of the TrobriandKinship Categories," *American Anthropologist* 67 (1965), 142-185.

4347   Loving, Richard, "Awa Kinship Terminology and Its Use," *Ethnology* 12 (1973), 429-436.

4348   Lundsgaarde, Henry P., "Some Legal Aspects of Gilbertese Adoption," *Adoption in Eastern Oceania,* ed. Vern Carroll (Honolulu, 1970), 236-260.

4349   Lundsgaarde, Henry P., and Martin G. Silverman, "Category and Group in Gilbertese Kinship: An Updating of Goodenough's Analysis," *Ethnology* 11 (1972), 95-110.

4350   Marshall, Donald S., "Notes on Rarotongan Kinship Terminology," *Journal of Austronesian Studies* 1 (1956), 8-19.

4351   Marshall, Mac [Keith M.], "The Structure of Solidarity and Alliance on Namoluk Atoll." Ph.D. Dissertation, University of Washington, 1972.

4352   Marshall, Mac, "Changing Patterns of Marriage and Migration on Namoluk Atoll," *Pacific Atoll Populations,* ed. Vern Carroll (Honolulu, 1975), 160-211.

4353   Marshall, Mac, "Solidarity or Sterility? Adoption and Fosterage on Namoluk Atoll," *Transactions in Kinship: Adoption and Fosterage in Oceania,* ed. Ivan Brady (Honolulu, 1976), 28-50.

4354   Marshall, Mac, "Incest and Endogamy on Namoluk Atoll," *Journal of the Polynesian Society* 85 (1976), 181-197.

4355   Maude, H. E., and H. C. Maude, "Adoption in the Gilbert Islands," *Journal of the Polynesian Society* 40 (1931), 225-235.

4356   McDowell, Nancy, "Kinship and Exchange: The *Kamain* Relationship in a Yuat River Village," *Oceania* 47 (1976), 36-48.

4357   Mead, Margaret, *Coming of Age in Samoa.* London, 1929.

4358   Mead, Margaret, "Kinship in the Admiralty Islands," *Anthropological Papers of the American Museum of Natural History* 34 (1934), 181-358.

4359   Meggitt, Mervyn J., "The Growth and Decline of Agnatic Descent Groups among the Mae Enga of the New Guinea Highlands," *Ethnology* 1 (1962), 158-165.

4360   Meggitt, Mervyn J., *The Lineage System of the Mae Enga of New Guinea.* Edinburgh, 1965.

4361   Meggitt, Mervyn J., "Introduction," *Pigs, Pearlshells, and Women: Marriage in the New Guinea Highlands,* ed. R. M. Glasse and M. J. Meggitt (Englewood Cliffs, 1969), 1-15.

4362   Monberg, Torben, "Determinants of Choice in Adoption and Fosterage on Bellona Island," *Ethnology* 9 (1970), 99-136.

4363 Monberg, Torben, "Ungrammatical 'Love' on Bellona (Mungiki)," *Journal of the Polynesian Society* 85 (1976), 243-255.

4364 Montague, Susan, "Trobriand Kinship and the Virgin Birth Controversy," *Man* 6 (1971), 353-368.

4365 Morton, Keith L., "Kinship, Economics, and Exchange in a Tongan Village." Ph.D. Dissertation, University of Oregon, 1972.

4366 Morton, Keith L., "Tongan Adoption," *Transactons in Kinship: Adoption and Fosterage in Oceania,* ed. Ivan Brady (Honolulu, 1976), 64-80.

4367 Murdock, George P., "Cognatic Forms of Social Organization," *Social Structure in Southeast Asia,* ed. George Peter Murdock (Chicago, 1960), 1-14. (See #4075)

4368 Nayacakalou, R. R., "The Fijian System of Kinship and Marriage," *Journal of the Polynesian Society* 64 (1955), 44-55; 66 (1957), 44-59.

4369 Needham, Rodney, "Lineal Equations in a Two-Section System: A Problem in the Social Structure of Mota (Banks Island)," *Journal of the Polynesian Society* 69 (1960), 23-30.

4370 Needham, Rodney, "The Mota Problem and Its Lessons," *Journal of the Polynesian Society* 73 (1964), 302-314.

4371 O'Brien, Denise, "Marriage among the Konda Valley Dani," *Pigs, Pearlshells, and Women: Marriage in the New Guinea Highlands,* ed. R. M. Glasse and M. J. Meggitt (Englewood Cliffs, 1969), 198-234.

4372 Ogan, Eugene, "Nasioi Marriage: An Essay in Model-Building," *Southwestern Journal of Anthropology* 22 (1966), 172-193.

4373 Oliver, Douglas L., *A Solomon Island Society. Kinship and Leadership among the Siuai of Bougainville.* Boston, 1967. Originally, Cambridge, 1955.

4374 Oliver, Douglas L., *Ancient Tahitian Society.* v. 2. Honolulu, 1974.

4375 Ottino, Paul, "Adoption on Rangiroa Atoll, Tuamotu Archipelago," *Adoption in Eastern Oceania,* ed. Vern Carroll (Honolulu, 1970), 88-118.

4376 Ottino, Paul, *Rangiroa: Parenté étendue, résidence et terres dans un atoll polynésien.* Paris, 1972.

4377 *Pacific Atoll Populations,* ed. Vern Carroll. Honolulu, 1975.

4378 Panoff, Michel, "Patrifiliation as Ideology and Practice in a Matrilineal Society," *Ethnology* 15 (1976), 175-188.

4379 Pollock, Nancy, J. M. Lalouel, and N. E. Morton, "Kinship and Inbreeding on Namu Atoll (Marshall Islands)," *Human Biology* 44 (1972), 459-474.

4380 Pospisil, Leopold, "The Kapauku Papuans and Their Kinship Organization," *Oceania* 30 (1960), 188-205.

4381 Pouwer, Jan, "A Social System in the Star Mountains: Toward a Reorientation of the Study of Social Systems," *American Anthropologist* 66 (1964), 133-161.

4382 Pouwer, Jan, "Towards a Configurational Approach to Society and Culture in New Guinea," *Journal of the Polynesian Society* 75 (1966), 267-286.

4383 Powdermaker, Hortense, "Vital Statistics of New Ireland (Bismarck Archipelago) as Revealed in Genealogies," *Human Biology* 3 (1931), 351–375.

4384 Powell, H. A., "Genealogy, Residence and Kinship in Kiriwina," *Man* 4 (1969), 177–202.

4385 Powell, H. A., "Territory, Hierarchy and Kinship in Kiriwina," *Man* 4 (1969), 580–604.

4386 Radcliffe-Brown, A. R., "The Regulation of Marriage in Ambrym," *Journal of the Royal Anthropological Institute of Great Britain and Ireland* 57 (1927), 343–348.

4387 Rappaport, Roy A., "Marriage among the Maring," *Pigs, Pearlshells, and Women: Marriage in the New Guinea Highlands,* ed. R. M. Glasse and M. J. Meggitt (Englewood Cliffs, 1969), 117–137.

4388 Read, Kenneth E., "Marriage among the Gahuku-Gama of Eastern Central Highlands, New Guinea," *South Pacific* 7 (1954), 864–870.

4389 Ryan, D'Arcy, "Marriage in Mendi," *Pigs, Pearlshells, and Women: Marriage in the New Guinea Highlands,* ed. R. M. Glasse and M. J. Meggitt (Englewood Cliffs, 1969), 159–175.

4390 Rynkiewich, Michael A., "Adoption and Land Tenure among Arno Marshallese," *Transactions in Kinship: Adoption and Fosterage in Oceania,* ed. Ivan Brady (Honolulu, 1976), 93–119.

4391 Sahlins, Marshall D., "Land Use and the Extended Family in Moala, Fiji," *American Anthropologist* 59 (1957), 449–462.

4392 Sahlins, Marshall D., *Moala: Culture and Nature on a Fijian Island.* Ann Arbor, 1962.

4393 Sahlins, Marshall D., "On the Ideology and Composition of Descent Groups," *Man* 65 (1965), 104–107.

4394 Salisbury, Richard F., "Unilineal Descent Groups in the New Guinea Highlands," *Man* 56 (1956), 2–7.

4395 Salisbury, Richard F., "New Guinea Highlands Models and Descent Theory," *Man* 64 (1964), 168–171.

4396 Scheffler, Harold W., "Kindred and Kin Groups in Simbo Island Social Structure," *Ethnology* 1 (1962), 135–157.

4397 Scheffler, Harold W., "Descent Concepts and Descent Groups: The Maori Case," *Journal of the Polynesian Society* 73 (1964), 126–133.

4398 Scheffler, Harold W., *Choiseul Island Social Structure.* Berkeley, 1965.

4399 Scheffler, Harold W., "Kinship and Adoption in the Northern New Hebrides," *Adoption in Eastern Oceania,* ed. Vern Carroll (Honolulu, 1970), 369–389.

4400 Scheffler, Harold W., "Ambrym Revisted: A Preliminary Report," *Southwestern Journal of Anthropology* 26 (1970), 52–66.

4401 Scheffler, Harold W., "Baniata Kin Classification: The Case for Extensions," *Southwestern Journal of Anthropology* 28 (1972), 350–381.

4402 Schneider, David M., "The Kinship System and Village Organization of Yap, West Caroline Islands, Micronesia." Ph.D. Dissertation, Harvard University, 1949.

4403 Schneider, David M., "Yap Kinship Terminology and Kin Groups," *American Anthropologist* 55 (1953), 215-236.

4404 Schneider, David M., "Political Organization, Supernatural Sanctions, and the Punishment for Incest on Yap," *American Anthropologist* 59 (1957), 791-800.

4405 Schneider, David M., "Double Descent on Yap," *Journal of the Polynesian Society* 71 (1962), 1-24.

4406 Schneider, David M., "Depopulation and the Yap *Tabinau,*" *Social Organization and the Applications of Anthropology,* ed. Robert J. Smith (Ithaca, 1974), 94-113.

4407 Schneider, David M., "The Meaning of Incest," *Journal of the Polynesian Society* 85 (1976), 149-169.

4408 Schwimmer, Erik, "Friendship and Kinship: An Attempt to Relate Two Anthropological Concepts," *The Compact: Selected Dimensions of Friendship,* ed. Elliott Leyton (Memorial University of Newfoundland, 1974), 49-70.

4409 Shaw, Daniel, "Samo Sibling Terminology," *Oceania* 44 (1974), 233-239.

4410 Shore, Bradd, "Incest Prohibitions and the Logic of Power in Samoa," *Journal of the Polynesian Society* 85 (1976), 275-296.

4411 Shore, Bradd, "Adoption, Alliance, and Political Mobility in Samoa," *Transactions in Kinship: Adoption and Fosterage in Oceania,* ed. Ivan Brady (Honolulu, 1976), 164-199.

4412 Sider, K. B., "Affinity and the Role of the Father in the Trobriands," *Southwestern Journal of Anthropology* 23 (1967), 65-109.

4413 Silverman, Martin G., "Banaban Adoption," *Adoption in Eastern Oceania,* ed. Vern Carroll (Honolulu, 1970), 209-235.

4414 Silverman, Martin G., *Disconcerting Issue: Meaning and Struggle in a Resettled Pacific Community.* Chicago, 1971.

4415 Smith, J. Jerome, "Rotanese Fosterage: Counterexample of an Oceanic Pattern," *Transactions in Kinship: Adoption and Fosterage in Oceania,* ed. Ivan Brady (Honolulu, 1976), 247-270.

4416 Spoehr, Alexander, "The Generation Type Kinship System in the Marshall and Gilbert Islands," *Southwestern Journal of Anthropology* 5 (1949), 107-116.

4417 Spoehr, Alexander, "Observations on the Study of Kinship," *American Anthropologist* 52 (1950), 1-15.

4418 Strathern, Andrew, *One Father, One Blood: Descent and Group Structure among the Melpa People.* London, 1972.

4419 Strathern, Andrew, and Marilyn Strathern, "Marriage in Melpa," *Pigs, Pearlshells, and Women: Marriage in the New Guinea Highlands,* ed. R. M. Glasse and M. J. Meggitt (Englewood Cliffs, 1969), 138-158.

4420 Swartz, Marc J., "The Social Organization of Behavior: Relations among Kinsmen on Romónum, Truk." Ph.D. Dissertation, Harvard University, 1958.

4421 Swartz, Marc J., "Situational Determinants of Kinship Terminology," *Southwestern Journal of Anthropology* 16 (1960), 393-397.

4422 Swartz, Marc J., "Recruiting Labor for Fissionary Descent Lines on Romónum, Truk," *Southwestern Journal of Anthropology* 18 (1962), 351-364.

4423 Tiffany, Sharon, "The Cognatic Descent Groups of Contemporary Samoa," *Man* 10 (1975), 430-447.

4424 Tonkinson, Robert, "Adoption and Sister Exchange in a New Hebridean Community," *Transactions in Kinship: Adoption and Fosterage in Oceania,* ed. Ivan Brady (Honolulu, 1976), 228-246.

4425 Wagner, Roy, *The Curse of Souw: Principles of Daribi Clan Definition and Alliance.* Chicago, 1967.

4426 Wagner, Roy, "Marriage among the Daribi," *Pigs, Pearlshells, and Women: Marriage in the New Guinea Highlands,* ed. R. M. Glasse and M. J. Meggitt (Englewood Cliffs, 1969), 56-76.

4427 Walter, Michael A.H.B., "Kinship and Marriage in Mualevu: A Dravidian Variant in Fiji?" *Ethnology* 14 (1975), 181-196.

4428 Webster, Steven, "Cognatic Descent Groups and the Contemporary Maori: A Preliminary Reassessment," *Journal of the Polynesian Society* 84 (1975), 121-152.

4429 Weckler, Joseph E., "Adoption on Mokil," *American Anthropologist* 52 (1950), 555-568.

4430 Weiner, Annette B., *Women of Value, Men of Renown. New Perspectives in Trobriand Exchange.* Austin, 1976.

4431 Wilson, Walter Scott, "Household, Land, and Adoption in Kusaie," *Transactions in Kinship: Adoption and Fosterage in Oceania,* ed. Ivan Brady (Honolulu, 1976), 81-92.

Australia and New Zealand

GENERAL SURVEYS AND COLLECTIONS

4432 *The Family in Australia,* ed. Jerzy Krupinski and Alan Stoller. Sydney, 1974.

4433 *The Family Today,* ed. Alan Stoller. Melbourne, 1962.

4434 *Fertility and Family Formation: Australasian Bibliography and Essays,* ed. Helen Ware. Canberra, 1973.

4435 *Marriage and the Family in Australia,* ed. Adolphus Peter Elkin. Sydney, 1957.

4436 *Marriage and the Family in New Zealand,* ed. Stewart Houston. Wellington, 1970.

BIBLIOGRAPHIES

4437 Barwick, D. E., J. Urry, and D. H. Bennett, "A Select Bibliography of Aboriginal History and Social Change. Theses and Published Research to 1976," *Aboriginal History* 1 (1977), 111–169.

4438 Smith, S. S., and B. A. English, "Bibliography of the Family in Australia, 1945–75," *Australian Family Research Bulletin* 3 (1976), 42–106.

AUSTRALIA

4439 Basavarajappa, K. G., "The Influence of Fluctuations in Economic Conditions on Fertility and Marriage Rates, Australia 1920–21 to 1937–38 and 1946–47 to 1966–67," *Population Studies* 25 (1971), 39–53.

4440   Borrie, W. D., "Australian Family Structure: Demographic Observations," *Marriage and the Family in Australia,* ed. Adolphus Peter Elkin (Sydney, 1957), 1–23. (See #4435)

4441   Brown, Morven S., "Changing Functions of the Australian Family," ibid., 82–114.

4442   Burns, Alisa, "Marital Breakdown and Divorce," *Search* 5 (1974), 309–314.

4443   Caldwell, J. C., and H. Ware, "The Evolution of Family Planning in Australia," *Population Studies* 27 (1973), 7–31.

4444   Cannon, Michael, *Australia in the Victorian Age.* v. 3: *Life in the Cities.* Melbourne, 1975.

4445   Coughlan, W. G., "Marriage Breakdown," *Marriage and the Family in Australia,* ed. Adolphus Peter Elkin (Sydney, 1957), 115–164. (See #4435)

4446   Dixson, Miriam, *The Real Matilda: Woman and Identity in Australia, 1788–1975.* Melbourne, 1976.

4447   Encel, Solomon, *Equality and Authority: A Study of Class, Status and Power in Australia.* Melbourne, 1970.

4448   Festy, Patrick, "Canada, United States, Australia and New Zealand: Nuptiality Trends (1830–1940)," *Population Studies* 27 (1973), 479–492.

4449   Finlay, Henry, "The Family and the Law," *The Family in Australia,* ed. Jerzy Krupinski and Alan Stoller (Sydney, 1974), 83–100. (See #4432)

4450   Kelly, Elizabeth, "Sociological Aspects of Family Life," ibid., 18–30.

4451   Kingston, Beverly, *My Wife, My Daughter, and Poor Mary Anne: Women and Work in Australia.* Melbourne, 1975.

4452   Krupinski, Jerzy, "Demographic Data on Marriage and the Family," *The Family in Australia,* ed. Jerzy Krupinski and Alan Stoller (Sydney, 1974), 5–17. (See #4432)

4453   McDonald, Peter F., *Marriage in Australia: Age at First Marriage and Proportions Marrying, 1880–1971.* Canberra, 1974.

4454   Ruzicka, L. T., "Age at Marriage and Timing of the First Birth," *Population Studies* 30 (1976), 527–538.

4455   Ruzicka, L. T., and L. Day, "Australian Patterns of Family Formation," *Search* 5 (1974), 300–305.

4456   Spencer, Geraldine, "Premarital Pregnancies and Exnuptial Births in Australia, 1911–1966. A Comment," *Australia and New Zealand Journal of Sociology* 5 (1969), 121–127.

4457   Spencer, Geraldine, "Recent Trends in Marriages in Australia," *Economic Record* 45 (1969), 206–217.

4458   Spencer, Geraldine, "Fertility Trends in Australia," *Demography* 8 (1971), 247–259.

4459   Summers, Anne, *Damned Whores and God's Police.* Melbourne, 1975.

NATIVE PEOPLES OF AUSTRALIA

4460 Barwick, Dianne E., "Changes in the Aboriginal Population of Victoria, 1863-1966," *Aboriginal Man and Environment in Australia,* ed. Derek J. Mulvaney and Jack Golson (Canberra, 1971), 288-315.

4461 Gale, Fay, "A Changing Aboriginal Population," *Settlement and Encounter,* ed. Fay Gale and Graham H. Lawton (Melbourne, 1969), 65-88.

4462 Huffer, V., "Australian Aboriginie. Transition in Family Grouping," *Family Process* 12 (1973), 305-315.

4463 Inglis, Judy, "Dispersal of Aboriginal Families in South Australia, 1860-1960," *Aboriginies Now,* ed. Marie Reay (Sydney, 1964), 115-132.

4464 Rowley, Charles D., *Outcasts in White Australia.* 2 v. Canberra, 1971.

NEW ZEALAND

4465 Alcock, Peter, "Eros Marooned: Ambivalence in Eden (The Family in New Zealand Literature)," *Marriage and the Family in New Zealand,* ed. Stewart Houston (Wellington, 1970), 242-275. (See #4436)

4466 Gilson, Mirian, "The Changing New Zealand Family: A Demographic Analysis," ibid., 41-65.

4467 Houston, Stewart, "The New Zealand Family: Its Antecedents and Origins," ibid., 21-40.

4468 Vosburgh, M. G., "Some Social and Demographic Influences on New Zealand Family Structure from 1886." Ph. D. Dissertation, Victoria University of Wellington, 1971.

4469 Vosburgh, M. G., "Changing Marriage Patterns in New Zealand," *New Zealand Society: Contemporary Perspectives,* ed. Stephen D. Webb and John Collette (Sydney, 1973), 202-216.

NATIVE PEOPLES OF NEW ZEALAND

4470 Biggs, Bruce G., *Maori Marriage: An Essay in Reconstruction.* Wellington, 60.

4471 Borrie, W. D., "Some Economic and Social Implications of Maori Population Growth in New Zealand," *Journal of the Polynesian Society* 70 (1961), 410-418.

4472 Heuer, Berys, "Maori Women in Traditional Family and Tribal Life, 1769-1840," *Journal of the Polynesian Society* 78 (1969), 448-494.

4473   Heuer, Berys, *Maori Women.* Wellington, 1972.

4474   Metge, Joan, "The Maori Family," *Marriage and the Family in New Zealand,* ed. Stewart Houston (Wellington, 1970), 110–141. (See #4436)

4475   Pool, D. I., "Post-War Trends in Maori Population Growth," *Population Studies* 21 (1967), 87–98.

China

BIBLIOGRAPHIES

4476 *Asian Studies Indexed Journal Reference Guide,* ed. University Center for International Studies. Pittsburgh, 1978.

4477 *Bibliography of Asian Studies,* ed. Association for Asian Studies. Pittsburgh, 1957-77.

4478 *Modern Chinese Society: An Analytical Bibliography:*
    v. 1 *Publications in Western Languages, 1644-1972,* ed. G. William Skinner. Stanford, 1973.
    v. 2 *Publications in Chinese, 1644-1969,* ed. G. William Skinner and Winston Hsieh. Stanford, 1973.
    v. 3 *Publications in Japanese 1644-1971,* ed. G. William Skinner and Shigeaki Tomita. Stanford, 1973.

IMPERIAL OR TRADITIONAL CHINA (TO 1911)

4479 Addison, James Thayer, *Chinese Ancestor Worship: A Study of Its Meaning and Its Relations with Christianity.* Shanghai, Tokyo, 1925.

4480 Baker, Hugh D. R., "Extended Kinship in the Traditional City," *The City in Late Imperial China,* ed. G. William Skinner (Stanford, 1977), 499-520.

4481 Chao, Lin, *Marriage, Inheritance and Lineage in Shang-Chou China.* Taipei, 1970.

4482 Chen, Ta, and John Knight Shryock, "Chinese Relationship Terms," *American Anthropologist* 34 (1932), 623-669.

4483   Cheng, Ch'eng-k'un, "Familism, the Foundation of Chinese Social Organization," *Social Forces* 23 (1944-45), 50-59.

4484   Chikusa, Tatsuo, "Succession to Ancestral Sacrifices and Adoption of Heirs to the Sacrifices: As Seen from an Inquiry into Customary Institutions in Manchuria," *Chinese Family Law...*, ed. David C. Buxbaum (Seattle and London, 1978), 151-175. (See #4554)

4485   Choi, Jai-seuk, "Comparative Study on the Traditional Families in Korea, Japan and China," *Families in East and West*, ed. Reuben Hill and René König (The Hague, 1970), 202-210. (See #76)

4486   Doolittle, Justus, *Social Life of the Chinese*. Taipei, 1966. Originally, New York, 1865.

4487   Dull, Jack L., "Marriage and Divorce in Han China: A Glimpse at 'Pre-Confucian' Society," *Chinese Family Law...*, ed. David C. Buxbaum (Seattle and London, 1978), 23-74. (See #4554)

4488   Escarra, Jean, "Das chinesische Familienrecht in der alten Gesetzgebung und in der neuen Kodifikation," *Sinica* 8 (1933), 97-109.

4489   Escarra, Jean, *La codification du droit de la famille et du droit des successions (livres IV et V du code civil de la république chinoise)*. Shanghai, 1931.

4490   Feng, Han-yi, "Teknonymy as a Formative Factor in the Chinese Kinship System," *American Anthropologist* 38 (1936), 59-66.

4491   Feng, Han-yi, "The Chinese Kinship System," *Harvard Journal of Asiatic Studies* 2 (1937), 141-276.

4492   Feng, Han-yi, and John Knight Shryock, "Marriage Customs in the Vicinity of I-ch'ang (Hupeh)," *Harvard Journal of Asiatic Studies* 13 (1950), 362-430.

4493   Hoang, Pierre, *Le mariage chinois au point de vue légal*. 2nd ed.; Shanghai, 1915.

4494   Hong Kong, Mui-tsai Committee, *Mui-tsai in Hong Kong: Report of the Committee Appointed by His Excellency the Governor, Sir William Peel*. London, 1936.

4495   Hoogers, Joseph, "Théorie et pratique de la piété filiale chez les Chinois," *Anthropos* 5 (1910), 1-15, 688-702.

4496   Hou You-ing, *Etude sur la parenté en droit chinois*. Paris, 1933.

4497   Houx, Koung-ou, *La famille et l'institution du mariage et du divorce en Chine*. Geneva, 1919.

4498   Hsu, Francis L. K., "Incest Tabu in a North China Village," *American Anthropologist* 42 (1940), 122-135.

4499   Hsu, Francis L. K., "Observations on Cross-Cousin Marriage in China," *American Anthropologist* 47 (1945), 83-103.

4500   Hsu, Francis L. K., "On a Technique for Studying Relationship Terms," *American Anthropologist* 49 (1947), 618-624.

4501   Hus, Francis L. K., "The Differential Functions of Relationship Terms," *American Anthropologist* 44 (1942), 248-256.

4502 Hsu, Francis L. K., *Under the Ancestors' Shadow: Kinship, Personality and Social Mobility in Village China.* 2nd ed.; Stanford, 1971.

4503 Hu, Hsien-chin, *The Common Descent Group in China and Its Functions.* New York, 1948.

4504 Jamieson, George, *Chinese Family and Commercial Law.* Taipei, 1968. Originally, Shanghai, 1921.

4505 Jamieson, George, "The History of Adoption and Its Relation to Modern Wills," *China Review* 18 (1889), 137-146.

4506 Koehn, Alfred, *Filial Devotion in China.* Peking, 1943.

4507 Kroeber, Alfred Louis, "Process in the Chinese Kinship System," *American Anthropologist* 35 (1933), 151-157.

4508 Lang, Olga, *Chinese Family and Society.* Hamden, Conn., 1968. Originally, New Haven, 1946.

4509 Levy, Marion, *The Family Revolution in Modern China.* New York, 1963. Originally, Cambridge, Mass., 1949.

4510 Liao, Bao-seing, "Die chinesischen Hochzeitsbräuche vor der Revolution 1911," *Sinica* 15 (1940), 173-180.

4511 Liu, Hui-chen Wang, *The Traditional Chinese Clan Rules.* Locust Valley, New York, 1959.

4512 Lo, Che-tsi, *La succession "ab intestat" dans le code civil chinois.* Toulouse, 1932.

4513 Mäding, Klaus, *Chinesisches traditionelles Erbrecht, unter besonderer Berücksichtigung südostchinesischen Gewohnheitsrechts vom Ende des 19. Jahrhunderts.* Berlin, 1966.

4514 Medhurst, Walter Henry, "Marriage, Affinity, and Inheritance in China," *Transactions of the China Branch of the Royal Asiatic Society* 4 (1853-54), 1-32.

4515 Mollendorff, Paul Georg von, *The Family Law of the Chinese.* Shanghai, 1896.

4516 Parker, Edward Harper, "Comparative Chinese Family Law," *China Review* 8 (1879), 67-107.

4517 Pasternak, Burton, "The Role of the Frontier in Chinese Lineage Development," *Journal of Asian Studies* 28 (1968-69), 551-561.

4518 Rivetta, Pietro Silvio, "Il matrimonio nel diritto cinese," *Rivista italiana di sociologia* 16 (1912), 175-214.

4519 Scherzer, Fernand, *La puissance paternelle en Chine: étude de droit chinois.* Paris, 1878.

4520 Schmitt, Erich, *Die Grundlagen der chinesischen Ehe.* Leipzig, 1927.

4521 Shiga, Shūzō, "Family Property and the Law of Inheritance in Traditional China," *Chinese Family Law...*, ed. David C. Buxbaum (Seattle and London, 1978), 109-150. (See #4554)

4522 Shih, Hung-shun, *Le testament dans le nouveau code civil chinois.* Nancy, 1936.

4523 Siao, T'ong, *De la succession et de l'adoption en droit chinois.* Shanghai, 1927.

4524 Simon, G. E., "The Family," *China: Its Social, Political, and Religious Life,* ed. G. E. Simon (London, 1887), 1–60.

4525 Su, Sing Ging, *The Chinese Family System.* New York, 1922.

4526 Suen, Peng-hien, *Les principes généraux du droit de succession en Chine, jusqu'à la fin du 1er quart du XXe siècle.* Nancy, 1929.

4527 Tai, Yen-hui, "Divorce in Traditional Chinese Law," *Chinese Family Law...,* ed. David C. Buxbaum (Seattle and London, 1978), 75–106. (See #4554)

4528 Tch'en, Si-tan, *L'adoption en droit chinois.* Shanghai, 1924.

4529 Topley, Marjorie, "Marriage Resistance in Rural Kwangtung," *Women in Chinese Society,* ed. Margery Wolf and Roxane Witke (Stanford, 1975), 67–88.

4530 Valk, Marius Hendrikus van der, *An Outline of Modern Chinese Family Law.* Taipei, 1969. Originally, Peiping, 1939.

4531 Valk, Marius Hendrikus van der, *Conservatism in Modern Chinese Family Law.* Leiden, 1956.

4532 Vannicelli, Luigi, *La famiglia cinese: studio etnologico.* Milan, 1943.

4533 Wang, Tse-sin, *Le divorce en Chine.* Paris, 1932.

4534 Wolf, Margery, "Women and Suicide in China," *Women in Chinese Society,* ed. Margery Wolf and Roxane Witke (Stanford, 1975), 111–141.

4535 Wu, Ching-chao, "The Chinese Family: Organization, Names, and Kinship Terms," *American Anthropologist* 29 (1927), 316–325.

4536 Yates, Matthew Tyson, *Ancestral Worship.* Shanghai, 1877.

4537 Yang, Kun, *Recherches sur le culte des ancêtres comme principe ordonnateur de la famille chinoise: la succession au culte, la succession au patrimonie.* Lyons, 1934.

4538 Yen, Chih-t'ui, *Family Instructions for the Yen Clan.* Leiden, 1968.

4539 Young, J. W. "Het huwelijk en de wetgeving dienaangaande in China," *Tijdschrift voor Indische taal-, land- en volkenkunde* 38 (1895), 1–190.

MODERN CHINA
(1911 TO THE PRESENT)

4540 Ahern, Emily M., *The Cult of the Dead in a Chinese Village.* Stanford, 1973.

4541 Aijmer, Lars Göran, "A Structural Approach to Chinese Ancestor Worship," *Bijdragen tot de taal-, land- en volkenkunde van Nederlandsch-Indië* 124 (1968), 91–98.

4542 Anderson, Eugene Newton, Jr., "Lineage Atrophy in Chinese Society," *American Anthropologist* 72 (1970), 363–365.

4543 Baker, Hugh David Roberts, *A Chinese Lineage Village: Sheung Shui.* Stanford, 1968.

4544 Baker, Hugh David Roberts, "Clan Organization and Its Role in Village Affairs: Some Differences between Single-Clan and Multiple-Clan Villages," *Aspects of Social Organization in the New Territories,* ed. Hong Kong Branch, Royal Asiatic Society (Hong Kong, 1964), 4–9.

4545   Befu, H., "Patrilineal Descent and Personal Kindred," *American Anthropologist* 65 (1963), 1328–1341.

4546   Buxbaum, David C., "A Case Study of the Dynamics of Family Law and Social Change in Rural China," *Chinese Family Law...,* ed. David C. Buxbaum (Seattle and London, 1978), 217–260. (See #4554)

4547   Buxbaum, David C., "Chinese Family Law in a Common Law Setting," *Journal of Asian Studies* 25 (1966), 621–644.

4548   Buxbaum, David C., "Family Law and Social Change: A Theoretical Introduction," *Chinese Family Law...,* ed. David C. Buxbaum (Seattle and London, 1978), 3–20. (See #4554)

4549   Chao, Paul Kwang-yi, "The Marxist Doctrine and the Recent Development of the Chinese Family in Communist China," *Journal of Asian and African Studies* 4 (1967), 161–173.

4550   Chao, Y. R., "Chinese Terms of Address," *Language* 32 (1956), 217–241.

4551   Chen, Chiyen, "The Foster Daughter-in-Law System in Formosa," *American Journal of Comparative Law* 6 (1957), 302–314.

4552   Chen, Theodore H. E., and Wen-hui C. Chen, "Changing Attitudes towards Parents in Communist China," *Sociology and Social Research* 43 (1958–59), 175–182.

4553   Chin, Ai-li S., *Modern Chinese Fiction and Family Relations.* Cambridge, Mass., 1966.

4554   *Chinese Family Law and Social Change in Historical and Comparative Perspective,* ed. David C. Buxbaum. Seattle and London, 1978.

4555   Chiu, Vermier Yantak, *Marriage Laws and Customs of China.* Hong Kong, 1966.

4556   Cohen, Myron, *House United, House Divided: The Chinese Family in Taiwan.* New York, 1976.

4557   Davis-Friedmann, Deborah, "Strategies for Aging: Interdependence between Generations in the Transition to Socialism," *Contemporary China* 1 (1976–77), 34–42.

4558   Eberhard, Wolfram, "Chinese Genealogies as a Source for the Study of Chinese Society," *Studies in Asian Genealogy,* ed. Spencer John Palmer (Provo, Utah, 1972), 27–37.

4559   Eberhard, Wolfram, "Research on the Chinese Family," *Settlement and Social Change in Asia* (Hong Kong, 1967), 28–42.

4560   Evans, David Meurig Emrys, "The New Law of Succession in Hong Kong," *Hong Kong Law Journal* 3 (1973), 7–50.

4561   *Family and Kinship in Chinese Society,* ed. Maurice Freedman. Stanford, 1970.

4562   Freedman, Maurice, "Ancestor Worship: Two Facets of the Chinese Case,"

Social Organization: Essays Presented to Raymond Firth, ed. Maurice Freedman (Chicago, 1967), 85-103.

4563 Freedman, Maurice, *Chinese Lineage and Society: Fukien and Kwangtung.* New York, 1966.

4564 Freedman, Maurice, *Lineage Organization in Southeastern China.* London, 1958.

4565 Freedman, Maurice, "Problems in the Analysis of the Chinese Family," *Philadelphia Anthropological Society Bulletin* 14 (1961), 21-23. (See #4561)

4566 Freedman, Maurice, "Ritual Aspects of Chinese Kinship and Marriage," *Family and Kinship in Chinese Society,* ed. Maurice Freedman (Stanford, 1970), 163-187. (See #4561)

4567 Fried, Morton Herbert, "Clans and Lineages: How to Tell Them Apart and Why, with Special Reference to Chinese Society," *Bulletin of the Institute of Ethnology* 29 (1970), 11-36.

4568 Fried, Morton Herbert, "Some Political Aspects of Clanship in a Modern Chinese City," *Political Anthropology,* ed. Marc Jerome Swartz, Victor W. Turner, and Arthur Tuden (Chicago, 1966), 285-300.

4569 Fried, Morton Herbert, "The Family in China: The People's Republic," *The Family: Its Functions and Destiny,* ed. Ruth Nanda Anshen. rev. ed. (New York, 1959), 146-166. (See #82)

4570 Fried, Morton Herbert, "Trends in Chinese Domestic Organization," *Symposium on Economic and Social Problems of the Far East,* ed. Edward Francieszek Szczepanik (Hong Kong, 1962), 405-414.

4571 Gallin, Bernard, "Cousin Marriage in China," *Ethnology* 2 (1963), 104-108.

4572 Gallin, Bernard, "Matrilateral and Affinal Relationships of a Taiwanese Village," *American Anthropologist* 62 (1960), 632-642.

4573 Goode, William J., "China," *World Revolution and Family Patterns* (New York, 1963), 270-320. (See #106)

4574 Ho, Ping-ti, "An Historian's View of the Chinese Family System," *Man and Civilization: The Family's Search for Survival,* ed. Seymour M. Farber, Piero Mustacchi, and Roger H. L. Wilson (New York, 1965), 15-30.

4575 Hsu, Francis L. K., "Chinese Kinship and Chinese Behavior," *China in Crisis,* v. 1: *China's Heritage and the Communist Political System,* ed. Ping-ti Ho and Tang Tsou (Chicago, 1968), 579-608.

4576 Hsu, Francis L. K., "Filial Piety in Japan and China: Borrowing, Variation and Significance," *Journal of Comparative Family Studies* 2 (1971), 67-74.

4577 Huang, Lucy Jen, *The Impact of the Commune on the Chinese Family.* Santa Barbara, 1962.

4578 Jordan, David Kinsey, *Gods, Ghosts, and Ancestors.* Berkeley and Los Angeles, 1972.

4579 Jordan, David Kinsey, "Two Forms of Spirit Marriage in Rural Taiwan," *Bijdragen tot de taal-, land- en volkenkunde van Nederlandsch-Indië* 127 (1971), 181-189.

4580 Lethbridge, Henry James, "Youth, Society, and the Family in China," *Youth in China,* ed. Edward Stuart Kirby (Hong Kong, 1965), 31–65.

4581 Lo, Hsiang-lin, "The History and Arrangement of Chinese Genealogies," *Studies in Asian Genealogy,* ed. Spencer John Palmer (Provo, Utah, 1972), 13–26.

4582 Madge, Charles, "The Relevance of Family Patterns to the Process of Modernization in East Asia," *Social Organization and the Applications of Anthropology: Essays in Honor of Lauriston Sharp,* ed. Robert J. Smith (Ithaca, 1974), 161–195.

4583 McCoy, William John, "Chinese Kin Terms of Reference and Address," *Family and Kinship in Chinese Society,* ed. Maurice Freedman (Stanford, 1970), 209–226. (See #4561)

4584 Meijer, Marinus Johan, *Marriage Law and Policy in the Chinese People's Republic.* Hong Kong, 1971.

4585 Meijer, Marinus Johan; "Marriage Law and Policy in the People's Republic of China," *Chinese Family Law...,* ed. David Buxbaum (Seattle and London, 1978), 426–483. (See #4554)

4586 Meskill, Johanna Menzel, "The Chinese Genealogy as a Research Source," *Family and Kinship in Chinese Society,* ed. Maurice Freedman (Stanford, 1970), 139–161. (See #4561)

4587 Morioka, K., "Life Cycle Patterns in Japan, China, and the United States," *Journal of Marriage and the Family* 29 (1967), 595–606.

4588 Müller-Freienfels, W., "Soviet Family Law and Comparative Chinese Developments," *Chinese Family Law...,* ed. David Buxbaum (Seattle and London, 1978), 323–399. (See #4554)

4589 Pasternak, Burton, "Atrophy of Patrilineal Bonds in a Chinese Village in Historical Perspective," *Ethnohistory* 15 (1968), 293–327.

4590 Pasternak, Burton, *Kinship and Community in Two Chinese Villages.* Stanford, 1972.

4591 Potter, Jack Michael, "Land and Lineage in Traditional China," *Family and Kinship in Chinese Society,* ed. Maurice Freeman (Stanford, 1970), 121–138. (See #4561)

4592 Pratt, Jean A., "Emigration and Unilineal Descent Groups: A Study of Marriage in a Hakka Village in the New Territories, Hong Kong," *Eastern Anthropologist* 13 (1960), 147–158.

4593 Ridehalgh, A., and J. C. McDouall, *Chinese Marriages in Hong Kong.* Hong Kong, 1960.

4594 Rohlen, Thomas P., "Father-Son Dominance: Tikopia and China," *Kinship and Culture,* ed. Francis L. K. Hsu (Chicago, 1971), 144–157.

4595 Sharma, Satya P., "Structural and Functional Characteristics of Lineages in Societies with Unilineal Descent Groups and Centralized Government: A Comparative Exploration," *Journal of Asian and African Studies* 6 (1971), 226–232.

4596   Tsao, W. Y., "The Chinese Family from Customary Law to Positive Law," *Hastings Law Journal* 17 (1966), 727-765.

4597   Wolf, Arthur Paul, "Adopt a Daughter-in-Law, Marry a Sister: A Chinese Solution to the Problem of the Incest Taboo," *American Anthropologist* 70 (1968), 864-874.

4598   Wolf, Arthur Paul, "Childhood Association, Sexual Attraction, and the Incest Taboo: A Chinese Case," *American Anthropologist* 68 (1966), 883-898.

4599   Wolf, Margery, "Child Training and the Chinese Family," *Family and Kinship in Chinese Society,* ed. Maurice Freedman (Stanford, 1970), 37-62. (See #4561)

4600   Wolf, Margery, *The House of Lim: A Study of a Chinese Farm Family.* New York, 1968.

4601   Wolf, Margery, *Women and the Family in Rural Taiwan.* Stanford, 1972.

4602   Yang, C. K., *The Chinese Family in the Communist Revolution.* Cambridge, Mass., 1959.

4603   Yang, Martin M. C., "Changes in Family Life in Rural Taiwan," *Journal of the China Society* 2 (1962), 68-79.

See also #4147.

Japan

GENERAL SURVEYS AND COLLECTIONS

4604 Ariga Kizaemon, "The Family in Japan," *Marriage and Family Living* 16 (1954), 362-368.

4605 Ariga Kizaemon, "Introduction to the Family System in Japan, China, and Korea," *Transactions of the Third World Congress of Sociology* 4 (1956), 199-207.

4606 Beardsley, Richard K., John W. Hall, and Robert E. Ward, *Village Japan*. Chicago, 1959.

4607 Befu, Harumi, *Japan: An Anthropological Introduction*. New York, 1971.

4608 Cornell, John B., "Dōzoku: An Example of Evolution and Transition in Japanese Village Society," *Comparative Studies in Society and History* 6 (1963-64), 449-480.

4609 Dore, Ronald P., *City Life in Japan: A Study of a Tokyo Ward*. Berkeley, 1958.

4610 Fujiki Norio, "The *Koseki* as a Source for Genetic Studies," *Studies in Asian Genealogy*, ed. Spencer J. Palmer (Provo, Utah, 1972), 129-138.

4611 Nakane Chie, *Kinship and Economic Organization in Rural Japan*. London, 1967.

4612 Smith, Robert J., *Ancestor Worship in Contemporary Japan*. Stanford, 1974.

4613 Smith, Thomas C., *The Agrarian Origins of Modern Japan*. Stanford, 1959.

4614 Taeuber, Irene B., *The Population of Japan*. Princeton, 1958.

4615 Yanase Toshiyuki, "The *Koseki* as a Source for the Scholar of Japan," *Studies in Asian Genealogy*, ed. Spencer J. Palmer (Provo, Utah, 1972), 114-128.

4616 Vogel, Ezra F., "The Japanese Family," *Comparative Family Systems*, ed. Meyer F. Nimkoff (Boston, 1965), 287-300. (See #49)

4617 Vogel, Ezra F., *Japan's New Middle Class: The Salary Man and His Family in a Tokyo Suburb*. 2nd ed.; Berkeley, 1971.

BIBLIOGRAPHIES AND REVIEW ESSAYS

4618 Allinson, Gary D., "Modern Japan: A New Social History," *Historical Methods Newsletter* 6 (1973), 100-110.

4619 Crawcour, Sidney, "Documentary Sources of Tokugawa Economic and Social History," *Journal of Asian Studies* 20 (1961), 345-351.

4620 Hall, John W., "Materials for the Study of Local History in Japan: Pre-Meiji Village Records," *Occasional Papers* of the Center for Japanese Studies, University of Michigan 3 (1952), 1-14.

4621 Hanley, Susan B., and Kozo Yamamura, "A Quiet Transformation in Tokugawa Economic History," *Journal of Asian Studies* 30 (1971), 373-384.

4622 Hayami Akira, "La démographie historique japonaise," *Annales de démographie historique* (1970), 327-349.

4623 Hiraga Noburu, "The Extent and Preservation of Original Historical Records in Japan," *Studies in Asian Genealogy,* ed. Spencer J. Palmer (Provo, Utah, 1972), 83-98.

4624 Koyano Shōgo, "Sociological Studies in Japan," *Current Sociology* 24 (1976), 5-201.

4625 Moore, Ray A., "Family Records and Social History in Tokugawa Japan," *Studies in Asian Genealogy,* ed. Spencer J. Palmer (Provo, Utah, 1972), 99-113.

4626 Nakane Chie, "Bibliography," *Kinship and Economic Organization in Rural Japan* (London, 1967), 173-197.

4627 Nakane Chie, "Cultural Anthropology in Japan," *Annual Review of Anthropology* 3 (1974), 57-72.

4628 Nakano Takashi, "Recent Studies of Change in the Japanese Family," *International Social Science Journal* 14 (1962), 527-538.

4629 Silberman, Bernard M., *Japan and Korea: A Critical Bibliography.* Tucson, 1962.

4630 Sofue Takao, "Anthropology in Japan: Historical Review and Modern Trends," *Biennial Review of Anthropology* (1961), 173-214.

4631 Yamamura, Kozo, and Susan B. Hanley, "Quantitative Data for Japanese Economic History," *The Dimensions of the Past,* ed. Val R. Lorwin and Jacob M. Price (New Haven, 1972), 503-530.

ARCHAIC AND ANCIENT PERIODS
(TO 1000 A.D.)

4632   Borgen, Robert, "The Origins of the Sugawara: A History of the Haji Family," *Monumenta Nipponica* 30 (1975), 405–422.

4633   Hall, John W., *Government and Local Power in Japan 500 to 1700: A Study Based on Bizen Province.* Princeton, 1966.

4634   Hirota Kōji, "Kodai sekichō ni arawareta nōmin no kon'in keitai ne tsuite," *Shigaku Zasshi* 74 (1965), 1580–1612. [The Marital Form of Peasants Recorded in the Ancient Family Registers]

4635   Hurst, G. Cameron III, "The Structure of the Heian Court," *Medieval Japan: Essays in Institutional History,* ed. John W. Hall and Jeffrey P. Mass (New Haven, 1974), 39–59.

4636   Kiley, Cornelius J., "A Note on the Surnames of Immigrant Officials in Nara Japan," *Harvard Journal of Asiatic Studies* 29 (1969), 177–189.

4637   Kiley, Cornelius J., "State and Dynasty in Archaic Yamato," *Journal of Asian Studies* 33 (1973), 25–49.

4638   McCullough, W. H., "Japanese Marriage Institutions in the Heian Period," *Harvard Journal of Asiatic Studies* 27 (1967), 103–167.

4639   Miller, Richard J., *Ancient Japanese Nobility and the Kabane Ranking System.* Berkeley, 1974.

4640   Morris, Ivan, *The World of the Shining Prince: Court Life in Ancient Japan.* New York, 1964.

4641   Nanbu Noboru, "Kodai sekichō yori mita kyōdai sōzoku," *Shigaku Zasshi* 79 (1970), 1569–1612. [Brother Inheritance as Observed in Ancient Census Registers, in Connection with the Problems of Female Householder and Empress]

4642   Nunomura Kazuo, "Kamigami no kekkon," *Minzokugaku Kenkyū* 24 (1960), 60–74. [Dual Organization and Marriage between Different Generations in Ancient Japan]

4643   Sekiguchi Hiroko, "Ritsuryō kokka ni okeru chakusaishōsei ni tsuite," *Shigaku Zasshi* 81 (1972), 1–31.

MEDIEVAL PERIOD
(1000–1600)

4644   Katsumata Shizuo, "Chūsei buke mikkaihō no tenkai," *Shigaku Zasshi* 81 (1972), 899–925. [Development of the Regulations on Adultery for the Medieval Warriors' Families]

4645   Solomon, Michael, "Kinship and the Transmission of Religious Charisma: The Case of Hoganji," *Journal of Asian Studies* 33 (1974), 403–413.

EARLY MODERN PERIOD
(1600–1868)

4646 Ackroyd, Joyce, "Women in Feudal Japan," *Transactions of the Asiatic Society of Japan* 3rd series 7 (1959), 31–68.

4647 Befu, Harumi, "Ecology, Residence, and Authority: The Corporate Household in Central Japan," *Ethnology* 7 (1968), 25–42.

4648 Befu, Harumi, "Origin of Large Households and Duolocal Residence in Central Japan," *American Anthropologist* 70 (1968), 309–319.

4649 Blayo, Y., "Un village japonais à l'époque Tokugawa," *Population* 25 (1970), 142–147.

4650 Eng, Robert Y., and Thomas C. Smith, "Peasant Families and Population Control in Eighteenth-Century Japan," *Journal of Interdisciplinary History* 6 (1975–76), 417–445.

4651 Fruin, W. Mark, "Farm Family Migration: The Case of Echizen in the Nineteenth Century," *Keio Economic Studies* 10 (1973), 37–46.

4652 Hanley, Susan B., "Toward an Analysis of Demographic and Economic Change in Tokugawa Japan: A Village Study," *Journal of Asian Studies* 31 (1972), 515–537.

4653 Hanley, Susan B., "Migration and Economic Change in Okayama during the Tokugawa Period," *Keio Economic Studies* 10 (1973), 19–35.

4654 Hanley, Susan B., "Fertility, Mortality and Life Expectancy in Pre-Modern Japan," *Population Studies* 28 (1974), 127–142.

4655 Hanley, Susan B., and Kozo Yamamura, *Economic and Demographic Change in Preindustrial Japan*. Princeton, 1977.

4656 Hayami Akira, "The Population at the Beginning of the Tokugawa Period," *Keio Economic Studies* 4 (1967), 1–28.

4657 Hayami Akira, "The Demographic Analysis of a Village in Tokugawa Japan: Kando-Shinden of Owari Province, 1778–1871," *Keio Economic Studies* 5 (1968), 50–88.

4658 Hayami Akira, "Aspects démographiques d'un village japonais 1671–1871," *Annales E.S.C.* 24 (1969), 617–639.

4659 Hayami Akira, "Demographic Aspects of a Village in Tokugawa Japan," *Population and Economics*, ed. Paul Deprez (Winnipeg, 1970), 109–125.

4660 Hayami Akira, "Labor Migration in a Pre-Industrial Society: A Study Tracing the Life Histories of the Inhabitants of a Village," *Keio Economic Studies* 10 (1973), 1–17.

4661 Hayami Akira and Uchida Nobuko, "Size of household in a Japanese county throughout the Tokugawa era," *Household and Family...*, ed. Peter Laslett and Richard Wall (Cambridge, England, 1972), 473–515. (See #156)

4662 McMullen, I. J., "Non-Agnatic Adoption: A Confucian Controversy in Seventeenth and Eighteenth Century Japan," *Harvard Journal of Asiatic Studies* 35 (1975), 133–189.

4663 Moore, Ray A., "Adoption and Samurai Mobility in Tokugawa Japan," *Journal of Asian Studies* 29 (1970), 617–632.

4664 Naito Kanji, "Kinsei shoki Nagasaki no kazoku dotai," *Shakaigaku Hyoron* 73 (1968), 83–104. [Family Dynamics in Nagasaki City, Seventeenth Century]

4665 Nakane Chie, "An Interpretation of the Size and Structure of the Household in Japan over Three Centuries," *Household and Family...*, ed. Peter Laslett and Richard Wall (Cambridge, England, 1972), 517–543. (See #156)

4666 Smith, Robert J., "Aspects of Mobility in Pre-Industrial Japanese Cities," *Comparative Studies in Society and History* 5 (1962–63), 416–423.

4667 Smith, Robert J., "Town and City in Pre-Modern Japan: Small Families, Small Households, and Residential Instability," *Urban Anthropology*, ed. Aidan Southall (New York, 1973), 163–210.

4668 Smith, Thomas C., "Farm Family By-Employments in Pre-Industrial Japan," *Journal of Economic History* 29 (1969), 687–715.

4669 Smith, Thomas C., *Nakahara: Family Farming and Population in a Japanese Village, 1717–1830.* Stanford, 1977.

4670 Sugiyama S., and W. J. Schull, "Consanguineous Marriages in Feudal Japan," *Monumenta Nipponica* 15 (1959–60), 126–141.

4671 Yamamura, Kozo, *A Study of Samurai Income and Entrepreneurship.* Cambridge, Mass., 1974.

MODERN PERIOD (1868 TO THE PRESENT)

4672 Fukushima Masao, "*Zaibatsu* and the Japanese Family System Seen Through Their Family Constitutions," *Proceedings of the 25th International Congress of Orientalists* 5 (1963), 414–420.

4673 Goode, William J., "Japan," *World Revolution and Family Patterns* (New York, 1963), 321–365. (See #106)

4674 Johnson, Erwin, "The Stem Family and Its Extension in Present Day Japan," *American Anthropologist* 66 (1964), 839–851.

4675 Kawashima Takeyoshi, and Kurt Steiner, "Modernization and Divorce Rate Trends in Japan," *Economic Development and Cultural Change* 9 (1961), 213–239.

4676 Kitano Seiichi, "*Dōzoku* and Kindred in a Japanese Rural Society," *Families in East and West*, ed. Reuben Hill and René König (The Hague, 1970), 248–269. (See #76)

4677 Koyama Takashi, *The Changing Position of Women in Japan.* Paris, 1961.

4678 Koyama Takashi, "Changing Family Structure in Japan," *Japanese Culture: Its Development and Characteristics,* ed. Robert J. Smith and Richard K. Beardsley (Chicago, 1962), 47–54.

4679 Koyama Takashi, "Changing Family Composition and the Position of the Aged in the Japanese Family," *International Journal of Comparative Sociology* 5 (1964), 155–161.

4680 Koyama Takashi, "Technology and the Disintegration of the Large Extended Family in Japan," *Explorations in the Family and Other Essays,* ed. Dhirendra Narain (Bombay, 1975), 359–368.

4681 Koyano Shogo, "Changing Family Behavior in Four Japanese Communities," *Journal of Marriage and the Family* 26 (1964), 149–159.

4682 Kurokawa Minako, "Lineal Orientation in Child Rearing among Japanese," *Journal of Marriage and the Family* 30 (1968), 129–136.

4683 Matsubara H., "The Family and Japanese Society after World War Two," *Developing Economics* 7 (1969), 499–526.

4684 Matsumoto, Y. Scott, "Notes on Primogeniture in Postwar Japan," *Japanese Culture: Its Development and Characteristics,* ed. Robert J. Smith and Richard K. Beardsley (Chicago, 1962), 55–69.

4685 Morioka Kiyomi, "Life Cycle Patterns in Japan, China, and the United States," *Journal of Marriage and the Family* 29 (1967), 595–606.

4686 Nagai Michio, "*Dōzoku:* A Preliminary Study of the Japanese 'Extended Family' Group and Its Social and Economic Functions," *Report* of the Research Foundation, Ohio State University 7 (1953).

4687 Okada Y., "Changing Family Relationships of Older People in Japan during the Last Fifty Years," *Social and Psychological Aspects of Aging,* ed. C. Tibbitts and W. Donahue (New York, 1942), 454–458.

4688 Sano, Chiye, *Changing Values of the Japanese Family.* Washington, D.C., 1958. Reprint, New York, 1973.

4689 Smith, Robert J., "Japanese Kinship Terminology: The History of a Nomenclature," *Ethnology* 1 (1962), 349–359.

4690 Smith, Robert J., *Kurusu: The Price of Progress in a Japanese Village, 1951–1975.* Stanford, 1978.

4691 Steiner, Kurt, "The Revision of the Civil Code of Japan: Provisions Affecting the Family," *Far Eastern Quarterly* 9 (1950), 169–184.

4692 Suenari Michio, "First Child Inheritance in Japan," *Ethnology* 11 (1972), 122–126.

4693 Vogel, Ezra F., "Kinship Structure, Migration to the City and Modernization," *Aspects of Social Change in Modern Japan,* ed. R. P. Dore (Princeton, 1967), 91–112.

4694 Watanabe Yozo, "The Family and the Law: The Individualistic Premise and Modern Japanese Family Law," *Law in Japan,* ed. Arthur Taylor Von Mehren (Cambridge, Mass., 1963), 364–398.

4695 Wimberley, Howard, "On Living with Your Past: Style and Structure among Contemporary Japanese Merchant Families," *Economic Development and Cultural Change* 21 (1973), 423–428.

4696 Yamamura, Kozo, and Susan B. Hanley, "*Ichi hime, ni Tarō:* Educational

Aspirations and the Decline in Fertility in Postwar Japan," *Journal of Japanese Studies* 2 (1975), 83–125.

4697 Yamamura Masae, "Chokkeiseika ni okeru kakubunri," *Shakaigaku Hyōron* 102 (1975), 18–35. [An Analysis of Separation of Nuclear Units within a Stem Family in a Rural Community]

4698 Yamane Tsuneo, "Nihon ni okeru kakukazokuka no genzai to mirai ni kansuru ichi kōsatsu," *Shakaigaku Hyōron* 98 (1974), 18–36. [Nucleation of the Family in Japan: Present and Future]

4699 Yamane Tsuneo and Nonoyama Hisaya, "Isolation of the Nuclear Family and Kinship Organization in Japan," *Journal of Marriage and the Family* 29 (1967), 783–796.

4700 Yokoe, Katsumi, "Historical Trends in Home Discipline," *Families in East and West,* ed. Reuben Hill and René König (The Hague, 1970), 175–186. (See #76)

Korea

GENERAL SURVEYS AND COLLECTIONS

4701 Akiba Takashi, "A Study on Korean Folkways," *Folklore Studies* 16 (1957), 1-106.

4702 Biernatzki, William E., "Varieties of Korean Lineage Structure." Ph.D. Dissertation, St. Louis University, 1967.

4703 Brandt, Vincent Selden Randolph, *A Korean Village between Farm and Sea.* Cambridge, Mass., 1971.

4704 Ch'oe Chae-sok, *Han'guk Kajok Yon'gu.* Seoul, 1966. [A Study of the Korean Family]

4705 Choi Syn-duk and Kim Chaeyoon, "A Traditional Clan Village: Hyo-ri, Kyongsang-Namdo," *Munhwa Illyuhak* 5 (1972), 269-302.

4706 Eisuke Zensho, "The Family System in Korea," *Transactions of the Third World Congress of Sociology* 4 (1956), 222-230.

4707 *Ethno-sociological Reports of Four Korean Villages,* ed. John E. Mills. San Francisco: U.S. Operations Mission to Korea, 1960.

4708 Han Chung-nim C., "Social Organization of Uppen Han Hamlet in Korea." Ph.D. Dissertation, University of Michigan, 1949.

4709 Han Sang-Bok, "Socio-Economic Organization in Korean Fishing Villages." Ph.D. Dissertation, Michigan State University, 1972.

4710 Janelli, Roger L., "Anthropology, Folklore and Korean Ancestor Worship," *Korea Journal* 15 (1975), 34-43.

4711 Kim Taik-Kyoo, *The Cultural Structure of a Consanguineous Village.* Taegu, 1964.

4712 Kwon Tai Hwan et al., *The Population of Korea.* Seoul, 1975.

4713 Lee Jung-Young, "Shamanistic Thought and Traditional Korean Homes," *Korea Journal* 15 (1975), 43-51.

4714 Lee Kwang-Kyu, *The Kinship System in Korea.* New Haven,1976.

4715 Lee Kwang-Kyu and Y. K. Harvey, "Teknonymy and Geononymy in Korean Kinship Terminology," *Ethnology* 12 (1973), 31-46.

4716 Lee Mangap, "Consanguineous Group and Its Function in the Korean Community," *Families in East and West,* ed. Reuben Hill and René König (The Hague, 1970), 338-347. (See #76)

4717 McBrian, Charles D., "Kinship and Community in a Korean Village." Ph.D. Dissertation, Harvard University, 1973.

4718 Osgood, Cornelius, *The Koreans and Their Culture.* New York, 1951.

4719 Park Sang-Youl, "The Social Structure of a Korean Village under the Control of Consanguinity," *Bulletin of the Korean Research Center* 27 (1967), 70-98.

4720 Yi Kwang-Gyu, "Comparative Study of Rule of Descent in East Asia: China, Korea, and Japan," *Han'guk Kajok ŭi Kujo Punsŏk,* ed. Yi Kwang-Gyu (Seoul, 1975), 382-400.

See also #4605.

BIBLIOGRAPHIES AND REVIEW ESSAYS

4721 Choi Kyong-Rak, "Compilation and Publication of Korean Historical Materials under Japanese Rule," *Developing Economies* 7 (1969), 380-391.

4722 Henthorn, William E., *A Selected and Annotated Bibliography of Korean Anthropology.* Seoul, 1968.

4723 Koh Hesung Chun, *Social Science Resources on Korea: A Preliminary Computerized Bibliography.* New Haven, 1968.

4724 *Korean Population and Family Planning Bibliography,* ed. National Population Clearing House. Seoul, 1974.

4725 Silberman, Bernard M., *Japan and Korea: A Critical Bibliography.* Tucson, 1962.

ANCIENT PERIOD (TO 918 A.D.)

4726 Grayson, James H., "Some Structural Patterns of the Royal Families of Ancient Korea," *Korea Journal* 16 (1976), 27-32.

4727 Inoue Hideo, "Shiragi Bokushi ōkei no seiritsu," *Chōsen Gakuhō* 47 (1968), 1-36. [On the Royal Line of the Bag Family of Silla—A Review of Golpumjei]

4728 Takeda Yukio, "Shiragi no sonraku shihai ichi Shōsōin Shozō monjo no tsuiki o megutte," *Chōsen Gakuhō* 81 (1976), 211-257. [The Ruling System of the

Sillan Village Community, through the Postscript Written into the Document Treasured in Shōsōin]

KORYO PERIOD (918–1392)

4729 Okada H., "The Royal Genealogical Charts of the Koryo Dynasty," *Chōsen Gakuhō* 9 (1956), 253–274.

4730 Unruh, Ellen Salem, "The Landowning Slave: A Korean Phenomenon," *Korea Journal* 16 (1976), 27–34.

YI DYNASTY (1392–1910)

4731 Ha Hyon-Kang, "Preference for Male Issue in Korean History," *Korea Journal* 15 (1975), 44–53.

4732 Hahm Pyong-Choon, "A Historical Study of Discriminatory Legislation against the Descendents of Concubines in Korea, 1415–1894," *Transactions of the Royal Asiatic Society, Korea Branch* 42 (1966), 27–48.

4733 Han Yeong-Kuk, "Jūshichi-hachi seiki Taikyū chi-iki no shakai henka ni kan-suru ichi shikō," *Chōsen Gakuhō* 61 (1971), 45–67. [A Study of the Social Change in the Taegu District in the Eighteenth and Nineteenth Centuries—with Special Reference to the 'New Family Registers' of the Taegu Prefectural Government]

4734 Hiraki Makoto, "Jūshichi-hachi seiki ni okeru doryōsaishosei no kizoku ni tsuite," *Chōsen Gakuhō* 61 (1971), 45–76. [On the Standing of Slaves (Mean Class), Wives of Common People and Their Children in Seventeenth and Eighteenth Centuries]

4735 Hulbert, Homer B., *The Passing of Korea.* New York, 1906.

4736 Joe, Wanne J., *Traditional Korea: A Cultural History.* Seoul, 1972.

4737 Kawashima Fujiya, "Clan Structure and Political Power in Yi Dynasty Korea: A Case Study of the Munhwa Yu Clan." Ph.D. Dissertation, Harvard University, 1972.

4738 Kawashima Fujiya, "Bunkaryushi ni mirareru shizoku no ido to sono seikaku," *Chosen Gakuho* 70 (1974), 43–74. [Clan Residence and Geopolitics: A Case Study of the Munhwa Yu Clan during the Choson Dynasty]

4739 Park Pyong-Ho, "Characteristics of Traditional Korean Law," *Korea Journal* 16 (1976), 4–16.

4740 Peterson, Mark, "Adoption in Korean Genealogies: Continuation of Lineages," *Korea Journal* 14 (1974), 28–35, 45.

4741 Shin, S. S., "The Social Structure of Kumwha County in the Late Seventeenth Century," *Occasional Papers on Korea* 1 (1974).

4742 Somerville, John N., "Stability in Eighteenth Century Ulsan," *Korean Studies Forum* 1 (1976), 1-18.

4743 Song Jun-Ho, "The Government Examination Rosters of the Yi Dynasty," *Studies in Asian Genealogy*, ed. Spencer J. Palmer (Provo, Utah, 1972), 153-176.

4744 Yim Seong Hi, *Die Grundlage und die Entwicklung der Familie in Korea.* Köln, 1961.

4745 Wagner, Edward W., "The Korean *Chokpo* as a Historical Source," *Studies on Asian Genealogy*, ed. Spencer J. Palmer (Provo, Utah, 1972), 141-252.

4746 Wagner, Edward W., "Seventeenth Century Social Stratification," *Occasional Papers on Korea* 1 (1974).

MODERN PERIOD (1910 TO THE PRESENT)

4747 *Aspects of Social Change in Korea*, ed. Kim C. I. Eugene and Ch'angboh Chee. Kalamazoo, Michigan, 1969.

4748 Chang Yunshik et al., *A Study of the Korean Population, 1966.* Seoul, 1974.

4749 Che Je Seuk, "Kankoku nōson ni okeru shinzoku no han'i," *Minzokugaku Kenkyū* 27 (1963), 541-555. [A Study of Kinship in Korean Villages]

4750 Cho Lee-Jay, "Economic and Demographic Influences on the Family in Korea," *Fogarty International Center Proceedings* 3 (1969), 139-153.

4751 Choi Syn-duk, "Social Change and the Korean Family," *Korea Journal* 15 (1975) 4-13.

4752 *A City in Transition: Urbanization in Taegu, Korea*, ed. Lee Man-Gap and H. R. Barringer. Seoul, 1971.

4753 Kim Chu-Su, "The Marriage System in Korea," *Korea Journal* 16 (1976), 17-29.

4754 Kim Taek Il, John A. Ross, and George C. Worth, *The Korean National Family Planning Program.* New York, 1972.

4755 Koh Kap-Suk and Jung Keun Cha, "The Influence of Increased Age at First Marriage upon Fertility in Korea," *Journal of Population Studies* [Seoul] 10 (1970), 174-177.

4756 Kwak Yoon-Chik, "The Korean New Civil Code," *Bulletin of the Korean Research Center* 17 (1962), 1-23.

4757 Lee Chong-Sik, "Social Change in North Korea: A Preliminary Assessment," *Journal of Korean Affairs* 6 (1976), 17-28.

4758 Lee Hyo-Chai, "Size and Composition of Korean Families on the Basis of Two

Recent Sample Studies," *Bulletin of the Korean Research Center* 15 (1961), 56–75.

4759 Lee Hyo-Jae, "Life in Urban Korea," *Transactions of the Royal Asiatic Society, Korea Branch* 46 (1971).

4760 Lee Mun Woong, *Rural North Korea under Communism: A Study of Socio-cultural Change.* Houston, 1976.

4761 Moon Seung Gyu, "Ancestor Worship in Korea: Tradition and Transformation," *Journal of Comparative Family Studies* 5 (1974), 71–87.

4762 Pak Ki-Hyuk and Sidney D. Gamble, *The Changing Korean Village.* Seoul, 1975.

4763 Park Hyoung Cho, "The Urban Middle Class Family in Korea." Ph.D. Dissertation, Harvard University, 1974.

4764 Park Hyoung Cho, "The Kin Network of the Urban Middle Class Family in Korea," *Korea Journal* 15 (1975), 22–33.

4765 Roh Chang Shub and Ralph R. Ireland, "Recent Changes in Korean Family Life Patterns," *Journal of Comparative Family Studies* 3 (1972), 217–227.

4766 Tsche Chong-Kil, *Die Scheidung im koreanischen materiellen und internationalen Privatrecht.* Köln, 1961.

4767 Yi Kwang-Gyu, "Women's Status in the East Asian Patriarchal Family," *Han'guk Kajok ŭi Kujo Punsŏk,* ed. Yi Kwang-Gyu (Seoul, 1975), 401–419.

4768 Yoon Jong-Joo, *A Study on Fertility and Out-Migration in a Rural Area.* Seoul Women's College, 1971.

4769 Yoon Jong-Joo, *A Study on Rural Population.* Seoul, 1974.

4770 Yun Young-Koo, "Factors Affecting Mate Selection in Korea," *Bulletin of the Korean Research Center* 17 (1962), 24–45.

Canada

GENERAL SURVEYS AND COLLECTIONS

4771   Bouvier, Léon, "The Spacing of Births among French-Canadian Families: An Historical Approach," *Canadian Review of Sociology and Anthropology* 4 (1968), 17–26.

4772   Charbonneau, Hubert, *Vie et mort de nos ancêtres*. Montreal, 1975.

4773   *Family, School and Society in 19th Century Canada*, ed. Alison Prentice and Susan Houston. Toronto, 1976.

4774   Garigue, Philippe, *La vie familiale des Canadiens-français*. Montreal, 1962.

4775   Garigue, Philippe, "The French-Canadian Family," *La Dualité Canadienne/ Canadian Dualism*, ed. Mason Wade (Quebec, 1960), 181–200.

4776   Griffiths, N.E.S., *Penelope's Web*. Toronto, 1976.

4777   Henripin, Jacques, "From Acceptance of Nature to Control: The Demography of the French-Canadians since the Seventeenth Century," *The Canadian Journal of Economics and Political Science* 23 (1957), 10–19.

4778   Henripin, Jacques, *Trends and Factors of Fertility in Canada*. Ottawa, 1972.

4779   Henripin, Jacques, and Yves Peron, "La transition démographique de la Province de Québec," *La population du Québec*, ed. Hubert Charbonneau (Québec, 1973), 23–44. (See #4781)

4780   Langlois, Georges, *Histoire de la population Canadienne-française*. Montreal, 1935.

4781   *La Population du Québec: études rétrospectives*, ed. Hubert Charbonneau. Québec, 1973.

4782   *Never Done: Three Centuries of Women's Work in Canada*, ed. The Corrective Collective. Toronto, 1974.

4783   Poulin, Gonzalve, *Brève histoire de la famille canadienne*. Montreal, 1940.

4784   *Privilege of Sex: A Century of Canadian Women*, ed. Eva Zaremba. Toronto, 1971.

4785 Sutherland, Neil, *Children in English-Canadian Society: Framing the Twentieth-Century Consensus.* Toronto, 1976.

4786 *The Family in the Evolution of Agriculture,* ed. Vanier Institute of the Family. Ottawa, 1968.

4787 *The Proper Sphere: Women's Place in Canadian Society,* ed. Ramsay Cook and Wendy Mitchinson. Toronto, 1976.

4788 *Women at Work: Ontario, 1850–1930,* ed. Janice Acton, Penny Goldsmith, and Bonnie Shepard. Toronto, 1974.

BIBLIOGRAPHIES AND REVIEW ESSAYS

4789 Armstrong, F. H., "The Family: Some Aspects of a Neglected Approach to Canadian Historical Studies," *Historical Papers,* Canadian Historical Association (1971), 112–123.

4790 Atnikov, P., et al., *Out from the Shadows: A Bibliography of the History of Women in Manitoba.* Winnipeg, 1975.

4791 Dumont-Johnson, Micheline, "Peut-on fair l'histoire de la femme?" *Revue d'histoire de l'Amérique française* 29 (1975–76), 421–428.

4792 Hamel, R., *Bibliographie sommaire sur l'histoire de l'écriture féminine au Canada 1769–1961.* Montreal, 1974.

4793 Strong-Boag, Veronica, "Cousin Cinderella: A Guide to Historical Literature Pertaining to Canadian Women," *Women in Canada,* ed. Marylee Stephensen (Toronto, 1973), 245–274.

NEW FRANCE

4794 Bosher, John F., "The Family in New France," *In Search of the Visible Past,* ed. Barry M. Gough (Waterloo, Ontario, 1975), 1–13.

4795 Dechêne, Louise, *Habitants et marchands de Montréal au XVIIe siècle.* Paris, 1974.

4796 Foulché-Delbose, Isabel, "Women of New France; Three Rivers: 1651–1663," *Canadian Historical Review* 21 (1940), 132–149.

4797 Henripin, Jacques, *La population canadienne au début du XVIIIe siècle.* Paris, 1954.

4798 Leclerc, Paul-André, "Le mariage sous le régime français," *Revue d'histoire de l'Amérique française* 13 (1959–60), 230–246.

4799 Sabagh, Georges, "The Fertility of French-Canadian Women during the Seventeenth Century," *American Journal of Sociology* 47 (1942), 680–689.

4800   Séguin, Robert-Lionel, "La Canadienne, aux XVIIe et XVIIIe siècles," *Revue d'histoire de l'Amérique française* 13 (1959-60), 492-508.

4801   Trudel, Marcel, *La population du Canada en 1663*. Montreal, 1973.

4802   Van Kirk, Sylvia, "Women and the Fur Trade," *The Beaver* 303 (1972), 4-21.

BRITISH NORTH AMERICA

4803   Acheson, T. W., "A Study in the Historical Demography of a Loyalist County," *Histoire sociale/Social History* 1 (1968), 53-65.

4804   Bale, Rosemary R., "A Perfect Farmer's Wife: Women in 19th-Century Rural Ontario," *Canada: An Historical Magazine* 3 (1975), 2-21.

4805   Brun, R. S., "Histoire socio-démographique du sud-est du Nouveau-Brunswick: Migrations acadiennes et seigneuries anglaises, 1760-1810," *Société historique acadienne* 3 (1969), 58-88.

4806   Gagan, David, "The Historical Identity of the Denison Family of Toronto 1792-1860," *Historical Papers*, Canadian Historical Association (1971), 124-137.

4807   Gagan, David, "The Prose of Life: Literary Reflections of the Family, Individual Experience and Social Structure in Nineteenth-Century Canada," *Journal of Social History* 9 (1975-76), 367-381.

4808   Gagan, David, and Herbert Mays, "Historical Demography and Canadian Social History: Families and Land in Peel County, Ontario," *Canadian Historical Review* 54 (1973), 27-47.

4809   Houston, Susan, "The Victorian Origins of Juvenile Delinquency," *History of Education Quarterly* 12 (1973), 254-280.

4810   Johnson, Leo, "The Political Economy of Ontario Women in the Nineteenth Century," *Women at Work...*, ed. Janice Acton, Penny Goldsmith, and Bonnie Shepard (Toronto, 1974), 13-31. (See #4788)

4811   Katz, Michael, *The People of Hamilton, Canada West: Family and Class in a Mid-Nineteenth Century City*. Cambridge, Mass., 1975.

4812   Prentice, A., "Education and the Metaphor of the Family: An Upper Canadian Example," *History of Education Quarterly* 12 (1972), 281-303.

4813   Prentice, Alison, "The Feminization of Teaching in British North America and Canada, 1845-1875," *Histoire sociale/Social History* 7 (1975), 5-20.

POST-CONFEDERATION CANADA

4814   Bliss, Michael, " 'Pure Books on Avoided Subjects': Pre-Freudian Sexual Ideas in Canada," *Historical Papers,* Canadian Historical Association (1970), 89-108.

4815 Bock, P. K., "Patterns of Illegitimacy on a Canadian Indian Reserve: 1860-1960," *Journal of Marriage and the Family* 26 (1964), 142-148.

4816 Bouchard, Gérard, "L'histoire de la population et l'étude de la mobilité sociale au Saguenay, XIXe-XXe siècles," *Recherches sociographiques* 17 (1976), 353-372.

4817 Bouchard, Gérard, "L'histoire démographique et le problème des migrations. L'exemple de la terrière," *Histoire sociale/Social History* 7 (1975), 21-33.

4818 Charles, E., *The Changing Size of the Family in Canada.* Ottawa, 1948.

4819 Churcher, C. S., and N. A. Kenyon, "The Tabor Hill Ossuaries: A Study in Iroquois Demography," *Human Biology* 22 (1960), 249-273.

4820 Cross, Suzanne, "The Neglected Majority: The Changing Role of Women in Nineteenth-Century Montreal," *Histoire sociale/Social History* 6 (1973), 202-223.

4821 Denton, F. T., and P. J. George, "The Influence of Socio-Economic Variables on Family Size in Wentworth County, Ontario, 1871," *Canadian Review of Sociology and Anthropology* 10 (1973), 334-350.

4822 Fortin, Gérald, "Women's Role in the Evolution of Agriculture in Quebec," *The Family in the Evolution of Agriculture,* ed. Vanier Institute of the Family (Ottawa, 1968), 25-31.

4823 Gagan, David, "Indivisibility of Land: A Microanalysis of the System of Inheritance in Nineteenth-Century Ontario," *Journal of Economic History* 36 (1976), 126-141.

4824 Gagnon, Mona-Josée, *Les Femmes vues par le Québec des hommes: 30 ans d'histoire des idéologies 1940-1970.* Montreal, 1974.

4825 Gérin, Léon, "La Famille canadienne-française, sa force, ses faiblesses. Le paysan de Saint-Irénée, hier et aujourd'hui," *Revue trimestrielle canadienne* 19 (1932), 37-63.

4826 Kohland, Seena, and John W. Bennet, "Kinship, Succession, and the Migration of Young People in a Canadian Agricultural Community," *International Journal of Comparative Sociology* 6 (1965), 95-116.

4827 Morrison, T., " 'Their Proper Sphere': Feminism, the Family and Child-Centered Social Reform in Ontario, 1875-1900," *Ontario History* 68 (1976), 45-74.

4828 Pelletier, A. J., F. D. Thompson, and A. Rochon, *The Canadian Family.* Ottawa, 1938.

4829 Romaniuk, Anatole, and Victor Piche, "Natality Estimates for the Canadian Indians by Stable Population Models, 1900-1969," *Canadian Review of Sociology and Anthropology* 9 (1972), 1-20.

4830 Royce, Marion, "Arguments over the Education of Girls: Their Admission to Grammar Schools in this Province," *Ontario History* 67 (1975), 1-13.

4831   Stoddart, J., and V. Strong-Boag, "...And Things Were Going Wrong at Home," *Atlantis* 1 (1975), 38–44.

4832   Tepperman, L., "Ethnic Variations in Marriage and Fertility: Canada 1871," *Canadian Review of Sociology and Anthropology* 11 (1974), 324–343.

4833   Trofimenkoff, Susan Mann, "Henri Bourassa and 'The Woman Question,' " *Journal of Canadian Studies* 10 (1975), 3–11.

4834   Wargon, J., "Using the Census for Research on the Family in Canada," *Journal of Comparative Family Studies* 3 (1972), 148–167.

The United States

GENERAL BIBLIOGRAPHIES, REVIEW ESSAYS, SURVEYS, AND COLLECTIONS

4835 Adams, Bert N., *The American Family: A Sociological Interpretation.* Chicago, 1971.

4836 *The American Family in Social-Historical Perspective,* ed. Michael Gordon. New York, 1973. 2nd ed.; New York, 1978.

4837 *Anonymous Americans: Explorations in Nineteenth-Century Social History,* ed. Tamara K. Hareven. Englewood Cliffs, N.J., 1971.

4838 Bardis, Panos D., "Changes in the Colonial and Modern American Family Systems," *Social Science* 38 (1963), 103–114.

4839 Blake, Nelson Manfred, *The Road to Reno: A History of Divorce in the United States.* New York, 1962.

4840 Boatright, Mody C., Robert B. Downs, and John T. Managan, *The Family Saga and Other Phases of American Folklore.* Urbana, Ill., 1958.

4841 Brownlee, W. Elliot, and Mary H. Brownlee, *Women in the American Economy: A Documentary History, 1675–1929.* New Haven, Conn., 1976.

4842 Burgess, Ernest W., and Paul Wallin, *Engagement and Marriage.* Philadelphia, Pa., 1953.

4843 Cable, Mary, *The Little Darlings: A History of Child Rearing in America.* New York, 1975.

4844 Calhoun, Arthur Wallace, *A Social History of the American Family from Colonial Times to the Present.* 3 v. Cleveland, 1917.

4845 *Children and Youth in America: A Documentary History,* ed. Robert H. Bremner, John Barnard, Tamara K. Hareven, and Robert Mennel. 3 v. Cambridge, Mass., 1970–74.

4846 Christensen, Harold T., "Development of the Family Field of Study," *Handbook of Marriage and the Family,* ed. Harold T. Christensen (Chicago, 1964), 3–32. (See #124)

4847 Clarke, Helen I., *Social Legislation: American Laws Dealing with the Family, Child, and Dependent.* New York, 1940.

4848 *Clio's Consciousness Raised: New Perspectives on the History of Women,* ed. Mary Hartman and Lois Banner. New York, 1974.

4849 Cremin, Lawrence A., *The Family as Educator.* New York, 1974.

4850 Davis, Glenn, *Childhood and History in America.* New York, 1976.

4851 Davis, Lenwood G., *The Black Family in the United States: A Selected Bibliography of Annotated Books, Articles, and Dissertations on Black Families in America.* New York, 1978.

4852 Davis, Lenwood G., *The Black Family in Urban Areas in the United States.* 2nd ed.; Monticello, Ill., 1975.

4853 Demos, John, "The American Family in Past Time," *American Scholar* 43 (1974), 422–446.

4854 Ditzion, Sidney, *Marriage, Morals, and Sex in America: A History of Ideas.* New York, 1961.

4855 *Emerging Conceptual Frameworks in Family Analysis,* ed. Francis Ivan Nye and Felix M. Berardo. New York, 1966.

4856 *Family and Kin in Urban Communities: 1700–1930,* ed. Tamara K. Hareven. New York, 1977.

4857 *The Family, Communes, and Utopian Societies,* ed. Sallie McFague TeSelle. New York, 1972.

4858 Farber, Bernard, *Family: Organization and Interaction.* San Francisco, 1964.

4859 Felmley, Jenrose, *Working Women: Homemakers and Volunteers: An Annotated Selected Bibliography.* Washington, D.C., 1975.

4860 Gildrie, Richard, "Family Structure and Local History in America," *History of Education Quarterly* 13 (1973), 433–439.

4861 Groves, Ernest R., *The American Family.* Philadelphia, 1934.

4862 Groves, Ernest R., and William F. Ogburn, *American Marriage and Family Relationships.* New York, 1928.

4863 Handlin, Oscar, and Mary F. Handlin, *Facing Life: Youth and the Family in American History.* Boston, 1971.

4864 Hareven, Tamara K., "The Historical Study of the Family in Urban Society," *Journal of Urban History* 1 (1974–75), 259–267.

4865 Jeffrey, Kirk, "Varieties of Family History," *American Archivist* 38 (1974–75), 521–532.

4866 Lorimer, Frank, and Frederick Osborn, *Dynamics of Population.* New York, 1934.

4867 McCormick, C. O., "The History of Birth Control in America," *Journal of the Indiana Medical Association* 27 (1934), 385–391.

4868   Medicine, Beatrice, "The Role of Women in Native American Societies: A Bibliography," *The Indian Historian* 8:3 (1975), 50–54.

4869   Monahan, Thomas Patrick, *The Pattern of Age at Marriage in the U.S.* 2 v. Philadelphia, 1951.

4870   Nimkoff, Meyer F., *Marriage and the Family*. Boston, 1947.

4871   Potter, David M., *People of Plenty: Economic Abundance and the American Character*. Chicago, 1954.

4872   Ruthstein, Pauline Marcus, "Women: A Selected Bibliography of Books," *Bulletin of Bibliography and Magazine Notes* 32:2 (1975), 45–54, 76.

4873   Ryan, Mary P., *Womanhood in America: From Colonial Times to the Present*. New York, 1975.

4874   Saveth, Edward N., "The American Patrician Class: A Field for Research," *Kinship and Family Organization*, ed. Bernard Farber (New York, 1966), 157–168. (See #162)

4875   Saveth, Edward N., "The Problem of American Family History," *American Quarterly* 21 (1969), 311–329.

4876   *Sex, Marriage, and Society*, ed. Charles Rosenberg and Caroll Smith-Rosenberg. New York, 1974.

4877   Soltow, Martha Jane, *Women in American Labor History, 1825–1935: An Annotated Bibliography*. East Lansing, Mich., 1972.

4878   Stein, Stuart J., "Common-Law Marriage: Its History and Certain Contemporary Problems," *Journal of Family Law* 9 (1970), 271–299.

4879   Stewart, Philip, "Toward a History of Childhood," *History of Education Quarterly* 12 (1972), 198–209.

4880   *Themes in the History of the Family*, ed. Tamara K. Hareven. Worcester, Mass., 1978.

4881   Thwing, Charles Franklin, and Carrie F. Butler Thwing, *The Family: An Historical and Social Study*. Boston, 1886.

4882   United States Treasury Department, *Digest of the Law Relating to Common Law Marriage in the States, Territories, and Dependencies of the United States*. Washington, D.C., 1919.

4883   Vann, Richard T., "Quaker Family Life," *Journal of Interdisciplinary History* 5 (1974–75), 739–749.

4884   Vernier, Chester G., *American Family Laws*. 5 v. Stanford and London, 1931–38. Reprint, Westport, Conn., 1971.

4885   Vinovskis, Maris A., "Recent Trends in American Historical Demography— Some Methodological and Conceptual Considerations," *Annual Review of Sociology* 4 (1978), 603–627.

4886   *The Voices of Children, 1700–1914*, ed. Irina Strickland. New York, 1973.

4887   Wells, Robert V., "Family History and Demographic Transition," *Journal of Social History* 9 (1975–76), 1–19.

4888   *Willard W. Waller on the Family, Education, and War; Selected Writings*, ed.

by William J. Goode, Frank F. Furstenberg, Jr., and Larry R. Mitchell. Chicago, 1970.

4889 Williams, Faith M., and Carle C. Zimmerman, *Studies of Family Living in the United States and Other Countries.* Washington, D.C., 1935.

4890 Wimmer, Larry T., and Clayne L. Pope, "The Genealogical Society Library of Salt Lake City: A Source of Data for Economic and Social Historians," *History Methods Newsletter* 8 (1975), 51-58.

4891 Winch, Robert F., "Permanence and Change in the History of the American Family and Some Speculations as to Its Future," *Journal of Marriage and the Family* 32 (1970), 6-15.

4892 Winch, Robert F., and Rae Lesser Blumberg, "Societal Complexity and Familial Organization," *Selected Studies in Marriage and the Family,* ed. Robert F. Winch and Louis W. Goodman (New York, 1968), 70-92.

See also #55, #67, #68, #85, #106, #107, #108, #125, #126, #130, #131, and #262.

TO 1790

4893 Adams, Charles Francis, "Some Phases of Sexual Morality and Church Discipline in Colonial New England," *Proceedings of the Massachusetts Historical Society* 2nd series 6 (1891), 477-516.

4894 Alexander, John K., "The Philadelphia Numbers Game: An Analysis of Philadelphia's Eighteenth-Century Population," *Pennsylvania Magazine of History and Biography* 98 (1974), 314-324.

4895 Allen, Nathan, "The New England Family," *The New Englander* 41 (1882), 137-159.

4896 Aurand, A. Monroe, *Little Known Facts about Bundling in the New World.* Harrisburg, Pa., 1938.

4897 Auwers, Linda, "Fathers, Sons, and Wealth in Colonial Windsor, Connecticut," *Journal of Family History* 3 (1978), 136-149.

4898 Axtell, James, *The School upon a Hill: Education and Society in Colonial New England.* New Haven, 1974.

4899 Bailyn, Bernard, "The Beekmans of New York: Trade, Politics, and Families," *William and Mary Quarterly* 14 (1957), 598-608.

4900 Bailyn, Bernard, *Education in the Forming of American Society.* Chapel Hill, 1960.

4901 Barker-Benfield, Ben, "Anne Hutchinson and the Puritan Attitude toward Women," *Feminist Studies* 1 (1972), 65-96.

4902 Beales, Ross W., Jr., "In Search of the Historical Child: Miniature Adulthood and Youth in Colonial New England," *American Quarterly* 27 (1975), 379-398.

4903 Benson, Mary Sumner, *Women in Eighteenth Century America: A Study of Opinion and Social Usage.* New York, 1935.

4904 Billings, Warren M., "The Case of Fernando and Elizabeth Key: A Note on the Status of Blacks in Seventeenth-Century Virginia," *William and Mary Quarterly* 30 (1973), 467–474.

4905 Blumenthal, Walter Hart, *Brides from Bridewell: Female Felons Sent to Colonial America.* Rutland, Vt., 1962.

4906 Brower, Merle G., "Marriage and Family Life among Blacks in Colonial Pennsylvania," *Pennsylvania Magazine of History and Biography* 99 (1975), 368–372.

4907 Brown, Richard D., *Mondernization: The Transformation of American Life 1600–1865.* New York, 1976.

4908 Bushman, Richard, *From Puritan to Yankee: Character and Social Order in Connecticut, 1690–1765.* Cambridge, Mass., 1967.

4909 Caley, Percy B., "Child Life in Colonial Western Pennslyvania," *Western Pennsylvania Historical Magazine* 9 (1926), 33–49, 104–121, 188–201.

4910 Calhoun, Arthur Wallace, "The Early American Family," *Annals of the American Academy of Political and Social Science* 160 (1932), 7–12.

4911 Carr, Lois Green, and L. S. Walsh, "The Planter's Wife: The Experience of White Women in Seventeenth-Century Maryland," *William and Mary Quarterly* 34 (1978), 542–571.

4912 Caulfield, Ernest, *The Infant Welfare Movement in the Eighteenth Century.* New York, 1931.

4913 Caulfield, Ernest, "Some Common Diseases of Colonial Children," *Transactions of the Colonial Society of Massachusetts* 35 (1942–46), 4–65.

4914 *Child-Rearing Concepts, 1628–1861: Historical Sources,* ed. Philip J. Greven. Ithaca, Ill., 1973.

4915 Cobbledick, M. R., "The Property Rights of Women in Puritan New England," *Studies in the Science of Society,* ed. George Murdock (New Haven, 1937), 107–116.

4916 Cohen, Ronald D., "Socialization in Colonial New England," *History of Education Quarterly* 13 (1973), 73–82.

4917 Cohn, Henry S., "Connecticut's Divorce Mechanism, 1636–1969," *American Journal of Legal History* 14 (1970), 35–54.

4918 Cott, Nancy F., *The Bonds of Womanhood: "Woman's Sphere" in New England, 1780–1835.* New Haven, Conn., 1977.

4919 Cott, Nancy F., "Divorce and the Changing Status of Women in Eighteenth-Century Massachusetts," *William and Mary Quarterly* 33 (1976), 586–614.

4920 Crandall, Ralph J., "New England's Second Great Migration: The First Three Generations of Settlement, 1630–1700," *New England Historical Genealogical Register* 129 (1975), 347–360.

4921 Cremin, Lawrence A., *American Education: The Colonial Experience.* New York, 1970.

4922 Daniels, Bruce C., "Family Dynasties in Connecticut's Largest Towns, 1700–1760," *Canadian Journal of History* 8 (1973), 99–110.

4923 Dart, Henry P., "Marriage Contracts of French Colonial Louisiana," *Louisiana Historical Quarterly* 17 (1934), 229–241.

4924 DeLong, Thomas A., *The DeLongs of New York and Brooklyn: A Huguenot Family Portrait*. Southport, Conn., 1972.

4925 Demos, John, "Demography and Psychology in the Historical Study of Family-Life: A Personal Report," *Household and Family...*, ed. Peter Laslett and Richard Wall (Cambridge, England, 1972), 561–570. (See #156)

4926 Demos, John, "Families in Colonial Bristol, R.I.: An Exercise in Historical Demography," *William and Mary Quarterly* 25 (1968), 40–57.

4927 Demos, John, *A Little Commonwealth: Family Life in Plymouth Colony*. New York, 1970.

4928 Demos, John, "Notes on Life in Plymouth Colony," *William and Mary Quarterly* 22 (1965), 264–286.

4929 Demos, John, "Underlying Themes in the Witchcraft of Seventeenth Century New England," *American Historical Review* 75 (1970), 1311–1326.

4930 Dow, George Francis, *Domestic Life in New England in the 17th Century*. Topsfield, Mass., 1925.

4931 Dunn, Richard S., *Puritans and Yankees: The Winthrop Dynasty of New England, 1630–1717*. Princeton, 1962.

4932 Earle, Alice Morse, *Colonial Dames and Good Wives*. New York, 1924. Originally 1895.

4933 Earle, Alice Morse, *Home Life in Colonial Days*. New York, 1896.

4934 Earle, Alice Morse, "Old Time Marriage Customs in New England," *Journal of American Folklore* 6 (1893), 97–102.

4935 Ellet, Elizabeth F., *Domestic History of the American Revolution*. New York, 1850.

4936 Farber, Bernard, *Guardians of Virtue: Salem Families in 1800*. New York, 1972.

4937 Flaherty, David H., *Privacy in Colonial New England*. Charlottesville, 1972.

4938 Fleming, Sandford, *Children and Puritanism: The Place of Children in the Life and Thought of the New England Churches, 1620–1847*. New Haven, 1933. Reprint, 1969.

4939 Frost, Jerry W., "As the Twig Is Bent: Quaker Ideas of Childhood," *Quaker History* 60 (1971), 67–86.

4940 Frost, Jerry W., *The Quaker Family in Colonial America*. New York, 1973.

4941 Gladwin, Lee, "Tobacco and Sex: Some Factors Affecting Non-Marital Sexual Behavior in Colonial Virginia," *Journal of Social History* 12 (1978–79), 57–75.

4942 Gollin, Gillian Lindt, *Moravians in Two Worlds: A Study of Changing Communities*. New York, 1967.

4943 Gollin, Gillian Lindt, "Family Surrogates in Colonial America: The Moravian

Experiment," *Journal of Marriage and the Family* 31 (1969), 650–658.

4944   Gordon, Ann D., and Mari Jo Buhle, "Sex and Class in Colonial and 19th-Century America," *Liberating Women's History*, ed. Berenice A. Carrol (Urbana, 1976), 278–300.

4945   Gould, Mary Earle, *The Early American House: Household Life in America, 1620–1850.* Rutland, Vt., 1965.

4946   Greven, Philip J., Jr., "The Average Sizes of Families and Households in the Province of Massachusetts in 1764 and in the United States in 1790; An Overview," *Household and Family...*, ed. Peter Laslett and Richard Wall (Cambridge, England, 1972), 545–560. (See #156)

4947   Greven, Philip J., Jr., "Family Structure in Seventeenth-Century Andover, Massachusetts," *William and Mary Quarterly*, 23 (1966), 234–256. Now in *The American Family in Social-Historical Perspective*, ed. Michael Gordon (New York, 1973), 77–99.

4948   Greven, Philip J., Jr., *Four Generations: Population, Land, and Family in Colonial Andover, Massachusetts.* Ithaca, N.Y., 1970.

4949   Greven, Philip J., Jr., "Historical Demography and Colonial America: A Review Article," *William and Mary Quarterly* 24 (1967), 438–454.

4950   Greven, Philip J., Jr., "Old Patterns in the New World: The Distribution of Land in 17th-Century Andover," *Essex Institute Historical Collections* 101 (1965), 133–148.

4951   Greven, Philip J., Jr., *The Protestant Temperament: Patterns of Child-Rearing, Religious Experience, and the Self in Early America.* New York, 1977.

4952   Gutman, Herbert G., *The Black Family in Slavery and Freedom, 1750–1925.* New York, 1976.

4953   Hancock, Harold B., "The Indenture System in Delaware, 1681–1921," *Delaware History* 16 (1974), 47–59.

4954   Haskins, George, "The Beginnings of Partible Inheritance in the American Colonies," *Essays in the History of Early American Law*, ed. David Flaherty (Chapel Hill, 1969), 204–225.

4955   Hecht, Irene W. D., "The Virginia Muster of 1624-5 as a Source of Demographic History," *William and Mary Quarterly* 30 (1973), 65–92.

4956   Hedges, James B., *The Browns of Providence Plantations.* 2 v. Providence, R.I., 1968.

4957   Henretta, James A., *The Evolution of American Society, 1700–1815: An Interdisciplinary Analysis.* Lexington, Mass., 1973.

4958   Henretta, James A., "The Morphology of New England Society in the Colonial Period," *Journal of Interdisciplinary History* 2 (1971–72), 379–398. Now in *The Family in History*, ed. Theodore K. Rabb and Robert I. Rotberg (New York, 1973), 191–210. (See #80)

4959   Higgs, Robert, and H. Louis Stettler, "Colonial New England Demography: A Sampling Approach," *William and Mary Quarterly* 27 (1970), 282–294.

4960 Hiner, N. Ray, "Adolescence in Eighteenth-Century America," *History of Childhood Quarterly* 3 (1975–76), 253–280.

4961 Holdsworth, William K., "Adultery or Witchcraft: A New Note on an Old Case in Connecticut," *New England Quarterly* 48 (1975), 394–409.

4962 Holliday, Carl, *Woman's Life in Colonial Days.* Boston, 1922. Reprint, New York, 1960.

4963 Houdaille, J., "Démographie de la Nouvelle Angleterre aux XVIIe et XVIIIe siècles," *Population* 26 (1971), 963–966.

4964 Illick, Joseph E., "Child-Bearing in 17th Century England and America," *The History of Childhood,* ed. Lloyd DeMause (New York, 1974), 303–350. (See #154)

4965 Ironside, Charles Edward, *The Family of Colonial New York.* New York, 1942.

4966 Jaffe, A. J., "Differential Fertility in the White Population in Early America," *Journal of Heredity* 31 (1940), 407–411.

4967 Jester, Annie Lash, *Domestic Life in Virginia in the Seventeenth Century.* Williamsburg, Va., 1957.

4968 Keim, C. Ray, "Primogeniture and Entail in Colonial Virginia," *William and Mary Quarterly* 25 (1968), 545–586.

4969 Kenny, Alice P., *The Gansevoorts of Albany: Dutch Patricians in the Upper Hudson Valley.* Syracuse, 1969.

4970 Keyssar, Alexander, "Widowhood in Eighteenth-Century Massachusetts: A Problem in the History of the Family," *Perspectives in American History* 8 (1974), 83–122.

4971 Kiefer, Monica, *American Children through Their Books, 1700–1835.* Philadelphia, 1948.

4972 Kimball, Sidney Fiske, *Domestic Architecture of the American Colonies and New Republic.* New York, 1922.

4973 Klein, Randolph Shipley, *Portrait of an Early American Family: The Shippens of Pennsylvania across Five Generations.* Philadelphia, 1975.

4974 Kolb, Avery E., *The Grand-Families of America, 1776–1976: Patterns of Origin, Settlement and Growth of Families with Predominant Surnames.* Baltimore, 1974.

4975 Konig, David Thomas, "Community Custom and the Common Law: Social Change and the Development of Land Law in Seventeenth-Century Massachusetts," *American Journal of Legal History* 18 (1974), 137–177.

4976 Ktorides, Irene, "Marriage Customs in Colonial New England," *Historical Journal of Western Massachusetts* 2 (1973), 5–21.

4977 Kulikoff, Allan, "The Beginnings of the Afro-American Family in Maryland," *Law, Society, and Politics in Early Maryland,* ed. Aubrey C. Land, Lois Green Carr, and Edward C. Papenfuse (Baltimore, 1977), 171–196.

4978 Kulikoff, Allan, " 'Throwing the Stocking,' a Gentry Marriage in Provincial Maryland," *Maryland Historical Magazine* 71 (1976), 516–521.

4979   Lantz, Herman R., *Marital Incompatibility and Social Change in Early America*. Beverly Hills, Calif., 1976.

4980   Lantz, Herman R., Jane Keyes, and Morten Schultz, "The American Family in the Preindustrial Period: From Base Lines in History to Change," *American Sociological Review* 40 (1975), 21–36.

4981   Lantz, Herman R., Margaret Britton, Raymond Schmidt, and Eloise C. Snyder, "The Preindustrial Family in America: A Further Examination of Early Magazines," *American Journal of Sociology* 79 (1973), 566–588.

4982   Lantz, Herman R., Margaret Britton, Raymond Schmidt, and Eloise C. Snyder, "The Preindustrial Patterns in the Colonial Family in America: A Content Analysis of Colonial Magazines," *American Sociological Review* 33 (1968), 413–426.

4983   Lemon, James T., "Household Consumption in Eighteenth-Century America and Its Relationship to Production and Trade: The Situation among Farmers in Southeastern Pennsylvania," *Agricultural History* 41 (1967), 59–70.

4984   Lockridge, Kenneth, "Land, Population, and the Evolution of New England Society 1630–1790," *Past and Present* 39 (1968), 62–80.

4985   Lockridge, Kenneth, "The Population of Dedham, Mass., 1636–1736," *Economic History Review* 2nd series 19 (1966), 318–344.

4986   Lotka, Alfred J., "The Size of American Families in the Eighteenth Century and the Significance of the Empirical Constants in the Pearl-Reed Law of Population Growth," *Journal of American Statistical Association* 22 (1927), 154–170.

4987   Lumpkin, William L., "The Role of Women in 18th-Century Virginia Baptist Life," *Baptist Historical Heritage* 8 (1973), 158–167.

4988   McGovern, James R., *Yankee Family*. New Orleans, 1975.

4989   Marietta, Jack D., "Quaker Family Education in Historical Perspective," *Quaker History* 63 (1974), 3–16.

4990   Mathé, Alain, "L'immigration française en Louisiane, 1718–1721," *Revue d'histoire de l'Amérique française* 28 (1974–75), 555–564.

4991   Meehan, Thomas R., "Not Made Out of Levity: Evolution of Divorce in Early Pennsylvania," *Pennsylvania Magazine of History and Biography* 92 (1968), 441–456.

4992   Menard, Russell R., "From Servant to Freeholder: Status Mobility and Property Accumulation in Seventeenth-Century Maryland," *William and Mary Quarterly* 30 (1973), 37–64.

4993   Menard, Russell R., "Immigration to the Chesapeake Colonies in the Seventeenth Century: A Review Essay," *Maryland Historical Magazine* 68 (1973), 323–329.

4994   Menard, Russell R., "The Maryland Slave Population, 1658 to 1730: A Demographic Profile of Blacks in Four Counties," *William and Mary Quarterly* 32 (1975), 29–54.

4995 Menard, Russell R., and Lorena S. Walsh, "Death in the Chesapeake: Two Life Tables for Men in Early Colonial Maryland," *Maryland Historical Magazine* 59 (1974), 211-229.

4996 Moller, Herbert, "Sex Composition and Correlated Culture: Patterns of Colonial America," *William and Mary Quarterly* 2 (1945), 113-153.

4997 Morgan, Edmund S., *The Puritan Family: Religion and Domestic Relations in Seventeenth-Century New England.* rev. ed.; New York, 1966.

4998 Morgan, Edmund S., "The Puritans and Sex," *New England Quarterly* 15 (1942) 591-607. Now in *The American Family in Social-Historical Perspective,* ed. Michael Gordon (New York, 1973), 282-295.

4999 Morgan, Edmund S., *Virginians at Home: Family Life in the Eighteenth Century.* Williamsburg, Va., 1952.

5000 Morris, Richard B., "Women's Rights in Early American Law," *Studies in the History of American Law* (New York, 1930), 126-200.

5001 Murrin, John M., "Review Essay," *History and Theory* 11 (1972), 226-275.

5002 Nash, Gary B., and Billy G. Smith, "The Population of Eighteenth-Century Philadelphia," *Pennsylvania Magazine of History and Biography* 99 (1975), 362-368.

5003 Norton, Susan L., "Marital Migration in Essex County, Massachusetts, in the Colonial and Early Federal Periods," *Journal of Marriage and the Family* 35 (1973), 406-418.

5004 Norton, Susan L., "Population Growth in Colonial America: A Study of Ipswich, Massachusetts," *Population Studies* 25 (1971), 433-452.

5005 O'Keefe, Doris, "Marriage and Migration in Colonial New England: A Study in Historical Population Geography," *Discussion Paper* 16, Department of Geography, Syracuse University (1976).

5006 Osterud, Nancy, and J. Fulton, "Family Limitation and Age at Marriage: Fertility Decline in Sturbridge, Massachusetts 1730-1850," *Population Studies* 30 (1976), 481-494.

5007 O'Toole, Dennis A., "Democratic Balance—Ideals of Community in Early Portsmouth," *Rhode Island History* 32 (1973), 3-17.

5008 Parkes, Henry Bamford, "Morals and Law Enforcement in Colonial New England," *New England Quarterly* 5 (1932), 431-452.

5009 Pope, Robert G., *The Half-Way Covenant: Church Membership in Puritan New England.* Princeton, 1969.

5010 Porter, Dorothy B., "Family Records, a Major Resource for Documenting the Black Experience in New England," *Old-Time New England* 63 (1973), 69-72.

5011 Potter, James, "The Growth of Population in America, 1700-1860," *Population in History,* ed. David V. Glass and D.E.C. Eversley (London, 1965), 631-688. (See #214)

5012 Powell, Chilton L., "Marriage in Early New England," *New England Quarterly* 1 (1928), 323-334.

5013 Powell, Sumner Chilton, *Puritan Village: the Formation of a New England Town.* Middletown, Conn., 1963.

5014 Rothenberg, Charles, "Marriage, Morals and the Law in Colonial America," *New York Law Review* 74 (1940), 393–398.

5015 Rothman, David J., "A Note on the Study of the Colonial Family," *William and Mary Quarterly* 23 (1966), 627–634.

5016 Rovet, Jeanine, "Des Puritains aux Yankees: l'évolution des communautés rurales en Nouvelle-Angleterre aux XVIIe siècles," *Annales E.S.C.* 28 (1973), 1131–1142.

5017 *Rural Household Inventory: Establishing the Names, Uses, and Furnishings of Rooms in the Colonial New England Home, 1675–1775,* ed. Abbott L. Cummings. Boston, 1964.

5018 Rutman, Darrett G., *Husbandmen of Plymouth: Farms and Villages in the Old Colony, 1620–1692.* Boston, 1967.

5019 Rutman, Darrett G., "People in Process: The New Hampshire Towns of the Eighteenth Century," *Journal of Urban History* 1 (1974–75), 268–292. Now in *Family and Kin...,* ed. Tamara K. Hareven (New York, 1972), 16–37. (See #4850)

5020 Ryerson, Alice, "Medical Advice on Childrearing 1550–1900," *Harvard Educational Review* 31 (1961), 302–323.

5021 Savitt, Todd L., "Smothering and Overlaying of Virginia Slave Children: A Suggested Explanation," *Bulletin of the History of Medicine* 49 (1975), 400–404.

5022 Seward, Rudy Ray, "The Colonial Family in America: A Socio-Historical Restoration of Its Structure," *Journal of Marriage and the Family* 35 (1973), 58–70.

5023 Smith, Abbot E., "Indentured Servants: New Light on Some of America's 'First' Families," *Journal of Economic History* 2 (1942), 40–53.

5024 Smith, Daniel Blake, "Mortality and Family in the Colonial Chesapeake," *Journal of Interdisciplinary History* 8 (1977–78), 403–428.

5025 Smith, Daniel Scott, "The Demographic History of Colonial New England," *Journal of Economic History* 32 (1972), 165–183. Now in *The American Family in Social-Historical Perspective,* ed. Michael Gordon (New York, 1973), 397–415.

5026 Smith, Daniel Scott, "Parental Power and Marriage Patterns: An Analysis of Historical Trends in Hingham, Mass.," *Journal of Marriage and the Family* 35 (1973), 419–428.

5027 Smith, Daniel Scott, "Underregistration and Bias in Probate Records: An Analysis of Data from Eighteenth Century Hingham, Massachusetts," *William and Mary Quarterly* 32 (1975), 100–110.

5028 Smith, Daniel Scott, and Michael S. Hindus, "Premarital Pregnancy in America 1640–1971: An Overview and Interpretation," *Journal of Interdisciplinary History* 5 (1974–75), 537–570.

5029 Somerville, James K., "Family Demography and the Published Records: An Analysis of the Vital Statistics of Salem, Massachusetts," *Essex Institute Historical Collections* 106 (1970), 243-251.

5030 Somerville, James K., "The Salem (Mass.) Women in the Home, 1660-1770," *Eighteenth-Century Life* 1 (1974), 11-14.

5031 Spalletta, Matteo, "Divorce in Colonial New York," *New York Historical Society Quarterly* 39 (1955), 422-440.

5032 Spruill, Julia Cherry, *Woman's Life and Work in the Southern Colonies.* New York, 1972.

5033 Stannard, David E., "Death and Dying in Puritan New England," *American Historical Review* 78 (1973), 1305-1330.

5034 Stannard, David E., "Death and the Puritan Child," *American Quarterly* 26 (1974), 456-476.

5035 Stannard, David E., *The Puritan Way of Death: A Study in Religion, Culture, and Social Change.* New York, 1977.

5036 Stiles, Henry Reed, *Bundling: Its Origins, Progress and Decline in America.* Albany, 1869.

5037 Tjarks, Alicia V., "Comparative Demographic Analysis of Texas, 1777-1793," *Southwest Historical Quarterly* 77 (1974), 291-338.

5038 Tompsett, Christine H., "A Note on the Economic Status of Widows in Colonial New York," *New York History* 55 (1974), 319-332.

5039 Towner, Lawrence W., " 'A Fondness for Freedom': Servant Protest in Puritan Society," *William and Mary Quarterly* 19 (1962), 201-219.

5040 Tryon, Rolla M., *Household Manufactures in the United States, 1640-1860.* Chicago, 1917.

5041 Vinovskis, Maris A., "Angels' Heads and Weeping Willows: Death in Early America," *Themes...*, ed. Tamara K. Hareven (Worcester, Mass., 1978), 25-54. (See #4880)

5042 Vinovskis, Maris A., "The Field of Early American Family History: A Methodological Critique," *The Family in Historical Perspective* 7 (1974), 2-8.

5043 Vinovskis, Maris A., "Mortality Rates and Trends in Massachusetts before 1860," *Journal of Economic History* 32 (1972), 184-213.

5044 Walzer, John F., "A Period of Ambivalence: Eighteenth-Century American Childhood," *The History of Childhood,* ed. Lloyd DeMause (New York, 1974), 351-382. (See #154)

5045 Waters, John J., Jr., *The Otis Family in Provincial and Revolutionary Massachusetts.* Chapel Hill, 1968.

5046 Weisberg, D. Kelly, " 'Under Greet Temptations Heer': Women and Divorce in Puritan Massachusetts," *Feminist Studies* 2 (1975), 183-193.

5047 Wells, Robert Vale, "Demographic Change and the Life Cycle of American Families," *Journal of Interdisciplinary History* 2 (1971-72), 273-282. Now in *The Family in History,* ed. Theodore K. Rabb and Robert I. Rotberg (New York, 1973), 85-94. (See #80)

5048 Wells, Robert Vale, "Family Size and Fertility Control in Eighteenth-Century America: A Study of Quaker Families," *Population Studies* 25 (1971), 73–82.

5049 Wells, Robert Vale, "Household Size and Composition in the British Colonies in America, 1675–1775," *Journal of Interdisciplinary History* 4 (1973–74), 543–570.

5050 Wells, Robert Vale, "Quaker Marriage Patterns in a Colonial Perspective," *William and Mary Quarterly* 29 (1972), 415–442.

5051 Wertenbaker, Thomas Jefferson, *The First Americans, 1607–1690.* New York, 1927.

5052 White, Philip L., *The Beekman Family of New York in Politics and Commerce, 1647–1877.* New York, 1956.

5053 Withey, Lynne E., "Household Structure in Urban and Rural Areas: The Case of Rhode Island, 1774–1800," *Journal of Family History* 3 (1978), 37–50.

5054 Wolf, Stephanie Grauman, *Urban Village: Community and Family in Germantown, Pennsylvania, 1683–1800.* Princeton, 1976.

5055 Wolfe, A. B., "Population Censuses before 1790," *Journal of the American Statistical Association* 27 (1932), 357–370.

5056 Woodson, Carter G., "The Beginnings of Miscegenation of the Whites and Blacks," *Journal of Negro History* 3 (1918), 335–353.
       See also #840 and #841.

1790–1890

5057 Abzug, Robert H., "The Black Family during Reconstruction," *Key Issues in the Afro-American Experience,* v. 2, ed. Nathan Huggins (New York, 1971), 26–41.

5058 Allmendinger, David F., Jr., "The Dangers of Ante-Bellum Student Life," *Journal of Social History* 7 (1973–74), 75–85.

5059 Allmendinger, David F., Jr., *Paupers and Scholars: The Transformation of Student Life in New England 1760–1860.* New York, 1974.

5060 Anderson, Harry H., "Fur Traders as Fathers: The Origins of the Mixed-Blood Community among the Rosebud Sioux," *South Dakota History* 3 (1973), 233–270.

5061 Andrews, Edward Deming, *The People Called Shakers.* New York, 1953.

5062 Andrews, William D., and Deborah C. Andrews, "Technology and the Housewife in Nineteenth-Century America," *Women's Studies* 2 (1974), 309–328.

5063 Arrington, Leonard J., "The Economic Role of Pioneer Mormon Women," *Western Humanities Review* 9 (1955), 145–164.

5064 Arrington, Leonard J., and Dean May, "A Different Mode of Life: Irrigation and Society in 19th-Century Utah," *Agricultural History* 49 (1975), 3–20.

5065 Austin, Anne L., *The Woolsey Sisters of New York: A Family's Involvement in the Civil War and a New Profession (1860–1900)*. Philadelphia, 1971.

5066 Bakan, David, "Adolescence in America: From Idea to Social Fact," *Daedalus* 100 (1971), 979–995.

5067 Banner, Lois W., "Religion and Reform in the Early Republic: The Role of Youth," *American Quarterly* 23 (1971), 677–695.

5068 Barker, Howard F., "The Family Names of American Negroes," *American Speech* 14 (1939), 163–174.

5069 Barker-Benfield, Ben, *The Horrors of the Half-known Life: Male Attitudes toward Women and Sexuality in Nineteenth-Century America*. New York, 1976.

5070 Barker-Benfield, Ben, "The Spermatic Economy: A 19th-Century View of Sexuality," *Feminist Studies* 1 (1972), 45–74.

5071 Barnett, James Harwood, *Divorce and the American Divorce Novel, 1858–1937*. New York, 1968.

5072 Barton, H. Arnold, "Scandinavian Immigrant Women's Encounter with America," *Swedish Pioneer Historical Quarterly* 25 (1974), 37–42.

5073 Bash, Wendell H., "Changing Birth Rates in Developing America: New York State, 1840–1875," *Milbank Memorial Quarterly* 41 (1963), 161–182.

5074 Bash, Wendell H., "Differential Fertility in Madison County, New York, 1865," *Milbank Memorial Quarterly* 33 (1955), 161–186.

5075 Beijbom, Ulf, *Swedes in Chicago: A Demographic and Social Study of the 1846–1880 Immigration*. Stockholm, 1971.

5076 Bek, W. G., "Survivals of Old Marriage Customs among the Low Germans of Missouri," *Journal of American Folklore* 21 (1908), 60–67.

5077 Bieder, Robert E., "Kinship as a Factor in Migration," *Journal of Marriage and the Family* 35 (1973), 429–439.

5078 Blackburn, George M., and Sherman L. Ricards, "A Demographic History of Slavery: Georgetown County, South Carolina, 1850," *South Carolina Historical Magazine* 76 (1975), 215–224.

5079 Blackmore, J. S., and F. C. Mellonie, "Family Endowment and the Birth Date in the Early Nineteenth Century," *Economic History* 1:2 (1927), 205–213; 1:3 (1928), 412–418.

5080 Blassingame, John W., "Before the Ghetto: The Making of the Black Community in Savannah, Ga. 1865–1880," *Journal of Social History* 6 (1972–73), 463–488.

5081 Blassingame, John W., *The Slave Community: Plantation Life in the Antebellum South*. New York, 1972.

5082 Blassingame, John W., "The Slave Family in America," *American History Illustrated* 7 (1972), 10–17.

5083 Blegen, Theodore C., *Norwegian Migration to America 1825–1860*. Northfield, Minn., 1931.

5084 Bloomberg, Susan, et al., "A Census Probe into Nineteenth-Century Family

History: Southern Michigan, 1850-1880," *Journal of Social History* 5 (1971-72), 26-45.

5085 Blumin, Stuart N., "Rip Van Winkle's Grandchildren: Family and the Household in the Hudson Valley, 1800-1860," *Journal of Urban History* 1 (1974-75), 293-315.

5086 Bodnar, John E., "Socialization and Adaptation: Immigrant Families in Scranton, 1880-1890," *Pennsylvania History* 43 (1976), 147-163.

5087 Bowie, Lucy, "Young Men in Love, 1795-1823," *Maryland Historical Magazine* 41 (1946), 219-234.

5088 Bridges, William, "Family Patterns and Social Values in America, 1825-1875," *American Quarterly* 17 (1965) 3-11.

5089 Brink, Pamela, "Prviotso Child Training," *The Indian Historian* 4 (1971), 47-50.

5090 Brooks, Carol Flora, "The Early History of the Anti-Contraceptive Laws in Massachusetts and Connecticut," *American Quarterly* 18 (1966), 3-23.

5091 Brown, Judith K., "Economic Organization and the Position of Women among the Iroquois," *Ethnohistory* 17 (1970), 151-167.

5092 Bunkle, Phillida E., "Sentimental Womanhood and Domestic Education, 1830-1870," *History of Education Quarterly* 14 (1974), 13-30.

5093 Bushman, Claudia L., *Mormon Sisters: Women in Early Utah.* Cambridge, Mass., 1976.

5094 Cannon, Charles A., "The Awesome Power of Sex: The Polemical Campaign against Mormon Polygamy," *Pacific Historical Review* 43 (1974), 61-82.

5095 Carden, Maren Lockwood, *Oneida.* Baltimore, 1969.

5096 Carter, Gregg L., "Social Demography of the Chinese in Nevada, 1870-1880," *Nevada Historical Society Quarterly* 18 (1975), 72-89.

5097 *The Children of Pride,* ed. Robert Manson Myers. New Haven, 1972.

5098 Chudacoff, Howard, "New Branches on the Tree: Household Structure in Early Stages of the Family Cycle in Worcester, Massachusetts, 1860-1880," *Themes...,* ed. Tamara K. Hareven (Worcester, Mass., 1978), 55-72. (See #4880)

5099 Chudacoff, Howard P., "Newlyweds and Family Extension: The First Stage of the Family Cycle in Providence, Rhode Island, 1864-1865 and 1879-1880," *Family and Population...,* ed. Tamara K. Hareven and Maris Vinovskis (Princeton, N.J., 1978), 179-205. (See #5127)

5100 Chudacoff, Howard P., and Tamara K. Hareven, "Family Transitions and Household Structure in the Later Years of Life," *Transitions,* ed. Tamara K. Hareven (New York, 1978), 217-244. (See #261)

5101 Cirillo, Vincent J., "Birth Control in Nineteenth Century America: A View from Three Contemporaries," *Yale Journal of Biology and Medicine* 47 (1974), 260-267.

5102 Cirillo, Vincent J., "Edward Foote's *Medical Common Sense:* An Early American Comment on Birth Control," *Journal of the History of Medicine* 25 (1970), 341–345.

5103 Clarke, John Henrik, "The Black Family in Historical Perspective," *Journal of Afro-American Issues* 3 (1975), 336–342.

5104 Coale, Ansley J., and Norfleet W. Rives, "A Statistical Reconstruction of the Black Population of the United States, 1880–1970: Estimates of True Numbers by Age and Sex, Birth Rates, and Total Fertility," *Population Index* 39 (1973), 3–36.

5105 Coale, Ansley J., and Melvin Zelnik, *New Estimates of Fertility and Population in the United States: A Study of Annual White Births from 1855 to 1960 and of Completeness of Enumeration in the Censuses from 1880 to 1960.* Princeton, N.J., 1963.

5106 Connor, Paul, "Patriarchy: Old World and New," *American Quarterly* 17 (1965), 48–62.

5107 Cook, Sherburne F., "The Stability of Indian Custom Marriage," *The Indian Historian* 7 (1974), 33–34.

5108 *The Cult of Youth in Middle-Class America,* ed. Richard L. Rapson. Lexington, Mass., 1971.

5109 Davis, Angela, "Reflections on the Black Woman's Role in the Community of Slaves," *Black Scholar* 3: 10 (1971), 2–16.

5110 Degler, Carl N., "What Ought to Be and What Was: Women's Sexuality in the Nineteenth Century," *American Historical Review* 79 (1974), 1468–1490.

5111 Del Castillo, Richard Griswold, "La Familia Chicana: Social Changes in the Chicano Family of Los Angeles, 1850–1880," *Journal of Ethnic Studies* 3 (1975), 41–58.

5112 Del Castillo, Richard Griswold, "Preliminary Comparison of Chicano, Immigrant, and Native-Born Family Structures, 1850–1880," *Aztlan* 6 (1975), 87–96.

5113 *The Demographic and Social Pattern of Emigration from Southern European Countries,* ed. Massimo Livi-Bacci. Florence, 1972.

5114 Demos, John, and Virginia Demos, "Adolescence in Historical Perspective," *Journal of Marriage and the Family* 31 (1969), 623–638. Now in *The American Family in Social-Historical Perspective,* ed. Michael Gordon (New York, 1973), 209–221.

5115 "Dislocation and Emigration: The Demographic Background of American Immigration." Special Issue of *Perspectives in American History* 7 (1973).

5116 Donegan, Jane Bauer, "Man-Midwifery and the Delicacy of the Sexes," *'Remember the Ladies': New Perspectives on Women in American History,* ed. Carol V. R. George (Syracuse, N.Y., 1975), 90–109.

5117 Dubovik, Paul N., "Housing in Holyoke and Its Effects on Family Life, 1860–1910," *Historical Journal of Western Massachusetts* 4 (1975), 40–50.

5118 Duvall, Severn, "Uncle Tom's Cabin: The Sinister Side of the Patriarchy," *New England Quarterly* 36 (1963), 3–22.

5119 Easterlin, Richard A., "Factors in the Decline of Farm Family Fertility in the United States: Some Preliminary Research Results," *Journal of American History* 63 (1976), 600–614.

5120 Eblen, Jack E., "An Analysis of Nineteenth-Century Frontier Populations," *Demography* 11 (1965), 399–413.

5121 Edeen, Martin, "Frontier Marriage and the Status Quo," *Westpoint Historical Quarterly* 10 (1975), 99–108.

5122 Engerman, Stanley, "Changes in Black Fertility, 1880–1940," *Family and Population...*, ed. Tamara K. Hareven and Maris Vinovskis (Princeton, N.J., 1978), 69–93. (See #5127)

5123 Engerman, Stanley, "Economic Perspectives on the Life Course," *Transitions,* ed. Tamara K. Hareven (New York, 1978), 271–286. (See #261)

5124 Erickson, Charlotte, *Invisible Immigrants: The Adaptation of English and Scottish Immigrants in Nineteenth-Century America.* Coral Gables, 1972.

5125 Ernst, George A. O., *The Legal Status of Married Women in Massachusetts.* Boston, 1895.

5126 Fairbanks, L. S., *Marriage and Divorce Laws of Massachusetts.* Boston, 1881.

5127 *Family and Population in 19th-Century America,* ed. Tamara K. Hareven and Maris Vinovskis. Princeton, N.J., 1978.

5128 Farber, Bernard, "Women, Marriage, and Illness: Consumptives in Salem, Massachusetts, 1785–1819," *Journal of Comparative Family Studies* 4 (1973), 36–48.

5129 Farley, Reynolds, "The Demographic Rates and Social Institutions of the Nineteenth-Century Negro Population: A Stable Population Analysis," *Demography* 2 (1965), 386–398.

5130 Farley, Reynolds, *Growth of the Black Population: A Study of Demographic Trends.* Chicago, 1970.

5131 Finkelstein, Barbara, "Pedagogy as Intrusion: Teaching Values in Popular Primary Schools in Nineteenth-Century America," *History of Childhood Quarterly* 2 (1974–75), 349–378.

5132 Fogel, Robert, and Stanley Engerman, *Time on the Cross: The Economics of American Negro Slavery.* Boston, 1974.

5133 Foster, Colin, and G.S.L. Tucker, *Economic Opportunity and White American Fertility Ratios, 1800–1860.* New Haven, 1972.

5134 Frazier, E. Franklin, *The Free Negro Family.* Nashville, 1932.

5135 Frazier, E. Franklin, "The Impact of Urban Civilization upon Negro Family Life," *American Sociological Review* 2 (1937), 609–618.

5136 Frazier, E. Franklin, "The Negro Slave Family," *Journal of Negro History* 15 (1930), 198–259.

5137 Friedberger, Mark, "Cohorting with the State Census: The Concept of the Cohort, and Its Use in Manuscript Census Research," *Historical Methods Newsletter* 6 (1972), 1–3.

5138 Friedman, Lawrence M., "Patterns of Testation in the Nineteenth Century: A

Study of Essex County (New Jersey) Wills," *American Journal of Legal History* 8 (1964), 34–53.

5139 Furstenberg, Frank F., Jr., "Industrialization and the American Family: A Look Backward," *American Sociological Review* 31 (1966), 326–337.

5140 Furstenberg, Frank F., Jr., et al., "The Origins of the Female-Headed Black Family: The Impact of the Urban Experience," *Journal of Interdisciplinary History* 6 (1975–76), 211–233.

5141 Genovese, Eugene D., *Roll, Jordon, Roll: The World the Slaves Made.* New York, 1974.

5142 Giffen, Jerena East, " 'Add a Pinch and a Lump': Missouri Women in the 1820's," *Missouri Historical Review* 65 (1971), 478–504.

5143 Glanz, Rudolf, *The Jewish Woman in America: Two Female Immigrant Generations, 1820–1929.* New York, 1976.

5144 Glasco, Laurence A., "The Life Cycles and Household Structure of American Ethnic Groups: Irish, Germans, and Native-born Whites in Buffalo, New York, 1885," *Journal of Urban History* 1 (1974–75), 339–364. Now in *Family and Kin...*, ed. Tamara K. Hareven (New York, 1977), 122–143. (See #4856)

5145 Glasco, Laurence A., "Migration and Adjustment in the Nineteenth-Century City: Occupation, Property, and Household Structure of Native-Born Whites, Buffalo, New York, 1855," *Family and Population...*, ed. Tamara K. Hareven and Maris Vinovskis (Princeton, N.J., 1978), 154–178. (See #5127)

5146 Glassie, Henry, *Folk Housing in Middle Virginia: A Structural Analysis of Historical Artifacts.* Knoxville, 1975.

5147 Goodsell, Willystine, "The American Family in the 19th Century," *Annals of the American Academy of Political and Social Science* 160 (1932), 13–22.

5148 Gordon, Linda, *Woman's Body, Woman's Right: A Social History of Birth Control in America.* New York, 1976.

5149 Gordon, Linda, "Voluntary Motherhood: The Beginnings of Feminist Birth Control Ideas in the United States," *Feminist Studies* 1:3/4 (1973), 5–22. Now in *Clio's Consciousness Raised*, ed. Mary Hartman and Lois Banner (New York, 1974), 54–71. (See #4848)

5150 Gordon, Michael, "From an Unfortunate Necessity to a Cult of Mutual Orgasm: Sex in American Marital Education Literature, 1830–1940," *Studies in the Sociology of Sex,* ed. James Henslin (New York, 1971), 53–77.

5151 Gordon, Michael, and M. Charles Bernstein, "Mate Choice and Domestic Life in the Nineteenth Century Marriage Manual," *Journal of Marriage and the Family* 32 (1970), 665–675.

5152 Graff, Harvey J., "Patterns of Dependency and Child Development in the Mid-Nineteenth-Century City: A Sample from Boston 1860," *History of Education Quarterly* 13 (1973), 129–143.

5153 Griffen, Clyde, and Sally Griffen, "Family and Business in a Small City: Poughkeepsie, New York, 1850–1880," *Journal of Urban History* 1 (1975),

316–338. Now in *Family and Kin...*, ed. Tamara K. Hareven (New York, 1977), 144–163. (See #4856)

5154   Gutman, Herbert G., "Persistent Myths about the Afro-American Family," *Journal of Interdisciplinary History* 6 (1975–76), 181–210. Originally in French in *Annales E.S.C.* 27 (1972), 1197–1218.

5155   Hall, G. Stanley, *Adolescence: Its Psychology and Its Relations to Physiology, Anthropology, Sociology, Sex, Crime, Religion, and Education.* 2 v. New York, 1904.

5156   Haller, John S., Jr., "From Maidenhood to Menopause: Sex Education for Women in Victorian America," *Journal of Popular Culture* 6 (1972), 49–69.

5157   Haller, John S., Jr., and Robin M. Haller, *The Physician and Sexuality in Victorian America.* Urbana, Ill, 1974.

5158   Haller, Mark Hughlin, *Eugenics: Heriditarian Attitudes in American Thought.* New Brunswick, N.J., 1963.

5159   Hamilton, W. B., "Mississippi, 1817: A Sociological and Economic Analysis," *Journal of Mississippi History* 29 (1967), 270–292.

5160   Handlin, Oscar, *Boston's Immigrants, 1790–1880: A Study in Acculturation.* Cambridge, Mass., 1941.

5161   Handlin, Oscar, *The Uprooted.* New York, 1951.

5162   Hareven, Tamara K., and Maris A. Vinovskis, "Marital Fertility, Ethnicity, and Occupation in Urban Families: An Analysis of South Boston and the South End in 1880," *Journal of Social History* 8 (1974–75), 69–93.

5163   Hareven, Tamara K., and Maris A. Vinovskis, "Patterns of Childbearing in Late Nineteenth-Century America: The Determinants of Marital Fertility in Five Essex County Towns in 1880," *Family and Population...*, ed. Tamara K. Hareven and Maris Vinovskis (Princeton, N.J., 1978), 85–125. (See #5127)

5164   Harris, William, "Work and the Family in Black Atlanta, 1880," *Journal of Social History* 9 (1975–76), 319–330.

5165   Hawes, Joseph M., *Children in Urban Society: Juvenile Delinquency in Nineteenth-Century America.* New York, 1971.

5166   Herman, Sondra R., "Loving Courtship or the Marriage Market? The Ideal and Its Critics, 1871–1911," *American Quarterly* 25 (1973), 235–252.

5167   Hershberg, Theodore, "Free Blacks in Ante-Bellum Philadelphia: A Study of Ex-Slaves, Free-Born and Socio-Economic Decline," *Journal of Social History* 5 (1971–72), 183–209.

5168   Hershberg, Theodore, "A Method for the Computerized Study of Family and Household Structure Using the Manuscript Schedules of the U.S. Census of Population," *Family in Historical Perspective* 3 (1973), 6–20.

5169   Hirsh, Joseph, "Sex Attitudes and Venereology in New York City One Hundred Years Ago," *Journal of Social Hygiene* 38 (1952), 212–219.

5170   "History of the Family in American Urban Society," ed. Tamara K. Hareven. Special Issue of the *Journal of Urban History* 1:3 (1975).

5171   Hogeland, Ronald W., "Coeducation of the Sexes at Oberlin College: A Study of Social Ideas in Mid-Nineteenth Century America," *Journal of Social History* 6 (1972–73), 160–176.

5172   Hogeland, Ronald W., "The Female Appendage: Feminine Life-Styles in America, 1820–1960," *Civil War History* 17 (1971), 102–114.

5173   Holland, C. G., "The Slave Population on the Plantation of John C. Cotton, Jr., Nanesmond County, Virginia, 1811–1863," *Virginia Magazine of History and Biography* 80 (1972), 331–340.

5174   Horton, James Oliver, "Generations of Protest: Black Families and Social Reform in Ante-Bellum Boston," *The New England Quarterly* 49 (1976), 242–256.

5175   Horwitz, Richard P., "Architecture and Culture: The Meaning of the Lowell Boarding House," *American Quarterly* 25 (1973), 64–82.

5176   Jeffrey, Kirk, "The Family as a Utopian Retreat from the City: The Nineteenth Century," *Soundings* 55 (1972), 21–41.

5177   Jeffrey, Kirk, "Marriage, Career, and Feminine Ideology in Nineteenth-Century America: Reconstructing the Marital Experience of Lydia Maria Child, 1828–1874," *Feminist Studies* 2:2/3 (1975), 113–130.

5178   Jentsch, Theodore W., "Old Order Mennonite Family Life in the East Penn Valley," *Pennsylvania Folklife* 24 (1974), 18–27.

5179   Johnson, Guion Griffis, "Courtship and Marriage Customs in Antebellum North Carolina," *North Carolina Historical Review* 8 (1931), 384–402.

5180   Katz, Michael B., *The Irony of Early School Reform.* Cambridge, Mass., 1968.

5181   Kelly, R. Cordon, *Mother Was a Lady: Self and Society in Selected American Children's Periodicals, 1865–1890.* Westport, Conn., 1974.

5182   Kennedy, Ruby Jo Reeves, "Single or Triple Melting-Pot? Intermarriage Trends in New Haven, 1870–1940," *American Journal of Sociology* 49 (1944), 331–339.

5183   Kennedy, Ruby Jo Reeves, "Single or Triple Melting-Pot? Intermarriage in New Haven, 1870–1950," *American Journal of Sociology* 58 (1952), 56–59.

5184   Kephart, William M., "Experimental Family Organization: An Historico-Cultural Report on the Oneida Community," *Journal of Marriage and the Family* 25 (1963), 261–271.

5185   Kett, Joseph F., "Adolescence and Youth in Nineteenth-Century America," *Journal of Interdisciplinary History* 2 (1971–72), 283–299. Now in *The Family in History*, ed. Theodore K. Rabb and Robert I. Rotberg (New York, 1973), 95–110. (See #80)

5186   Kett, Joseph F., "Growing Up in Rural New England, 1800–1840," *Anonymous Americans*, ed. Tamara K. Hareven (Englewood Cliffs, N.J., 1971), 1–16. (See #4837)

5187   Kett, Joseph F., *Rites of Passage: Adolescence in America, 1790 to the Present.* New York, 1977.

5188   Kleinberg, Susan J., "Technology and Women's Work: The Lives of Working-

Class Women in Pittsburgh, 1870–1900," *Labor History* 17 (1976), 58–72.

5189 Kobrin, Frances E., "The American Midwife Controversy: A Crisis of Professionalization," *Bulletin of the History of Medicine* 49 (1966), 350–363.

5190 Kuhn, Anne Louise, *The Mother's Role in Childhood Education: New England Concepts, 1830–1860*. New Haven, 1947.

5191 Labinjok, Justin, "The Sexual Life of the Oppressed: An Examination of the Family Life of Ante-Bellum Slaves," *Phylon* 35 (1974), 375–397.

5192 Ladner, Joyce, "Racism and Tradition: Black Womanhood in Historical Perspective," *Liberating Women's History: Theoretical and Critical Essays,* ed. Berenice A. Carroll (Urbana, 1976), 179–193.

5193 Lammermeier, Paul J., "The Urban Black Family of the Nineteenth Century: A Study of Black Family Structure in the Ohio Valley, 1850–1880," *Journal of Marriage and the Family* 35 (1973), 440–456.

5194 Larrabee, Harold A., "New England Family: The Kennedys," *New England Quarterly* 42 (1969), 436–445.

5195 Larson, T. A., "Women's Role in the American West," *Montana Magazine of Western History* 24 (1974), 3–11.

5196 Lasch, Christopher, " 'Selfish Women': The Campaign to Save the American Family, 1880–1920," *Columbia Forum* 4 (1975), 24–31.

5197 Laslett, Barbara, "The Family as a Public and Private Institution: An Historical Perspective," *Journal of Marriage and the Family* 35 (1973), 480–494.

5198 Laslett, Barbara, "Household Structure on an American Frontier: Los Angeles, Calif., in 1850," *American Journal of Sociology* 81 (1975), 109–128.

5199 Laslett, Barbara, "Social Change and the Family: Los Angeles, California, 1850–1870," *American Sociological Review* 42 (1977), 268–291.

5200 Leet, Don R., "Population Pressure and Human Fertility Response: Ohio, 1810–1860," *Journal of Economic History* 34 (1974), 286–288.

5201 Lerner, Gerda, "The Lady and the Mill Girl: Changes in the Status of Women in the Age of Jackson," *Midcontinent American Studies Journal* 10 (1969), 5–14.

5202 Lyman, Stanford M., "Marriage and the Family among Chinese Immigrants to America, 1850–1960," *Phylon* 29 (1968), 321–330.

5203 Mann, Ralph, "A Decade after the Gold Rush: Social Structure in Grass Valley and Nevada City, California, 1850–1860," *Pacific Historical Review* 46 (1972), 484–504.

5204 May, Dean L., "People on the Mormon Frontier: Kanabis Families of 1974," *Journal of Family History* 1 (1976), 169–192.

5205 McLachlan, James, *American Boarding Schools: A Historical Study*. New York, 1970.

5206 McLaughlin, Virginia Yans, *Family and Community: Italian Immigrants in Buffalo, 1880–1930*. Ithaca, New York, 1977.

5207 McLaughlin, Virginia Yans, "A Flexible Tradition: South Italian Immigrants

Confront a New York Experience," *Journal of Social History* 7 (1973–74), 429–445.

5208   McLaughlin, Virginia Yans, "Patterns of Work and Family Organization: Buffalo's Italians," *Journal of Interdisciplinary History* 2 (1971–72), 299–314.

5209   McLoughlin, William G., "Evangelical Child-Rearing in the Age of Jackson: Francis Wayland's View on When and How to Subdue the Wilfulness of Children," *Journal of Social History* 9 (1975–76), 20–34.

5210   Mechling, Jay E., "Advice to Historians on Advice to Mothers," *Journal of Social History* 9 (1975–76), 44–63.

5211   Modell, John, "Family and Fertility on the Indiana Frontier, 1820," *American Quarterly* 23 (1971), 615–634.

5212   Modell, John, Frank Furstenberg, and Douglas Strong, "The Timing of Marriage in the Transition to Adulthood: Continuity and Change, 1860–1975," *Turning Points,* ed. John Demos and Sarane Spence Boocock (Chicago, 1978), 120–151. (See #262)

5213   Modell, John, Frank Furstenberg, and Theodore Hershberg, "Social Change and Transition to Adulthood in Historical Perspective," *Journal of Family History* 1 (1976), 7–32.

5214   Modell, John, and Tamara K. Hareven, "Transitions: Patterns of Timing," *Transitions,* ed. Tamara K. Hareven (New York, 1978), 245–269. (See #261)

5215   Modell, John, and Tamara K. Hareven, "Urbanization and the Malleable Household: An Examination of Boarding and Lodging in American Families," *Journal of Marriage and the Family* 35 (1973), 467–479. Now in *Family and Kin...,* ed. Tamara K. Hareven (New York, 1977), 164–186. (See #4856)

5216   Monahan, Thomas Patrick, "One Hundred Years of Marriage in Massachusetts," *American Journal of Sociology* 56 (1951), 534–545.

5217   Morgan, Lewis H., *Houses and House-Life of the American Aborigines.* Chicago, 1966.

5218   Mott, Frank L., "Portrait of an American Mill Town: Demographic Response in Mid-Nineteenth Century Warren, Rhode Island," *Population Studies* 26 (1972), 147–157.

5219   Muncy, Raymond Lee, *Sex and Marriage in Utopian Communities: Nineteenth-Century America.* Bloomington, Ind., 1973.

5220   Nelsen, Anne K., and Hart M. Nelsen, "Family Articles in Frontier Newspapers: An Examination of One Aspect of Turner's Frontier Thesis," *Journal of Marriage and the Family* 31 (1969), 644–650.

5221   Nordhoff, Charles, *Communistic Societies of the United States.* New York, 1875. Reprint, New York, 1966.

5222   Nostrand, Richard L., "Mexican Americans circa 1850," *Annals of the Association of American Geographers* 65 (1975), 378–390.

5223   Noyes, Hilda Herrick, and George Wallingford Noyes, "The Oneida Community Experiment in Stirpiculture," *Eugenics, Genetics, and the Family, Scientific Papers of the Second International Congress of Eugenics* (Baltimore, 1923), I, 374–386.

5224   Oblinger, Carl D., "Vestiges of Poverty: Black Families and Fragments of Black Families in Southeastern Pennsylvania, 1830–1860," *Family in Historical Perspective* 4 (1973), 9–14.

5225   O'Neill, W. L., "Divorce as a Moral Issue: A Hundred Years of Controversy," *'Remember the Ladies': New Perspectives on Women in American History,* ed. Carol V. R. George (Syracuse, New York, 1975), 127–143.

5226   Papashvily, Helen Waite, *All the Happy Endings: A Study of the Domestic Novel in America, The Women Who Wrote It, The Women Who Read It, in the 19th Century.* New York, 1956.

5227   Parkhurst, Jessie W., "The Role of the Black Mammy in the Plantation Household," *Journal of Negro History* 23 (1938), 349–369.

5228   Partridge, Bellamy, and Otto Bettmann, *As We Were, Family Life, 1850–1900.* New York, 1946.

5229   Pauly, Thomas H., "Ragged Dick and Little Women: Idealized Homes and Unwanted Marriages," *Journal of Popular Culture* 9 (1975), 583–592.

5230   Pessen, Edward, "The Marital Theory and Practices of the Antebellum Urban Elite," *New York History* 53 (1972), 380–410.

5231   Pickens, Donald K., *Eugenics and the Progressives.* Nashville, 1968.

5232   Pivar, David J., *The Purity Crusade: Sexual Morality and Social Control, 1868–1900.* Westport, Conn., 1973.

5233   Pleck, Elizabeth H., "The Two-Parent Household: Black Family Structure in Late Nineteenth-Century Boston," *Journal of Social History* 6 (1972–73), 3–31. Now in *The American Family in Social-Historical Perspective,* ed. Michael Gordon (New York, 1973), 152–177.

5234   Pleck, Elizabeth H., "Two Worlds in One: Work and Family," *Journal of Social History* 10 (1976–77), 178–195.

5235   Potter, James, "American Population in the Early National Period," *Population and Economics: Proceedings of Section V of the Fourth Congress of the International Economic History Association, 1968* (Winnipeg, 1970), 55–69.

5236   Prentice, Allison, "Education and the Metaphor of the Family: The Upper Canadian Example," *History of Education Quarterly* 12 (1972), 281–303.

5237   *Primers for Prudery: Sexual Advice to Victorian America,* ed. Ronald G. Walters. Englewood Cliffs, N.J., 1974.

5238   Provine, Dorothy, "The Economic Position of Free Blacks in the District of Columbia, 1800–1860," *Journal of Negro History* 58 (1973), 61–72.

5239   Pryor, Edward T., Jr., "Rhode Island Family Structure, 1875 and 1960," *Household and Family...,* ed. Peter Laslett and Richard Wall (Cambridge, England, 1972), 571–589. (See #156)

5240   Rapson, Richard L., "The American Child as Seen by British Travelers: 1845–1935," *American Quarterly* 17 (1965), 520–534. Now in *The American Fam-*

ily in Social-Historical Perspective, ed. Michael Gordon (New York, 1973), 192–208.

5241 Rawick, George P., "The Black Family under Slavery," *The American Slave: A Composite Autobiography,* ed. George P. Rawick (Westport, Conn., 1972), I, 77–94.

5242 Rawick, George P., *From Sundown to Sunup: The Making of the Black Community.* New York, 1972.

5243 Reistein, Eleanor Fein, "Minutes of the West Grove Housekeepers Association as Source Material for Folklife Studies," *Pennsylvania Folklife* 21 (1971), 16–25.

5244 Riegel, Robert E., "Dr. Knowlton: American Pioneer in the Birth Control Movement," *New England Quarterly* 6 (1933), 470–490.

5245 Riley, Glenda Gates, "The Subtle Subversion: Changes in the Traditional Image of the American Woman," *The Historian* 22 (1970), 210–227.

5246 Ripley, C. Peter, "The Black Family in Transition: Louisiana, 1860–1865," *Journal of Southern History* 41 (1975), 369–380.

5247 Robertson, Constance Noyes, *Oneida Community: An Autobiography, 1851–1876.* Syracuse, N.Y., 1970.

5248 Robertson, Constance Noyes, *Oneida Community: The Breakup, 1876–1881.* Syracuse, N.Y., 1972.

5249 Roemer, Kenneth M., "Sex Roles, Utopia and Change: The Family in Late Nineteenth-Century Utopian Literature," *American Studies* 13 (1972), 33–48.

5250 Rosenberg, Charles E., "Sexuality, Class and Role in Nineteenth-Century America," *American Quarterly* 25 (1973), 131–153.

5251 Rostch, Melvin M., "The Home Environment," *Technology in Western Civilization,* ed. Melvin Kranzberg and Carroll W. Pursell (New York, 1967), 217–233.

5252 Rubin, Ernest, "The Demography of Immigration to the United States," *Annals of the American Academy of Political and Social Science* 367 (1966), 15–22.

5253 Ruchames, Louis, "Race, Marriage and Abolition in Massachusetts," *Journal of Negro History* 40 (1955), 250–273.

5254 Rugoff, Milton Allan, *Prudery and Passion.* New York, 1971.

5255 Sauer, R., "Attitudes to Abortion in America, 1800–1973," *Population Studies* 28 (1974), 53–67.

5256 Schlenker, Jon A., "An Historical Analysis of the Family Life of the Choctaw Indians," *Southern Quarterly* 13 (1975), 323–334.

5257 Schmitt, Robert C., and Rose C. Strombel, "Marriage and Divorce in Hawaii before 1870," *Hawaii Historical Review* 2 (1966), 267–271.

5258 Schweninger, Loren, "A Slave Family in the Ante-Bellum South," *Journal of Negro History* 60 (1975), 29–44.

5259   Scott, Ann Firor, *The Southern Lady: From Pedestal to Politics, 1830–1930*. Chicago, 1970.

5260   Scott, Anne Firor, "Women's Perspective on the Patriarchy in the 1850's," *Journal of American History* 61 (1974), 52–64.

5261   Sears, Hal D., "The Sex Radicals in High Victorian America," *Virginia Quarterly Review* 48 (1972), 377–392.

5262   Sennett, Richard, *Families against the City: Middle Class Homes of Industrial Chicago, 1872–1890*. Cambridge, Mass., 1971.

5263   Sennett, Richard, "Middle-Class Families and Urban Violence: The Experience of a Chicago Community in the 19th Century," *Nineteenth-Century Cities: Essays in the New Urban History*, ed. Stephan Thernstrom and Richard Sennett (New Haven, 1969), 386–420. Now in *The American Family in Social-Historical Perspective*, ed. Michael Gordon (New York, 1973), 111–134.

5264   Sharpless, John, and Ray M. Shortridge, "Biased Underenumeration in Census Manuscripts: Methodological Implications," *Journal of Urban History* 1 (1974–75), 409–439.

5265   Shifflet, Crandall A., "The Household Composition of Rural Black Families: Louisa County, Virginia, 1880," *Journal of Interdisciplinary History* 6 (1975–76), 235–260.

5266   Showers, Susan, "A Weddin' and a Buryin' in the Black Belt," *The Negro and His Folklore in Nineteenth Century Periodicals*, ed. Bruce Jackson (Austin, Texas, 1967), 293–301.

5267   Sides, Sudie Duncan, "Slave Weddings and Religion: Plantation Life in the Southern States before the American Civil War," *History Today* 24 (1974), 77–78.

5268   Simmons, Adele, "Education and Ideology in Nineteenth-Century America: The Response of Educational Institutions to the Changing Role of Women," *Liberating Women's History*, ed. Berenice A. Carroll (Urbana, 1976), 115–126.

5269   Simon, Roger D., "Housing and Services in an Immigrant Neighborhood: Milwaukee's Ward 14," *Journal of Urban History* 2 (1975–76), 435–458.

5270   Sklar, Kathryn Kish, *Catharine Beecher: A Study in American Domesticity*. New Haven, 1973.

5271   "The Slaveholder and the Abolitionist: Binding Up a Family's Wounds," ed. Frank Otto Gatell, *Journal of Southern History* 27 (1961), 368–391.

5272   Smith, Daniel Scott, "Family Limitation, Sexual Control, and Domestic Feminism in Victorian America," *Feminist Studies* 1:3/4 (1973), 40–57. Now in *Clio's Consciousness Raised*, ed. Mary Hartman and Lois Banner (New York, 1974), 119–136. (See #4848)

5273   Smith, J. E., and P. R. Kunz, "Polygymy and Fertility in Nineteenth-Century America," *Population Studies* 30 (1976), 465–480.

5274 Smith, Thelma, "Feminism in Philadelphia, 1790–1850," *Pennsylvania Magazine of History and Biography* 68 (1944), 243–268.

5275 Smith-Rosenberg, Carroll, "Beauty, the Beast and the Militant Woman: A Case Study in Sex Roles and Social Stress in Jacksonian America," *American Quarterly* 23 (1971), 562–584.

5276 Smith-Rosenberg, Carroll, "The Hysterical Woman: Sex Roles and Role Conflict in Nineteenth-Century America," *Social Research* 39 (1972), 652–678.

5277 Smith-Rosenberg, Carroll, "Puberty to Menopause: The Cycle of Femininity in Nineteenth-Century America," *Clio's Consciousness Raised*, ed. Mary Hartman and Lois Banner (New York, 1974), 23–37. (See #4848)

5278 Smith-Rosenberg, Carroll, and Charles Rosenberg, "The Female Animal: Medical and Biological Views of Woman and Her Role in Nineteenth-Century America," *Journal of American History* 60 (1973), 332–356.

5279 Spengler, Joseph J., "Notes on Abortion, Birth Control, and Medical and Sociological Interpretations of the Decline of the Birth Rate in Nineteenth-Century America," *Marriage Hygiene* [Bombay, India] (1935), 159–160.

5280 Spengler, Joseph J., "Values and Fertility Analysis," *Demography* 3 (1966), 109–130.

5281 Sprague, William, *Women and the West*. Boston, 1940.

5282 Stoeltje, Beverly J., "A Helpmate for Man Indeed: The Image of the Frontier Woman," *Journal of American Folklore* 88 (1975), 25–41.

5283 Strickland, Charles, "A Transcendentalist Father: The Child-Rearing Practices of Bronson Alcott," *History of Childhood Quarterly* 1 (1973–74), 4–51. See also comments, ibid. 52–61.

5284 Strong, Floyd Brian, "Toward a History of the Experiential Family: Sex and Incest in the Nineteenth Century Family," *Journal of Marriage and the Family* 35 (1973), 457–466.

5285 Sunley, Robert, "Early Nineteenth-Century American Literature on Child-Rearing," *Childhood in Contemporary Cultures*, ed. Margaret Mead and Martha Wolfenstein (Chicago, 1955), 150–167. (See #44)

5286 Taylor, William R., "Toward a Definition of Orthodoxy: The Patrician South and the Common Schools," *Harvard Educational Review* 36 (1966), 412–426.

5287 Taylor, William R., and Christopher Lasch, "Two Kindred Spirits: Sorority and Family in New England, 1839–46," *New England Quarterly* 36 (1963), 231–241.

5288 Thernstrom, Stephan, *The Other Bostonians*. Cambridge, Mass., 1973.

5289 Thernstrom, Stephan, *Poverty and Progress: Social Mobility in a Nineteenth-Century City*. Cambridge, Mass., 1964.

5290 Thernstrom, Stephan, and Peter R. Knights, "Men in Motion: Some Data and Speculations about Urban Population Mobility in Nineteenth-Century America," *Anonymous Americans*, ed. Tamara K. Hareven (Englewood Cliffs, N.J., 1971), 17–47. (See #4837)

5291 T'ien, H. Yuan, "A Demographic Aspect of Interstate Variation in American Fertility, 1800–1860," *Milbank Memorial Fund Quarterly* 37 (1959), 49–59.

5292 Travis, Anthony R., "The Origins of Mothers' Pensions in Illinois," *Journal of the Illinois State Historical Society* 68 (1975), 421–428.

5293 Uhlenberg, Peter, "A Study of Cohort Life Cycles: Cohorts of Native Born Massachusetts Women, 1830–1920," *Population Studies* 23 (1969), 407–420.

5294 Uhlenberg, Peter, "Cohort Variations in Family Life Cycle Experiences of U.S. Females," *Journal of Marriage and the Family* 36 (1974), 284–292.

5295 Uhlenberg, Peter, "Changing Configurations of the Life Course," *Transitions,* ed. Tamara K. Hareven (New York, 1978), 65–97. (See #261)

5296 Veysey, Lawrence, *The Communal Experience: Anarchist and Mystical Counter-Cultures in America.* New York, 1973.

5297 Vinovskis, Maris A., "The Demography of the Slave Population in Antebellum America," *Journal of Interdisciplinary History* 5 (1974–75), 459–467.

5298 Vinovskis, Maris A., "Socioeconomic Determinants of Interstate Fertility Differentials in the United States in 1850 and 1860," *Journal of Interdisciplinary History* 6 (1975–76), 375–396.

5299 Vinovskis, Maris A., "Trends in Massachusetts Education, 1826 to 1860," *History of Education Quarterly* 12 (1972), 501–530.

5300 Vinyard, Jo Ellen, "Inland Urban Immigrants: The Detroit Irish, 1850," *Michigan History* 57 (1973), 121–139.

5301 Walkowitz, Daniel J., "Working-Class Women in the Gilded Age: Factory, Community and Family Life among Cohoes, New York, Cotton Workers," *Journal of Social History* 5 (1971–72), 464–490.

5302 Walters, Ronald G., "The Family and Ante-bellum Reform: An Interpretation," *Societas* 3 (1973), 221–232.

5303 Wasserstrom, William, *Heiress of All the Ages: Sex and Sentiment in the Genteel Tradition.* Minneapolis, Minn., 1959.

5304 Wein, Roberta, "Women's Colleges and Domesticity, 1875–1918," *History of Education Quarterly* 14 (1974), 31–48.

5305 Welter, Barbara, "The Cult of True Womanhood: 1820–1860," *American Quarterly* 18 (1966), 151–174. Now in *The American Family in Social-Historical Perspective,* ed. Michael Gordon (New York, 1973), 224–250.

5306 *What Everyone Knew about Sex: Explained in the Words of Orson Squire Fowler and Other Victorian Moralists,* ed. William M. Dwyer. London, 1973.

5307 White, John, "Whatever Happened to the Slave Family in the Old South?" *Journal of American Studies* 8 (1974), 383–390.

5308 Williams, Blaine T., "Demographic Characteristics of the Pioneer Family in the North Central Texas Area of 1850," *Proceedings of the Southwest Sociological Association* 15 (1965), 80–88.

5309 Williams, Blaine T., "The Frontier Family: Demographic Fact and Historical

Myth," *Essays on the American West,* ed. Harold M. Hollingsworth and Sandra L. Meyers (Austin, Texas, 1969), 40-65.

5310 Wires, Richard, *The Divorce Issue and Reform in Nineteenth-Century Indiana.* Muncie, Ind., 1967.

5311 Wishy, Bernard, *The Child and the Republic: The Dawn of Modern American Child Nurture.* Philadelphia, 1967.

5312 Woodson, Carter G., *Free Negro Heads of Families in the United States.* Washington, 1925.

5313 Wright, Carroll D., *A Report on Marriage and Divorce in the U.S., 1867-1886.* Washington, D.C., 1897.

5314 Yasuba, Yasukichi, *Birth Rates of the White Population of the U.S., 1800-1860: An Economic Study.* Baltimore, 1962.

5315 Zelnik, Melvin, "The Fertility of the American Negro in 1830 and 1850," *Population Studies* 20 (1966), 77-83.

1890 TO THE PRESENT

5316 Aberle, Sophie, and George W. Corner, *Twenty-Five Years of Sex Research: History of the National Research Council Committee for Research in Problems of Sex, 1922-1947.* Philadelphia, 1953.

5317 *Abortion in a Changing World,* ed. Robert E. Hall. New York, 1970.

5318 Abrams, R. H., "Residential Propinquity as a Factor in Marriage Selection: Fifty Year Trends in Philadelphia," *American Sociological Review* 18 (1943), 288-317.

5319 Acker, Joan, "Women and Social Stratification: A Case of Intellectual Sexism," *American Journal of Sociology* 78 (1973), 936-945.

5320 Adamic, Louis, "Family Life and the Depression," *My America: 1928-38* (New York, 1938), 283-293.

5321 Alexis, Marcus, "Patterns of Black Consumption, 1935-1960," *Journal of Black Studies* 1 (1970), 55-74.

5322 Alvarez, Rodolfo, "The Psychohistorical and Socioeconomic Development of the Chicano Community in the United States," *Social Science Quarterly* 53 (1973), 920-942.

5323 *The American Sexual Dilemma,* ed. William L. O'Neill. New York, 1972.

5324 Anderson, Barbara, and Margaret Clark, *Culture and Aging.* Springfield, Ill., 1964.

5325 Anderson, John E., "Child Development: An Historical Perspective," *Child Development* 27 (1956), 181-196.

5326 Anderson, W. A., "Some Characteristics of Rural Families on Relief in New York State," *Rural Sociology* 1 (1936), 322-331.

5327   Angell, Robert Cooley, *The Family Encounters the Depression*. New York, 1936.

5328   Babchuck, Nicholas, and John A. Ballweg, "Black Family Structure and Primary Relations," *Phylon* 33 (1972), 334-347.

5329   Banner, Lois W., *Women in Modern America: A Brief History*. New York, 1974.

5330   Barnes, John A., "Marriage and Residential Continuity," *American Anthropologist* 62 (1960), 850-866.

5331   Barnett, James Harwood, and Rhoda Guren, "Recent American Divorce Novels, 1938-1945: A Study in the Sociology of Literature," *Social Forces* 26 (1948), 322-327.

5332   Baron, Milton L., *People Who Intermarry. Intermarriage in a New England Industrial Community*. Syracuse, 1946.

5333   Barton, Joseph J., *Peasants and Strangers: Italians, Rumanians, and Slovaks in an American City, 1890-1950*. Cambridge, Mass., 1975.

5334   Beaver, M. W., "Population, Infant Mortality, and Milk," *Population Studies* 27 (1973), 243-254.

5335   Becker, Gary S., *The Economic Approach to Human Behavior*. Chicago, Ill., 1976.

5336   Becker, Gary S., "On the Relevance of the New Economics of the Family," *American Economic Review* 64 (1974), 317-319.

5337   Becker, Gary S., "Theory of Marriage," *Journal of Political Economy* 81 (1973), 813-846; 82 (1974), S 11-S 26.

5338   Bell, Daniel, "The Breakup of Family Capitalism: On Changes of Class in America," *The End of Ideology* (New York, 1961), 39-45.

5339   Bell, Robert R., *Premarital Sex in a Changing Society*. Englewood Cliffs, N.J., 1966.

5340   Belville, Catharine R., *The Commercialization of the Home through Industrial Home Work*. Washington, D.C., 1935.

5341   Bernard, Jessie, "Age, Sex, and Feminism," *Annals of the American Academy of Political and Social Science* 415 (1974), 120-137.

5342   Bernard, Jessie, *The Future of Marriage*. New York, 1973.

5343   Bernard, Jessie, *Marriage and Family among Negroes*. Englewood Cliffs, N.J., 1966.

5344   Bigner, Jerry J., "Parent Education in Popular Literature: 1950-1970," *Family Coordinator* 21 (1972), 313-319.

5345   Billingsley, Andrew, and Amy Tate Billingsley, *Black Families in White America*. Englewood Cliffs, N.J., 1968.

5346   Billingsley, Andrew, and Amy Tate Billingsley, "Negro Family Life in America," *Social Service Review* 39 (1965), 310-319.

5347   Billingsley, Andrew, and Jeanne M. Giovannoni, *Children of the Storm: Black Children and American Child Welfare*. New York, 1972.

5348 Bradshaw, Benjamin S., and Frank D. Bean, "Trends in the Fertility of Mexican-Americans," *Social Science Quarterly* 53 (1973), 688-696.

5349 Bremer, Richard G., "Patterns of Spatial Mobility: A Case Study of Nebraska Farmers 1890-1970," *Agricultural History* 48 (1974), 529-542.

5350 Bressier, Marvin, "Selected Family Patterns in W. I. Thomas' Unfinished Study of the Bintl' Brief," *American Sociological Review* 17 (1952), 563-571.

5351 Bronfenbrenner, Urie, *Two Worlds of Childhood: U.S. and USSR.* New York, 1969.

5352 Broom, Leonard, and John I. Kitsusi, *The Managed Casualty: The Japanese-American Family in World War II.* Berkeley and Los Angeles, 1956.

5353 Brown, J. S., and H. K. Schwarzweller, "Kentucky Mountain Migration and the Stem Family: An American Variation on a Theme by LePlay," *Rural Sociology* 28 (1963), 68-69.

5354 Burch, Thomas K., "The Size and Structure of Families: A Comparative Analysis of Census Data," *American Sociological Review* 32 (1967), 347-363.

5355 Burnham, John C., "The Progressive Era Revolution in American Attitudes toward Sex," *Journal of American History* 59 (1973), 885-908.

5356 Byington, Margaret, "The Family in a Typical Mill Town," *American Journal of Sociology* 14 (1909), 648-659.

5357 Byington, Margaret, *Homestead: The Households of a Mill Town.* Pittsburgh, 1974.

5358 Cahen, A., *Statistical Analysis of American Divorce.* New York, 1932.

5359 Cain, Glen G., *Married Women in the Labor Force.* Chicago, 1966.

5360 Cain, Leonard D., "Political Factors in the Emerging Legal Age Status of the Elderly," *Annals of the American Academy of Political and Social Science* 415 (1974), 70-79.

5361 Carr, Malcolm, Katherine Spencer, and Doriane Woolley, "Navaho Clans and Marriage at Pueblo Alto," *American Anthropologist* 41 (1939), 245-257.

5362 Carter, Hugh, and Paul C. Glick, *Marriage and Divorce: A Social and Economic Study.* Cambridge, Mass., 1970. Rev. ed., 1976.

5363 Cary, Eve, "Pregnancy without Penalty," *Civil Liberties Review* 1 (1973), 31-48.

5364 Cavan, Ruth Shonle, and Katherine Howland Ranck, *The Family and the Depression.* Freeport, New York, 1969.

5365 Centers, Richard, "Marital Selection and Occupational Strata," *American Journal of Sociology* 54 (1949), 530-538.

5366 Chafe, William H., *The American Woman: Her Changing Social, Economic, and Political Roles, 1920-1970.* New York, 1972.

5367 Child, Irvin L., *Italian or American? The Second Generation in Conflict.* New Haven, 1943.

5368 Choldin, Harvey M., "Kinship Networks in the Migration Process," *International Migration Review* 7 (1973), 163-175.

5369 Ciocco, Antonio, "The Trend of Age at Marriage in Washington County,

Maryland, from 1897 to 1938," *Human Biology* 12 (1940), 59-76.

5370   Clark, John G., David M. Katzman, Richard D. McKinzie, and Theodore A. Wilson, *Three Generations in Twentieth-Century America: Family, Community, and Nation.* Homewood, Ill., 1976.

5371   Codere, Helen, "A Genealogical Study of Kinship in the United States," *Psychiatry* 18 (1955), 65-79.

5372   Coleman, James S., *The Adolescent Society.* Glencoe, Ill., 1961.

5373   Coleman, James S., et al., *Youth: Transition to Adulthood.* Chicago, 1974.

5374   Comhaire, J. L., "Economic Change and the Extended Family," *Annals of the American Academy of Political and Social Sciences* 305 (1956), 45-52.

5375   Conard, Laetitia M., "Some Effects of the Depression on Family Life," *Social Forces* 15 (1936-37), 76-81.

5376   Connor, John, "Acculturation and Family Continuities in Three Generations of Japanese Americans," *Journal of Marriage and the Family* 36 (1974), 159-165.

5377   Coser, R. L., *Life Cycle and Achievement in America.* New York, 1969.

5378   Cowan, Ruth Schwartz, "The 'Industrial Revolution' in the Home: Household Technology and Social Change," *Technology and Culture* 17 (1976), 1-23.

5379   Cowles, May L., "Changes in Family Personnel, Occupational Status, and Housing Occurring over the Farm Family's Life Cycle," *Rural Sociology* 18 (1953), 35-44.

5380   Cuber, John F., "Changing Courtship and Marriage Customs," *Annals of the American Academy of Political and Social Science* 229 (1943), 30-38.

5381   Cumming, Elaine, and David M. Schneider, "Sibling Solidarity: A Property of American Kinship," *American Anthropologist* 63 (1961), 489-507.

5382   Cutright, Phillips, "Components of Change in the Number of Female Family Heads Aged 15-44: United States, 1940-1970," *Journal of Marriage and the Family* 36 (1974), 714-721.

5383   Cutright, Phillips, "Illegitimacy in the United States, 1920-1968," *Demographic and Social Aspects...*, ed. Charles F. Westoff and Robert Parke, Jr. (Washington, D.C., 1972), 375-438. (See #5389)

5384   Davis, Katherine B., *Factors in the Sex Life of Twenty-Two Hundred Women.* New York, 1929.

5385   Davis, Kingsley, "The American Family in Relation to Demographic Change," *Demographic and Social Aspects...*, ed. Charles F. Westoff and Robert Parke, Jr. (Washington, D.C., 1972), 235-265. (See #5389)

5386   Degler, Carl N., "Revolution without Ideology: The Changing Place of Women in America," *Daedalus* 93 (1964), 653-670.

5387   De Jong, Gordon F., *Applachian Fertility Decline.* Lexington, Ky., 1968.

5388   Demeny, Paul, and Paul Gingrich, "A Reconsideration of Negro-White Mortality Differentials in the United States," *Demography* 4 (1967), 820-837.

5389   *Demographic and Social Aspects of Population Growth*, ed. Charles F. Westoff and Robert Parke, Jr. Washington, D.C., 1972.

5390 Dennis, Wayne, *The Hopi Child*. New York, 1965.

5391 Diones, C. Thomas, *Law, Politics, and Birth Control*. Urbana, Ill., 1972.

5392 Driver, Harold E., "Girls' Puberty Rites in Western North America," *University of California Anthropology Records* 6 (1941), 21–90.

5393 Driver, Harold E., "Reply to Opler on Apachean Subsistence, Residence, and Girls' Puberty Rites," *American Anthropologist* 74 (1972), 1147–1151.

5394 Du Bois, William E. B., *The Philadelphia Negro*. Philadelphia, 1899. Most recent reissue: Millwood, N.Y., 1973.

5395 Dyer, William G., and Richard Urban, "The Institutionalization of Equalitarian Family Norms," *Marriage and Family Living* 20 (1958), 53–58.

5396 Easterlin, Richard A., "Does Human Fertility Adjust to the Environment?" *American Economic Review* 61 (1971), 399–407.

5397 Easterlin, Richard A., "Relative Economic Status and the American Fertility Swing," *Family Economic Behavior: Problems and Prospects*, ed. Eleanor B. Sheldon (Philadelphia, 1973), 170–223.

5398 Ehrich, Ira F., "The Aged Black in America: The Forgotten Person," *Journal of Negro Education* 44 (1975), 12–23.

5399 Elder, Glen H., Jr., *Children of the Great Depression: Social Structure and Personality*. Chicago, 1974.

5400 Elder, Glen H., Jr., and Charles E. Bowerman, "Family Structure and Child-Rearing Patterns: The Effect of Family Size and Sex Composition," *American Sociological Review* 28 (1963), 891–905.

5401 Elder, Glen H., Jr., and Richard C. Rockwell, "Marital Timing in Women's Life Patterns," *Journal of Family History* 1 (1976), 34–53.

5402 Ellis, Albert, *The Folklore of Sex*. New York, 1961.

5403 England, R. W., Jr., "Images of Love and Courtship in Family Magazine Fiction," *Marriage and Family Living* 22 (1960), 162–165.

5404 Enterline, P. E., "Causes of Death Reponsible for Recent Increases in Sex Mortality Differentials in the United States," *Milbank Memorial Fund Quarterly* 39 (1961), 312–338.

5405 *Ethnic Families in America*, ed. Charles H. Mindel and Robert W. Habenstein. New York, 1976.

5406 *The Family and Sexual Revolution*, ed. Edwin M. Schur. Bloomington, Ind., 1964.

5407 *The Family Life of Black People*, ed. Charles Vert Willie. Columbus, 1970.

5408 Farber, Bernard, *Kinship and Class, a Midwestern Study*. New York, 1971.

5409 Feldman, Egal, "Prostitution, the Alien Woman and the Progressive Imagination, 1910–1915," *American Quarterly* 19 (1967), 192–206.

5410 Ferguson, Leonard W., "The Cultural Genesis of Masculinity-Femininity," *Psychological Bulletin* 38 (1941), 584–585.

5411 Ferriss, Abbott L., *Indicators of Change in the American Family*. New York, 1970.

5412 Filene, Peter Gabriel, *Him/Her/Self: Sex Roles in Modern America.* New York, 1975.

5413 Frank, Lawrence K., "The Beginning of Child Development and Family Education in the Twentieth Century," *Merrill-Palmer Quarterly* 8 (1962), 207–227.

5414 Frazier, E. Franklin, *The Negro Family in Chicago.* Chicago, 1932.

5415 Frazier, E. Franklin, *The Negro Family in the United States.* Chicago, 1966.

5416 Frazier, E. Franklin, *Negro Youth at the Crossways: Their Personality Development in the Middle States.* Washington, D.C., 1940.

5417 Freedman, Estelle B., "The New Woman: Changing Views of Women in the 1920's," *Journal of American History* 61 (1974), 372–393.

5418 Freedman, Ronald, et al., *Family Planning, Sterility, and Population Growth.* New York, 1959.

5419 Friedan, Betty, *The Feminine Mystique.* New York, 1963.

5420 Friedenberg, Edgar Z., *Coming of Age in America.* New York, 1965.

5421 Friedenberg, Edgar Z., *The Vanishing Adolescent.* Boston, 1959.

5422 Gans, Herbert J., *The Urban Villagers: Group and Class in the Life of Italian-Americans.* New York, 1962.

5423 *The Ghetto and Beyond: Essays on Jewish Life in America,* ed. Peter I. Rose. New York, 1969.

5424 Gilmore, Harlan W., "Family-Capitalism in a Community of Rural Louisiana," *Social Forces* 15 (1936–37), 71–75.

5425 Glick, Paul C., *American Families.* New York, 1957.

5426 Glick, Paul C., "A Demographer Looks at American Families," *Journal of Marriage and the Family* 37 (1975), 15–26.

5427 Glick, Paul C., "The Family Cycle," *American Sociological Review* 12 (1947), 164–174.

5428 Glick, Paul C., "Family Trends in the U.S., 1890–1940," *American Sociological Review* 7 (1942), 505–514.

5429 Glick, Paul C., "The Life Cycle of the Family," *Marriage and Family Living* 17 (1955), 3–9.

5430 Glick, Paul C., "Types of Families: An Analysis of Census Data," *American Sociological Review* 6 (1941), 830–838.

5431 Glick, Paul C., "Updating the Life Cycle of the Family," *Journal of Marriage and the Family* 39 (1977), 5–13.

5432 Glick, Paul C., and Robert Parke, Jr., "New Approaches in Studying the Life Cycle of the Family," *Demography* 2 (1965), 187–202.

5433 Goldscheider, Calvin, and Sidney Goldstein, "Generational Changes in Jewish Family Structure," *Journal of Marriage and the Family* 29 (1967), 269–276.

5434 Gordon, Linea, "The Politics of Birth Control, 1920–1940: The Impact of Professionals," *International Journal of Health Services* 5 (1975), 253–277.

5435 Gordon, Linea, "The Politics of Population: Birth Control and the Eugenics Movement," *Radical America* 8 (1974), 61–97.

5436 Grabill, Wilson H., Clyde V. Kiser, and Pascal K. Welpton, *The Fertility of American Women.* New York, 1958.

5437 Grabill, Wilson H., Clyde V. Kiser, and Pascal K. Welpton, "A Long View," *The American Family in Social-Historical Perspective,* ed. Michael Gordon (New York, 1973), 374-396.

5438 Graebner, Alan, "Birth Control and the Lutherans: The Missouri Synod as a Case Study," *Journal of Social History* 2 (1968-69), 302-332.

5439 Hagood, Margaret Jarman, *Mothers of the South: Portraiture of the White Tenant Farm Women.* Chapel Hill, 1939.

5440 Hamasy, Laila Shakry, "The Role of Women in a Changing Navaho Society," *American Anthropologist* 59 (1957), 101-111.

5441 Handlin, David P., "Efficiency and the American Home," *Architectural Quarterly* 5 (1972), 50-54.

5442 Handy, E. S. Craighill, and Elizabeth Green Handy, "Personality, Family, and History," *Virginia Magazine of History and Biography* 51 (1943), 55-70.

5443 Hareven, Tamara K., "The Dynamics of Kin in an Industrial Community," *Turning Points,* ed. John Demos and Sarane Spence Boocock (Chicago, 1978), 151-182. (See #262)

5444 Hareven, Tamara K., "Family Time and Industrial Time: Family and Work in a Planned Corporation Town, 1900-1924," *Journal of Urban History* 1 (1974-75), 365-389. Now in *Family and Kin...,* ed. Tamara K. Hareven (New York, 1977), 187-206. (See #4856)

5445 Hareven, Tamara K., "The Laborers of Manchester, New Hampshire, 1912-1922: The Role of Family and Ethnicity in Adjustment to Industrial Life," *Labor History* 16 (1975), 249-265.

5446 Hareven, Tamara K., "The Last Stage: Historical Adulthood and Old Age," *Daedalus* 105 (1976), 13-27.

5447 Hareven, Tamara K., and Randolph Langenbach, *Amoskeag: Life and Work in an American Factory-City.* New York, 1978.

5448 Hastings, Donald W., C. H. Reynolds, and R. R. Canning, "Mormonism and Birth Planning: The Discrepancy between Church Authorities' Teaching and Lay Attitudes," *Population Studies* 26 (1972), 19-28.

5449 Hastings, Donald W., and J. Gregory Robinson, "Incidence of Childlessness for U.S. Women, Cohorts Born 1891-1945," *Social History* 21 (1974), 178-184.

5450 Hauser, Rita E., "Adoption and Religious Control," *American Bar Association Journal* 54 (1968), 771-773.

5451 Havens, Elizabeth M., "Women, Work, and Wedlock: A Note on Female Marital Patterns in the United States," *American Journal of Sociology* 78 (1973), 975-981.

5452 Havighurst, Robert J., et al., *Growing Up in River City.* New York, 1962.

5453 Hays, Samuel P., "History and Genealogy: Patterns of Change and Prospects for Cooperation," *Prologue* 7 (1975), 39-43, 81-84, 187-191.

5454 Hellman, Louis M., "Family Planning Comes of Age," *American Journal of Obstetrics and Gynecology* 109 (1971), 214-224.

5455 Henri, Florette, *Black Migration: 1900-1920*. New York, 1974.

5456 Hilger, M. Inez, *Arapaho Child Life and Its Cultural Background*. Washington, D.C., 1952.

5457 Hilger, M. Inez, *Chippewa Child Life and Its Cultural Background*. Washington, D.C., 1952.

5458 Hilger, M. Inez, "Chippewa Pre-natal Food and Conduct Taboos," *Primitive Man* 9 (1936), 46-48.

5459 Hill, Reuben, *Families under Stress: Adjustment to the Crises of War Separation and Reunion*. New York, 1949.

5460 Hill, Reuben, J. Joel Moss, and Claudine G. Wirths, *Eddyville's Families: A Study of Personal and Family Adjustments Subsequent to the Rapid Urbanization of a Southern Town*. Chapel Hill, 1953.

5461 Hochstrasser, Donald L., Gerry Arthur, and Michael Lewis, "Fertility Decline in Southern Appalachia: An Anthropological Perspective," *Human Organization* 32 (1973), 331-336.

5462 Hoffer, Charles R., "The Impact of War on the Farm Family," *Rural Sociology* 10 (1945), 151-156.

5463 Holder, Stephen C., "The Family Magazine and the American People," *Journal of Popular Culture* 7 (1973), 264-279.

5464 Hole, Judith, and Ellen Levine, *Rebirth of Feminism*. New York, 1971.

5465 Hollinghead, A. B., *Elmtown's Youth*. New York, 1949.

5466 Honigmann, Irma, and John Honigmann, "Child Rearing Patterns among the Great Whale River Eskimo," *Anthropological Papers of the University of Alaska* 2 (1953), 31-50.

5467 Hostetler, John A., *Hutterite Society*. Baltimore, Md., 1974.

5468 Hostetler, John A., and Gertrude Enders Huntington, "Socialization and Family Patterns," *The Hutterites in North America* (New York, 1967), 57-91.

5469 Hunter, Robert, *Poverty*. New York, 1904.

5470 Hutchinson, E. P., *Immigrants and Their Children, 1900-1950*. New York, 1956.

5471 *The Italian Experience in the United States*, ed. Silvano M. Tomasi and Madeline H. Engel. Staten Island, N.Y., 1970.

5472 Ivins, Stanley, "Notes on Mormon Polygamy," *Western Humanities Review* 10 (1956), 229-239. Also in *Utah History Quarterly* 35 (1967), 309-321.

5473 Jaco, E. Gartly, and Ivan Belknap, "Is a New Family Form Emerging in the Urban Fringe?" *American Sociological Review* 18 (1953), 551-557.

5474 Jacobson, Paul H., *American Marriage and Divorce*. New York, 1959.

5475 Jensen, Richard, "Family, Career, and Reform: Women Leaders of the Progressive Era," *The American Family in Social-Historical Perspective*, ed. Michael Gordon (New York, 1973), 267-280.

5476 Johnson, Charles S., *Growing Up in the Black Belt: Negro Youth in the Rural South*. Washington, 1941.

5477 Kanowitz, Leo, *Women and the Law: The Unfinished Revolution*. Albuquerque, N.M., 1969.

5478 Kaut, Charles R., "Western Apache Clan and Phratry Organization," *American Anthropologist* 58 (1956), 140-146.

5479 Keller, Suzanne Infeld, *The American Lower-Class Family*. Albany, 1968.

5480 Kenniston, Kenneth, "Social Change and Youth in America," *Daedalus* 91 (1962), 145-171.

5481 Kenniston, Kenneth, *The Uncommitted: Alienated Youth in American Society*. New York, 1965.

5482 Kenniston, Kenneth, *Young Radicals: Notes on Committed Youth*. New York, 1968.

5483 Kenniston, Kenneth, "Youth as a 'New' Stage of Life," *The American Scholar* 39 (1970), 631-654.

5484 Kenniston, Kenneth, and the Carnegie Council on Children, *All Our Children: The American Family under Pressure*. New York, 1977.

5485 Kennedy, Anne, "History of the Development of Contraceptive Materials in the United States," *American Medicine* 41 (1935), 159-161.

5486 Kennedy, David M., *Birth Control in America: The Career of Margaret Sanger*. New Haven, 1970.

5487 Kinsey, Alfred C., Wardell B. Pomeroy, and Clyde E. Martin, *Sexual Behavior in the Human Male*. Philadelphia, 1948.

5488 Kinsey, Alfred C., Wardell B. Pomeroy, Clyde E. Martin, and Paul H. Gebhard, *Sexual Behavior in the Human Female*. Philadelphia, 1953.

5489 Kitagawa, Evelyn M., "Differential Fertility in Chicago, 1920-40," *American Journal of Sociology* 58 (1952-53), 481-492.

5490 Kluckhohn, Clyde K., *The Navaho*. Cambridge, Mass., 1946.

5491 Knudsen, D. D., "The Declining Status of Women: Popular Myths and the Failure of Functionalist Thought," *Social Forces* 48 (1969), 183-193.

5492 Kobrin, Frances E., "The Fall in Household Size and the Rise of the Primary Individual in the United States," *Demography* 13 (1976), 127-138.

5493 Kobrin, Frances E., "Household Headship and Its Changes in the United States, 1940-1960, 1970," *Journal of the American Statistical Association* 68 (1973), 793-800.

5494 Koller, Marvin, "Some Changes in Courtship Behavior in Three Generations of Ohio Women," *American Sociological Review* 16 (1951), 365-370.

5495 Komarovsky, Mirra, *Blue-Collar Marriage*. New York, 1964.

5496 Kraditor, Aileen S., *The Ideas of the Woman Suffrage Movement: 1890-1920*. New York, 1965.

5497 Kraus, Philip E., *Yesterday's Children: A Longitudinal Study from Kindergarten into the Adult Years*. New York, 1973.

5498 Lantis, Margaret, *Eskimo Childhood and Interpersonal Relationships: Nunivak Biographies and Genealogies.* Seattle, Wash., 1960.

5499 Lasch, Christopher, "Divorce and the Family in America," *Atlantic Monthly* 218:5 (1966), 57–61.

5500 Lasch, Christopher, "Ideology and Sexual Emancipation and Its Domestication, 1900–1935," *Katallagete* 5 (1975), 19–24.

5501 Lasch, Christopher, *Haven in a Heartless World: The Family Besieged.* New York, 1977.

5502 Leff, Mark H., "Consensus for Reform: The Mother's Pension Movement in the Progressive Era," *Social Service Review* 47 (1973), 397–417.

5503 Leichter, Hope J., "Some Perspectives on the Family as Educator," *Teachers College Record* 76 (1974), 175–217.

5504 Lewis, Claudia, *Indian Families of the Northwest Coast: The Impact of Change.* Chicago, 1970.

5505 Liberty, Margot, "Population Trends among Present-Day Omaha Indians," *Plains Anthropologist* 20 (1975), 225–230.

5506 Lindermann, Frank B., *Red Mother.* New York, 1932.

5507 Lipman-Blumen, Jean, "Crisis Framework Applied to Microsociological Family Changes: Marriage, Divorce, and Occupational Trends Associated with World War II," *Journal of Marriage and the Family* 37 (1975), 889–902.

5508 Litwak, Eugene, "Extended Kin Relations in an Industrial Democratic Society," *Social Structure and the Family,* ed. Ethel Shanas and Gordon F. Streib (n.p., 1965), 290–325. (See #243)

5509 Litwak, Eugene, "Geographical Mobility and Extended Family Cohesion," *American Sociological Review* 25 (1960), 385–394.

5510 Litwak, Eugene, "Occupational Mobility and Extended Family Cohesion," *American Sociological Review* 25 (1960), 9–21.

5511 Locke, Harvey J., "Contemporary American Farm Families," *Rural Sociology* 10 (1945), 142–151.

5512 Lynd, Robert, and Helen Lynd, *Middletown.* New York, 1929.

5513 Lynd, Robert, and Helen Lynd, *Middletown in Transition.* New York, 1937.

5514 Lynes, Russell, *The Domesticated Americans.* New York, 1963.

5515 McPharlin, Paul, *Love and Courtship in America.* New York, 1946.

5516 *Marriage and the Family,* ed. Reuben Hill and Howard Becher. Boston, 1942.

5517 Marriott, Alice, *Ten Grandmothers.* Norman, Okla., 1948.

5518 Marshall, Douglas G., "The Decline in Farm Fertility and Its Relationship to Nationality and Religious Background," *Rural Sociology* 15 (1950), 42–49.

5519 Masnick, George S., and Joseph A. McFalls, Jr., "A New Perspective on the Twentieth-Century American Fertility Swing," *Journal of Family History* 1 (1976), 217–244.

5520 Mason, K. O., J. L. Czajka, and S. Arber, "Change in U.S. Women's Sex-Role Attitudes, 1964–1974," *American Sociological Review* 41 (1976), 573–596.

5521 Matthews, Elmore Messer, *Neighbor and Kin: Life in a Tennessee Ridge Community*. Nashville, Tenn., 1965.

5522 May, Henry F., *The End of American Innocence: A Study of the First Years of Our Time, 1912–1917*. New York, 1959.

5523 Meade, J. E., et al., "Demography and Economics," *Population Studies* Supplement 24 (1970), 25–31.

5524 McGovern, James R., "The American Woman's Pre-World War I Freedom in Manners and Morals," *Journal of American History* 55 (1968), 315–333.

5525 Merrill, Francis E., and Andrew G. Truxal, *Marriage and Family in American Culture*. New York, 1953.

5526 Middleton, Russell, "Fertility Values in American Magazine Fiction, 1916–1956," *Public Opinion Quarterly* 24 (1960), 139–143.

5527 Miller, Daniel, and Guy Swanson, *The Changing American Parent*. New York, 1958.

5528 Mirande, Alfred M., "The Isolated Nuclear Family Hypothesis: A Reanalysis," *The Family and Change*, ed. John N. Edwards (New York, 1969), 153–163.

5529 Modell, John, "Japanese American Family: A Perspective for Future Investigations," *Pacific Historical Review* 37 (1968), 67–81.

5530 Modell, John, "Patterns of Consumption, Acculturation, and Family Income Strategies in Late Nineteenth Century America," *Family and Population*, ed. Tamara K. Hareven and Maris Vinovskis (Princeton, N.J., 1978), 206–240. (See #5127)

5531 Modell, John, "Tradition and Opportunity: The Japanese Immigrant in America," *Pacific Historical Review* 40 (1971), 163–182.

5532 Mogey, John, "Century of Declining Paternal Authority," *Marriage and Family Living* 19 (1957), 234–239.

5533 Mogey, John, "Family and Community in Urban-Industrial Societies," *Handbook of Marriage...*, ed. Harold T. Christensen (Chicago, 1964), 501–534. (See #124)

5534 Monahan, Thomas Patrick, "The Number of Children in American Families and the Sharing of Households," *Marriage and Family Living* 18 (1956), 201–203.

5535 Monahan, Thomas Patrick, "Premarital Pregnancy in the United States: A Critical Review and Some New Findings," *Eugenics Quarterly* 7 (1960), 133–147.

5536 Morgan, Winona Louise, *The Family Meets the Depression*. Minneapolis, 1939.

5537 Morrill, R. L., and F. R. Pitts, "Marriage, Migration and the Mean Information Field: A Study in Uniqueness and Generality," *Annals of the Association of American Geographers* 57 (1967), 401–422.

5538 Moss, Leonard W., and Walter H. Thomson, "The South Italian Family: Literature and Observation," *Human Organization* 18 (1959), 35–41.

5539 Moynihan, Daniel Patrick, "Employment, Income, and the Ordeal of the Negro Family," *Daedalus* 94 (1965), 745–770.

5540 Moynihan, Daniel Patrick, *The Negro Family in America: The Case for National Action.* Washington, D.C., 1965. Also in *The Moynihan Report and the Politics of Controversy,* ed. Lee Rainwater and William L. Yancey (Cambridge, Mass., 1967), 41–124.

5541 *The Negro American,* ed. Talcott Parsons and Kenneth B. Clark. Boston, 1970.

5542 *The Negro American Family,* ed. William E. B. Dubois. Atlanta, 1908. Reprint, Cambridge, Mass., 1970.

5543 "Nellie Kedsie Jones' Advice to Farm Women: Letters from Wisconsin, 1912–1916," ed. Jeanne Hunnicutt Delgado, *Wisconsin Magazine of History* 57 (1973), 2–27.

5544 Nelson, Lowry, "Education and the Changing Size of Mormon Families," *Rural Sociology* 17 (1952), 335–342.

5545 Neugarten, Bernice L., "Age Groups in American Society and the Rise of the Young-Old," *Annals of the American Academy of Political and Social Science* 415 (1974), 187–198.

5546 Nobles, Wade W., "Africanity: Its Role in Black Families," *Black Scholar* 5 (1974), 10–17.

5547 Norton, Eleanor Holmes, "Population Growth and the Future of Black Folk," *Crisis* 80 (1973), 151–153.

5548 Notestein, Frank W., "The Decrease in the Size of Families from 1890 to 1910," *Milbank Memorial Fund Quarterly Bulletin* 9 (1931), 181–188.

5549 Notestein, Frank W., "The Differential Rate of Increase among the Social Classes of the American Population," *Social Forces* 12 (1933–34), 17–33.

5550 Nye, F. Ivan, "Emerging and Declining Family Roles," *Journal of Marriage and the Family* 36 (1974), 238–245.

5551 Ogburn, William F., "Changing Family Functions," *Recent Social Trends* (New York, 1933), 661–708.

5552 Ogburn, William F., and Meyer F. Nimkoff, *Technology and the Changing Family.* Cambridge, Mass., 1955.

5553 O'Neill, William L., *Divorce in the Progressive Era.* New Haven, 1967.

5554 O'Neill, William L., *Everyone Was Brave: The Rise and Fall of Feminism in America.* Chicago, 1969.

5555 Oppenheimer, Valerie Kincade, "Demographic Influence on Female Employment and the Status of Women," *American Journal of Sociology* 78 (1973), 946–961.

5556 Oppenheimer, Valerie Kincade, *The Female Labor Force in the United States: Demographic and Economic Factors Governing Its Growth and Changing Composition.* Westport, Conn., 1976. Originally, Berkeley, 1966.

5557 Ostergren, Robert C., "Cultural Homogeneity and Population Stability among

Swedish Immigrants in Chicago County," *Minnesota History* 43 (1973), 255–269.

5558 Park, Robert E., and Herbert A. Miller, *Old World Traits Transplanted*. New York, 1969.

5559 Parsons, Elsie Clews, "Tewa Mothers and Children," *Man* 24 (1924), 148–151.

5560 Parsons, Talcott, "Age and Sex in the Social Structure of the United States," *American Sociological Review* 7 (1942), 604–616.

5561 Parsons, Talcott, "The Incest Taboo in Relation to Social Structure and the Socialization of the Child," *British Journal of Sociology* 5 (1954), 101–117.

5562 Parsons, Talcott, "The Kinship System of the Contemporary United States," *American Anthropologist* 45 (1943), 22–38.

5563 Pearlin, Leonard I., and Melvin L. Kohn, "Social Class, Occupation, and Parental Values: A Cross-National Study," *American Sociological Review* 31 (1966), 466–479.

5564 Rainwater, Lee, *Behind Ghetto Walls: Black Families in a Federal Slum*. Chicago, 1970.

5565 Rainwater, Lee, "Crucible of Identity: The Negro Lower Class Family," *Daedalus* 95 (1966), 172–216.

5566 Rainwater, Lee, Richard Coleman, and Gerald Handel, *Workingman's Wife: Her Personality, World, and Life Style*. New York, 1959.

5567 Rainwater, Lee, and Karol Kane Weinstein, *And the Poor Get Children: Sex, Contraception, and Family Planning in the Working Class*. Chicago, 1960.

5568 Raphael, Marc Lee, "European Jewish and Non-Jewish Marital Patterns in Los Angeles, 1910–1913," *Western States Jewish Historical Quarterly* 6 (1974), 100–106.

5569 Reiss, Ira L., *Premarital Sexual Standards in America*. Glencoe, Ill., 1960.

5570 Reyes, Ramos, "A Case in Point: An Ethnomethodological Study of a Poor Mexican American Family," *Social Science Quarterly* 53 (1973), 905–919.

5571 Richards, Cara E., "Matriarchy or Mistake: The Role of Iroquois Women through Time," *Cultural Stability and Cultural Change*, ed. Verne Frederick Ray (Seattle, 1957), 30–45.

5572 Richardson, Herbert, *Nun, Witch, and Playmate: The Americanization of Sex*. New York, 1971.

5573 Riedl, Norbert F., and Carol K. Buckles, "House Customs and Beliefs in East Tennessee," *Tennessee Folklore Society Bulletin* 41 (1975), 47–56.

5574 Robins, Lee N., and Miroda Tomanec, "Closeness to Blood Relatives Outside the Immediate Family," *Kinship and Family Organization*, ed. Bernard Farber (New York, 1966), 134–141. (See #162)

5575 Robinson, Paul A., *The Modernization of Sex*. New York, 1976.

5576 Rolle, A. F., *The Immigrant Upraised; Italian Adventures and Colonists in an Expanding America*. Norman, Okla., 1968.

5577 Rollins, Mable A., "Monetary Contributions of Wives to Family Income in 1920 and 1960," *Marriage and Family Living* 25 (1963), 226–227.

5578   Romanofsky, Peter, "To Save...Their Souls: The Care of Dependent Children in New York City, 1900-1905," *Jewish Social Studies* 36 (1974), 253-261.

5579   Rosen, Bernard C., "Family Structure and Achievement Motivation," *American Sociological Review* 26 (1961), 574-585.

5580   Rosen, Harvey S., "The Monetary Value of a Housewife: A Replacement Cost Approach," *American Journal of Economics and Sociology* 33 (1974), 65-73.

5581   Rosenwaike, Ira, *Population History of New York City.* Syracuse, N.Y., 1972.

5582   Rosenwaike, Ira, "Two Generations of Italians in America (1940-1960): Their Fertility Experience," *International Migration Review* 7 (1973), 271-280.

5583   Ross, Heather L., and Isabel V. Sawhill, *Time of Transition: The Growth of Families Headed by Women.* Washington, D.C., 1975.

5584   Rossi, Alice S., "Family Development in a Changing World," *American Journal of Psychiatry* 128 (1972), 1057-1066.

5585   Rossi, Alice S., "Naming Children in Middle-Class Families," *American Sociological Review* 30 (1965), 499-513.

5586   Rossi, Alice S., "Transition to Parenthood," *Journal of Marriage and the Family* 30 (1968), 26-39.

5587   Ryder, Norman B., "The Emergence of a Modern Fertility Pattern: United States, 1917-1966," *Fertility and Family Planning: A World View,* ed. Samuel J. Behrman (Ann Arbor, 1969), 99-123.

5588   Safilios-Rothschild, Constantina, "The Study of Family Power Structure: A Review 1960-1969," *Journal of Marriage and the Family* 32 (1970), 539-552.

5589   Sanderson, Warren, "The Fertility of American Women Since 1920," *Journal of Economic History* 30 (1970), 271-288.

5590   Scanzoni, John, *The Black Family in Modern Society.* Boston, 1971.

5591   Schneider, David M., *American Kinship: A Cultural Account.* Englewood Cliffs, N.J., 1968.

5592   Schneider, David M., and George Homans, "Kinship Terminology and the American Kinship System," *American Anthropologist* 57 (1955), 1194-1208.

5593   Schneider, David M., and Raymond Smith, *Class Differences and Sex Roles in American Kinship and Family Structure.* Englewood Cliffs, N.J., 1973.

5594   Schnepp, Gerald J., and Agnes Masako Yui, "Cultural and Marital Adjustment of Japanese War Brides," *American Journal of Sociology* 61 (1955), 48-50.

5595   Schwarzeweler, Harry K., James S. Brown, and J. J. Mangalam, *Mountain Families in Transition: A Case Study of Appalachian Migration.* University Park, Pa., 1971.

5596   Searcy, Ann McElroy, *Contemporary and Traditional Prairie Potawatomi Child Life.* Lawrence, Kansas, 1965.

5597   Seidenberg, Robert, *Marriage in Life and Literature.* New York, 1970.

5598   Shanas, Ethel, et al., *Old People in Three Industrial Societies.* New York, 1968.

5599   Sharet, Stephen, "The Three-Generation Thesis and the American Jews," *British Journal of Sociology* 24 (1973), 151-164.

5600 Sherif, Muzafer, *Problems of Youth: Transition to Adulthood in a Changing World*. Chicago, 1965.

5601 Shiloh, Arlon, *By Myself I'm A Book! An Oral History of the Immigrant Jewish Experience in Pittsburgh*. Waltham, Mass., 1972.

5602 Sinclair, Andrew, *The Emancipation of the American Woman*. New York, 1965.

5603 Sirjamaki, John, *The American Family in the Twentieth Century*. Cambridge, Mass., 1953.

5604 Smigel, Edwin O., and Rita Seiden, "The Decline and Fall of the Double Standard," *Annals of the American Academy of Political and Social Science* 376 (1968), 6-17.

5605 Smith, Daniel Scott, "The Dating of the American Sexual Revolution: Evidence and Interpretation," *The American Family in Social-Historical Perspective*, ed. Michael Gordon (New York, 1973), 321-335.

5606 Smith, Raymond, "The Nuclear Family in Afro-American Kinship," *Journal of Comparative Family Studies* 1 (1970-71), 55-70.

5607 Smuts, Robert W., *Women and Work in America*. New York, 1971.

5608 Sorokin, Pitirim A., *The American Sex Revolution*. Boston, 1956.

5609 Speck, Ross V., and Carolyn L. Attneave, *Family Networks*. New York, 1973.

5610 Spengler, Joseph J., "The Fecundity of Native and Foreign-Born Women in New England," *Brookings Institution Pamphlet Series* 2:1 (1930).

5611 Stack, Carol B., *All Our Kin: Strategies for Survival in a Black Community*. New York, 1974.

5612 Stack, Carol B., "Sex Roles and Survival Strategies in an Urban Black Community," *Woman, Culture, and Society*, ed. Michelle Zimbalist Rosaldo and Louise Lamphere (Stanford, 1974), 113-128.

5613 Staples, Robert, *The Black Family: Essays and Studies*. Belmont, Calif., 1971.

5614 Staples, Robert, "The Mexican-American Family: Its Modification over Time and Space," *Phylon* 32 (1971), 179-192.

5615 Steere, Geoffrey Hazard, "Freudianism and Child-Rearing in the Twenties," *American Quarterly* 20 (1968), 759-767.

5616 Steinfels, Margaret O'Brien, *Who's Minding the Children? The History and Politics of Child Care in America*. New York, 1974.

5617 Stetson, Dorothy M., and Gerald C. Wright, "The Effects of Laws on Divorce in American States," *Journal of Marriage and the Family* 37 (1975), 537-547.

5618 Stoddard, Ellwyn R., "The Adjustment of Mexican American Barrio Families to Forced Housing Relocation," *Social Science Quarterly* 53 (1973), 749-759.

5619 Stouffer, Samuel A., and Paul F. Lazarsfeld, *The Family in the Depression*. New York, 1937.

5620 Strauss, Anselm, "Strain and Harmony in American-Japanese War-Bride Marriages," *Marriage and Family Living* 16 (1954), 99-106.

5621 Streib, Gordon F., and Clement J. Schneider, *Retirement in American Society.* Ithaca, New York, 1971.

5622 Strong, Floyd Brian, "Ideas of the Early Sex Education Movement in America, 1890-1920," *History of Education Quarterly* 12 (1972), 129-161.

5623 Sussman, Marvin B., "Family Continuity: Selective Factors Which Affect Relationships between Families at General Levels," *Marriage and Family Living* 16 (1954), 112-120.

5624 Sussman, Marvin B., "The Help Pattern in the Middle Class Family," *American Sociological Review* 18 (1953), 22-28.

5625 Sussman, Marvin B., "The Isolated Nuclear Family: Fact or Fiction," *Social Problems* 6 (1959), 333-347.

5626 Sussman, Marvin B., "Parental Participation in Mate Selection and Its Effect on Family Continuity," *Social Forces* 32 (1953), 76-81.

5627 Sweet, James A., *Women in the Labor Force.* New York, 1973.

5628 Sweet, James A., and Larry L. Bumpass, "Differentials in Marital Instability of the Black Population: 1970," *Phylon* 35 (1974), 323-331.

5629 Sweetser, Frank L., and Paavo Piepponen, "Postwar Fertility Trends and Their Consequences in Finland and the United States," *Journal of Social History* 1 (1967-68), 101-118.

5630 Taeuber, Conrad, and Irene B. Taeuber, *The Changing Population of the United States.* New York, 1958.

5631 Taeuber, Irene B., "Change and Transition in Family Structure," *The Family in Transition: Proceedings of the Fogarty International Center* (Bethesda, Md., 1971), 35-98.

5632 Taeuber, Irene B., "Demographic Transitions and Population Problems in the United States," *Annals of the American Academy of Political and Social Science* 369 (1967), 131-140.

5633 Taeuber, Irene B., *Population Trends in the United States, 1900-1960.* Washington, D.C., 1964.

5634 Temply-Trujillo, Rita E., "Conceptions of the Chicano Family," *Smith College Studies in Social Work* 45 (1974), 1-20.

5635 Ten Houten, Warren D., "The Black Family Myth and Reality," *Psychiatry* 33 (1970), 145-173.

5636 Thomas, Dorothy Swaine, "Migration, Marriage, and Divorce," *Rural Sociology* 4 (1939), 155-165.

5637 Thompson, Laura, and Alice Joseph, *The Hopi Way.* Chicago, 1945.

5638 Trattner, Walter I., *Crusade for the Children: A History of the National Child Labor Committee and Child Labor Reform in America.* Chicago, 1970.

5639 Twombly, Robert C., "Saving the Family: Middle Class Attraction to Wright's Prairie House, 1901-1909," *American Quarterly* 27 (1975), 57-72.

5640 Uhlenberg, Peter R., "Changing Configurations of the Life Course," *Transitions,* ed. Tamara K. Hareven (New York, 1978), 65-97. (See #261)

5641 Uhlenberg, Peter R., "Cohort Variation in Family Life Cycle Experiences of

U.S. Families," *Journal of Marriage and the Family* 36 (1974), 284-292.

5642 Uhlenberg, Peter R., "A Study of Cohort Life Cycles: Cohorts of Native Born Massachusetts Women, 1830-1920," *Population Studies* 23 (1969), 407-420.

5643 Uminski, Sigmund H., *The Polish Pioneers in Virginia*, v. 2 of *The Poles in the Americas*. New York, 1974.

5644 Waller, Willard, *The Family: A Dynamic Interpretation*. New York, 1938.

5645 Warner, W. Lloyd, and P. Lunt, *The Social Life of a Modern Community*. New Haven, 1941.

5646 Warner, W. Lloyd, and Leo Srole, *The Social Systems of American Ethnic Groups*. New Haven, 1945.

5647 Weigley, Emma Seifrit, "It Might Have Been Euthenics: The Lake Placid Conferences and the Home Economics Movement," *American Quarterly* 26 (1974), 79-96.

5648 Weisbord, Robert G., *Genocide. Birth Control and the Black American*. Westport, Conn., 1975.

5649 Weslager, W. A., "Name-Giving among the Delaware Indians," *Names* 19 (1971), 268-282.

5650 Whelpton, Pascal K., *Cohort Fertility*. Princeton, N.J., 1954.

5651 Williams, Phyllis H., *South Italian Folkways in Europe and America*. New Haven, 1938.

5652 Wolfenstein, Martha, "Fun Morality: An Analysis of Recent American Child-Training Literature," *Childhood in Contemporary Cultures,* ed. Margaret Mead and Martha Wolfenstein (Chicago, 1955), 168-178. (See #44)

5653 Young, Christabel M., "Factors Associated with the Timing and Duration of the Leaving-Home Stage of the Family Life Cycle," *Population Studies* 29 (1975), 61-73.

5654 Young, Virginia Heyer, "Family and Childhood in a Southern Negro Community," *American Anthropologist* 72 (1970), 269-288.

5655 Zelditch, Morris, Jr., "Statistical Marriage Preferences of the Ramah Navaho," *American Anthropologist* 61 (1950), 470-491.

5656 Zimmerman, Carle C., and Merle E. Frampton, *Family and Society: A Study of the Sociology of Reconstruction*. New York, 1935.

5657 Zuckerman, Michael, "Dr. Spock: The Confidence Man," *The Family in History,* ed. Charles E. Rosenberg (Philadelphia, 1975), 179-207. (See #79)

See also #147, #212, #224, #243, #255, #3290, #4448, #6037, and #6048.

Latin America

GENERAL SURVEYS AND COLLECTIONS

5658 Azevedo, Fernando de, *Brazilian Culture,* tr. William R. Crawford. New York, 1950.

5659 Burch, Thomas K., "Comparative Family Structure: A Demographic Approach," *Estadística* 26 (1968), 285-293.

5660 Burch, Thomas K. "The Size and Structure of Families: A Comparative Analysis of Census Data," *American Sociological Review* 32 (1967), 347-363.

5661 Burch, Thomas K., "Some Demographic Determinants of Average Household Size: An Analytical Approach," *Demography* 4 (1970), 61-69.

5662 Bush, A. C., "Latin Kinship Extension: An Interpretation of the Data," *Ethnology* 19 (1971), 409-432.

5663 Cabrera Ypina de Corse, Matilde, *La familia Hernández Soto de San Luis Potosí.* San Luis Potosí, 1966.

5664 Cafferata, José Ignacio, et al., *La familia.* Córdoba, Argentina, 1973.

5665 Candido, Antônio, "The Brazilian Family," *Brazil: Portrait of Half a Continent,* ed. T. Lynn Smith and Alexander Marchant (Westport, Conn., 1972), 291-312.

5666 Corredor, Berta, *La familia en América Latina.* Madrid, 1962.

5667 Costa Pinto, L. A., *Lutas de famílias no Brasil: introdução ao seu estudo.* São Paulo, 1949.

5668 Cutright, P., M. Hout, and D. R. Johnson, "Structural Determinants of Fertility in Latin America, 1800-1970," *American Sociological Review* 41 (1976), 511-526.

5669 Dirks, R., and V. Kerns, "Mating Patterns and Adaptive Change in Rum Bay, 1823-1970," *Social and Economic Studies* 25 (1976), 34-54.

5670 *The Family in the Caribbean: Proceedings of the First Conference on the*

Family in the Caribbean, St. Thomas, V.I., 1968, ed. Standford N. Gerber. Río Piedras, 1968.

5671 *The Family in the Caribbean: Proceedings of the Second Conference on the Family in the Caribbean, Aruba, Netherlands Antilles, December 1–5, 1969,* ed. Stanford N. Gerber. Río Piedras, 1973.

5672 Foster, George M., "The Dyadic Contract: A Model for the Social Structure of a Mexican Peasant Village," *American Anthropologist* 63 (1961), 1173–1192.

5673 Foster, George M., "The Dyadic Contract in Tzintzuntzán; II: Patron-Client Relationship," *American Anthropologist* 65 (1963), 1280–1294.

5674 Freyre, Gilberto, "The Patriarchal Basis of Brazilian Society," *Politics of Change in Latin America*, ed. Joseph Maier and Richard W. Weatherhead (New York, 1964), 155–173.

5675 González, Elda R., and Rolando Mellafe, "La función de la familia en la historia social hispanoamericana colonial," *Anuario del Instituto de Investigaciones Históricas* 8 (1965), 57–71.

5676 González, Nancie K. Solien, "The Consanguineal Household and Matrifocality," *American Anthropologist* 67 (1965), 1541–1549.

5677 Goode, William J., "Illegitimacy, Anomie and Cultural Penetration," *American Sociological Review* 26 (1961), 910–925.

5678 Gudeman, Stephan, "The *Compadrazgo* as a Reflection of the Natural and Spiritual Person," *Proceedings of the Royal Anthropological Institute of Great Britain and Ireland* 101 (1971), 45–71.

5679 Herrmann, Lucila, "Evolucao da estrutura de Guaratingueta num periodo de trezentos anos," *Revista de Administracao* 2 (1948), 3–320.

5680 Hunt, Eva, "The Meaning of Kinship in San Juan: Genealogical and Social Models," *Ethnology* 8 (1969), 37–53.

5681 Hutchinson, Carmelita J. A., "Notas preliminares ao estudo da família no Brasil," *Segunda Reunião Brasileira de Antropologia* (Bahia, 1955), 261–274.

5682 Ingham, John M., "The Asymmetrical Implications of Godparentage in Tlayacapan, Morelos," *Man* 5 (1970), 281–289.

5683 *Journal of Family History* 3:4 (1978): "The Family in Latin America," ed. Francesca M. Cancian, Louis Wolf Goodman, and Peter H. Smith.

5684 Kubler, George, *The Indian Caste of Peru, 1795–1940: A Population Study Based upon Tax Records and Census Reports*. Westport, Conn., 1952.

5685 Kumstadter, Peter, "A Survey of the Consanguine or Matrifocal Family," *American Anthropologist* 65 (1963), 56–66.

5686 Lauterbach, Albert, *Enterprise in Latin America*. New York, 1966.

5687 Lewis, Oscar, "An Anthropological Approach to Family Studies," *American Journal of Sociology* 55 (1950), 468–475.

5688 Lewis, Oscar, "The Extended Family in Mexico," *Readings in Family and Society*, ed. William Goode (Englewood Cliffs, N.J., 1964), 180–183.

5689   López, D. E., "The Structure of *Compadrazgo* in Latin America," *Cornell Journal of Social Relations* 4 (1969), 82-95.

5690   Mintz, Sidney W., and Eric Wolf, "An Analysis of Ritual Co-Parenthood *(Compadrazgo)*," *Southwestern Journal of Anthropology* 6 (1950), 341-368.

5691   Nutini, Hugo G., "A Synoptic Comparison of Mesoamerican Marriage and Family Structure," *Southwestern Journal of Anthropology* 23 (1967), 383-404.

5692   Peñalosa, Fernando, "Mexican Family Roles," *Journal of Marriage and the Family* 30 (1968), 680-689.

5693   Rodman, Hyman, "Illegitimacy in the Caribbean Social Structure: A Reconsideration," *American Sociological Review* 31 (1966), 673-683.

5694   Rodman, Hyman, "Lower-Class Attitudes toward 'Deviant' Family Patterns: A Cross-Cultural Study," *Journal of Marriage and the Family* 31 (1969), 315-321.

5695   Segre, Sandro, "Family Stability, Social Classes and Values in Traditional and Industrial Societies," *Journal of Marriage and the Family* 37 (1975), 431-436.

5696   Solien, Nancie L., "Household and Family in the Caribbean: Some Definitions and Concepts," *Social and Economic Studies* 9 (1960), 101-106.

5697   Thompson, Richard A., "A Theory of Instrumental Social Networks," *Journal of Anthropological Research* 29 (1973), 244-265.

5698   Torres-Ríoseco, A., "The Family in Latin America," *The Family: Its Function and Destiny,* ed. Ruth Nanda Anshen. rev. ed. (New York, 1959), 85-103. (See #82)

5699   Vieira, Oldegar Franco, *Sociología educacional da família.* Bahia, 1957.

5700   Wolf, Eric, "Kinship, Friendship, and Patron-Client Relations," *The Social Anthropology of Complex Societies,* ed. Michael Banton (London, 1966), 1-22.

BIBLIOGRAPHIES AND REVIEW ESSAYS

5701   Carlos, Manuel L., and Lois Sellers, "Family, Kinship Structure, and Modernization in Latin America," *Latin American Research Review* 7 (1972), 95-124.

5702   Davidson, William, "Rural Latin American Culture," *Social Forces* 25 (1947), 249-252.

5703   Florescano, Enrique, "Bibliografía de historia demográfica de México: época prehispánica-1910," *Historia Mexicana* 21 (1972), 525-537.

5704   *Handbook of Latin American Studies,* v. 1-38. Gainesville, 1935-1976.

5705 Knaster, Meri, *Women in Spanish America: An Annotated Bibliography from Pre-Conquest to Contemporary Times.* Boston, 1977.

5706 Lockhart, James, "The Social History of Colonial Spanish America: Evolution and Potential," *Latin American Research Review* 7 (1972), 6-45.

5707 Schlesinger, Benjamin, "Family Patterns in Jamaica: Review and Commentary," *Journal of Marriage and the Family* 30 (1968), 136-148.

5708 Schlesinger, Benjamin, *The One-Parent Family: Perspectives and Annotated Bibliography.* Buffalo, 1969.

5709 Smith, Raymond T., "Culture and Social Structure in the Caribbean: Some Recent Work on Family and Kinship Studies," *Comparative Studies in Society and History* 6 (1963-64), 24-46.

5710 TePaske, John J., "Quantification in Latin American Colonial History," *The Dimensions of the Past,* ed. Val R. Lorwin and Jacob M. Price (New Haven, 1972), 431-476.

5711 Trujillo, María Salete Zulzke, "A família brasileira," *Notícia bibliográfica e histórica* 7 (1975), 139-146.

THEORY, SOURCES, AND METHODOLOGIES

5712 "Archivo antiguo cedido por Bernardo J. Caycedo al Archivo Nacional de Bogotá," *Archivos. Academia Colombiana de Historia* 3 (1971), 211-254.

5713 Arriaga, Eduardo E., *New Life Tables for Latin American Populations in the Nineteenth and Twentieth Centuries.* Berkeley, 1968.

5714 Bender, Donald R., "A Refinement of the Concept of Household Families," Co-Residence, and Domestic Functions," *American Anthropologist* 69 (1967), 493-504.

5715 Borah, Woodrow, and Sherburne F. Cook, "La demografía histórica de América Latina: necesidades y perspectivas," *Historia Mexicana* 21 (1971), 312-327.

5716 Bourde, Guy, "Sources et methodes de l'histoire démographique à Cuba: XVIIIe et XIXe siècles," *Annales de démographie historique* (1972), 385-424.

5717 Brady, Trent M., "The Application of Computers to the Analysis of Census Data: The Bishopric of Caracas, 1780-1820, a Case Study," *Population and Economics,* ed. Paul Deprez (Winnepeg, 1970), 271-274.

5718 Bromley, Rosemary D. F., "Parish Registers as a Source in Latin American Demographic and Historic Research," *Bulletin of the Society for Latin American Studies* 19 (1974), 14-21.

5719 Bueno, Clodoaldo, "Os cartórios como fonte primária para a história: os cartórios de Marília," *Revista de História* 35 (1967), 215-228.

5720   Cardoso, Clotilde de Santa Clara Medina, "Arrolamento das fontes históricas do município de Batatais," *Revista de História* 37 (1968), 447–459.

5721   Carlinger, Geoffrey, "Determinants of Household Headship," *Journal of Marriage and the Family* 37 (1975), 28–38.

5722   Castro, Jeanne B. de, and José S. Witter, "Arrolamento das fontes primárias de Rio Claro," *Revista de História* 28 (1964), 427–453.

5723   Diaz Vial, R., "Situación de los libros parroquiales," *Revista de Estudios Históricos* 10 (1962), 109–122.

5724   Eisenstadt, S. N., "Ritualized Personal Relations: Blood Brotherhood, Best Friends, Compadre etc.; Some Comparative Hypotheses and Suggestions," *Man* 56 (1956), 90–95.

5725   Elder, Glen H., "Role Relations, Sociocultural Environments and Autocratic Family Ideology," *Sociometry* 28 (1965), 173–196.

5726   Feinberg, Stephen E., "A Statistical Technique for Historians: Standardizing Tables of Counts," *Journal of Interdisciplinary History* 1 (1970–71), 305–315.

5727   Glick, Paul C., and R. Glick, "New Approaches in Studying the Life Cycle of the Family," *Demography* 2 (1965), 187–202.

5728   Goody, Jack R., "Marriages, Prestations, Inheritance and Descent in the Pre-Industrial Societies," *Journal of Comparative Family Studies* 1 (1970), 37–54.

5729   Greenfield, Sidney, "Industrialization and the Family in Sociological Theory," *American Journal of Sociology* 67 (1961–62), 312–322.

5730   Jowdy, E. William, "Archival Note: Archivo del Duque del Infante," *Hispanic American Historical Review* 51 (1971), 128–129.

5731   Konetzke, Richard, "Documentos para la historia y crítica de los registros parroquiales en las Indias," *Revista de Indias* 7 (1946), 581–586.

5732   Lodolini, Elio, "Los libros parroquiales y de estado civil en América Latina," *Archivum* 8 (1958), 95–113.

5733   Marcília, María Luisa, "A aplicação de computadores na análise histórica quantitativa no Brasil," *Trabalho livre e trabalho escravo: anais do VI Simpósio Nacional dos Professôres Universitários de História,* ed. Eurípedes Simões de Paula (São Paulo, 1973), 51–65.

5734   Marcília, María Luisa, "Dos registros paroquiais à demográfia histórica no Brasil," *Anais de História* 2 (1970), 81–100.

5735   Mayer, Enrique, "Censos insensatos: evaluación de los censos campesinos en la historia de Tangor," *Visita de la provincia de León de Huánuco en 1562* (Huánuco, 1972), 341–365.

5736   Mendirichago Cueva, Tomás, "Breve reseña del archivo parroquial de la catedral de Monterrey," *Humanitas* 3 (1962), 377–388; 4 (1963), 427–444.

5737   Morin, Claude, "Los libros parroquiales como fuente para la historia demográfica y social novohispana," *Historia Mexicana* 21 (1972), 389–418.

5738   Paula, María Regina de Cunha R. S. de, "As fontes primárias existentes no

Arquivo da Cúria Metropolitana de São Paulo, capital," *Revista de História* 32 (1966), 437-493.

5739   Razzell, P. E., "The Evaluation of Baptism as a Form of Birth Registration through Cross-Matching Census and Parish Register Data," *Population Studies* 26 (1972), 121-146.

5740   Riley, Lawrence E., and Elmer A. Spreitzer, "A Model for the Analysis of Lifetime Marriage Patterns," *Journal of Marriage and the Family* 36 (1974), 64-70.

5741   Rocha, María Helena Degani, "Arrolamento das fontes históricas de Jundiaí," *Revista de História* 34 (1967), 555-567.

5742   Sánchez-Albornoz, Nicolás, "Les registres paroissiaux en Amérique Latine: quelques considérations sur leur exploitation pour la démographie historique," *Revue suisse d'histoire* 17 (1967), 60-71.

5743   Thompson, Richard A., "Structural Statistics and Structural Mechanics: The Analysis of *Compadrazgo*," *Southwestern Journal of Anthropology* 27 (1971), 381-403.

5744   Vianna, Hélio, *Sao Paulo no Arquivo de Mateus*. Rio de Janeiro, 1969.

5745   Witter, José S., and Maria Lúcia Hildorf, "Arrolamento das fontes históricas de Piracicaba," *Revista de Historia* 30 (1965), 379-422.

5746   Zeitlin, Maurice, and Richard E. Ratcliff, "Research Methods for the Analysis of the Internal Structure of Dominant Classes," *Latin American Research Review* 10 (1975), 5-61.

COLONIAL PERIOD

5747   Acevedo, Edberto Oscar, "Situación social y religiosa de Catamarca en 1770-1771," *Revista de Historia Americana y Argentina* 2 (1958-59), 237-340.

5748   Apolant, Juan Alejandro, *Los primeros pobladores españoles de la Colonia del Sacramento*. Montevideo, 1971.

5749   Arcaya, Pedro M., "Familias de Coro: población de origen europeo de Coro en la época colonial," *Boletín de la Academia Nacional de la Historia* 48 (1965), 169-211.

5750   Arcaya, Pedro M., *Población de origen europeo de Coro en la época colonial*. Caracas, 1972.

5751   Barbier, Jacques A., "Elites and Cadres in Bourbon Chile," *Hispanic American Historical Review* 52 (1972), 416-435.

5752   Barnadas, Josep M., *Charcas: orígenes históricos de una sociedad colonial, 1535-1565*. La Paz, 1973.

5753   Barrett, Ward, *The Sugar Hacienda of the Marqueses del Valle de Oaxaca*. Minneapolis, 1970.

5754 Bazant, Jan, "Los bienes de la familia de Hernán Cortés y su venta por Lucas Alamán," *Historia Mexicana* 19 (1969), 228-242.

5755 Blanco, José A., "El censo del Departamento del Atlántico, Partido de Tierradentro en el año 1777," *Boletín de la Sociedad Geográfica de Columbia* 27 (1972), 287-324.

5756 Blank, Stephanie, "Patrons, Clients, and Kin in Seventeenth-Century Caracas: A Methodological Essay in Colonial Spanish American Social History," *Hispanic American Historical Review* 54 (1974), 260-283.

5757 Blank, Stephanie, *Social Integration and Social Stability in a Colonial Spanish American City: Caracas, 1595-1627.* Bloomington, 1972.

5758 Borah, Woodrow W., *The Population of Central Mexico in 1548: An Analysis of the Suma de Visitas de Pueblos.* Berkeley, 1960.

5759 Borah, Woodrow W., and Sherburne F. Cook, "Marriage and Legitimacy in Mexican Culture: Mexico and California," *California Law Review* 54 (1966), 946-1008.

5760 Boyd-Bowman, Peter, "Patterns of Spanish Emigration to the Indies until 1600," *Hispanic American Historical Review* 56 (1976), 580-604.

5761 Brading, David A., "Los españoles en México: 1790," *Historia Mexicana* 23 (1973), 126-144.

5762 Brading, David A., "Government and Elite in Late Colonial Mexico," *Hispanic American Historical Review* 53 (1973), 389-414.

5763 Brading, David A., "Grupos étnicos: clases y estructura ocupacional en Guanajuato, 1792," *Historia Mexicana* 21 (1972), 460-480.

5764 Brading, David A., *Miners and Merchants in Bourbon Mexico, 1763-1810.* Cambridge, England, 1971.

5765 Brading, David A., and Celia Wu, "Population Growth and Crisis: León, 1720-1860," *Journal of Latin American Studies* 5 (1973), 1-36.

5766 Braithwaite, Edward, *Folk Culture of the Slaves in Jamaica.* London, 1970.

5767 Brito Figueroa, Federico, "La población y la estructura social de Venezuela en la primeras décadas del siglo XIX," *Bulletin hispanique* 69 (1967), 347-364.

5768 Bronner, Fred, "Peruvian Encomenderos in 1630: Elite Circulation and Consolidation," *Hispanic American Historical Review* 57 (1977), 633-659.

5769 Burkholder, Mark, "From Creole to Peninsular: The Transformation of the Audiencia of Lima," *Hispanic American Historical Review* 52 (1972), 395-415.

5770 Campbell, Leon, "A Colonial Establishment: Creole Domination of the Audiencia of Lima," *Hispanic American Historical Review* 52 (1972), 1-25.

5771 Calvo, Thomas, "Démographie historique d'une paroisse mexicaine: Acatzingo, 1606-1810," *Cahiers des Amériques latines* 6 (1972), 7-41.

5772 Carmagnani, Marcello, "Colonial Latin American Demography: Growth of Chilean Population, 1700-1830," *Journal of Social History* 1 (1967-68), 179-191.

5773 Carmagnani, Marcello, "Demografía y sociedad: la estructura social de los centros mineros del norte de México, 1600-1720," *Historia Mexicana* 21 (1972), 419-459.

5774 Carmagnani, Marcello, and Herbert S. Klein, "Demografía histórica: la población del obispado de Santiago, 1777-1778," *Boletín de la Academia Chilena de la Historia* 32 (1965), 57-74.

5775 Carrasco, Pedro, "El barrio ya la regulación del matrimonio en un pueblo del Valle de México en el siglo XVI," *Revista Mexicana de Estudios Antropológicos* 17 (1961), 7-26.

5776 Carrasco, Pedro, "Family Structure of Sixteenth-Century Tepotzlán," *Process Pattern in Culture: Essays in Honor of Julian H. Steward*, ed. Robert A. Manners (Chicago, 1964), 185-210.

5777 Carroll, Patrick, "Estudio sociodemográfico de personas de sangre negra en Jalapa, 1791," *Historia Mexicana* 23 (1972-73), 111-125.

5778 Casañas, Ofelia, Beatriz Rasini, and Dante Ruggeroni, "La población de Santa María," *Anuario del Instituto de Investigaciones Históricas* 6 (1962-63), 41-118.

5779 Cervera, Felipe J., and Mabel Gallardo, "Sante Fe, 1765-1830: historia y demografía," *Anuario del Instituto de Investigaciones Históricas* 9 (1966-67), 39-66.

5780 Chao, María del Pilar, "La población de Potosí en 1779," *Anuario del Instituto de Investigaciones Históricas* 8 (1965-66), 171-180.

5781 Colmares, Germánn, *La provincia de Tunja en el Nuevo Reino de Granada: ensayo de historia social, 1539-1800.* Bogotá, 1970.

5782 Comadrán Ruiz, Jorge, *Evolución demográfica argentina durante el período hispano, 1535-1810.* Bueno Aires, 1969.

5783 Comadrán Ruiz, Jorge, "La población de la ciudad de Catamarca y su jurisdicción al crearse el virreinato," *Revista de Historia Americana y Argentina* 2 (1958-59), 125-144.

5784 Cook, Sherburne F., "The Population of Mexico in 1793," *Human Biology* 14 (1942), 499-515.

5785 Cook, Sherburne F., and Woodrow Borah, *Essays in Population History: Mexico and the Caribbean.* Berkeley, 1971.

5786 Cook, Sherburne F., and Woodrow Borah, *The Indian Population of Central Mexico, 1531-1610.* Berkeley, 1960.

5787 Cook, Sherburne F., and Lesley B. Simpson, *The Population of Central Mexico in the Sixteenth Century.* Berkeley, 1948.

5788 Cousins, W. M., "Slave Family in the British Colonies: 1800-1834," *The Sociological Review* 27 (1935), 35-55.

5789 Dobyns, Henry F., "Demographic Changes in the Mining Community of Muzo after the Plague of 1629," *Hispanic American Historical Review* 47 (1967), 338-343.

5790 Dutra, Francis A., "Duarte Coelho Pereira, First Lord-Proprietor of Pernambuco: The Beginnings of a Dynasty," *The Americas* 29 (1972-73), 415-441.

5791 Ellis, Alfredo, "Os prieiros troncos paulistas e o cruzamento Euro-Americano," *Revista do Instituto Histórico e Geográfico de São Paulo* 29 (1929), 93-142.

5792 Endrek, Emiliano, *El mestizaje en el Tucumán: siglo XVIII-demografía comparada.* Cordoba, 1967.

5793 Espejo, Juan Luis, "Discordias coloniales: las familias de Larraínes," *Revista Chilena de Historia y Geografía* 9 (1919), 134-148.

5794 Espinoza Soriano, Waldemar, "Los señoríos étnicos del Valle de Condebamba y provincia de Cajabamba," *Anales Científicos de la Universidad del Centro del Perú* 3 (1974), 11-374.

5795 Floyd, Troy, "The Guatemalan Merchants, the Government, and the Provincianos, 1750-1800," *Hispanic American Historical Review* 41 (1961), 90-110.

5796 Freyre, Gilberto, *The Masters and the Slaves: A Study in the Development of Brazilian Civilization,* tr. Samuel Putnam. New York, 1956.

5797 García Belsunce, César A., "Prohibición de matrimonio entre españoles y americanas, 1817," *Revista del Instituto de História del Derecho* 14 (1963), 47-58.

5798 García Bernal, Manuela Cristina, *La sociedad de Yucatán, 1700-1750.* Seville, 1972.

5799 Gibson, Charles, "The Aztec Aristocracy in Colonial Mexico," *Comparative Studies in Society and History* 2 (1959-60), 169-196.

5800 Góngora, Mario, "Los grupos de conquistadores de Tierra Firme (1509-1530): fisionomía histórico-social de un tipo de conquista," *Lotería* 2nd series 10 (1965), 56-85.

5801 Graham, Richard, "Slave Families on a Rural Estate in Colonial Brazil," *Journal of Social History* 9 (1975-76), 382-402.

5802 Gurgel, Hector, *Uma família carioca do século XVI.* Rio de Janeiro, 1964.

5803 Handler, Jerome S., "An Archaeological Investigation of the Domestic Life of Plantation Slaves in Barbados," *Journal of the Barbados Museum and Historical Society* 34 (1972), 64-72.

5804 Harth-Terré, Emilio, *Cauces de españolización en la sociedad indoperuana de Lima virreinal.* Lima, 1964.

5805 Higman, B. W., "Household Structure and Fertility on Jamaican Slave Plantations: A Nineteenth Century Example," *Population Studies* 27 (1973), 527-550.

5806 Higman, B. W., "The Slave Family and Household in the British West Indies, 1800-1834," *Journal of Interdisciplinary History* 6 (1975-76), 261-287.

5807 Hoberman, Louisa Schell, "Merchants in Seventeenth-Century Mexico City: A Preliminary Portrait," *Hispanic American Historical Review* 57 (1977), 479-503.

5808 Houdaille, Jacques, "Trois paroisses de Saint-Domingue au XVIIIe siècle," *Population* 18 (1963), 93-110.

5809 Jaen Suárez, Omar, *El hombre y la tierra en Natá de 1700 a 1850.* Panamá, 1971.

5810 Kennedy, John N., "Bahian Elites, 1750-1822," *Hispanic American Historical Review* 53 (1973), 415-439.

5811 Kinsbruner, Jay, "The Political Status of the Chilean Merchants at the End of the Colonial Period: the Concepción Example, 1790-1810," *The Americas* 29 (1972-73), 30-56.

5812 Konetzke, Richard, "La emigración de las mujeres españolas a América durante la época colonial," *Revista Internacional de Sociología* 3 (1945), 123-150.

5813 Lisanti Filho, Luis, "La población de la capitanía de São Paulo entre la segunda mitad del siglo XVIII y el comienzo del siglo XIX," *Anuario del Instituto de Investigaciones Históricas* 6 (1962-63), 13-26.

5814 Lisanti Filho, Luis, and Marcilio, Maria Luisa, "Estrutura demográfica, social, e econômica da Vila de Lajes, 1798-1808," *Estudios Históricos* 8 (1969), 9-52.

5815 Lockhart, James, *The Men of Cajamarca: A Social and Biographical Study of the First Conquerors of Peru.* Austin, Texas, 1972.

5816 Lockhart, James, *Spanish Peru, 1532-1560: A Colonial Society.* Madison, 1968.

5817 Love, Edgar F., "Marriage Patterns of Persons of African Descent in a Colonial Mexico City Parish," *Hispanic American Historical Review* 51 (1971), 79-91.

5818 Maeder, Ernesto J. A., "El censo de 1812 en la historia demográfica de Catamarca," *Anuario del Instituto de Investigaciones Históricas* 10 (1968-69), 217-248.

5819 Maeder, Ernesto J. A., "La estructura demográfica y ocupacional de Corrientes y Entre Ríos en 1820," *Trabajos y Comunicaciones* 12 (1964), 111-138.

5820 Malvido, Elsa, "Factores de despoblación y de reposición de la población de Cholula, 1641-1810," *Historia Mexicana* 23 (1973), 52-110.

5821 Marcílio, María Luisa, "A cidade de São Paulo: povoamento e populaçaõ, 1750-1850," *Revista da Universidade Católica de São Paulo* 33 (1967) 413-418.

5822 Marcílio, María Luisa, "População, sociedade e econômia de uma comunidade pré-Malthusiana brasileira," *Estudos Históricos* 10 (1971), 9-20.

5823 Marcílio, María Luisa, "Tendences et structures des ménages dans la capitainerie de São Paulo (1765-1868) selon les listes nominatives d'habitantes," *L'histoire quantitative du Brésil de 1800 à 1930* (Paris, 1973), 157-165.

5824 Marzahl, Peter, "Creoles and Government: The Cabildo of Popayán," *Hispanic American Historical Review* 54 (1974), 636-656.

5825 Mesquita, E., "Uma contribuiçao ao estudo da estrutura familiar em São Paulo durante o período colonial: a família agregada em Itu de 1780 a 1830," *Revista de História* 53 (1976), 33-46.

5826   Moreno, José Luis, "La estructura social y demográfica de la ciudad de Buenos Aires en el año 1778," *Anuario del Instituto de Investigaciones Históricas* 8 (1965-66), 151-171.

5827   Morín, Claude, "Population et épidémies dans une paroisse méxicaine: Santa Inés Zacalteco, XVIIIe-XIXe siècles," *Cahiers des Amériques Latines* 6 (1972), 43-73.

5828   Phelan, John L., *The Kingdom of Quito in the Seventeenth Century: Bureaucratic Politics in the Spanish Empire*. Madison, 1967.

5829   Phelan, John L., *The People and the King: The Comunero Revolution in Columbia, 1781*. Madison, 1977.

5830   Ramos, Donald, "Marriage and the Family in Colonial Vila Rica," *Hispanic American Historical Review* 55 (1975), 200-225.

5831   Rasini, Beatriz, "El censo de 1771 (Chile)," *Anuario del Instituto de Investigaciones Históricas* 7 (1963-64), 43-57.

5832   Rasini, Beatriz, "Estructura demográfica de Jujuy: siglo XVIII," *Anuario del Instituto de Investigaciones Históricas* 8 (1965-66), 119-150.

5833   Rodríguez Crespo, Pedro, "Sobre parentescos de los oidores con los grupos superiores de la sociedad limeña (a comienzos del siglo XVII)," *Mercurio Peruano* 447-450 (1950), 3-15.

5834   Salinas Mexa, René, "Caracteres generales de la evolución demográfica de un centro urbano chileno: Valparaíso, 1685-1830," *Historia* 10 (1971), 177-204.

5835   Salinas Mexa, René, *La población de Valparaíso en la segunda midad del siglo XVIII: estudio preliminar del empadronamiento de 1779*. Valparaíso, 1970.

5836   Schwartz, Stuart B., "Magistracy and Society in Colonial Brazil," *Hispanic American Historical Review* 50 (1970), 715-730.

5837   Schwartz, Stuart B., *Sovereignty and Society in Colonial Brazil: The High Court of Bahia and Its Judges, 1607-1751*. Berkeley, 1973.

5838   Smith, Clifford T., "Depopulation of the Central Andes in the 16th Century," *Anales Científicos* 11 (1970), 453-464.

5839   Soares de Souza, J. A., "A população de Sao Paulo em 1766 e 1772," *Revista do Instituto de História e Geografia do Brasil* 223 (1954), 3-15.

5840   Solano, Francisco de, "Tierra, comercio y sociedad: un análisis de la estructura social agraria centroamericana durante el siglo XVIII," *Revista de Indias* 31 (1971), 311-365.

5841   Spalding, Karen, "Kurakas and Commerce: A Chapter in the Evolution of Andean Society," *Hispanic American Historical Review* 53 (1973), 581-599.

5842   Tanzi, Héctor José, "Estudio sobre la población del Virreinato del Río de la Plata en 1790," *Revista de Indias* 27 (1967), 143-156.

5843   Thayer Ojeda, Tomás, *Formación de la sociedad chilena y censo de la pobla-*

ción de Chile en los años 1540 y 1565, con datos estadísticos, biográficos, étnicos y demográficos. 3 v. Santiago, 1939-41.

5844 Tibesar, Antonine S., "The Lima Pastors, 1750-1820: Their Origins and Studies as Taken from Their Autobiographies," *The Americas* 28 (1971-72), 39-51.

5845 Tjarks, Alicia V., "Comparative Demographic Analysis of Texas, 1777-1793," *Southwestern Historical Quarterly* 77 (1974), 291-338.

5846 Volmer, Gunther, "La evolución cuantitativa de la población indígena en la región de Puebla: 1570-1810," *Historia Mexicana* 23 (1973), 43-51.

5847 Warren, Dave, "Some Demographic Considerations of the Matricula of Huexotzinco," *The Americas* 27 (1970-71), 252-270.

NINETEENTH CENTURY

5848 Arrom, Silvia M., *La mujer mexicana ante el divorcio eclesiástico (1800-1857).* Mexico City, 1976.

5849 Bello, Julio, *Memórias de um Senhor de Engenho.* Rio de Janeiro, 1938.

5850 Comadrán Ruiz, Jorge, "Algunos aspectos de la estructura demográfica y socioeconómica de Mendoza hacia 1822-1824," *Historiografía y Bibliografía Americanista* 16 (1972), 1-28.

5851 Felstiner, Mary Lowenthal, "Kinship Politics in the Chilean Independence Movement," *Hispanic American Historical Review* 56 (1976), 58-80.

5852 Freyre, Gilberto, *The Mansions and the Shanties: The Making of Modern Brazil,* tr. Harriet de Onís. New York, 1963.

5853 Freyre, Gilberto, *Order and Progress: Brazil from Monarchy to Republic,* tr. Rod W. Horton. New York, 1970.

5854 Freyre, Gilberto, "Social Life in Brazil in the Middle of the Nineteenth Century," *Hispanic American Historical Review* 5 (1922), 597-630.

5855 García de la Concha, José, *Reminiscencias: vida y costumbres de la vieja Caracas.* Caracas, 1962.

5856 Garrigós, Zelmira, *Memorias de mi lejana infancia: el barrio de La Merced en 1880.* Buenos Aires, 1964.

5857 Haigh, Roger M., *The Formation of the Chilean Oligarchy, 1810-1821.* Salt Lake City, 1972.

5858 Hamerly, Michael T., "La demografía histórica del distrito de Cuenca, 1778-1838," *Boletín de la Academia de Historia* 116 (1970), 203-229.

5859 Hamerly, Michael T., *Historia social y económica de la antigua Provincia de Guayaquil, 1763-1842.* Guayaquil, 1973.

5860 Harris, Charles H., *The Sánchez Navarros: A Socio-Economic Study of a Coahuilan Latifundio, 1846-1853.* Chicago, 1964.

5861 Ladd, Doris M., *The Mexican Nobility at Independence, 1780–1826.* Austin, Texas, 1976.

5862 Lattes, Alfredo E., and Raúl Poczter, *Muestra del censo de población de Buenos Aires de 1855.* Buenos Aires, 1968.

5863 Levi, Darrell Erville, *Os prado de São Paulo.* São Paulo, 1977.

5864 Machado Neto, Antônio Luiz, *Estrutura social da república das letras: sociologia da vida intelectual brasileira, 1870–1930.* São Paulo, 1973.

5865 Maeder, Ernesto J. A., *Evolución demográfica argentina de 1810 a 1869.* Buenos Aires, 1969.

5866 Maeder, Ernesto J. A., "Historia y resultados del censo confederal de 1857," *Trabajos y Comunicaciones* 18 (1968), 137–162.

5867 Martínez-Alier, Verena, "Color, clase y matrimonio en Cuba en el siglo XIX," *Revista de la Biblioteca Nacional 'José Martí'* 2 (1968), 47–112.

5868 Martínez-Alier, Verena, "Elopement and Seduction in Cuba," *Past and Present* 55 (1972), 91–129.

5869 Martínez-Alier, Verena, *Marriage, Class, and Color in Nineteenth-Century Cuba: A Study of Racial Attitudes and Sexual Values in a Slave Society.* New York, 1974.

5870 Martínez-Alier, Verena, "Virginidad y machismo: el honor de la mujer en Cuba en el siglo XIX," *Cuadernos de Ruedo Ibérico* 30 (1971), 51–79.

5871 Martínez, C., Pedro Santos, et al., "Mendoza a mediados del siglo XIX: aportaciones socioculturales," *Revista de la Junta de Estudios Históricos de Mendoza* 2 (1972), 647–668.

5872 Mikielievich, Wladimir C., "Rosario en 1816," *Anuario del Instituto de Investigaciones Históricas* 9 (1966–67), 183–204.

5873 Safford, Frank, "Social Aspects in Politics in Nineteenth Century Spanish America: New Granada, 1825–1850," *Journal of Social History* 5 (1971–72), 344–370.

5874 Smith, M. G., "Some Aspects of Social Structure in the British Caribbean about 1820," *Social and Economic Studies* 1 (1953), 55–79.

5875 Somoza, Jorge L., *La mortalidad en la Argentina entre 1869 y 1960.* Buenos Aires, 1971.

5876 Somoza, Jorge L., and Alfredo E. Lattes, *Muestras de los dos primeros censos nacionales de población: 1869 y 1895.* Buenos Aires, 1967.

5877 Sousa, José Antônio Soares de, "O barão de Vila Bela e a história de uma família," *Revista Trimestral do Instituto Histórico e Geográfico Brasileiro* 294 (1972), 179–189.

5878 Stein, Stanley J., *Vassouras: A Brazilian Coffee Country, 1850–1890.* New York, 1974.

5879 Viglione de Arrastía, Hebe, "Demografía histórica: análisis del censo de población de la Provincia de Santa Fe, año 1858," *Anuario del Instituto de Investigaciones Históricas* 10 (1968–69), 291–330.

TWENTIETH CENTURY

5880 Adams, Richard N., *A Community in the Andes: Problems and Progess in Muquiyauyo*. Seattle, 1959.

5881 Adams, Richard N., "Family, Household and Kinship," *The Second Sowing, Power and Secondary Development in Latin America* (San Francisco, 1967), 149–160.

5882 *Allpanchis Phuturinqa*. Special Issues 4 (1972) and 5 (1973).

5883 Alvarez Andrews, Oscar, "El problema de la familia en Chile," *Revista Mexicana de Sociología* 20 (1958), 413–428.

5884 Araujo, Alceu Maynard, "A família numa comunidade alagoana," *Sociologia* 17 (1955), 113–131.

5885 Arriaga, Eduardo E., "Some Aspects of Family Composition in Venezuela," *Eugenics Quarterly* 15 (1968), 177–190.

5886 Ashcraft, N., "Domestic Group in Mahogany, British Honduras," *Social and Economic Studies* 15 (1966), 266–274.

5887 Avila, Manuel, *Tradition and Growth: A Study of Four Mexican Villages*. Chicago, 1969.

5888 Azevedo, Thales de, "As regras do namôro no Brasil: um padrão tradicional," *América Latina* 13 (1970), 128–153.

5889 Azevedo, Thales de, "Family, Marriage and Divorce in Brazil," *Contemporary Cultures and Societies in Latin America*, ed. Dwight Heath and Richard Adams (New York, 1965), 288–310.

5890 Azevedo, Thales de, *Social Change in Brazil*. Gainesville, 1963.

5891 Bastide, Roger, *A monografia familiar no Brasil*. São Paulo, 1941.

5892 Beales, Ralph L., *Cherán: A Sierra Tarascan Village*. Washington, 1946. Reprint, New York, 1973.

5893 Bastien, Remy, *La familia rural haitiana: Valle de Maribal*. México, 1951.

5894 Bastien, Remy, "Haitian Rural Family Organization," *Social and Economic Studies* 10 (1961), 478–510.

5895 Beckford, George, "Plantation Society: Toward a General Theory of Caribbean Society," *Savacou* 5 (1971), 7–22.

5896 Bell, Robert R., "Marriage and Family Differences among Lower-Class Negro and East Indian Women in Trinidad," *Race* 12 (1970), 59–73.

5897 Berlinck, Manuel Tosta, *The Structure of the Brazilian Family in the City of São Paulo*. Ithaca, 1969.

5898 Bermúdez, María Elvira, *La vida familiar del mexicano*. México, 1955.

5899 Biesanz, John, and Mavis Biesanz, "Costa Rican Courtship and Marriage," *Costa Rican Life*, ed. John and Mavis Biesanz (New York, 1944), 46–72.

5900 Biesanz, John, and Mavis Biesanz, "Costa Rican Family Life," ibid., 73–107.

5901 Biesanz, John, and Mavis Biesanz, *The People of Panama*. New York, 1955.

5902 Blake, Judith, "Family Instability and Reproductive Behaviour in Jamaica," *Current Research in Human Fertility* (New York, 1955), 24–41.

5903 Blake, Judith, Mayone Stycos, and Kingsley Davis, *Family Structure in Jamaica: The Social Context of Reproduction.* New York, 1961.

5904 Bock, E. Wilbur, and Sugiyama Iutaka, "Social Status, Mobility and Premarital Pregnancy: The Case of Brasil," *Journal of Marriage and the Family* 32 (1970), 284-292.

5905 Bock, E. Wilbur, Sugiyama Iutaka, and F. M. Berardo, "Maintenance of the Extended Family in Urban Areas of Argentina, Brazil, and Chile," *Journal of Family Studies* 6 (1975), 31-45.

5906 Bourricaud, François, "Structure and Function of the Peruvian Oligarchy," *Studies in Comparative International Development* 11 (1966), 17-31.

5907 Brand, Donald, *Quiroga: A Mexican Municipio.* Washington, 1951.

5908 Brazelton, T. B., "Implications of Infant Development among the Mayan Indians of Mexico," *Human Development* 15 (1972), 90-111.

5909 Brush, Stephen B., *Mountain, Field, and Family: The Economy and Human Ecology of an Andean Valley.* Phliadelphia, 1977.

5910 Bryce-Laporte, Roy S., "Family Adaptation of Relocated Slum Dwellers in Puerto Rico: Implications for Urban Research and Development," *Journal of Developing Areas* 2 (1968), 533-539.

5911 Buitrago Ortiz, Carlos, *Estructura social y orientaciones valorativas en Esperanza, Puerto Rico y el Mediterráneo.* Río Piedras, 1970.

5912 Buitrago Ortiz, Carlos, "Estructura y problema en las ciencias sociales y en el estudio de la familia en Puerto Rico," *Revista de Ciencias Sociales* 11 (1967), 337-346.

5913 Bunzel, Ruth, *Chichicastenango: A Guatemalan Village.* Washington, D.C., 1952.

5914 Buschkens, Willem F. L., *The Family System of the Paramaribo Creoles.* The Hague, 1974.

5915 Bushnell, John H., and Donna D. Bushnell, "Sociocultural and Psychodynamic Correlates of Polygyny in a Mexican Village," *Ethnology* 10 (1971), 44-55.

5916 Butterworth, Douglass, "A Study of the Urbanization Process among the Mixtec Migrants from Tilantongo in Mexico City," *América Indigena* 22 (1962), 257-274.

5917 Camargo, C. P. de, et al., "Marriage Patterns and Fertility in São Paulo," *Social Biology* 17 (1970), 260-268.

5918 Cancian, Francesca M., "The Effect of Patrilocal Households on Nuclear Family Interaction in Zinacantan," *Estudios de Cultura Maya* 5 (1965), 300-315.

5919 Cancian, Francesca M., "Interaction Patterns in Zinacanteco Families," *American Sociological Review* 29 (1964), 540-550.

5920 Cândido, Antonio, "A vida familial do Caipira," *Sociologia* 16 (1954), 341-367.

5921 Carlos, Manuel L., "Fictive Kinship and Modernization in Mexico," *Anthropological Quarterly* 46 (1973), 75-91.

5922 Chance, John K., "Kinship and Urban Residence: Household and Family Organization in a Suburb of Oaxaca, Mexico," *Journal of the Steward Anthropological Society* 2 (1971), 122-147.

5923 Clarke, Edith, "Land Tenure and the Family," *Social and Economic Studies* 1 (1953), 81-118.

5924 Clarke, Edith, *My Mother Who Fathered Me: A Study of the Family in Three Selected Communities in Jamaica.* London, 1966.

5925 Cochran, Thomas C., and Reuben E. Reina, *Entrepreneurship in Argentine Culture.* Philadelphia, 1962.

5926 Cohen, Yehudi, "Four Categories of Interpersonal Relationships in the Family and Community in a Jamaican Village," *Anthropological Quarterly* 28 (1955), 121-147.

5927 Cohen, Yehudi,"The Social Organization of a Selected Community in Jamaica," *Social and Economic Studies* 2 (1954), 104-133.

5928 Cohen, Yehudi, "Structure and Function: Family Organization and Socialization in a Jamaican Community," *American Anthropologist* 58 (1966), 664-686.

5929 Colby, Benjamin N., and Pierre L. van den Berghe, *Ixil Country: A Plural Society in Highland Guatemala.* Berkeley, 1969.

5930 Collier, George A., "Familia y tierra en varias communidades Mayas," *Estudios de Cultura Maya* 6 (1966), 301-335.

5931 Collier, George A., *Fields of the Tzotzil: The Ecological Basis of Tradition in Highland Chiapas.* Austin, Texas, 1975.

5932 Collier, Jane F., *Courtship and Marriage in Zinacantan, Chiapas, Mexico.* New Orleans, 1968.

5933 Comhaire-Sylvain, S., "Courtship, Marriage and Plasaj at Kenscoff, Haiti," *Social and Economic Studies* 7 (1958), 210-233.

5934 Cortés Ruiz, Efraín C., *San Simón de la Laguna: la organización familiar y lo mágico-religioso en el culto al oratorio.* Mexico City, 1972.

5935 Costa, Edras Borges, *Cerrado e retiro: cidade e fazenda no Alto São Francisco.* Rio de Janeiro, 1960.

5936 Costa, Edras Borges, "Relações de família em Cerrado e Retiro," *Sociologia* 17 (1955), 132-146.

5937 Coy, Peter, "An Elementary Structure of Ritual Kinship: A Case of Prescription in the Compadrazgo," *Man* 9 (1974), 470-479.

5938 Cruz, Levy, "Aspectos de formação e destinegração da família em Rio Rico," *Sociologia* 16 (1954), 390-412.

5939 Cumper, George E., "The Fertility of Common-Law Unions in Jamaica," *Social and Economic Studies* 15 (1966), 189-202.

5940 Cumper, George E., "Household and Occupation in Barbados," *Social and Economic Studies* 10 (1961), 386-419.

5941 Cumper, George E., "The Jamaican Family: Village and Estate," *Social and Economic Studies* 7 (1958), 76-108.

5942 Davango, Julie, *The Determinants of Family Formation in Chile, 1960: An Econometric Study of Female Labor Force Participation, Marriage, and Fertility Decisions.* Santa Monica, 1972.

5943 Davenport, William, "The Family System of Jamaica," *Social and Economic Studies* 10 (1961), 420-455.

5944 Dehoyos, A., "The Amigo System and Alienation of the Wife in the Mexican Family," *Kinship and Family Organization,* ed. Bernard Farber (New York, 1966), 102-115.

5945 Deshon, Shirley K., "Compadrazgo on a Henequen Hacienda in Yucatán: A Structural Re-Evaluation," *American Anthropologist* 65 (1963), 574-583.

5946 Díaz, May N., "Opposition and Alliance in a Mexican Town," *Ethnology* 3 (1964), 179-184.

5947 Díaz Guerrero, Rogelio, *Estudios de psicología del mexicano.* Mexico City, 1961.

5948 Díaz Guerrero, Rogelio, "La mujer y las premisas histórico-socioculturales de la familia mexicana," *Revista Latinoamericana de Psicología* 6 (1974), 7-16.

5949 Díaz Guerrero, Rogelio, "Neurosis and the Mexican Family Structure," *American Journal of Psychiatry* 6 (1955), 411-417.

5950 Dirks, Robert, "Networks, Groups, and Adaptation in an Afro-Caribbean Community," *Man* 7 (1972), 565-585.

5951 Dobyns, Henry F., *The Social Matrix of Peruvian Indigenous Communities.* Ithaca, 1964.

5952 Doob, C. B., "Family Background and Peer Group Development in a Puerto Rican District," *Sociological Quarterly* 11 (1970), 523-532.

5953 Dubreuil, Guy, "La famille martiniquaise: analyse et dynamique," *Anthropologica* 7 (1965), 103-129.

5954 Early, John D., "Demographical Profile of a Maya Community: The Atitecos of Santiago Atitlán," *Milbank Memorial Fund Quarterly* 48 (1970), 167-178.

5955 Elder, Glen H., "Family Structure and Achievement Motivation in Brazil," *American Sociological Review* 27 (1962), 612-624.

5956 Esteva Fabregat, Claudio, "Familia y matrimonio en México: el patrón cultural," *Revista de Indias* 115-116 and 117-118 (1969), 173-278.

5957 Fals Borda, Orlando, *Peasant Society in the Columbian Andes: A Sociological Study of Saucio.* Gainesville, 1962.

5958 Faron, Louis G., "Marriage, Residence, and Domestic Groups among the Chocó," *Ethnology* 1 (1962), 13-38.

5959 Fernández Marina, R., E. D. Maldonado-Sierra, and R. D. Trent, "Three Basic Themes in Mexican and Puerto Rican Family Values," *Journal of Social Psychology* 48 (1958), 167-181.

5960 Ferrari, Alfonso Trujillo, "A família em Potengi," *Sociologia* 17 (1955), 147-162.

5961 Ferrari, Alfonso Trujillo, *Potengi, encruzilhada no Vale do São Francisco.* São Paulo, 1960.

5962 Flinn, William L., "Family Life of Latin American Urban Migrants: Three Case Studies in Bogotá," *Journal of Inter-American Studies and World Affairs* 16 (1974), 326-349.

5963 Folan, William J., and Paul C. Weigand, "Fictive Widowhood in Rural-Urban Mexico," *Anthropologia* 10 (1968), 119-128.

5964 Forman, Shepard, *The Raft Fishermen: Tradition and Change in the Brazilian Peasant Economy.* Bloomington, 1970.

5965 Foster, George M., "Godparents and Social Networks in Tzintzuntzán," *Southwestern Journal of Anthropology* 25 (1969), 261-278.

5966 Foster, George M., *Tzintzuntzán.* Boston, 1967.

5967 Frazier, E. Franklin, "The Negro Family in Bahia, Brazil," *American Sociological Review* 7 (1942), 465-478.

5968 Freilich, Morris, "Social Polygyny, Negro Peasants, and Model Analysis," *American Anthropologist* 63 (1961), 955-973.

5969 Freire-Maia, Newton, "Consanguineous Marriages in Brazil," *Eugenics Quarterly* 5 (1958), 105-114.

5970 Freire-Maia, Newton, "Frequencies of Consanguineous Marriages in Brazilian Populations," *American Journal of Human Genetics* 4 (1952), 194-203.

5971 Freire-Maia, Newton, "In-Breeding Levels in American and Canadian Populations: A Comparison with Latin America," *Eugenics Quarterly* 15 (1968), 22-33.

5972 Freire-Maia, Newton, "Recherches sur les mariages consanguins au Brésil," *Population* 24 (1969), 941-950.

5973 Freire-Maia, Newton, and J.B.C. Azecedo, "The Inbreeding Load in Brazilian Whites and Negroes as Estimated with Sib and Cousin Controls," *American Journal of Human Genetics* 23 (1971), 1-7.

5974 Freire-Maia, Newton, and A. Freire-Maia, "The Structure of Consanguineous Marriages and Its Implications," *Annals of Human Genetics* 25 (1961), 29-39.

5975 Freyre, Gilberto, *Tempo morto e outros tempos: trechos de um diário de adolescência e primeira mocidade, 1915-1930.* Rio de Janeiro, 1975.

5976 Fried, Jacob, "Social Organization and Personal Security in a Peruvian Hacienda Indian Community: Vicos," *American Anthropologist* 64 (1962), 771-780.

5977 Friedrich, Paul, *Agrarian Revolt in a Mexican Village.* Englewood Cliffs, N.J., 1970.

5978 Friedrich, Paul, "A Mexican Cacicazgo," *Ethnology* 4 (1965), 190-209.

5979 Ganon, I., "Sobre la familia uruguaya," *Revista Mexicana de Sociología* 26 (1964), 173-190.

5980 Gans, Marjorie, José Pastore, and Eugene A. Wilkening, "A mulher e a modernização da família brasileira," *Pesquisa e Planejamento* 12 (1970), 97-139.

5981   Gardner, Richard E., and Aaron M. Podolefsky, "Some Further Considerations on West Indian Conjugal Patterns," *Ethnology* 16 (1977), 299-308.

5982   Gendell, M., and Jean van der Tak, "The Size and Structure of Residential Families, Guatemala City, 1964," *Population Studies* 27 (1973), 302-322.

5983   Germani, Gino, "Inquiry into the Social Effects of Urbanization in a Working Class Sector of Greater Buenos Aires," *Urbanization in Latin America*, ed. Philip M. Hauser (New York, 1961), 206-233.

5984   Gibaja, R. E., "Actitudes hacia la familia entre obreros industriales argentinos," *Revista Latinoamericana de Sociología* 3 (1967), 411-432.

5985   Gillin, John, *Moche: A Peruvian Coastal Community.* Washington, D.C., 1947.

5986   Goldschmidt, Walter, and Evalyn J. Kunkel, "The Structure of the Peasant Family," *American Anthropologist* 73 (1971), 1058-1076.

5987   González, Nancie K. Solien, *Black Caribbean Household Structure: A Study of Migration and Modernization.* Seattle, 1969.

5988   González, Nancie K. Solien, "Changes in Black Carib Kinship Terminology," *Southwestern Journal of Anthropology* 16 (1960), 144-159.

5989   González, Nancie K. Solien, "Childrearing Practices, Nutrition and Health Status," *Milbank Memorial Fund Quarterly* 44 (1966), 77-96.

5990   González, Nancie K. Solien, "Family Organization in Five Types of Migratory Wage Labor," *American Anthropologist* 63 (1961), 1264-1280.

5991   González, Nancie K. Solien, "Some Aspects of Child-Bearing and Child-Rearing in a Guatemalan Ladino Community," *Southwestern Journal of Anthropology* 19 (1963), 411-423.

5992   Goode, Judith G., "Latin American Urbanism and Corporate Groups," *Anthropological Quarterly* 43 (1970), 146-167.

5993   Goode, William, "Illegitimacy in the Caribbean Social Structure," *American Sociological Review* 25 (1960), 21-30.

5994   Greenfield, Sidney M., "Households, Families and Kinship Systems in the West Indies," *Anthropological Quarterly* 35 (1962), 121-133.

5995   Greenfield, Sidney M., "Socio-Economic Factors and Family Forms: A Bahian Case Study," *Social and Economic Studies* 10 (1961), 72-85.

5996   Griffing, C. D., "Size of Superior Families in Brazil," *Sociology and Social Research* 24 (1940), 203-215.

5997   Guiteras, Calixta, "Clanes y sistema de parentesco de Canus (México)," *Acta Americana* 15 (1947), 1-17.

5998   Gutiérrez de Pineda, Virginia, *La familia en Colombia.* Bogotá, 1962.

5999   Gutiérrez de Pineda, Virginia, *Familia y cultura en Colombia: Tipologías, funciones y dinámica de la familia.* Bogotá, 1968.

6000   Hamburger, Adelaide, "A família numa pequena comunidade paulista," *Sociologia* 16 (1954), 284-292.

6001   Hammel, Eugene A., "The Family Cycle in a Coastal Peruvian Slum Village," *American Anthropologist* 6 (1961), 939-1005.

6002 Hammel, Eugene A., "Territorial Patterning of Marriage Relationships in a Coastal Peruvian Village," *American Anthropologist* 66 (1964), 67–74.

6003 Harris, Marvin, *Town and Country in Brazil*. New York, 1956.

6004 Hayner, Norman S., "Notes on the Changing Mexican Family," *American Sociological Review* 7 (1942), 489–497.

6005 Heckscher, Bridget T., "Household Structure and Achievement Orientation in Lower-Class Barbadian Families," *Journal of Marriage and the Family* 29 (1967), 521–526.

6006 Heintz, Peter, "La familia de clase baja en transición y el autoritarismo obrero," *Revista Latinoamericana de Sociología* 3 (1967), 433–447.

6007 Henriques, Fernando, *Family and Colour in Jamaica*. London, 1953.

6008 Henriques, Fernando, "West Indian Family Organization," *Caribbean Quarterly* 13 (1967), 31–40.

6009 Hernández Alvarez, Lilia Inés de, *Matrimonio en Puerto Rico: estudio sociodemográfico, 1910–1968*. Río Piedras, 1971.

6010 Herskovits, Melville J., "The Negro in Bahia, Brazil: A Problem in Method," *American Sociological Review* 8 (1943), 394–404.

6011 Hill, Reuben, "El noviazgo en Puerto Rico: período de transición," *Revista de Ciencias Sociales* 2 (1958), 87–104.

6012 Hill, Reuben, "Courtship in Puerto Rico: An Institution in Transition," *Marriage and Family Living* 17 (1955), 26–35.

6013 Hopkins, Nicholas A., "A Formal Account of Chalchihuitán Tzotzil Kinship Terminology," *Ethnology* 8 (1969), 85–102.

6014 Hopkins, Nicholas A., "Some Aspects of Social Organization in Chalchihuitán, Chiapas, Mexico," *Anthropology Tomorrow* 11 (1967–68), 13–33.

6015 Horowitz, Michael M., "A Decision Model of Conjugal Patterns in Martinique," *Man* 2 (1967), 445–453.

6016 Horowitz, Michael M., *Morne-Paysan: Peasant Village in Martinique*. New York, 1967.

6017 Hotchkiss, J. C., "Children and Conduct in a Ladino Community of Chiapas, Mexico," *American Anthropologist* 69 (1967), 711–718.

6018 Hugan, Paul, *Demografia brasileira: ensaio de demoeconomia brasileira*. São Paulo, 1973.

6019 Humphrey, Norman David, "Family Patterns in a Mexican Middletown," *Social Service Review* 26 (1952), 195–201.

6020 Hunt, Robert, "The Developmental Cycle of the Family Business in Rural Mexico," *Essays in Economic Anthropology*, ed. June Helm (Seattle, 1969), 54–79.

6021 Hutchinson, Bertram, "The Patron-Dependent Relationship in Brazil," *Sociologia Ruralis* 6 (1964), 3–30.

6022 Hutchinson, Harry W., *Village and Plantation Life in Northeastern Brazil*. Seattle, 1957.

6023 Iutaka, Sugiyama, and E. Wilbur Bock, "Social Status, Mobility and

Premarital Pregnancy: A Case of Brazil," *Journal of Marriage and the Family* 32 (1970), 284-292.

6024   Jaramillo, Alfredo, *Estructura familiar: estudio sobre los sectores populares de Quito, Ecuador*. Santiago, 1972.

6025   Jayawardena, Chandra, "Family Organization in Plantations in British Guiana," *International Journal of Comparative Sociology* 3 (1962), 43-64.

6026   Jayawardena, Chandra, "Marital Stability in Two Guianese Sugar Estates and Communities," *Social and Economic Studies* 9 (1960), 76-100.

6027   Kahl, J. A., "Modern Values and Fertility Ideals in Brazil and Mexico," *Journal of Social Issues* 23 (1960), 99-114.

6028   Keith Alvarado, Henry M., *Historia de la familia Alvarado Barroeta*. San José, 1972.

6029   Kottak, Conrad Philip, "Kinship and Class in Brazil," *Ethnology* 6 (1967), 427-443.

6030   Kubat, Daniel, and Santa Elena Bosco, "Marital Status and Ideology of the Family Size: Case of Young Men in Urban Brazil," *América Latina* 12 (1969), 17-34.

6031   Landy, David, *Tropical Childhood: Cultural Transmission and Learning in a Rural Puerto Rican Village*. New York, 1965.

6032   Lazo, B., et al., "Consanguinity in the Province of Valparaíso, Chile, 1917-1966," *Social Biology* 17 (1970), 167-179.

6033   Legerman, Caroline J., "Kin Groups in a Haitian Market," *Man* 62 (1962), 145-149.

6034   Leñero Otero, Luis, *Investigación de la familia en México: presentación y avance de resultados de una encuesta nacional*. Mexico City, 1968.

6035   Leridon, Henri, "Fertility in Martinique," *Natural History* 79 (1970), 57-59.

6036   Leridon, Henri, Elisabeth Zucker, and Maite Cazenove, *Fecondité et famille en Martinique: faites, attitudes et opinions*. Paris, 1970.

6037   Lewis, Oscar, *The Children of Sánchez: Autobiography of a Mexican Family*. New York, 1961.

6038   Lewis, Oscar, "La cultura de vecindad en la ciudad de México," *Ciencias Políticas y Sociales* 5 (1959), 350-364.

6039   Lewis, Oscar, "A Day in the Life of a Mexican Peasant Family," *Marriage and Family Living* 18 (1956), 3-13.

6040   Lewis, Oscar, *A Death in the Sánchez Family*. New York, 1969.

6041   Lewis, Oscar, "Family Dynamics in a Mexican Village," *Marriage and Family Living* 21 (1959), 218-226.

6042   Lewis, Oscar, *Five Families: Mexican Case Studies in the Culture of Poverty*. New York, 1954.

6043   Lewis, Oscar, "Husbands and Wives in a Mexican Village: A Study of Role Conflict," *American Anthropologist* 51 (1949), 602-610.

6044   Lewis, Oscar, *Life in a Mexican Village*. Urbana, 1951.

6045 Lewis, Oscar, *Pedro Martínez: A Mexican Peasant and His Family.* New York, 1964.

6046 Lewis, Oscar, "Urbanización sin desorganización: las familias tepoztecas en la ciudad de México," *América Indigenista* 17 (1957), 231-246.

6047 Lewis, Oscar, "Urbanization with Breakdown: A Case Study," *Scientific Monthly* 75 (1952), 31-41.

6048 Lewis, Oscar, *La Vida: A Puerto Rican Family in the Culture of Poverty—San Juan and New York.* New York, 1966.

6049 Leyburn, James C., *The Haitian People.* New Haven, 1966.

6050 Lobb, John, "Family Life in Brazil," *Marriage and Family Living* 10 (1948), 8-10.

6051 Lomnitz, Larissa, *Como sobreviven los marginados.* México City, 1975.

6052 Loomis, Charles P., "Visiting Patterns and Miscegenation at Oxapama, Peru," *Rural Sociology* 9 (1944), 68.

6053 Loomis, Charles P., et al., *Turrialba: Social Systems and Social Change.* Chicago, 1953.

6054 Lowrie, Samuel H., "Racial and National Inter-Marriage in a Brazilian City," *American Journal of Sociology* 44 (1939), 684-707.

6055 MacDonald, John Stuart, and Leatrice D. MacDonald, "Transformations of African and Indian Family Traditions in the Southern Caribbean," *Comparative Studies in Society and History* 15 (1973), 171-196.

6056 Mace, David Robert, and Vera Mace, *Sex, Love and Marriage in the Caribbean.* New York, 1965.

6057 Macewen, Alison M., "Kinship and Mobility on the Argentine Pampa," *Ethnology* 12 (1973), 135-151.

6058 Maeyama, Takashi, *Familialization of the Unfamiliar World: The Familia, Networks and Groups in a Brazilian City.* Ithaca, 1975.

6059 Maldonado Sierra, E. D., R. D. Trent, and R. F. Marina, "Neurosis and Traditional Family Beliefs in Puerto Rico," *International Journal of Social Psychiatry* 7 (1960), 237-246.

6060 Marino, Anthony, "Family Fertility and Sex Ratios in the British Caribbean," *Population Studies* 24 (1970), 154-172.

6061 Martínez, H., "Compadrazgo en una comunidad indígena altiplánica," *América Indigenista* 23 (1963), 127-139.

6062 McGinn, Noel F., "Marriage and Family in Middle-Class Mexico," *Journal of Marriage and the Family* 28 (1966), 305-313.

6063 McGinn, Noel F., Ernest Harburg, and Gerald P. Ginsburg, "Dependency Relations with Parents and Affiliative Responses in Michigan and Guadalajara," *Sociometry* 28 (1965), 305-321.

6064 Medina, Carlos Alberto de, *Família e mudança: o familismo numa sociedade arcaica em transformação.* Petropolis, 1947.

6065 Mendoza, A., "The Rural Family in Argentina," *Marriage and Family Living* 4 (1942), 14.

6066   Metzger, Duane, and Gerald E. Williams, "A Formal Ethnographic Analysis of Tenejapa Ladino Weddings," *American Anthropologist* 65 (1963), 1076-1101.

6067   Michielutte, R., C. E. Vincent, and C. M. Cochran, "Consensual and Legal Marital Unions in Costa Rica," *International Journal of Comparative Sociology* 14 (1973), 119-128.

6068   Mintz, Sidney, *Worker in the Cane: A Puerto Rican Life History.* New Haven, 1960.

6069   Mitchell, Simon, "The Influence of Kinship in the Social Organization of Northeast Brazilian Fisherman: A Contrast in Case Studies," *Journal of Latin American Studies* 6 (1974), 301-313.

6070   Moraes, Maria A. S., *História de uma oligarquia: os Bulhões.* Goiana, 1974.

6071   Moore, Alexander, *Life Cycles in Atchalán: The Diverse Careers of Certain Guatemalans.* New York, 1973.

6072   Mortara, Giorgio, "The Development and Structure of Brazil's Population," *Population Studies* 8 (1954), 121-139.

6073   Mortara, Giorgio, *Le Unioni Conjugali Ligere Nell'America Latina.* Rome, 1961.

6074   Moxley, Robert L., "Family Solidarity and Quality of Life in an Agricultural Peruvian Community," *Journal of Marriage and the Family* 35 (1973), 497-504.

6075   Murra, John W., "Studies in Family Organization in the French Caribbean," *Transactions of the New York Academy of Sciences* 19 (1957), 372-378.

6076   Nash, June C., *In the Eyes of the Ancestors.* New Haven, 1970.

6077   Nerlove, Marc, and T. Paul Schultz, *Love and Life between the Censuses: A Model of Family Decision Making in Puerto Rico, 1950-1960.* Santa Monica, 1970.

6078   Nogueira, Oracy, *Família e comunidade: um estudo sociológico de Itapétininga.* Rio de Janeiro, 1962.

6079   Nogueira, Oracy, "A organizacão da família no municipio de Itapétininga," *Educação e Ciencias Sociais* 5 (1959), 61-112.

6080   Núñezdel Prado, Oscar, "El hombre y la familia: su matrimonio y organización político-social en Q'ero," *Allpanchis Phuturinqa* 1 (1969), 5-27.

6081   Nutini, Hugo G., *San Bernardino Contla, Marriage and Family Structure in a Tlaxcalan Municipio.* Pittsburgh, 1968.

6082   Nutini, Hugo G., "Polygyny in a Tlaxcalan Community," *Ethnology* 4 (1965), 123-147.

6083   Nutini, Hugo G., and Timothy D. Murphy, "Labor Migration and Family Structure in the Tlaxcala-Puebla Area, Mexico," *The Social Anthropology of Latin America,* ed. Walter Goldschmidt and Harry Haijer (Los Angeles, 1970), 80-103.

6084   Nutini, Hugo G., and Douglas R. White, "Community Variations and Network Structure in the Social Functions of Compadrazgo in Rural Tlaxcala, Mexico," *Ethnology* 16 (1977), 353-384.

6085 Okraku, I. O., "The Family Life-Cycle and Residential Mobility in Puerto Rico," *Sociology and Social Research* 55 (1971), 324-340.

6086 Ordóñez Chipin, Martín, "Estudio sobre la poliginia en Santa María Chiquimula, municipio del Departmento de Totonicapán," *Guatemala Indígena* 6 (1971), 154-159.

6087 Osborn, Ann, "Compadrazgo and Patronage: A Colombian Case," *Man* 3 (1968), 593-608.

6088 Otterbein, Keith F., *The Andros Islanders: A Study of Family Organization in the Bahamas*. Lawrence, Kans., 1966.

6089 Otterbein, Keith F., "Caribbean Family Organization: A Comparative Analysis," *American Anthropologist* 67 (1965), 66-79.

6090 Otterbein, Keith F., "The Household Composition of the Andros Islanders," *Social and Economic Studies* 12 (1963), 78-83.

6091 Otterbein, Keith F., and Charlotte S. Otterbein, "A Stochastic Process Analysis of the Developmental Cycle of the Andros Household," *Ethnology* 16 (1977), 415-426.

6092 Parsons, Elsie C., *Mitla: Town of the Souls*. Chicago, 1936.

6093 Parsons, Elsie C., *Peguche: A Study of Andean Indians*. Chicago, 1945.

6094 Paul, B. D., "Symbolic Rivalry in a Guatemalan Indian Village," *American Anthropologist* 52 (1950), 205-218.

6095 Paul, Lois, and Benjamin D. Paul, "Changing Marriage Patterns in a Highland Guatemalan Community," *Southwestern Journal of Anthropology* 19 (1963), 131-148.

6096 Paz Soldán, Carlos Enrique, "La política demográfica del mariscal Castillia," *Revista del Instituto Libertador Ramón Castilla* 6 (1961), 1-12.

6097 Peattie, Lisa Redfield, *The View from the Barrio*. Ann Harbor, 1968.

6098 Pierson, Donald, *Cruz das Almas: A Brazilian Village*. Washington, D.C., 1951.

6099 Pierson, Donald, "Família e compadrio numa comunidade rural paulista," *Sociologia* 16 (1954), 368-389.

6100 Pierson, Donald, "The Family in Brazil," *Marriage and Family Living* 16 (1954), 308-314.

6101 Plattner, Stuart, "Occupation and Marriage Trading Community," *Southwestern Journal of Anthropology* 28 (1972), 193-206.

6102 Price, Richard, "Saramaka Emigration and Marriage: A Case Study of Social Change," *Southwestern Journal of Anthropology* 26 (1970), 157-189.

6103 Price, W. J., "Getting Married in Todos Santos," *Practical Anthropology* 12 (1965), 281-286.

6104 Puffer, Ruth R., and Carlos V. Serrano, *Patterns of Mortality in Childhood: Report of the Inter-American Investigation of Mortality in Childhood*. Washington, D.C., 1973.

6105   *Race and Class in Rural Brazil,* ed. Charles Wagley. New York, 1952.

6106   Ramírez, Santiago, and Ramón Parres, "Some Dynamic Patterns in the Organization of the Mexican Family," *International Journal of Social Psychiatry* 3 (1957), 18-21.

6107   Redfield, Robert, *Chan Kom: A Maya Village.* Washington, D.C., 1962.

6108   Redfield, Robert, *The Folk Culture of Yucatan.* Chicago, 1941.

6109   Redfield, Robert, "Marriage in a Maya Village," *Mexican Folklore* 7 (1932), 154-159.

6110   Redfield, Robert, *Tepoztlan: A Mexican Village.* Chicago, 1930.

6111   Reina, Rubén, *Paraná: Social Boundaries in an Argentine City.* Austin, 1973.

6112   Reina, Rubén, "Two Patterns of Friendship in a Guatemalan Community," *American Anthropologist* 61 (1959), 44-50.

6113   Ribeiro, René, "On the Amaziado Relationship and Other Aspects of Family in Recife (Brazil)," *American Sociological Review* 10 (1945), 44-51.

6114   Rios, José Arthur, "Classe e familia no Brasil," *Digesto Económico* 6 (1950), 127-134.

6115   Riviere, P. G., "The Honor of Sanchez-Honor and Shame-Family as Basis for Morality," *Man* 2 (1967), 569-583.

6116   Roberts, Bryan, "The Social Organization of Low-Income Families," *Masses in Latin America,* ed. Irving Louis Horowitz (New York, 1970), 345-382.

6117   Roberts, George W., *The Population of Jamaica.* Cambridge, England, 1957.

6118   Roberts, George W., "Some Aspects of Mating and Fertility in the West Indies," *Population Studies* 8 (1955), 199-227.

6119   Roberts, George W., and Lloyd Braithwaite, "Fertility Differentials by Family Type in Trinidad," *Annals of the New York Academy of Sciences* 84 (1960), 963-980.

6120   Roberts, George W., and Lloyd Braithwaite, "A Gross Mating Table for a West Indian Population," *Population Studies* 14 (1961), 198-217.

6121   Roberts, George W., and Lloyd Braithwaite, "Mating among East Indian and Non-East Indian Women in Trinidad," *Social and Economic Studies* 11 (1962), 203-240.

6122   Roberts, Lydia J., and Rosa Luisa Stefani, *Patterns of Living in Puerto Rican Families.* Rio Piedras, 1949.

6123   Rocha, José Martinho de, *Virginidade, sexo, família.* Rio de Janeiro, 1972.

6124   Rodman, Hyman, *Lower-Class Families: The Culture of Poverty in Negro Trinidad.* New York, 1971.

6125   Rogers, William B., "Household Atomism and Change in the Out Island of Bahamas," *Southwestern Journal of Anthropology* 23 (1967), 244-260.

6126   *Les rôles familiaux dans les civilisations différentes,* ed. Séminaire d'étude des rôles familiaux, Brussels. Brussels, 1971.

6127   Romanucci-Ross, Lola, *Conflict, Violence, and Morality in a Mexican Village.* Palo Alto, 1973.

6128   Romney, K., and R. Romney, "The Mixtecans of Juxtlahuaca, Mexico: Family

Organization and Kinship," *Six Cultures: Studies of Child Rearing*, ed. B. B. Whiting (New York, 1963), 586-601.

6129 Rosario, C., "Dos tipos de amor romántico: Estados Unidos y Puerto Rico," *Revista de Ciencias Sociales* 2 (1958), 349-368.

6130 Rosen, Bernard C., "Social Change, Migration and Family Interaction in Brazil," *American Sociological Review* 38 (1973), 198-212.

6131 Rosen, Bernard C., and Manoel T. Berlinck, "Industrialization, Family, and Fertility: A Structural-Psychological Analysis of the Brazilian Case," *Demography* 8 (1971), 49-70.

6132 Rosen, Bernard C., and Manoel T. Berlinck, "Modernization and Family Structure in the Region of São Paulo, Brazil," *América Latina* 2 (1968), 75-96.

6133 Rosen, Bernard C., and Anita La Raia, "Modernity in Women: An Index of Social Change in Brazil," *Journal of Marriage and the Family* 34 (1972), 353-360.

6134 Rosenberg, Terry J., "Industrialization and Regional Influences on the Employment of Colombian Women," *Journal of Marriage and the Family* 38 (1976), 339-353.

6135 Rosenthal, Celia S., "Lower Class Family Organization on the Caribbean Coast of Colombia," *Pacific Sociological Review* 3 (1960), 12-17.

6136 Russell-Wood, A.J.R., *Fidalgos and Philanthropists: The Santa Casa da Misericórdia of Bahia, 1550-1755*. Berkeley, 1968.

6137 Sanders, Andrew, "Family Structure and Domestic Organization among Coastal Amerindians in Guyana," *Social and Economic Studies* 22 (1973), 440-478.

6138 Sayres, William C., "Ritual Kinship and Negative Effect," *American Sociological Review* 21 (1956), 348-352.

6139 Schlesinger, Benjamin, "Family Patterns in the English-Speaking Caribbean," *Journal of Marriage and the Family* 30 (1968), 149-154.

6140 Schulman, S., "Family Life on a Colombian 'Turgurio,' " *Sociological Analysis* 28 (1967), 184-195.

6141 Scott, J. W., "Sources of Social Change in Community, Family and Fertility in a Puerto Rican Town," *American Journal of Sociology* 72 (1967), 520-530.

6142 Seigel, Morris, "Effects of Culture Contact on the Form of the Family in a Guatemalan Village," *Journal of the Royal Anthropological Institute* 72 (1942), 55-68.

6143 Service, Elman R., and Helen S. Service, *Tobatí: Paraguayan Town*. Chicago, 1954.

6144 Shirley, Robert W., *The End of a Tradition: Culture Change and Development in the Município of Cunha, São Paulo*. New York, 1970.

6145 Silva, Fernando Altenfelder, *Xique-Xique e Marrecas: duas comunidades do médio São Francisco*. Rio de Janeiro, 1961.

6146   Simpson, George E., "Sexual and Family Institutions in Northern Haiti," *American Anthropologist* 44 (1942), 655-674.

6147   Simpson, M. L., "Ideal Family Size in Monterrey, Mexico," *Human Mosaic* 3 (1968), 105-123.

6148   Smith, Michael Garfield, *Kinship and Community in Carrioucou*. New Haven, 1962.

6149   Smith, Michael Garfield, *West Indian Family Structure*. Seattle, 1962.

6150   Smith, Raymond T., "Aspects of Family Organization in a Coastal Negro Community in British Guiana," *Social and Economic Studies* 1 (1953), 87-111.

6151   Smith, Raymond T., "The Family in the Caribbean," *Caribbean Studies: A Symposium,* ed. Vera Rubin (Kingston, 1957), 67-75.

6152   Smith, Raymond T., *The Negro Family in British Guiana: Family Structure and Social Status in the Villages*. New York, 1956.

6153   Smith, Raymond T., *The Negro Family in the Caribbean*. London, 1956.

6154   Smith, Raymond T., "The Nuclear Family in Afro-American Kinship," *Journal of Comparative Family Studies* 1 (1970), 58-70.

6155   Smith, Raymond T., and Chandra Jayawardena, "Marriage and the Family amongst East Indians in British Guiana," *Social and Economic Studies* 8 (1959), 321-376.

6156   Smith, Suzanne, E. A. Wilkening, and José Pastore, "Interaction of Sociological and Ecological Variables Affecting Women's Satisfaction in Brasilia," *International Journal of Comparative Sociology* 12 (1971), 114-127.

6157   Smith, T. Lynn, *Brazil: People and Institutions*. Baton Rouge, 1963.

6158   Smith, T. Lynn, Justo Rodríguez Díaz, and Luis Roberto García, *Tabio: A Study in Rural Social Organization*. Washington, 1945.

6159   Solien, Nancie L., "The nonunilineal Descent Group in the Caribbean and Central America," *American Anthropologist* 61 (1959), 578-583.

6160   Somoza, Jorge L., "Algunos efectos sociales y económicos derivados de la baja de la mortalidad en la República Argentina entre 1900 y 1960," *Desarrollo Económico* 41 (1971), 113-123.

6161   Stein, William, *Hualcan: Life in the Highlands of Peru*. Ithaca, 1961.

6162   Staley, A. J., "Racial Democracy in Brazilian Marriage," *American Catholic Sociological Review* 21 (1960), 146-163.

6163   Stavenhagen, María Eugenia de, "El compadrazgo en una comunidad Zapoteca," *Ciencias Políticas y Sociales* 5 (1959), 365-402.

6164   Stern, Lilo, "Inter-Household Movement in a Ladino Village of Southern Mexico," *Man* 8 (1973), 393-415.

6165   Stewart, Julian H., et al., *The People of Puerto Rico: A Study in Social Anthropology*. Urbana, 1956.

6166   Strickon, Arnold, "Class and Kinship in Argentina," *Ethnology* 1 (1962), 500-515.

6167 Stoffle, Richard W., "Industrial Impact on Family Formation in Barbados, West Indies," *Ethnology* 16 (1977), 253-267.

6168 Stross, Brian, "Tzeltal Marriage by Capture," *Anthropological Quarterly* 47 (1974), 328-346.

6169 *Structure and Process in Latin America: Patronage, Clientage, and Power Systems,* ed. Arnold Strickon and Sidney M. Greenfield. Albuequrque, 1972.

6170 Stycos, J. Mayone, "Culture and Differential Fertility in Peru," *Population Studies* 16 (1963), 257-270.

6171 Stycos, J. Mayone, "Family and Fertility in Puerto Rico," *American Sociological Review* 17 (1952), 572-580.

6172 Stycos, J. Mayone, *Family and Fertility in Puerto Rico: A Study of the Lower Income Group.* New York, 1955.

6173 Stycos, J. Mayone, "Haitian Attitudes toward Family Size," *Human Organizations* 23 (1964), 42-47.

6174 Stycos, J. Mayone, "Social Class and Preferred Family Size in Peru," *American Journal of Sociology* 70 (1965), 651-658.

6175 Sum Sacalxot, María Amelia, *El matrimonio indígena en Quezaltenango.* Quezaltenango, Guatemala, 1965.

6176 Szuchman, Mark D., "The Limits of the Melting Pot in Urban Argentina: Marriage and Integration in Córdoba, 1869-1909," *Hispanic American Historical Review* 57 (1977), 24-50.

6177 Taggert, James M., "The Fissiparous Process in Domestic Groups of a Nahuatl-Speaking Community," *Ethnology* 11 (1972), 132-149.

6178 Thompson, Richard A., *The Winds of Tomorrow: Social Change in a Maya Town.* Chicago, 1974.

6179 Turner, P. R., "Tequistlatecon Kinship and Limitations on Choice of Spouse," *Ethnology* 5 (1966), 245-250.

6180 van den Berghe, Gwendoline, and Pierre L. van den Berghe, "Compadrazgo and Class in Southwestern Mexico," *American Anthropologist* 68 (1966), 1237-1244.

6181 van den Berghe, Pierre L., and Benjamin N. Colby, "Ladino-Indian Relations in the Highlands of Chiapas, Mexico," *Social Forces* 40 (1961), 63-71.

6182 Vernez, G., "Residential Movements of Low Income Families: The Case of Bogotá, Colombia," *Land Economics* 50 (1974), 421-428.

6183 Villa Rojas, Alfonso, "Kinship and Nogualism in a Tzeltal Community, Southern Mexico," *American Anthropologist* 49 (1947), 578-587.

6184 Vogt, Evon Z., *Zincantan: A Maya Community in the Highlands of Chiapas.* Cambridge, England, 1970.

6185 Wilkening, E. A., João Bosco Pinto, and José Pastore, "Role of the Extended Family in Migration and Adaptation in Brazil," *Journal of Marriage and the Family* 30 (1968), 689-695.

6186 Wagley, Charles, *Amazon Town: A Study of Man in the Tropics.* New York, 1964.

6187 Wagley, Charles, "Luzo-Brazilian Kinship Pattern: The Persistence of a Cultural Tradition," *Politics of Change in Latin America,* ed. J. Maier and R. Weatherhead (New York, 1964), 174-189.

6188 Wagley, Charles, *The Social and Religious Life of a Guatemalan Village.* Menasha, Wis., 1948.

6189 Whetten, Nathan L., *Rural Mexico.* Chicago, 1948.

6190 Whitten, Norman E., Jr., *Class, Kinship, and Power in an Ecuadorian Town: The Negroes of San Lorenzo.* Stanford, 1965.

6191 Whiteford, Andrew H., *Two Cities of Latin America: A Comparative Description of Social Classes.* Garden City, 1964.

6192 Willems, Emílio, "Intermarriage among German-Brazilians," *Migration News* 5 (1956), 10-18.

6193 Willems, Emílio, "The Structure of the Brazilian Family," *Social Forces* 31 (1953), 339-345.

6194 Willems, Emílio, *Uma vila brasileira: tradição e transição.* São Paulo, 1961.

6195 Williamson, Robert C., "Some Variables of Middle and Lower Classes in Two Central American Cities," *Social Forces* 41 (1962), 195-207.

6196 Williamson, Robert C., "Social Class and Orientation to Change: Some Relevant Variables in a Bogotá Sample," *Social Forces* 46 (1968), 317-328.

6197 Wilson, Peter J., "Caribbean Crews: Peer Groups and Male Society," *Caribbean Studies* 10 (1971), 18-34.

6198 Wilson, Peter J., "Household and Family on Providencia," *Social and Economic Studies* 10 (1961), 511-527.

6199 Wilson, Peter J., and John Buettner-Janush, "Demography and Evolution on Providencia Island, Colombia," *American Anthropologist* 63 (1961), 940-954.

6200 Yaukey, D., "Differential Female Age at First Marriage in Six Latin American Cities," *Journal of Marriage and the Family* 34 (1972), 375-379.

6201 Yaukey, D., T. Thorsen, and A. T. Onala, "Marriage at an Earlier than Ideal Age in Six Latin American Capital Cities," *Population Studies* 26 (1972), 263-272.

6202 Young, Frank W., and Ruth C. Young, "The Differentiation of Family Structure in Rural Mexico," *Journal of Marriage and the Family* 30 (1968), 154-161.

6203 Young, Philip D., *Ngwabe: Tradition and Change among the Western Guaymi of Panama.* Urbana, 1971.

6204 Zarate, A. O., "Differential Fertility in Monterrey, Mexico: Prelude to Transitions," *Milbank Memorial Fund Quarterly* 45 (1967), 93-108.

6205 Zannonia, E. A., "Institutional Control and the Family in Latin America, Conjugal Illegitimacy," *Revista de Estudios Políticos* 158 (1968), 168-202.

Index of Names